GREECE'S NORTHERN FRONTIER

COLLOQUIA ANTIQUA

Supplements to the Journal ANCIENT WEST & EAST

FOUNDER

GOCHA R. TSETSKHLADZE (†) (UK)

EDITORIAL BOARD

M. Dana (France), J. Hargrave (UK),
M. Kazanski (France), A. Mehl (Germany),
M. Manoledakis (Greece), A. Podossinov (Russia), J. Wiesehöfer (Germany)

ADVISORY BOARD

S. Atasoy (Turkey), L. Ballesteros Pastor (Spain), A. Baralis (France),
Sir John Boardman (UK), H. Bru (France), S. Burstein (USA), B. d'Agostino (Italy),
J. de Boer (The Netherlands), A. Domínguez (Spain), O. Doonan (USA),
S. Günther (Germany/China),S. Kovalenko (Russia), R. Morais (Portugal),
M. Pearce (UK), D. Potts (USA), R. Rollinger (Austria), N. Theodossiev (Bulgaria),
M. Tiverios (Greece), C. Ulf (Austria), J. Vela Tejada (Spain)

Colloquia Antiqua is a refereed publication

For proposals and editorial and other matters, please contact the Series Editors:

The Gallery
Spa Road
Llandrindod Wells
Powys LD1 5ER
UK
E-mail: g.tsetskhladze63@gmail.com
afcoltd@btinternet.com

COLLOQUIA ANTIQUA
—— 38 ——

GREECE'S NORTHERN FRONTIER

Studies in the History of the Ancient Greek
Experience in the Black Sea

By

STANLEY M. BURSTEIN

PEETERS
LEUVEN – PARIS – BRISTOL, CT
2024

A catalogue record for this book is available from the Library of Congress.

ISBN 978-90-429-5060-3
eISBN 978-90-429-5061-0
D/2024/0602/19
© 2024, Peeters, Bondgenotenlaan 153, B-3000 Leuven, Belgium

No part of this book may be reproduced in any form or by any electronic or mechanical means, including information storage or retrieval devices or systems, without prior written permission from the publisher, except the quotation of brief passages for review purposes.

TABLE OF CONTENTS

SERIES EDITOR'S PREFACE IX

LIST OF STANLEY BURSTEIN'S PUBLICATIONS XI

AUTHOR'S PREFACE... XIX

ABBREVIATIONS AND CONVENTIONS XXIII

PERMISSIONS XXI

INTRODUCTION.. 1

PART I: Book
Outpost of Hellenism: The Emergence of Heraclea on the Black Sea

PREFACE 21

INTRODUCTION.. 23
    Sources 23
    Geography... 28
    The Mariandynoi 31

I. SETTLEMENT 43
    Greek Colonization in the Black Sea...................... 43
    Possible Milesian Colony at Heraclea 44
    Organization and Departure 48
    Government.. 54

II. FROM THE FOUNDATION TO THE END OF THE PELOPONNESIAN WAR:
    560 TO 404... 61
    The Fall of the Democracy.............................. 61
    Heraclea and Persia to 480............................. 65
    The Conquest of the Mariandynoi 69
    Heraclea and Athens to 404............................. 73
    Internal Developments to 404 84

III. FROM THE END OF THE PELOPONNESIAN WAR TO THE REFORM OF THE
    DEMOCRACY: 404 TO *CA.* 370 89
    Power Vacuum in the Pontus............................. 89

Heraclea and the Ten Thousand	90
Foreign Relations: The Aegean and Persia	92
Foreign Relations: The Struggle with the Spartocids	95
Internal Developments: The Reform of the Democracy	98

IV. CLEARCHUS AND SATYRUS: *CA.* 370 TO 346 103

The Crisis	103
Seizure of Power	109
From Tyranny to Monarchy	113
Foreign Affairs	114
Heracleote Society and Government during the Reign of Clearchus	120
Repression and Assassination	129
The Regency of Satyrus: 352 to 346	131

V. TIMOTHEUS AND DIONYSIUS: 346 TO 305 135

The Reign of Timotheus: A New Era: 346 to 337	135
Foreign Affairs	139
Internal Developments	141
The Reign of Dionysius: 337 to 305	143
Foreign Affairs: Alexander and the Exiles: 334 to 323	143
Foreign Affairs: Dionysius and the Diadochi: 323 to 305	147
Internal History and the Death of Dionysius	152

VI. AMASTRIS, CLEARCHUS II, AND OXATHRES: THE END OF THE TYRANNY:

305 TO 281	157
The Regency of Amastris: 305 to *ca.* 300	157
The Government of Clearchus II and Oxathres: 301 to 284	160
The Administration of Heracleides of Cyme: 284/3 to 281	166
An End and a Beginning	167

CONCLUSION	171
APPENDIX : THE DATE OF LYSIMACHUS' OCCUPATION OF HERACLEA	173
BIBLIOGRAPHY	177

PART II: Articles

Fragment 53 of Callisthenes and the Text of *Iliad* 2. 850–55.	191
Heraclea Pontica: The City and Subjects.	195
The Black Sea: An Achaemenid Frontier Zone.	203

TABLE OF CONTENTS VII

The Greek Cities of the Black Sea.............................. 213

IG 1³ 61 and the Black Sea Grain Trade........................ 233

Chersonesus between Greece and Scythia'...................... 241

The Origin of the Athenian Privileges at Bosporus: a Reconsideration. 251

The Date of Amage, Queen of the Sarmatians: A Note on Polyaenus,
  Strategemata 8. 56... 255

The War between Heraclea Pontica and Leucon I of Bosporus....... 261

Sceptre or Thunderbolt: Plutarch, *Moralia* 338B................. 279

IG II² 653, Demosthenes and Athenian Relations with Bosporus in the
  Fourth Century B.C. 283

Menander and Politics: The Fragments of the *Halieis*............. 293

Lysimachus and the Cities: The Early Years. 301

IG II² 1485A and Athenian Relations with Lysimachus............ 311

Syriskos of Chersonesus: A New Interpretation of *IOSPE* 1² 344..... 317

The Aftermath of the Peace of Apamaea: Rome and the Pontic War. . 323

Go-Betweens and the Greek Cities of the Black Sea. 335

INDEX 343

SERIES EDITOR'S FOREWORD

When originally conceived, almost 25 years ago, this was to have been a volume in my previous series *Colloquia Pontica*. It had the enthusiastic backing of the then editor for Classics at Brill. But events (including my move to Melbourne), changes of personnel and relatively primitive technology conspired against it. Thus, I am very pleased to see this volume brought to press, making more readily available than hitherto Stanley Burstein's 1976 book *Outpost of Hellenism: The Emergence of Heraclea on the Black Sea*, and complementing it with numerous articles, written by him over the course of almost half a century, on the Black Sea, my first and abiding great interest.

Stanley is Professor Emeritus of History at California State University, Los Angeles, where he taught from 1968 to 2004. He received his BA, MA and Ph.D. degrees in Ancient History from the University of California at Los Angeles. He was president of the Association of Ancient Historians. His field of research is Greek history and historiography, with particular emphasis on the encounter between Greeks and non-Greek peoples in the Black Sea basin and ancient Northeast Africa, fields in which he remains active.

I should like to thank all those publications and publishers which readily granted permission to republish Stanley's articles and book, our own publisher, Peeters, especially Bert Verrept, for work converting texts and formats, and Stanley himself, in response to my enthusiastic prodding, for returning to the fray and pursuing the project to completion. His new Introduction provides a *tour d'horizon* of major developments in the field over 50 years, and it seems meet to detail Stanley's productivity across all spheres of activity in those years by including a full list of his publications in this one.

Gocha Tsetskhladze (†)

PUBLICATIONS
(excluding book reviews)

Books and Monographs

Outpost of Hellenism: The Emergence of Heraclea on the Black Sea (Classical Studies 14) (Berkeley 1976).

The Babyloniaca of Berossus (Sources from the Ancient Near East, vol. 1, fasc. 5) (Malibu 1978).

Panhellenica: Essays in Ancient History and Historiography in Honor of T.S. Brown, ed. with L.A. Okin (Lawrence, KN 1980).

Ancient History, Selected Reading Lists and Course Outlines from American Colleges and Universities, vol. 1, ed. with S.B. Pomeroy (New York 1984; 2nd ed. 1986).

The Hellenistic Age from the Battle of Ipsos to the Death of Kleopatra VII (Translated Documents of Greece and Rome, vol. 3) (Cambridge 1985).

Agatharchides of Cnidus, On the Erythraean Sea, ed. and trans. (Hakluyt Society, 2nd ser. 172) (London 1990).

Graeco–Africana: Studies in the History of Greek Relations with Egypt and Nubia (New Rochelle, NY 1995).

The Ancient World: Readings in Social and Cultural History, with D.B. Nagle (Hoboken, etc., 1995; 2nd ed. 2002; 3rd ed. 2005; 4th ed. 2009; 5th ed. 2014).

Ancient African Civilizations: Kush and Axum (Princeton 1998; 2nd ed. 2009).

Ancient Greece: A Political, Social, and Cultural History, with S. Pomeroy, J. Roberts and W. Donlan (Oxford 1999; 2nd ed. 2008; 3rd ed. 2012; 4th ed. 2017). Spanish translation 2001; Polish translation 2010; Chinese translation 2010.

Land of Enchanters: Egyptian Short Stories from the Earliest Times to the Present Day, with B. Lewis (Princeton 2001).

Ancient Greece: A Brief History, with S. Pomeroy, J. Roberts and W. Donlan (Oxford 2003; 2nd ed. 2009; 3rd ed. 2014; 4th ed. 2020).

The Lords of Kush (Artesian Press, 2004) (Elementary school textbook).

The Reign of Cleopatra (Westport, CT 2004; paperback: Norman, OK 2007), Polish translation 2009.

Ancient Civilizations, with R. Shek (Austin, TX 2006) (Sixth grade textbook).

Medieval and Early Modern Times, with R. Shek (Austin, TX 2006) (Seventh grade textbook).

World History, with R. Shek (Austin, TX 2006) (Middle school textbook).

Readings in Greek History: Sources and Interpretations, with D.B. Nagle (New York 2007; 2nd ed. 2013).

The World from 1000 BCE to 300 CE (New York 2017), German translation 2022.

The Essential Greek Historians (Indianapolis 2022).

XII   PUBLICATIONS

Chapters in Books, Articles, etc.

'The Recall of the Ostracized and the Themistocles Decree'. *California Studies in Classical Antiquity* 4 (1971), 93–110.

'The War between Heraclea Pontica and Leucon I of Bosporus'. *Historia* 23 (1974), 401–16.

'Sceptre or Thunderbolt: Plutarch, *Moralia* 338B'. *California Studies in Classical Antiquity* 7 (1974), 89–92.

'Alexander, Callisthenes and the Sources of the Nile'. *Greek, Roman, and Byzantine Studies* 17 (1976), 135–46.

'Fragment 53 of Callisthenes and the Text of *Iliad* 2.850–855'. *Classical Philology* 71 (1976), 339–41.

'*IG* II^2 561 and the Court of Alexander IV'. *Zeitschrift für Papyrologie und Epigraphik* 24 (1977), 223–25.

'The Date of the Athenian Victory over Pleistarchus'. *Classical World* 71 (1977), 128–29.

'*IG* II^2 1485A and Athenian Relations with Lysimachus'. *Zeitschrift für Papyrologie und Epigraphik* 31 (1978), 181–85.

'*IG* II^2 653, Demosthenes and Athenian Relations with Bosporus in the Fourth Century B.C.'. *Historia* 27 (1978), 428–36.

'Heraclea Pontica: The City and Subjects'. *The Ancient World* 2 (1979), 25–28.

'The Nubian Campaigns of C. Petronius and G. Reisner's Second Meroitic Kingdom of Napata'. *Zeitschrift für Ägyptische Sprache und Altertumskunde* 106 (1979), 95–105.

'Lysimachus and the Greek Cities of Asia: The Case of Miletus'. *The Ancient World* 3 (1980), 73–79.

'Menander and Politics: The Fragments of the *Halieis*'. In S.M. Burstein and L.A. Okin (eds.), *Panhellenica: Essays in Ancient History and Historiography in Honor of Truesdell S. Brown* (Lawrence, KN 1980), 69–76.

'Bithys, Son of Cleon from Lysimachia: A Reconsideration of the Date and Significance of *IG* II^2, 808'. *California Studies in Classical Antiquity* 12 (1980), 39–50.

'The Aftermath of the Peace of Apamaea: Rome and the Pontic War'. *American Journal of Ancient History* 5 (1980), 1–12.

'Herodotus and the Emergence of Meroe'. *Journal of the Society for the Study of Egyptian Antiquities* 11 (1981), 1–5.

'Axum and the Fall of Meroe'. *Journal of the American Research Center in Egypt* 18 (1981), 47–50.

'Two Inscribed Dedications in the J. Paul Getty Museum'. *Journal of the J. Paul Getty Museum* 9 (1981), 99–100.

'Ancients Help Historians'. *Coin World International* (December 23, 1982), 64.

'Arsinoe II: A Revisionist View'. In E. Borza and W.L. Adams (eds.), *Philip II, Alexander the Great and the Macedonian Heritage* (Washington, DC 1982), 197–212.

'The Tomb of Philip II and the Succession of Alexander the Great'. *Classical Views* 26 (1982), 141–63 (reprinted in J. Roisman [ed.], *Alexander the Great: Ancient and Modern Perspectives* [Lexington, MA 1995], 40–49).

'The Axumite Inscription from Meroe and Late Meroitic Chronology'. *Meroitica* 7 (1984), 220–21.

PUBLICATIONS   XIII

'Lysimachus the Gazophylax: A Modern Scholarly Myth?'. In W. Heckel and R. Sullivan (eds.), *Ancient Coins of the Graeco-Roman World* (Waterloo, Ont. 1984), 57–68.
'Callisthenes and Babylonian Astronomy: A Note on *FGrH* 124 T3'. *Classical Views* 28 (1984), 71–74.
'A New *Tabula Iliaca* in the J. Paul Getty Museum: The Vasek Polak Chronicle'. *Journal of the J. Paul Getty Museum* 12 (1984), 153–62.
'Psamtek I and the End of Nubian Domination in Egypt'. *Journal of the Society for the Study of Egyptian Antiquities* 14 (1985), 31–34.
'The Ethiopian War of Ptolemy V: An Historical Myth?'. *Beiträge zur Sudanforschung* 1 (1986), 17–23.
'Lysimachus and the Cities: The Early Years'. *The Ancient World* 14 (1986), 19–24.
'Lysimachus and the Cities: A Problem in Interpretation'. In *Ancient Macedonia IV: Papers read at the Fourth International Symposium* (Thessalonica 1986), 133–38.
'Cornelius Gallus and Aethiopia'. *The Ancient History Bulletin* 2 (1988), 16–20.
'Greek History: Bibliography'. In *Books for College Libraries*, 3rd ed. (Chicago 1988), 121–27.
'Greek Class Structures and Relations'. In M. Grant and R. Kitzinger (eds.), *Civilizations of the Ancient Mediterranean*, vol. 1 (New York 1988), 529–47.
'The Greek Tradition from Alexander to the End of Antiquity'. In C.G. Thomas (ed.), *Paths from Ancient Greece* (Leiden 1988), 28–50.
'Berossus'. *Encyclopedia Iranica*, vol. 4.2 (London 1989), 165–66.
'Kush and the External World: A Comment'. *Meroitica* 10 (1989), 226–30.
'*SEG* 33.802 and the Alexander Romance'. *Zeitschrift für Papyrologie und Epigraphik* 77 (1989), 275–76.
'Hellenistic Culture: Recent Resources: 1960–1989'. *Choice* 27 (1990), 1634–43.
'Pharaoh Alexander: A Scholarly Myth?', *Ancient Society* 22 (1991), 139–45.
Introduction to: *The Origins of Greek Civilization: From the Bronze Age to the Polis ca. 2500–600 B.C.* (Los Angeles 1991).
Introduction to: *The Golden Age of Greece: Imperial Democracy 500–400 B.C.: A Unit of Study for Grades 6–12* (Los Angeles 1991).
'Hecataeus of Abdera's History of Egypt'. In J.H. Johnson (ed.), *Life in a Multi-Cultural Society: Egypt from Cambyses to Constantine* (Chicago 1992), 45–49.
'An Elephant for Anastasius'. *Ancient History Bulletin* 6 (1992), 55–57.
'Egypt and Kush'. In *Lessons from History: Essential Understandings and Historical Perspectives Students Should Acquire* (Los Angeles 1992), 202–07.
'Arms Control in Antiquity'. In R.D. Burns (ed.), *Encyclopedia of Arms Control*, vol. 2 (New York 1993), 551–61.
'The Origins of the Athenian Privileges at Bosporus: a Reconsideration'. *Ancient History Bulletin* 7 (1993), 81–83.
'The Hellenistic Fringe: The Case of Meroe'. In P. Green (ed.), *Hellenistic History and Culture* (Berkeley 1993), 38–54.
'Introducing Kush: A Mini-Guide to an Ancient African Kingdom'. *Social Studies Review* 33.1 (1993), 22–30.
'Sayce's Axumite Inscription from Meroe: Observations on a New Edition'. *Meroitic Newsletter* 25 (September 1994), 39–43.
'The Challenge of *Black Athena*: An Interim Assessment'. *Ancient History Bulletin* 8 (1994), 11–17.

'Greece, Rome, and the American Republic'. *Laetaberis: The Journal of the California Classical Association* n.s. 10 (1993–94), 1–24 (reprinted with revisions in *The History Teacher* 30 [1996], 29–44 as 'The Classics and the American Republic').

'Alexander in Egypt: Continuity or Change?'. In H. Sancisi-Weerdenburg *et al.* (eds.), *Achaemenid History 8: Continuity and Change* (Leiden 1994), 381–87.

'Truesdell Sparhawk Brown'. *In Memoriam* (Academic Senate, University of California, 1993) 7–8. Reprinted with revisions in *The Biographical Dictionary of North American Classicists* (Westport, CT 1994), 66–68.

'Athena–Svart eller Kvit?'. In O. Andersen and T. Hägg (eds.), *I Skyggen av Akropolis* (Bergen 1994), 225–44.

'Egypt and the Fabrication of European Identity: Commentary'. In I.A. Bierman (ed.), *Egypt and the Fabrication of European Identity* (Los Angeles 1995), 87–95.

'Greek Contact with Egypt and the Levant, ca. 1600–500 BC. An Overview'. *The Ancient World* 27 (1996), 20–28.

'Ivory and Ptolemaic Exploration of the Red Sea: The Missing Factor'. *Topoi* 6 (1996), 799–807.

'Meroë'. *Calliope* (November/December 1996), 13–16.

'The Debate over Black Athena'. *Scholia* 5 (1996), 3–16.

'Images of Egypt in Greek Historiography'. In A. Lopreino (ed.), *Ancient Egyptian Literature: History and Forms* (Leiden 1996), 591–604.

The Hellenistic Period in World History (Essays on Global and Comparative History, American Historical Association, Washington, DC, 1996). Reprinted with revisions in M. Adas (ed.), *Agricultural and Pastoral Societies in Ancient and Classical History* (Philadelphia 2001), 275–307.

'Egypt and Greece: Afrocentrism and Greek History'. In *Were the Achievements of the Ancient Greeks Borrowed from Africa?* (Society for the Preservation of the Greek Heritage, 1997), 21–33.

'The Hellenistic Age'. In C.G. Thomas (ed.), *Ancient History: Recent Work and New Directions* (Claremont, CA 1997), 37–54.

'Paccius Maximus: A Greek Poet in Nubia or a Nubian Greek Poet'. In *Actes de la VIIIe Conférence internationale des études nubiennes: Lille, 11–17 septembre 1994* (Lille 1998), 47–52.

'The Roman Withdrawal from Nubia: A New Interpretation'. *Symbolae Osloenses* 73 (1998), 125–32.

'Afrocentrism and the Greeks: A Contested History'. *The History Teacher* 31 (1998), 403–04.

'World Civilization: Eurasia to 500 CE'. In S. Adams, M. Adas and K. Reilly (eds.), *World History: Selected Course Outlines and Reading Lists from American Colleges and Universities* (Princeton 1998), 149–51.

'The New AP World History Course: How Will it Compare with College World History Courses?'. *The History Teacher* 32 (1999), 283–88.

'The New California History–Social Science Standards in World History: How do They Measure Up?'. *Social Studies Review* 38.2 (1999), 18–19.

'Word-Order Transference between Latin and Greek: The Relative Position of the Accusative Direct Object and the Governing Verb in Cassius Dio and Other Greek and Roman Prose Authors'. *Harvard Studies in Classical Philology* 99 (1999), 357–90 (member of coauthor team).

PUBLICATIONS   XV

'Roman Egypt'. In K.A. Bard (ed.), *Encyclopedia of the Archaeology of Ancient Egypt* (London/New York 1999), 73–77.

'*IG* 1³ 61 and the Black Sea Grain Trade'. In R. Mellor and L.A. Tritle (eds.), *Text and Tradition: Studies in Greek History and Historiography in Honor of Mortimer Chambers* (Claremont, CA 1999), 93–104.

'Cleitarchus in Jerusalem: A Note on the *Book of Judith*'. In F.B. Tichener and R.F. Morton (eds.), *The Eye Expanded: Life and the Arts in Greco-Roman Antiquity* (Berkeley 1999), 105–12.

'The Origins of the Napatan State in Classical Sources'. In S. Wenig (ed.), *Studien zum antiken Sudan* (Wiesbaden 1999), 118–26.

'The Legacy of Alexander'. *Encarta Reference Suite 2000* (electronic).

'Ptolemaic Exploration and Hellenistic Ethnography'. *The Ancient World* 31 (2000), 31–37.

'A Soldier and His God in Lower Nubia: The Mandulis Hymns of Paccius Maximus'. *Graeco-Arabica* 7–8 (1999–2000), 45–50.

'A New Kushite Historiography: Three Recent Contributions to Nubian Studies'. *Symbolae Osloenses* 75 (2000), 190–97.

'Map: 81: Triakontaschoinos'. In *The Barrington Atlas of the Greek and Roman World* (Princeton 2000).

'Prelude to Alexander: The Reign of Khababash'. *The Ancient History Bulletin* 14 (2000), 149–54.

'The Kingdom of Meroe'. In E.M. Yamauchi (ed.), *Africa and Africans in Antiquity* (Lansing, MI 2001), 132–58.

'Le relazioni dei Greci con Kush e Aksum'. In *I Greci 3* (Turin 2001), 471–98.

'A Contested History: Egypt, Greece, and Afrocentrism'. In C.G. Thomas (ed.), *Current Issues and the Study of Ancient History* (Claremont, CA 2002), 9–30.

'Current Trends in Ancient History in American Schools'. *The Occasional Papers of the American Philological Association's Committee on Ancient History* 1 (2002), 1–12 (electronic).

'State Formation in Ancient Northeast Africa and the Indian Ocean Trade'. *Interactions: Regional Studies, Global Processes, and Historical Analysis*, February 28 through March 3, 2001, Library of Congress, Washington DC (electronic).

'Aithiopia: The Southern Periphery of the Graeco-Roman World'. *Ancient West and East* 1.1 (2002), 55–58.

'The Date of Amage, Queen of the Sarmatians: A Note on Polyaenus, *Strategemata* 8. 56'. *Ancient West and East* 1.1 (2002), 173–77.

'Kush, Axum and the Ancient Indian Ocean Trade'. In T.A. Bacs (ed.), *A Tribute to Excellence. Studies Offered in Honor of Erno Gaál, Ulrich Luft, Lázló Török* (Budapest 2002), 127–37.

'Greek Identity in the Hellenistic Age'. In L.A. Tritle and W. Heckel (eds.), *Crossroads of Empire* (Claremont, CA 2003), 217–42 (reprinted in K. Zacheria [ed.], *Hellenisms: Culture, Identity, and Ethnicity from Antiquity to Modernity* [Aldershot 2008], 59–78).

'Three Milestones in the Historiography of Ancient Nubia: Review Article'. *Symbolae Osloenses* 78 (2003), 137–41.

'History in the Age of Standards'. *Social Studies Review* 43 (2004), 5–7.

'From Blameless Ethiopians to Faithless Blemmyes: Nonracial Stereotypes in Greek and Roman Accounts of Kush'. In C. Fleur-Lobban and K. Rhodes (eds.), *Race and Identity in the Nile Valley: Ancient and Modern Perspectives* (Trenton, NJ 2004), 71–85.

XVI PUBLICATIONS

'Rome and Kush: A New Interpretation'. In T. Kendall (ed.), *Nubian Studies 1998* (Boston 2004), 13–23.

'Richard Brett (1567–1637)'. In *The Dictionary of British Classicists* (Bristol 2004), 104–05.

'The Greek Cities of the Black Sea'. In K. Kinzl (ed.), *A Companion to the Classical Greek World* (Oxford 2006), 137–52.

'When Greek was an African Language' (the *Frank M. Snowden, Jr. Lectures, Howard University*) http://chs.harvard.edu/publications.sec/online_print_books.ssp/frank_m._snowden_jr. (Center for Hellenic Studies, Washington, DC. August 2006).

'Silko's Bad Conscience: A New Interpretation of the Silko Inscription (*FHN* 317)'. In I. Caneva and A. Roccati (eds.), *Acta Nubica: Proceedings of the X International Conference of Nubian Studies* (Rome 2006), 447–50.

Cambridge Dictionary of Classical Civilization (Cambridge 2006): Agatharchides of Cnidus, Berossus, Lysimachus, Manetho.

'Ancient History and the Challenge of World History'. *Syllecta Classsica* 18 (2007), 225–40.

Introduction to W. Heckel and P. Wheatley (eds.), *Alexander's Empire: From Formulation to Decay* (Claremont, CA 2007), xi–xv.

'The Gardener became King or Did He?: the Case of Abdalonymus of Sidon'. In W. Heckel and P. Wheatley (eds.), *Alexander's Empire: From Formulation to Decay* (Claremont, CA 2007), 139–49.

'When Greek was an African Language: The Role of Greek Culture in Ancient and Medieval Culture'. *Journal of World History* 19 (2008), 41–61 [revised version of the Snowden lecture].

'Trogodytes=Blemmyes=Beja?: The Misuse of Ancient Ethnography'. In H. Barnard and W. Wendrich (eds.), *The Archaeology of Mobility: Old World and New World Nomadism* (Los Angeles 2008), 250–63.

The Encyclopedia of Ancient Natural Science: The Greek Tradition and its Many Heirs (London/New York 2008): Agatharchides of Cnidus, Berossus.

'Elephants for Ptolemy II: Ptolemaic Policy in Nubia in the Third Century BC.' In P.R. McKechnie and P. Guillaume (eds.), *Ptolemy II Philadelphus and his World* (Leiden 2008), 135–46.

'Alexander's Organization of Egypt: A Note on the Career of Cleomenes of Naucratis'. In T. Howe and J. Reames (eds.), *Macedonian Legacies: Papers on Macedonian Culture and History in Honor of Eugene N. Borza* (Claremont, CA 2009), 183–94.

The Oxford Encyclopedia of Ancient Greece and Rome (Oxford 2009): Africans in Antiquity, Ethiopia.

'The Origin of the Utopian Alphabet: A Suggestion'. *Notes and Queries* 56 (2009), 26–27.

'Another Nubian Prince in Constantinople: New Light on the Last Days of Meroë'. *Beiträge zur Sudanforschung* 10 (2009), 5–8.

'Hecataeus of Miletus and the Greek Encounter with Egypt'. *Ancient West and East* 8 (2009), 133–46.

'New Light on the Fate of Greek in Ancient Central and South Asia'. *Ancient West and East* 9 (2010), 181–92.

'Changing Greek Views of Achaemenid Persia in the Classical Period'. *Nam-ye Iran-e Bastan: The International Journal of Ancient Iranian Studies* 10 (2010–11), 3–14.

PUBLICATIONS

Berkshire Encyclopedia of World History (Great Barrington, MA 2011): Aksum (reprinted in *Africa in World History*), Alexander the Great, Herodotus, Macedonian Empire, Meroë (reprinted in: *Africa in World History*).

'Whence the Women? The Origin of the Bactrian Greeks'. *Ancient West and East* 11 (2012), 97–104.

'Agatharchides of Cnidus, *On the Erythrean Sea* F 20: A Note on the History of Cavalry in Kush'. *Beiträge zur Sudanforschung* 11 (2012), 15–19.

'An Egyptian Source of Tacitus' Sarapis Narrative (*Histories* 4.84)'. *Zeitschrift für Papyrologie und Epigraphik* 183 (2012), 37–38.

Dictionary of African Biography (Oxford 2012): Agatharchides of Cnidus, Alexander the Great, Cleomenes of Naucratis, Khababash, Manetho, Paccius Maximus, Chaeremon.

'Go-Betweens and the Greek Cities of the Black Sea'. *World History Connected* 10.3 (October 2013) (electronic).

'A Peltast Among Hoplites: Ernst Badian and Athenian History'. In *The Legacy of Ernst Badian* (Association of Ancient Historians, 2013), 33–49.

'The Satrap Stela and the Struggle for Lower Nubia'. In J.R. Anderson and D.A. Welsby (eds.), *The Fourth Cataract and Beyond* (Leuven 2014), 573–76.

Foreword to S.Y. Auyang, *The Dragon and the Eagle: The Rise and Fall of the Chinese and Roman Empires* (Armonk, NY 2014), xi–xiii.

'States, Empires and Connections: Africa, ca. 1200 BCE–ca. 900 CE'. In C. Benjamin (ed.), *Cambridge History of the World Vol. 4* (Cambridge 2015), 631–61.

'Alexander's Unintended Legacy: Borders'. In T. Howe *et al.* (eds.), *Greece, Macedon and Persia: Studies in Social, Political and Military History in Honour of Waldemar Heckel* (Oxford/Philadelphia 2015), 118–26.

'Ptolemy III and the Dream of Reuniting Alexander's Empire'. *The Ancient History Bulletin* 31 (2016), 77–86 (electronic).

'Chersonesus between Greece and Scythia'. *World History Connected* 14.1 (February 2017) (electronic).

'*P. Michigan 281* and the Roman Occupation of Qasr Ibrim'. *Proceedings of the Fifth Day for Nubian Studies* (Rome 2017), 61–68.

'Ctesias' Sources: A Suggestion'. *Dabir* 5 (2018), 17–20.

'A 2,000-year-old view of old age'. *Nature* 430 (23 August 2018), 430 (with C. Finch).

'Werner Jaeger Comes to Chicago'. *International Journal of the Classical Tradition* 26 (2019), 319–32.

'"A Friend in Foreign Lands": The Friendship of Alfonso Reyes and Werner Jaeger'. In R. Cantú (ed.), *A Scholiast's Quill: New Critical Essays on Alfonso Reyes* (Newcastle-upon-Tyne 2019), 32–42.

'The War Elephant: East and West'. *World History Connected* 17.2 (June, 2020) (electronic).

'"The Essence of Classical Culture": Werner Jaeger's First Public Address in the United States'. *History of Classical Scholarship* 2 (2020), 115–30.

Lexicon of Argead Macedonia (Berlin 2020): Egypt.

'The Subject of *P. Oxy.* 4458: A Suggestion'. *Zeitschrift für Papyrologie und Epigraphik* 216 (2020), 53–54.

'Plato on Kings and Priests in Egypt'. *Göttinger Miszellen* 262 (2020), 9–12.

'The Phonen Letter: A Reconsideration'. *Beiträge zur Sudanforschung* 13 (2021), 39–45.

XVIII PUBLICATIONS

'Egypt and the Kingdom of Kush'. *Ancient Egypt* 124 (March/April 2021), 28–35.
'The African Encounter with Greece: The Case of Kush'. *Acta Classica* 64 (2021), 48–71.
'Greek and Roman Views of Nubia'. In G. Emberling and B. Williams (eds.), *The Oxford Handbook of Ancient Nubia* (Oxford 2021), 697–712.
'The Black Sea: An Achaemenid Frontier Zone'. In T. Daryaee and R. Rollinger (eds.), *Iran and its Histories: From Earliest Times through the Achaemenid Empire* (Wiesbaden 2021), 369–78.
'A View from the Fringe: Heraclea Pontica in the Age of Alexander'. In J. Boardman, J. Hargrave, A. Avram and A. Podossinov (eds.), *Connecting the Ancient West and East. Studies Presented to Prof. Gocha R. Tsetskhladze* (Leuven 2022), 185–93.
'Lead Poisoning in Ancient Rome: The State of the Question'. *Journal of Ancient Civilizations* 37 (2022), 225–46 (with C. Finch).
'Syriskos of Chersonesus: A New Interpretation of *IOSPE* 1^2.344'. *Ancient West and East* 21 (2022), 273–78.
'Alexander and Arabia: The Voyage of Anaxikrates'. *Ancient West and East* 22 (2023).
'The Seleucid Conquest of Koile Syria and the Incense Trade'. *Proceedings of the Payravi Conference on Seleucid History* (forthcoming).
'Agatharchides'. In G.J. Shipley (ed.), *Geographers of the Ancient Greek World: Selected Texts in Translation* (Cambridge) (forthcoming).
'Ptolemy III'. In *Oxford Classical Dictionary* (Oxford) (forthcoming).

Miscellaneous

D.S. Wiesen, 'Cicero's Image in America and the Discovery of *De Republica*', ed. by S.M. Burstein, *History of Classical Scholarship* 2 (2020), 150–79.
Brill's New Jacoby (Leiden 2006–): *FGrH* 86, 622–625, 642, 652–657, 662, 666–673 (electronic).

PREFACE

This book has had a long gestation. Planning for it began over two decades ago in a conversation with Gocha Tsetskhladze during a visit by him to Los Angeles. The initial contract was signed in 2004, and permissions for reprinting my first book, *Outpost of Hellenism: The Emergence of Heraclea on the Black Sea*, and later related articles were quickly obtained, but then progress ground to a halt. The main problem was technological. Early scanners were inefficient, so the scans of my book and articles were difficult to use, abounding in errors, sometimes dozens per page. As a result, the volume regretfully was put aside, while I concentrated on other projects, until Gocha encouraged me to take it up again a few years ago. The delay, as it turned out, has been beneficial. Scanners have improved greatly, scholarship has progressed, and I have been able to include additional articles, so that this is a better book than it would have been had it been published 20 years ago.

Compiling a volume like this one is an interesting and revealing experience, permitting, as it does, a retrospective look over a person's whole career, a career in my case spanning half a century. My involvement with the history of the Greeks in the Black Sea was accidental, the result of my failure to successfully complete a PhD thesis on a different topic. My thesis advisor suggested as a substitute the history of Heraclea Pontica.

Every work of scholarship is a product of its own time. Since I completed my thesis in 1972, my approach in it and my subsequent studies during my subsequent career reflected the scholarship of that time, focusing on issues I encountered in the works of scholars such as M.I. Rostovtzeff, D M. Pippidi, and A.J. Graham to name only a few. As the title of my thesis – *A Political History of Heraclea Pontica to 281 BC* – indicates, that focus concerned the history of Greek *poleis* founded in a frontier zone of the greater Greek world, their relations with each other and the Greek homeland, and contact with their non-Greek neighbors from the late Archaic Period to the Hellenistic Period. It is a huge topic, but my hope is that the studies dealing with the ancient Greek experience in the Black Sea collected in this volume contribute to a better understanding of a chapter of one of the most remarkable stories in world history, a story whose plot is well summed up in the title of an excellent recent book: *The Greeks: A Global History*.[1]

---

[1] R.M. Beaton, *The Greeks: A Global History* (New York 2021).

XX   PREFACE

Over the course of a half-century-long career, I have accumulated a multitude of debts to scholars, who have kindly answered my questions and generously sent me copies of their publications, far too many to acknowledge here. Four, however, do stand out and need to be acknowledged. First and foremost, is my thesis advisor, Dr T.S. Brown, Professor of History at the University of California, Los Angeles, who suggested to me that Heraclea Pontica was worth studying and without whose continuous supervision and advice, I would not have been able to complete my project. Second, is the great Romanian scholar D.M. Pippidi, who kindly spent an afternoon discussing Greek settlement in the Dobruja with me in his office in Bucharest and who arranged for me to tour the sites of the principal Greek cities of the region barely a month after the crisis of the great earthquake of spring, 1977. Third and finally are the two scholars without whom this volume could not have been completed, Gocha Tsetskhladze, who first suggested it and has encouraged and guided it at every stage of its development, and James Hargrave who generously undertook the formidable task of standardizing the format of my book and articles and reviewing and correcting the scans of them.

ABBREVIATIONS AND CONVENTIONS

AJPh *American Journal of Philology.*

APIH S. Mekler, *Academicorum philosophorum index Herculanensis* (Berlin 1902; repr. 1958).

ATL B.D. Meritt, H.T. Wade-Gery and M.F. McGregor, *The Athenian Tribute Lists*, 4 vols. (Cambridge/Princeton 1939–53).

AWE *Ancient West and East.*

BCH *Bulletin de correspondance hellénique.*

BCO *Bibliotheca Classica Orientalis.*

BNJ *Brill's New Jacoby.*

CAH *The Cambridge Ancient History.*

CIA A. Kirchhoff (ed.), *Corpus Inscriptionum Atticarum*, 4 vols. (Berlin 1873–97).

CIRB V.V. Struve *et al.* (eds.), *Corpus Inscriptionum Regni Bosporani* (Moscow 1965).

FGrH F. Jacoby, *Die Fragmente der griechischen Historiker*, 3 vols. in 15 (Leiden 1926–58).

FHG C. Mueller (ed.), *Fragmenta Historicorum Graecorum*, 5 vols. (Paris 1841–70).

GGM C. Mueller (ed.), *Geographi Graeci Minores*, 2 vols. (Paris 1855–61; repr. Hildesheim 1965).

GHI M.N. Tod (ed.), *A Selection of Greek Historical Inscriptions*, 2nd ed., 2 vols. (Oxford 1946–48).

IG *Inscriptiones Graecae.*

IGB G. Mihailov, *Inscriptiones Graecae in Bulgaria repertae*, 5 vols. (Sofia 1956–97); I² (Sofia 1970).

IGRRP R. Cagnat, J. Toutain, P. Jouguet and G. Lafaye (eds.), *Inscriptiones Graecae ad res Romanas pertinentes*, 3 vols. (Paris 1901–27; repr. 1964).

IOSPE V.V. [Basilius] Latyschev (ed.), *Inscriptiones Antiquae Orae Septentrionalis Ponti Euxini Graecae et Latinae*, 3 vols. (St Petersburg 1885–1901; I²: Petrograd 1916; repr. Hildesheim 1965).

JHS *Journal of Hellenic Studies.*

LSJ H.G. Liddell, R. Scott and H.S. Jones, *A Greek-English Lexicon*, 9th ed. (Oxford 1940).

NC *Numismatic Chronicle.*

OGIS W. Dittenberger (ed.), *Orientis Graeci Inscriptiones Selectae*, 2 vols. (Leipzig 1903; 1905).

RE A. Pauly and G. Wissowa, *Realencyclopädie der klassischen Altertums-wissenschaft.*

Recueil W.H. Waddington, E. Babelon and T. Reinach (eds.), *Recueil général des monnaies grecques d'Asie Mineure*, 1 vol. in 3 (Paris 1904–10).

SEG *Supplementum Epigraphicum Graecum.*

SGDI H.O. Collitz, F. Bechtel *et al.* (eds.), *Sammlung der griechischen Dialekt-Inschriften*, 4 vols. (Göttingen 1884–1915).

XXII ABBREVIATIONS AND CONVENTIONS

SIG   W. Dittenberger (ed.), *Sylloge Inscriptionum Graecarum*, 3rd ed., 4 vols. (Leipzig 1915–24).
TAPA   *Transactions of the American Philological Association.*
VDI   *Vestnik Drevnei Istorii.*

The spelling of proper names has been standardized (usually on the Romanized forms used in *Outpost of Hellenism*), this applies particularly to the article 'The Greek Cities of the Black Sea' where the volume editor adopted Germanic practices. The text references from that chapter have here been replaced by footnotes. The style(s) of footnotes and bibliographies of all pieces have been standardized according to the editorial norms of *Colloquia Antiqua*, but the footnote numbering in the original pieces has been retained. Likewise, citations of ancient sources, corpora, etc. have been unified and the above combined list of abbreviations compiled. Unless otherwise stated or the context makes clear, dates are BC. American English has been used as the default (though with occasional minor modifications to punctuation) to reflect the author's origins and practice and the language of most of the publications reproduced below.

PERMISSIONS

I would like to express my gratitude to the following publishers and individuals for generously granting permission to reprint the following publications in this book:

Ares Publishers, Inc.
'Heraclea Pontica: The City and Subjects', *The Ancient World* 2 (1979), 25–28.
'Lysimachus and the Cities: The Early Years', *The Ancient World* 14 (1986), 19–24.

Prof. Ernst Badian
'The Aftermath of the Peace of Apamaea: Rome and the Pontic War', *The American Journal of Ancient History* 5 (1980), 1–12.

Blackwell Publishing, Ltd
'The Greek Cities of the Black Sea', in K. Kinzl (ed.), *A Companion to the Classical Greek World* (Oxford 2006), 137–52.

Brill Academic Publishers
'The Date of Amage, Queen of the Sarmatians: A Note on Polyaenus *Strategemata* 8. 56', *Ancient West and East* 1.1 (2002), 173–77.

Coronado Press
'Menander and Politics: The Fragments of the *Halieis*', in S.M. Burstein and L.A. Okin (eds.), *Panhellenica: Essays in Ancient History and Historiography in Honor of Truesdell S. Brown* (Lawrence, Kansas 1980) 69–76. Copyright owned by author.

Dr. Rudolf Habelt
'*IG* II² 1485A and Athenian Relations with Lysimachus', *Zeitschrift für Papyrologie und Epigraphik* 31 (1978), 181–85.

Franz Steiner Verlag
'The War between Heraclea Pontica and Leucon I of Bosporus', *Historia* 23 (1974), 401–16.
'*IG* II² 653, Demosthenes and Athenian Relations with Bosporus in the Fourth Century B.C.', *Historia* 27 (1978), 428–36.

Harrassowitz Verlag
'The Black Sea: An Achaemenid Frontier Zone', in T. Daryaee and R. Rollinger (eds.), *Iran and its Histories: From Earliest Times through the Achaemenid Empire* (Wiesbaden 2021), 369–78.

Prof. Timothy Howe
'The Origins of the Athenian Privileges at Bosporus: a Reconsideration', *Ancient History Bulletin* 7 (1993), 81–83.

Prof. Ronald Mellor and Prof. Lawrence Tritle
'*IG* 1³ 61 and the Black Sea Grain Trade', in R. Mellor and L. Tritle (eds.), *Text and Tradition: Studies in Greek History and Historiography in Honor of Mortimer Chambers* (Regina Press, Claremont 1999), 93–104.

Peeters Publishers
'Syriskos of Chersonesus: A New Interpretation of *IOSPE* 1² 344', *Ancient West and East* 21 (2022), 273–78.

University of California Press
'Sceptre or Thunderbolt: Plutarch, *Moralia* 338B', *California Studies in Classical Antiquity* 7 (1974), 89–92.
Outpost of Hellenism: The Emergence of Heraclea on the Black Sea (University of California Press, Berkeley 1976). Copyright owned by author.

University of Chicago Press
'Fragment 53 of Callisthenes and the Text of *Iliad* 2. 850–55', *Classical Philology* 71 (1976), 339–41.

University of Illinois Press
'Go-Betweens and the Greek Cities of the Black Sea', *World History Connected* 10.3 (October 2013 [electronic]).
'Chersonesus between Greece and Scythia', *World History Connected* 14.1 (February 2017 [electronic]).

INTRODUCTION

Tempus fugit as the cliché holds. It has been half a century since I completed my PhD. thesis in History in early 1972, *A Political History of Heraclea Pontica to 281 B.C.*, at the University of. California, Los Angeles. It was not my first choice of thesis topic, but when insuperable difficulties forced me to change the subject of my thesis, the history of Heraclea Pontica was the subject that my advisor, the Hellenistic historian T.S. Brown, believed would be appropriate for me, and he was right. Four years later in 1976 a revised version of my thesis became my first book under the title *Outpost of Hellenism: The Emergence of Heraclea on the Black Sea*. Since then, my interests and publications have ranged widely over the ancient Greek world, but as the articles collected in this volume make clear, my interest in the experience of the Greeks in the Black Sea has never flagged.

I could not have known that, of course, when I began work on my thesis in 1969. Heraclea Pontica, as it turned out, had both advantages and disadvantages as a thesis subject. On the positive side, it had been almost a century since the publication of the last comprehensive studies of Heraclea, namely, the two brief monographs of H. Schneiderwirth,[1] which surveyed the history of the city from its founding until 200 BC and the 1910 Halle dissertation of H. Apel[2] on the 4th-century BC tyrants of Heraclea. Other than the detailed discussion of Heracleote historiography in Richard Laqueur's 1927 article on 'Lokalchronik' in the thirteenth volume of the *Realencyclopädie*[3] and the two monographs of P. Desideri,[4] scholarship on the historians of Heraclea was virtually non-existent. Moreover, the sources for the history of the city were primarily textual, and those sources were both readily accessible and of high quality. As a result, it was possible to reconstruct the internal history of Heraclea with a level of detail that was unique for a colonial city located outside the Aegean. On the other hand, research by an American graduate student on a Black Sea topic like the history of Heraclea was not easy during the Cold War.

---

[1] Schneiderwirth 1882; 1885.
[2] Apel 1910.
[3] Laqueur 1927.
[4] Desideri 1967; 1970–71.

2 INTRODUCTION

Lack of potentially relevant scholarship on the history of the Greeks in the
region as a whole was not the problem. Scholarship on the Greek cities of the
Black Sea, particularly those of the north coast, was extensive and dated back
to well before the 20th century. Moreover, authoritative summaries of pre-
Soviet-era scholarship were available in the classic works of E.H. Minns[5] and
M.I. Rostovtzeff.[6] Comparable and readily accessible syntheses of Soviet-era
scholarship, however, were lacking. Thus, while the extent of Soviet and east
European scholarship was clear from the invaluable bibliographical guide of
E. Bellin de Ballu[7] and the brief surveys of current excavations published
occasionally in *The Journal of Hellenic Studies*, relevant works were overwhelmingly written in Russian and published in journals and books that didn't
circulate widely in the west. The situation with regard to the cities of the west
coast of the Black Sea including Heraclea's colony of Callatis, modern Mangalia, was less dire thanks to the works of scholars such as the Romanian and
Bulgarian historians D.M. Pippidi[8] and C.M. Danov.[9]

The problems with scholarship concerning the cities of the south coast of the
Black Sea were different but equally serious. The main difficulty was that excavation of potentially relevant sites was minimal because the principal ancient
cities including Heraclea – modern Ereğli – were overbuilt by contemporary
cities.[10] The situation at Heraclea was particularly unfortunate since a Turkish
military base had been built on the site of the ancient acropolis, during the construction of which most of the visible ancient remains were destroyed. As a
result, relevant archaeological evidence was almost non-existent except for accidental finds and scattered architectural remains, which were summarized in the
valuable monograph of W. Hoepfner[11] on the evidence for the city's architec-
ture. Such was the situation when my book was published in 1976. Much has
changed since then, and in the remainder of this introduction I will try to review
the highlights of those developments and how they would affect the views
I expressed in my book and the related articles were I writing them now.

Scholarship, of course, does not stand still, and that cliché holds true for
scholarship concerning the history of the Greeks in the Black Sea in general

---

[5] Minns 1913.

[6] Rostovtzeff 1922; 1931.

[7] Bellin de Ballu 1965.

[8] Pippidi 1962; 1967; 1971.

[9] Danov 1962; 1976.

[10] For a lucid overview of the state of the archaeology of the Greek cities of the south coast
of the Black Sea, see Tsetskhladze 2007, 160–80. An exception is Heraclea's eastern neighbor
Tium, but current excavation at the site of the ancient city has not produced pre-Roman material
(*cf.* Öztürk 2013).

[11] Hoepfner 1966. For subsequent finds see Akkaya 1994.

INTRODUCTION

3

and Heraclea Pontica in particular. The intellectual context in which my book was written unexpectedly disappeared a little over a decade after its publication in 1976 with the end of the Cold War in 1989. The barriers that had hindered interaction between Western and East European and Soviet scholarship ceased to exist with dramatic results. Suddenly co-operation between scholars representing the two scholarly traditions became possible and manifested itself in a flood of publications in new journals, proceedings of conferences, and books synthesizing the results of Soviet and East European scholarship, particularly archaeological scholarship.[12] These developments inevitably were reflected in scholarship concerning the history of Heraclea Pontica that was published after the end of the Cold War.

As was true of other Black Sea cities, the volume of publications concerning Heraclea expanded significantly. A brief but comprehensive guide to this new scholarship was provided by A. Avram, J.G.F. Hind and G.R. Tsetskhladze in the invaluable *An Inventory of Archaic and Classical Poleis*[13] which was compiled under the auspices of the Copenhagen Polis Center. In addition, Heraclea was well served by the publication of three important monographs. Two were general histories of the city that appeared in the decades following the publication of *Outpost of Hellenism* in 1976, namely, S.J. [S.Y.] Saprykin's 1997 study, *Heraclea Pontica and Tauric Chersonesus before Roman Domination (VI–I Centuries B.C.)*[14] and A. Bittner's[15] 1998 monograph *Gesellschaft und Wirtschaft in Herakleia Pontike: Eine Polis zwischen Tyrannis und Selbstverwaltung.* A distinctive feature of both works was that they carried the narrative of Heracleote history from the end of the city's tyranny in 281 BC, where my monograph ended, through the Hellenistic period to the Roman conquest in 70 BC. Their other distinguishing characteristic was that both authors drew on the extensive Soviet and East European scholarship on the classification and distribution of Heracleote amphorae published during the Cold War with the result that they confirmed and added welcome detail to the more general analysis of Heracleote trade in the Black Sea during the 4th and early 3rd centuries BC that I was able to provide in my book on the basis of the evidence available to me in the early 1970s. The third of these new works was A. Robu's[16] magisterial study *Mégare et les établissements mégariens de Sicile, de la Propontide et du Pont-Euxin: Histoire et Institutions*, which was published in 2014 and

---

[12] Several surveys of publications on the Black Sea have bene provided by G. Tsetskhladze in *AWE*.

[13] Hansen and Nielsen 2004, no. 715. See also the survey by Erçiyas 2003.

[14] Saprykin 1997. See also his important article, Saprykin 1991.

[15] Bittner 1998.

[16] Robu 2014.

4 INTRODUCTION

replaced K. Hanell's[17] classic but outdated 1934 monograph *Megarische Studien* and placed study of the Megarian foundations of Heraclea's constitutional structure on a firm foundation.

One thing, unfortunately, has not changed since the end of the Cold War, the lack of significant new sources for the history of Heraclea. So, while archaeological evidence for Heraclea's principal colonies, Callatis[18] in the Dobruja and Chersonesus[19] in the Crimea, has continued to steadily increase, conditions for excavation at Ereğli have continued to be unfavorable. As a result, historically significant new finds relevant to the history of Heraclea have either come from excavations at other locations in the Black Sea or, if they were from Ereğli, they lacked secure archaeological contexts. This situation finally has begun to change with the excavations in the İnönü Cave at the base of the Acherousian Peninsula that are currently being conducted by Dr H. Ekmen and his team under the auspices of Bülent Ecevit University.[20] Only preliminary reports on the excavations carried out in 2017 and 2018 have been published, but they already have made clear that occupation near Heraclea began as early as the 5th millennium BC.

The situation is similar with regard to new epigraphic evidence. So, while we now have a well edited corpus of Heracleote inscriptions known as of 1994 in Lloyd Jones's[21] *The Inscriptions of Heraclea Pontica*, the number of inscriptions contained in the corpus remains small and only one is pre-Roman in date.[22] Significant pieces of new epigraphic evidence have been discovered, but they are the result of discoveries made at other Pontic cities, most notably at Sinop, ancient Sinope, and Phanagoria.

The situation is more complicated, however, with regard to the textual evidence for the history of Heraclea. When I was writing and revising my thesis in the early 1970s, the principal primary sources for the history of the city were the fragments of the local historians of Heraclea collected and edited by Felix Jacoby in the third volume of *Die Fragmente der Griechischen Historiker*, and scholarship on these texts was limited to Jacoby's brief commentary, an unpublished doctoral dissertation completed in 1963 by M. Janke,[23] and the already mentioned articles of Laqueur and Desideri. In one sense, nothing has changed, since no new fragments of the Heracleote historians have been discovered since

---

[17] Hanell 1934.
[18] Hansen and Nielsen, Nr. 686. See also the survey by Avram 2007.
[19] Hansen and Nielsen, Nr. 695. For a good introduction to the site see *Crimean Chersonesos* 2003.
[20] Ekmen *et al.* 2020; 2021; Yalçin *et al.* 2021.
[21] Jonnes 1994. *I. Heraclea* 70 is a Hellenistic boundary marker for a sanctuary.
[22] Öztürk and Sonmez 2009; 2011; Öztürk 2016.
[23] Manfred Janke 1963.

INTRODUCTION 5

Jacoby published his edition in 1964. However, while the corpus of the fragments of the Heracleote historians has remained the same, new editions have been published online in *Brill's New Jacoby* with excellent English translations and detailed historical commentaries by S. Blakely, M. Cuypers, R. Billows, A. Keaveny, and J.A. Madden,[24] and these new editions have made the fragments of Heracleote historiography more accessible to students and scholars than was the case in the 1970s. Relevant scholarship has also increased. Important studies by C. Higbie[25] and R. Thomas[26] have expanded understanding of the nature of local historiography and its place in the development of Greek historiography. Important studies by Desideri,[27] W. Ameling,[28] and W.G. Thalmann[29] have clarified the role of mythography in the development of Heracleote historiography in the 4th century BC and cleared away long entrenched speculative analyses of the role of the history of Domitius Kallistratos as the source of the Roman sections of Memnon's history of Heraclea, while L.M. Yarrow[30] explicated the late Roman Republican context of Memnon's history in her fine monograph, *End of the Republic: Provincial Perspectives on Roman Rule.*

Not surprisingly, the impact of these developments on my book were I writing it today would be significant but uneven. The most far-reaching changes would be in my account of the pre-Greek inhabitants of the Heracleotis, the Mariandynoi. According to Strabo (12. 3. 4), nothing was known about the identity or origin of the Mariandynoi, although he noted that their culture was similar to that of the Bithynians. Presumably, he meant that it was Thracian in character. Drawing on essentially the same evidence as Strabo – myths and the fragments of the Heracleote historians – I was hardly able to improve on his conclusions. From this evidence, I was able to show that Heracleote historians had constructed a prehistory of Heraclea which connected the Mariandynoi with the Argonaut saga and served as a charter myth for the later Greek settlement of Heraclea and their subsequent conquest of the Mariandynoi. Beyond that I could only suggest that the Mariandynoi probably were one of a number of Anatolian peoples inhabiting the area around Heraclea and that by the 4th century BC, when Heracleote historiography began, their culture was

---

[24] Herodorus (*BNJ* 31) was edited by Blakely; Promathidas (*BNJ* 430), Amphitheus (*BNJ* 431), and Timogenes of Miletus (*BNJ* 435) were all edited by Cuypers; Nymphis (*BNJ* 433) was edited by Billows; and Memnon (*BNJ* 434) was edited by Keaveny and Madden.

[25] Higbie 2003.

[26] Thomas 2019.

[27] Desideri 1991.

[28] Ameling 1995.

[29] Thalmann 2011.

[30] Yarrow 2006.

6   INTRODUCTION

similar to that of the Bithynians, that is, it was essentially Thracian in character as Strabo had already suggested two thousand years ago.

Although they have barely begun, the excavations in the Inönü Cave have changed this picture dramatically, establishing that peoples relying on a mixed agricultural and pastoral economy had occupied the Heracleotis continuously from as early as the 5th millennium BC. Equally important, pottery and metal finds dating to the Late Bronze and Early Iron Ages have close parallels with material from Troy, Gordion, and Hattusas in Anatolia and Thrace in the Balkans, suggesting, therefore, that the pre-Greek inhabitants of the Heracleotis had connections with peoples throughout northwest and central Anatolia and the Balkans. Beyond these tentative conclusions, it is not possible to go at present. Certainly, proposed identifications with specific peoples mentioned in Hittite texts such as the Kaska have to be considered as possible but still speculative, but the new evidence suggests that conditions in the area of Heraclea before Greek settlement were far more complex than the sources available to me half a century ago allowed.

New evidence also would permit me to add welcome detail to my account of the early history of Heraclea,[31] particularly with regard to its relations with the Persian Empire. While I was able to show in my book that both Heraclea and the Mariandynoi recognized the suzerainty of Persia, the available evidence only permitted a general account of the implications of that fact. Three new discoveries have altered that situation: a marble head found near Heraclea, a fragment of an Old Persian inscription discovered at Phanagoria on the Taman Peninsula, and an inscription found during the construction of a building at Sinop.[32] The discovery of an Old Persian inscription on the north coast of the Black Sea memorializing the construction of some sort of building during the reign of the Persian king Darius I was totally unexpected, and its implications were dramatic since it left no doubt that, at a minimum, for an undetermined period of time during the late 6th and early 5th century BC Persian authority extended throughout the Black Sea.[33]

How Heraclea reacted to that fact is illuminated by the already mentioned sculpted marble head. Published by the Turkish archaeologist Ekrem Akurgal[34] in

---

[31] Recent attempts to rehabilitate Strabo's (12. 3. 4) identification of Miletus as the founder of Heraclea (Saprykin 1997, 23–27; Vinogradov 2007) are unconvincing. It should be noted that by qualifying his references to Miletus as the founder of Heraclea and responsible for subduing the Mariandynoi with 'they say (*phasi*)' and 'it is said (*eiretai*)' Strabo indicated that he did not take responsibility for this account. Similarly unconvincing is the proposed removal of the Boeotians as co-founders of Heraclea by N. Erhardt (1996).

[32] *I. Sinope* 1, published in French 2004, 1–4.

[33] On this inscription and its implications see Tsetskhladze 2019; and Burstein 2021.

[34] Akurgal 1986. The fullest analysis of this sculpture and its significance is Summerer 2005. For possible numismatic evidence concerning Heraclea and the Persians, see Fischer-Bossert 2020.

INTRODUCTION 7

the mid-1980s, the head was from a life size statue and represented a bearded man wearing a diadem over a pointed cap that left the face open but covered both ears and the back of the head to the neck. Stylistically it can be dated to the last decades of the 6th century BC, probably *ca.* 520 BC to 510 BC while the iconography indicates that the subject of the statue was a high Persian official, very likely a satrap with connections to Heraclea. Commissioning and setting up such a statue in the city indicates, moreover, that the government of Heraclea did not just officially recognize Persian overlordship but publicly celebrated it. But that is not the end of the implications of this remarkable sculpture for the history of Heraclea.

Stylistic analysis suggests that the statue was the product of an Aegean workshop, possibly Ionian or mainland Greek, and that implies that the city had both the connections and wealth to commission such a statue and that its urban development had progressed far enough to properly display it. The implications of Heraclea's subjection to Persia were difficult to explain, however, in the absence of evidence of satrapal authority in the Black Sea, although Memnon (*BNJ* 434 F 4.1) referred to restraint exercised on the actions of cities such as Heraclea by the Great King. It is this puzzle that the new inscription from Sinop, which dates to the mid-4th century BC, would have allowed me to explain since it revealed that cities such as Heraclea had great freedom in the use of their military forces except in cases of disputes with Persian agents and their forces, which had to be referred to the Great King for decision, who functioned, therefore, as the chief arbiter of disputes in the region with the right to intervene in its affairs at will.

Unfortunately, the progress of scholarship does not always bring with it increased clarity. That is the case with regard to our understanding of two of the most important events in the early history of Heraclea: the foundation of its two principal colonies, Callatis, modern Mangalia, in the Dobruja and Chersonesus in the south-western Crimea at the northern terminus of the shortest sailing route between the northern and southern coasts of the Black Sea. As already mentioned, unlike their metropolis, the archaeological and epigraphic evidence for Callatis and Chersonesus is rich, steadily increasing, and accessible. This is particularly true of the inscriptions which have been collected in excellent corpora, those of Callatis in the third volume of *Inscriptions de Scythie Mineure* superbly edited by A. Avram[35] and those of Chersonesus in the first volume of V.V. Latyschev's[36] old but still indispensable *Inscriptiones antiquae orae septentrionalis Ponti Euxini Graecae et Latinae (IOSPE)*.

---

[35] Avram 1999.
[36] Latyschev 1916. A new edition is being prepared by Dr Igor Makarov.

8 INTRODUCTION

The picture that emerges from this evidence is clear and consistent. By the second half of the 4th century BC Callatis and Chersonesus were fully developed *poleis*. They had well-established urban centers supported by the agricultural produce of extensive *chorae*[37] in which the primary source of labor probably was dependent native populations[38] as was also the case at Heraclea.[39] Their institutions and cults also revealed numerous similarities with those of Megarian colonies ultimately derived from Megara, and they both used Doric for public purposes, all of which was to be expected in colonies founded by Heraclea. What is surprising, therefore, is that a principal theme of scholarship published after the appearance of *Outpost of Hellenism* in 1976 has been questioning the role of Heraclea in the foundation of Callatis and Chersonesus as presented in my book.

At issue are seeming conflicts between archaeological evidence for the date and character of the earliest Greek settlements at Callatis and Chersonesus. The problem first became apparent in scholarship concerning the foundation of Callatis. The principal source for the foundation of Callatis is lines 761–764 (= F 4 Marcotte) of the *Periodos Ges* of Ps.-Scymnus: 'Callatis, a colony of the Heracleotes, founded in accordance with an oracle. They founded it, when Amyntas assumed rule of the Macedonians.'

In my book I followed the existing consensus of scholarship and assumed that Ps.-Scymnus' source, the late 3rd-century BC historian Demetrius of Callatis, meant Amyntas I (*ca.* 540 BC to *ca.* 495 BC) and dated, therefore, the foundation of Callatis to the 'third quarter of the 6th century BC'. Already in the 1970s some Romanian scholars had begun to question this view.[40] The problem was twofold. The earliest reference to the existence of Callatis was in the mid-4th-century BC *Periplus* of Ps.-Scylax and archaeology had produced no finds that could be dated earlier than the beginning of the 4th century BC. As a result, it was suggested that the Macedonian king Amyntas mentioned by Ps.-Scymnus should be identified with Amyntas III (393 BC to 370 BC) instead of Amyntas I and that the foundation of Callatis should be re-dated to the early 4th century BC.

To date no consensus has emerged about whether Ps.-Scymnus' reference was to Amyntas I or Amyntas III,[41] but in the meantime a new complication has appeared. While most sources identify Heraclea as the metropolis of Callatis, the 1st-century AD geographer Pomponius Mela (*De Chorographia* 2. 22) assigned

---

[37] Callatis: Avram 1991; 2001, 612–32. Chersonesus: Saprykin 1994; Nikolaenko 2003.
[38] For dependent labor in the Black Sea as a whole, see Pippidi 1962, 60–74.
[39] The fullest recent discussion of the dependent status of the Mariandynoi is Avram 1984.
[40] Ulanici 1974.
[41] The principal defender of a 6th-century BC date is Avram (1996, 292–93; 1999, 9–11).

INTRODUCTION

it to Miletus. Mela's evidence has been routinely dismissed as a simple error, but new evidence has raised the possibility of another and more positive explanation. Excavations in the southern portion of Callatis' *chora* near Cape Shabla has produced Late Archaic Ionian pottery, particularly Chian amphorae. Although these findings are preliminary, they raise the possibility of the existence of a Late Archaic settlement near Callatis that could have been founded during the reign of Amyntas I as I suggested, but which might have been Milesian instead of Heracleote.[42]

A similar controversy has arisen also concerning the date and character of the foundation of Chersonesus. The sole literary evidence for the foundation of Chersonesus is Ps.-Scymnus' statement (lines 827–828 = F 12 Marcotte) that in the territory of the Taurians 'there was a Greek *polis*, which the Heracleotes and Delians settled'. In *Outpost of Hellenism* I followed what was then the accepted view concerning the date of the foundation of Chersonesus, placing it specifically in the year 422/1 BC, when Delians were in exile as a result of the purification of Delos by Athens. Although as early as 1922 Rostovtzeff[43] had posited the existence of an Ionian emporium at Chersonesus as early as the late 6th century BC on the basis of a small number of Ionic pottery sherds discovered there, his position found no supporters for most of the 20th century as the archaeology seemed to support a date in the 420s BC since, other than the few Ionic sherds just mentioned, the earliest finds from the site dated to the late 5th and early 4th centuries BC. This consensus, however, was upended in 1990 with the publication of an important article jointly written by J.G. Vinogradov and M. Zolotarev.[44] On the basis on new finds of Ionic pottery in the northeast sector of Chersonesus dated to the late 6th and early 5th centuries BC and ostraca written in the Ionian alphabet but containing primarily Dorian names, Vinogradov and Zolotarev revived Rostovtzeff's theory but in a modified form, arguing that the late 5th-century BC colony of Chersonesus was preceded by a small but fully fledged *polis* at the same location that was founded jointly by Heraclea and Sinope in the late 6th century BC.

Thorough and convincing critiques of Vinogradov's and Zolotarev's thesis have since been provided independently by Saprykin[45] and J.G.F. Hind.[46] At the same time, however, Hind[47] also introduced a new complication in the

[42] Bîrzescu and Ionescu 2016.
[43] Rostovtzeff 1922, 63.
[44] Vinogradov and Zolotarev 1990.
[45] Saprykin 1997, 54–71.
[46] Hind 1998, 141–43.
[47] Hind 1998, 144–46.

10 INTRODUCTION

argument by suggesting that Ps.-Scymnus mistakenly confused Delos and Delion in Boeotia, a dependency of Tanagra which was one of the original participants in the settlement of Heraclea, in identifying Delos as her partner in the colonization of Chersonesus, a suggestion which, if correct, would mean that Chersonesus could have been founded any time between *ca.* 424 BC and the mid-370s BC. At present, no new consensus has emerged concerning the history of Chersonesus before the 4th century BC, when its existence is securely attested, although the finds of Late Archaic Ionic pottery at the site makes it likely that some sort of still undetermined interaction between Ionians and local populations such as the Tauri occurred in the late 6th and early 5th centuries BC, and that is where the controversy stands at present.

The situation is different with regard to the history of Heraclea in the 4th and 3rd centuries BC. The evidence available to me in the 1970s was limited to the same literary sources that as those that had been used by my predecessors. As a result, while scholarship has added detail to the narrative of Heracleote history, it has by and large not changed the narrative as a whole. So, for example, the background to the seizure of power by Clearchus has been clarified by the identification of the Persian named Mithridates with whom he served before becoming tyrant with an ancestor of Mithridates Ctistes of Pontus and ruler of a substantial kingdom that included Mysia and the hinterland of the Heracleotis.[48] Similarly understanding of Heraclea's economic history has been clarified by improvements in our knowledge of the chronology and distribution in the Black Sea of Heracleote amphorae and roof tiles,[49] but the basic narrative remains unchanged. There is one exception, however, the already mentioned new inscription from Sinop now published as *I. Sinope* 1, which is the most important addition to our sources for the history of Heraclea discovered in the 20th and 21st centuries. As this important text is still too little known, I have appended a translation of it below:[50]

> (line 1) On these (terms) the Sinopeans and Satyros and the sons of Klearchos made an oath and alliance:
> That if anyone attacks Satyros or the son of Heraklia or its territory, except the King, the Sinopeans are to help with all their strength according to their ability and if anyone attacks Sinope or its territory, except the King, Satyros and the (line 5) sons of Klearchos are to help with all their strength according to their ability;
> And if the one who is attacking Satyros or the sons of Klearkhos or Heraklia or its (line 10) territory or Sinope or its territory says that he is attacking with the

[48] Bosworth and Wheatley 1998.
[49] See in particular Kac 2003; Monakhov and Kuznetsova 2017.
[50] Translated by Burstein 2021, 373–74.

INTRODUCTION

King, (the parties to the treaty) are to send, jointly with the attacker, envoys to the King and to request him (the attacker) to leave the territory;
And if the attacker does not choose to send envoys and to leave the territory, (the parties) are to help one another with all their strength according to their
(line 15) ability; that the pay of the soldiers is to be 2½ staters a month; and those who are giving help are to provide in advance one month's pay;
And repayment of the expenses is (to come) from the party requesting help within 6 months after peace has been made;
That as many as have fled Sinope or Heraklia, to them it is permitted to remain in (line 20) the cities if they do no wrong;
And if they in any way seem to do wrong from the [time] when the treaty has come into being, the (parties) are to send envoys and to banish them, provided that it is decided by the Sinopeans and Satyros and the sons of Klearkhos to banish them;
That the people of Kromna and Sesamos are (included) in the treaty, if they wish;
(line 25) That each party is to [maintain] the alliance, if on the one hand [anyone attacks] within twenty days from the days when those in charge call for help;
If on the other hand anyone of those [in the cities] works to overthrow the people of Sinope or [to divide them], or conspires against Satyros or the sons of Klearkhos, (the parties) [are to help one another]
(line 30) With all their strength according to their ability within ten days of the day when those in charge call for help; ...[51]

Even a cursory examination of this remarkable inscription reveals the importance of the evidence it provides for a wide range of issues in the history of the Greek cities of the Black Sea in the 4th century BC. Its implications for understanding how Persian power was exercised in the region have already been mentioned. Its most important contribution, however, is the light it throws on Heraclea during the six-year reign of Clearchus' brother Satyrus from 352 BC to 346 BC. Memnon's account of the tyranny of Satyrus is little more than a stereotypical picture of a typically brutal tyrant who died an appropriately gruesome death. Other than admitting that the worst of Satyrus' violence was limited to the beginning of his reign and that he was devoted to assuring the succession of Clearchus' sons Timotheus and Dionysius, his reign was essentially a blank when I wrote my book. *I. Sinope* 1 has changed that situation, allowing no doubt that the impression created by Memnon that nothing of importance occurred during Satyrus' reign is seriously misleading. Quite the contrary, it leaves no doubt that significant changes in Heracleote affairs that strengthened the tyranny were already in place during his reign including the

---

[51] The final three lines (lines 31–33) seem to deal with the procedure for mobilizing troops and amending the treaty, but they are too fragmentary for certain translation. French (2004, 4) suggests: That [the call-up] is to be made by both parties from [the ages from] 20 to [39], and it is permitted (for it) to be amended in whatever way [is decided by the Sinopeans and Satyros and] the sons of Klearkhos...

12 INTRODUCTION

suppression of the last vestiges of the Heracleote democracy, reorganization of the method of organizing the military, establishment of good relations with other cities in the region, and, most important, neutralization of the threat to the regime posed by the oligarchs exiled by Clearchus and living in other Pontic cities.

Re-reading work written during a career that has spanned half a century is a strange and even disconcerting experience. This is particularly true with regard to *Outpost of Hellenism*, the book with which my career began. As I said at the beginning of this introduction, the beginning of my involvement with the history of Heraclea Pontica in particular and that of the Greeks in the Black Sea in general was somewhat accidental, and were I writing that book today, there is no doubt that it would be different in many ways. Still, it is reassuring how little I would have to change after 50 years. There would be differences, of course, but, as the above review of scholarship since the 1970s indicates, those differences would be in every case the result of the discovery of new evidence that was not available to me 50 years ago. The situation with regard to the other papers collected in this volume is different. Unlike *Outpost of Hellenism*, they are based on close readings of texts – literary and epigraphic – and in the absence of new evidence their validity has to rest on the judgment of readers concerning the quality of my analyses.

Bibliography

Akkaya, T. 1994: *Herakleia Pontike (Karadeniz Erğlisi)'nin Tarihî Gelişimi ve Eski Eserleri* (Istanbul).

Akurgal, E. 1986: 'Neue archaische Skulpturen aus Anatolien'. In Kyrieleis, H. (ed.), *Archaische und klassische griechische Plastik* (Akten des internationalen Kolloquiums vom 22.–25. April 1985 im Athen) (Mainz), 1–14.

Ameling, W. 1995: 'Domitius Kallistratos, *FGrHist* 433'. *Hermes* 94, 373–76.

Apel, H. 1910: *Das Tyrannis von Heraklea* (Dissertation, Halle).

Avram, A. 1984: 'Bemerkungen zu den Mariandynern von Herakleia am Pontos'. *Studii Clasice* 22, 19–28.

—. 1991: 'Untersuchungen zur Geschichte des Territoriums von Kallatis in Griechischer Zeit'. *Dacia* n.s. 35, 103–37.

—. 1996: 'Les cités grecques de la côte Ouest du Pont-Euxin'. In Hansen, M.H. (ed.), *Introduction to an Inventory of Poleis* (Acts of the Copenhagen Polis Centre 3; Historisk-filosofiske meddelelser 74) (Copenhagen), 288–316.

—. (ed.) 1999: *Inscriptions de Scythie Mineure III: Callatis et son Territoire* (Bucharest).

—. 2001: 'Les Territoires d'Istros et de Callatis'. In *Problemi della 'Chora' Coloniale dall'Occidente al Mar Nero* (Atti del quarantesimo convegno di studi sulla Magna Grecia Taranto 29 settembre–3 ottobre 2000) (Taranto), 593–632.

—. 2007: 'Kallatis'. In Grammenos, D.V. and Petropoulos, E.K. (eds.), *Ancient Greek Cities of the Black Sea 2* (BAR International Series 1675) (Oxford), 239–86.

INTRODUCTION 13

Bellin de Ballu, E. 1965: *L'histoire des colonies grecques du littoral nord de la Mer Noire* (Leiden).

Bîrzescu, I. and Ionescu, M. 2016: 'Recherches sur la fondation de Callatis: l'apport de la documentation archéologique'. In Robu, A. and Bîrzescu, I. (eds.), *Mégarika: Nouvelles recherches sur Mégare, les cités de la Propontide et du Pont-Euxin* (Actes du colloque de Mangalai, 8–12 juillet 2012) (De l'archéologie à l'histoire 66) (Paris), 381–91.

Bittner, A. 1998: *Gesellschaft und Wirtschaft in Herakleia Pontike: Eine Polis zwischen Tyrannis und Selbstverwaltung* (Asia Minor Studien 30) (Bonn).

Bosworth, A.B. and Wheatley, P.V. 1998: 'The origins of the Pontic house'. *JHS* 118, 155–64.

Burstein, S.M. 2021: 'The Black Sea: An Achaemenid Frontier Zone'. In Daryaee, T. and Rollinger, R. (eds.), *Iran and Its Histories: From the Beginnings through the Achaemenid Empire* (Classica et Orientalia 29) (Wiesbaden), 369–78.

Crimean Chersonesos 2003: *Crimean Chersonesos: City, Chora, Museum, and Environs* (Austin).

Danov, C.M./K.M. 1962: 'Pontos Euxinos'. *RE* Suppl. 9, 865–1176.

—. 1976: *Altthrakien* (Berlin).

Desideri, P. 1967: 'Studi di storiographia eracleota, I: Promathidas e Nymphis'. *Studi classice et Orientali* 16, 366–416.

—. 1970–71: 'Studi di storiographia eracleota, II: La guerra con Antioco il Grande'. *Studi classice et Orientali* 19–20, 487–537.

—. 1991: 'Cultura Eracleota: Da Erodoro a Eraclide Pontico'. In Rémy, B. (ed.), *Pontica I: Recherches sur l'histoire du Pont dans l'Antiquité* (Istanbul), 7–24.

Ekmen, H., Gülden Ekmen, F. and Güney, A. 2020: 'Inönü Cave: New Results of the Early Iron Age Culture in the Western Black Sea Region'. *Olba* 28, 35–56.

—. 2021: 'A New Prehistoric Settlement near Heraclea Pontica on the Western Black Sea Coast, Inönü Cave'. *Arkeoloji Dergisi* 26.1 (April), 23–46.

Erçiyas, D.B. 2003: 'Heracleia Pontica – Amastris'. In Grammenos, D.V. and Petropoulos, E.K. (eds.), *Ancient Greek Cities of the Black Sea* (Thessaloniki), 1403–31.

Erhardt, N. 1996. 'Ilias B 508 und die Gründer von Heraclea Pontica'. *Hermes* 12, 101–03.

Fischer-Bossert W. 2020. 'Die Elektronhekten mit dem Herakleskopf', *Numismatische Zeitschrift* 26, 15–164.

French, D.H. (ed.). 2004: *The Inscriptions of Sinope, Part I: Inscriptions* (Inschriften Griechischer Städte Kleinasiens 64) (Bonn).

Hanell, K. 1934: *Megarische Studien* (Lund).

Hansen, M.H. and Nielsen, T.H. (eds.) 2004: *An Inventory of Archaic and Classical Poleis* (Oxford).

Higbie, C. 2003: *The Lindian Chronicle and the Greek Creation of their Past* (Oxford).

Hind, J.G.F. 1998: 'Megarian Colonisation of the Western Half of the Black Sea (Sister- and Daughter-Cities of Herakleia)'. In Tsetskhladze, G.R. (ed.), *The Greek Colonisation of the Black Sea Area* (Historia Einzelschriften 121) (Wiesbaden), 131–52.

Hoepfner, W. 1966: *Herakleia Pontike – Ereğli: Eine Baugeschichliche Untersuchung* (Forschungen an der Nordküste Kleinasiens 2.1) (Vienna).

Janke, M. 1963: *Historische Untersuchungen zu Memnon von Herakleia: Kap. 18–40, FGrHist Nr. 434* (Dissertation, Würzburg).

14 INTRODUCTION

Jonnes, L. 1994: *The Inscriptions of Heraclea Pontica* (Inschriften Griechischer Städte Kleinasiens 47) (Bonn).

Kac, V.A. 2003: 'A New Chronology for the Ceramic Stamps of Herakleia Pontike'. In Bilde, P.G., Højte, J.M.H. and Stolba, V.F. (eds.), *The Cauldron of Ariantas: Studies Presented to A.N. Ščeglov on the Occasion of his 70th Birthday* (Black Sea Studies 1) (Aarhus), 261–78.

Laqueur, R. 1927: 'Lokalchronik'. *RE* 13, 1083–1110.

Latyschev, V.V. 1916: *Inscriptiones antiquae orae septentrionalis Ponti Euxini Graecae et Latinae*, vol. 1, 2nd edition (Petrograd).

Minns, E.H. 1913: *Scythians and Greeks: A Survey of Ancient History and Archaeology on the North Coast of the Euxine from the Euxine to the Caucasus* (Cambridge).

Monakhov, S.I. and Kuznetsova, E.V. 2017: 'Overseas Trade of the Black Sea Region from the Archaic to the Hellenistic Period'. In Kozlovskaya, V. (ed.), *The Northern Black Sea in Antiquity: Networks, Connectivity, and Cultural Interactions* (Cambridge), 59–99.

Nikolaenko, G.M. 2003: 'The Chersonesean Chora in Light of the New Investigations in the Herakleian Peninsula (1991–2003)'. In Bilde, P.G., Højte, J.M.H. and Stolba, V. F. (eds.), *The Cauldron of Ariantas: Studies Presented to A.N. Ščeglov on the Occasion of his 70th Birthday* (Black Sea Studies 1) (Aarhus), 131–44.

Öztürk, B. 2013: 'The History of Tieion/Tios [Eastern Bithynia] in the Light of Inscriptions'. In Manoledakis, M. (ed.), *Exploring the Hospitable Sea* (Proceedings of the International Workshop on the Black Sea in Antiquity held in Thessaloniki, 21–23 September 2012) (BAR International Series 2013) (Oxford), 147–64.

—. 2016: 'New Inscriptions from the Karadeniz Ereğli Museum III (Herakleia Pontike and Tieion/Tios)'. *Tyche* 31, 227–34.

Öztürk, B. and Sonmez, I.F. 2009: 'New Inscriptions from the Karadeniz Ereğli Museum I'. *Arkeoloji ve Sanat Dergusi* 132, 129–38.

—. 2011: 'New Inscriptions from the Karadeniz Ereğli Museum II'. *Arkeoloji ve Sanat Dergusi* 137, 155–66.

Pippidi, D.M. 1962: *Epigraphische Beiträge zur Geschichte Histrias in Hellenistischer und Römischer Zeit* (Deutsche Akademie der Wissenschaften zu Berlin. Sektion für Altertumswissenschaft. Schriften 34) (Berlin).

—. 1967: *Contibutii la Istoria Veche a Români* (Bucharest).

—. 1971: *I Greci nel Basso Danubio: dall'età arcaica alla conquista romana* (Biblioteca storica dell'antichità 8) (Milan).

Robu, A. 2014: *Mégare et les établissements mégariens de Sicile, de la Propontide et du Pont-Euxin: Histoire et Institutions* (Berne etc.).

Rostovtzeff, M.I. 1922: *Iranians and Greeks in South Russia* (Oxford).

—. [Rostowzew] 1931: *Skythien und der Bosporus I: Kritische Übersicht der schriftlichen und archäologischen Quellen* (Berlin).

Saprykin, S.J. [S.Y.] 1991: 'Héraclée du Pont et Chersonésos Taurique: Institutions publiques et rapports fonciers'. *Dialogues d'Histoire Ancienne* 17, 103–17.

—. 1994: *Ancient Farms and Land-plots on the Khora of Khersonesos Taurike (Research in the Herakleian Peninsula, 1974–1990)* (Antiquitates Proponticae, Circumponticae et Caucasicae 1; McGill University Monographs in Classical Archaeology and History 16) (Amsterdam).

—. 1997: *Heraclea Pontica and Tauric Chersonesus before Roman Domination (VI–I Centuries B.C.)* (Amsterdam).

INTRODUCTION 15

Schneiderwirth, H. 1882: *Heraclea am Pontus* (Heiligenstadt).
—. 1885: *Das Pontische Heraklea* (Heiligenstadt).
Summerer, L. 2005: 'Achämeniden am Schwarzen Meer: Bemerkungen zum spät-archaischen Marmorkopf aus Herakleia Pontike'. *Ancient Near Eastern Studies* 42, 231–52.
Thalmann, W.G. 2011: *Apollonius of Rhodes and the Spaces of Hellenism* (Oxford).
Thomas, R. 2019: *Polis Histories, Collective Memories and the Greek World* (Cambridge).
Tsetskhladze, G.R. 2007: 'Greeks and Locals in the Southern Black Sea Littoral: A Re-Examination'. In Herman, G. and Shatzman, I. (eds.), *Greeks between East and West: Essays in Greek Literature and History in Memory of David Asheri* (Jerusalem), 160–95.
—. 2019: 'An Achaemenid Inscription from Phanagoria: Extending the Boundaries of Empire'. *AWE* 18, 113–51.
Ulanici, A. 1974. 'Cu Privire la Data Intemeirii Orasului Callatis'. *Muzeul National* 1, 191–95.
Vinogradov, J.G. [Y.G.] 2007: 'Milet und Megara erschliessen den Pontos Euxeinos'. In Cobet, J., von Graeve, V., Niemeier, W.-D. and Zimmermann, K. (eds.), *Frühes Ionien: eine Bestandsaufnahme* (Panionion-Symposion Güzelçamli, 26. September–1. Oktober 1999) (Milesische Forschungen 5) (Mainz), 465–73.
Vinogradov, J. [Y.G.] and Zolotarev, M. 1990: 'La Chersonèse de la fin de l'Archaïsme'. In Lordkipanidzé, O. and Lévêque, P. (eds.), *Le Pont-Euxin vu par les Grecs: Sources écrites et archéologie* (Symposium de Vani [Colchide], septembre–octobre 1987) (Annales littéraires de l'Université de Besançon 427) (Paris), 85–119.
Yalçin, Ü., Gülden Ekman, F. and Ekman, H. 2021: 'Chalcolithic Gold Beads from Inönü Cave, Zonguldak'. *Anatolica* 47, 277–98.
Yarrow, L.M. 2006: *End of the Republic: Provincial Perspectives on Roman Rule* (Oxford).

PART I

OUTPOST OF HELLENISM:
THE EMERGENCE OF HERACLEA
ON THE BLACK SEA*

* First published by the University of California Press (Berkeley/Los Angeles/London 1976) as University of California Publications: Classical Studies Volume 14 (Approved for publication 18 October 1974). ISBN 0-520-09530-8; Library of Congress Catalog Card No. 74-620189.

To
MY WIFE
Who suffered through it thrice

PREFACE

Few of the hundreds of ancient Greek cities were of more than local significance. Heraclea Pontica was one of those few. From the time of her foundation about 560 (unless otherwise noted, all dates in this study are to be understood as BC) until the Roman conquest of the city in 70 ended her history as an independent state, Heraclea played a leading role in the political affairs of northern Anatolia and the Black Sea basin. Moreover, from her foundation until her capture by the Ottoman Sultan Murad I in AD 1360, a period of almost 1800 years, Heraclea was an important outpost of Hellenism on the Black Sea. Throughout her long history, Heraclea, virtually alone of the Pontic cities, produced a series of intellectuals who made notable contributions to the development of Greek thought, men such as the philosophers Heracleides Ponticus and Chamaeleon and the mathematicians Bryson and Amyclas.

Despite her ancient fame and importance, Heraclea has received little attention from modern scholars. No general study of the city has appeared since the 1880s when H. Schneiderwirth sketched her history to 70 in two brief monographs, *Heraclea am Pontus* and *Das pontische Heraklea*. These works were hardly more than chronicles based on an uncritical use of the ancient literary evidence, however, and were devoid of any attempt to view the history of Heraclea against the broader background of that of northern Anatolia and the Pontus. There has long been a need for a new study of the city's past, and the present is opportune for such a reconsideration. The publication of the third volume of Felix Jacoby's great collection of the fragments of the Greek historians has provided us for the first time with a reliable picture of Heraclea's own historical tradition, and the survey work of F.K. Dörner and W. Hoepfner has resulted in an accurate description of the remains of the ancient city now rapidly disappearing because of the industrialization of modern Ereğli. The present monograph deals with the political history of the period covered by Schneiderwirth in *Heraclea am Pontus*, namely, the three centuries from the city's foundation to her emergence at the end of the wars of Alexander's successors in 281 as the most powerful of the Greek cities of the south coast of the Pontus. Little is known of the histories of most of the Greek cities of the Black Sea. In the case of Heraclea, however, the sources enable us to reconstruct in considerable detail the story of the city's internal development and her relations with her various Greek and non-Greek neighbors during these centuries and to thus gain a unique insight into the problems faced by cities founded in a frontier area such as the Pontus.

22   PART I: BOOK

Two matters must be dealt with. First, a question of form, the spelling of Greek names. Although there has been a tendency for scholars to employ exact transcriptions of Greek names, such as Platon, Herodotos, Thoukydides, and so on, I have never found this practice congenial. Accordingly, I use the Latinized forms, throughout this study.

Second, acknowledgment must be made of my debts to those persons without whose assistance this monograph could not have been completed. First and foremost of these is Prof. T.S. Brown, who provided guidance and advice during all stages of the preparation of the dissertation on which it is based. A special vote of thanks must also be extended to Prof. Spyros Vryonis, Jr, of the Department of History at UCLA and Miss Sharon Breit, who are responsible for the translations of the Turkish and most of the Russian material cited below. Beyond these I should like to express my gratitude to those scholars who so kindly answered my questions concerning their work: Dr Nezih Fıratlı of the Arkeoloji Müzeleri at Istanbul, Dr Wolfram Hoepfner of the Deutsches archäologisches Institut at Athens, Dr Eberhard Reschke of the University of Erlangen, Dr F.K. Dörner of the University of Münster, Dr Otto Mørkholm of the National Museum at Copenhagen, Mr David Wilson, Dr Margaret Thompson, Chief Curator of the American Numismatic Society, and Dr J.G.F. Hind of the University of Leeds. Finally, I should like to thank Prof. David Asheri of the Hebrew University of Jerusalem for providing me with a copy of his stimulating paper on the early history of Heraclea in time for me to profit from it in the revision of my thesis.

S.M.B.

INTRODUCTION

SOURCES

Except for numismatic evidence[1] the history of Heraclea in the Hellenic and early Hellenistic periods rests almost entirely on literary sources. The archaeological exploration of the south Pontic cities is still in its infancy and no excavations have as yet been undertaken at Heraclea. For the pre-Turkish city, therefore, we are dependent on a number of 19th- and 20th-century travelers' accounts[2] and the surveys of the area produced by Friedrich Dörner and his student Wolfram Hoepfner.[3] The value of this material for the present study, however, is limited, because the continued occupation of the city until the present has effaced all surface remains of pre-Roman Heraclea. Likewise, the few Heracleote inscriptions discovered and published to date are of little use, since virtually all of them are of Roman or Byzantine date.[4]

Fortunately, the literary evidence bearing on the history of Heraclea, although relatively small in quantity, is exceptional, both for its scope and quality. In time, the sources extend over a period of at least nineteen hundred years, from the 7th century BC to the 14th century AD and include representatives of almost every genre of classical literature from epic to lexicography. Since the Black Sea formed throughout antiquity a distinct political and economic region, whose affairs impinged on those of the Aegean only intermittently, many of these texts contain little more than mentions of Heraclea, or references to those few aspects of its history that attracted general Greek interest: oddities of provincial Greek culture,[5] its writers,[6] the 4th-century tyranny, or the helot-like status of the Mariandynoi under Heracleote rule.[7] Alone of the

---

[1] For Heraclea's coinage, see *Recueil* I.2, 343–83; Wroth 1889, 139–48; and Six 1885, 51–65.

[2] I have consulted the following travelers' accounts: Jaubert 1821, 408–13; Bore 1840 I, 208–17; Ainsworth 1842 I, 25–45; Hommaire 1854 II, 324–29; Perrot, Guillaume, and Delbet 1872 II, 15–19; v. Diest 1889, 79–81; and Robert 1937, 245–59.

[3] Dörner 1962; 1963; Dörner and Hoepfner 1962; Hoepfner 1966; and Asheri *et al.* 1972.

[4] In the absence of an *IG* volume for Anatolia the inscriptions of Heraclea have to be traced through various journals and monographs, of which the most important are: Hirschfeld 1888, 881–85; Pargoire 1898; Kalinka 1933, 96–102; and Robert 1937, 245–59.

[5] Plutarch *Quaestiones conviviales* 1. 3,619B. Wehrli 1967–69 IX, F3 (2nd ed.).

[6] Strabo 12. 3. 1. *Cf.* the work of Timogenes (?) of Miletus on Heraclea and its writers (*FGrH* 3B, 435, and Jacoby's comments in *FGrH* 3B *Texte*, 283).

[7] *Cf.* Rostovtzeff 1941, 591–92.

24   PART 1: BOOK

Pontic cities, however, Heraclea produced a distinguished series of local historians – the names of five are known, Promathidas, Amphitheus, Nymphis, Domitius Callistratus, and Memnon – whose works covered the history of the city and its environs from its mythical beginnings until at least the second half of the 1st century.[8] Although now lost in their original form, the works of these writers nevertheless form the basis of our knowledge of Heracleote history because of their use by a number of still-surviving authors, of whom the most important are Apollonius Rhodius and his scholiasts, Justin, the epitomizer of the *Philippica* of Trogus Pompeius, and Photius, the brilliant 9th-century AD scholar and Patriarch of Constantinople. In the case of Heraclea, therefore, we are in the almost unique position of being able to view its history, so to speak, from within. At the same time, of course, allowance must be made for the distortion caused by the patriotic and political biases of these historians, which are readily apparent in the sources.

The founder of the historiographic tradition, however, was not a historian but a late 5th-century sophist and mythographer, Herodorus, who compiled an important monograph on Heracles and possibly others on the Argonauts and the Pelopids.[9] Although, as Felix Jacoby pointed out,[10] his main interest was to use the myths as vehicles to propound his scientific and ethical theories, Herodorus incidentally also produced the first literary account of the pre-Greek history of Heraclea. Because the site of Heraclea had previously been of little importance in Greek mythical tradition, Herodorus was able to create a prominent place for it in the Heracles and Argonaut sagas only by introducing modifications in the generally accepted versions of these legends. The fragments reveal, however, that in making the necessary changes Herodorus was not arbitrary. Rather, he altered the myths so that they agreed with local Heracleote tradition, which had already identified various landmarks near the city – a cave, some tumuli – with such incidents of these sagas as the capture of Cerberus by Heracles[11] and the deaths of the Argo's seer Idmon and its pilot Tiphys.[12]

---

[8] The fragments of Memnon end during the '40s (*FGrH* 3B, 434 F40. 4). On Heracleote historiography, see Jacoby *FGrH* 3B *Texte*, 254–56; and Desideri 1967; 1970–71.

[9] Herodorus *FGrH* 1A, 31T3–4. For his date and works, see Jacoby *FGrH* 1a, 502.

[10] Jacoby *FGrH* 1a, 502.

[11] Herodorus *FGrH* 1A, F31. The cave was pointed out to the Ten Thousand in 400 (Xenophon *Anabasis* 6. 2. 2); for an ancient description of it, see Quintus of Smyrna *Posthomerica* 6, lines 470–490. Its recent exploration by Wolfram Hoepfner (1966, 40–46) has revealed no evidence of pre-Greek use; as Erwin Rohde suggested (1881, 556, n. 1), the cave was probably the site of the oracle of the dead mentioned by Plutarch (*Cimon* 6. 4–6; *De sera numinis vindicta* 10. 555C).

[12] *FGrH* 1A, 31 F31, 51, 54. The supposed tombs of Idmon and Tiphys were presumably Mariandynian tumuli. In a letter of January 5, 1971 Prof. Nezih Fıratlı of the Istanbul Archaeological Museum informed me that there is a large unexcavated tumulus near Heraclea. To localize Idmon's death at Heraclea, Herodorus had to modify the Argonaut tradition which portrayed him

INTRODUCTION 25

Promathidas[13] and Amphitheus,[14] the two earliest Heracleote historians, are little more than names. The surviving fragments, six of Promathidas and one of Amphitheus, which all concern the pre-Greek period, are too few to permit a reconstruction of their works, although they suggest that while preserving the main outlines of Herodorus' version of Heracleote prehistory they added further detail and elaboration to it.[15]

Unlike his predecessors, the third of the Heracleote historians, Nymphis, who wrote during the second half of the 3rd century, is a comparatively well-known figure. Scion of one of the city's great houses, Nymphis was a statesman as well as a scholar. An exile himself, he was responsible for the return to Heraclea in 281 of the descendants of the families exiled by the tyrant Clearchus and his successors. Thereafter he continued to play an important role in political affairs until about the middle of the 3rd century, when he probably retired only to continue advocating his political views in his two histories.[16] Of these, the huge history of Alexander, the Diadochi, and the Epigoni, in 24 books, has almost completely disappeared.[17] Numerous fragments, however, remain of the second, a history of Heraclea in 13 books down to the reign of Ptolemy III, which quickly became the standard work on the city's past and was used extensively by Apollonius Rhodius[18] and Memnon[19] so that it is, in fact, the ultimate source for much of the knowledge of Heraclea's history.

Nymphis' fragments and the work of Memnon reveal clearly that the work was a true history and not a chronicle. The annalistic organization favored by the atthidographers, in which events were entered under the appropriate archon year, was eschewed by Nymphis, who instead preferred to group events into large,

---

as alive in Colchis (Eumelus *FGrH* 3B, 451 F3; C. Wendel [ed.], *Scholia in Apollonium Rhodium vetera* [Berlin 1935], 234 *ad* 2. 523–524) and placed his death during the return voyage. Herodorus accomplished this by following the version of the Argonaut legend known to the composer of the *Odyssey* (12, lines 69–70) in which the Argo returned to Greece by way of the Bosporus instead of Ocean.

[13] *FGrH* 3B, 430. On the basis of his use by Apollonius of Rhodes (*FGrH* 3B, 430 T1) Jacoby (*FGrH* 3B *Texte*, 256) dates him to the 4th or first half of the 3rd century.

[14] *FGrH* 3B, 431. Schwartz (1894, 1963) suggested that he should be dated to the Hellenistic period. Jacoby (*FGrH* 3B *Texte*, 258) prefers the 4th century.

[15] Promathidas (*FGrH* 3B, 430 F4–5) identified the place where Orpheus dedicated his lyre as being near Heraclea.

[16] *FGrH* 3B, 432 T14. For discussion, see Jacoby *FGrH* 3B *Texte*, 259; Laqueur 1937, 1608; and Desideri 1967, 395–97.

[17] The only surviving fragment (*FGrH* 3B, 432 F17) concerns the size of turtles in the Red Sea.

[18] *FGrH* 3B, 432 F3 (= Apollonius Rhodius 2, lines 729–735) and F14 (= Apollonius Rhodius 2, lines 786–787). For the extent of Apollonius' debt to Nymphis, see Desideri 1967, 380–87.

[19] *FGrH* 3B, 432 F10 (= Memnon *FGrH* 3B, 434 F4. 7). *Cf.* Jacoby *FGrH* 3B *Texte*, 269–70.

26   PART 1: BOOK

thematically unified blocks that were dated by synchronisms with Greek or Near Eastern history.[20] At the same time, Nymphis constantly sought to place Heracleote history within a broader historical context so that his work became, in effect, a general history of Anatolia and the Pontus, as viewed from the perspective of Heraclea.[21] The conception was excellent, but not its execution, which was marred by the limitations of the sources available to Nymphis and, more importantly, by his own biases. That Nymphis, like most Greek historians, was an original authority only for his own time, and essentially a complier and synthesizer of other people's work for previous periods, is only to be expected, although it is unfortunate that the fragments allow us to say only that he used his predecessors for the mythical period while permitting no similar determination of his sources for the rest of Heraclea's history. The fragments also reveal, however, that Nymphis interpreted his sources in the light of his own political sympathies, modifying, for example, the city's prehistory to bolster Heracleote pretensions in the 3rd century.[22] The situation is most serious with regard to his treatment of the tyranny that ruled the city from 364 to 284. His exile deprived him of access to local informants who were present in Heraclea and supported the tyranny for all but the last phase of its rule. When this was combined with an evident desire on his part to emphasize the benefits won for Heraclea by the compromise settlement he arranged between the exiles and those who had remained in the city during the tyranny, the result was a somewhat superficial and tendentious account of much of this critical 80-year period in Heracleote history which must be used with extreme care.[23]

Little is known about the next Heracleote historian, Domitius Callistratus, who wrote most likely in the 1st century, about 200 years after Nymphis.[24] The nine fragments that survive of his history of Heraclea show that it was at least seven books in length and included an unusually full account of the mythical period,[25] but they are otherwise too scant – seven are brief notes from

[20] See the reconstruction of his work by Jacoby *FGrH* 3B *Texte*, 260. For the use of synchronisms by Nymphis, see Memnon *FGrH* 3B, 434 F1. 4, 2. 5.

[21] Nymphis *FGrH* 3B, 432 F7, 9; Memnon *FGrH* 3B, 434 F4 with Jacoby's note at *FGrH* 3B *Texte*, 273 *ad* F4.

[22] Apollonius Rhodius, following Nymphis (*cf.* Nymphis *FGrH* 3B, 432 F14), lists the boundaries of the territory conquered for the Mariandynoi by Heracles as the Rhebas River and Mt Colone on the west and the Billaeus River on the east. Allowing for confusion on Apollonius' part between the Rhebas River and the district Rhebantia, which included the area from it eastward to the Psilis River (Arrian *FGrH* 2B, 156 F77a; Kämmel 1869, 8), these limits parallel the political situation of Heraclea in the decades after 281 (*cf.* Memnon *FGrH* 3B, 434 F9.4; Desideri 1967, 403).

[23] *Cf.* Memnon *FGrH* 3B, 434 F1. 1, 2. 1, 7. 4.

[24] *FGrH* 3B, 433. For his date, see Jacoby *FGrH* 3B *Texte*, 265. Desideri's redating (1970–71, 495–96) of Callistratus to the 2nd century is arbitrary.

[25] *FGrH* 3B, 433 F1–3, indicates that it covered at least two books.

INTRODUCTION   27

the geographical lexicon of Stephanus of Byzantium – to permit a reconstruction or evaluation of the work. But if Jacoby's suggestions are correct, namely, that it was essentially a continuation of Nymphis and the main source for Memnon after Nymphis broke off, its value for our period can, in any case, only have been slight.[26]

The situation is different with regard to Memnon, the last of the known historians of Heraclea in antiquity. His date is disputed but he probably belongs to the first or, more likely, the 2nd century AD, when Heraclea's growing prosperity and prominence among the cities of northern Anatolia fostered pride in her glorious past and the second sophistic was encouraging interest in local history in general.[27] Oddly, although Memnon himself is only a name, his history of Heraclea, in more than 16 books, is better known than that of any of his predecessors – it is the principal source for the history of the city from the mid-4th to the mid-1st century – because a copy survived until the 9th century AD, when Photius read it and made an epitome of it which now constitutes codex 224 of his *Bibliotheca*.[28] Analysis, however, has shown clearly that the work, despite its length and importance to modern scholars, was only a compilation drawn from a few sources – Nymphis certainly and possibly Callistratus – which he seems simply to have juxtaposed. Memnon's own share seems to have been limited to selection and abridgment without any attempt to remedy the deficiencies of his sources, or even to impose a unified organization on his material.[29] Accordingly, like Diodorus, Memnon is important not for himself, but because he preserves information from earlier, better informed sources. It is, therefore, unfortunate that Photius' own interest in the Roman sections of Memnon resulted in his offering only a brief paraphrase of books 9 to 13, which concern our period, in contrast to his very full excerpts from books 14 to 16, which are almost entirely devoted to Heraclea's role in the Mithridatic wars.[30]

---

[26] Jacoby *FGrH* 3B *Texte*, 266, 270.

[27] Bowie 1970. Another example of this trend at Heraclea is probably the collection of letters ascribed to Chion, the assassin of Clearchus, the city's first tyrant. Ingemar Düring (*Chion of Heraclea: A Novel in Letters* [Acta universitatis gotoburgensis, Göteborgs högskolasarsskrift 7.5] [Gothenburg 1951] 15, 22–25) dates them to the 1st century AD on the basis of linguistic evidence.

[28] Decisive for the length of the work is Photius' statement (*FGrH* 3B, 434 T1) that he had not seen the books after the sixteenth. For Memnon, see Jacoby *FGrH* 3B *Texte*, 267–71; Laqueur 1927; and Janke 1963, 1–8.

[29] Memnon *FGrH* 3B, 434 F18.1, with Jacoby's comment at *FGrH* 3B *Texte*, 268. For the differences in organization between chapters 1 to 17 and 18 to 40 of Memnon, see Janke 1963, 136.

[30] Desideri 1967, 370–72.

28 PART 1: BOOK

Although the general features of the Heracleote tradition on which we depend for our information are clear, special problems are raised by one of the sources, the 45th letter of Nicephorus Gregoras.[31] Written between AD 1330 and 1335 to another Heracleote, Maximus, the abbot of the Chortaitus monastery near Thessalonica, the letter is essentially an elegant compliment built around the theme that Gregoras was glad to be born a man in what was not only the most beautiful country in the world, but also the birthplace of a person as illustrious as Maximus. The bulk of the letter, however, is devoted to the recounting, in rhetorical language, of various episodes of Heracleote history extending from before the foundation of the city to approximately the 8th century AD. As it is with all late texts, the question of Gregoras' sources is critical – but this is precisely the problem. His immediate source was probably his own now lost panegyric on Heraclea, but beyond that little is clear. Gregoras was perhaps the most learned scholar of his day, and there is no way of estimating what material was still available at Heraclea and Constantinople.[32] All that can be said with confidence, therefore, is that since literary sources, which he followed closely, albeit somewhat carelessly, can be identified for many of his statements, the presumption must be that he also used similar sources, either of ancient or Byzantine date, that are now lost and whose quality is unknown for those statements for which he is the only authority.[33] Accordingly, Gregoras' evidence on those matters for which he is the sole source must be treated cautiously, but also with respect.

GEOGRAPHY

Geography provides the key to much of Heraclea's long history.[34] The south coast of the Black Sea is of relatively recent origin, the result of the same upward movement of the northern edge of the Anatolian land block that also created the Pontic mountain chain.[35] Thus, although the coast trends eastward from the Bosporus in a gradually undulating curve for over 700 miles, it

[31] The letter was first published by C.N. Sathas (1880). I cite it according to Guilland 1927, 156–65. For Gregoras, see Guillland 1926.
[32] Gregoras mentions the panegyric in a letter to Demetrius Cabasilas dated by Guilland (1927, 19) to 1325.
[33] For the identifiable literary sources, see Guilland's notes to letter 45. The only certain error in the letter is Gregoras' reference to Craterus being a satrap in 319 (letter 45. 161). On the other hand, patriotic distortion is apparent in his account of Heraclea's relations with the Ten Thousand (letter 45. 159) and Alexander (letter 45. 159).
[34] For geographical conditions in the Pontus and northern Anatolia, see Danov 1962; Wilson 1960; *Turkey* 1942–43; Nowack 1931; and Sölch 1925.
[35] Linton and Moseley 1970, 28–29.

INTRODUCTION   29

presents a smooth and unfriendly face to the mariner. Throughout its length
the Pontic mountains stand near the coast, at many points, indeed, reaching the
sea where they terminate abruptly in sheer cliffs. Beaches and anchorages
exist, which offer no protection against the sudden storms of the Pontus, but
good harbors are few. At Heraclea, however, there is such a harbor. About
135 miles, or, according to Xenophon, one day's sail east of the Bosporus and
two days west of Sinope,[36] the coast abruptly ceases its eastward run and
curves north in a great semicircle that ends in the sharp point of Cape Baba,
the ancient Acherousian Peninsula, thus creating a sheltered bay that attracted
a steadily increasing volume of shipping to Heraclea as the commerce of the
Black Sea grew.

Likewise, by rendering land communications between Heraclea and the surrounding areas difficult, the Pontic mountains determined, to a large extent the
character of the city's relations with her Anatolian hinterland. Thus, movement
eastward toward Paphlagonia was possible only by following a difficult and cir-
cuitous route through the mountains, so that the city was protected from a sudden attack from that direction.[37] The mountains also tended to isolate Heraclea
from events transpiring in the interior of Anatolia because of the difficulty of
north-south communication across them. Contact with the plain of Bolu, the
ancient Salonian Plain, was of course possible via the valley of the Lycus River,[38]
but the route was difficult and subject to flash flooding,[39] as was also the valley
of the Cales River further to the west.[40] To be sure, an easy path to the interior
did exist via the Hypius River valley, but that was 18 miles to the west of Heraclea and could be reached only by crossing the Kizil Tepe Mountains.[41]

---

[36] Strabo 12. 3. 6. For modern descriptions of the harbor, see Lehman-Hartleben 1923, 130–
31; Wilson 1960, 149; and Hoepfner 1966, 22–23. For the distances, see Xenophon *Anabasis* 6.
2. 1; 6. 4. 2. In miles it is 205 to Sinope (*Turkey* 1942–43 I, 41) and 135 to the Bosporus (*Turkey*
1942–43 I, 39).

[37] Wilson 1960, 341–43. For the difficulty in going eastward by land, see v. Diest 1889,
75–76. The Roman road listed in the *Peutinger Table* (K. Miller [ed.], *Die Peutingerische Tafel*
[Stuttgart 1916], 11 *ad* section IX) presumably went inland as v. Diest pointed out.

[38] The existence of the route is mentioned by no ancient source but is probably implied by
Diodorus (20. 109. 6). Ainsworth (1842 I, 42–47) followed it as far as the juncture with the Billaeus. *Cf.* Nowack 1931, 77.

[39] Ainsworth 1842 I, 41, 43. He notes that both its ancient name, the Lycus or Wolf River,
and its modern name, Kilij Irmak or Sword River, probably refer to its sudden rises.

[40] Thucydides 4. 75. 2; Diodorus 12. 72. 4; and Justin 16. 3. 10.

[41] Nowack 1931, 77–78; Wilson 1960, 341. Sölch (1925, 170) notes that the Roman road
from Nicomedia to Heraclea ran through the Hypius Valley. The route westward over the Kizil
Tepe Mountains went inland rather than along the coast (Xenophon *Anabasis* 6. 2. 18; Wilson
1960, 341). At present none of the Pontic rivers are navigable (*Turkey* 1942–43 I, 103–04),
although the Sangarius may have been in antiquity (Arrian *FGrH* 2B, F78a; Anonymous *Periplus Ponti Euxini*, in Diller 1952, 118–38, 8v5).

30 PART 1: BOOK

Combined with the predominantly east to west orientation of communications south of the Pontic ranges, her geographical situation therefore ensured that Heraclea's own political activity would be limited in the main to the coasts of the Pontus and that her relations with the various powers that controlled central and western Anatolia would be comparatively loose and infrequent.[42]

Location thus dictated Heraclea's basic political orientation, but her growth and prosperity depended on the rich natural resources of her site. The moisture-laden winds that blow off the Pontus and strike the Pontic mountains result in an abundant rainfall which is spread throughout the year[43] and is responsible for the thick forests that cloak the mountains surrounding the city; in antiquity they furnished her with abundant timber for her fleet and other uses.[44] Similarly, rain and the fertile soil of the narrow coastal plain near Heraclea – as well as of the valleys of the Lycus, Cales, and, eventually, the Hypius rivers – provided the city with agricultural riches.[45] The sources indicate that the Heracleotes grew barley,[46] grapes,[47] and olives,[48] and that these domesticated plants were supplemented by a number of wild plant products such as nuts,[49] aconite,[50] origanum,[51] and honey,[52] of which the last three were supposedly of medicinal value. The Pontus itself furnished the city with an abundant source of food as well as a valuable export product in its fish, particularly the great schools of tunny that passed by the city during

[42] *Cf.* Werner 1957.

[43] Wilson (1960, 29), gives a figure of 1267 mm or 50.68 inches a year for Zonguldak some 30 miles east of Heraclea.

[44] Strabo 12. 3. 12. *Cf.* Ainsworth 1842 I, 36–37; Hommaire 1854 II, 319; v. Diest 1889, 78; *Turkey* 1942–43 I, 233; Nowack 1931, 77–78; and Wilson 1960, 145. Among the trees mentioned by the travelers are beech, oak, chestnut, pistachio, elm, hornbeam, and conifers of various types.

[45] Apollonius Rhodius 2, line 723. I have not been able to find the proverb *mariandyniorum terra semper virens* credited by M. Allier de Hauteroche (*apud* Jaubert 1821, 412 n.) to Pliny and cited also by Schneiderwirth 1885, 28.

[46] Xenophon *Anabasis* 6. 2. 3.

[47] Quintus of Smyrna *Posthomerica* 6, lines 473–474; Athenaeus 1. 32b; *Geoponica* 5. 2. 10. *Cf.* Xenophon *Anabasis* 6. 2. 3.

[48] Ps.-Aristotle *Oeconomica* 2. 2. 8. 1347b5, may refer to imported olive oil, but the mentions of wild olives in the area (Apollonius Rhodius 2, lines 848–850; *Schol. Ap. Rhod.* 192 *ad* 2. 848–850a) point to cultivation of the domestic olive at Heraclea since the wild variety is only a feral form of the domestic (Wilson 1960, 26, 29; *cf.* Robert 1937, 265, n. 3).

[49] Theophrastus *HP* 3. 15. 1–2; Athenaeus 2. 53b–54c; Macrobius *Saturnalia* 3. 187. 7.

[50] Because of the localization of Heracles' eleventh labor at Heraclea, references to the presence of aconite, which was supposed to have originated from the vomit of Cerberus, are common. See, for example, Theophrastus *HP* 9. 14. 4–5; Strabo 12. 3. 7; Pliny *NH* 27. 4; Herodorus *FGrH* 1A, 31 F21; Theopompus *FGrH* 2B, 115 F181; Arrian *FGrH* 2B, 156 F76a.

[51] Pliny *NH* 20. 170, 177.

[52] Pliny *NH* 21. 74; Dioscorides 2. 103, 138.

INTRODUCTION   31

their annual migration to the Mediterranean from their breeding grounds in the Sea of Azov.[53]

Heraclea also enjoyed substantial mineral resources. To be sure, the great coal fields of the area were not worked in antiquity,[54] but the forests undoubtedly supplied whatever fuel was necessary. Likewise, gold and silver were lacking,[55] but on the other hand the iron deposits of the Kizil Tepe Mountains were apparently being worked.[56] Further, Sandarace, the name of a small anchorage east of Heraclea, suggests that realgar, a red mineral pigment with an arsenic base, was being mined in the vicinity.[57] Finally, although Heraclea had no source of marble, the mountains furnished her with a plentiful supply of building stone,[58] and the existence of Heracleote pottery points to the presence of good quality clay near the city.[59]

THE MARIANDYNOI

A site as excellent as that of Heraclea did not remain unoccupied. Greek colonies were normally founded in already inhabited areas and Heraclea was not an exception to this rule.[60] In Strabo's phrase, Heraclea was established among the Mariandynoi,[61] and Heracleote tradition points to its having been built near a previously existing Mariandynian settlement.[62] Despite their close association with Heraclea from the beginning of its history, however, little is known of the Mariandynoi.

By the 4th century, scholars ranked them among the principal non-Greek populations of northern Anatolia and ascribed to them a territory called Mariandynia,[63] which extended from the Sangarius River in the west to

---

[53] Aelian *NA* 15. 5; Strabo 7. 6. 2. See also Pliny *NH* 9. 176–178. Athenaeus 8. 331c; Ps.-Aristotle, *De mirabilibus auscultationibus* 73, 835b15–23. *Epistles of Chion* 6 should also be mentioned; as emended by Düring, it lists as Heracleote products pickled fish, wine, and honey.

[54] *Cf.* Hoepfner 1966, 102–03.

[55] For Anatolian sources of precious metals, see Broughton 1938, 620–21.

[56] Apollonius Rhodius 2, line 141. *Cf.* Robert 1972, 454; and Nowack 1931, 77–78.

[57] Anonymous *Periplus* 8v14; *Menippi Pergameni Periplus*, in Diller 1952, 151–56, D5723; Arrian *Periplus Ponti Euxini* 13. 4. *Cf.* Broughton 1938, 623.

[58] Hoepfner 1966, 19.

[59] Zeest 1948.

[60] Wasowicz 1966, 556–71.

[61] Strabo 12. 3. 4; *cf.* Xenophon *Anabasis* 6. 2. 1.

[62] Apollonius Rhodius 2, line 760. *Schol. Ap. Rhod.* 187 *ad* 2.780–783a, suggests that its name was Tition.

[63] Ephorus *FGrH* 2A, 70 F162 (= Strabo 14. 5. 23); Ps.-Scymnus *Fragmenta periegeseos ad Nicomedem regem*, in Diller 1952, 165–76, line 977 (= line 936). Mariandynia: Stephanus of Byzantium *s.v. Mariandunia*; Ammianus Marcellinus 22. 8. 14; Eusebius, *Chronicorum libri duo*, ed. A. Schoene (Berlin 1866; reprinted Zurich 1967) II, 24–35. It is implied in Theopompus *FGrH*

32 PART 1: BOOK

somewhere near the Billaeus River in the east.[64] Moreover, although Strabo was to complain about the lack of reliable information concerning the origin and ethnic affinities of the Mariandynoi,[65] mythographers at least as early as the 7th century had connected them with the Argonaut saga, a connection that presupposed their presence in Anatolia before the Trojan War.[66] Likewise, various genealogies linking Mariandynus, the eponym of the people, with different mythical figures were proposed in order to locate them securely within the framework of prehistory that Greek scholars were constructing from the sagas. Thus, someone who held closely to the link with the Argonaut legend suggested Phrixus[67] as the father of Mariandynus, others supported Cimmerius,[68] but the genealogy that achieved the widest acceptance outside Heraclea was one that made Mariandynus and Thynus brothers and the sons of Phineus, the son of Phoenix and grandson of Agenor.[69] In other words, since Agenor was supposedly a contemporary of Minos, it accepted the pre-Trojan date for the

2B, 115 F388, and the name was already current in the 5th century as can be seen from its use by Eupolis F279 Edmonds.

[64] Western border at the Sangarius: Apollonius Rhodius 2, line 722; Strabo 12. 4. 1; Arrian *FGrH* 2B, 156 F76a; Solinus 43. 1. This is not contradicted by the 4th-century geographer called Ps.-Scylax (dated *ca.* 350–335 by C. Mueller [*GGM* I, XLIII–XLIV]) who places the Sangarius within Bithynia and the Hypius within Mariandynia (*GGM* I, 67, 34 [91]). Rather, he is probably reflecting the fact that the territories of the Bithynians and the Mariandynoi shaded into each other instead of being neatly divided by a river. Eastern border at the Billaeus: Apollonius Rhodius 2, lines 790–791; Strabo 12. 3. 5; Pliny *NH* 6. 5. Ptolemy's borders (*Geographia* 5. 7. 11), Heraclea to Cytorus, cannot at present be explained. The Pontic mountains probably formed the southern boundary of Mariandynia. In this connection the statement of Constantine Porphyrogenitus (*De thematibus* 6. 22) that Bithynium-Claudiopolis was the metropolis of the Mariandynoi is not relevant, since it probably reflects the ecclesiastical organization of Byzantine Anatolia when Heraclea was within the jurisdiction of the metropolitan of Claudiopolis (*cf.* Vryonis 1971, 293). In antiquity the territory around Bithynium was considered part of Bithynia (Strabo 12. 4. 7; Ernst Meyer 1925a, 109).

[65] Strabo 12. 3. 4.

[66] *Fragmenta Hesiodea*, ed. R. Merkelbach and M.L. West (Oxford 1967), F157 (= *Schol. Ap. Rhod.* 140 *ad* 178–182a). The generally accepted *terminus ante quem* for the composition of the *Catalogue* is *ca.* 600 (*cf.* Schmid and Stahlin 1929, 266–69). As Albin Lesky pointed out (1966, 104), however, the loose structure of the work facilitated interpolation so that the inclusion of the story of Cyrene in it does not provide a *terminus post quem* of *ca.* 630 for the composition of the *Catalogue* as a whole.

[67] *Schol. Ap. Rhod.* 187 *ad* 2. 780–783a.

[68] Domitius Callistratus *apud* Promathidas *FGrH* 3B, 430 F1; *Schol. Ap. Rhod.* 136 *ad* 2. 140a; 183 *ad* 2. 723; 187 *ad* 2. 780–783a.

[69] In the 5th century the genealogy was accepted by Sophocles (*apud Schol. Ap. Rhod.* 141 *ad* 2. 178–182b) and possibly by Pherecydes (*FGrH* 1A, 3 F27; *cf.* Jacoby's corrigenda *ad FGrH* 1A, 68, line 30). Apollonius Rhodius, however, always refers to him as the son of Agenor (2, lines 178, 237, 240, 293, 426, 490, and 618), perhaps following Hellanicus (*FGrH* 1A, 4 F95; *cf. Schol. Ap. Rhod.* 140 *ad* 2. 178–182ab).

INTRODUCTION   33

Mariandynoi's being in Anatolia and posited in addition a relationship between them and their Bithynian neighbors.[70]

Although the Heracleote historians seem to have rejected the genealogy tracing the origin of the Mariandynoi back to Phineus, they agreed in assuming that they were in Anatolia prior to the Trojan War. That 'fact' became the central point in the prehistory they created for the city with the aid of Greek legends and material gathered from the Mariandynoi themselves. Only fragments now remain of this account – a reference to numerous defeats of the Mariandynoi at the hands of the Bebrycians before Heracles assisted them,[71] the gracious reception offered by them to the Argonauts,[72] and the death of two Mariandynian heroes fighting for Troy during the last phase of the Trojan War[73] – but it is clear from these that the prehistory placed the Mariandynoi in Anatolia at least three generations before the Trojan War, and that it emphasized the friendly relations between them and the Greek heroes before the outbreak of that war. Further, the fragments of Nymphis indicate that according to the chronology followed by the Heracleotes, the presence of the Mariandynoi in Anatolia antedated the appearance of the Phrygians, the first of the Thracians Greek scholars believed invaded Anatolia toward the end of the 2nd millennium.[74] Both traditions, the Heracleote and the mythographic, are, however, manifestly late and artificial, the former only achieving its authoritative form in the third century and the latter almost certainly not antedating the beginning of Ionian exploration of the Black Sea, an event probably to be placed in the 8th century.[75] Not surprisingly, therefore, the majority of modern scholars have refused to accept the presence of the Mariandynoi in Anatolia

---

[70] Arrian *FGrH* 2B, 156 F58. Eusebius (2. 35) dates Phoenix's appearance in northern Anatolia to *anno Abraham* 593 or 1424.

[71] Apollonius Rhodius 2, lines 138–141, 792–795; *Schol. Ap. Rhod.* 186 *ad* 2. 758; 187 *ad* 2. 780–783a (*cf.* Valerius Flaccus *Argonautica* 4, lines 162–173); Ps.-Apollodorus *Bibliotheca* 2. 5. 9; and John Tzetzes *Chiliades* 3. 806–817.

[72] Apollonius Rhodius 2, lines 750–899 (*cf.* Valerius Flaccus *Argonautica* 4, lines 733–762); Ps.-Apollodorus *Bibliotheca* 1 .9. 23. 1; Herodorus *FGrH* 1A, 31 F49; Nymphis *FGrH* 3B, 432 F4. The above texts ascribe the friendly reception to the common hostility of the Mariandynoi and the Argonauts toward the Bebrycians. Another version accounted for it by the supposed kinship of the Mariandynian Lycus and the Argonauts through the former's uncle Pelops (*Schol. Ap. Rhod.* 185–186 *ad* 2. 752).

[73] Quintus of Smyrna *Posthomerica* 6, lines 465–473. Probably part of the same account is the story in Antoninus Liberalis (*Metamorphoseon synagoge*, ed. I. Cazzaniga [Milan 1962], 3) that Hierax, a noble and just Mariandynus, was turned into a hawk by Poseidon because he assisted the Teucrians.

[74] Implied by the fact that Nymphis (*FGrH* 3B, 432 F14) listed the Phrygians among the peoples conquered for the Mariandynoi by Heracles.

[75] For the possibility of Greek navigation of the Black Sea in the 8th century, see Labaree 1957; Graham 1958; and Burstein 1976.

34 PART 1: BOOK

during the 2nd millennium and have, instead, sought to connect them with the later Thracian migrations. More specifically, they are believed to have been a Bithynian tribe that entered Anatolia with the other Bithynians in the 7th century following the invasion of the Cimmerians.[76]

Nevertheless, the sources do not in fact support this theory. Its weakest link is the 7th century date for the invasion. For those who support it, the genealogy making Mariandynus and Thynus the sons of Phineus presents a major difficulty. Phineus' original home was in south-western Anatolia, so the genealogy implies an Anatolian origin for both the Mariandynoi and the Bithynians, a fact difficult to explain had the invasions of these two peoples taken place in the 7th century when the Greeks were in constant contact with the whole north Aegean and Pontic areas.[77] Actually, however, the theory rests largely on the mistaken belief that the genealogy making Mariandynus the son of Cimmerius alluded to the Mariandynian invasion being connected with that of the Cimmerians, just as Arrian's statement that the Bithynians drove the Cimmerians from Bithynia was assumed to refer to events of the 7th century.[78] Although the Cimmerians did raid this area in the 7th century,[79] the Heracleote tradition (and probably Arrian also) concerned, as Erwin Rohde[80] recognized, not the historical invaders of Anatolia, but the mythical people mentioned in the *Odyssey* in whose land lay the entrance to Hades.[81]

On the other hand, there is some ancient support for the other limb of this thesis, the contention that the Mariandynoi were ethnically Thracian. The genealogy linking Mariandynus and Thynus could be taken as pointing toward that conclusion. More to the point, Pherecydes, writing in the 5th century, stated that Phineus ruled a kingdom that extended from Paphlagonia to the Bosporus and encompassed all the Thracians in Asia.[82] Similarly, Xenophon described Asiatic Thrace as beginning at the Bosporus and ending at Heraclea.[83] Finally, in the

---

[76] Ed. Meyer 1897, 510–11; Reinach 1888, 93; Ruge 1930.

[77] Lessen 1884–1937 III.2, 2369. For his southwest Anatolian connections, see *Schol. Ap. Rhod.* 140 *ad* 2.178–182a.

[78] Beside the texts cited above in n. 68, see also Heracleides Ponticus (Wehrli 1967–69 VII, F129): *Kimmerious: Phēsin Herakleidēs ho Pontikos hupokatō tou Pontou einai*; and Arrian *FGrH* 2B, 156 F76a. For the Bithynians and the Cimmerians, see Arrian *FGrH* 2B, 156 F60, 76b.

[79] Strabo 1. 3. 21. On this group, see Cozzoli 1968, 71–72; and Wirth 1967.

[80] Rohde 1881, 556, n. 1. *Cf.* Cozzoli 1968, 100, n. 9.

[81] Homer *Odyssey* 11. 13–19. For the Homeric Cimmerians, see Cozzoli 1968, 17–33. That Arrian cannot have been referring to the historical Cimmerians is indicated by his identification of the Bithynians with the Homeric Halizones (*Iliad* 2, line 856; *FGrH* 2B, 156 F97), i.e. he dated the Bithynian invasion to the period before the Trojan War.

[82] Pherecydes *FGrH* 1A, 3 F27.

[83] Xenophon *Anabasis* 6. 4. 1.

INTRODUCTION   35

first century AD, Strabo concluded that the Mariandynoi were Thracians because
there appeared to be no significant differences of either language or culture
between them and the Bithynians.[84]

The discussion of the Mariandynoi has hitherto been based on the assumption that Mariandynia was inhabited in the historical period by the Heracleotes and a single non-Greek people, the Mariandynoi, whose place of origin
and the date they left it to migrate to their later home were the questions to
be resolved. Given the tendency of the Greek geographers to concentrate
their attention on the major non-Greek populations of Anatolia, and the
unfortunate silence of the Hittite records on this area,[85] the adoption of
this approach is understandable. Nevertheless, as is shown below, the evidence suggests that this is an oversimplification and that the Mariandynian
population of historical times was not a unity but the result of the fusion of
several originally distinct ethnic groups some time during the first half of the
1st millennium.

The combined evidence of Pherecydes, Xenophon, and Strabo proves that
from the 5th century on Mariandynian culture was predominantly Thracian in
character. This, however, is probably to be accounted for by the influence of
not one but at least two distinct Thracian peoples settled within the confines of
classical Mariandynia: Mysians, who according to Nymphis[86] occupied the
Hypius River valley, and Thynians, whose territory, according to Arrian,[87]
who is supported by the evidence of toponymy,[88] extended from the Cales
River near Heraclea westward across the Sangarius to the Psilis River. At the
same time, several items – the existence of a town named Arkiroessa, with its
distinctive Anatolian (-ss-) termination,[89] and the Mariandynian names Sagaris

---

[84] Strabo 12. 3. 4. Strabo (7. 3. 2; 14. 5. 23) did suggest that the Mariandynoi were Thracians
who migrated to Anatolia after the time of Homer, but this was only an attempt to blunt Apollodorus' charge (*FGrH* 2B, 244 F157; F170) that Homer's silence about them vitiated the claim
that he was a reliable authority on geography.

[85] Except for a brief period during the Hittite old kingdom the Hittites were always cut off
from the Pontus by the hostile Kaskas who occupied the area of later Paphlagonia (Goetze 1957,
178–79).

[86] Nymphis *FGrH* 3B, 432 F2. These are probably the Mysians Apollonius Rhodius (2, line 786)
says Heracles conquered for the Mariandynoi.

[87] Arrian *FGrH* 2B, 156 F78a.

[88] Ps.-Scymnus, lines 1023–1024 (= 977–978), and Anonymous *Periplus* 8v6–7, place the
Sangarius River within Thynias, thus implying that the region extended east of that river, a view
confirmed by *Schol. Ap. Rhod.* 189 *ad* 2. 794–795b, which also locates the Hypius River within
Thynias. *Cf.* Kämmel 1869, 8–10.

[89] Stephanus of Byzantium *s.v. Arkiroessa*. For these place names, see now Hester 1957,
107–19.

36   PART 1: BOOK

and Priolas, which both appear to be of Anatolian origin –[90] point to the presence of a non-Thracian element among the Mariandynoi.

Despite the prominence of the Thracian elements of the population and the tendency to identify the Mariandynoi with the Thynian segment of it, it is probable that it was this non-Thracian group that was politically dominant, unified the area, and gave its name to the region's inhabitants. Particularly significant in this regard is a seemingly unnoticed fact connected with the genealogy linking Mariandynus and Thynus to Phineus. The Heracleote historians seem to have ignored it, preferring to make Mariandynus the son of Cimmerius or to connect him with a Mariandynian hero, Titias, the son of Zeus – that is, the native high god,[91] and its probative value with regard to their being Thracian is, in any event, slight since the Thracian origin of the Bithynians was clearly unknown to its creator. At most, it proves that the Mariandynoi and the Thynians were separate tribes occupying contiguous territories in Anatolia when the Ionians first came into contact with them. What has been overlooked hitherto, is that after the Thracian origin of the Bithynians and Thynians was established, Greek scholars outside Heraclea also seem to have severed the genealogical tie between Mariandynus and Thynus and to have instead accepted the Heracelote contention that the Mariandynoi were in Anatolia before the arrival of their Thracian neighbors.[92] This development is most likely to be explained by their believing that the Mariandynoi were not Thracians.

Fortunately, although the genealogies offered by the Heracleote historians are uninformative, other aspects of their account of the city's prehistory

---

[90] Sagaris: Clearchus of Soli (Wehrli 1967–69 III, F53). For the name as Anatolian, see Robert 1963, 536–38. Priolas: Apollonius Rhodius 2, line 780; *Schol. Ap. Rhod.* 187 *ad* 2. 780–783a; *Scholia vetera in Nicandri Alexipharmica*, ed. E. Abel (Budapest 1891) *ad* line 15; Pollux 4. 55 (*Iolla* is probably an error for *Priola* as suggested by van der Kolf [1954, 2315]). There was a settlement named Priola near Heraclea (Stephanus of Byzantium *s.v. Priola*). For the name as Anatolian, see van der Kolf 1954, 2315.

[91] Domitius Callistratus *apud* Promathidas *FGrH* 3B, 430 F1; Nymphis *FGrH* 3B, 432 F5a; Theophanes *FGrH* 2B, 188 F2. The identification of him with the Titias said by Apollonius Rhodius to have been an Idaean Dactyl and *paredros* of Rhea at Miletus (1, lines 1125–1126) proposed by modern scholars (e.g. Hemberg 1952, 53–55; Jacoby *FGrH* 3B *Texte*, 257 *ad* 430 F1) rests only on *Schol. Ap. Rhod.* 187 *ad* 2.780–783a ('some say that Titias is the son of Zeus, one of the Idaean Dactyls, and some the eldest son of Mariandynus') and this cannot stand against the clear statement of Callistratus that he was a native hero. The root *Tit-* is too common for certain attribution to any linguistic stock, but it could be Anatolian (*cf.* Zgusta 1964, 516–17, nos. 1567–1575). On the other hand, the suggestion that it is Thracian (Pohlenz 1916, 584–85) is probably to be rejected since the only example of a Thracian root *Tit-* listed by D. Detschew (1957, 506–07) is the personal name *Titha* which Zgusta (1964) has shown to be Greek.

[92] See the genealogy cited by Arrian (*FGrH* 2B, 156 F77a) according to which Thynus and Bithynus (but not Mariandynus) were the sons of Odrysus and the adopted sons of Phineus, whose legitimate son was Paphlagon.

INTRODUCTION   37

suggest that they believed the Mariandynoi came from western Anatolia. Primary among these is the presence of Dascylus, the son of Tantalus, in their kinglist of the Mariandynoi with its implication that they tried to connect the Mariandynian royal family with the mythical Tantalid dynasty of Lydia.[93] Further support is found in a story attested only in the *Bibliotheca* of Ps.-Apollodorus[94] and the *Chiliades* of John Tzetzes[95] but clearly derived from a Heracleote source, most likely Herodorus.[96] According to this narrative the Mariandynoi lived in Mysia before Heracles conquered the site of the later Heraclea and its environs for them from the Bebrycians. Admittedly, the Heracleote tradition is only a construct, but Mariandynian legend was used in its formation and this fact, together with the other evidence adduced above, creates a strong presumption that the account of the Mariandynoi, migrating to their later home from north-western Anatolia, was based on native tradition and should be accepted.[97]

On the other hand, the pre-Trojan War, or 2nd millennium, date for their migration lacks authority since it is clearly based on the connection of the Mariandynoi with events of Greek mythology. The genealogy of the Ps.-Hesiodic *Catalogue* provides a *terminus ante quem* of the 7th century with the implication of a considerably earlier actual date because of its author's ignorance of the Thynians being Thracian. A *terminus post quem* is still lacking, but in view of the confusion that must have attended the repeated Thracian invasions of north-western Anatolia at the end of the 2nd and the beginning of the 1st millennium, it is a plausible hypothesis that it belongs to this period, that is, it occurred some time between the 12th and the 9th or 8th century.[98]

If the date of the appearance of the Mariandynoi in the area of Heraclea must remain conjectural for the present, toponymy allows an insight into

---

[93] For Dascylus, see Apollonius Rhodius 2, line 776; *Schol. Ap. Rhod.* 185 *ad* 2. 752.

[94] Ps.-Apollodorus *Bibliotheca* 2. 5. 9.

[95] John Tzetzes *Chiliades* 3. 806–817. Tzetzes mistakenly refers the story to Heraclea-Perinthus instead of Pontica.

[96] The Heracleote origin of the story is indicated by the presence of Lycus the son of Dascylus in it and its purpose of explaining how the area of Heraclea came into Mariandynian hands through the help of Heracles. The source is probably earlier than Nymphis, who portrayed Heracles as assisting Dascylus when the latter was already settled at Heraclea (Apollonius Rhodius 2, lines 775–776). Herodorus is the most likely candidate since Ps.-Apollodorus is known to have used him elsewhere (*Bibliotheca* 1. 118 [= *FGrH* 1A, 31 F41a]; 3.45 [= *FGrH* 1A, 31 F56]; *cf. FHG* 2, 32 F15).

[97] In addition to the presence of such Mariandynian heroes as Titias and Priolas in Heracleote tradition, note the reference to native informants in Nymphis *FGrH* 3B, 432 F5b. As for their residence in western Anatolia, Theopompus (*FGrH* 2B, 115 F388) seems to have known of it, although he explained it as the result of a migration by Mariandynus from Mariandynia to Bebrycia.

[98] *Cf.* Goetze 1957, 185.

38   PART 1: BOOK

events subsequent to their arrival. The point of interest is an apparent contradiction in ancient accounts of the western boundary of Mariandynia. Although the geographers regularly placed the beginning of Mariandynian territory at the Sangarius, the fact that they also called the area from the Cales to the Psilis *Thynias* must indicate that when the Greeks first 'mapped' that area it was occupied by Thynians and not Mariandynoi. Presumably, the latter's territory at that time began near the Cales and extended eastward to about the Billaeus. From these considerations it follows that the Sangarius boundary reflects a later expansion of the Mariandynoi toward the west in the course of which they would have conquered the Mysian and Thynian settlements within the confines of the later Mariandynia. Subsequent assimilation of the Mariandynoi, and their presumably more numerous Thracian subjects, would then account for the predominantly Thracian character of the area's population and culture by the 5th century. Although a date for the completion of the process of assimilation is lacking, the apparent disappearance of the Thynians from history after the first half of the 6th century and the time necessary to produce the cultural situation existing in the 5th century suggest it must have been over well before the end of the 6th century.[99]

The loss of the bulk of Heracleote historiography has deprived us of the evidence necessary to form a clear picture of Mariandynian culture, either before or after the foundation of Heraclea. As far as their society is concerned, the fertility of Mariandynia, references to a harvest festival in the sources, and their later position as state agricultural slaves all point to the Mariandynoi having been a settled farming population. As it was elsewhere in Anatolia under such conditions, a considerable proportion of them seem to have lived in villages scattered throughout Mariandynia,[100] although there were apparently also settlements, including one on approximately the site of Heraclea, which were of sufficiently large size for the Greeks to refer to them as *poleis*.[101] Little information survives concerning either the military or the political aspects of

---

[99] The only mention of them as a separate people by a 5th-century author is Herodotus 1. 28, and already his source for the Persian army list seems only to have known the Bithynians (7. 75. 2; *cf.* Thucydides, 4. 75. 2).

[100] One village, Akonai, is mentioned in the sources (Theophrastus *HP* 9. 16. 4; Stephanus of Byzantium *s.v. Akonai* refers to it as a *polichnion*). Pliny (*NH* 6. 4) suggests that it was a port east of Heraclea. Villages are also implied by Aristotle's reference to *perioeci* at Heraclea (*Politics* 7. 5. 7. 1327M4–16). *Cf.* Hoepfner 1966, 39.

[101] Stephanus of Byzantium *s.v. Priola* (*cf.* Nicander *Alexipharmica* line 15, and *Schol. Nic. Alex ad* line 15). The Mariandynian *polis* named Stephanis mentioned by Hecataeus of Miletus (*FGrH* 1A, 1 F198) is probably not to be identified with the *Stephane limen* of Ps.-Scylax (*GGM* I, 66, 90), as proposed by C. Mueller (*GGM* I, 66, n. *ad loc.*) and Ruge (1930, 1749), since the latter appears to have been in eastern Paphlagonia. For the *polis* near the site of Heraclea itself, see above n. 62.

INTRODUCTION 39

their culture. In the early 5th century they seem to have fought as light infantry, with equipment similar to that used by the Paphlagonians, but nothing is known about the organization of their forces.[102] As for their political system, all that can be said is that the fact that the Heracleote historians constructed a king-list for the Mariandynoi probably reflects their having been ruled by chieftains in the 6th century when Heraclea was founded.

Little but scattered hints remain to attest the existence once of a rich Mariandynian spiritual culture. Thus, the mention of Titias, the son of Zeus, who was deified for his services to the Mariandynoi, illustrates the disappearance of a body of oral saga about the past of the Mariandynoi. Likewise, except for the cult of Bormus discussed below, our evidence is too limited to permit more than the listing of a few Mariandynian deities, such as the hero the Greeks called Agamestor,[103] a high god identified with Zeus, the god of the river Lycus,[104] nymphs,[105] and, judging from the existence of a place named *Metroen* east of Heraclea, some form of the Great Mother.[106] In addition, we should probably see in the stories of a number of Greek gods and heroes, such as Demeter,[107] Dionysus,[108] and the Tyndaridae,[109] being worshipped by the Mariandynoi before the foundation of Heraclea further evidence of the identification of native deities with Greek divinities by the Heracleotes.

[102] Herodotus 7. 72. 1.

[103] Apollonius Rhodius 2, lines 844–847 (= Promathidas *FGrH* 3B, 430 F3). *Cf.* Quintus of Smyrna *Posthomerica* 6, line 464. Jacoby's suggestion (*FGrH* 3B *Noten*, 168, n. 15) that Agamestor was the heroized leader of Heraclea's Boeotian settlers is improbable, since the cult of a founder would have preserved his identity. The identification of his tomb with that of Idmon, however, was apparently still arguable in the 4th century because Chamaeleon (Wehrli 1967–69, F15) ascribed it to Thestor, a descendant of Nestor.

[104] *Schol. Ap. Rhod.* 184 *ad* 2. 724; 185–186 *ad* 2. 752.

[105] The evidence for nymphs is, in fact, relatively weak. *Schol. Ap. Rhod.* 184 *ad* 2. 724; 185–186 *ad* 2. 752, mention Anthemoeisia, the daughter of the river Lycus, presumably the eponym of the Anthemoeisian Lake (Apollonius Rhodius 2, line 724; Stephanus of Byzantium *s.v. Anthemous*), and Quintus of Smyrna (*Posthomerica* 6, line 472) says that the Acherousian cave was sacred to nymphs. The nymphs of Apollonius Rhodius 2, line 821, may only be literary embellishment. Note also the place name Nymphaeum east of Heraclea (Anonymous *Periplus* 8v14; Arrian *Periplus* 13. 4).

[106] Anonymous *Periplus* 8v13; Arrian *Periplus* 13. 3. Note also the association of Heracleote worshippers of Cybele at Callatis revealed by a 3rd-century AD inscription (Rădulescu 1964, 148–53).

[107] Antoninus Liberalis *Metamorphoseon synagoge* 3; and possibly also Hesychius *s.v. Pampanon: he Dēmētēr en Herakleiai*.

[108] Apollonius Rhodius 2, lines 904–910; *Schol. Ap. Rhod.* 193–194 *ad* 2. 904–910a; Valerius Flaccus *Argonautica* 5, lines 74–76; Ammianus Marcellinus 22. 8. 23. *Cf.* Amphitheus *FGrH* 3B, 431 F1, and Jacoby *FGrH* 3B *Texte*, 258.

[109] Apollonius Rhodius 2, lines 806–810.

40 PART 1: BOOK

Because it attracted interest among the Greeks living outside Heraclea, the harvest festival in honor of Bormus or Borimus, which the Mariandynoi celebrated annually until early in the Christian Era, is fairly well documented in the sources.[110] As early as the 5th century, the dirges associated with the rites were familiar in Athens,[111] but the festival itself is known to us only in its third century form when Nymphis described it in the first book of his history of Heraclea.[112] According to him, at the time of reaping in the height of summer, the Mariandynoi wandered through the countryside calling Bormus by name and chanting a dirge to the accompaniment, as we know from other sources, of wailing flutes.[113]

Probably because of its long survival, the sources contain several different versions of the cult legend. According to Nymphis' Mariandynian informants, Bormus was the handsome son of Titias, a rich landowner, who disappeared while getting water for the reapers working on his father's estate.[114] On the other hand, Domitius Callistratus, although agreeing that Bormus was the son of Titias, maintains that he disappeared while hunting,[115] and the same account is given by Pollux who, however, calls him the son of King Oupius.[116] Finally, Hesychius refers to Bormus as the son of Mariandynus and says that he was seized by a nymph.[117] That any of these preserve the original myth is doubtful. Titias is known to have been a great hero and if the suggestion that Pollux's Oupius is an error for Titias is correct,[118] probably a king as well, so that the fact that Nymphis describes him as merely a rich landowner brands his version, despite its being collected from the Mariandynoi themselves, as a late variant in which the legend's heroic background has disappeared under the

---

[110] Domitius Callistratus (*FGrH* 3B, 433 F3) refers to the rites as current in the 1st century. On the other hand, the confusion about the character of the dirges – whether they were mournful or mocking – in the 5th-century AD lexicographer Hesychius (M279–280; for his date, see Lesky 1966, 832) indicates that they had ceased to be celebrated considerably before his time. The mourning rites for Priolas mentioned by Apollonius (2, lines 780–782) are, *contra* Hemberg (1952, 54), an invention by Apollonius (*cf. Schol. Ap. Rhod.* 187 *ad* 2. 780–783b).

[111] Aeschylus, *Persians*, line 939. The dirge was called the Bormus, presumably because it consisted of the repeated calling of the deity's name (Pollux 4. 54; Hesychius B1394; Nymphis *FGrH* 3B, 432 F5).

[112] Nymphis *FGrH* 3B, 432 F5.

[113] Domitius Callistratus *FGrH* 3B, 433 F3a. It was probably the flutes that inspired the story that Mariandynus was the teacher of Marsyas (Domitius Callistratus *FGrH* 3B, 433 F3a; Eustathius *GGM* II, 355 *ad* Dionysius Perigetes, line 787).

[114] Nymphis *FGrH* 3B, 432 F5.

[115] Domitius Callistratus *FGrH* 3B, 433 F3a.

[116] Pollux 4. 55.

[117] Hesychius B1394.

[118] The emendation was proposed by Kämmel 1869, 32–33, and accepted by van der Kolf 1954, 2315.

INTRODUCTION 41

influence of the historical experience of the Mariandynoi, who had worked the estates of the Heracleote aristocracy since the 5th century. Likewise, although Hesychius' statement that Bormus was seized by a nymph may preserve the mechanism of his disappearance, the substitution of Mariandynus for Titias raises doubts and renders attractive the suggestion that his version is not native but rather the result of contamination with the legend of Hylas.[119] Similar objections, admittedly, cannot be made against those of Callistratus and Pollux, but their lateness and the clear evidence of changes during the process of oral transmission provided by that of Nymphis allow us to accept it only as one of the versions of the legend current in the 1st century. But if the details of the original cult legend cannot be recovered, its purpose is not in doubt. Central to all the versions is the annual search for a divinity who had disappeared, a feature that recalls the cults of Attis and Adonis. Like them, Bormus clearly was a god of vegetation, and the timing of the rites to coincide with the harvest indicates that Tomaschek was correct in identifying him with the '*genius* of the harvest'.[120]

The result of this investigation can be briefly summarized. Prior to the foundation of Heraclea the future site of the city and its environs was occupied by a population of mixed Thracian and Anatolian origin. The Mariandynoi are to be identified with the Anatolian component of it and were politically dominant. Despite this, they were being gradually assimilated by their Thracian neighbors, a process that was already complete by the 5th century when the whole population of Mariandynia impressed the Greeks as being Thracian.

[119] Turk 1895, 7.

[120] Tomaschek 1894, 42. Kämmel's identification (1869, 22–27) of Bormus with the water that disappears in the summer is impossible given the climatic conditions at Heraclea (see above n. 43).

CHAPTER I

SETTLEMENT

Greek Colonization in the Black Sea

The Black Sea basin was the last important area settled by the Greeks. Tradition credited Miletus with the colonization of its shores, but little remains to attest to that achievement except the few foundation dates preserved by Eusebius and Ps.-Scymnus.[1] These indicate that although exploration of its waters may have begun as early as the 8th century, actual settlement did not begin until about the middle of the 7th century.[2] This delay is not surprising. Reports of the Pontus' harsh weather and its harborless coasts inhabited by hostile natives early led the Greeks to equate its Iranian name *Axsăina*, 'dark', with *Axeinos*, 'inhospitable'.[3] Only the pressure applied to the East Greek cities by the kings of Lydia sufficed to make the Ionians forget the Pontus' evil reputation and look on it instead as a region with the potential for profitable exploitation.

Conquest of the coastal cities was a major goal of the Mermnad dynasty from its establishment by Gyges about 680. Sustained as it was for much of the rest of the 7th century, the Lydian push westward amounted to a virtual siege of the Ionian cities which not only prevented their expansion but at times also made the feeding of their growing populations difficult.[4] Land for emigrants and food for their *mētropolis* were the twin objectives of the colonies resulting from this pressure. The Cimmerian invasions, despite their disruption of the important overland trade with the metal-working centers of Urartu and the Caucasus, did not last long enough to significantly alter the essentially agricultural orientation of Pontic colonization.[5] Thus, although Sinope with its easy access to the iron mines of the Chalybes was among the earliest colonies

---

[1] For Miletus' colonial activity in general the classic text is Pliny *NH* 5. 112. For the Black Sea colonies, see Ephorus *FGrH* 2A, 70 F183 and Strabo 14. 1. 6. For the individual colonies, see Bilabel 1920, 13–66.

[2] For these dates, see Burn 1935, 132–36, and his more recent reconsideration of the problem in Burn 1960, 403–08; and Roebuck 1959, 119–21.

[3] Danov 1962, 951–54. The Greek attitude toward the Pontus can be seen in Herodotus 4. 28; Diodorus 3. 34. 7; and Strabo 7. 3. 18. For the dates, see Archilochus F97a Edmonds.

[4] Herodotus 1. 14. 4–22. *Cf.* Roebuck 1959, 105, 128–29.

[5] Birmingham 1961.

44 PART I: BOOK

founded (631, Eusebius), it was the fertile land of the west and north coasts of the Black Sea which primarily attracted the Ionians.[6] By the middle of the 6th century, a string of cities, Apollonia, Istros, Tyras, Olbia, and Panticapaeum, stretched along the route from the Bosporus to the Straits of Kerch.[7]

The establishment of Heraclea belongs to a later phase of the colonization of the Pontus. The exact date of its foundation is unknown, but Ps.-Scymnus synchronized it with the conquest of Media by Cyrus I.[8] Eusebius assigned the conquest of Media to 560; a recent study indicates that the correct date was 554.[9] Since, however, we have no way of determining the date intended by Ps.-Scymnus' source, we can only say that the evidence points to Heraclea's having been founded sometime around 560. More important, this means that the Boeotians and the Megarians occupied the last remaining good harbor on the south coast of the Pontus at a time when excavation shows that trade on a steadily increasing scale already existed between the Pontic cities and various East Greek centers, as well as such cities of the Greek mainland as Athens and especially Corinth.[10] Together with the good fishing and rich farm land of Heracleotis, this assured the rapid growth and future prosperity of the new city.

POSSIBLE MILESIAN COLONY AT HERACLEA

Previous historians of Heraclea have maintained that the Milesians had not overlooked the city's excellent site, but that they had established a colony there before the Boeotians and Megarians.[11] Certainly, the genealogy linking

---

[6] Roebuck 1959, 116–30. For the agricultural nature of the settlement on Berezan, see Lapin 1965.

[7] Boardman 1964, 255–64.

[8] Ps.-Scymnus, line 1019 (= 975). Anonymous *Periplus* 8v10.

[9] Eusebius 2. 95, col. 55, 1. Drews 1969, 1–4.

[10] In the 6th century the dominant imported pottery is East Greek, with small amounts of Corinthian (Roebuck 1959, 124–26, and Boardman 1964, 251). Attic pottery appeared as early as the second quarter of the 6th century but only became at all common toward the end of the century (Brashinskii 1968, 103). At Sinope, Akurgal and Budde (1956, 9) report Corinthian as not uncommon, with the oldest example being an aryballus dated to *ca.* 600. As for Heraclea, Prof. E. Reschke of the University of Erlangen informed me in a letter dated April 15, 1970 that the oldest sherd so far discovered is a piece of Attic Red Figure ware, which gives us a provisional *terminus post quem* of *ca.* 530 for the beginning of trade with Athens (*cf.* Cook 1960, 165–71).

[11] Accepted by Schneiderwirth 1882, 8–9; and considered possible by Hanell (1934, 135). Denied by Beloch (1912–27 I.1, 259, n. 5) and Bilabel (1920, 43, n. 1). No evidence supports Schneiderwirth's theory (1882, 8–9) that there was a Phoenician settlement at Heraclea prior to the Milesians. Likewise, Kämmel's theory (1869, 46–48) of a Carian settlement rests on a misinterpretation of Pliny's reference (*NH* 16. 239) to altars of Zeus Stratius *in Ponto citra Heracleam* (*cf.* Herodotus 5. 119. 2 for Zeus Stratius in Caria). Actually, Pliny's further remark that *in eodem tractu portus Amyci est* (*cf.* Pliny *NH* 5. 150; Ammianus Marcellinus 22. 8. 14; and *Schol. Ap. Rhod.* 137 *ad* 2. 159–160b) show that they were located on the Asiatic shore of the Bosporus.

I. SETTLEMENT

Thynus and Mariandynus to Phineus allows no doubt that the Ionians were familiar with the Mariandynoi and their neighbors well before the middle of the 6th century. Eduard Meyer's claim that the Milesians deliberately avoided colonizing Bithynia because of the savagery of the natives is, therefore, untenable, and the possibility of a Milesian settlement at Heraclea must be carefully examined.[12]

The literary evidence for a Milesian Heraclea is limited to the following two passages of Strabo:

> ... for Heraclea, they say [*phasi*], is situated in the country of the Mariandynoi, and was founded by the Milesians...
> This, too, has been said [*eirētai*], that the Milesians who were first to found Heraclea forced the Mariandynoi, who held the place before them, to serve as helots, so that they made them subject to sale, but not beyond the boundaries of their country (for the two peoples came to an agreement on this), just as the Mnoan class, as it is called, worked the land [*ethēteuen*] of the Cretans and the Penestae that of the Thessalians.[13]

These texts cannot be dismissed with the assertion that Strabo wrote *Milesians* out of habit instead of *Megarians*.[14] His double reference to a Milesian foundation excludes that possibility. Furthermore, his use of *phasi* and *eirētai* clearly indicates that he is repeating information found in an earlier source.[15] That source did not contradict the tradition that made Heraclea a joint foundation of the Boeotians and Megarians by sponsoring a rival Milesian claim. Rather it supplemented that version: the Milesians were supposed to have been the *first*, not the sole colonizers of Heraclea. A later settlement is clearly implied. Strabo's source, therefore, stated that Heraclea was founded twice, first by Miletus, and then later by Megara and Boeotia.

No confirmation of this account is to be found in the fragments of the Heracleote historians. The only piece of solid evidence that seemed to support the theory of a Milesian colony at Heraclea, an inscription purportedly proving the presence of the Ionic tribe Boreis there, has been shown by Louis Robert to actually belong to Heraclea Perinthus.[16] Likewise, Felix Jacoby's connection of Titias with a Milesian claim to have been the *mētropolis* of Heraclea fails because it is based on the fallacious identification of the Mariandynian hero

---

[12] Ed. Meyer 1965–69 III, 421.

[13] Strabo 12. 3. 4.

[14] Burn 1960, 120, n. 65.

[15] Ed. Meyer (1965–69 III, 627, n. 1), Jacoby (*FGrH* 2D, 400 *ad* 115 F389) and Asheri (1972, 12) suggest Theopompus as Strabo's source. This identification is rendered highly probable by Strabo's citing him for a similar statement concerning Amisus (*FGrH* 2B, 115 F389 [= Strabo 12. 3. 14]).

[16] Robert 1936, 113–22. The inscription was originally published by G. Doublet (1889, 316–17).

46 PART I: BOOK

with the companion of Rhea attested at Miletus.[17] One fact, however, that Heraclea's own colony of Chersonesus was founded on the site of an abandoned Ionian settlement, makes it impossible to simply dismiss Strabo's account of an initial Milesian colony at Heraclea.[18]

The tradition of a double foundation is not an isolated one. Besides Heraclea, similar traditions exist for Sinope[19] and Amisus[20] and probably for Cyzicus[21] in the Propontis. A circumstantial account is preserved only in the case of Sinope. According to Ps.-Scymnus, Sinope was first established by a certain Habrondas only to be destroyed by Cimmerian raiders. The historical city was refounded at the time of the great Cimmerian invasion of Anatolia, that is, about the middle of the 7th century.[22] As to the date of these early colonies, Eusebius dates both Cyzicus and Trapezus to the year 756, and the latter implies a still earlier date for the first Sinope since Trapezus was a Sinopean colony.[23] On the basis of this evidence scholars have developed the theory that these early colonies were part of a chain of trading stations established in the 8th century which were wiped out by Cimmerian raiders.[24] A Milesian Heraclea could easily have belonged to such a series of settlements, and it could have met the same fate as the others since the Cimmerians are known to have been active in Paphlagonia.[25]

The possibility of such early colonization of the Black Sea is strengthened somewhat by references in Homer,[26] Hesiod,[27] Eumelus,[28] Archilochus,[29] and the *Cypria*,[30] which indicate that by the early 7th century the Greeks were

[17] Jacoby *FGrH* 3B *Texte*, 257 *ad* 430 F1. For Miletus' claims in the Roman period to be the founder of many cities, see Robert 1937, 247–48.

[18] Danov 1962, 1106. Boardman 1963, 44.

[19] Ps.-Scymnus, lines 992–993 (= 947–948). For discussion, see Bilabel 1920, 32–33.

[20] Theopompus *FGrH* 2B, 115 F389 (= Strabo 12. 3. 4. 14). Ps.-Scymnus, line 956 (= 918).

[21] Suggested by the fact that Eusebius gives two foundation dates for Cyzicus: 756 (2. 8) and 680 (2. 86–87).

[22] Ps.-Scymnus, lines 992–997 (= 947–953).

[23] Eusebius 2. 80. For an interesting attempt to prove that Eusebius' text is corrupt at this point and that he actually dated Sinope and not Trapezus to 756, see M. Miller 1970, 19–20.

[24] The most important statement of this position is Miltner 1939, 191–95.

[25] Strabo 1. 3. 21.

[26] *Iliad* 2, lines 850–855. Graham 1958, 37–38, has shown that the passage in the *Odyssey* (12, lines 59–72) concerning the Argo passing through the Cyanean Rocks refers to the Bosporus.

[27] Hesiod *Theogony* (M. West 1966), lines 339–340, 344. For Hesiod and the Black Sea in general, see Gissinger 1929, 318. West (1966, 40–47) dates Hesiod to the 8th century. Kirk (1962, 63–64) more cautiously proposes 675 as the *terminus post quem* for the composition of the *Theogony*.

[28] Eumelus *FGrH* 3B, 451 F2b, 5. Eumelus probably should be dated to the last quarter of the 8th century (*cf.* Huxley 1969, 62). Jacoby (*FGrH* 3B [297–607] *Kommentar*, 297) believes that the fragments derive from a 4th-century prose adaptation of Eumelus' epic.

[29] Archilochus F97a Edmonds.

[30] *Cypria* F 1: Evelyn-White 1936, 492–95. Date unknown but Lesky (1966, 83) suggests the mid-6th century for the completion of the epic cycle.

I. SETTLEMENT

familiar with almost the entire circuit of the Black Sea and had even made contact with some of the nomadic peoples of southern Russia. The archaeological evidence, unfortunately, is incomplete and hence ambiguous. Nothing Greek earlier than the middle of the 7th century has been found anywhere in the Pontus,[31] and the south coast has not produced anything earlier than the beginning of the 6th century.[32] The problem is that only the cities of the west and north coasts have been thoroughly excavated. That the earliest objects found in these cities date from the second half of the 7th century has no bearing on the possibility of an abortive colonization of the south coast starting sometime in the 8th century because none of the west and north coast cities have foundation dates earlier than the second quarter of the 7th century. Moreover, the recent discovery that Ionian activity in the Propontis *ca.* 700 was sufficiently intense for them to have colonized the inland site of Dascyleum shows clearly that they could also have settled in the Pontus at that time had they so desired.[33]

On the other hand, the double foundation tradition, especially as it relates to Heraclea, has two suspicious features. Miletus' primacy in the colonization of the Pontus was generally accepted by the Greeks, and what the double foundation tradition does is to eliminate such important exceptions to her claims as Heraclea and Amisus by providing them with Milesian pedigrees. This by itself raises doubts about the tradition which are confirmed by a consideration of the rest of Strabo's account of the activities of the Milesians at Heraclea. Not only had they founded the city, but they had also conquered the Mariandynoi and reduced them to a status similar to that of the Cretan Mnoa and the Thessalian Penestae. The servile status of the Mariandynoi was well-known and was frequently cited by theorists in discussing the origins and varieties of slavery.[34] Strabo's source, as is revealed by the comparison with the Mnoa and the Penestae, was familiar with this debate, and the whole account suggests that it supported the position that this type of slavery arose from conquest. There was, however, another version of the subjection of the Mariandynoi which ignored the Milesians and denied that any conquest had taken place. According to Posidonius, who followed this tradition, the Mariandynoi voluntarily surrendered

---

[31] Pippidi (1971, 37) reports the recent discovery of pottery dating from the second half of the 7th century at Istrus.

[32] For the material from Sinope, see Akurgal and Budde 1956, 5–7. The results of the excavations at Amisus are known to me only through Akurgal and Budde 1956, 4–5. Boysal 1959 goes too far in concluding that the finds from Sinope prove that colonization began in the 7th century since, as Graham points out (1958, 33), there is no proof that the earliest graves have yet been discovered.

[33] Akurgal 1956, 24.

[34] *Cf.* Plato *Laws* 6. 776C; and Athenaeus 6. 263c–264b. For the use of Heraclea in the discussion of the origins of slavery, see v. Wilamowitz-Moellendorff and Niese 1910, 37–38.

48   PART I: BOOK

their freedom to the intellectually superior Hearacleotes in return for the establishment of a benevolent paternalism that was secured by a pledge that no Mariandynus should be sold out of his homeland.[35] Now Strabo reports that the
Milesians made this same concession to the Mariandynoi. The occurrence of
this rule in two such divergent accounts clearly indicates that Strabo and Posidonius' sources have here incorporated into their accounts a regulation that did
exist at Heraclea. Acceptance of Strabo's explanation of its origin, however,
requires us to believe the following implausible sequence of events: namely,
that the Milesians conquered the Mariandynoi, the latter regained their freedom
and then lost it again to the later colonists, who imposed on them the same
terms as had the Milesians. More likely, the later situation has been retrojected
to the supposed earlier colonization in order to add substance to the claim that
Miletus was the original founder of Heraclea. Taken in combination with the
fact that there is no trace of Ionian influence at Heraclea,[36] these objections
indicate that the existence of a Milesian colony at Heraclea should be rejected.

Organization and Departure

The historical founders of Heraclea were the Boeotian League and Megara.[37]
On this point most of the sources agree, although they disagree strongly as to
which of the partners was responsible for organizing the colony. Justin[38] and
Euphorion[39] assigned the credit to the Boeotians. On the other hand, Xenophon,
the earliest source, ignored them completely and simply referred to Heraclea

---

[35] Posidonius *FGrH* 2A, 87 F8. Wilhelm Capelle (1932, 99–100) believes that Posidonius is
developing ideas of his teacher Panaetius which derive ultimately from Aristotle.

[36] Asheri (1972, 15–17) makes it clear that Ionian influence begins at Tium. His attempt to
evade the implications of this fact by arguing that Strabo's source actually said that the Milesians
were the first to settle the area controlled by Heraclea in the late 4th century is unconvincing,
especially since his thesis presupposes a total misunderstanding of his source by Strabo.

[37] See below, nn. 38–41, for the texts. That it was a league foundation is indicated by the
constant reference to the Boeotians as cofounders. The theory of Glotz and Cohen (1925–38 I,
168) that Heraclea was founded by Byzantium has no support in the sources and is rendered
virtually impossible by the fact that the eponymous official at Byzantium was an *hieromnamon*
and not a *basileus* as at Heraclea (Polybius 4. 52; Walbank 1957–79 I, 506, n. *ad loc.*).

[38] Justin 16. 3. 4–8. Trogus' source was probably Nymphis' history of Alexander and his successors (Desideri 1967, 391, n. 6).

[39] Euphorion (J.U. Powell 1925 F177 = *Schol. Ap. Rhod.* 155 *ad* 2. 351–352a = Ephorus
FGrH 2A, 70 F44b). The ascription of this fragment to Ephorus is questionable. F44a does not
correspond to the proposed F44b in the following points: (1) it portrays Heraclea as a joint foundation of the Boeotians and Megarians while 44b indicates that it was a Boeotian colony with a
Megarian *oecist*; (2) F44a omits the name of the *oecist* unlike F44b; and (3) the neutral term
ektisan used in F44a cannot be considered a synonym for *kateschon* in F44b. Since Powell's
fragments 37 and 78 show that Euphorion did deal with Heraclea, the implications of the above
differences should be accepted and the fragment should again be assigned to Euphorion.

I. SETTLEMENT

49

as a Megarian foundation.[40] Pausanias described it as a Megarian project in which some Boeotians participated[41] and others, such as Ephorus, evaded the problem entirely by merely mentioning the city's two founders without further defining their respective roles.[42] The ancient bias in favor of Megara is understandable. Gnesiochus, Heraclea's *oikistēs*, was from Megara, and the city's institutions and dialect were overwhelmingly Megarian in character.[43] The correctness of Justin and Euphorion's version, however, is indicated by the fact that Heracles was the patron divinity of the city. Since Heracles had no cult in Megara but was at home in Boeotia, the Boeotians must have taken the initiative in founding a city in his honor.[44]

Justin provides the only account of the circumstances that led the Boeotian League to decide to found a colony in the Black Sea area. His account is as follows:

> When the Boeotians were suffering from a plague, the oracle at Delphi in answer to their inquiry told them that they should found a colony dedicated to Heracles in the region of the Pontus. When the charge was not fulfilled by them, who preferred death in their own country because of the fear of the long and dangerous trip by sea, the Phocians conducted a war against them. When the Boeotians suffered defeats, they again turned to the oracle. The response was that the remedy would be the same for the war as for the plague. Therefore, after having enrolled a body of colonists, they transported them into the Pontus and founded the city of Heraclea...[45]

Exact dating of these events is not possible.[46] Clearly, however, the war with Phocis and the second consultation must have taken place shortly before the foundation of Heraclea about 560, that is, they probably should be dated to the second half of the 560s. The interval between the first and the second oracle is not

---

[40] Xenophon *Anabasis* 6. 2. 1. Xenophon is probably the source of the similar remarks in Diodorus 14. 31. 3; Arrian *Periplus* 13. 3; and Anonymous *Periplus* 8v10. The Boeotians are also omitted at Apollonius 2, lines 748–749, but probably for metrical reasons since they are mentioned at 2, lines 846–847 (*cf.* Asheri 1972, 23).

[41] Pausanias 5. 26. 7.

[42] Ephorus *FGrH* 2A, 70 F 44a. Apollonius 2, lines 846–847. *Schol. Ap. Rhod.* 185 *ad* 2. 743–749c; 191 *ad* 2. 844–847a. Ps.-Scymnus, lines 1016–1017 (= 972–973).

[43] Hanell 1934, 141–42, 152–55. Magie 1950 II, 1191, n. 23.

[44] Heracles and his exploits form the most common type on the coins of Heraclea (*cf.* Head 1911, 514–16, for the basic types). A statue of him stood in the *agora* (Memnon *FGrH* 3B, 434 F35. 8) and Heraclean games were held during the Roman period (Moretti 1953, no. 80). He also had a month devoted to him in the calendars of Heraclea and her colonies (Hanell 1934, 191; *IOSPE* 1 402, line 7). For Heracles' absence from Megara, see Hanell 1934, 30, who points out that his place was taken by Alcathous. For Heracles in Boeotia, see Cloché n.d., 29; and Nilsson 1906, 446.

[45] Justin 16. 3. 4–7.

[46] Asheri (1972, 24), connects this war with Phocis with the events leading up to the battle of Ceressus, which he dates to *ca.* 571. The battle of Ceressus, however, should probably be dated to the early 5th century as has been shown by Sordi 1953, 256–58.

50   PART I: BOOK

specified, but the narrative implies that it was not long. The whole sequence of events, therefore, probably should be placed in the decade between 570 and 560.

By the middle of the 6th-century consultation of Delphi was a regular part of the procedure for founding a colony.[47] Its role in Justin's account therefore raises no difficulties, and the oracle itself with its lack of ambiguity is unobjectionable. Justin, however, does not tell the whole story. Someone had to ask Delphi if founding a colony sacred to Heracles in the Pontus would be satisfactory expiation for the plague.[48] In other words, there must have been a faction within Boeotia which desired to colonize in the Pontus. Equally clearly, despite Delphi's positive response, it roused little enthusiasm among the states of the Boeotian League. In fertile Boeotia there was little incentive to emigrate, and the member states of the League lacked the experience in Black Sea navigation and trade essential to the successful establishment of a city in that area. Only the defeat by Phocis and the second Delphic oracle sufficed to overcome the League's reluctance to approve the dispatch of the colony.

The motives behind the movement to found Heraclea are obscure, but one circumstance is suggestive. Mariandynia and Bithynia had recently been brought under Lydian authority by Alyattes.[49] As early as Gyges, Lydian kings had used Greek colonies to help control the outlying provinces of their kingdom;[50] Alyattes himself founded a city in Bithynia, Alyatta, to secure that region.[51] Thebes enjoyed good relations with Alyattes' successor Croesus, and there is evidence that suggests that Thebes contributed the largest single contingent of Boeotian colonists.[52] Accordingly, it is a likely hypothesis that the plan to found Heraclea originated in a request from a Lydian king, most likely Alyattes, that Thebes sponsor a colony in Mariandynia.

Be that as it may, when the League finally did authorize the enrollment of colonists, the task of organizing the colony was entrusted to Thebes' close ally Tanagra.[53] Although each state was apparently asked to furnish a body of volunteers led by one of their fellow citizens, the sources have preserved only

[47] Parke and Wormell 1956 I, 78–79. Forrest 1957.

[48] Amandry (1950, 149–59), showed that the answer of the oracle was determined by the form in which the inquirer submitted his question.

[49] Herodotus 1. 28. Herodotus credits Croesus with these conquests, but Ed. Meyer (1965–69 III, 166) pointed out that they were probably the work of Alyattes.

[50] Strabo 13. 1. 22.

[51] Stephanus of Byzantium *s.v. Aluatta*.

[52] Thebes and Lydia: Herodotus 1. 46, 49, 52. Cloché n.d., 18–19. The importance of the Theban contingent is suggested by the presence of a tribe Thebais at Prusias ad Hypium, the successor city of the Heracleote colony of Cierus (Dörner 1952, 10–11, no. 4, line 22). For the Heracleote foundation of Cierus, see Magie 1950 II, 1190, n. 21; and Dörner 1957, 1135–36.

[53] Pausanias 6. 26. 7. For Tanagra and Thebes, see Herodotus 5. 79. 2.

I. SETTLEMENT 51

the name of the leader of the Theban group, Damis, the ancestor of Heracleides Ponticus.[54]

Besides Thebes and Tanagra, Wilamowitz was able to identify the small city of Siphae as having sent some colonists to Heraclea on the grounds that Tiphys, her eponymous hero, had a cult there.[55] To these three cities we can probably also add Thespiae, another ally of Thebes, since Siphae served as her port.[56] That other Boeotian cities contributed settlers is probable, but they can no longer be identified.

Although some members of the Boeotian nobility joined,[57] the total number of Boeotian colonists appears to have been small, since it would be hard to explain otherwise the lack of significant Boeotian influence at Heraclea. Only a few place names, the cult of Heracles, the inclusion of a month *Hērakleios* in the city's calendar, and the probable existence of a tribe Thebais attest to the Boeotian role in her foundation.[58] To obtain additional colonists the League may have sought volunteers in northern Greece and particularly in Thessaly.[59] Even so, the number of prospective settlers was apparently still inadequate, so the League seems to have asked Megara to assume joint responsibility for the colony. This would, at least, seem the most likely explanation for the fact that Gnesiochus, its *oikistēs*, was a Megarian.

The choice was a natural one. Relations between Boeotia and Megara were close during the archaic period[60] and individual Boeotians had previously participated in the founding of Megarian colonies.[61] Megara, moreover, had the

[54] Heracleides Ponticus (Wehrli 1967–69 VII, F2 = *Suda s.v. Herakleidēs Euphronos*).

[55] v. Wilamowitz-Moellendorff 1886, 111, n. 3. For Tiphys in general, see Pherecydes *FGrH* 1A, 3 F107.

[56] Pherecydes *FGrH* 1A, 3 F107. The significance of Siphae and Thespiae was pointed out by Asheri 1972, 26. His further identifications of Potniae and Aphormion on the grounds that they also were connected with Tiphys are doubtful. For Thebes and Thespiae, see Herodotus 5. 79. 2.

[57] This is suggested by the claim of heroic ancestry by a Boeotian settler named Panelus (Stephanus of Byzantium *s.v. Panelos*). Panelus was one of the leaders of the Boeotian force in the *Iliad* (2, line 494).

[58] For toponyms of Boeotian origin near Heraclea, see Asheri 1972, 14–15. For the month *Herakleios*, see Hanell 1934, 202.

[59] This is suggested by Cierus, the name of one of Heraclea's colonies, since the only other city of this name was in Thessaly (Strabo 9. 5. 14; Pape and Benseler 1875 I, 658, *s.v. Kieros*; Dörner 1957, 1135–36). The Thessalian city was also called Arne (Stephanus of Byzantium *s.v. Arnē*).

[60] Ernst Meyer 1925b, 181; and Hanell 1934, 23. For Boeotian influence on Megara's dialect, see Köppner 1892, 559–61.

[61] Byzantium: Boeotian influence is indicated by the presence of a cult of Amphiareus (Hesychius *FGrH* 3B, 390 F1. 16; Dionysius of Byzantium, *Anaplus Bospori*, ed. R. Gingerich [Berlin 1927], 34). Constantine Porphyrogenitus (*De Thematibus* 1. 45) lists the Boeotians as one of the founders of Byzantium. Chalcedon: Hanell 1934, 143. Astacus: Memnon *FGrH* 3B, 434 F12. 2 (named after one of the Spartoi).

52 PART I: BOOK

experience needed for the undertaking. She seems to have been on good terms with Miletus,[62] and her own colonies of Selymbria, Byzantium, and Chalcedon together with Chalcedon's foundation of Astacus dominated the upper Propontis and the Bosporus.[63] Also, conditions in Megara about 560 were such that the Boeotians had no reason to anticipate difficulties in attracting a sufficient number of potential colonists.

The decades between 600 and 560 had been difficult for Megara. Although the chronology of these years is obscure, the main trends are clear. Military reverses, which resulted in the conquest of Salamis and the temporary occupation of Nisaia by Athens and the loss of the mountainous district of Gerania to Corinth, undermined the credit of the aristocratic oligarchy that had governed the city since the end of Theagenes' tyranny in the late 7th century.[64] During these same years, the economic position of the Megarian *dēmos*, always precarious because of the poor quality of the city's small territory, worsened considerably. Those who had had farms on Salamis or had exploited its fishing grounds were the hardest hit, but they were not the only ones to suffer. Plutarch indicates that debt was widespread among Megara's poor and that the resulting discontent sometimes led to assaults on the property of their creditors.[65] Finally, sometime before 560 a coalition composed of rich non-nobles and members of the less prosperous aristocratic families managed to seize power by exploiting the unrest of the poor and to establish in place of the existing oligarchy a government the sources refer to as a democracy.[66] It was this democracy that received and accepted the Boeotian appeal for assistance in the founding of Heraclea.

The Heracleote historians apparently provided a circumstantial narrative of the events surrounding the actual settlement of Heraclea, but only two probable fragments of it remain. Unfortunately, these suggest that much of its detail

[62] This is indicated by Megara's ability to freely colonize in the Propontis and Pontus (*cf.* Burn 1960, 92–93; Highbarger 1927, 109). Megara may have participated in the foundation of Cyzicus: John Lydus (*De Magistratibus populi romani* 3. 70, p. 163 [Wuensch]), lists Megara as founder, and some support is given this by a Megarian decree recognizing *sungeneia* between Megara and Cyzicus (Hollaux 1897; *cf.* Hanell 1934, 131–32, and Bilabel 1920, 47, n. 1).

[63] For these colonies, see Hanell 1934, 119–28.

[64] Ernst Meyer 1925b, 185–87. For the date of Theagenes, see Schachermeyr 1934, 1342–44.

[65] Plutarch *Greek Questions* 18, 295C–D. For economic conditions at Megara, see Trever 1925.

[66] Theognis, lines 39–60, 183–196. For the democracy, see Ernst Meyer 1925b, 184–85; Highbarger 1927, 138–43; and most recently Burn 1960, 247–57. I follow Burn (1960, 255) in rejecting the year 560 for the end of the democracy and instead extending its life beyond 550, a date suggested by the ancient floruit for Theognis (Eusebius 2. 99, ol. 59, 4 [= 541/40]; *Suda* s.v. *Theognis*, ol. 59 [= 544–540]). The date 560, on the other hand, is based solely on the assumption that Heraclea was founded as a refugee colony for the partisans of the democracy.

I. SETTLEMENT

was more romance than authentic tradition. Thus, Plutarch mentions Gnesiochus in a list of *oikistai* who required special evidence to identify the land assigned them by Apollo.[67] That Megara consulted Delphi before accepting the Boeotian proposal by itself is not unlikely, but the riddling character of the oracle given them points to its being a late invention designed to connect Delphi with Megara, the city commonly believed to have been Heraclea's *mētropolis*.[68] Likewise, the story that the Megarian colonists gained refuge from a storm by sailing up the river Acheron which they henceforth called the Soonautes is obviously an etiological story intended to explain a popular local name for the river.[69] The following passage of Justin, however, reveals that the Greek settlers did not receive a hostile reception from the Mariandynoi at the time of their arrival:

> ... they founded a city, Heraclea, and since they had been conveyed to this site by the auspices of the Fates, they acquired great power in a short time. Afterwards [*deinde*] there were many wars of this city against its neighbors.[70]

Despite the lack of detail, Justin does not obscure the important fact that relations between Heraclea and the Mariandynoi only became unfriendly when the city had grown in size and power to the degree that the natives considered it a threat to themselves. The settlement itself, therefore, had taken place peacefully with the consent of the Mariandynoi, who probably saw in the colony a useful ally against their Thynian enemies to the west and an *emporion* through which they might more easily obtain luxury goods from passing Greek ships.[71]

The Mariandynoi allowed Gnesiochus to build his city around the tomb of a local hero whom the Greeks called Agamestor, the good counselor, and worshipped as Heraclea's divine protector. Nothing is so indicative of the initially good relations between the two peoples as this adoption of a native patron for the new city. Nevertheless, the seeds of future conflict had already been sown. As the Mariandynoi had not been conquered, the settlers had at their disposal only the land conceded them by their native hosts. This was probably good farmland in the plain of the Lycus River south of the city.[72] Two factors, however,

---

[67] Plutarch *De Pythiae oraculis* 27, 407. Parke (1939, 63, n. 2) made the identification. *Cf.* Parke and Wormell 1956 I, 80, n. 38.

[68] Pease 1917, 12–13. The oracle in question is probably that in which the Boeotians and Megarians were told to build their city around the wild olive growing on the tomb of Idmon (Apollonius 2, lines 841–850; Herodorus *FGrH* 1A, 31 F51; Promathidas *FGrH* 3B, 430 F3; *Schol Ap. Rhod.* 191 *ad* 2. 843).

[69] *Schol. Ap. Rhod.* 191 *ad* 2. 843.

[70] Justin 16. 3. 7–8.

[71] The pattern is similar to that attested for Lampsacus where the Bebrycians invited the Greeks to settle as allies (Charon *FGrH* 3A, 262 F7).

[72] Memnon *FGrH* 3B, 434 F34. 2.

54 PART I: BOOK

reduced the amount of this land they could actually use. First, *temenoi* had to be set aside for the city's gods and heroes.[73] Second, the Mariandynian settlement near Heraclea probably continued to exist for some time, so that the Heracleotes must have had to share the plain of the Lycus with their native neighbors. Accordingly, hostilities between the Greeks and the Mariandynoi were almost inevitable, since any significant increase in Heraclea's population would result in serious overcrowding of its available land. Moreover, as Aristotle's reference to *gnōrimoi* indicates, Gnesiochus aggravated this situation by ignoring the tradition that the lots of all colonists should be equal and took the status of the individual colonists into account when he made the division of the city's land.[74]

GOVERNMENT

The sources do not permit a systematic description of the constitution of Heraclea and the manner in which its institutions functioned. Direct evidence is confined to a few notes in Aristotle's *Politics* and isolated passages in Aeneas Tacticus, Polyaenus, Justin, and Memnon. Although inscriptions have rectified similar deficiencies for other cities, those of Heraclea are few in number and relatively uninformative, if not misleading, since they largely date from the early centuries AD and refer to the institutions of the city after its reestablishment following its sack in 70. Because the organization of a colony tends to reproduce that of its *mētropolis*, however, it is possible to identify some of Heraclea's institutions if their existence can be documented at one of her own colonies and at Megara or another Megarian colony.

Although Heraclea's history included long periods of oligarchic and tyrannical rule, the city was founded as a democracy. Perhaps because of preconceptions about the nature of democracy, Aristotle's statement to this effect has been disregarded and it has been asserted instead that Heraclea was originally ruled by an oligarchy of large landholders.[75] Such a situation, however, is most

---

[73] The earliest known Heracleote inscription (Hirschfeld 1888, no. 51) is a boundary stone of a *temenos*. F. Sokolowski (1955, 185–86), dates it to the 4th century. A *temenos* of the Tyndaridae is mentioned by Apollonius Rhodius (2, lines 809–810). Apollonius seems to locate this shrine near Heraclea, but if it is the same as the Tyndaridae of Arrian (*Periplus* 13. 4) and the Todaridae of Anonymous *Periplus*, 8v13, then it was some distance to the east of the city (160 stades according to Arrian; 165 according to Anonymous *Periplus*) and, hence, could not belong to the earliest years of its history.

[74] Aristotle *Politics* 5. 4. 2, 1304b33. *Cf.* Asheri 1972, 29. For the principle of equality in the size of colonial lots, see Asheri 1966, 13–16.

[75] Aristotle *Politics* 5. 4. 2, 1304b31. For an oligarchy at the founding, see, for example, Glotz and Cohen 1925–38 I, 168; and Ed. Meyer 1965–69 III, 628. That this passage of Aristotle does refer to Heraclea Pontica was made clear by W.L. Newman (1887–1902 IV, 337).

I. SETTLEMENT

55

unlikely to have arisen at the foundation of a colony. Every settler had to receive a *klēros*,[76] and even allowing for Gnesiochus' failure to observe the principle of equality in their distribution, the disparity among them cannot have been so great as to result in the division of the population into a few large landholders and an impoverished *dēmos*. Moreover, Gnesiochus is unlikely to have granted fewer privileges to the Heracleotes, none of whom were landless, than were enjoyed by the poorer citizens of Megara about 560. These included the right to attend the assembly and to sit as jurors, and this latter privilege is in fact attested for the Heracleote *dēmos*,[77] There is, therefore, no reason to reject Aristotle's statement that Heraclea was initially organized as a democracy, even though it is likely the powers of her assembly were limited to ratifying or rejecting proposals laid before it by the city's magistrates or *boulē*.[78]

Decrees of Heraclea and her colonies always state that they are decisions of *ha boula kai ho damos*.[79] This formula establishes the fact that Heraclea had a *boulē* but tells us nothing about its character. Unfortunately, our earliest detailed evidence for a council at Heraclea concerns the Council of 300 which was overthrown by Clearchus, the city's first tyrant, in 364. This, however, was not a *probouleutic* council of the usual type, but instead the ruling body of the city, its members drawn only from the richest citizens and able to act independently of the assembly.[80] It had come into existence about 370 as a result of an oligarchic revolution, which overthrew a democratic government that had itself been established during the late 5th century. The Council of 300, therefore, cannot be used as evidence for the original council of the city.

Indirect evidence for that council, however, is provided by the information we have about the office of *aisumnētēs*. The office itself has not yet been documented at either Heraclea or its colonies, but the inscriptions of Chersonesus and Callatis do mention a *proaisumnon* who should be the head of a body

---

[76] Gwynn 1918, 100, 106–07. Asheri 1966, 9, 11.

[77] Theognis, lines 53–60; Plutarch *Greek Questions* 18, 295D. That the Heracleote *dēmos* originally possessed judicial authority is indicated by Aristotle *Politics* 5. 5. 5, 1305b34–37, which shows that they exercised this power even during the period of oligarchic rule.

[78] For 6th-century democracy, see especially Butler 1962; and Sealey 1969.

[79] Pargoire 1898, 492, no. 1 (= Kalinka 1933, 95–96, no. 67); Robert 1937, 250; Memnon *FGrH* 3B, 434 F18. 8. For Chersonesus: *IOSPE* 1 340, line 2; 344, lines 9–10; 352, lines 47–48; and *passim*. *Cf.* Latyschev 1885, 279–80. For Callatis: *SEG* 18, 289, line 1; *SEG* 24, 1021, lines 7–8.

[80] For the Council of 300, see Polyaenus 2. 30. 2. The interpretation in the text is based on the account of its actions in Justin 16. 4. 2–4, 18. The supposed existence of a council of 600 (Schneiderwirth 1882, 19) or an assembly of 600 (Ehrenberg 1960, 53), is based on a misinterpretation of Aristotle (*Politics* 5. 5. 2, 1305b2–13), where '600' refers to the number of Heracleotes eligible to hold office and not to an organized body.

56   PART I: BOOK

of *aisumnetai*.[81] At both cities the *proaisumnōn*, and therefore the body of which he was chairman, served for only one month. At Chalcedon likewise the *aisumnetai* had one-month terms, and their chairman, moreover, was *hagemōn boulas*, that is, he presided over Chalcedon's council.[82] Accordingly, Hanell was correct in concluding that the *aisumnetai* and their chairman corresponded to the Athenian *prutaneis* and *epistates*.[83] Since this office existed at Callatis, which was founded in the second half of the 6th century,[84] it must also have been found in Heraclea. A committee of a council with a term of only one month suggests that Heraclea's original council was an annually elected rather than a permanent body. Beyond its probable *probouleutic* function nothing is known concerning its powers.

For most of the magistrates of Heraclea only the titles of their offices remain.[85] The head of state was an eponymous *basileus* whose duties were most likely religious in nature;[86] a recently discovered inscription reveals that in the Roman period, at least, the office could be held by a woman as well as by a man.[87] The actual executive power of the city was wielded by the members of a college of officials called *damiourgoi*. Their number and manner of selection are unknown, but it is clear from the 3rd-century citizens' oath of Chersonesus that they possessed broad responsibility for the welfare of the city and that plots against it and similar matters were to be reported to them.[88] The last of the nonmilitary secular officials that can be assumed to have formed part of the original government of Heraclea are two bodies of judicial magistrates, *nomophulakes* and *prodikoi*, but nothing is known about their duties.[89]

---

[81] For Callatis: Sauciuc-Saveanu 1924, 128, 133; *SEG* 24, 1021, line 9. For Chersonesus: *IOSPE* 1 352, line 57; 690; *GDI* 3, 3052, line 12; Hanell 1934, 150.

[82] *GDI* 3, 3053, 3054.

[83] Hanell 1934, 150. Pippidi 1971, 82–83, suggests that the *proaisumnon* also presided over the assembly at Callatis.

[84] For the date, see chapter 2.

[85] Some magistrates attested only in the late 5th or 4th centuries cannot with certainty be referred to Heraclea's original constitution. These include: (1) the *stratēgoi*, Ps.-Aristotle *Oeconomica* 2. 2. 8, 1347b13 (Van Groningen 1933); (2) the *agoranomoi*, Hirschfeld 1888, 884, no. 50; V. Canarache 1957, 15, 196, no. 459; and (3) the mint officials who reveal themselves by their emission marks on the city's coins (e.g. *Recueil* I.2, 346, no. 5, 348, no. 21, 351, no. 44; Franke 1966).

[86] Hirschfeld 1888, 883, no. 45; Kalinka 1933, 97, no. 69, lines 9–10.

[87] Dörner 1962, 34.

[88] *IOSPE* 1 401 (= *SIG*[4] 1 360, lines 17–19, 47–48).

[89] *Nomophulakes*: *IOSPE* 1 342, line 1; 343, line 2; 351, line 1. Aristotle (*Politics* 6. 5. 13, 1323a9) refers to them as an aristocratic body (*cf.* Hanell 1934, 154–55). *Prodikoi*: *IOSPE* 1 359, line 35. Minns (1913, 541), suggests that they may have represented the council in legal affairs as a similarly named body did at Corcyra.

I. SETTLEMENT

57

Only one body of religious officials can be shown to have probably existed at Heraclea, the *summnamones*, that is, a college of *mnamones*, who are found both at Megara and Chersonesus.[90] Their known functions involve the public recitation of decrees and the preparation of stelae containing decrees connected with religious affairs.[91]

Citizenship in all Greek cities depended on membership in one or more kinship or residential groups. At Heraclea two such are known, tribes and *hekatostues*. In contrast to the sketchiness of our knowledge concerning the city's magistrates, a relatively clear idea of these bodies can be won from the following passage of Aeneas Tacticus:

> Similarly, in Heraclea Pontica, when the democracy was in power and the rich were conspiring against it and about to make an attack, the leaders of the *demos*, who knew what was imminent, persuaded the people to establish a division into 60 *hekatostues* in place of their former three tribes and four *hekatostues* so that the rich should do both guard duty and the other services in the new divisions. The result was that here, too, the rich were scattered in each *hekatostus*, few among many of the supporters of the democracy.[92]

The reform described by Aeneas was instituted about 370, but the existence of *hekatostues* at Megara and other Megarian colonies proves that these groups formed part of the original organization of Heraclea.[93]

The three tribes were obviously kinship groups of the type usual in Greek cities. As far as those at Heraclea are concerned, only one question about them has to be answered: their identity. Scholars have generally identified the three Heracleote tribes with the three Doric tribes known to have existed at Megara.[94] This identification, however, ignores the important role played by the Boeotian League in the founding of Heraclea. In such circumstances it is possible that a colony's tribal structure would not repeat that of either of its metropoleis but would instead be based on the regional origins of the various groups of settlers.[95] In the absence of evidence from Heraclea, only data concerning the tribes of her daughter colonies can resolve this question. Although such information has not yet been furnished by the excavations of Callatis and Chersonesus, a 3rd century AD inscription from Prusias ad Hypium, the later name of Heraclea's colony of Cierus, contains a list of that city's twelve

---

[90] *IOSPE* 1 344, line 21; 346, line 5; 349, line 17; 352, line 49. Hanell 1934, 154.

[91] *IOSPE* 1 352, line 49; perhaps 353, line 4. Syriscus *FGrH* 3B, 807 T1, lines 16–17. Minns 1913, 542.

[92] Aeneas *On Siegecraft* 11. 10–11 (Hunter 1927).

[93] Hanell 1934, 140–44.

[94] E.g. Schneiderwirth 1882, 19, and Hanell 1934, 141.

[95] *Cf.* the cases of Cyrene (Herodotus 4. 161. 3) and Thurii (Diodorus 12. 11. 3).

58 PART I: BOOK

tribes.[96] Nine are clearly of Hellenistic or Roman origin, but three, Megaris, Thebais, and Dionysias, probably date from the founding of Cierus. Their presence there implies their existence in Cierus' metropolis also and thus strongly points to Heraclea's tribes being organized according to the places of origin of her colonists. The first two tribes, Megaris and Thebais, would have contained the settlers from Megara and Thebes, the cities that probably provided the largest contingents. The remaining Boeotians and whatever northern Greeks may have joined the colony would have been placed in the third tribe dedicated to the god Dionysus, a most suitable patron for them since his cult was widespread in Boeotia and northern Greece.

The nature of the *hekatostues* is more difficult to determine. The institution is not peculiar to Megara since they are also found at Lampsacus and Samos.[97] The name, 'hundreds', suggests that the *hekatostues* like the Roman centuries formed part of a military system in which a *hekatostus* was either a kinship or a residence group that was supposed to furnish a force of 100 men to the city's army.[98] Scholars have generally assumed that the Megarian *hekatostues* were kinship groups that functioned as subdivisions of the city's tribes. Accordingly, they have interpreted Aeneas' reference to three tribes and four *hekatostues* at Heraclea to mean that there were three tribes with four *hekatostues* in each.[99] There are, however, serious objections to this view. First, if the analysis of Heraclea's tribal structure offered above is correct, it is difficult to understand why the city would have preserved the subdivisions of the Megarian tribes while rejecting the tribes themselves. Second and more important, it is questionable whether the *hekatostues* at Megara were kinship groups. The name of one of them, Kynosouris, is known and it is the same as that of one of the five villages that made up Megara.[100] The implication is that each of the villages made up one *hekatostus* or, in other words, that Megara contained five *hekatostues*, and there is no way that five *hekatostues* can be evenly allotted among three tribes. A similar situation may also have existed at Chalcedon where to date 16 *hekatostues* have been identified.[101] This strongly suggests that the Megarian *hekatostues* were residence units and not subdivisions of her tribes. If this is so, then it is likely that the same would be true at Heraclea.

---

[96] Dörner 1962, 10–11, no. 4, lines 30 (Megaris), 22 (Thebais), 38 (Dionysias).

[97] Samos: *SIG*⁴ 1 312, line 30; 333, line 29. Lampsacus: Busolt and Swoboda 1926 I, 261, n. 1. In both places they are subdivisions of the tribes.

[98] Hanell 1934, 141.

[99] E.g. Hunter 1927, 140. Busolt and Swoboda (1926 I, 261, n. 1) suggest that *en hekastēi* be inserted before *hekatostuōn* in the text of Aeneas.

[100] *IG*² 4 42. This was pointed out by Cary (1935) in a review of K. Hanell, *Megarische Studien*. For the village names, see Plutarch *Greek Questions* 17, 295B.

[101] Hanell 1934, 142.

I. SETTLEMENT 59

Aeneas' text should, therefore, probably be interpreted to mean that Heraclea contained only four *hekatostues* before the reform.[102] Unfortunately, only the discovery of new evidence can completely settle this question.

But if the character of the *hekatostues* is in doubt, their importance is not. They were the basic organizational unit of the Heracleote government. Evidence from Megara and Byzantium indicates that enrollment in a *hekatostus* was required of all fully privileged citizens,[103] and this is confirmed for Heraclea by Aeneas whose account shows that the citizens met in their *hekatostues* to perform their civic and military duties. As to the age at which a Heracleote began to fulfill these obligations, we can only say that a citizen seems to have been eligible for military service from the age of 16 until he reached 65.[104]

[102] If correct, this has important implications for the size of the original colony at Heraclea. Assuming that the *hekatostues* each contained 100 men at the time they were established, the fact that there were only four of them points to the first settlement containing about 400 men, a figure that is in line with recent scholarship which suggests that most Greek colonies were small, being composed of only a few hundred individuals (Bérard 1960, 81; Andrewes 1967, 99–100).

[103] At Megara a citizen was identified by giving his name, his father's name, and that of his *hekatostus* (IG^2 4 42, lines 18–20). At Byzantium a man being granted citizenship was allowed to enroll in whatever *hekatostus* he desired (*GDI* 3, 3059, line 30). Presumably there were registers of the members of each *hekatostus* and proof of citizenship was provided by a person's name appearing on such a list. For the similar function of *deme* registers at Athens, see Aristotle *Ath. Pol.* 42. 1.

[104] Polyaenus 2. 30. 3.

CHAPTER II

FROM THE FOUNDATION TO THE END
OF THE PELOPONNESIAN WAR: 560 TO 404

The Fall of the Democracy

Heraclea grew rapidly during the second half of the 6th century. Although the increase of the original settlers was probably responsible for some of this growth, its rapidity suggests that much of it should be ascribed to the arrival of new immigrants, most likely from Megara following the replacement of that city's democratic government by an oligarchy. The added population strengthened Heraclea, but it also led to serious problems in the new *polis'* relations with the Mariandynoi and in her own internal life.[1]

At the root of her difficulties was the city's need for land to satisfy her expanding population. Had the Mariandynoi been conquered at the time of Heraclea's foundation, this would not have been a major problem. With the full territory of Mariandynia at their disposal, the Heracleotes could have dealt with this situation as other colonies did, namely, by setting aside a considerable portion of their land as a reserve from which new lots could be made as the need for them arose.[2] Possessing, however, only the limited land given them by the Mariandynoi, this course was not open to the Heracleotes, and what little reserve they may have been able to establish must have been quickly exhausted by the swift rise of Heraclea's population. The result was that her citizens seem to have begun early to enviously eye the territory of their native neighbors.

When the Mariandynoi belatedly recognized their error in permitting the Greeks to settle among them and perceived the serious danger posed by the growth of Heraclea, open warfare broke out between the two peoples.[3] No details are preserved concerning the course of the struggle, but it was clearly long and bitter with neither side winning a decisive victory until some time

---

[1] Justin 16. 3. 8. Heraclea's ability to colonize in the 6th century suggests an unusually rapid increase in her population for which additional immigration is the most likely explanation. The weakness of the Boeotian element in her culture points to Megara as the source of any new settlers.

[2] Asheri 1966, 10–11.

[3] Justin 16. 3. 7–8.

62   PART I: BOOK

after 480.[4] Unambiguous evidence of the severity of the threat to Heraclea's survival presented by the hostility of the Mariandynoi is, however, provided by the city's walls, walls that were formidable enough to intimidate the Ten Thousand in 400.[5]

Meanwhile, the land problem resulted first in the appearance of *stasis* within Heraclea, and then in the fall of the democracy and its replacement by an oligarchy shortly after the foundation of the city. According to Aristotle, our only source for these events, the democracy fell because of the insolence of the democratic leaders (*tōn dēmagōgōn*) who unjustly brought about the exile of various members of the upper class (*hoi gnōrimoi*). After a time, however, the number of exiles rose to the point where they were able to unite, return to Heraclea by force, and overthrow the democracy, much as had happened at Megara where the democratic leaders had driven out the aristocrats in order to confiscate their property.[6]

Despite Aristotle's brevity, the implications of his account are clear. When the aggressive attitude of the Mariandynoi foreclosed the possibility of gaining more land at their expense, a disturbed period ensued during which the leaders of the democracy looked to the estates of the aristocrats to satisfy the needs of their followers. Such a course of action was likely to be popular. Bitterness over Gnesiochus' favoring of the aristocrats in the original allotment probably rose as the land shortage worsened, and this feeling may well have been magnified by resentment on the part of Heraclea's Megarian majority at the prominence of members of the city's Boeotian minority in the aristocracy.[7] Trials took place and, although the charge is unknown, in the heated atmosphere the aristocrats were condemned to exile and their property confiscated. Before the democrats could exploit their success, however, the exiled aristocrats returned and drove them from power.

Once in power and again in possession of their property, the exiles quickly moved to ensure their continued control of Heraclea. The democracy was suppressed and an oligarchy established in its place, organized on the principle that the city was composed of a number of *oikoi* or households whose political privileges varied according to their wealth.[8] Thus, although the institutional structure remained unchanged, henceforth only the rich enjoyed the privilege

---

[4] That the Mariandynoi had not been subdued by 480 is indicated by their providing a contingent in Xerxes' army (Herodotus 7. 72. 2).

[5] Xenophon *Anabasis* 6. 2. 8; Athenaeus 8. 351d. The oldest surviving segment of Heraclea's walls dates only from the 4th or 3rd century (Hoepfner 1966, 21, 37–38).

[6] Aristotle *Politics* 5. 4. 2–3, 1304b31–39.

[7] Asheri 1972, 27, 29–30.

[8] For the *oikos* principle in general, see Lacey 1968, 52–53.

II. FROM THE FOUNDATION TO THE END OF THE PELOPONNESIAN WAR   63

of holding office while the rest of the Heracleotes retained only the right to sit on juries[9] and, presumably, to attend the assembly. We have no information specifically concerning the manner in which these changes were implemented, but the passage of Aeneas Tacticus discussed in the previous chapter suggests that the key measure was the imposition of a high property qualification for membership in the *hekatostues*, the bodies in which a citizen had to be enrolled if he was to enjoy full political privileges. This would then have been followed by a revision of the citizen rolls in which all those Heracleotes who could not meet this criterion were allowed to retain their membership in the city's three tribes but were stricken from the lists of those belonging to the *hekatostues*.[10] These measures by themselves would have limited political influence to a small minority of the Heracleotes, but application of the *oikos* principle further reduced the number of those who actually governed the city, since under it only the head of an *oikos*, the father, or in the event of his death his eldest son, was entitled to hold office.[11]

Although Heraclea was to be under oligarchic rule until 424, it is clear from Justin and Aristotle that the fall of the democracy was followed not by internal stability but by renewed disturbances which eventually resulted in fundamental changes in the form and character of the oligarchy. Dissension, however, was centered now not among the poorer Heracleotes but within the ranks of the ruling class itself. The protests were directed against the *oikos* principle, and its exclusion of all but the heads of the wealthiest families from office. What form they took and how long they lasted is not known, but the protests did succeed in forcing the oligarchs to abandon the *oikos* principle and to gradually widen the number of the rich able to hold office to include, first, the eldest son during the lifetime of his father and then, finally, all of a man's sons.[12]

Following, as it probably did, the outbreak of hostilities with the Mariandynoi, the establishment of an oligarchy dominated by the returned exiles can only have exacerbated the already existing tension between them and the rest of the Heracleotes, especially when the latter saw their political rights and their hopes for land lost as a result. If the first challenges to the new oligarchy came from its

---

[9] Aristotle *Politics* 5. 5. 5, 1305b34–36. As can be seen from *Politics* 6. 4. 5, 1321a27–31, *politeuma* in this passage means 'those qualified to hold office'. Newman (1887–1902 IV, 35, nn. 3–4) is probably correct in suggesting that Aristotle means that juries were drawn from the whole citizen body and not that the oligarchs were excluded from jury service.

[10] As George Grote (1907 XII, 363) recognized, Aeneas Tacticus 11. 10. 2 implies that only the rich were enrolled in the *hekatostues* at the time of the planned *coup*.

[11] Aristotle *Politics* 5. 5. 2–4, 1305b2–22.

[12] Justin 16. 3. 8; 16. 4. 1. Aristotle *Politics* 5. 5. 2, 1305b2–12.

64   PART I: BOOK

own excluded members and not the populace, that is probably to be ascribed in part to the demoralization of the populace, but in the main to the fact that the oligarchs resorted during the third quarter of the 6th century to the traditional Greek remedy for land hunger, colonization. The sources refer to two Heracleote colonies, Panelus and Callatis, whose foundations belong to this period.

The earliest was probably Panelus, but of this settlement, which seems never to have attained any importance, we know only that it was located in the Pontus and that Panelus, its *oikistēs*, was a member of the original contingent of Boeotian colonists of Heraclea.[13]

More important was the foundation of Callatis, the first of Heraclea's two trans-Pontic colonies. According to Ps.-Scymnus, our main source, Callatis was founded by the Heracleotes on the instructions of an oracle, probably Delphi, when Amyntas ascended the throne of Macedon.[14] Although Amyntas III, the father of Philip II, has been suggested,[15] scholars generally agree that the reference is to Amyntas I, whose accession Eusebius dated to the year 540.[16] In view of our ignorance concerning the evidence on which this synchronism is based, however, we should probably disregard its seeming exactness and treat it only as indicating a date sometime during the third quarter of the 6th century for the establishment of Callatis.

Although the exact date of Callatis' foundation thus remains uncertain, the site chosen by its *oikistēs*, present-day Mangalia in Romania, allows no doubt that it was land and not trade that attracted its Heracleote colonists. Trade along the west coast of the Pontus and with its hinterland had already attained some volume, but Callatis had the poorest location of any of the west Pontic cities to exploit these opportunities since it neither possessed a safe anchorage for ships nor controlled any significant trade route to the interior. Although Callatis drew some advantage from the coastal trade, it was clearly the rich harvests promised by the 'black-earth steppe' country,[17] a promise whose

---

[13] Stephanus of Byzantium *s.v. Panelos*.

[14] Ps.-Scymnus, lines 760–764. Anonymous *Periplus* 15r6–10. See also Memnon *FGrH* 434 F13; Strabo 7. 6. 1; Orus, *apud Etymologicum Magnum*, ed. C.T. Gaisford (Oxford 1848), 486, line 41, who remarks that it was named after a nearby lake. Mela (2. 22) lists Miletus as the *mētropolis*, but this is probably the result of confusion with Tomis as suggested by Bilabel 1920, 17. On the other hand, Ovid's characterization of the founders of Callatis as *quos Alcathoi memorant e moenibus ortos/ sedibus his profugos constituisse Larem* (*Tristia* 1. 10, lines 39–40) may reflect a local tradition at Callatis (*memorant*) crediting Megara with a direct role in the city's establishment. Hanell (1934, 130) suggests confusion with Mesembria.

[15] *ATL* 1, 539, n. 1.

[16] For discussion, see Pippidi 1971, 63–64. The discovery of a late 5th or early 4th century Athenian cup which was dedicated to Zeus Soter tends to support the early date, since it presupposes the existence of a shrine and, thus, the city prior to the reign of Amyntas III (Popescu 1964).

[17] Short 193, 146–48.

II. FROM THE FOUNDATION TO THE END OF THE PELOPONNESIAN WAR 65

fulfillment is evident from the ear of wheat and the head of Demeter that appears on her coinage,[18] that determined the site of the colony.

Our evidence for the first centuries of Callatis' existence is limited, but the city clearly prospered. Callatis probably early reduced to subjection the inhabitants of Cerbatis,[19] the Thracian settlement that had occupied the site of the colony before the arrival of the Greeks, and by the early Hellenistic period it had gained control of a sizable territory and assumed a position of leadership among the west Pontic cities.[20] Nevertheless, unlike the situation that prevailed with Heraclea's other trans-Pontic colony, Chersonesus, the indications are that relations between Callatis and her *mētropolis*, although probably cordial, were never particularly close. The two cities may have jointly founded a short-lived settlement named Heraclea south of Callatis,[21] and Callatis did honor Heracles as *ktistēs*,[22] but her appeal to Heraclea for aid against Byzantium about 260 was unsuccessful.[23] Such coolness toward her colony should not be considered surprising. Trade between Heraclea and the west coast of the Pontus existed throughout much of her history, but it was always of minor importance compared to that with the north coast or the Aegean.[24] Moreover, since none of the Greek cities or native populations of the area were important naval powers, Callatis' political affairs held little interest for Heraclea.

HERACLEA AND PERSIA TO 480

Until the defeat of Croesus by Cyrus in 547 Mariandynia formed the most northerly possession of the kingdom of Lydia.[25] If, as was suggested in the previous chapter, Heraclea was founded at the instigation of Lydia, it is possible that the city recognized Croesus as her overlord and maintained friendly relations with him until the conquest of his kingdom by the Persians. If such relations existed, however, they are unlikely either to have been particularly close or to have imposed serious burdens on Heraclea. The organization of the

---

[18] Pick and Regling 1898–1910, 97–98, nos. 196–205; and Head 1911, 273.

[19] Pliny *NH* 4. 44. For its Thracian character, see Detschew 1957, 223, 240.

[20] Callatis' prominence is indicated by the leading role it took in the revolt against Lysimachus in 313 (Diodorus 19. 73; Preda 1968, 7–8). For her territory, see Pippidi 1971, 210.

[21] Pliny *NH* 4. 44.

[22] Pick and Regling 1898–1910, 111, nos. 290–296. Head 1911, 274.

[23] Memnon *FGrH* 3B, 434 F13.

[24] Menippus *Periplus* 5715–5716, and Anonymous *Periplus* 8v11, both give the distance between Heraclea and Apollonia as 1000 stades, which suggests the existence of a sailing route between the two cities. For the volume of the trade, see Canarache 1957, 357–59.

[25] Smith 1944, 36, 135. The date is based on the so-called Nabonidus Chronicle which places the fall of Lydia in the ninth year of Nabonidus (Pritchard 1955, 306).

66 PART I: BOOK

Lydian Empire was loose and the authority of its monarch limited, especially in its more distant provinces where the various local rulers, although recognizing his suzerainty, seem to have continued to govern their peoples much as they had done before becoming subjects of Lydia.[26]

Although close relations with Persia were at the heart of Heraclea's foreign policy until the last third of the 4th century, the city probably did not immediately recognize Cyrus. When it did is not known, but Heraclea is unlikely to have been under serious pressure to do so before the early years of the reign of Darius. At the time of his accession in 521 Persian authority was weak or non-existent throughout much of northern Anatolia. The only representative of the Persian crown in the area was the satrap of Dascyleum and his power was confined to Aeolis and the Asiatic coast and hinterland of the Hellespont and Propontis, the area the Greeks called Hellespontine Phrygia and the Persians *tyaiy drayahyā*, or 'those on the sea'.[27] Alone of the Pontic peoples the Paphlagonians had voluntarily recognized Cyrus, but they had received in return the privilege of neither having a satrap appointed for their territory nor being placed under the authority of the satraps of either Dascyleum or Cappadocia.[28] Sometime before 513, however, most likely as part of the preparations for Darius' Scythian expedition, this situation changed. The Bithynians and the Mariandynoi recognized the overlordship of Persia[29] and they, together with the Paphlagonians and Cappadocians, were placed under the authority of the satrap of Dascyleum.[30] The year 513, therefore, should be considered the *terminus ante quem* for the establishment of formal relations between Heraclea and Persia. The actual date may have been a few years earlier since Ctesias' account of the raid into Scythia conducted early in Darius' reign by Ariaramnes, the satrap of Cappadocia, implies that at least some of the south Pontic cities were already under Persian authority.[31]

---

[26] Radet 1892, 221.

[27] For the extent of Persian holdings in northern Anatolia before Darius, see Xenophon *Cyropaedia* 8. 6. 7–8, 21, and 8. 8. 1. *Contra* the wholesale condemnation of the *Cyropaedia* as a source by, for example, Ed. Meyer 1965–69 III, 130, n. 1, and Breitenbach 1967, 1790–1817, see the comments of Smith 1944, 24–28. For *tayaiy drayahyā*, see Kent 1953, DB 1. 13; DSe 28; XPh 23. For its identification with the satrapy of Dascyleum, see R. Schmitt 1972. Herodotus (3. 126) confirms the existence of the satrapy of Dascyleum before Darius.

[28] Xenophon *Cyropaedia* 8. 6. 8. For Cappadocia as a satrapy, see Ctesias *FGrH* 3C1, 688 F13. 20; Xenophon *Cyropaedia* 8. 6. 7; and the comments of Beloch 1912–27 III.2, 132, and Lehmann-Haupt 1921, 121.

[29] From Herodotus (4. 85) it is clear that Darius' line of march to the Bosporus ran through Bithynia. For the date of the Scythian expedition, see Cameron 1943, 313; and Burn 1962, 128, n. 4.

[30] Herodotus 3. 90. 2.

[31] Ctesias *FGrH* 3C1, 688 F13. 20 (the 30 penteconters must have been provided by the cities of northern Anatolia).

II. FROM THE FOUNDATION TO THE END OF THE PELOPONNESIAN WAR 67

From the last decades of the 6th century, therefore, Heraclea and the other south Pontic cities belonged to the Persian Empire – but in what status? According to Strabo, who provides a compressed history of Heraclea in his twelfth book, the city was *autonomos* prior to the establishment of Clearchus' tyranny in 364.[32] Although *autonomos* can simply mean independent, Strabo's similar characterization of Sinope,[33] an undoubted Persian subject, suggests that his source used the word to describe a status established by a treaty: the Great King granted Heraclea not only the privilege of retaining its own laws, institutions, and defenses, but also freedom from interference in her internal life by his satraps and other officials; Heraclea, in return, recognized his sovereignty and promised to pay tribute and perform military service when summoned by him.[34] This has been doubted, and the status of the Pontic cities assimilated to that of the cities of the west coast, but the cases are not parallel.[35] The former most likely accepted Persian rule voluntarily whereas the latter, except for Miletus, were forcibly subdued and their status determined by Cyrus in his capacity as their conqueror. But, as the example of Miletus shows, the Persian kings granted autonomous status to cities that freely accepted their rule and the existence of such a relationship between Heraclea and Persia is not only suggested by Strabo but also implied by Justin's reference to her not joining the Delian League *ob amicitiam regum Persicorum*.[36]

Recognition of Persia imposed few burdens or serious restrictions on Heraclea, and it did bring the city distinct advantages. Her tribute probably was not oppressively high and, except for possibly furnishing a few of the 30 penteconters used by Ariaramnes for his Scythian raid, the Persians seem to have

---

[32] Strabo 12. 3. 6.

[33] LSJ *s.v. autonomos*. For Sinope: Strabo 12. 3. 11.

[34] For the terms, see Xenophon *Cyropaedia* 7. 4. 9. For Sinope in the 4th century the status is implied by Polyaenus 7. 21. 5. The visible symbol of the status was the retention of its walls by a city (*cf.* Herodotus 1. 164; Xenophon *Cyropaedia* 3. 1. 10, for the leveling of walls as a symbol of subjection). Heraclea (above n. 5) and Sinope (Polyaenus 7. 21. 2) both meet this criterion for autonomous status. For the status itself, see H. Schaefer 1963, 256–59.

[35] Maksimova 1956, 96–97.

[36] Justin 16. 3. 9 (the plural *regum* suggests a policy extending over several reigns). Nymphis *FGrH* 3B, 432 F6, may also be relevant in this connection (see the comments of Jacoby *FGrH* 3B *Texte*, 263 *ad* F 6). For the right of conquest as the basis of Persian authority in Ionia, see Hampl 1939, 26–28. Justin's statement (38. 7. 2) that Paphlagonia, Cappadocia, Bithynia, Pontus, and Armenia were never touched by a foreign conqueror, although incorrect as far as Cappadocia and Armenia are concerned, probably does reflect a lack of references to Persian actions in northern Anatolia in the historical tradition, as may also Nicephorus Gregoras' remark (Letter 45. 159) that the Medes and Persians stayed away from Heraclea. Lack of Persian activity in the Pontus is also implied by Arrian's statement (*FGrH* 2B, 156 F71) that Phanagoria was founded by Teans fleeing the Persians. For Miletus' treaty, see Herodotus 1. 41. 4 (*cf.* the terms offered Athens by Mardonius at 8. 140a2).

68   PART I: BOOK

demanded no significant military service from Heraclea before the late 480s.[37] At the same time, although no Persian garrisons or officials were placed in Bithynia or Mariandynia,[38] Heraclea gained a potentially useful ally in the satrap of Dascyleum should she be attacked by her neighbors. Not surprisingly, therefore, Heraclea did not participate either in the revolt of the Greek cities of northwest Anatolia that broke out after Darius' defeat by the Scythians or in the more serious Ionian revolt, but instead remained consistently loyal to Persia.

During the second half of the 480s, however, Heraclea's isolation from events occurring outside the Bosporus ended. Xerxes had begun to gather a great fleet for his projected invasion of European Greece, and Heraclea and the other cities of northern Anatolia received orders to build warships for it.[39] In 480, according to Herodotus, these cities furnished a contingent of 100 triremes with crews armed in Greek fashion.[40] The size of Heraclea's squadron is not attested, but it was probably small since the bulk of the force must have been contributed by the long-established cities of the Hellespont and the Propontis and the major Pontic naval power at this time was Sinope, not Heraclea.[41] Nothing is known of its exploits, although it presumably took part in the battles of Artemisium and Salamis before being ordered to return home.[42]

[37] No Pontic city seems to have provided Darius with ships for his Scythian expedition. The only surviving reference to Persian activity in the Pontus prior to the 480s is an obscure passage of Ctesias (*FGrH* 3C1, 688 F13. 22) stating that Datis had been there before the Marathon campaign.

[38] Suggested by the activity of Doedalsus in the 5th century (Memnon *FGrH* 3B, 434 F12. 3; Strabo 12. 4. 2). See also Ed. Meyer 1965–69 IV.1, 50–51. Probably indicative of the limitations of Persian power in northern Anatolia is the fact that no Pontic people is mentioned in any of the lists of subject peoples put up by the Persian Kings (that the so-called satrapy lists are really lists of peoples ruled by the Persians has been shown by Cameron 1973, 47–50).

[39] Diodorus 11. 2. 1.

[40] I take Herodotus 7. 95. 2, as Ephorus apparently did (Diodorus, 11. 3. 8, where the strength is given as 80 ships) to refer to contingents from both the Pontus and Hellespontine regions. Stein (1893–1908 IV, 94 *ad* 7. 95, line 10) denied this, asserting instead that *Pontus* uniquely in this passage designated the whole Hellespontine area (i.e. the Hellespont, Propontis, and Bosporus) instead of the Euxine as is usual in Herodotus (*cf.* J.E. Powell 1938, *s.v. Pontos*, c). Such an *ad hoc* explanation for Herodotus' failure to mention the contingents from the Propontis is, however, unlikely. More probably, Hellespont here includes the Propontis, a usage that is found elsewhere in his work Legrand 1954, *s.v. Hellespontos*) and attested by Strabo (7. 57) as not unusual in early geographic literature.

[41] Strabo 12. 3. 11. D. Robinson 1906a, 153.

[42] Tarn 1908, 214–16, suggested that these northern units were among the ships lost trying to go around Euboea. This reconstruction, however, is based on his theory that the Persian fleet was divided into five regional squadrons of 120 ships each, a view whose weaknesses have been clearly pointed out by Hignett (1963, 345–50). Hignett's own suggestion (1963, 246) that the Greek units were sent home after Salamis has been adopted in the text as the most likely account of the final disposition of the Pontic ships.

II. FROM THE FOUNDATION TO THE END OF THE PELOPONNESIAN WAR   69

Equally unknown is the fate of the troop of Mariandynoi, who, along with the Ligyes, Matienoi, and Cappadocians, served in the light infantry corps commanded by Gobryes, the son of Darius and Arty-stone.[43]

THE CONQUEST OF THE MARIANDYNOI

Their participation in the Persian invasion of Greece temporarily halted the long struggle between the Heracleotes and the Mariandynoi. It resumed, however, with the return of their forces and lasted until some time in the second or third quarter of the 5th century, when the Mariandynoi were decisively defeated, their lands were confiscated, and they themselves became the subjects of Heraclea. Although the initial Heracleote victory may only have extended the city's territory westward to the Cales River,[44] by 424 the Heracleotes had pushed across the Hypius River to the borders of Bithynia, that is, to the Sangarius River where the boundary between the two peoples seems to have stood in 400.[45] Mistress of the largest and richest territory ruled by any south Pontic city and able to man a formidable fleet by using her Mariandynian subjects as rowers, Heraclea had achieved a position of preeminence among the cities of the Pontus by the end of the century.[46] At the same time, although the threat from the Mariandynoi disappeared, Heraclea's victory raised new problems for the city. Despite their hostility, the Mariandynoi had served as a buffer between Heraclea and the more powerful and aggressive Bithynians. With the conquest of Mariandynia the buffer disappeared and the Heracleotes and Bithynians faced each other across the Sangarius. Only the fact that the Bithynian rulers were preoccupied until the late 3rd century with expanding their power westward to the Propontis saved Heraclea from a new and even more serious conflict on her western border. As it was, despite the gradual development of trade between Heraclea and Bithynia, it is clear that relations between the two peoples became increasingly strained as the century

---

[43] Herodotus 7. 72. 1.

[44] The *terminus ante quem* is 424 (Thucydides 4. 75. 2). The Cales as the limit of the initial conquest was proposed by Desider 1967, 397–98.

[45] That the Sangarius was the border in 400 is indicated by the fact that Xenophon (*Anabasis* 6. 2. 19) places the boundary of Heracleotis at the beginning of Bithynian territory but does not, as Wilson (1960, 424) pointed out, mention crossing this major river. Xenophon (*Anabasis* 6. 4. 1–2) cited by Desideri (1967, 398, n. 165), in support of his view that the Cales was the limit of Heracleote territory in 400, is irrelevant since it refers to geographical and ethnic rather than political conditions.

[46] *Cf.* Xenophon *Anabasis* 5. 6. 10, and the account of the Ten Thousand's stay at Heraclea in *Anabasis* 6. 2. For the use of the Mariandynoi as rowers, see Aristotle *Politics* 7. 5. 7, 1327b7–16.

70 PART I: BOOK

progressed, although there is no evidence of actual fighting between them.[47] A more important and pressing problem immediately after the conquest of the Mariandynoi was the organization of Heraclea's new territory.

The land itself was dealt with quickly. The oligarchs appropriated the best of the land near the city and carved it into estates for themselves. The more distant, or perhaps the later conquered, areas – such as the valley of the river Hypius and, probably, the more rugged and mountainous regions of Mariandynia – became, on the other hand, part of Heraclea's territory (*chora*).[48]

As for the Mariandynoi themselves, conquest had made them subjects of Heraclea but it did not end their existence as a people. They continued to live in their villages and work their land while preserving their language and culture more or less intact.[49] The only difference was that the land now often formed part of the estate of one or another of the oligarchs to whom – as the Heracleote term for the Mariandynoi, *dorophoroi* or 'gift bearers', indicates – they paid a tribute, presumably a fixed percentage of their crops and other produce.[50] The sources describe their legal status, and that of several other peoples such as the Helots or Penestae, as slavery.[51] Although modern scholars have preferred to call them serfs on the basis of Pollux's definition of their condition as lying 'between free and slave [*metaxu de elutherōn kai doulōn*]'.[52] Detlef Lotze has convincingly shown that the ancient description of them as

---

[47] Xenophon *Anabasis* 6. 4. 23, but notice the aid the Heracleote merchant renders the Ten Thousand in raiding Bithynian villages and the assistance afforded the Arcadians in their plans to raid in Bithynia by Heraclea (Xenophon *Anabasis* 6. 2. 17).

[48] Specific evidence bearing on the distribution of the conquered land is lacking, but Justin 16. 4. 2 suggests that the aristocrats controlled most of it in the early 360s. That the Hypius Valley was not included in the initial division is indicated by the foundation of Cierus. The date of Cierus' foundation is not known. At present the *terminus ante quem* is the early 3rd century (Memnon *FGrH* 3B, 434 F9. 4); the *terminus post quem* is the Heracleote conquest of the area in the 5th century. For numismatic evidence of its existence in the early 4th century, see E. Robinson 1921, 4–7; and for possible archaeological evidence for the late 5th century, see Dörner 1957, 1134–35. For the advantages of Cierus' location, see Dörner 1957, 1134.

[49] Nymphis (*FGrH* 3B, 432 F5) and Domitius Callistratus (*FGrH* 3B, 433 F3) attest to the performance of the rites in honor of Bormus in their day, and Strabo (12. 5. 4) indicates that their language still survived in the 1st century AD.

[50] Euphorion F78 = Athenaeus 6. 263; *dōrophoroi kaleoiath' hupophrissontes anaktas*; Hesychius D27 (Latte), *s.v. dōrophorous tous oiketas. Mariandunoi*; Callistratus *FGrH* 3B, 348 F4. In view of these texts the reference in Pollux (3. 83) to *Mariandunōn dōrophoroi* should be interpreted as an error on Pollux's part and not as evidence for a class of nontributary Mariandynoi as suggested by Asheri 1972, 18.

[51] Plato *Laws* 6. 776c–d; Callistratus *FGrH* 3B, 348 F4; Strabo 12. 3. 4; Photius *Lexicon s.v. Klarōtai*; *Suda s.v. Kallikurioi*; Eustathius, *Commentarii ad Homeri Iliadem et Odysseam*, ed. G. Stallbaum, 7 vols. in 4 (Leipzig 1825–30; repr. Hildesheim 1960), 295, lines 30–32.

[52] Pollux 3. 83. For modern opinion see, for example, Rostovtzeff 1941 I, 591; Neumann 1906, 27; and Burn 1960, 120.

II. FROM THE FOUNDATION TO THE END OF THE PELOPONNESIAN WAR   71

slaves is correct. The distinction between them and other slaves implied by Pollux was not based on a difference in their respective legal positions but on the fact that conquest made peoples such as the Mariandynoi the slaves of another people, that is, their true master was the *polis* of Heraclea and not the various individuals whose estates they worked and to whom they paid their tribute.[53] According to Strabo and Posidonius, the servitude of the Mariandynoi was established by an agreement between them and the Heracleotes; although the circumstances described by them are clearly unhistorical, the tradition itself reflects the fact that their condition was defined by an official act of the Heracleote government and, hence, could only be altered by a similar decision.[54] Moreover, the description of the terms of the Mariandynoi's servitude found in Strabo and Posidonius agrees with our other evidence and seems to be based on fact. From them it is clear that the Mariandynoi were bound to the soil they worked and that their condition and obligations were hereditary. On the other hand, as partial compensation for their subjection the Heracleotes did guarantee that no Mariandynus could be sold outside of Mariandynia.[55]

A special problem, however, is presented by a passage of Aristotle's *Politics*, which clearly implies that there were not one, but two nonfree populations at Heraclea, 'perioeci and those working the land (*perioikōn kai tōn tēn chōran geōrgountōn*)'[56] Ethnically, both groups were probably Mariandynoi, and the latter surely are to be identified with those Mariandynoi who lived on the estates of the Heracleote oligarches. But who are the *perioeci*? They cannot be dependent free communities of the Spartan type because of the contrast Aristotle draws between them and Heraclea's free population. Lotze saw the difficulty, but he could only suggest that Aristotle had Anatolian conditions in mind and that if the Mariandynoi were of Anatolian stock, *perioikoi* might indicate a status similar to that of the *laoi* of the Hellenistic period.[57] This, however, is unsatisfactory since it makes a legal situation dependent on race and ignores the fact that, whatever the origin of the Mariandynoi, their status

---

[53] Lotze 1959, 77. *Cf.* Theopompus FGrH 2B, 115 F122.

[54] Strabo 12. 3. 4; Posidonius *FGrH* 2A, 87 F8. For similar treaties in connection with the Helots and the Penestae, see Ephorus *FGrH* 2A, 70 F117, and Archemachus *FGrH* 3B, 424 F1. Treaty, of course, is a euphemism since what was involved was a unilateral decision of the conquering people, as can be seen from Tyrtaeus' comments (Ff 6–7 Edmonds) apropos of the Messenians.

[55] The provision occurs in all the supposed 'treaties' and was a significant concession in the case of the Mariandynoi, at least, because of the importance of the Pontic slave trade (*cf.* Finley 1962), although the Mariandynian servant in Pherecrates *Coriano* F68 Edmonds (= Athenaeus 14. 653a), indicates that an occasional Mariandynus found his way to the Aegean slave markets.

[56] Aristotle *Politics* 7. 5. 7, 1327b7–13.

[57] Lotze 1959, 57.

72 PART I: BOOK

was one devised by and imposed on them by Greeks, not Anatolians. Another solution must be found, and one is available if we recall that Aristotle sometimes uses the term *perioikos* in its geographical sense to designate a population living around a city.[58] As already mentioned, some of the land taken from the Mariandynoi became part of Heraclea's *chora*, and some of their villages such as the port of Aconae east of the city or those in the Hypius River valley prior to the foundation of Cierus must have been located on such land.[59] If these were the *perioeci* mentioned by Aristotle, then the distinction between them and 'those working the land' is clear. Although both groups were legally the slaves of Heraclea, they differed in that the latter paid their tribute to individual masters whereas the former, living on city land, had no such masters but instead paid their tribute directly to the government of Heraclea.[60]

Once the conquest and enslavement of the Mariandynoi was complete, Heraclea, like Sparta, found herself faced with the difficult and continuing task of maintaining her ascendancy over an ethnically homogeneous population reduced to servitude in its home territory. The ever-present danger of revolt was made all the more serious by the fact that the Mariandynoi clearly outnumbered the Heracleotes, although by how much cannot now be determined.[61] Nothing definite is known about the measures Heraclea took to deal with this situation, but probably among them was the foundation of a number of settlements at strategic points throughout Mariandynia of which the most important

---

[58] On the basis of *Politics* 2. 7. 3, 1272a2 and 2. 7. 8, 1272b18, Lotze (1959, 8–9) claims that Aristotle uses *perioikos* to characterize the slave status of the Cretan Aphamiotai. This, however, ignores the fact that in these places and in *Politics* 2. 7. 1, 271b31, Aristotle writes *hoi perioikoi* with the definite article, which suggests that he is here using a Cretan term for these people (*cf.* the similar interpretation of van Effenterre 1948, 94–95). For possible epigraphical evidence of this usage in Crete, see *SGDI* 4490, lines 9–10. For the geographical use of *perioikos*, see *Politics* 7. 8. 5, 1329a26 and 7. 9. 9, 1330a28, passages that Lotze (1959, 9) suggested referred to Anatolian conditions and Newman (1887–1902 III, 394 *ad* 1330a28) connected with Heraclea.

[59] For these cities, see the Introduction.

[60] The possibility exists that *kai* in *Politics* 7. 5. 7, 1327b12–13, is explanatory. In that case 'those working the land' would merely be a descriptive phrase lending greater specificity to the term *perioeci*, and the distinction I have drawn between the statuses of two groups of Mariandynoi would have to be abandoned. Decisive evidence to settle this point of interpretation is lacking. The description of the town of Arkiroessa as being *Herakleias hupotelēs* by Domitius Callistratus (*FGrH* 3B, 433 F6) does, however, tend to support the interpretation offered in the text since it suggests the existence of a type of tributary non-Greek settlement near Heraclea whose inhabitants could be called *perioeci*. For a similar view, see Burn 1960, 120.

[61] Beloch 1912–27 III.1, 302, pointed out that Aeneas Tacticus (11. 10. 2) implies that Heraclea's population *ca.* 370 was about 6000. On the other hand, the mobilization of 40 triremes about the same period (Ps.-Aristotle *Oeconomica* 2. 2. 8, 1347b3) indicates that 6800 Mariandynoi were drafted as rowers. This, however, gives us only a minimum, not a maximum, figure for the Mariandynoi. Their actual population may have been considerably higher.

II. FROM THE FOUNDATION TO THE END OF THE PELOPONNESIAN WAR   73

was the city of Cierus dominating the Hypius River valley.[62] Despite our ignorance about the details, it is clear that the precautions taken by the Heracleotes achieved their purpose since their domination of the Mariandynoi lasted until at least the 1st century. Moreover, the city seems to have largely escaped the repeated uprisings of her subjects that plagued the Spartans and the Thessalians.[63] Indeed, if there is any truth to Posidonius' fanciful picture of the Mariandynoi as the happy slaves of the benevolent Heracleotes, the extreme bitterness that characterized similar situations elsewhere would have been absent at Heraclea.[64]

HERACLEA AND ATHENS TO 404

During the first century or so of Heraclea's history, her commercial relations with Athens steadily increased.[65] Nevertheless, while the Delian League was driving Persian power from virtually the entire western seaboard of Anatolia during the years between 480 and 449, Heraclea and the other south Pontic cities continued to remain loyal to Persia. On the other hand, except for a

---

[62] The fact that Prusias ad Hypium had *paroikoi* in the Roman period (*IGRRP* III, 69, lines 26–27) suggests that the Mariandynoi in the Hypius Valley were assigned to Cierus. The conversion of state slave status to that of *paroikos* often occurred during the Hellenistic and Roman periods (Rostovtzeff 1910, 309; Broughton 1938, 638–39). The settlement of Hodioupolis mentioned by Domitius Callistratus (*FGrH* 3B, 433 F8) may also have been intended as a stronghold against the Mariandynoi. Less likely is v. Diest's identification (1889, 81–82) of the remains of a settlement in the forest along the Alaply-Su River southwest of Heraclea as a similar stronghold, since they may instead represent internal colonization of this area in the Roman period when surface remains indicate that the region was thickly settled (Dörner and Hoepfner 1962, 580).

[63] This is the most probable explanation for Aristotle's relatively favorable estimate of the system at Heraclea (nn. 56 and 58 above) in contrast to his remarks about the situation in Sparta and Thessaly and potentially in Crete (*Politics* 2. 6. 2, 1269a37–1269b14). For Heraclea's territory, see Memnon *FGrH* 3B, 434 F39. 4. The western border was probably at the Hypius where Ptolemy (5. 1. 11) places its boundary in the 2nd century AD and just east of which Dörner (1962, 32–33) reports the discovery of a boundary stone of a *polis*.

[64] Posidonius *FGrH* 2A, 87 F8. Plato's remark (*Laws* 6. 776c–d) that the system at Heraclea was less controversial than those at Sparta or in Thessaly does not refer (*pace* Lotze 1959, 52) to the Heracleotes' being good masters but to the fact that the Mariandynoi were not Greeks enslaved by other Greeks (*cf.* Plato *Republic* 4. 469b–471c).

[65] In a letter dated April 4, 1970, Prof. E. Reschke of the University of Erlangen informed me that the oldest pottery so-far discovered at Heraclea are some early Attic red-figure sherds which would indicate commercial contact at least from the last third of the 6th century (*cf.* Cook 1960, 165). Close contact is implied for the early 5th century by Aeschylus' offhand reference (*Persians*, lines 935–940; *cf. Schol. ad 940 apud* Domitius Callistratus *FGrH* 3B, 433 F3) to the Mariandynian mourning chants for Bormus. For general familiarity with the Paphlagonian coast near Heraclea, see Sophocles' statement (*apud Schol. Ap. Rhod.* 141 *ad* 2. 178–182b) that the sons of Phineus were Carambis and Parthenius.

74 PART I: BOOK

mission to the Pontus by Aristides about 468 that seems to have produced no significant results,[66] Athens and her allies made no attempt to extend their offensive against Persia beyond the Bosporus. Indeed, by specifying in the Peace of Callias that the Great King's ships might sail as far as the Cyanean Rocks, that is, to the Pontic entrance of the Bosporus, they implicitly recognized that the Pontus and its cities belonged to the Persian sphere of influence.[67] The situation changed dramatically, however, with the deterioration of the position of the Pontic cities after 450.

Despite the lack of actual fighting in the Pontus, the Delian League's successes in the Aegean probably worked to the disadvantage of the Pontic cities. The defection of the majority of his Greek subjects and the loss of much of his revenue weakened the satrap of Dascyleum and thereby lessened his ability to maintain order in his vast satrapy and to restrain the Pontic cities' native neighbors.[68] It was probably during the 440s that the Bithynians began to threaten Astacus,[69] and a minor Cappadocian dynast seized control of Amisus.[70] Meanwhile, the powerful Odrysian and Scythian kings were extending their authority over the Greek cities of the west and north coasts of the Pontus.[71] Sometime during this same decade Pericles, probably in response to an appeal for help from one or more of the Pontic cities, led a powerful fleet beyond the Bosporus for the first time and cruised along the coasts of the Pontus, where he 'accomplished whatever the Greek cities asked and treated them graciously' while displaying Athenian might and daring to the rulers of the various non-Greek populations of the area.[72] Amisus was freed from its Cappadocian ruler

[66] Plutarch *Aristides* 26. 1. For the date, see Lenardon 1959, 26–27. Similarly lacking in results was a visit to Heraclea by Pausanias during the 470s (Plutarch *Cimon* 6. 4–6; *De sera numinis vindicta* 10. 555C).

[67] For the northern limit as the Pontic entrance to the Bosporus, see Oliver 1957, 254–55. Pericles also excluded the Pontic cities from his call for a Panhellenic congress (Plutarch *Pericles* 17; on this project, see Meiggs 1972, 512–15).

[68] According to the tables in Meiggs 1972, 542–46, 45 cities, including all the major cities of the Troad and the Asiatic shores of the Hellespont, Propontis, and Bosporus, were members of the Delian League.

[69] Memnon *FGrH* 3B, 434 F12. 3; Strabo 12. 4. 2. This may be reflected in the fact that from 442 on Astacus is absent from the Athenian tribute lists (*cf.* the tables in Meiggs 1972, 544–45). For Astacus and the Bithynians in general, see Toepffer 1896, 124–27.

[70] Theopompus *FGrH* 2B, 115 F389.

[71] Olbia seems to have become a dependent of the Scythians (Herodotus 4. 78–80; Rostovtzeff 1922, 64–65). Odrysian control of Greek cities is first attested during the last quarter of the 5th century (Thucydides 2. 97), but see Danov 1960, 75–80.

[72] Plutarch *Pericles* 20. 1–2. For the date adopted in the text, see Dunker 1885, 537–42. Plutarch appears to date the expedition before 440, but, unfortunately, the account occurs in an *eidographic* context (*Pericles* 15–22) where chronology may not be preserved. In support of a date in the 440s, however, is the fact pointed out by Gomme *et al.* 1944–70 I, 378, that all the other examples in these chapters are to be dated before 443. Those scholars who disregard

II. FROM THE FOUNDATION TO THE END OF THE PELOPONNESIAN WAR 75

and then, while Pericles and the bulk of the fleet returned to Athens, a squadron of 13 ships under the command of Lamachus remained in order to overthrow the tyranny of Timesilaus at Sinope. Upon receipt of the news of his success at Athens, 600 settlers were dispatched to Sinope where the Sinopeans welcomed them and gave them the lands of the tyrant and his supporters. Probably about the same time Athens refounded Amisus under the name Piraeus.[73] Thus, although no Pontic city entered the Delian League as a result of Pericles' expedition, an Athenian sphere of influence had been established in Paphlagonia and useful diplomatic contacts had been made elsewhere.

Geography requires us to assume that both Pericles and the later Athenian settlers stopped at Heraclea during their voyages. The city's government cannot have been uninterested in this sudden appearance of Athenian power in the Pontus, but the sources are silent concerning its attitude toward this development. Scholars, however, have tended to believe that Heraclea's reception of Pericles was hostile.[74] Glotz, indeed, went so far as to maintain that this was only the climax to a long, ultimately unsuccessful attempt by Heraclea (with Persian support) to wrest control of the Pontic trade from Athens during the decades after 480.[75] This reconstruction is most improbable. Not only is there no evidence of any attempt by Persia to restrict Athenian commerce,[76] but the theory itself is based on a misunderstanding of the respective roles of Athens

---

Plutarch's apparent date and place the expedition about 438/7 rely mainly on two considerations: (1) the unsupported and probably erroneous view that the expedition resulted in a commercial treaty with Spartocus I who seized control of Panticapaeum that year (Gomme *et al.* 1944–70 I, 368, n. 3; Rostovtzeff 1922, 68–69; Glotz and Cohen 1925–38 II, 211; and Meiggs 1972, 198; on this, see below n. 98); and (2) the belief that Lamachus who served with Pericles and shared the command of the Sicilian expedition in 416 must still have been relatively young in 426 since Aristophanes (*Acharnians*, lines 600–601) calls him *neanias* (Beloch 1912–27 II.2, 216; Gomme *et al.* 1944–70 I, 368, n. 3; Meiggs 1972, 197–98). Beloch, however, who first called attention to this also noted that *neanias* need only mean that Lamachus was less than 50 years old in 426, and a glance at the context of Aristophanes' remark indicates that his caution was well advised. Far from being an objective characterization of Lamachus, it is part of an *ad hominem* appeal to the chorus of Acharnians, who are *Marathonomachoi* (lines 181, 698–699) and very old (line 610), by Dicaeopolis (described as an old man in lines 1129–1130) to the effect that the 'old' always serve (line 600) while the 'young' like Lamachus (lines 601–606) always draw the soft and profitable assignments. In such a context *neanias* need only mean that Lamachus belonged to the post-Persian war generation and, hence, is insufficient evidence on which to reject the implied date of Plutarch.

[73] Theopompus *FGrH* 2B, 115 F389; Plutarch *Lucullus* 19. 7; Appian *Mithridatica* 83; Anonymous *Periplus* 9r1. Connection of the liberation of Amisus with the Pontic expedition is to a degree conjectural since the only indication of a date for it is Plutarch's statement that it took place during Athens' thalassocracy. For coins of Amisus with the name Piraeus in the 4th century, see *Recueil* I.1, 4, 46–47, nos. 1–6.

[74] E.g. Ed. Meyer 1965–69 IV.1, 726; Dunker 1885, 542–43; Schneiderwirth 1882, 12.

[75] Glotz and Cohen 1925–38 II, 210.

[76] On this, see Brashinskii 1967.

76 PART I: BOOK

and Heraclea in the economy of the Pontus. Their interests were complementary, not antagonistic. Far from discouraging Athenian trade, Heraclea can only have welcomed it because like the other Pontic cities, her revenues depended largely on the use of her harbor by foreign shipping and the export of the surplus produce of her territory, grain, nuts, and fish, for which Athens was the single largest consumer. As far as Athens was concerned, the Pontus was as yet only one of several sources of grain and other foodstuffs to supplement the yield of her own land. Her interests in this region did not conflict with those of any Pontic city since they required only that free passage through the Hellespont and Bosporus be assured to ships bound for Athens, and this had been assured by Cimon's campaigns in the 470s.[77] But if the existence of long-term hostility between Heraclea and Athens is to be discounted, Heraclea's oligarchic government still is unlikely to have welcomed Athens' intervention in the affairs of the Pontus. It clearly represented a violation of the terms of the Peace of Callias, and Heraclea, no longer threatened by the Mariandynoi, would have had less incentive to risk compromising her relations with Persia than the less fortunate cities to the east of her. Moreover, the oligarchs cannot have been pleased by the support the Athenians gave to the democratic factions at Sinope and Amisus and perhaps elsewhere in the Pontus.[78] Most likely, therefore, Heraclea accorded Pericles' fleet and the subsequent bodies of Athenian colonists diplomatically correct welcomes – Plutarch's source clearly knew of no rebuffs by any Pontic city – but no official ties between the two cities or other changes in their previous policies towards each other resulted from these visits.

Except for evidence indicating that trade with Athens continued,[79] the sources are silent concerning Heraclea's subsequent relations with Athens down to 425. Although the *argumentum ex silentio* is always suspect, it is probable that in this case it reflects the fact that Pericles, despite his initial successes at Amisus and Sinope, had to abandon any plans for the further expansion of Athenian influence in the Pontus in order to strengthen Athens' position in the Aegean in the face of growing difficulties caused first by the revolts

---

[77] On the basis of literary evidence L. Gernet (1909, 314–19), maintained that Pontic grain only became vital to Athens in the 4th century. This has now been confirmed by excavation which shows that the 4th century was the great period for the importation of Attic pottery to South Russia (Rostovtzeff 1931, 173–76; Brashinskii 1968, 105–07).

[78] Pippidi (1971, 62–63) suggests that the democratic revolution at Histria mentioned by Aristotle (*Politics* 5. 5. 2, 1305b5–11) may have been connected with Pericles' Pontic expedition.

[79] Pherecrates *Coriano* F68 Edmonds (= Athenaeus 14. 653a); Hermippus *Phormophoroi* F63 Edmonds (= lines 20–21 = Athenaeus 1. 27de). The reference to Sitalces as Athens' ally in lines 7–8 dates the play to the early years of the Peloponnesian War since he died in 424 (Thucydides 4. 101. 5).

II. FROM THE FOUNDATION TO THE END OF THE PELOPONNESIAN WAR   77

of Byzantium and Samos in 440 and then by the worsening of relations with the Peloponnesian League during the 430s.[80] The outbreak of the Peloponnesian War in 431 brought no change in this trend since Pericles' essentially defensive strategy of avoiding a direct confrontation with Sparta while concentrating on preventing revolts by Athens' subjects precluded any Athenian adventures in the Pontus. But in the summer of 425 the situation changed.

Pericles was dead, and six years of war had strained Athenian resources to the point that new revenue had to be obtained if Athens was to continue the struggle.[81] At the same time, morale was high and a renewed expansionist spirit was current at Athens following Cleon's victory at Sphacteria in the spring. Major gains were anticipated from the fleet then operating in Sicilian waters[82] and preparations may already have been under way for the campaign later in the year that was to result in the conquest of Cythera.[83] In this atmosphere, Thoudippus, probably a supporter of Cleon,[84] carried a bill authorizing a general assessment of the empire that resulted in the tribute of the allies being raised to about 1460 talents. Although Thoudippus' motion only mentioned the four previously existing districts of the empire, the appearance in the assessment lists of a group of over 40 Pontic cities organized in a new district with the rubric 'Cities from the Euxine' shows that Cleon and his followers used the assessment to expand the empire into the Pontus by the simple expedient of having the *taktai* add new cities to the lists.[85]

The names of only four of the Pontic cities admit of relatively secure identification, but these – Heraclea,[86] Apollonia,[87] Niconia on the Dniester River,[88] and Cimmeri(-con?) near the Straits of Kerch[89] – suffice to show that the new district included at least the south, west, and north coasts, if not the whole circuit of

---

[80] For the effect of these revolts on Athenian policy, see Kagan 1969, 179–82. On relations between Athens and the Peloponnesian League from 440 to 432, see now de Ste Croix 1972, 73–74, 200–05.

[81] For Athenian finances in this period, see Meiggs and Lewis 1969, 72, with their commentary (pp. 214–217); Gomme *et al.* 1944–70 II, 432–36; and Meiggs and Lewis 1969, 69, lines 16–17 (= *ATI* 2.A9 = *IG* I² 63 [in what follows the text of the decree is cited as edited by Meiggs and Lewis]).

[82] Thucydides 4. 65. 3–4.

[83] Thucydides 4. 53–54. For the date, see Gomme *et al.* 1944–70 III, 507.

[84] Meiggs and Lewis 1969, 197.

[85] *ATL* 2A9, IV, line 126. *ATL* assigns 43 cities to the district (2A9, IV, lines 127–170) of which there remain parts of the names and assessments of 26, but Dow (1941, 78–80), showed that as many as seven more spaces for city names should be assumed in restoring the Euxine Panel.

[86] *ATL* 2A9, IV, line 127. *Cf. ATL* 1, 489–90.

[87] *ATL* 2A9, IV, line 128. *Cf. ATL* 1, 469.

[88] *ATL* 2A9, IV, line 167. *Cf. ATL* 1, 526.

[89] *ATL* 2A9, IV, line 166. *Cf. ATL* 1, 502.

78   PART I: BOOK

the Pontus.[90] The assessment of the new district is not known. The figures preserved on the stone plus the one talent that Craterus[91] says Nymphaeum paid
amount to only 32 talents. Meritt and West, however, point out in their edition
of the assessment decree that this does not include the tributes of the larger cities
such as Heraclea and suggest accordingly that 50 talents should be considered
the minimum possible figure.[92] As for Heraclea's assessment, despite the loss of
the relevant figures, we can safely assume that it was considerably more than the
four talents that is the highest tribute now preserved on the inscription since
Heraclea headed the list which was drawn up with the largest cities first.[93] This
is all the more likely because the evidence of Athenian comedy indicates that
Heraclea and her territory were considered to be among the chief prizes to be
gained by the inclusion of the Pontic cities in the empire.[94]

Because the establishment of the Euxine district had been affected by
administrative fiat, Heraclea and the other Pontic cities probably first learned
of it when an Athenian herald, most likely one of those assigned to the Thracian district,[95] arrived at the city and announced to its government that it was
to send ambassadors to Athens during the month of Maimakterion to learn the
amount of the city's assessment.[96] We hear of no resistance elsewhere to the
Athenian demands. Sinope and Amisus, after all, had been centers of Athenian
influence for close to a decade,[97] and the other cities, under pressure from the
Odrysian kings, the aggressive new tyrants of Panticapaeum,[98] or merely their

---

[90] Less certain restorations are Patrasus (*ATL* 2A9, IV, line 168; *cf. ATL* 1, 532), Cerasus
(*ATL* 2A9, IV, line 169; *cf. ATL* 1, 500–01), and Callatis (*ATL* 2A9, IV, line 165; *cf.* Pippidi
1971, 64).

[91] Craterus *FGrH* 3B, 342 F8.

[92] Meritt and West 1934, 87–88. They suggest that the figure may actually have been as high as
150 or even 200. Meiggs (1972, 328) more conservatively places the maximum at about 100 talents.

[93] *ATL* 2A9, IV, line 142. Meritt and West 1934, 87–88.

[94] Eupolis *The Golden Race* F270 Edmonds: *A. horō B. theō nun tēnde Mariandunian.* The
play appears to have been a satire on Cleon's management of Athens (F290) and to have been
produced about 424 or 423 (Edmonds 1957–61 I, 410 n. a).

[95] Suggested by the fact that the Pontic list appears as an appendix to the list of the Thracian
district. Two heralds were sent to each district (Meiggs and Lewis 1969, 69, line 5).

[96] Meiggs and Lewis 1969, 69, lines 6–7.

[97] Athenian influence at Sinope: Robert 1937, 296–97; Maksimova 1956, 99–100. No trace
of their names remains on the stone although their membership in the district is probable. The
fact that Amisus had been colonized by Athens, however, may have freed it from the obligation
of tribute (Gomme *et al.* 1944–70 I, 368, but *cf.* 375, n. 3).

[98] Athenian control of Nymphaeum (Aeschines 3. 171; Craterus *FGrH* 3B, 342 F8) blocked
Spartocid ambitions in the Crimea. This implies that Athenian relations with the Spartocids in the
5th century were not originally friendly. Support for this view is provided by Aeschines' characterization (3. 171) of them as enemies and by the fact that the earliest indications of cordial
relations between Athens and Panticapaeum date from the last years of the Peloponnesian War
(Lysias 16. 4) and the early 4th century (Isocrates *Trapeziticus* 57; *GHI* 2 167, lines 21–23, with

II. FROM THE FOUNDATION TO THE END OF THE PELOPONNESIAN WAR 79

own native neighbors, might easily consider the protection afforded them by Athenian might adequate compensation for their acquiescence. At Heraclea, however, the herald's proclamation met defiance. The city's government refused to abandon its traditional policy of loyalty to Persia by accepting Heraclea's enrollment in the Delian League.[99]

Heraclea's refusal to pay her tribute was clearly unacceptable to Athens. Accordingly, when Lamachus, a veteran of Pericles' Pontic expedition, led a squadron of ten triremes into the Pontus in the summer of 424 to collect the district's tribute, he apparently had specific orders to secure Heraclea's compliance by force. On reaching Heracleote territory, therefore, he anchored his ships in the mouth of the Cales River southwest of the city and immediately began devastating the estates in the area. But hardly had he begun to apply this pressure when nature intervened. A sudden storm over the coastal mountains turned the Cales into a swollen torrent which swamped the Athenian ships and inflicted heavy casualties on their crews. Lamachus and the other survivors were stranded, facing the equally unpleasant alternatives of awaiting a possible Heracleote attack or trying to reach Chalcedon by marching through hostile Bithynian territory without guides or provisions. They were probably very much relieved when the Heracleote government, instead of attacking them, adopted a conciliatory attitude, and then provided them with supplies and an armed escort for their march to Chalcedon.[100]

Trogus, following Nymphis, ascribed this development to the Heracleotes' magnanimous willingness to overlook the injuries they had sustained in the hope of winning the friendship of the Athenians by their kindness. Presumably, less edifying considerations also played a part in their decision. Heraclea's position was considerably weaker in the summer of 424 than a year earlier when she had rejected Athens' demands. She might defeat Lamachus, but then a new attack by a stronger Athenian force later was likely, and no help could be expected from the other Pontic cities. More importantly, Heraclea could also hope for little aid from her Persian overlord since the death of Artaxerxes I in the winter of 425/4 and the subsequent struggle over the succession had thrown the empire into confusion.[101] Moreover, there was

---

reference to Satyrus during his period of sole rule from 393/2 to 389/8; *cf.* Werner 1955, 418–21). As for a treaty between Athens and Panticapaeum, the evidence points toward one being concluded at the earliest during the second half of the 4th century (H. Schmitt 1969, commentary *ad* no. 401 [= *SIG*³ 1, 370, lines 17–20]).

[99] Justin 16. 3. 9.

[100] Thucydides 4. 75. 2; Justin 16. 3. 9–12; Diodorus 12. 72. 4.

[101] Ctesias *FGrH* 3C1, 688 F15. 47–49; Diodorus 12. 64. 1; 12. 71. Andrewes (1961, 2–5) notes that Darius II cannot have consolidated his power before December 424. For the importance of Persian weakness in the formation of the Euxine district, see Meiggs 1972, 330.

80 PART I: BOOK

always the danger that the Athenians might try to incite the Mariandynoi to revolt. Hastening their departure, therefore, was clearly in Heraclea's interest. But since there is reason to believe that Heraclea paid tribute in one of the following years,[102] and hence that her government had not merely refrained from attacking Lamachus but had also agreed to her becoming subject to Athens, it is likely that the true explanation for her behavior in the summer of 424 is that an upheaval occurred within the city at that time which resulted in the overthrow of the oligarchy and the establishment of the democracy that ruled the city until the early 360s.[103] Support for this dating of the fall of the oligarchy may perhaps be found in a proxeny decree for a Heracleote named Sotimus, if West's placement of it in early 423 is correct, since it shows that Athens had influential friends in Heraclea at that time, and in the fact that Heraclea's colony of Chersonesus appears to have been founded as a democracy.[104]

With the departure of Lamachus from the area the sources almost completely ignore Heraclea, leaving us to infer the further course of Heracleote-Athenian relations from a few disconnected facts. These facts, however – the above mentioned proxeny decree for Sotimus, the existence of a Heracleote *proxenus* at Athens in the early 4th century,[105] and the surprising fact that Spintharus, a Heracleote tragedian, apparently had plays of his produced at Athens during the last quarter of the 5th century –[106] combine to suggest that relations between the two cities became closer and more friendly after 424. Since neither the Athenians nor their enemies extended their military operations beyond the Bosporus, this growing friendship did not result in Heraclea becoming directly involved in any actual fighting, but it was probably an important factor in the decision to found the second and more important of

---

[102] Eupolis *Poleis* F216 Edmonds. The play was produced *ca.* 422 (Edmonds 1957–61 I, 388, n. 3). Simon appears to have been an official tried for misuse of public money in a notorious trial marked by suspicions of perjury (Aristophanes *Clouds*, lines 35, 399–400; *Schol. ad* 351). The Eupolis fragment suggests he was accused of mishandling tribute money.

[103] For a similar view, see Tyumenev 1938, 256–57. Democratic rule is also indicated for the late 5th century by the coins with the inscription *DAM[OS]* issued at that time (*Recueil* I.2, 345, no. 2). The attempt by Head (1911, 244) to ascribe them to Heraclea Sintica may now be considered to have failed as a result of the discovery of one of these coins at Heraclea Pontica (Thompson 1962, no. 914).

[104] *IG* I² 145. A. West 1935, 74–75, who suggested that Sotimus was honored for assisting Lamachus' men in the summer of 424. Chersonesus: Latyschev 1885, 278–80; Belov 1948, 66.

[105] Ps.-Demosthenes 52. 5.

[106] *Suda s.v. Spintharos*; Diogenes Laertius 5. 92. He is probably to be identified with the Spintharus satirized by Aristophanes (*Birds*, line 761). Further: Diehl 1929, 1813. The supposed friendship of Socrates and Matris, the father of Chion (*Epistles of Chion* 5) would, if true, belong to this period.

II. FROM THE FOUNDATION TO THE END OF THE PELOPONNESIAN WAR 81

Heraclea's trans-Pontic colonies, Chersonesus, in the Crimea near the site of the present city of Sevastopol.[107]

According to Ps.-Scymnus, our most important source for the foundation of Chersonesus, Heraclea colonized the city jointly with Delians at the behest of an oracle, presumably Delphi.[108] Although Ps.-Scymnus gives no date, the reference to Delian participation allows us to place it with a high degree of certainty in the year 422/1, when the Delians were living in exile at Atramyttium after being expelled from Delos by the Athenians during a purification of the island.[109] The Athenians restored the Delians to their home the following year, so it was only in the year 422/1, especially after the exiles had been treacherously attacked by Arsaces, the satrap of Sardis, that a small number of them could have been persuaded to participate in the establishment of a colony on the north coast of the Black Sea.[110] Excavation supports this conclusion since, except for a few Ionic sherds of the 6th century, the earliest remains at Chersonesus belong to the late 5th century.[111]

Although agriculture formed the basis of Chersonesus' economy during most of antiquity,[112] commercial considerations appear to have been of primary importance in the decision to found the city and in the choice of its site.[113] During the 5th century, ships sailing to the grain ports of southern Russia followed two main routes: the preferred one, which followed the west and north coasts as far as Olbia, Theodosia, Nymphaeum and Panticapaeum, and then a shorter one, which ran along the south coast as far as Cape Carambis, then cut across the open sea to Criumetopon, the southernmost point of the

---

[107] For the location, see Strabo 7. 4. 2. His statement, however, that the city was moved to the present location of its ruins from a site he calls Old Chersonesus has been disproved by excavation (v. Stern 1909, 146–47). Pliny's reference (*NH* 4. 85) to the city being called Heraclea appears to be the result of his confusing it with its metropolis (Brandis 1899, 2265; Minns 1913, 493).

[108] Ps.-Scymnus, lines 826–831 (= 822–827). Anonymous *Periplus* 12v19–22; 12v25–29. For Heraclea as sole founder, see Strabo 7. 4. 2; 12. 3. 6; Menippus *Periplus* 12v6.

[109] Thucydides 5. 1; Diodorus 12. 73. 1. Schneiderwirth (1882, 15) recognized the significance of the purification of Delos in dating the colony. *Contra* the suggestion of Brandis (1899, 2262), that Delians is an error for Delphians, Delian participation is supported by the celebration of a festival called the Chersonesia on Delos during the Hellenistic period, most likely in commemoration of Delos' only colonial venture (Homolle 1890, 492, 492, n. 6, 496, n. 7; Deonna 1908, 127, n. 1), and by Chersonesus' dedication of vases at Delos beginning in 276 (*Délos* 313a74; 386, lines 8–9; 399B16). For further discussion, see Tyumenev 1938, 253–56; and Pečirka 1970, 463–64.

[110] Thucydides 5. 23. 1. Attack by Arsaces: Thucydides 8. 108. 4.

[111] Ionic remains: Minns 1913, xl, addenda; Rostovtzeff 1922, 363–64; Danov 1962, 1106; Neubauer 1960, 142. Late 5th-century finds: v. Stern 1909, 146–47; Boardman 1964, 272.

[112] v. Stern 1915, 175; Danov 1962, 1107.

[113] Ps.-Scylax 30 (68) *GGM* I, 57, refers to the city as *Cherronēsos emporion*.

82 PART I: BOOK

Crimea, and finally either northwest to Olbia or northeast to Panticapaeum.[114] On either route, however, the coasts of the Crimea from Kerkinitis to Theodosia constituted an area of particular danger to ships since, prior to the foundation of Chersonesus, there were no friendly ports in which they could take refuge from storms and they were exposed to the piratical attacks of the Tauri, whose hostility to foreigners was proverbial.[115] It was probably to remedy this situation that Heraclea and the Delians, most likely with the approval and encouragement of Athens, founded Chersonesus.[116] Similarly, the need to protect the new colony from the Tauri and then from the expansionist tendencies of the Spartocid rulers of Panticapaeum probably accounts for the close political relations that, unlike the situation with Callatis, Heraclea maintained with Chersonesus from the time of her foundation.[117]

Aside from these matters, the history of Heraclea's relations with the Aegean in the 5th century is obscure. As the western Greek colonies did, Heraclea patronized the Panhellenic shrines of Delphi and Olympia. Indeed, at the latter she dedicated a notable statue group representing a number of Heracles' labors – the Nemean lion, the Hydra, the Erymanthean boar, and Cerberus – to commemorate her great victory over the Mariandynoi.[118] Contact was also probably maintained with Megara and Boeotia,[119] and the existence of a Heracleote

[114] For the routes, see Rostovtzeff 1922, 62-64. Maksimova (1959) argued that the short route only came into use in the 4th century, but the increasing evidence for trade between Heraclea and the north coast prior to the 4th century (see below n. 130) and the recent discovery of a 5th-century Olbian proxeny decree for a citizen of Sinope (Boultounova 1969, 300) indicate that use of the route dates from at least the 5th century. On the other hand, Euripides (*Iphigenia in Tauris*, lines 421–438) suggests that the western route was still the one most familiar to Athenians during the last quarter of the 5th century (for the date of the *Iphigenia in Tauris*, see Lesky 1965, 385–89).

[115] Herodotus 4. 103; Euripides *Iphigenia in Tauris*, *passim*; Diodorus 3. 43. 5; 20. 25. 2; Strabo 7. 4. 2. See also Belov 1948, 26–31; and Leskow 1960, 346–49.

[116] This is suggested by the ending of Euripides' *Iphigenia in Tauris* (lines 1475–1485) where Athena forces the King of the Tauri to cease his hostility to the Greeks and he in turn agrees to release his Greek slaves. For Chersonesus' importance on the short trade route, see Roebuck 1959, 124.

[117] According to Neubauer (1960, 142) Soviet scholars believe that Heracleotes 'ohne weiteres volles Bürgerrecht im Chersonesos genossen', and *isopoliteia* between Heraclea and Chersonesus is in fact indicated by a decree of the 1st or 2nd century AD (*IOSPE* 1 357, lines 11–12). For the 4th century close contact between the two cities is suggested by the fact that 50% of the 4th-century pottery found at Chersonesus is of Heracleote origin (Pečirka 1970, 465). For the possibility that Chersonesus was politically dependent on Heraclea in the 4th century, see Niese 1893–1903 I, 408.

[118] Pausanias 5. 26. 7. In addition to probably consulting Delphi in connection with founding her colonies Heraclea also at some unknown date dedicated there a statue of Apollo (Pausanias 10. 51. 1).

[119] For relations between Heraclea and Megara and Thebes, see chapter 4. Ties with Tanagra may be indicated by *IG* 7 1565, if the individual is from Heraclea Pontica.

II. FROM THE FOUNDATION TO THE END OF THE PELOPONNESIAN WAR 83

proxenus at Argos may indicate the establishment of ties with that city as well during the 5th century.[120] It is possible that Heraclea's entrance into the Delian League may have resulted in an interruption of some of these contacts, but if this happened they most likely were quickly resumed after the relatively brief period of Athenian domination ended.

Officially, Heraclea probably remained a member of the Delian League until at least 410/9 when the Pontic cities seem to have been included in the general assessment of the empire made during that year,[121] but Athenian control of her is likely to have lapsed sometime before that date. Despite the occupation of Nymphaeum[122] and perhaps other strong points in the Pontus,[123] Athenian power in the region was probably always relatively weak, and it can only have deteriorated further after the Sicilian disaster and the resumption of the war by Sparta made it difficult to spare the ships needed to maintain her influence beyond the Bosporus.[124] Even before that date, it seems, Seuthes, the Odrysian king, had wrested control of the west Pontic cities from Athens.[125] Under these circumstances, therefore, the establishment by Alcibiades of a station at Chrysopolis to collect a 10% toll on shipping through the Bosporus in 410/9 suggests that the inclusion of the Pontic cities in the assessment of that year may have been little more than a formality.[126] Certainly, whatever threads

[120] Ps.-Demosthenes 52. 10.

[121] Craterus *FGrH* 3B, 342 F8 (= *ATL* 2A13). For the date, see Jacoby *FGrH* 3B *Texte*, 102 *ad* F 6–8. For the possibility that the Pontic cities were included in the assessment of 420, see Meiggs 1972, 329.

[122] Aeschines 3. 171; Craterus *FGrH* 3B, 342 F8. There is no evidence to support the common belief (Ed. Meyer 1965–69 IV.1, 728; Dunker 1885, 544–45; Minns 1913, 561) that Athenian occupation or even foundation (Rostovtzeff 1922, 67) dates from Pericles' Pontic expedition.

[123] Rostovtzeff 1922, 67, suggested that the Athenians also occupied Athenaeum near Theodosia (Anonymous *Periplus* 12v5) and Stratocleia in the Taman Peninsula (Pliny *NH* 6. 18).

[124] Since Heraclea issued silver coins during the late 5th century (above n. 103) the recent discovery of a copy of the coinage decree in the Odessa Museum, if it originated in the Black Sea (*SEG* 21 [1965] no. 18; Mattingly 1966, 193–95), suggests that Athens did not strictly enforce its prohibition on local silver coinages (Meiggs and Lewis 1969, 45, 12) in the Pontus at that late period, i.e. after 420. For the possibility, however, that the Odessa copy of the decree is of Delian origin, see *SEG* 23 (1968) no. 8.

[125] The west Pontic cities were presumably among those Thucydides says (2. 97. 3) paid Seuthes a total of 400 talents per year. Gomme *et al.* (1944–70 II, 244–45) suggest they may also have paid Athens tribute by arrangement with Seuthes as was done in the 4th century (*GHI* 2 151, lines 4–9). This, however, is unlikely in view of the hostile relations that generally prevailed between Athens and Seuthes (Thucydides 2. 101. 5–6; Polyaenus 7. 38).

[126] Xenophon *Hellenica* 1. 1. 22; Diodorus 13. 64. 2; Polybius 4. 44. 3–4. The supposed Pontic expedition of Alcibiades (v. Stern 1909, 145; Rostovtzeff 1922, 67) is a modern invention for which there is no ancient evidence (Gundel 1942–43, 127, n. 22). The surrender of Nymphaeum by Gylon to the Spartocids (Aeschines 3. 171), usually dated toward the end of the Peloponnesian War (v. Stern 1915, 182; Minns 193, 561; Werner 1955, 414), probably reflects this Athenian withdrawal from the Pontus.

84   PART I: BOOK

may have continued to bind Heraclea to Athens after that year would have
been severed by Lysander's victory at Aegospotami in 405 and his subsequent
actions, so that the city would have regained her full independence before the
fall of Athens in 404.

                        INTERNAL DEVELOPMENTS TO 404

Situated on an established trade route and possessed of the only good harbor
between the Bosporus and Sinope, Heraclea prospered from her foundation.
Except for a brief period during the first quarter of the 5th century when trade
between the Aegean and the Pontus seems to have temporarily slackened,[127] a
steadily increasing number of ships entered her port bringing her revenue in
the form of harbor and market tolls, along with manufactured goods from the
homeland, and taking away the fish and other produce of Mariandynia. As the
short route to the north coast, that via Cape Carambis, came into more frequent
use during the second half of the 5th century, the role played by this shipping
in Heraclea's economy became still more important. Moreover, if two important but undated Heracleote actions – namely, the construction of a temple to
the Tyndaridae on a prominent point east of the city where it functioned as a
beacon to sailors[128] and the seizure of the island of Thynias which provided a
safe haven for ships sailing along the otherwise hostile Bithynian coast –[129]
belong to this period, Heraclea clearly not only profited from this trade but
actively sought to encourage and facilitate it.

     Meanwhile, the annexation of Mariandynia and the subjection of the Mari-
andynoi dramatically increased Heraclea's resources. Judging from Xenophon's account of the reception the city prepared for the Ten Thousand in 400,
Heraclea enjoyed considerable agricultural surpluses at that time. With the
labor provided by the Mariandynoi, Heracleote landowners were raising vines
and barley and running herds of cattle and flocks of sheep on their estates in
addition to the nuts, wheat, and olives that are indicated by other sources. The
result was that, while benefiting from the general growth in the Pontic trade
during the 5th century, Heraclea developed her own foreign trade. By the end
of the century it had only attained a moderate volume but its geographical
extent was notable. Heracleote merchants or Heracleote wine could then be

     [127] Brashinskii 1967, 60.
     [128] Apollonius 2, lines 806–808.
     [129] Herodorus *FGrH* 1A, 31 F48, suggests Heracleote occupation of Thynias during the 5th
century (Jacoby *FGrH* 1a, 502, dates Herodorus *ca.* 400). The reported discovery of black-figure
sherds there (Dörner 1963, 136) indicates that commercial use of the island may already have
begun in the 6th century (*cf.* Cook 1960, 62–90).

II. FROM THE FOUNDATION TO THE END OF THE PELOPONNESIAN WAR 85

found almost everywhere in the Pontus, in the cities of the north and south coasts,[130] the villages of Bithynia,[131] and probably also those of Paphlagonia.[132] In addition, the evidence indicates that Heracleote merchants were already venturing outside the Bosporus to visit the cities of northern Greece,[133] as well as Athens and probably other major centers of European Greece.

These developments also stimulated the growth of Heraclea's internal economic life. Details are lacking, but the fact that when Heraclea first minted coins in the last quarter of the century the issues were limited to small denominations, diobols, obols, and hemiobols struck on the Persian standard, indicates that a considerable proportion of the city's daily business was then being conducted on a cash basis.[134] Likewise, the existence of a large number of ships at Heraclea in 400 and the construction of a fleet of warships presuppose the appearance of a shipbuilding industry.[135] Similarly, the export of her wine required the development of a small ceramic industry to provide the necessary containers in addition to the pottery used by the citizens in their daily lives.

Despite Heraclea's economic growth and prosperity, her political life continued to be troubled in the 5th century as it had been in the 6th. Even after the rule limiting the right to hold office to heads of *oikoi* had been dropped, those citizens enjoying full political privileges under the oligarchy remained a small minority of the Heracleotes, their numbers reaching only some 600 men or little

---

[130] I.B. Zeest (1951, 106–09) dated the beginnings of trade between Heraclea and the north coast to the second half of the 4th century. The discovery of Heracleote amphorae in late 5th-century contexts at Nymphaeum and Olbia (Skudnowa 1961; 1959), and of a 5th-century Olbian proxeny decree for a Heracleote (Knipovich and Levi 1968, no. 2), indicate that this is too late by over half a century. For the amphorae, see Zeest 1948 and Brashinskii 1965. Brashinskii (1965, 27) places the earliest series of Heracleote stamped amphorae *ca.* 400–370. South coast: Xenophon *Anabasis* 5. 6. 19 (although these merchants had gone to meet the Ten Thousand, there is no reason to believe their presence in the area was unusual).

[131] Xenophon *Anabasis* 6. 4. 23.

[132] Direct evidence is lacking, but contact is suggested by the observation v. Gall (1966, 29–33, 54–55) that a Paphlagonian tomb of the late 5th or early 4th century bears an image of a charging bull similar to those on contemporary Heracleote coins (*Recueil* I.2, 344, no. 5).

[133] Head's ascription of Heraclea's earliest coins to Heraclea Sintica (above n. 103) reflects the fact that they were modeled on the issues of northern Greek cities such as Amphipolis or the kingdom of Macedon (Head 1911, 215, 219).

[134] For this issue, see above n. 103. On small change: Kraay 1964. Heraclea's coinage was for local circulation primarily (*cf.* Golenko and Shelov 1965, who report the presence of only one Heracleote coin among the 1000 discovered). For foreign trade Heraclea probably used Cyzicene staters, as did other Pontic cities (Xenophon *Anabasis* 6. 2. 4–5; Belin de Ballu 1972, 66–67). It should, however, be noted that the ascription by J.P. Six (1885, 51 nos. 1-2) of some early 5th-century electrum hectae has not yet been verified (*cf.* the criticisms of Wroth 1889, xi–xii).

[135] Xenophon *Anabasis* 5. 6. 10, for ships at Heraclea, although, of course, not all of them necessarily need have been Heracleote. By his own estimate (Xenophon *Anabasis* 5. 7. 8) Heraclea would have had to furnish about 100 ships if she were to transport the Ten Thousand by sea to Byzantium. For her fleet, see Ps.-Aristotle *Oeconomica* 2. 2. 8, 1347b3.

86 PART I: BOOK

more than 10% of the total citizen body.[136] Meanwhile, as indicated by the foundations of Cierus and Chersonesus – the latter, admittedly, and the former possibly organized after the fall of the oligarchy – the land hunger of the Heracleote poor reappeared as a significant force during the second half of the 5th century; its intensity had probably been heightened by the failure of the general citizenry to profit significantly from the conquest of Mariandynia. Thus, although the Athenian attack in the summer of 424 apparently provided the occasion for the revolution that toppled the oligarchy, the potential for broad popular support of it already existed. The movement itself, however, originated not in the discontents of the populace but in the fierce internal divisions of the oligarchs themselves, whose factions conducted their struggles for influence through lawsuits in the popular courts. According to Aristotle, the spark that set off the revolution was just such a prosecution. The leader of the revolution was a certain Eurytion, who seized power with the aid of his supporters after he had been prosecuted by his enemies for adultery and, on being convicted, had been forced to submit to the humiliating punishment of being placed in stocks and then exposed to public mockery in the agora of Heraclea.[137]

Later Heracleote tradition unfairly vilified Eurytion as a tyrant,[138] since the actual results of his actions were comparatively limited. An aristocrat himself and a loyal member of the oligarchy prior to his humiliation, Eurytion desired revenge, not the destruction of his class and its privileges. Accordingly, far from establishing a tyranny, he used his victory to establish a moderate democracy. The aristocratic monopoly of office was broken, such democratic institutions as pay for military and, possibly, political service were instituted,[139] and the authority of the assembly, which was open to all citizens on an equal basis, was increased.[140] On the other hand, he left unchanged the high property qualification required for membership in the *hekatostues* and made no attempt to

---

[136] Aristotle *Politics* 5. 5. 2–4, 1305b5–13. For Heraclea's population, see above n. 61.

[137] Aristotle *Politics* 5. 5 .5, 1305b33–37; 5. 5. 10, 1306a38–1306b3.

[138] Identifying Eurytion with Euopius (*Suda s.v. Klearchos* = Aelian F86 [Hercher 1866]) who is called *palaios Herakleōtōn turannos* as did Apel (1910, 23, n. 1). Against the theory of Schneiderwirth (1882, 19) and Helmut Berve (1967 I, 315) are two considerations: (1) the notes in Aristotle's *Politics* indicate that Heraclea's government developed from democracy to narrow oligarchy and then to a broadened oligarchy which was finally overthrown, a sequence which seems to have no room for an early tyranny; and (2) Memnon (*FGrH* 3B, 434 F1. 1) and Justin (16. 4. 1) both maintain that Clearchus was the city's first tyrant. For a recent attempt to identify Euopius with a figure of Mariandynian mythology used by Clearchus as part of a propaganda program aimed at the Mariandynoi, see Asheri 1972, 30.

[139] Ps.-Aristotle *Oeconomica* 2. 2. 8, 1347b3–14. Griffith (1935, 270) recognized that citizen and not mercenary soldiers were involved. Pay for political office is not attested, but it is possible that the small denominational coinage with its *dam(os)* inscription was put into circulation this way.

[140] Implied by Aeneas Tacticus 10. 11. 2.

II. FROM THE FOUNDATION TO THE END OF THE PELOPONNESIAN WAR   87

confiscate and redistribute the property of the former oligarchs to the general citizenry.

Of the history of the democracy subsequent to its establishment by Eurytion we only know for certain that it continued to govern Heraclea until the early 360s. Eurytion's refusal to break the social and economic power of Heraclea's rich was ultimately to prove fatal to the democracy, and even in the short run it probably caused bitterness among the Heracleote poor. Conceivably, one of the reasons for Heraclea's interest in the founding of Chersonesus was to ease this situation by providing land for some of the *demos*. On the other hand, the close relations that seem to have existed between Heraclea and Athens after 424 may have restrained the ex-oligarchs from attempting a counterrevolution and the withdrawal of Athens from the Pontus prior to Aegospotami and the consequent lack of Spartan action in the area deprived them of the Spartan support that led to the overthrow of democracies friendly to Athens in the Aegean.[141] Thus, although the seeds of future trouble existed, the democracy survived the end of the Peloponnesian War without, in all likelihood, as yet having faced any serious challenge to its government of the city.

---

[141] For the lack of Spartan action against Athens' friends in the Pontus, see Xenophon *Hellenica* 1. 2. 1 (Athenian supporters in Byzantium flee to the Pontus) and note the survival of the Athenian colony at Amisus as indicated by the fact that in the 4th century the city continued to mint coins under the name Piraeus (*Recueil* I.1, 44–48, nos. 1–8).

CHAPTER III

FROM THE END OF THE PELOPONNESIAN WAR
TO THE REFORM OF THE DEMOCRACY: 404 TO *CA*. 370

POWER VACUUM IN THE PONTUS

The defeat of Athens officially meant a return to the political situation that had existed in northern Anatolia prior to 424. Having recognized the Great King's claims in Asia in 411, the Spartans surrendered the Greek cities of Ionia and Aeolis to the Persians after their victory and concentrated their own efforts on establishing Sparta's hegemony in European Greece.[1] As far as the Pontus is concerned, it is clear from Xenophon's description of conditions on its south coast in 400 that the Spartans made no attempt to extend their influence east of the Bosporus. Instead they adopted Athens' old policy of controlling shipping to and from the Black Sea by holding the Hellespont. For this purpose they stationed a squadron of ships in Hellespontine waters and placed garrisons in the cities of Byzantium and Chalcedon. All these forces were under the command of a harmost resident in Byzantium, whose political and military responsibilities ended at the Bosporus.[2]

The new arrangement was advantageous for Heraclea and her neighbors to the east. Officially, the Persian government might claim that its authority had been restored on both the west and south coasts of the Pontus, but it was a restoration in name only.[3] In Thrace, Persian rule existed only on paper,[4] and in the Pontic districts of Armenia and Hellespontine Phrygia the government

---

[1] Thucydides 8. 58. 2. Limitation of Spartan interest to Europe is implied by the appeal of the Ionians that they extend their concern to Asia (Xenophon *Hellenica* 3. 1. 3–4).

[2] Lysander had established a harmost at Byzantium after Aegospotami (Xenophon *Hellenica* 2. 2. 2; Diodorus 14. 3. 5), but this was apparently only temporary since there was no harmost there when Clearchus was sent in 403/2 (Diodorus 14. 12. 2). For the harmost's control of forces in Chalcedon, see Xenophon *Anabasis* 7. 1. 20. From *Anabasis* 5. 1. 4 and 6. 6. 12–13 it is clear that Cleander had no military or political responsibilities in the Pontus.

[3] For the extent of Persian claims, see Deinon *FGrH* 3C1, 690 F23b, who mentions as the official boundaries of the empire the Ister and the Nile.

[4] For Persian claims in Thrace, see Ps.-Xenophon *Anabasis* 7. 8. 25: *tōn en Eurōpēi Thraikōn archōn Seuthēs*. This is confirmed by the fact that Skudra (i.e. Thrace) appears as one of the throne bearers on the tomb of Artaxerxes II or III at Persepolis (see Kent 1953, *A?P*, line 25). For the problems connected with the satrapy list contained in the *Anabasis*, see the discussions of Leuze (1935, 165–83) and Ed. Meyer (1965–69 IV.1, 8).

90   PART I: BOOK

was able to exact merely a formal acknowledgment of its authority from the various tribes inhabiting the territory east of Amisus and from Corylas, the dynast of Paphlagonia.[5] In Bithynia, the area of most immediate concern to Heraclea, Boteiras refused to make even this token submission.[6] Thus, although the cities probably also made the gesture of a formal recognition of Persian rule in return for confirmation of their former autonomous status, this action can have had little practical significance.[7] Contrary to what had happened in Greece and western Anatolia, the Spartan victory did not merely result in a change of masters for Heraclea and her neighbors, but in their virtual freedom from all foreign domination.

HERACLEA AND THE TEN THOUSAND

Barely four years after Heraclea had thus gained her freedom, her government was faced with the difficult and dangerous situation created by the unexpected arrival of the Ten Thousand at Trapezus in the spring of 400. It was a staggering task to simply feed this moving *polis*, whose fighting men alone probably outnumbered the citizen bodies of even the largest south Pontic city.[8] Worse, however, it quickly became obvious that the soldiers had little understanding or sympathy for the complex relationships that existed between the various cities and their native neighbors. Provided only that it might be a source of loot or of value in hastening their return home, the troops did not hesitate to disrupt the profitable coasting trade by seizing ships,[9] to raid friendly and hostile natives alike,[10] or even to attack their Greek hosts and their property.[11]

---

[5] For the status of Pontic Armenia, see Ps.-Xenophon *Anabasis* 7. 8. 25. For that of Paphlagonia, Ps.-Xenophon *Anabasis* 7. 8. 25; Xenophon *Anabasis* 5. 6. 8; 6. 1. 2; *Agesilaus* 3. 4; and Nepos *Datames* 2. 2. 3.

[6] Ps.-Xenophon *Anabasis* 7. 8. 25 shows that Bithynia was officially under the jurisdiction of the satrap of Hellespontine Phrygia, but that this was only nominal is clear from *Anabasis* 6. 4. 24. That Bithynia formed part of the satrapy of Hellespontine Phrygia is also implied by Xenophon *Hellenica* 3. 2. 2, as was pointed out by Krumbholtz (1883, 58). For Boteiras, see Memnon *FGrH* 3B, 434 F12. 4. Beloch (1912–27, IV.2, 212) and Ed. Meyer (1897, 515) place his death in 277.

[7] Isocrates *Panegyricus* 162, shows that the area from Cnidus to Sinope was Persian in the 380s (the *Panegyricus* was published in 380, but its composition seems to have occupied much of the previous decade; *cf*. Isocrates, *Discours*, ed. G. Mathieu and É. Brémond, vol. 2 [Paris 1938], 5–6). Sinope's autonomy is implied by Polyaenus 7. 21. 5, and that of Heraclea by Justin 16. 4. 7.

[8] The review of the army at Cerasus (Xenophon *Anabasis* 5. 3. 2; *cf*. 5. 6. 15) showed its strength to be 8600 soldiers, which is to be compared with the approximately 6000 citizens of Heraclea in the early 4th century (Beloch 1912–27 III.1, 302).

[9] Xenophon *Anabasis* 5. 1. 11–12, 16.

[10] Xenophon *Anabasis* 5. 12.

[11] Xenophon *Anabasis* 5. 5. 6, 7, 19–21. Note also Xenophon's threat that the army might join forces with Corylas against Sinope (*Anabasis* 5. 5. 22–23).

III. FROM THE END OF THE PELOPONNESIAN WAR 91

But since the army was only to be in the Pontus for a brief time, Heraclea, just like the other cities, seems at first to have done little more than make preparations for its arrival and speedy departure. In the meantime, Heracleote merchants sailed east to meet the army and exploit the possibilities for trade offered by the soldiers and their camp followers.[12]

The situation changed, however, during the army's stay at Cotyora. The rapacity of the soldiers was already well-known, and now merchants brought to Heraclea the disquieting news that Xenophon was planning to use the army to found a new city in the Pontus. In fact his plan had little or no support among the soldiers and had only been leaked to merchants from Heraclea and Sinope by two of Xenophon's enemies, Timasion of Dardanus and a Boeotian named Thorax, in order to blackmail these cities into providing pay for the soldiers.[13] The device worked. Informed of the proposed colony, the two cities' governments quickly notified Timasion that they would furnish the shipping needed to transport the army out of the Pontus and, according to Xenophon, they offered him a bribe to persuade the soldiers to reject the idea of founding a colony.[14] Their offer was accepted, and shortly thereafter Sinopean ships disembarked the Ten Thousand on the shore north of Heraclea.[15]

On their arrival they found that the Heracleotes had provided for their immediate needs 3000 *medimnoi* of barley, 2000 jars of wine, 20 cattle, and 100 sheep.[16] Nevertheless, relations between the soldiers and the city quickly became tense. Almost home, but with little or nothing to show for all their toil, the soldiers rebelled against their generals. At an assembly called to consider the last leg of the army's journey, it was decided over the vehement objections of Chirisophus, its Spartan commander, and Xenophon to send an embassy to Heraclea to demand a large sum of money for the army. The Heracleotes received the ambassadors politely, told them that the matter would have to be considered at greater length, and then dismissed them. Instead of deliberating further, however, its government quickly readied Heraclea to withstand a possible assault. The citizens' properties were brought within the walls, the gates closed, and the battlements manned.[17]

The appearance of armed men on the city walls first revealed to the troops that their demands had been rejected. Its bluff called, the army, instead of

---

[12] Xenophon *Anabasis* 5. 6. 19. For the camp followers, see Xenophon *Anabasis* 5. 4. 33.
[13] Xenophon *Anabasis* 5. 6. 18–20.
[14] Xenophon *Anabasis* 5. 6. 21, 31.
[15] Xenophon *Anabasis* 6. 2. 2. Neither Diodorus (14. 31. 3) nor Nicephorus Gregoras (Letter 45. 159 [Guilland]) adds anything to Xenophon's account of the Ten Thousand's stay at Heraclea.
[16] Xenophon *Anabasis* 6. 2. 3.
[17] Xenophon *Anabasis* 6. 2. 4–8.

92 PART I: BOOK

attacking Heraclea, disintegrated. The Arcadians and Achaeans, 4500 strong, seceded and elected ten generals from their own ranks. The approximately 4000 other soldiers then broke into two separate forces of about equal strength, one under Chirisophus and the other under Xenophon.[18] The Heracleotes quickly took advantage of the division among their 'guests'. An agreement was arranged with the Arcadians and Achaeans in accordance with which Heracleote ships transported them to Bithynia where they hoped to plunder the native settlements near the coast. Later, ships bearing supplies for them were sent from Heraclea to the free harbor of Calpe.[19] With the largest group gone, the remainder of the army was easily dealt with. Chirisophus and his men were allowed to march through Heracleotis to Bithynia and the city's ships disembarked Xenophon's force just across the Sangarius River in Bithynian territory.[20]

FOREIGN RELATIONS: THE AEGEAN AND PERSIA

The confrontation with the Ten Thousand, despite its danger, was an isolated incident which had no significant consequences. Xenophon's account of it in the *Anabasis* does, however, show that Heraclea in 400 was strong, prosperous, and in full control of her territory. Moreover, his references to the not uncommon sighting of ships during the army's march indicates that the commercial traffic on which a large part of Heraclea's revenue depended had again attained a considerable volume.[21] In particular, this meant that commercial contact between Heraclea and Athens, now increasingly dependent on grain imported from southern Russia, had been restored following the lifting of the Spartan blockade imposed after Lysander's victory at Aegospotami.[22] But Athenian ships brought more than merchants to Heraclea. The mathematician and philosopher Theaetetus taught there for a time,[23] and even Anytus, the

---

[18] Xenophon *Anabasis* 6. 2 .9–16. Chirisophus had 1400 hoplites and 700 peltasts and Xenophon 1700 hoplites, 300 peltasts, and 40 cavalry.

[19] Xenophon *Anabasis* 6. 2. 17. That the Heracleotes had agreed to furnish them supplies at Calpe is indicated by the arrival there later of a ship from Heraclea bearing sacrificial animals (Xenophon *Anabasis* 6. 5. 1).

[20] Xenophon *Anabasis* 6. 2. 18–19. For the Sangarius as the boundary between Heracleotis and Bithynia about 400, see chapter 2.

[21] Xenophon *Anabasis* 5. 1. 11–12, 16; 5. 7. 15.

[22] For the growing Athenian dependence on the Pontic grain trade in the early 4th century, see Xenophon *Hellenica* 5. 1. 28. Lysias (22. 14), Demosthenes (20. 31), and Xenophon (*Oeconomica* 20. 27), however, show that the Pontus was still not Athens' sole source of grain.

[23] *Suda s.v. Theaitētos Athēnaios; Theaitētos Herakieias Pontou.* K v. Fritz (1934, 1351–52) points out that the *Suda* mistakenly distinguishes a Heracleote philosopher from the student of Plato. V. Fritz dates his stay at Heraclea between *ca.* 390 and 369.

III. FROM THE END OF THE PELOPONNESIAN WAR 93

moving force behind the prosecution of Socrates, died there.[24] Heraclea may also have hosted the prominent lyre player Stratonicus during these decades.[25]

Nor was the traffic all in one direction. Ps.-Demosthenes' oration *Against Callippus* provides a vivid picture of the life at Athens of a Heracleote merchant named Lycon. This reveals that men like him were common visitors to Athens and played a significant role in the life of its metic community.[26] The fact, moreover, that the Heracleote *proxenos* at Athens was a figure of the stature of Isocrates' friend Callippus, together with the account of Lycon's social relations that we find in Ps.-Demosthenes, also illustrate the close and cordial relations that existed between them and their Athenian hosts.[27] At the same time, the sons of Heraclea's aristocracy, men such as Clearchus, the future tyrant, his relative and assassin Chion, and the later philosophers Heracleides Ponticus and Amyclas, were to be found among the students of Plato and Isocrates.[28]

Although relations were closest with Athens, the sources show that Heracleotes and their friends could be found throughout European Greece. Thus, the maintenance of friendly relations between Heraclea and her founders is indicated by the presence of Bryson, the son of the mythographer Herodorus, among the associates of Eucleides at Megara[29] and by the epitaph of a Heracleote who died

---

[24] Diogenes Laertius 2. 43 says that the Heracleotes drove him out of the city on the day he arrived. Themistius 20. 239c (Dindorff) says they stoned him to death because of their respect for Socrates and that his tomb was still to be seen *en tōi proasteiōi*. Judeich (1894, 2656) accepts the exile. Ed. Meyer (1965–69 V, 222, n. 1), is somewhat skeptical. As to the date, it must have been after his term as *sitophylax* in 388/7 (Lysias 22. 8; Ed. Meyer 1965–69 V, 222, n. 1).

[25] For Stratonicus and Heraclea, see Athenaeus 8. 351c–d. The date may, however, have been later than 370, since he visited Panticapaeum after 348 (Rostovtzeff 1930, 577; and Werner 1955, 443).

[26] Ps.-Demosthenes 52. The speech was delivered by Pasion's son Apollodorus soon after his father's death in 370 (H. Schaefer 1949, 2065). According to Ps.-Demosthenes, Lycon had been the partner of a metic named Cephisiades who lived in the deme of Skiros (52. 3, 9). In 52. 20 Ps.-Demosthenes referes to an earlier incident in which Lycon had advanced 40 *minae* to some merchants for a trading voyage to Phoenicia.

[27] For Callipus, see Ps.-Demosthenes 52. 5, 14; and Isocrates *Antidosis* 93–94. For his influence, Ps.-Demosthenes 52. 1, 25; and Isocrates *Antidosis* 93–94. For Lycon's other Athenian connections, see Ps.-Demosthenes 52. 3, 7.

[28] For Clearchus and Chion, see chapter 4. For Heracleides Ponticus, see Ff 1–9 (Wehrli). For Amyclas (the spelling varies), see *APIH* VI. 1–2 (Amyntas); Diogenes Laertius 3. 46 (Amyklos); Aelian *VH* 3. 19 (Amyklas); Proclus, *In primum Euclidis Elementorum librum commentarii*, ed. G. Friedlein (Leipzig 1873), 67. As the example of Diogenes of Sinope indicates, Heraclea was not the only Pontic city whose citizens participated in the intellectual life of Athens (*cf*. Isocrates *Antidosis* 224; Diogenes Laertius 6. 3, 9).

[29] Bryson: Herodorus *FGrH* 1A, 31 T3. *Suda s.v. Purrōn; Sōkratēs*. His being the teacher of Pyrrhon makes impossible the tradition that Bryson was a student of Socrates. He was, however, associated with Plato (Theopompus *FGrH* 2B, 115 F259; Ephippus *apud* Athenaeus 11. 509c; Plato [?] *Epistles* 13. 360c). Aristotle *Posterior Analytics* 75b40. *Cf*. Natrop 1899.

94 PART I: BOOK

at Thebes.[30] Likewise, the existence of a Heracleote *proxenos* at Argos reveals that there were social and economic relations between that city and Heraclea.[31] The importance of these contacts and those with Athens as well should, however, not be overestimated. They ensured that Heraclea was not isolated from developments in the Aegean basin, but since there is no evidence that they were matched by the establishment of formal political ties, and indeed could not have been after the signing of the King's Peace in 386, they can have had little or no effect on Heraclea's foreign policy.[32]

On the other hand, relations with Persia were of the utmost importance to any Heracleote government. It is, therefore, unfortunate that the deficiencies of the sources obscure our understanding of this vital aspect of Heraclea's foreign affairs. The city's position was delicate. Persian weakness allowed her almost total freedom despite her recognition of the Great King's sovereignty, but that situation could change and any overt action against her overlord's interests might ultimately result in a worsening of her favorable status. A cautious and correct attitude toward Persia was required, and the sources suggest that such an attitude did, in fact, characterize Heraclea's policy toward her sovereign between 400 and 370, particularly during the years between 400 and 394 when the Spartans invaded Anatolia in order to support the resistance of the Ionian and Aeolian cities to the demands of Tissaphernes and Pharnabazus. Direct evidence concerning Heraclea's reaction to Sparta's intervention in western Anatolia is lacking, but one circumstance is suggestive. In 395, after arranging a marriage between the daughter of his Persian ally Spithridates and Otys, the current ruler of Paphlagonia, Agesilaus ordered that the bride be transported to her new home on a Spartan trireme.[33] Since the ship would not only have to pass Heraclea during its cruise to Paphlagonia but also probably have to spend a night beached in Heracleote territory, the fact that Agesilaus considered this voyage safe indicates that he had reason to believe that the city was sympathetic to the Spartan cause, despite her failure hitherto to render him any active assistance.[34] Agesilaus' recall from Asia in 394, however, prevented Heraclea from seriously compromising herself, and after the signing of the King's Peace in 386 she probably sought to maintain good relations with the Persian government.

[30] *IG* 7. 2531.

[31] Ps.-Demosthenes 52. 10.

[32] The subjects of the Great King were specifically excluded from membership in the Second Athenian League which took the King's Peace as its foundation (*GHI* 2 123, lines 12–18).

[33] Xenophon *Hellenica* 4. 1. 15.

[34] Avoiding direct involvement was easy for the south Pontic cities because the fighting did not touch the Euxine after Dercylidas' Bithynian raid in 399 (Xenophon *Hellenica* 3. 2. 2–6; Diodorus 14. 38. 3; Theopompus *FGrH* 2B, 115 Ff 15–16. For the reference of these fragments to this campaign, see Jacoby *FGrH* 2D, 357 *ad* Ff 15–17).

III. FROM THE END OF THE PELOPONNESIAN WAR   95

Foreign Relations: The Struggle with the Spartocids

Heraclea's noninvolvement in the troubled affairs of western Anatolia contrasted sharply with her active participation in those of the north coast of the Euxine during the first third of the 4th century. The dissolution of the Athenian empire and Sparta's lack of interest in the Pontus had resulted in a power vacuum which Heraclea sought to fill. Moreover, the existence of her colony Chersonesus and the need to protect it gave her a vital interest in the way events developed on the opposite coast – her fleet of 40 triremes,[35] probably the strongest in the Pontus, enabled her to take decisive action should Chersonesus seem threatened.

For tracing the spread of Heracleote influence on the north coast of the Pontus, we are dependent on the indications provided by one type of numismatic evidence, namely, the issuance of coins by a number of mints in that area bearing types that copy those of Heraclea. Although this phenomenon might merely indicate the existence of economic contacts, two considerations, the limited circulation of Heraclea's own coinage outside her immediate home territory and the fact that all the issues in question were composed of the relatively small denominations intended primarily for internal use, strongly suggest that the issuing governments adopted Heracleote types for the specific purpose of publicizing to their own citizens the establishment of close political relations between them and Heraclea.

The earliest example of this type of coin dates from the late 5th century and comes from the Taman Peninsula, where the kings of the Sindoi struck coins bearing a head of Heracles in lion-skin helmet similar to that on the earliest Heracleote issues.[36] Heraclea's influence in Sindica, however, was only of brief duration; early in the 4th century the Sindoi came under the authority of Panticapaeum.[37] But since similar minting policies were followed by the cities of Phanagoria,[38] Theodosia,[39] and Tyras,[40] as well as by her own colony of

---

[35] Ps.-Aristotle *Oeconomica* 2. 2 .8, 1347b3–15.

[36] Zograf 1951, pl. 39, no. 39. Zograf (1951, 244) dates these coins to 425–400. At the same time, the Sindoi struck coins bearing as their type the Athenian owl (Zograf 1951, pl. 39, nos. 38 and 244), so that the spread of Heracleote influence in Sindica was contemporary with and perhaps facilitated by the spread of that of Athens.

[37] For Panticapaean influence in Sindica, see Polyaenus 8. 55.

[38] Zograf 1951, pl. 39, no. 44, which he dates (p. 244), to the period 400–350. The coin is a diobol.

[39] Zograf 1951, pl. 39, nos. 3–4, which (p. 244) he dates to the mid-4th century. Minns (1913, 559) first suggested that the adoption of the charging bull type, which also appears on the contemporary coins of Chersonesus (Zograf 1951, pl. 35, nos. 4–9, and p. 242) indicated an alliance between the three cities. The coins may be hemidrachmae and, according to Shelov (1950, 175–76), they are very rare.

[40] Zograf 1951, pl. 28, no. 2, which he dates (p. 240), to about 360–350.

96   PART I: BOOK

Chersonesus,[41] it is clear that this was only a temporary setback in the development of a network of political ties that centered on Chersonesus and extended from the Taman Peninsula in the east to the Dniester River in the west. Indeed, of the cities on the north coast that minted in the 4th century, only Olbia and Panticapaeum did not employ Heracleote types. This is of particular interest with regard to Panticapaeum because, as the developments in Sindica suggest, the expansion of Heracleote influence among the cities of southern Russia, especially those in the Crimea and Taman Peninsula, interfered with the expansionist plans of the Spartocids and made an eventual confrontation between them and Heraclea virtually unavoidable.

The collision seems to have been precipitated by the attempt of the Spartocids to conquer the city of Theodosia, the center of the Crimean grain trade[42] and a refuge for political malcontents and exiles from Panticapaeum.[43] Control of the city would place the bulk of the profitable grain trade in Spartocid hands and eliminate at the same time a potential base for the activities of their enemies. It would also, however, open the way for further expansion westward in the Crimea and, eventually, for an attack on Chersonesus itself. Accordingly, sometime between the death of Satyrus I in 389, during an unsuccessful siege of Theodosia,[44] and 370 Heraclea fought a major war with Panticapaeum.[45]

The sources, limited as they are to a note in the Ps.-Aristotelian *Oeconomica* and three anecdotes in Polyaenus' collection of stratagems, do not permit a detailed account of this war. They throw light on some of its highlights – the trick by which the Heracleote general Tynnichus lifted the siege of Theodosia, the extraordinary fiscal measures adopted by Heraclea to finance its war effort, and the devices employed by Leucon I, Heraclea's main opponent,[46] to cope with disaffection among his Greek subjects – but a framework in which to place these incidents is lacking. Only the most general reconstruction of the war's course is therefore possible. The striking contrast between the tiny force entrusted to Tynnichus, one trireme, a single merchantman, and as many troops

---

[41] Zograf 1951, pl. 35, nos. 4–9, and p. 242.

[42] For Theodosia's commercial advantages, see Strabo 7. 4. 4, 6; and Demosthenes 20. 33. *Cf.* Minns 1913, 556–57.

[43] Anonymous *Periplus* 12v4: *en tautēi de Theudosiai legetai pote kai phugadas ek tōn Bosporou oikēsai*. Rostovtzeff (1931, 65) connects this with the hostilities between the Spartocids and Heraclea. Shelov (1950, 170) is somewhat skeptical.

[44] Harpocration *s.v. Theudosia.* The date of Satyrus' death in Diodorus 14. 93. 1 is four years too early. For discussion, see Werner 1955, 418–19.

[45] I have discussed the problems connected with this war fully in Burstein 1974.

[46] This is implied by Polyaenus 6. 9. 3.

III. FROM THE END OF THE PELOPONNESIAN WAR 97

as these ships could carry,[47] and the powerful Heracleote forces mentioned elsewhere[48] suggests that his exploit belongs to the early stages of the war. This, in turn, makes it likely that Leucon began the war with a surprise attack on Theodosia, since he was able to complete his siege lines around the city and bring it to the point of surrender before Heraclea could mount a full scale relief expedition. The small size of Tynnichus' force also makes it likely that his actual mission was to reinforce Theodosia until the Heracleotes could arrive in strength and that his relief of the city was an unexpected success. Beyond this we can only say that the Heracleotes apparently followed up his achievement by carrying the war into Leucon's own territory where their fleet of 40 ships gave them naval superiority and enabled them to land and raid at will, while disaffection among Leucon's Greek troops following his humiliation at Theodosia forced him to rely on the support of his Scythian allies to blunt the Heracleote offensive.[49] The duration of this second phase of the war is unknown, but it clearly lasted more than one month and probably extended over several since Ps.-Aristotle states that the Heracleotes paid their troops' *misthos* more than once.[50]

Unfortunately, the sources contain no indication of the outcome of the war. Clearly, Leucon was able to beat off at least one Heracleote landing in his territory with the aid of his Scythian troops;[51] equally clearly, any Heracleote hopes that their successes might enable the anti-Spartocid elements in Panticapaeum to overthrow Leucon proved to be unfounded.[52] This, however, does not justify Rostovtzeff's contention that Leucon emerged from the war victorious and in control of Theodosia while Heraclea was in turmoil as a result of her defeat.[53] Since the war centered on Theodosia, its outcome can be inferred from the date that city came under Spartocid control. Although this event cannot yet be given an exact date, Fernando Bosi has shown that it must be placed in the period after 370 and before 354,[54] when Demosthenes refers to Theodosia as a possession of Leucon.[55] Since the war between him and Heraclea is to be dated between 389 and 370, it is clear that Heraclea,

---

[47] Polyaenus 5. 23.

[48] Ps.-Aristotle *Oeconomica* 2. 2. 8, 1347b3–15.

[49] Polyaenus 6. 9. 4.

[50] Ps.-Aristotle *Oeconomica* 2. 2. 8, 1347b13–15. *Misthos* was normally paid monthly (Griffith 1935, 265–66).

[51] Polyaenus 6. 9. 4.

[52] Polyaenus 6. 9. 3.

[53] Rostovtzeff 1930, 569–70.

[54] Bosi 1967, 134–35. It should be noted that Heracleote coins of this period commemorate a military victory (Franke 1966, 132–37; Kraay and Hirmer n.d., no. 726).

[55] Demosthenes 20. 33. For the date, see Lesky 1966, 599.

98 PART I: BOOK

far from suffering a defeat as suggested by Rostovtzeff, accomplished her main military objective, the frustration of the Spartocid attempt to annex Theodosia.

Heraclea's success marked the peak of her influence on the north coast of the Euxine. The relief of Theodosia assured the security of Chersonesus and seemingly established Heraclea as the successor to Athens as the champion of the smaller Pontic cities. Probably soon afterwards Tyras, Phanagoria, and perhaps even Theodosia established the formal relations with Heraclea that are implied by their coins. Despite these ties, however, it seems clear that Heraclea made no attempt to assist either Theodosia or Phanagoria when Leucon finally did succeed in bringing them under his control.[56] Heraclea's reason for failing to support her allies is unknown, but speculation is possible. Ps.-Aristotle leaves no doubt that her victorious campaign severely strained Heraclea's financial resources, and that may have been a factor in discouraging any further such expeditions. Also Leucon may have attacked at a time when local problems such as those connected with the seizure of power by Clearchus in 364 made her intervention impossible. Two facts, though, the Spartocids' concentration of their imperial activity north and east of the Straits of Kerch after the fall of the Theodosia[57] and the good relations between them and Heraclea's colonies of Callatis and Chersonesus that existed in the late 4th and 3rd centuries, suggest another explanation.[58] Since Heraclea had probably fought Leucon because of fear for the safety of Chersonesus, a guarantee of her independence is likely to have formed part of the terms on which the hostilities were brought to an end. Such a guarantee would also remove the grounds for further Heracleote anxiety about Leucon's plans and, hence, would most satisfactorily account for her readiness to abandon her allies when he renewed his attacks on them.

Internal Developments: The Reform of the Democracy

The first three decades of the 4th century were a period of growth and change in Heraclea's internal life also. At the same time that she was expanding her political influence on the north coast of the Pontus, the acceleration of her economic development which had begun in the second half of the 5th century proceeded apace, with results that can be seen from the fact that her government was able to provide for the war against the Spartocids a sum of money

---

[56] Implied by the fact that Heraclea only fought one war with Leucon.

[57] Rostovtzeff 1930, 570–71.

[58] Callatis: Diodorus 20. 25. 1. Chersonesus: *IOSPE* 1 344, lines 4–7, 17–19 (= Syriscus *FGrH* 3C2, 807 T1).

III. FROM THE END OF THE PELOPONNESIAN WAR

99

that may have exceeded 50 talents.[59] Although not sufficient to fully fund that war, it still compares favorably with the figure of 130 talents which, according to Demosthenes, constituted the whole of Athens' annual revenue during some of the years prior to 341,[60] and it thus gives a fair picture of Heraclea's wealth at this time. During this same period the Heracleote economy seems to have increasingly come to resemble that of the larger commercial cities of the Aegean. An unknown but probably significant proportion of her land was used to grow grain, vines, and olives for both domestic consumption and export to various places within and without the Bosporus. Moreover, the extraordinary development of Heraclea's small denominational coinage, which by the end of the period ranged from less than a hemiobol to a drachma, clearly indicates that day-to-day economic affairs within the city were more and more being conducted on a cash basis.[61]

During these decades the democratic government established in the 420s continued to rule Heraclea. Of the internal history of these years, however, only one incident is known – a plot formed about 370 by the rich to overthrow the democracy, which was only barely foiled by the democracy's leaders.[62] But this is sufficient to show that the period was also marked by growing

[59] The figure is that of Van Groningen (1933, 84) who assumed a *misthos* of four obols per day for the crews, both citizen and Mariandynian, and followed Kirchhoff (1878, 139–40) in emending Ps.-Aristotle *Oeconomica* 2. 2. 8, 1347b9–10 to read as follows: *Ekeinoi te diadontes dimēnou misthon.* ... For a restoration implying a much lower figure, see Griffith 1935, 270, n. 2.

[60] Demosthenes 10. 37. For the date, see Lesky 1966, 604, and Demosthenes, *Harangues*, ed. M. Croiset (Paris 1925) II, 111–19: Although the figure of 130 talents may have been a deliberate underestimate of Athenian revenues by Demosthenes, its use as comparative evidence is still valid since he cannot have vitiated his argument at this point by advancing a total so low that his audience would not accept it as plausible.

[61] For the sake of convenience I cite the coins only as they appear in *Recueil*: eighth-drachma and less, 347, no. 15, 349, no. 31; obol, 349, nos. 26, 27, 29, 30; quarter-drachma, 346, nos. 6–7, 347, nos. 12–14, 349, no. 28; diobol, 349, nos. 23–25; hemidrachma, 346–47, nos. 8–11; drachma, 346, no. 5. These are all struck on the Persian standard. A winged Nike issue that has weights varying from 6.37 to 6.88 g. (Six 1885, 62, no. 65; Kraay and Hirmer n.d., 370, no. 726) is considerably heavier than the drachma on this standard but would fit the Aeginetan standard.

[62] Aeneas Tacticus 11. 10a. The date is based on Aeneas' statement (11. 2) that the plots in chapter 11 will be copied in order (*hrēthēsontai de hexēs hai epiboulai*) from another of his works. That *hexēs* means in chronological rather than merely textual order is indicated by the following facts: 11. 2 refers to the disturbances at Argos in 370 (*cf.* Diodorus 57. 3, and *Aeneas Tacticus, Asclepiodotus, Onasander*, ed. The Illinois Greek Club [London 1923], 67, n. l); 11. 13–15 refers to Chares' role in the revolution at Corcyra in 361; and Aeneas specifically notes that his refer nce to the revolt of the Parthenioi (11. 12) disturbs the chronological order by describing it as happening *palai*. This gives us 370 as the *terminus post quem* and 361 as the *terminus ante quem* for the plot at Heraclea. Aeneas' dating it to a period of democratic rule (*ousēs dēmokratias*) narrows the limits to between 370 and 364 and the fact – to be discussed in the next chapter – that an oligarchy seems to have been in power already by 364 points to *ca.* 370 as the most probable date.

100   PART I: BOOK

tension between the comparatively few large landholders who made up Heraclea's aristocracy and the remainder of the citizen body.

An analysis of the conditions responsible for this situation must be somewhat speculative, but the root of the problem seems to have been the progressive concentration of the city's agricultural land in the hands of these men and the consequent impoverishment and indebtedness of the city's smaller landowners.[63] This was, of course, not a new problem. Previously its impact had been eased by the foundation of Heraclea's colonies, and in the 4th century those colonies probably offered escape to those Heracleotes who chose to emigrate to them. Likewise, the expansion of Heraclea's trade enabled another small group of individuals to support themselves by embracing the *emporos'* life of semi-exile.[64] For the majority who remained in Heraclea, however, life can hardly have been easy. The profits derived from the increased export of the city's agricultural produce must have gone largely to the aristocrats on whose estates they were grown. The poor, on the other hand, who apparently could not survive on the produce of the land in their possession, had to cope with an economy that was increasingly currency-oriented in a small nonindustrial city that can have offered few opportunities for an individual to earn his own living. The payments and distributions of the democracy probably helped these people somewhat,[65] but many of them clearly could not avoid falling in debt to their more wealthy fellow citizens. The result was the bitter division among the Heracleotes which the sources show existed about 370 and later.

About 370 the growing tensions in Heracleote society found expression in the unsuccessful oligarchic *coup d'état* mentioned above. The oligarchs' plan was based on the fact that Eurytion had not lowered the high property requirements necessary for a person to become a member of one the city's four

---

[63] Implied by the demands for the cancellation of debts and the redistribution of the lands of the rich which the *dēmos* raised during the 360s (Justin 16. 4. 2). This section owes much to Mossé's discussion (1962a, 216–33) of the deterioration of the economic position of Greece's small farmers and its political repercussions during the 4th century.

[64] For the life of a Heracleote merchant in this period, see Ps.-Demosthenes 52 *passim*. For the position of the merchant, see Hasebroek 1933, 1–43; and Xenophon *Poroi* 4.6 for the reasons some farmers might choose to become merchants.

[65] One factor may have seriously limited the revenues available to the city for such purposes. Menippus *Periplus* D5709–5803, Anonymous *Periplus* 8v6–8v15 and Arrian *Periplus* 13. 2–5, list a string of *emporia* and anchorages for ships extending from the Sangarius River to Tium. The omission of these places in Ps.-Scylax (*GGM* I, 67, 91–92) and the surface studies of Dörner and Hoepfner (1962, 580) suggest that the *emporia* were founded in the Hellenistic period, but the anchorages could have been used earlier by merchants to purchase agricultural products directly from the estates of Heracleotis. This would spare the merchants' payment of Heraclea's harbor and market fees and enable the growers to escape the difficulties and high cost involved in moving their produce to Heraclea by land (*cf.* Mitchell 1957, 252). For an attempt by Chersonesus to control such direct export of grain, see *IOSPE* 1 401, lines 47–50.

III. FROM THE END OF THE PELOPONNESIAN WAR   101

hekatostues. This meant that when the citizens were summoned to meet by tribes and *hekatostues*, the rich formed a compact group with a military potential out of all proportion to their small numbers. Accordingly, the oligarchs had intended to stage their uprising on such an occasion, but the leaders of the democracy were informed of their plan before it could be executed. In order to frustrate it, they managed to quickly persuade the assembly to approve a radical reorganization of Heraclea's institutions which swept away this last vestige of the predemocratic regime. The city's three tribes were probably retained, but the four existing *hekatostues* were replaced by 60 new ones.[66] The Heracleotes were then enrolled in these new *hekatostues* without consideration for their wealth. The result was that when these new units met, the rich were now scattered among the mass of the population which supported the democracy and were thus rendered, for the time being, impotent.

---

[66] Pippidi's suggestion (1969, 238) that the reform was modeled on that of Cleisthenes, with ten residence-based tribes replacing Heraclea's three kinship-based tribes, is possible but not supported by Aeneas' text.

CHAPTER IV

CLEARCHUS AND SATYRUS: *CA.* 370 TO 346

THE CRISIS

The victory of the democratic faction was only temporary. How the oligarchs managed to seize power we do not know, but the sources leave no doubt that they had already done so by 364. At that time, although the *dēmos* was still formally supreme,[1] control of the city's affairs was in the hands of a body called the Council of Three Hundred, which had complete authority to administer Heraclea, conduct foreign affairs, and function as a court.[2] Of its procedures we know nothing. Whether or not membership was for life is not stated, but subsequent events make it clear that a high property qualification was required and that this actually meant that the Council was dominated by members of Heraclea's landholding aristocracy.

While the Council was still in the process of consolidating its power, relations between it and the *dēmos* moved steadily toward *stasis*. The root of the developing crisis was more economic than social. Substantial numbers of the poorer Heracleotes were in debt and threatened with eventual pauperization because the concentration of the bulk of Heraclea's best agricultural land in the hands of a small number of individuals left them too little land to subsist on. As I indicated in the last chapter, however, this was by no means a new problem. Moreover, there is no reason to believe that a dramatic worsening of the real economic position of the Heracleote poor took place during the first half of the 360s, which might have explained why their debt problem suddenly seemed unbearable to them and to many of their more fortunate fellow citizens. At most, the fall of the democracy and the consequent end of pay for public service and similar benefits may have pushed their backs somewhat closer to the wall by depriving them of a source of income that was small and sporadic, but useful. Rather, the new element in the situation was probably psychological. As in other 4th-century Greek cities, the hopes of the poor for relief centered on the establishment of a new and more just economic system through a cancellation of all debts and the breaking up and redistribution of the

---

[1] Clear from Justin 16. 4. 12–16. See also the reference in Polyaenus 2. 30. 1.
[2] Polyaenus 2. 30. 2; Justin 16. 4. 2–5.

104   PART I: BOOK

lands presently occupied by the rich among the whole citizen body.[3] Under the democracy there had probably been as little chance of this happening as there was now under the Council of Three Hundred's regime. The difference, and indeed the probable source of their desperation, was that with a government dominated by their creditors in power they now knew that relief, in any form, was an empty dream.

The situation was ideally suited for exploitation by the Council's political enemies, the leaders of the overthrown democracy. They had previously made ineffectual attempts to resist their loss of influence, which had only succeeded in provoking strong countermeasures from the Council, such as the condemnation to exile of the future tyrant Clearchus.[4] When, however, they sought to capitalize on the *dēmos'* discontent by adopting as their own program the poor's dreams of debt cancellation and land redistribution, the result was the outbreak of *stasis* late in the year 365 or early 364.[5]

The Council's predicament allowed no simple solutions. The councilors obviously could not grant the demands as presented since that would cost them their estates and their power. Furthermore, to attempt to appease the populace by offering just the cancellation of debts (as was to be later recommended by Aeneas Tacticus) had the drawback that it would only enhance their opponents' popular support.[6] Still, with emotion running so high on the issue, the dangers of a definitive rejection must have been apparent to all. What made their problem doubly difficult was that by choosing to force the issue when they did, the democratic leaders paralyzed Heraclea at a time when the collapse of royal authority in the satrapies of northern Anatolia exposed Heraclea to attack by the rebellious satraps.

Such an attack was not unlikely. Mithridates, the son of Ariobarzanes, the satrap of Hellespontine Phrygia,[7] had made no attempt to conceal his ambition to bring Heraclea under his personal authority, much as another Mithridates, perhaps his uncle, had already done in the case of the city of Cius on the

---

[3] Justin 16. 4. 1.

[4] Justin 16. 4. 4–6; *Suda s.v. Klearchos* (= Aelian F86 Hercher).

[5] According to the *Suda* (*s.v. Klearchos*), the *stasis* broke out *ou mēn meta makron* after Clearchus' exile. Justin's (16. 4. 2) *impotenter flagitarent* suggests violence in the city.

[6] Aeneas Tacticus 14.

[7] Justin 16. 4. 7; *Suda s.v. Klearchos*. Identification of the Mithridates of Justin and the *Suda* with the son of Ariobarzanes rests on the following three considerations: (1) he is likely to have been militarily active as is implied by the *Suda* since his father is known to have been in revolt during the period in question; (2) Ariobarzanes did appoint mercenary officers as governors of cities (Demosthenes 23. 141–142) just as Mithridates proposed to do in the case of Heraclea; and (3) geographical considerations make it unlikely that Mirthridates of Cius (see below n. 8) had ambitions of annexing Heraclea.

IV. CLEARCHUS AND SATYRUS

Propontis.[8] Because of the outbreak of *stasis* within Heraclea he now had the opportunity, and the improvement in his father's fortunes during 365 gave him the freedom to act if he so chose.

The decade of the 360s was, in fact, a dangerous period not only for Heraclea but for all of the autonomous cities of northern Anatolia. Almost continuously during these years there was rebellion in the neighboring satrapies of Hellespontine Phrygia and Cappadocia. In these rebellions the satraps sought to assure their access to the sea and possible allies and revenue by occupying the Greek cities and imposing their own officers on them as tyrants, but with the official title of *huparchos*. Even before his revolt became public in the summer of 366,[9] Ariobarzanes had succeeded in bringing a number of the Hellespontine cities under his control in this way,[10] and his ally Datames, the satrap of Cappadocia, had achieved similar successes over Sinope[11] and possibly also Amisus.[12] Fortunately for Heraclea, however, their plans for a coordinated revolt against Artaxerxes II failed, so that Datames had already agreed to a truce in central Anatolia just at the time that Ariobarzanes began his revolt.[13]

Free now to concentrate their forces against Ariobarzanes, Artaxerxes' chief supporters, Autophradates of Lydia and Mausolus of Caria, quickly forced him back into the city of Assos and then laid siege to it.[14] The complete collapse of

---

[8] Diodorus 15. 90. 3. That he ruled Cius follows from Diodorus 20. 111. 4. For his relationship to Mithridates the son of Ariobarzanes, see Beloch 1912–27 III.2, 150–51, who suggests that he was a younger brother of Pharnabazus.

[9] The date is based on the fact that Ariobarzanes' revolt was contemporary with the beginning of Timotheus' siege of Samos (Demosthenes 15. 9). Since that siege lasted for ten months (Isocrates *Antidosis* 111) and the restoration of the Samian exiles in 322 took place 43 years after their expulsion by the Athenians (Diodorus 18. 18. 9), the beginning of Ariobarzanes' rebellion can be placed in the middle of 366.

[10] Demosthenes 23. 141–42. *Cf.* Isocrates Letter 9. 8–10.

[11] Diodorus 15. 91. 2. By the mid-360s he had also taken control of Paphlagonia (Trogus Prologue 10; Judeich 1892, 192).

[12] An initial attempt to reduce Sinope by siege failed (Polyaenus 7. 21. 2, 5; Aeneas Tacticus 40. 4), but it did leave him with a strong fleet which must have made him a potential danger to Heraclea. Judeich (1892, 194) dates this siege to the beginning of the 360s. That Datames did ultimately gain control of Sinope is indicated by the appearance of his name on her coins (Six 1885, 26, nos. 34–36, and *Recueil* I.1, 183, no. 21). For further discussion, see Six 1885, 24–25, and D. Robinson 1906b, 245–47.

[13] Polyaenus 7. 21. 1; Ps.-Aristotle *Oeconomica* 2 .2. 24a, 1350b27–28. Since the coins of Amisus do not bear his name (*Recueil* I.1, 44–48, nos. 1–8), Datames may not have actually occupied the city.

[14] Alliance of Ariobarzanes and Datames: Nepos *Datames* 5. 6 The betrayal of his plans by his son Sysinas (Nepos *Datames* 7. 1) forced Datames to act before his ally was ready. For the peace with Artaxerxes, see Nepos *Datames* 8. 5–6. As Judeich (1892, 196) saw, it was probably the outbreak of Ariobarzanes' revolt that induced Autophradates to arrange the peace.

106 PART I: BOOK

the revolt was in sight and with it restoration of royal authority in Anatolia and security for the autonomous cities such as Heraclea.

A year later and shortly before Heraclea's internal crisis broke, however, the situation once more became threatening. Mausolus and Autophradates had lifted the siege of Assos in the summer of 365, thus freeing Ariobarzanes, as a result of the intervention on his behalf of Athens and Sparta in the persons of Timotheus and Agesilaus. They then ceased all hostilities and returned to their own satrapies.[15] The royal cause had virtually collapsed in western Anatolia, and the debacle there seems to have been quickly followed by an outbreak of new fighting by Datames in central Anatolia.[16] As the only still unsubdued Pontic city, Heraclea was now vulnerable and isolated from all support.

Such was the situation, *stasis* within Heraclea and a hostile political environment abroad, when the Council began to consider how best to cope with their problem. Its debates and the crisis both lasted into the summer of 364 without any solution being found.[17] Of the actual course of the discussion we know nothing. Conceivably there may have been some councilors who favored compromise, but subsequent events indicate that the majority would accept nothing less than the complete submission of the *dēmos* and its leaders without the oligarchs having to grant any concessions. The prolongation of the debate only reflected their inability to devise a policy that would achieve that result. The opportunity they were waiting for, however, arrived when Timotheus returned to the Propontis with an Athenian fleet in order to relieve the besieged city of Cyzicus.[18]

Since Callippus, the Heracleote *proxenus* at Athens, was, like the general, a student and close friend of Isocrates, Timotheus and his generally conservative views were probably well known to the councilors.[19] Nevertheless, he rejected their appeal that he extend his cruise to Heraclea and use his forces against the *dēmos* and instead departed from the Propontis for the Chalcidice.[20] The

[15] Xenophon *Agesilaus* 2. 26; Nepos *Timotheus* 1. 3.

[16] *Nepos* Datames 9.

[17] Justin 16. 4. 2–3.

[18] Diodorus 15. 81. 6; Nepos *Timotheus* 1. 2; Justin 16. 4. 3. Lenk (1927, 78), dated the appeal to Timotheus to 366, but this is improbable for two reasons. First, it presupposes an interval of a year between the approaches to Timotheus and Epaminondas, and second, it ignores Justin's statement that the Council asked for their help only when all other expedients had failed (*cum exitus rei non inveniretur, ad postremum auxilia … petivere*). The only serious obstacle to the chronology proposed in the text is the belief that Laches and Timotheus had been assigned the Hellespontine area for the year 364/3 (Judeich 1892, 201, n. 1). Diodorus (15. 79. 1), however, indicates that Laches' commission was not limited to the Hellespontine area but rather was a more general order to hinder the activities of the Theban fleet wherever it went.

[19] Callippus: Demosthenes 52. 5, 9; Isocrates *Antidosis* 93–94. On Timotheus' conservatism and opposition to revolution: Isocrates *Antidosis* 121, 127, 138.

[20] Justin 16. 4. 3; Diodorus 15. 81. 6; Isocrates *Antidosis* 113.

IV. CLEARCHUS AND SATYRUS 107

unexpected arrival at Byzantium of a Boeotian fleet under the command of Epaminondas that same summer offered them once more a chance to gain foreign aid. This time, moreover, their plea would be supported not only by the personal ties that existed between the aristocracies of the two cities,[21] but also by the traditional obligation of Thebes and the other Boeotians, as cofounders of Heraclea, to assist their colony. But again their request was rejected.[22]

The failure of their approaches to Timotheus and Epaminondas forced the councilors to change their tactics. In place of their former intransigence, they now affected a more conciliatory tone by offering to submit the dispute between them and the *dēmos* to arbitration. For this purpose they turned to the democratic politician they had previously exiled, Clearchus, then serving as an officer in the employ of Mithridates, the son of Ariobarzanes.[23] His sentence of exile was revoked and he was invited to return together with a body of mercenaries in order to assume the post of *ephoros tēs authis homonoias* (*arbiter civilis discordiae* in Trogus/Justin's translation).[24] Ostensibly, *Clearchus* was to consider impartially the problem and then impose a solution on both parties; meanwhile he would have full authority to administer Heraclea with the aid of his mercenaries.[25] This, however, was only the declared purpose for his recall. There had in fact been no change in the Council's ultimate goal; only the means were new.

Although Clearchus was publicly to act the role of a neutral arbiter, he was to use his men to suppress the Council's main opponents and demoralize their followers, or, as Trogus/Justin put it, he was to be *defensor senatoriae causae*.[26] Undoubtedly, the oligarchs were aware of the danger of this stratagem: as Aristotle was later to point out and Clearchus' behavior to confirm, such appointments were ideal stepping stones to a tyranny.[27] At the time, however, the oligarchs were desperate, and Clearchus must have seemed to be an almost

---

[21] For relations between Heraclea and Thebes in the 4th century, see *IG* 7 2531. The comment in line 3 of the epitaph that 'you, longing for it [*sc.* his homeland], die in the hands of friends' suggests that he may have belonged to one of the families exiled after the foundation of the tyranny.

[22] Justin 16. 4. 3. For Epaminondas' cruise in general, see Diodorus, 15. 79. 1; Isocrates *Philippus* 53; and Aeschines 2. 105.

[23] *Suda s.v. Klearchos*; Justin 16. 4. 7.

[24] *Suda s.v. Klearchos*; *Ephoros* (*contra* Schneiderwirth 1882, 23, only the first section of the latter article concerns Clearchus); Justin 16. 4. 4–5, 9; Aeneas Tacticus 12. 5. This is the post Aristotle *Politics* 5. 5. 9, 1306a28, calls *archōn mesidios*.

[25] The scope of his authority follows from his offer in Polyaenus 2. 30. 2, *tēi boutēi ... paradounai ta pragmata*.

[26] Justin 16. 4. 10.

[27] Aristotle *Politics* 5. 5. 9, 1306a27–32, apropos of Iphiades of Abydus and Simus of Larissa. The only reference to Clearchus in the Aristotelian corpus occurs in the probably spurious (Lesky 1966, 564) *Magna Moralia* (2. 6. 33, 1203a22–23), a surprising fact in view of the interest in Heraclea Aristotle reveals in the *Politics*.

108 PART I: BOOK

ideal tool. His record of past opposition to their rule climaxing in his exile would make him acceptable to the democrats. On the other hand, his background and, we must assume, secret communications with him during the crisis probably gave them reason to believe that he would betray his former political allies in exchange for inclusion in the oligarchy on his return to Heraclea.[28]

Our knowledge of Clearchus' life before his recall is admittedly scant. Forty-six years of age and obviously a member of the city's upper class, he had, as can be seen from his being exiled, attained some prominence in Heraclea's political life as a democratic politician. This was not, however, the result of any devotion on his part to democratic principles. It is clear from Isocrates' description of him before he became tyrant that Clearchus' manner and attitudes were essentially those of a typical *kalos kai agathos*,[29] Rather, like Eurytion, the founder of the Heracleote democracy, he had become a democrat because his personal enemies were influential oligarchs, so the belief that he might be induced to support the interests of his own class was by no means unreasonable.[30] The Council's error was that they underestimated the extend of his ambitions.

As far as other aspects of Clearchus' life are concerned, the sources only provide information on his stay in Athens during the middle and late 370s. An intellectual, he had largely devoted those years to the pursuit of his education, spending four years as a student of Isocrates and then attending the lectures of Plato for a brief time just before his return to Heraclea.[31] Also referred to this same period should be the establishment of his friendship with another of Isocrates's students, Timotheus, a relationship that had as an immediate result his becoming an Athenian citizen through the agency of the general on his return to Athens after his great success at Corcyra in 375.[32] This friendship, moreover, lasted at

[28] Suggested by Mossé 1962b, 7.

[29] Isocrates Letter 7. 12.

[30] For Eurytion, see Aristotle *Politics* 5. 5. 10, 1306a38–1306b3. For Clearchus, see the comment in the *Suda* (*s.v. Klearchos*) that his exile was caused by his being *phthonói de epiklustheis*.

[31] Memnon *FGrH* 3B, 434 F1. 1; *Suda s.v. Klearchos*; Isocrates Letter 7. 12. His intellectual interests are also alluded to in *Epistles of Chion* 16. 4. That he studied with Isocrates for four years means that he took the full course. His career as tyrant embarrassed both the Platonists and Isocrates, as can be seen from the dream in the *Suda* in which Philosophy declares him an enemy and from the passage of Isocrates Letter 7, just cited. For the hostility to Plato and Isocrates for supposedly training tyrants, see Isocrates *Antidosis* 30, and Athenaeus 11. 508e–509b.

[32] Demosthenes 20. 84. This is usually dated to the period after Clearchus became tyrant (e.g. Schneiderwirth 1882, 24; Apel 1910, 34; Berve 1967 I, 318) and is possible since Timotheus did sponsor Menelaus of Pelagonia for citizenship in 362 (*GHI* 2 143). Demosthenes, however, writes: *Timotheói didontes tén doreian, di' ekeinon edókate kai Klearchói kai tisin allois politeian*, that is, Clearchus was made a citizen when the Athenians honored Timotheus. Only one such occasion is known, namely, after Timotheus' return from Corcyra (Nepos *Timotheus* 2. 2–3; Aeschines 3. 243; Pausanias 1. 3. 2; *GHI* 2 128). Furthermore, Demosthenes at this point groups

IV. CLEARCHUS AND SATYRUS

least until 363 or 362, when Clearchus named his eldest son Timotheus after him,[33] and it was probably one of the factors that influenced Timotheus in his decision to reject the Council's request for assistance. The picture of Clearchus that emerges from these few facts, of an individual who was able, cultivated, but above all ambitious, is fully in accord with his subsequent career.

SEIZURE OF POWER

It was probably late in the summer of 364 that Clearchus, accompanied by a strong force of mercenaries furnished to him by Mithridates, entered Heraclea and was officially installed in his new position of *ephoros tēs authis homonoias*. Most likely to lessen the danger implicit in the presence of a large number of mercenaries within the city walls, they were billeted in homes throughout the city instead of being concentrated in a single camp.[34] The hopes of the *dēmos* and its leaders that Clearchus would show himself sympathetic to their cause, however, were quickly dispelled. The sources leave no doubt that during the period immediately following his return to Heraclea he allowed himself to become publicly identified with the Council and its objectives, and that the councilors, emboldened by his attitude, dropped all pretense of interest in a peaceful resolution of the *stasis*. Polyaenus gives us a brief glimpse of the deplorable conditions within Heraclea at this time, caused by Clearchus – surely with the tacit consent of the Council – allowing his men complete freedom to harass and intimidate the Heracleotes.[35] Seemingly, the Council's plan had worked, since they were able to easily arrange the murder of the chief democratic leaders amidst the then prevailing disorder and confusion.[36]

The Council, however, had seriously erred in its assessment of Clearchus and the reasons behind his acceptance of their offer of pardon. To him it was not a favor in return for which he should feel gratitude, but rather an unexpected

---

Timotheus' honors with those of Iphicrates and Chabrias, and it is clear from Demosthenes 23. 198, that this association was common, so that a reference to a gift to Timotheus at the same time that Iphicrates and Chabrias were mentioned would most naturally be connected to his great victory of the 370s. The nature of Clearchus' relationship to Timotheus is unclear, but Parke's suggestion (1933), 97, n. 5) that Clearchus served with him at Corcyra is attractive, especially in view of the displaced reference to a campaign in the *Suda* (*s.v. Klearchos*; *cf.* Hercher's apparatus *ad loc.*) which seems to refer to his Athenian period and the military experience implied by later service with Mithridates.

[33] For the date of Timotheus' birth, see below n. 105.

[34] This follows from Polyaenus 2. 30. 1. Such precautions were recommended by Aeneas Tacticus 12. 1; 13. 3.

[35] Polyaenus 2. 30. 1. *Cf.* Justin 16. 4. 12: *neque adfuturum se amplius grassanti in populum senatui ait* (*sc.* Clearchus).

[36] Aeneas Tacticus 12. 5.

110   PART I: BOOK

opportunity to establish his own personal ascendancy over Heraclea.[37] It was with this goal in mind that he had accepted their proposal and had, before leaving for Heraclea, arranged for Mithridates to assign a force of mercenaries to him in exchange for a promise to use them to seize control of the city in the Persian's name, surrender it to him personally on a mutually agreed date, and then rule it as his governor.[38] All the while, therefore, that he had co-operated with the oligarchs, he had at the same time been actively strengthening his own position in preparation for the moment when he would move against them. The violent removal of the democratic leaders was as beneficial to him as to the Council, for it meant that he would not have to contend with them as rivals or critics. Likewise, even the turbulence connected with their deaths worked to his advantage. While the Council reaped most of the blame for it, by his lax discipline he was probably able to increase his popularity among the mercenaries on whom his plans ultimately depended. Moreover, according to Polyaenus, he was even able to use the fear caused by the widespread disorders to force the Heracleotes to grant him permission to build a fortified camp on the acropolis in which to concentrate his soldiers, and thus to escape the obstacle to his freedom of action presented by the dispersal of his men throughout the city.[39] The result was that at the moment of their triumph the councilors found they had lost control of affairs to their own agent, who, accompanied already by a bodyguard[40] of mercenaries, was virtually tyrant of Heraclea.

Only two things still stood in his way, his agreement with Mithridates and his lack of sufficient funds to maintain the pay of his mercenaries. One bold act sufficed to remedy both problems. Whether or not he had ever intended to keep his bargain with the Persian we do not know, but as the development of events within Heraclea made it clear that he did not need him to rule the city, Clearchus, always the opportunist, turned on him without hesitation.

[37] That this was the attitude of the Council and of the later exiles is suggested by Memnon's characterization of Clearchus (*FGrH* 3B, 434 F1. 2) as *kai pros tous euergetas achariston*.

[38] Justin 16. 4. 7–9. Mossé's suggestion (1962b, 7) that Clearchus returned home at the head of a band of Heracleote exiles is most unlikely in view of the sources' insistence that the Council only recalled Clearchus.

[39] Polyaenus 2. 30. 1, 2; Justin 16. 4. 11; 16. 5.14; and Memnon *FGrH* 3B, 434 F9. 2. Presumably this is the *phrourion* mentioned in *Epistles of Chion* 13. 1.

[40] Bodyguard: Polyaenus 2. 30. 2, *doruphorōn* as opposed to *stratiōtas* later in this same passage, *misthophorous* in 2. 30. 1, and *xenon* and *misthophorōn* in 2. 30. 2. The normal meaning of *doruphoros* is bodyguard and not mercenary (*cf.* LSJ *s.v. doruphoros*, 2). The distinction between the rest of Clearchus' troops and his *doruphoroi* probably occurred in Polyaenus' source since, as Stadter (1965, 27–28) has shown, his practice was to reproduce the terminology of his sources as closely as possible. For Clearchus' continued possession of a bodyguard, see Justin 16. 5. 16; Memnon *FGrH* 3B, 434 F1. 5; and *Epistles of Chion* 13. 1.

IV. CLEARCHUS AND SATYRUS
111

When Mithridates and his personal entourage (*amici*) arrived at the agreed date to receive the submission of Heraclea, they were admitted into the city only to be placed immediately under arrest and then informed by Clearchus that their release was conditional on the immediate payment of a substantial ransom. The humiliated Persian had no choice but to pay. As Clearchus had promised, the release of Mithridates and his friends promptly followed, probably much to the dismay of the Heracleotes who, having enjoyed the discomfiture of their enemy, must have known that in the future his desire for revenge would make him a far more implacable foe.[41]

Once Clearchus was free of his ties to Mithridates and assured of the loyalty of his soldiers, the demise of the oligarchy quickly followed. Fortunately, by combining an anecdote in Polyaenus' collection of stratagems with the narrative of Justin, we can easily reconstruct the main outlines of his *coup d'état*.[42] His basic plan was simple enough. Despite his recent actions, he would assume the aspiring tyrant's traditional role of champion of the *dēmos* against the rich and in that capacity seize power without bloodshed by arresting at one time the entire membership of the Council. Accordingly, when he was ready, he let it be known to some of the councilors that he felt his work in Heraclea was over and that he, therefore, wished to resign his post, return the administration of the city to them, and then leave it. As he expected, they rose to the bait and hastily convened a meeting of the Council in order to accept his offer. Instead of making an appearance, however, he had his soldiers surround the Council building once their session had got under way, while he himself summoned an extraordinary sitting of the Heracleote assembly where he denounced the Council's past actions against the *dēmos*, disassociated himself from any similar activity by them in the future, and then dramatically offered to leave Heraclea with his men or, if the citizens wished, to stay and defend them against their oppressors. In a normal assembly the sincerity of his astonishing *volte-face* would hardly have been accepted without question, but in this confused and leaderless rump the ploy worked. His offer of protection was accepted immediately and a motion passed on the spot conferring on him what Justin calls *summum imperium*, a phrase that, as Berve suggests, should probably be interpreted to mean that the assembly appointed him *stratēgos autokratōr*, or general with extraordinary authority.[43]

---

[41] Justin 16. 4. 8–10.
[42] Justin 16. 4. 10–17; Polyaenus 2. 30. 2. *Cf.* Apel 1910, 29, n. 1.
[43] Justin 16. 4. 16; Berve 1967 I, 316. For the office in general, see Scheele 1932.

112 PART I: BOOK

Simple in concept, Clearchus' plan was only imperfectly executed. He had clearly anticipated that the whole Council would meet to accept his resignation, and had apparently made his dispositions on that assumption. But, in fact, only 60 of the councilors attended the session. These surrendered to Clearchus and were immediately imprisoned by him on the acropolis. The rest of the membership, even though they had to leave their families behind, managed to escape from Heraclea before Clearchus discovered the actual situation and could close the gates.[44]

With the escape of the councilors, Clearchus lost the initiative. He could do little to block effectively their efforts to obtain support, probably with the approval of Ariobarzanes, from the cities of Hellespontine Phrygia for an attack on him while his regime was new and still vulnerable.[45] In his 60 prisoners, and in the families and estates of the other councilors, however, he did have hostages, and he does seem to have sought to use them in an attempt, certainly doomed from the start, to affect a reconciliation with at least some of his enemies. Thus, while publicly promising death for his prisoners, he secretly offered them freedom in return for the payment of a ransom, and at the same time he took no overt action against either the women or the property of the other councilors. The ransom was paid, but when the progress of the oligarchs' preparations made it obvious that the gesture had otherwise failed, Clearchus finally acted to strengthen his own position within Heraclea by making the breach between himself and them complete. The prisoners, despite payment of their ransom, were executed. Likewise, the estates of the remaining councilors were then confiscated, some of their slaves freed and enfranchised to swell Clearchus' own following, and their wives and daughters forced to marry husbands of his choosing.[46] According to Justin, he compelled them to marry their own former slaves in order to further humiliate their families and to render his new citizens more loyal to himself. The motivation ascribed to Clearchus may have some truth in it, but his forcing them to marry their own slaves seems only to be part of the stock picture of the brutal tyrant. Although Heracleote tradition made much of the brave resistance of some of the women to such 'disgraceful' matches, examination of reports of similar measures by other tyrants makes it likely that,

[44] Justin 16. 4. 16–17; 16. 5. 2.

[45] Justin 16. 5. 1. Identification of Justin's vague *civitatibus* with the cities of Hellespontine Phrygia is probable because of Clearchus' hostile relations with the family of Ariobarzanes and the geographical difficulties of mounting an offensive against Heraclea from the cities to the east of her. If Astacus was one of the cities involved, that might explain Clearchus' later attack on it (Polyaenus 2. 30. 2).

[46] Justin 16. 5. 1–4.

IV. CLEARCHUS AND SATYRUS

although some such marriages may actually have taken place, the majority of the women probably found their new husbands among the tyrant's officers and supporters.[47]

The decisive battle with the forces of the Council and its allies probably took place toward the end of 364, or early in 363, and ended in a complete victory for Clearchus.[48] Those of the councilors and their friends who were able to escape from the debacle now entered a life in exile which only ended for their grandchildren in 281.[49] Moreover, during Clearchus' reign, at least, it was a life in which they had constantly to be on their guard against the assassins he employed to harass them and their more prominent supporters in other cities. As for those councilors unfortunate enough to fall into his hands, Clearchus had them paraded before the Heracleotes *in triumphi modum* as visual proof of the futility of any future attempt to challenge his power, and he then apparently executed them, and those of their sympathizers who had been discovered within Heraclea, during a brief period of violence following his victorious return to the city.[50]

FROM TYRANNY TO MONARCHY

From the date of his victory, until his assassination in the spring of 352, Clearchus was the undisputed ruler of Heraclea. At that moment he was, for the first time, securely ensconced in power with all opposition and criticism suppressed or driven underground and his popularity with the *dēmos* and his own men at its peak. For the modern historian of Heraclea, however, that event marks the beginning of obscurity. Henceforth, Nymphis' biographical approach and the limited evidence available to him at the time he wrote have resulted in

---

[47] The same charge is leveled against two other 4th-century tyrants, Dionysius I (Diodorus 14. 66. 5; Aeneas Tacticus 40. 2–3, apropos of a city other than Syracuse) and Chaeron of Pellene (*APIH* XI. 4–40; Athenaeus 11. 509b), and against Nabis (Polybius 16. 13. 1). That the new husbands were not chosen solely from ex-slaves, however, is indicated by Diodorus' description (14. 66. 5) of them as *[oiketais] kai migasin anthrōpois* and Polybius' identification elsewhere (13. 6. 3–4) of the men involved as *tois epiphanestatois kai tois misthophorois*.

[48] Justin 16. 5. 5.

[49] Memnon *FGrH* 3B, 434 F7. 3. The date is probably spring or early summer of 281 since we now know that Seleucus' death falls in August or September of 281 (Sachs and Wiseman 1954, 205–06). This discovery has important consequences for the chronology of the tyranny because it shows that Nymphis' figure of 84 years for the period from its establishment to the return of the exiles (Memnon *FGrH* 3B, 434 F6. 1; *cf.* Jacoby *FGrH* 3B *Texte*, 274 *ad* 434 F5) is reckoned inclusively, and, therefore, that his other statements concerning the duration of reigns are also probably inclusive.

[50] For the violence at the beginning of the reign, see Justin 16. 5. 6–7, and Theopompus *FGrH* 2B, 115 F28. *Epistles of Chion* 14. 1, and Memnon *FGrH* 3B, 434 F1. 2 are probably intended as general characterizations of Clearchus as a tyrant.

114 PART I: BOOK

our having little more than a character portrait of a typically brutal and arrogant tyrant.[51] From this and the mention of a few events, however, it is possible to establish the main features of his reign and to see that approximately the year 360 marked the transition from a policy of restraint at home and abroad to one that was more active and assertive.

FOREIGN AFFAIRS

Restraint, even though it meant abandoning Theodosia, Heraclea's ally in the eastern Crimea, to Leucon, was necessary during the closing years of the decade because they coincided with the last and most dangerous phase of the Satraps' Revolt.[52] As far as the decision whether to place Heraclea in the camp of the rebel satraps or in that of Artaxerxes II was concerned, the bitter enmity now existing between himself and the family of Ariobarzanes left Clearchus little choice. Early in his reign, therefore, he dispatched the first of several embassies to Artaxerxes II, which resulted in his obtaining recognition for his new regime and in the reestablishment of close relations between Heraclea and Persepolis.[53] Understandable though his move was, it left Heraclea completely isolated when the satraps Autophradates and Mausolus, who had supported the royal cause earlier in the decade, together with Orontes of Mysia, joined their forces to those of Ariobarzanes and Datames in late 363. The Greek cities of the west coast and the autonomous nations of southern Anatolia quickly followed the lead of the satraps so that, except for a few scattered strongholds, royal authority virtually disappeared from Anatolia.[54] But fortunately for Clearchus, the duration of the expanded revolt was brief. By 361, little more than a year after the satraps had formed their alliance, their inability to subordinate their personal ambitions to the good of their movement had led first to mutual betrayal and then to the complete collapse of the revolt.[55]

---

[51] For the biographical character of Nymphis' account of Clearchus and Satyrus, see Laqueur 1927, 1100. On Nymphis' possible sources, see Jacoby *FGrH* 3B *Kommentar*, 269–70, and Desideri 1967, 391–92.

[52] *Contra* Apel 1910, 36–37, and Maksimowa 1959, 117–18, there is no evidence for Heracleote activity on behalf of Theodosia after 370 (*cf.* Burstein1974a, 415).

[53] Memnon *FGrH* 3B, 434 F1. 4. The use of the word *pollakis* in connection with Artaxerxes II and Artaxerxes III requires us to date the opening of relations between Clearchus and Persepolis early in his reign, since Artaxerxes II was already dead by May 358 (Beloch 1912–27 III.2, 130; Judeich 1892, 230–31).

[54] Diodorus 15. 90 3–4; Trogus Prologue 10. On the discrepancy between Diodorus and Trogus, who calls Orontes *Praefectus Armeniae*, see now Osborne 1973, 538.

[55] Diodorus 15. 91. 1, 7; 15. 92. 1. *SIG*[3] 1 167, lines 17–18, show that Mausolus had made his peace with Artaxerxes by 361/60. Likewise, Artabazus had replaced Ariobarzanes in Hellespontine

IV. CLEARCHUS AND SATYRUS

115

The restoration of royal authority in northern Anatolia finally brought security and freedom of action to Clearchus. The two satraps who had dominated the region during the past decade, Ariobarzanes and Datames, were both dead, and Mithridates, his enemy and the man responsible for their deaths, had left the area in order to take up a post in the interior of the empire.[56] Moreover, the satraps' policies died with them. Autonomy was restored to Sinope[57] and Datames' personal empire, which had extended from the Taurus mountains to the Black Sea, was broken up. The area east of Sinope as far as Trapezus, roughly the area of the later kingdom of Pontus, was again formed into a separate satrapy and the same thing was done with Cappadocia.[58] Paphlagonia, on the other hand, was once more officially assigned to the satrapy of Hellespontine Phrygia, but all satrapal officials and garrisons were withdrawn so that the area became, in effect, autonomous. [59]

During the following years Clearchus continued to cultivate actively the close relations he had established with Artaxerxes II and then, after that monarch's death in 359/8, with his son and successor Artaxerxes III Ochus until his own death in 352.[60] His attempt to take advantage of this favorable situation to extend his power seems, however, to have been limited in both duration and result. Only one campaign, against the city of Astacus on the Propontis, is mentioned in the sources, and the manner in which Polyaenus introduces his account of it suggests that it was treated in his source as an isolated event, although one of unique importance and interest because of its scale and the

---

Phrygia before the death of the Odrysian king Cotys which occurred in 360 (Demosthenes 23. 153–155; on the date of Cotys' death, see Beloch 1912–27 III.2, 87).

[56] Mithridates and Datames: Nepos *Datames* 10–11; Polyaenus 7. 29. 1. Mithridates and Ariobarzanes: Xenophon *Cyropaedia* 8. 8. 4; Aristotle *Politics* 5 .8. 15, 1312a17; Valerius Maximus 9. 11. 2; Harpocration *s.v. Ariobarzanēs*. That the honors mentioned by Xenophon involved Mithridates leaving the Hellespontine area follows from the fact that his family's two posts in that region were held subsequently by other people, the satrapy of Hellespontine Phrygia by Artabazus and Cius by Ariobarzanes the son of Mithridates (Diodorus 16. 90. 2; for the rulers of Cius, see Beloch 1912–27 III.2, 150–51, and Sherman 1952, 202, n. 1).

[57] D. Robinson (1906b, 246–47) argued from the existence of a series of Sinopean coins with the Aramaic inscription *Abdusin* (*Recueil* I.1, 183–86, nos. 22–30; Six 1894, 302–05) that Sinope continued to be under direct Persian rule after the death of Datames. Further study, however, by E. Robinson (1920, 11–15), indicates that there was an interval of a decade or two between the coins of Datames and those of Abdusin during which Sinope issued coins bearing only the names of her own magistrates, that is, she was autonomous during that period.

[58] Cappadocia: Strabo 12. 1. 4. The limits are based on the kingdom of Ariarathes as determined from the boundaries of Eumenes' satrapy (Diodorus 18. 3. 1; Plutarch *Eumenes* 3. 2; Arrian *FGrH* 2B, 156 F1. 5; *cf.* Ernst Meyer 1925a, 10).

[59] Paphlagonia and Hellespontine Phrygia: Demosthenes 23. 155; Curtius Rufus 3. 1. 23; Krumbholtz 1883, 75.

[60] Memnon *FGrH* 3B, 434 F1. 4.

116 PART I: BOOK

impact it had on Clearchus' relations with the Heracleotes.[61] But since the most likely line of march to Astacus for an army leaving Heraclea is by way of the valley of the Hypius, geographical considerations indicate that prior to its being undertaken he had already obtained recognition of his authority by the city of Cierus which controlled that route.[62]

As for the campaign against Astacus itself, our knowledge is sketchy, but its importance in Clearchus' mind and his consciousness of its difficulty are well illustrated by the extraordinary scale of his preparations, which involved the mobilization not only of his mercenaries but also of the full citizen levy of Heraclea.[63] Despite this, it ended not in victory but in the inglorious abandonment of the siege because the citizen troops, who had been posted in a low-lying marshy area in order to prevent the city's defenses from being reinforced by its Bithynian subjects,[64] suffered disproportionately high casualties in comparison to his mercenaries as a result of an outbreak of swamp fever in their camp. Presumably, his operations against Cierus and Astacus were part of a plan to gain a foothold on the Propontis, but although he probably maintained control of Cierus the fiasco at Astacus marked the end of his plans for foreign expansion and of his honeymoon with the Heracleotes. As an explanation of his actions, that offered by Polyaenus' source, namely that he laid siege to Astacus only in order to cause the death of as many citizens as possible, may be dismissed as an example of the *post hoc, propter hoc* fallacy. It is, however, invaluable as an indication of the bitter complaints that circulated in Heraclea after the return of the survivors. The disarming of the Heracleotes and the conversion of his mercenaries into a force used solely to garrison Heraclea must have quickly followed.[65]

---

[61] Polyaenus 2. 30. 3: *boulomenos pollous ton politon apokteinai prophasin ouch echōn...*

[62] *Terminus ante quem* for the conquest of Cierus is the end of the 4th century (Memnon *FGrH* 3B, 434 F9. 4). There may, however, be some confirmation of the theory that it submitted to Clearchus in the fact that Cierus appears to have only coined for a brief time early in the 4th century and then never again under that name (E. Robinson 1921, 4–7).

[63] *Contra* Apel 1910, 36, n. 3, Isocrates Letter 7. 9, only indicates that Clearchus eventually disarmed Heraclea's citizen body and cannot, therefore, be used to discredit Polyaenus' account. It is worth noting in this connection that Dionysius I allowed the Syracusans to retain their arms for a short time before confiscating them (Diodorus 14. 10. 4; 14. 45. 5) and later would issue them weapons for particular campaigns (Diodorus 14. 64. 4).

[64] Sölch 1925, 145, n. 4, and Berve 1967 I, 318, identify the *Thraikes ... ek tēs chōras* of Polyaenus 2. 30. 3, with the Bithynians, and see in the passage evidence that Astacus was under Bithynian control at this time. The phase *ek tēs chōras*, however, suggests Bithynian helots since *chora* normally designates a city's rural territory and not an allied state (*cf.* Busolt and Swoboda 1926 I, 285, n. 1).

[65] Isocrates Letter 7. 9. There is no evidence for the conquests of Tium and part of the Paphlagonian coast ascribed to Clearchus by earlier scholars (e.g. Apel 1910, 36; Ed. Meyer 1965–69 V, 476; Beloch 1912–27 III.1, 138). Indeed, since Tium coined in her own name shortly after the middle of the 3rd century (*Recueil* I.3, 615, 616, nos. 1–3) her independence is assured. The basis for the earlier view probably was the belief that Memnon's reference to Clearchus'

IV. CLEARCHUS AND SATYRUS

The maintenance of good relations with the Persian government at Persepolis formed the core of Clearchus' foreign policy. Since Heraclea remained essentially a Pontic power throughout the 4th century with few if any political interests outside the Euxine basin, this was inevitable. During his reign, however, the already existing nonpolitical ties, both social and economic, which linked Heraclea and the cities of the Greek mainland, particularly Athens, became closer as Heracleotes continued to take up permanent or temporary residence abroad for a variety of reasons, now including political exile. At Athens this led to the growth in size and significance of the Heracleote colony,[66] at least two of whose more distinguished members, Heracleides Ponticus and the mathematician Amyclas, both students of Plato, became prominent figures in Athenian social and intellectual life.[67] Clearchus, at the time of his *coup*, as we have already seen, was an Athenian citizen with important personal contacts in Athenian political and intellectual circles. On the other hand, it seems clear that the violence at the beginning of his reign and the propaganda of the exiles and their sympathizers had, by the end of his reign, resulted in a generally hostile view of him current in Athens.[68] The dim light that a badly battered Athenian inscription (*IG* 2² 117) throws on the state of relations between his government and that of Athens is, therefore, of considerable interest.

Fragment a

```
['ΕΔΟΞΕΝ ΤΗΙ ΒΟΥΛΗΙ ΚΑΙ ΤΩΙ ΔΗΜΩ]Ι· Ε[Π]–
Ι ΤΗΣ ..........18..........ΠΡΥ]ΤΑ[Ν]–
[ΕΙ ΑΣ, ΗΙ ΧΑΙΡΙΩΝ ΧΑΡΙΝΑΫΤΟ ΦΑΛ]ΗΡ[Ε]–
]ΫΣ ΕΓΡΑΜΜΑΤΕΥΕΝ· ΤΕΤΑΡΤΗΙ ΚΑΙ] ΔΕ[Κ]–
5  [ΑΤΗΙ ΤΗΣ ΠΡΥΤΑΝΕΑΣ· ΤΩΝ ΠΡΟΕΔΡ]ΩΝ ΕΠ–
[ΕΨΗΦΙΖΕΝ..........16.......... ]Σ vacat
[....8... ΕΙΠΕΝ ΠΕΡΙ ΩΝ ΠΡΩΤΟΜ]ΑΧΟ–
[Σ ΛΕΓΕΙ --------------------------]
```

harshness *ei ti en allophulois polemion* (*FGrH* 3B, 434 F1. 2) concerned military activity. The parallel Memnon draws with his behavior toward the Heracleotes suggests instead that it actually refers to the murder of his supposed enemies (*cf. Epistles of Chion* 13. 1–2, probably not true but based on Clearchus' practices, and Polybius 13. 6. 7–9, on the use of assassins by Nabis).

[66] *IG* 2–3² pt 2, f. 3, contains the epitaphs of 24 Heracleotes dating from the 4th century, twelve of which belong to the period from the middle to the end of the century (8612, 8708, 8725, 8751, 8850, 8551, 8573, 8683, 8700, 8755, and 8792). That all come from Pontica cannot be proved but is likely in view of the unimportance of the majority of the other Heraclea's and the evidence for contact between Heraclea and Athens during this period (*cf.* Rostovtzeff 1941 III, 1455, n. 354). For examples of Heracleotes living abroad for business reasons, see the epitaph of a pilot who died at Athens (*IG* 2–3² pt. 2, f. 3, 8755) and record of a doctor's dedication at Delphi in 363 (*SIG*³ 1 239 IIIC, lines 15–20).

[67] Heracleides and Athens: Heracleides F3 Wehrli (= Diogenes Laertius 5. 86). Amyclas and the politics of the Academy: Aelian *VH* 3. 19.

[68] Isocrates Letter 7. 2.

118 PART I: BOOK

Fragment b

```
[ . . . . 7 . . . . ΑΓΑ]Θ[ΗΙ ΤΥΧΗΙ ΔΕΔΟΧΘΑΙ ΤΗ]–
Ι ΒΟΥΛΗΙ ΤΟΣ ΠΡ[ΟΕΔΡΟΣ ΟΪ ΑΝ ΛΑΧΩΣΙ]
ΠΡΟΕΔΡΕΥΕΝ ΕΙ[Σ ΤΗΝ ΠΡΩΤΗΝ ΕΚΚΛΗΣ]–
ΙΑΝ ΠΡΟΣΑΓΑΓΕ[Ν ΠΡΩΤΟΜΑΧΟΝ ΚΑΙ ΧΡ]–
5  ΗΜΑΤΙΣΑΙ ΑΥΤΩ̣ [ Ι, ΓΝΩΜΗΝ ΔΕ ΞΥΜΒΑΛΛ]–
ΕΣΘΑΙ ΤΗΣ ΒΟΛΗ[Σ ΕΙΣ ΤΟΝ ΔΗΜΟΝ ΟΤΙ Δ]–
ΟΚΕΙ ΤΗΙ ΒΟΥΛΗ[Ι · ΕΠΕΙΔΗ ΠΡΩΤΟΜΑΧΟ]–
Ν ΟΪ ΠΡΕΣΒΕΣ Ο[Ϊ ΠΑΡΑ . . . 9 . . . Απ]–
ΟΦΑΙΝΟΥ[ΣΙ]Ν [ΑΝΔΡΑ ΑΓΑΘΟΝ ΟΝΤΑ ΠΕΡ]–
10 Ι ΤΟΝ ΔΗΜ[ΟΝ Τ] Ο[Ν ΑΘΗΝΑΙΩΝ, ΕΙΝΑΙ ΠΡΩ]–
ΤΟΜΑΧΟΝ [ΑΡΙ]Σ[ΤΟ. . ; .15 . . . . ]
Ν ΠΡΟΞΕΝ[ΟΝ Κ]Α[Ι ΕΥΕΡΓΕΤΗΝ ΚΑΙ ΑΥΤΟ]–
Ν ΚΑΙ ΕΚΓΟ[ΝΟΥΣ ΤΟ ΔΗΜΟ ΤΟ ΑΘΗΝΑΙΩΝ].
ΚΑΙ ΑΝΑΓ[ΡΑΨΑΙ ΤΟΝ ΓΡΑΜΜΑΤΕΑ ΤΗΣ Β]–
15 ΟΛΗΣ ΤΟΔ[Ε ΤΟ ΨΗΦΙΣΜΑ ΕΝ ΣΤΗΛΗΙ ΛΙΘ]–
ΙΝΗΙ ΚΑΙ [ΣΤΗ]Σ[ΑΙ ΕΝ ΑΚΡΟΠΟΛΕΙ, ΕΙΣ Δ]–
Ε ΤΗΝ ΑΝΑΓ[ΡΑ]Φ[ΗΝ ΤΗΣ ΣΤΗΛΗΣ ΔΟΝΑΙ Τ]–
ΟΝ ΤΑΜΙΑΝ.Τ[Ο] Δ[ΗΜΟ. . . . ΔΡΑΧΜΑΣ ΤΩΙ]
ΓΡΑΜΜΑΤΕΙ [ΤΗΣ ΒΟΛΗΣ.·ΕΛΕΣΘΞΙ ΔΕ ΚΑ]–
20 Ι ΠΡΕΣΒΕΥΤ[Η]Ν [ΕΝΑ ΑΝΔΡΑ ΙΔΙΩΤΗΝ (?) ΤΗ]–
Ν ΒΟΛΗΝ ΕΞ [ΑΘ]Η[ΝΑΙΩΝ, ΟΣΤΙΣ ΑΦΙΚΟΜΕ]–
ΝΟΣ ΕΙΣ ΗΡΑ[ΚΛΕΙΑΝ ΑΞΙΩΣΕΙ ΗΡΑΚΛΕ]–
[Ι]ΩΤΑΣ ΑΠΟΔΟΝ[ΑΙ · · · · · · · · · · · · ]
. . .ΧΟΤ. . : Δ[ – ΔΡΑΧΜΑΣ? – – ]
. ΜΑΧΟΤ . .:– – – – – – – – ]
```

Letter forms date the inscription to the last years of the decade of the 360s.[69] As edited by Ulrich Kohler *(CIA* 2, 87) fragment *b*, the only part then known, was interpreted as a simple proxeny decree in honor of a Heracleote named Protomachus; this, together with the erroneous dating of the grant of citizenship to Clearchus to this same period, suggested that relations between the two cities were both cordial and close during his reign.[70] Although plausible since it would mean that Athens had managed to assure her merchants a friendly port on the southern leg of the critical grain route to Panticapaeum where they already enjoyed privileged status,[71] this interpretation left unexplained the *boulē's* recommendation (frag. *b*, lines 19–23) that an ambassador be appointed to go to Heraclea and ask that the Heracleotes return something to Protomachus. Surely a strange situation in which the Athenians must intercede on behalf of their proxenus with his own government!

---

[69] The lettering is identical to that of *IG* 2^2 116, which belongs to 361/60 (commentary to *IG* 2^2 117).

[70] A. Schaefer 1885 I, 122, n. 2. For close relations citing only the citizenship, see Judeich 1892, 276, and Glotz and Cohen 1925–38 I, 170.

[71] Demosthenes 20. 30–31.

IV. CLEARCHUS AND SATYRUS 119

Adolf Wilhelm, who also later identified fragment *a*,[72] provided the probably correct solution in 1892 when he called attention to the similarities between this inscription and *SIG*[3] 1 304, a decree in honor of a merchant named Heracleides from Cyprian Salamis, whose ship had been detained in Heraclea while he was transporting grain to Athens during the famine of 330.[73] Judging from the reference to previous services to Athens (frag. *b*, lines 8–10), Protomachus, like Heracleides, was probably also a merchant whose ship and cargo had been seized at Heraclea. Supported by an embassy from his home city (frag. *b*, lines 8–10), he had then appeared before the *boulē* (frag. *a*, lines 7–8) and asked for assistance in recovering his lost property. The result was a *probouleuma* (frag. *b*, lines 1–25) to the effect that the assembly should designate him a *proxenos* and then select an ambassador to go to Heraclea and plead his case before the Heracleote assembly (frag. *b*, lines 19–23).[74]

Unlike the contemporary situation in the Hellespontine area where Byzantium, Chalcedon, and Cyzicus were detaining wholesale grain ships bound for Athens to satisfy their own needs,[75] the incident involving Protomachus was clearly isolated, presumably the result of some dispute between him and the Heracleotes, and not part of an organized program of harassing shipping sailing past Heraclea.[76] As such it was, therefore, a matter of minor importance to both cities, and that is precisely its significance to us. Far from indicating any particular closeness of relations between Heraclea and Athens at this time, it suggests that relations were correct and moderately friendly but no more, exactly the situation one would expect in the case of two states for whom continued commercial contact was mutually profitable, but whose political interests touched at no point. However this affair was finally resolved, the important commercial relations between the two cities continued and so presumably did the cool and distant contact between their respective governments. Thus, although the decline in his personal reputation in the Aegean probably damaged Clearchus' prestige somewhat, this was of no great importance because of the minor role relations with Greek powers outside the Pontus played in his foreign policy.

---

[72] Wilhelm 1903, 783.

[73] Wilhelm 1892, 5, with reference to *SIG*[3] 1 304, lines 36–41.

[74] Wilhelm (1894, 37, n. 1) pointed out that *ten bolen* in line 21 is probably a mason's error for *ton dēmon*.

[75] Demosthenes 50. 6 (late summer 362), 17 (361).

[76] *Contra* Maksimowa 1959, 117–18. That this is true in the case of Heracleides of Salamis is obvious from *SIG*[3] 1 304, lines 41–43. For an idea of the sort of circumstances that might result in the detention of a single ship, see v. Premerstein 1911, 75 lines 14–16, where *ca.* 175 the population of an unidentified Pontic city tried to prevent the merchant in question from leaving their port with a cargo of olives because of a local shortage.

120   PART I: BOOK

HERACLEOTE SOCIETY AND GOVERNMENT
DURING THE REIGN OF CLEARCHUS

Clearchus' reign saw no fundamental innovations or advances in the area of foreign affairs, but the reverse was true as far as Heraclea's internal life was concerned. In addition to the establishment of a tyranny that was to last until about 284,[77] some 80 or so years, the opening days of his reign brought with them a radical redistribution of wealth and influence in Heracleote society which could, with some justice, be called a revolution. This had, of course, not been Clearchus' original intent. His actions, both before and after his initial seizure of power, show clearly enough that he had had no sympathy with the revolutionary demands of the poor and that his goal was not to destroy the existing order, but to rule it. It was only his own inadequate planning, and the resulting civil war, which forced him into the undesired role of revolutionary. Within the space of a few months almost the whole of Heraclea's upper class was swept away, leaving Clearchus in possession of much of Heraclea's wealth and facing the task of determining the future ownership of a large part of its agricultural land and the status of the Mariandynoi who worked it. He could not avoid coming to grips with this problem, but the manner in which he resolved it would be decisive for Heraclea's future social and economic life.

Examination of previous discussions of this question reveals a general agreement among scholars concerning the main features of Clearchus' solution. Basing their opinions largely on Clearchus' past role as a democratic leader, these scholars maintain that he made the basis of his policy the demands for a cancellation of debts and a general redistribution of land to the *dēmos* as a whole.[78] In addition, he would have probably made some grants to his mercenaries.[79] At the same time, he is supposed to have ended the servitude of the Mariandynoi, and by so doing to have transformed Heraclea into a state similar to that of Bosporus, that is, a military monarchy based on the reconciliation of the city's Greek and native populations.[80] A careful analysis of all the pertinent evidence suggests that this interpretation is to be rejected almost *in toto*. The only exception would be the cancellation of the debts of the poor, which would have been accomplished *de facto* by the death or exile of their principal creditors.

---

[77] Memnon *FGrH* 3B, 434 F5. 3. For the date, see the Appendix.

[78] Apel 1910, 32; Lenk 1927, 80; Mossé 1962b, 7–8.

[79] Apel 1910, 38.

[80] E.g. Mossé 1962b, 7–8, and 1960, 356–58; and Desideri 1967, 398–400. The political analysis is that of Rostovtzeff 1922, 68.

IV. CLEARCHUS AND SATYRUS

The key question is the status of the Mariandynoi, since freeing them would entail the complete reorganization of Heraclea's social and economic system. Belief in their emancipation is based on the identification of the slaves of the councilors that Justin says Clearchus freed with the Mariandynoi.[81] Against this, however, must be set Aristotle's description of Heraclea in the seventh book of the *Politics*, which he specifically qualifies as referring to the city at the time of writing, that is, sometime between 347 and 336.[82] There he describes the city's population as being composed of a small body of free men and two large unfree groups, the *perioeci* and 'those working the land'.

Two conclusions clearly follow from this passage. First and most important, Clearchus made no change in the relationship already existing between the Mariandynoi and the citizens except to give them new masters. P. Desideri has tried to minimize the significance of this text by interpreting it to mean that the Mariandynoi were now legally free, but not equal in status to the Greek population. Rather they existed in '*un tipo di rapporto che stava fra la soggezione e la collaborazione*'.[83] This suggestion, however, is most unlikely in view of the fact that Plato writing in the *Laws* less than two decades after Clearchus had seized power, with ready access to information about contemporary Heracleote affairs, still refers to their condition as *douleia*.[84] The more probable interpretation is that Justin's slaves are to be identified with the personal servants of the councilors. There may have been some individual Mariandynoi among these, but the people as a whole remained legally slaves and their labor continued to form the basis of the Heracleote economy. Second, since Aristotle notes that Heraclea's citizen population was comparatively small in his day the number of slaves freed cannot have been very large, although their enfranchisement probably did mean the introduction of a non-Greek element into the population.[85]

Direct evidence is lacking on the question of the land itself. It is worth noting, however, that less than 20 years later Clearchus' son Timotheus had to deal once again with the problem of widespread indebtedness among the citizenry.[86] This, and the continued servitude of the Mariandynoi, indicate that Clearchus left the landholding system in which the dominant feature was the existence of large estates worked by unfree labor fundamentally unchanged.

---

[81] Justin 16. 5. 1.

[82] Aristotle *Politics* 7. 5. 5, 1327b12–16. For the date of the seventh book of the *Politics*, see Jaeger 1948, 259–92; and Düring 1966, 51.

[83] Desideri 1967, 400.

[84] Plato *Laws* 6.776c–d. For the date of the *Laws*, see Lesky 1966, 511.

[85] For similar conclusions with regard to the enfranchisements of slaves by Dionysius I, see Stroheker 1958, 151, 240, n. 22.

[86] Memnon *FGrH* 3B, 434 F3. 1.

122 PART I: BOOK

As we have seen in the case of the Mariandynoi, the main result of Clearchus' becoming tyrant was a change at the top of society in which their new masters became also the new owners of the estates. The poor, as the rapid return of the debt problem shows, shared only to an insignificant degree, if at all, in the redistribution of the confiscated land. The bulk of it had gone, either by sale or grant, to Clearchus' own supporters, an amorphous group which certainly included his family, soldiers and officers, and probably also a number of Heracleotes of some means who had chosen his side in the revolution in order to gain the influence denied them under the regime of the Council of Three Hundred.[87]

Despite the fact that the establishment of the tyranny had not produced major changes in the basic structure of Heracleote society, its results were still of fundamental importance. In the freed slaves Clearchus had gained an important body of supporters who were personally obligated to him. But if the main change consisted only of the substitution of one narrow ruling class for another, there was one crucial difference. The councilors had been Heraclea's aristocracy. However much they may have been hated, tradition stretching back to the founding of the city had given legitimacy to both their wealth and their position. Their successors were new men whose status rested only on the favor of the tyrant and the exile or death of their predecessors. Creatures of the tyranny, they provided Clearchus and his successors with the officials and advisers necessary to the functioning and survival of their government. At the same time, however, their own self-interest, their desire, that is, to preserve their newly acquired wealth and status against the legitimate claims of the previous owners, made the members of this new ruling class the chief obstacle to any attempt by Clearchus, or his successors, to arrange a reconciliation with some or all of the exiles.[88]

In reorganizing Heracleote society, Clearchus sought political advantage rather than popularity. That the poor were disappointed by their exclusion from the process is likely, but the fact that Clearchus was later able to use confidently citizen troops in his attack on Astacus shows that he did retain considerable popular support for much of his reign. Part of the credit for this should probably be given to the care he took to avoid offending the political sensibilities of his subjects any more than was absolutely necessary.

---

[87] Sale of confiscated land: Isocrates Letter 7. 8–9. Some of the land may also have gone as dowries with the women of the exiled councilors, since the purpose of such enforced marriages was to prevent the wholesale extinction of households as has been shown by Asheri 1966, 32–36. The only individual Heracleote outside the family of the tyrant who can be identified with some probability as having preserved his property and position is Heracleides Ponticus, who Diogenes Laertius (5. 86) describes as wealthy and who was able to return to Heraclea and play a prominent role in its life during the reigns of Clearchus' sons Timotheus and Dionysius (*APIH* VI, IX–X; Diogenes Laertius 5. 91).

[88] Isocrates Letter 7. 8; and especially Memnon *FGrH* 3B, 434 F7. 3.

IV. CLEARCHUS AND SATYRUS 123

Clearchus had actually founded a military monarchy in which his true constituency consisted of his personal followers and the mercenaries on whom his power ultimately rested. His bodyguard and the fortress on the acropolis made concealment of the true situation impossible, but it was rendered less objectionable by the maintenance of an attitude of respect on his part for the traditional institutions of Heraclea. So far as appearances were concerned, the fall of the Council of Three Hundred was followed by the restoration of the democracy whose authority it had usurped. Accordingly, the citizens were allowed to possess arms,[89] magistrates were elected and performed the routine function of their offices;[90] and most importantly, the assembly met and, officially at least, dealt with public business.[91] As for himself, the only official position Clearchus occupied was the one the *dēmos* itself had conferred on him, that of *stratēgos autokratōr*. Its broad powers included sole command of Heraclea's armed forces and supervision of all government activities connected with military affairs. This office and his own prestige, therefore, gave him a position of enormous power and influence in Heraclea's public life which was still completely constitutional.[92]

The recent study of the coinage of Clearchus and Satyrus by P.R. Franke has shown that throughout their reigns they continued to rule Heraclea through the facade of the restored democracy.[93] Nevertheless, the sources clearly show that once Clearchus felt secure, the character of his public image and of the relationship between himself and his subjects changed radically. He proclaimed to the Heracleotes that he was a son of Zeus and that they, therefore, should accord him the honors granted to the Olympian gods. He also gave one of his sons, probably Timotheus, his eldest, the cognomen Ceraunus, which had obvious connections with Zeus.[94] Moreover, to further emphasize his unique and special relationship to the gods, he took a leading

[89] Polyaenus 2. 30. 3.

[90] Because of the lack of epigraphic material only two groups of minor officials can be definitely identified, namely, those in charge of the mint from their mint marks (*Recueil* I.2, 348, no. 21) and the *agoranomoi* from their identifying marks on Heracleote amphorae (Canarache 1957, 195–202).

[91] The prominent role played by the assembly under Clearchus is indicated by the fact that in 361 the Athenians instructed their ambassador to deal, not with the tyrant, but with 'the Heracleotes', i.e. the assembly of Heraclea, in attempting to obtain the return of the property of their *Proxenus* Protomachus (*IG* 2² 117, lines 21–22).

[92] Trogus' source (Justin 16. 41. 16) clearly considered Clearchus' obtaining this office to be the foundation of the tyranny proper (*his verbis sollicitata plebs summum ad eum imperium defert et … in servitutem se tyrannicae dominationis cum conjugis et liberis tradit*).

[93] Franke 1966, 138–39.

[94] Justin 16. 5. 9–11; *Suda s.v. Klearchos*; Memnon *FGrH* 3B, 434 F1. 1; Plutarch *De Alexandri magni fortuna aut virtute* 338B. For Ceraunus as a title of Zeus, see *IG* 5 2 288.

124 PART I: BOOK

role in the ritual aspects of the festivals devoted to them.[95] When he made an appearance among the people on these and other public occasions it was with all the trappings of a regal procession. His approach was heralded by an attendant bearing a gilt eagle, the symbol of his divine father, while he himself, his face heavily rouged, wore the costume used in tragedy to indicate the character of a king[96] – elevated shoes, purple robes, gold crown, and scepter.[97]

At the same time, his treatment of the Heracleotes took on a more openly autocratic cast.[98] The distance between himself and his subjects implied by his divine claims and adoption of regal dress came to characterize his whole style of living. Henceforth he lived apart from the populace within his fortress on the acropolis. There he held court in a manner whose rich and formal splendor is revealed by Memnon's reference to his practice of varying his dress depending on the impression he wished to make on his guests and by the requirement that those admitted to his presence perform *proskunesis*.[99] Access to his citadel was itself apparently a jealously guarded privilege granted only to a few individuals *iure familiaritatis,* probably Clearchus' family and closest associates, who thus constituted a virtual court nobility.[100]

Moreover, Clearchus' court, like that of Dionysius I on which it was modeled,[101] was to be a center of culture. The form his patronage took reflected his own intellectual interests and experience in the Athenian

---

[95] Clearchus was assassinated while taking part in the public sacrifices to Dionysus (Memnon *FGrH* 3B, 434 F1. 4; Diodorus 16. 36. 3, *Epistles of Chion* 17. 1).

[96] Justin 16. 5. 10. On the costume of the tragic king, see Alföldi 1955, who shows that the costume of the tragic king was based on that of the Persian Great King.

[97] Plutarch *De Alexandri magni fortuna aut virtute* 338B. For the reading *skeptron*, see Burstein 1974b.

[98] Memnon *FGrH* 3B, 434 F3. 1 (contrasting Timotheus with Clearchus): *ho de Timotheos paralabōn tēn archēn houtō tautēn epi to praoteron kai demokratikōteron meterruthmizen.* Democratic in this context refers to the manner in which a monarch deals with his subjects, his accessibility, graciousness in accepting petitions, etc. (*cf.* Plutarch *Demetrius* 42. 2). See also *Epistles of Chion* 15.1, and Aelian *NA* 5. 15.

[99] Dress: Memnon *FGrH* 3B, 434 F1. 1; *Suda s.v. Klearchos.* Proskynesis: *Suda s.v. Klearchos.* Proskynesis was primarily an act of subservience to a superior, not a recognition of divinity, as has been pointed out by Balsdon 1950, 374–76.

[100] Justin 16. 5. 14–15. Mossé 1962b, 8, n. 5. For a similar court nobility at Syracuse under Dionysius I, see Stroheker 1958, 158.

[101] Diodorus 15. 81. 4: *ezēlōse men tēn diagōgēn tēn Dionusiou tou Supakosiōn turannou.* In this context *diagōgē* probably means 'style of life' (LSJ. *s.v. diagōgē II*). The regal style was particularly associated with Dionysius I (Duris *FGrH* 2A, 76 F14; Livy 24. 5. 3–5) and he was the model for other tyrants (Livy 24. 5. 3–5; Stroheker 1958, 183). Schneiderwirth's suggestion (1882, 21) that clearchus was at Dionysius' court during his exile is unnecessary since his teacher Isocrates was interested in Dionysius (Letter 1.7; *Nicocles* 22) at the time he was studying with him.

IV. CLEARCHUS AND SATYRUS 125

schools. Anticipating the kings of the Hellenistic period, he founded a library[102] which, in all likelihood, played an important role in the vigorous intellectual activity at Heraclea that followed the return to the city of Heracleides Ponticus in 339.[103] But that was in the future. Meanwhile, his court did become the home of a small circle of Platonists who studied the teachings of their master under one of his own students, a relative of Clearchus by the name of Chion, who left the Academy for Heraclea sometime after the establishment of the tyranny.[104]

As far as the date of Clearchus' adoption of this new style and its accompanying claims, we have only an approximate *terminus post quem* in the birth of Timotheus, which can hardly be earlier than 363.[105] But since Clearchus seems to have played no public role in the negotiations involving Protomachus, we can probably lower our *terminus post quem* to about 360.[106] Unfortunately, our only exact *terminus ante quem* is 352, the date of Clearchus' death, but the fact that he named the son born in 361/60 Dionysius, obviously after the Sicilian tyrant, suggests that he was already thinking along these lines and that the change itself probably took place soon afterwards. The purpose behind it, however, is by no means clear.

The significance of the new style had already been lost by the middle of the 3rd century, when Nymphis viewed it as meaning that Clearchus was advancing a claim of actual divinity for himself. As to why Clearchus did this, Nymphis offered an interpretation not of his possible motives, but of the psychology which made such a claim possible, namely, that it resulted from his arrogance.[107] The notion of self-deification is an anachronism which was probably

---

[102] Memnon *FGrH* 3B, 434 F1. 2. In maintaining that Clearchus founded a library 'before others whom tyranny made famous', Nymphis was probably polemicizing against theories that credited Pisistratus and/or Polycrates with establishing the first libraries (Aulus Gellius *NA* 7. 17. 1–2; Athenaeus 1. 3A–B; Tertullian *Apology* 18. 5; Isidore *Etymologiarum* 6. 3. 3–5).

[103] *APIH* VII. 4–8. On the date of Speusippus' death, see Merlin 1959, 198.

[104] Chion and the Academy: *APIH* VI. 13; *Epistles of Chion passim*. The study circle: Justin 16. 5. 13; *Suda s.v. Klearchos*. Relationship to Clearchus: Memnon *FGrH* 3B, 434 F1. 3. From Isocrate (Letter 7. 12), it would appear that Clearchus also tried unsuccessfully to maintain his close relations with his teacher after he became tyrant.

[105] The *terminus ante quem* for the birth of Timotheus is that of his brother Dionysius in 360 (he was 55 at the time of his death in 306/5: Memnon *FGrH* 3B, 434 F4. 8; Diodorus 20. 77. 1). The *terminus post quem* is Clearchus' return to Heraclea in 364 since the fact that Timotheus had not yet come of age at the time of his uncle Satyrus' death in 346/5 (Memnon *FGrH* 3B, 434 F2. 3–4) indicates that he could not have been born before his father went into exile.

[106] *IG* 2² 117, lines 22–23. Compare the prominence of his son Dionysius in the similar negotiations about Heracleides of Salamis (*SIG*³ 1 304, lines 39–40). Another pointer to the year 360 as one marked by a major change in the tyranny is the fact that Theopompus (*FGrH* 2B, 115 F28) broke his account of Clearchus' reign at that date.

[107] Memnon *FGrH* 3B, 434 F1. 1; Justin 16. 5. 7–8; *Suda s.v. Klearchos*.

126 PART I: BOOK

suggested to Nymphis by the practices of his own day. In the 4th century, living men such as Lysander or Philip were deified, but it was as a result of the actions of cities which thus rewarded benefactors and not through their own actions.[108]

The only examples of self-deification known from the period before Alexander seem to have been limited to the followers of the mad Syracusan doctor Menecrates, who demanded that he be recognized as an incarnation of Zeus.[109] In fact, divine parenthood was an old myth motif which, by itself, carried no implication of divinity. Such a person stood close to the gods, accomplished great things with their aid, and might even be deified after his death, but during his lifetime he was still considered to be a man.[110] Therefore, although there were obvious religious overtones to his claims, we should not talk of Clearchus' attempting to use religion to free himself from the stigma of illegitimacy attached to a tyrant.[111] Indeed, and it is a point of considerable importance in this connection, the question of legitimacy could not arise in this sense because there was, strictly speaking, no tyrant. Heraclea was a democracy and Clearchus was its chief magistrate. Unofficially, of course – he was, like Augustus, much more than that.

The parallel with Augustus is, in fact, striking and useful. In much the same way, although on an infinitely smaller scale, Clearchus had established a system in which – despite the fact that his control of affairs rested on the overwhelming superiority of force provided him by his soldiers – the semblance of normal civic government was maintained because of the special relationship that existed between the *dēmos* and him as its leader.[112] That relationship, however, was personal and rested only on the enthusiasm generated by his destruction of the Council of Three Hundred. While it lasted, it assured him preeminent influence in the assembly, but it could be broken at any time and, most important, insofar as it was a personal tie between leader and followers it could not be automatically passed on to his successors. In short, although the

[108] For the civic character of the pre-Alexander cults, see Habicht 1956, 1–16, 160–71.

[109] On Menecrates, see Athenaeus 7. 289a–f; Clement *Protrepticus* 4. 48; *Suda s.v. Menekratēs.* The only example of a tyrant deifying himself was a member of Menecrates' circle, Nicagoras of Zela, who claimed to be an incarnation of Hermes (Baton *FGrH* 3A, 268 F2; Clement *Protrepticus* 4. 48; Berve 1967 I, 314).

[110] For this distinction between man and gods, see Isocrates *Panegyricus*, 60, 84; Agatharchides *GGM* I, 118; Arrian *Anabasis* 4. 11; Nilsson 1961–67 II, 139; and Badian 1961, 661.

[111] As does Berve 1967 I, and Apel 1910, 35. Desideri's suggestion (1967, 399–400) that Clearchus was attempting to conciliate the Mariandynoi can likewise be rejected since it rests on the fallacious belief that he significantly altered their condition for the better. In fact, the sources (especially Justin 16. 5. 9: [*sc. Clearcho*] *eunti per publicum*) leave no doubt that his claims were directed toward the Heracleotes themselves.

[112] *Cf.* Syme 1939, 322–23.

IV. CLEARCHUS AND SATYRUS

transfer of power would be easy since that was provided by the mercenaries who would support their paymaster, the delicate system of the restored democracy itself would not function unless the allegiance of the *dēmos* to Clearchus' successor was certain.

Now, if we keep in mind the three parts of his reform – the adoption of royal regalia and ceremonial, the claim to be the son of Zeus, and the association of his son in that claim – it becomes apparent that the principal effect of Clearchus' action was to redefine the basis of his relationship to the Heracleotes and to do it in such a way that the tie between the two parties became, in theory at least, a dynastic rather than a personal one. He was, in short, demanding that they accord to him the kind of obedience and loyalty they would pay a king because of his family's superior birth.[113] In a period when the praise of monarchy was a prominent theme in political thought and the tendency to exalt tyrants by referring to them as *isotheoi* was common, such a scheme was not out of place. If the Heracleotes accepted his pretensions, then the chances for an orderly succession and the continuation of the system he had devised would be greatly enhanced.[114]

To run the restored democracy and maintain his new image and style of living undoubtedly required the expenditure of considerable sums of money. Those expenses that were personal, such as the upkeep of his residence on the acropolis, he probably financed himself out of the vast fortune he had accumulated at the beginning of his reign from the ransoms and confiscations.[115] The rest, however, would have had to be paid for from the income of the Heracleote government, so that it is particularly unfortunate that we are so poorly informed about the economic side of his reign. Presumably, the city's main sources of revenue remained the same – its *chora* and the harbor. Toward the end of his reign the income derived from the latter must have increased noticeably because of the great growth in shipping between the Aegean and Bosporus following Leucon's refitting and opening of Theodosia about 356 as an emporium for the export of grain to complement Panticapaeum.[116] Otherwise we hear little in the literary sources about any measures taken by Clearchus to

---

[113] Note Justin 16. 5. 14: *veluti ad regem*. For the use of rich dress as a means of impressing on a ruler's subjects the distance between him and them, see Isocrates *To Nicocles* 32; Xenophon *Cyropaedia* 1. 3. 2 and 8. 3. 13–14. For the use of descent from Zeus as a dynastic claim, see Isocrates *To Nicocles* 42; *Evagoras* 12–18.

[114] Plato *Republic* 8. 568b.

[115] Isocrates Letter 7. 6; Memnon *FGrH* 3B, 434 F3. 1.

[116] Demosthenes 20. 32–33. Kocevalov 1932 showed that Demosthenes means that grain exports from Spartocid territory doubled with the opening of Theodosia by Leucon, an obvious exaggeration but still indicative of a sharp increase in volume of shipping between Athens and that area during the first half of the 350s.

128   PART I: BOOK

increase Heraclea's income, except for a vague reference by Isocrates to high taxes.[117] Heraclea's coinage, however, tells a different story.

Clearchus' reign seems to mark the beginning of a new era in the city's numismatic history. Hitherto, Heraclea had struck only silver coins on the Persian standard with denominations ranging from hemiobol to drachma. Now, however, a major change took place. Obols and diobols continued to be issued as before on the Persian standard, but in addition a uniform new series of coins – lightly bearded Heracles head in lion helmet on obverse and head of Hera in turreted crown on reverse – were struck on the Rhodian standard in denominations of hemidrachma, drachma, and, for the first time, tridrachma.[118]

The coinage reform was probably intended to increase the government's revenue from market and harbor tolls. During the first half of the 4th century, the Rhodian standard had largely replaced the Persian on the west and north-west coasts of Anatolia, so Heraclea's adoption of the former standard for her coinage would probably tend to encourage merchants from those areas to trade with her as opposed to merely using her harbor, and it would do this while still allowing Heraclea's coinage to be easily exchanged for coins struck on the Persian standard at Sinope and elsewhere in the Pontus.[119] At the same time, it would have had little effect on Heraclea's own commerce. Clearchus may have tried to encourage that by offering loans to local merchants, among others,[120] but if he did he achieved little since the analysis of the finds of Heracleote amphorae on the north and west coasts of the Pontus shows that her exports to those regions remained comparatively modest until the second half

---

[117] Isocrates Letter 7. 4. A tax in kind of Heraclea's agricultural produce may be implied by *IG* 2² 363, lines 9–12, which mentions a promise by Clearchus' son Dionysius (*cf*. Merit 1941, 47–49, no. 281) to give Athens 3000 *medimnoi* of grain in case of need, a gift equal to the three days supply Heraclea furnished the Ten Thousand in 400 (Xenophon *Anabasis* 6. 2. 3).

[118] *Recueil* I.2, 347–49: obol and diobol, nos. 23–28; hemidrachma (1.80–1.85 g.) no. 19; drachma (3.45–3.87 g.) no. 21; tridrachma (11.05–11.73 g.) nos. 16, 17, 20. For the date, see Franke 1966, 138. Le Rider (1963, 58, n. 1), pointed out that the denominations from hemidrachma to tridrachma were struck on the Rhodian standard. Clearchus may also have tried to increase the supply of small denominational coins in circulation if a unique type – obverse bearded Heracles in lionskin helmet, reverse club and quiver (*Recueil* I.2, 350, no. 32; Wroth 1889, 13, 140) – belongs to his reign.

[119] For the spread of the Rhodian standard in western Anatolia, see Le Rider 1963, 50–59. Heracleote commercial contact with that area, especially with the Propontis, is indicated by the striking of coins with Heracleote types by the city of Cyzicus (Seltman 1955, 181). P. Gardner (1918, 118) noted that Rhodian drachmae and tridrachmae might pass as Persian tetraobols and didrachmae.

[120] Memnon (*FGrH* 434 F3. 1) refers to Timotheus' cancelling debts owed to the tyrant and then offering new interest-free loans. The fact that Timotheus' new loans were interest-free indicates, however, that the tyrants were not the only moneylenders.

IV. CLEARCHUS AND SATYRUS

129

of the 4th century.[121] Overall, then, the impression is that Heraclea, under Clearchus, was relatively prosperous, but that this was mainly because, as before, of the exploitation of her superb location.

REPRESSION AND ASSASSINATION

Dates and references to specific events are almost totally lacking for the last part of Clearchus' reign. Nevertheless, the few items probably belonging to this period that are mentioned in our sources – such as the fiasco at Astacus and the subsequent disarming of the Heracleotes, Silenus' unsuccessful *coup* during which the rebels occupied the acropolis,[122] and a number of plots against Clearchus' life[123] – leave the clear impression of considerable unrest in Heraclea at this time. Not surprisingly, as his own fear for his security increased, the tyrant's rule became more openly 'tyrannical' as he sought to protect himself. And he had reason to be afraid. Silenus would never have achieved the success he did if he had not had considerable support and had the mercenaries guarding Clearchus' citadel been completely reliable. Plutarch's story[124] of Clearchus' sleeping in a chest like a snake in his hole because of his fear of his subjects is unlikely to be literally true, and the same is probably the case with regard to Theopompus' account[125] of the Heracleotes regularly taking the antidote for aconite before leaving their homes because Clearchus was using it to murder secretly their fellow citizens. But despite the obvious exaggeration of these lurid stories, there is no mistaking the atmosphere of fear and suspicion, with its rumors of mysterious arrests and execution of suspected traitors, which they reflect.

---

[121] Zeest 1951, 106.

[122] *Epistles of Chion* 13. 1. Düring (1966, 16, 97) contended that Silenus was invented by the author after the Heracleote politician of the 1st century (Memnon *FGrH* 3B, 434 F27. 5). This, however, is unlikely since, as Sykutris (1931, 214) argued and Doenges (1953, 147–85) confirmed, the authors of such epistolary novels tried to keep as close as possible to the known history of their period. As for the *Epistles of Chion*, Düring himself (1966, 12–13) has shown that where they can be checked they reflect the same tradition as do the other sources. Disarming of the Heracleotes: Isocrates Letter 7. 9.

[123] Memnon *FGrH* 3B, 434 F1. 3. This does not mean, of course, that plots against his life were confined to the later part of his reign.

[124] Plutarch *Ad principem ineruditem* 781D–E.

[125] Theopompus *FGrH* 2B, 115 F181. The fact that Theopompus discussed the source of aconite in Book 38 (assured by F181a) shows that he mentioned it there for the first time and, hence, that the story belongs to the period after 360 and not to the early years of Clearchus' tyranny which he had dealt with in Book 1 (F28). For the secrecy of the supposed murders, see F 181b: *Klearchou … peiromenou lanthanein.*

130   PART I: BOOK

Still, his security measures failed. In the end the danger came not from his subjects, but from Clearchus' own followers, many of whom must have resented his splendid life-style and pretensions which not only may have seemed arrogant, if not impious, but also cut them off from public glory while requiring humiliating displays of their dependence and even subservience to him. Not surprisingly, therefore, when his suspicions added danger to their already existing discontent, a substantial number of them – Justin says 52 – joined in the conspiracy that finally led to his death.[126]

The organizer and moving force behind the plot was Chion, Clearchus' relative and court philosopher, who may once have hoped to make a philosopher-king of him; but faced with the failure of that idea, he found in Plato's teachings the inspiration to free his city of the tyrant.[127] Despite the large number of fellow conspirators, the actual blow was struck by Chion in the company of several of his students while Clearchus was preparing to conduct the sacrifice during the festival of Dionysus in the spring of 352. On the second day after he was attacked, tormented, we are told, by visions of his victims, Clearchus died. He was 58 years of age and had ruled Heraclea for over eleven years.[128]

Although we know something of Clearchus' intellectualism and vigor and even of his charm, his individuality is largely lost in the portrait of a typical tyrant contained in the sources. That his reign was outwardly brilliant and that it marked the beginning of a new and important epoch in Heraclea's long and eventful history cannot be disputed.[129] During the century and a quarter that

---

[126] Justin 16. 5. 12–13: Chion and Leonides plus *L cognatos*. For the involvement of members of his court and family, see also Memnon *FGrH* 3B, 434 F1. 3, and *Epistles of Chion* 13. 3. Jacoby (*FGrH* 3B *Noten*, 168 *ad* 432 T2) cautiously suggests that the Nymphis mentioned in *Epistles of Chion* 13. 3, was the historian's grandfather. Laqueur (1937, 1609) and Düring (1966, 16) deny this.

[127] Justin 16. 5. 13; *Suda s.v. Klearchos*; *Epistles of Chion* 17; *APIH* VI. 13. For the attempt of Plato's students to implement the teachings of the *Republic*, see Gigon 1962, 209.

[128] Memnon *FGrH* 3B, 434 F1. 3–4; Justin 16. 5. 12–16; *Suda s.v. Klearchos*; *Epistles of Chion* 17; *APIH* VI. 13; Diodorus 16. 36. 3. Trogus' version of the assassination in which Clearchus is killed within his fortified residence by Chion and Leonides posing as petitioners probably does not represent a variant tradition as suggested by Apel (1910, 39, n. 1) but rather an adaptation by the Roman author for the purpose of drawing a parallel between the death of Clearchus and that of Julius Ceasar (*cf.* Nicolaos *FGrH* 2A, 90 F130. 24). The ambush (16. 5. 13) and the killing of the assassins by the bodyguard derive from an account similar to that of Memnon and the rest (the residence on the acropolis, etc.) probably from descriptions of Clearchus' court in Trogus' source. The slight variations in the lists of the actual assassins most likely result from incomplete excerpting of a longer list of the conspirators by the sources. On the other hand, the inclusion of Heracleides Ponticus in the plot by Demetrius of Magnesia (*apud* Diogenes Laertius 5. 89) most likely represents a confusion of him with another Platonist, Heracleides of Aenus, one of the assassins of Cotys (*APIH* VI. 15–20), as was suggested by F. Wehrli 1967–69 VII, 62 *ad* F11.

[129] Diodorus 15. 81. 5.

IV. CLEARCHUS AND SATYRUS

followed his seizure of power, Heraclea acquired a position of unchallenged preeminence among the Greek cities of northern Anatolia, mistress of an empire stretching from the Rhebas, or Psilis, to the Parthenius and center of a thriving economic and intellectual life. For almost 80 of those years, from 364 to about 284, members of Clearchus' family ruled the city. His own contribution to this was crucial, but limited. He founded the tyranny and preserved Heraclea's autonomy, and thereby made possible the achievements of his successors. Otherwise, however, his reign, despite his intelligence and considerable ability, presents a curious picture of failure and missed opportunities on which perhaps the best comment is that, like Caesar, Clearchus was killed by his friends and not his enemies.

THE REGENCY OF SATYRUS: 352 TO 346

The assassination of Clearchus accomplished nothing. There was discontent in Heraclea, but Chion and his associates had not thought to appeal to it. Just as was true of the assassins of Hipparchus or Julius Caesar, their act was that of a band of self-proclaimed liberators who assumed that freedom would automatically return once the tyrant was dead. Without popular support, the result was predictable. Far from defending their would-be champions, the Heracleotes passively looked on, first while Clearchus' bodyguard cut down on the spot the assassins themselves, and then during the next few days while the remaining members of the conspiracy were rounded up, tortured, and executed.[130] Meanwhile, the tyranny continued as the rest of Clearchus' followers, for whom 'liberation' would mean the return of the exiles and the loss of their wealth and influence, rallied to the support of his already designated heir and successor, Timotheus. Thus, despite the violent death of Clearchus, the formal transfer of power took place smoothly and without incident.

Both Timotheus and his brother Dionysius were still minors; indeed, neither had reached his early teens. So a long minority was inevitable, a prospect that raised the possibility that if Timotheus did not have a strong and loyal regent, he would be shunted aside by one of Clearchus' own followers in the ensuing struggle for power. The danger had not been lost on Clearchus, however, and he had moved to neutralize it before his death by appointing as his children's guardian his brother Satyrus.[131] Satyrus was 59 years of age when he undertook the task of ruling Heraclea on behalf of his nephew.[132]

---

[130] Memnon *FGrH* 3B, 434 F1. 5; Justin 16. 5. 16–17.
[131] Memnon *FGrH* 3B, 434 F2. 1.
[132] Memnon *FGrH* 3B, 434 F2. 5.

132   PART I: BOOK

Memnon, virtually the only source for his six years of rule, portrays Satyrus as a figure of incomparable wickedness.[133] Because of the widespread violence that followed his assumption of power, he is said to have surpassed not only Clearchus, but all other tyrants in his capacity for evil. According to Memnon, he was not satisfied with exacting vengeance for his brother's death from the actual conspirators, but he also pursued their innocent children, together with men who were guilty of no wrongdoing whatsoever. After this catalog of crime, it comes as something of a surprise to find Memnon saying that Satyrus became eventually glutted with murder and that he therefore desisted from further bloodshed.[134] This is the sum of his indictment, and it is clear that, although the facts are probably true, invocation of Satyrus' supposedly evil character is hardly sufficient to explain them.

Memnon's own narrative reveals two things essential to the interpretation of these events. First, Satyrus' actions were not random, but directed at the families of the conspirators and those he suspected of being in sympathy with them. And second, the actual period of open terror was short and confined to the first part of the reign. The conclusion to be drawn is obvious. The large scale of the conspiracy and the fact that it included members of Clearchus' own family had suddenly revealed the existence of widespread disaffection in Heraclea's new ruling class which had to be eradicated if the formation of similar plots against Satyrus and his nephews was to be avoided. In short, what Memnon is describing was not blind vengeance but a methodical purge of potentially disloyal members of the tyranny's own supporters, accompanied by the excesses normal in such situations – exile for those suspects able to flee Heraclea in time –[135] and death or imprisonment, with confiscation and redistribution of their property to seemingly more loyal men, for the rest. Once the purge was over, however, the remainder of Satyrus' years of power was free of large scale violence, although the security measures imposed at this time were maintained until his death.[136]

---

[133] Of Trogus' account of his reign (Prologue 16) Justin (16. 5. 17–18) has preserved only the following brief comment: *Qua re factum est ut tyrannus quidem occideretur, sed patria non liberaretur. Nam frater Clearchi, Satyrus, eadem via tyrannidem invadit...* Probably because he was officially only regent for Timotheus, Diodorus' kinglist ignored him and assigned his years of reign to the latter.

[134] Memnon *FGrH* 3B, 434 F2. 1–2. In view of this, Lenk's (1928, 14) proposed emendation of *eadem via* in Justin, 16. 5. 18, to *eadem vi* is attractive.

[135] If the Nymphis of *Epistles of Chion* 13. 3, was the historian's grandfather, then his family would have gone into exile at this time, a fact that might explain his extraordinary bitterness toward Satyrus.

[136] Memnon *FGrH* 3B, 434 F3. 1.

IV. CLEARCHUS AND SATYRUS

Otherwise, Satyrus' reign seems to have been relatively uneventful with no major departures from his brother's policies, except for his refusal to continue Clearchus' patronage of intellectual life for which he had no sympathy or interest.[137] This continuity with the past reflects the essentially caretaker character of his regime. Devoted to his brother, and childless himself, Satyrus followed one basic policy throughout, namely, that his function was to preserve the tyranny and its resources unimpaired until Timotheus came of age and could assume the responsibilities of power himself.[138] In this he succeeded, but his reluctance to break with his brother's policies meant that he did nothing to check the beginnings of a new and potentially serious socioeconomic crisis or to moderate the autocratic style of rule Clearchus had adopted, a style of rule that had been one of the principal reasons for the disaffection that had climaxed in his murder.[139] Still, when Satyrus died in 346 at the age of 65 at the end of a long and agonizing disease, apparently cancer of the groin, Timotheus, to whom he had already turned over most of the responsibility for governing Heraclea, easily assumed his position of sole ruler, although he was still a minor.[140]

---

[137] This is probably implied by Memnon *FGrH* 3B, 434 F2. 2. Jacoby (*FGrH* 3B *Texte*, 272–273 *ad* 434 F2. 5), however, did make the attractive suggestion that Memnon's dating of Satyrus' reign by reference to that of Archidamus III instead of that of a Persian king as in 434 F1. 4 may indicate the establishment of diplomatic ties between Heraclea and Sparta under Satyrus. Certainty is not possible, but the use of Archidamus instead of the more obvious Philip II if a European monarch was desired lends the theory some slight support.

[138] Memnon *FGrH* 3B, 434 F2. 3.

[139] Based on Memnon *FGrH* 3B, 434 F3. 1.

[140] Memnon *FGrH* 3B, 434 F2. 4.

CHAPTER V

TIMOTHEUS AND DIONYSIUS: 346 TO 305

THE REIGN OF TIMOTHEUS: A NEW ERA: 346 TO 337

In Heracleote tradition the death of Satyrus and the assumption of sole power by Timotheus was remembered as the beginning of a new era of prosperity and power for Heraclea. Timotheus inherited a demoralized city. Almost two decades of increasingly harsh rule by his predecessors had rooted the tyranny firmly in the city's political life, but the cost had been high – the creation of an atmosphere of fear and suspicion within Heraclea. On his accession Timotheus found the prisons filled with political prisoners as well as convicted criminals. Likewise, Clearchus and Satyrus had allowed debt to become again a major problem among the Heracleote poor.[1] Only drastic action could prevent the situation from deteriorating further.

Timotheus and his advisers fully understood the gravity of the situation. We do not know if he replaced Satyrus' counselors with new and more flexible men or if he himself had previously given any hint that he recognized the seriousness of the developing crisis. It is clear from the sources, however, that almost immediately on gaining power he decided to make major changes in the political and economic policies that had hitherto been followed by his predecessors.

Pursuant to this decision Timotheus implemented a number of dramatic measures calculated to ease Heraclea's disturbed conditions and to suggest that the 'bad old days' were finally over. A fresh beginning was to be made. Acting on his own authority, he proclaimed a general amnesty for all prisoners, the guilty as well as the innocent.[2] The debt problem, however, could not be resolved so simply. A general cancellation of debts was politically impossible, since the popularity Timotheus would gain among the city's poor would be more than offset by the hostility such action would create among their creditors, who were themselves members of the city's new aristocracy and supporters of the tyranny.

---

[1] Memnon *FGrH* 3B, 434 F3. 1. The hostility of Nymphis, Memnon's source, to Clearchus and Satyrus has probably resulted in a heightening of the contrast between their 'bad' reigns and that of Timotheus in the tradition. Nevertheless, the contemporary reference by Isocrates (Letter 7. 1) to Timotheus' making better use of his power than his father indicates that the distinction was based on fact.

[2] Memnon *FGrH* 3B, 434 F3. 1.

136 PART I: BOOK

But because of the fortune he had inherited from his father and uncle, Timotheus was able to forgive all debts owed to him personally and thus gain credit for his own generous gesture despite his leaving the general debt situation unchanged.[3]

More important, Timotheus took steps to improve the relations between himself and his subjects. The image of the aloof and stern monarch cultivated by Clearchus and Satyrus, along with their more offensive security measures, was abandoned and replaced by that of a gracious leader of his people. Claims of divine descent, the regal life-style, and the name Ceraunus, all these Timotheus seems to have dropped. Thenceforth, he made himself readily accessible to his subjects and strove at all times to appear genuinely interested in their welfare. And particularly in the area of law, where his predecessors' arbitrary actions had created especial bitterness, Timotheus took particular care to act the role of a benevolent and scrupulous judge.[4]

In a closely related development Timotheus adopted a policy of actively promoting his subjects' economic well-being. Canceling his own debts was a symbolic act, an important one no doubt, but no more. His long-range interest, however, was to eliminate the problem, or at least to significantly reduce it, and that could only be accomplished by enabling as many Heracleotes as possible to support themselves. Fortunately, an important passage in Memnon[5] not only shows that Timotheus did not shrink from this step, but also reveals the basic outlines of the policy he adopted: *kai tois chreizousi pros tas emporias kai ton allon bion tokōn aneu epērkese*. Again his action was made possible by the fortune amassed by Clearchus and Satyrus. Using this money, Timotheus, in effect, underwrote Heraclea's economy by offering interest-free loans to individuals desiring funds for commercial ventures (*pros tas emporias*) or any other need (*ton allon bion*), which presumably might include paying off outstanding debts. In this connection we should note that Ps.-Scylax, while describing conditions in the Pontus about this time, refers to the existence of a Heracleote settlement on the island of Thynias just off the Bithynian coast near Calpe Limen.[6] Although the island had been in Heracleote possession at least since the second half of the 5th century, the sources suggest that until the middle of the 4th century it had no population other than that necessary to

---

[3] Memnon *FGrH* 3B, 434 F3. 1; Isocrates Letter 7. 6.

[4] Memnon *FGrH* 3B, 434 F3. 1.

[5] Memnon *FGrH* 3B, 434 F3. 1.

[6] Ps.-Scylax *GGM* I, 67, 34(92). Unlike Ps.-Scylax, Ps.-Scymnus (lines 1025–1026 = 979–980) and Anonymous *Periplus* 8v2–4, refer to a *polis* founded by Heraclea on the island. This *polis* as opposed to the initial settlement was probably established during the Hellenistic period (*cf.* Fıratlı 1953, 15–16, who points out that the oldest remaining segments of the city wall appear to be of Hellenistic date).

V. TIMOTHEUS AND DIONYSIUS

137

manage the shrine of Apollo Eos that had been established on it.[7] It is therefore probable that Timotheus founded the settlement mentioned by Ps.-Scylax, most likely for the purpose of providing land for some of the poorer of his subjects.

Yet, as is usually the case in such seemingly complete breaks with the past, Timotheus' actions were only possible because Clearchus and Satyrus had prepared the ground for him by crushing all serious internal opposition to the tyranny and providing it with substantial financial resources. This is not, however, intended to deprecate the importance of his reforms. He did succeed in dissociating himself and his government from the most hated aspects of his predecessors' reigns. Far more important, he established for the first time a close relationship between the fortunes of the tyrant and those of his subjects, and that could only tend to strengthen the tyranny itself. Unquestionably, his readiness to underwrite generously his subjects' economic activities was central to this development. Beside the fact that this policy would tend to inhibit the trend dividing Heraclea's citizen body into the two mutually hostile groups of debtors and creditors, it also, and this was crucial, resulted in the creation of a considerable network of personal obligations between a fairly large number of Heracleotes and Timotheus, their patron and benefactor. Not unexpectedly, Timotheus' popularity and prestige within Heraclea rapidly increased, as can be seen from the local tradition preserved by Memnon and by the contemporary evidence provided by Isocrates.[8] Soon afterwards this new rapport between ruler and ruled received dramatic public expression. The Heracleote assembly voted Timotheus divine honors as *euergetēs* and *sōtēr* because of the benefactions he had conferred on the citizens.[9]

Shortly after Timotheus instituted his reforms he received a letter from Isocrates. Ostensibly it was intended to renew the ties between the sophist and his family that had existed before Clearchus became tyrant[10] and to introduce the bearer of the letter, a friend of Isocrates named Autocrator, and solicit hospitality for him.[11] But even a cursory reading of the text reveals this to be only a

---

[7] Wilson (1960, 446) suggested a date during the first half of the 4th century, but Callisthenes *FGrH* 2B, 124 F7 (*cf.* Pliny *NH* 5. 151) seems to rule out any Greek population. As Ziegler (1937, 720) noted, the presence of the *temenos* of Apollo Eos on the island makes it likely that the settlement was relatively small.

[8] Isocrates Letter 7. 1.

[9] Memnon *FGrH* 3B, 434 F3. 1. The epithets are those typical of civic cults and in the case of *sōtēr* imply actual cult (Habicht 1956, 156–59). Moreover, the statement that he received these epithets for what he did (*hois epratte ... onomazesthai*) is an accurate description of the motive for establishing such a cult and implies that the Heracleote assembly passed the necessary decree for its institution (*cf.* Habicht 1956, 162, 164).

[10] Isocrates Letter 7. 1, 12–13.

[11] Isocrates Letter 7. 10–11.

138   PART I: BOOK

pretext seized upon by Isocrates in order to assume his favorite role of adviser
to statesmen and in this capacity to urge Timotheus to adopt certain policies
which, he writes, would enable Timotheus to fulfill the promise of better days
for Heraclea held out by his initial actions. His recommendations are given
indirectly by offering for Timotheus' admiration and imitation the behavior of
the tyrant of Methymna on Lesbos, Cleommis, who recalled his exiles, returned
their property to them while compensating its present owners in full, and
rearmed his subjects.[12] If Timotheus would only take similar steps, Isocrates
implies, Heraclea would prosper and Timotheus would reveal himself as a
ruler who fully understands that his prime responsibility is to promote the
welfare of his state even at the cost of his own security.

The character of his advice makes it probable that Isocrates was attempting to
intercede with Timotheus on behalf of the Heracleote exiles. For them his accession and subsequent popular support can only have been profoundly discouraging, since they revealed just how unrealistic their hopes for an end to the tyranny
and their exile in the near future actually were. Clearly, although there were
undoubtedly many who would never compromise, some of the exiles were will-
ing to return to Heraclea if, and this was the difficult point, Timotheus would
agree to their resuming their former position at the top of Heracleote society.
These were the men whose cause Isocrates was espousing, but even he cannot
have been confident of the success of his efforts. Had this proposal been made
two decades earlier, while the tyranny was still new and comparatively weak,
Clearchus might have accepted it. Now, however, it was strong and the exiles no
longer posed any threat serious enough to justify Timotheus' arousing the wrath
of his own supporters by agreeing to their terms for a reconciliation. Although
unattested, his answer can only have been a firm negative. Nevertheless, not
long after rebuffing Isocrates' advances, Timotheus did rearm the Heracleotes.[13]
His confidence probably resulted from the favor he had gained among his subjects through his reforms, but Timotheus was impelled in any case to take this
step by the increasingly uncertain political situation in the Pontus and northern
Anatolia during the late 340s and the need for Heraclea to follow an energetic
foreign policy in order to cope with it.

---

[12] Isocrates Letter 7, 7–9. For Cleommis, see Berve 1967 I, 337. The interpretation of Letter
7 depends on the distinction between sections 1–6 and 7–9 of it. The former contains only
general reflections on the duties of a good monarch that were prompted by the news Isocrates
had received about the auspicious beginning of Timotheus' reign (cf. Letter 7. 1 in particular).
Section 7 then serves to introduce Isocrates' positive recommendations for the future.

[13] That he had not done so at the beginning of his reign is clear from Isocrates Letter 7. 9.
Aristotle *Politics* 7. 5. 7, 1327M0–16, implies that the citizens could bear arms.

V. TIMOTHEUS AND DIONYSIUS

139

FOREIGN AFFAIRS

Timotheus' reign coincides with a period of increased instability in the affairs of the Pontus. Royal authority in the eastern Mediterranean was strengthened after 346 by the suppression of long-standing revolts in Phoenicia and Egypt, but the pattern of political arrangements established in northern Anatolia in 360 began to deteriorate. The satrap of Hellespontine Phrygia lost the little influence he had possessed in Paphlagonia.[14] Further east, however, in Cappadocia satrapal power was again advancing to the detriment of the autonomous Pontic cities. The appearance of Sinopean coins with Aramaic legends shows that Sinope came once more under the direct control of the satraps of Cappadocia.[15] Meanwhile, Philip II rapidly made Macedon an important Pontic power by bringing under his control, between 343 and 339, all of Thrace as far as the Danube and a number of the Greek cities of the western Pontus.[16] As tensions increased between Macedon and Persia, despite the signing of a treaty between Philip and Artaxerxes III, Philip's aggressive action against Byzantium and his harassing of Pontic shipping can only have caused concern at Heraclea.[17]

Timotheus responded to the new situation, as already indicated, by adopting an active foreign policy but without abandoning his dynasty's close relations with Persepolis.[18] Rearming the Heracleotes furnished him with the necessary manpower, as can be seen from Aristotle's admiring comments on the strength of the Heracleote fleet in the late 340s and early 330s.[19] Memnon, unfortunately, refers only in the most general terms to Timotheus' wars, without identifying his enemies, but the praise he lavishes on him for his courage and ability to instill fear in his enemies indicates that they were victorious ones;[20] this is confirmed by the image of Heracles erecting a trophy that appears on the reverse of the coins Timotheus issued jointly with his brother Dionysius.[21] Despite our inability to identify Heraclea's foes, an

---

[14] Leuze 1935, 249.

[15] Based on the *Adbusin* coins (*Recueil* I.1, 183, no. 22). For their being dated *ca.* 345, see E. Robinson 1920, 11–14.

[16] Justin 9. 1. 9–9. 3. 3; Dion of Prusa *FGrH* 3C1, 707 F3; Arrian *Anabasis* 7. 9. 3. For discussion, see Momigliano 1933, 341–42; and Mihailov 1961, 35. Philip organized Thrace and the Pontus as a single administrative district under the control of a *stratēgos* (Bengtson 1937, 39–40).

[17] Theopompus *FGrH* 2B, 115 F292; Philochorus *FGrH* 3B, 328 F162.

[18] Clear from Memnon *FGrH* 3B, 434 F4. 1; *cf.* Jacoby *FGrH* 3B *Kommentar*, 273 *ad* 434 F2. 5.

[19] Aristotle *Politics* 7. 5. 7 1327b15–16.

[20] Memnon *FGrH* 3B, 434 F3. 2.

[21] *Recueil* I.2, 350, nos. 33–37.

140   PART I: BOOK

estimate of Timotheus' goals and achievements can still be formed. Two points are clear from Memnon's account, that he sought no territorial expansion and that he did affect a significant increase of Heracleote influence within the Pontus.

Once again it is only numismatic evidence, the imitation of Heracleote coin types by the mints of other cities, that permits us to trace the spread of Heraclea's influence. On a long series of Heracleote coins, whose first minting is usually dated to about 364,[22] the following figure appears on the reverse: profile head of a woman with hair rolled and pulled into a bun at the back of the head, wearing an earring consisting of a single horizontal bar from which dangle first a single pendant and then, in the coins that concern us, three pendants of equal length;[23] the woman also wears a crown surmounted by three knobs, the body of which is divided into three compartments by vertical lines and ornamented with a central palmette flanked on either side by a single ring. Shortly after the middle of the 4th century three cities – Kerkinitis[24] northwest of Chersonesus, and Cromna[25] and Amisus[26] east of Heraclea – issued coins bearing almost identical figures. The distribution of these coins indicates a spread of Heracleote influence along both the north and south coasts of the Euxine, which in the former area, however, was confined to a region in which no conflict with Panticapaeum could arise. Unfortunately, the impossibility of exactly dating these coins forbids our ascribing this development to Timotheus with certainty, but Memnon's account suggests that his reign was the most likely period for it to have taken place.

---

[22] Franke 1966, 138. *Cf.* Six 1885, 54–57.

[23] *Recueil* I.2, 348, no. 22. E. Robinson 1920, 12–13, showed that the triple pendant earring occurs only after the middle of the 4th century. It is worth noting that the Heracleote coin cited bears a three-quarter front beardless head of Heracles in lionskin helmet whose only analogue in Heraclea's coinage is the winged Nike issue that probably commemorated Heraclea's victory over Leucon. Conceivably Timotheus chose this rare type in order to arouse support for his foreign policy by recalling the earlier issue and the success connected with it.

[24] Zograf 1951, pl. 38, no. 16, which he dates *ca.* 340–330. The adoption of a Heracleote coin type was paralleled by the increasing predominance of pottery from Heraclea and Chersonesus at Kerkinitis (Tyumenev 1956, 173–74; Pečirka 1970, 468). By the early 3rd century Chersonesus had annexed Kerkinitis (*IOSPE* 1 401, line 20 = *SIG*³ 1 360, line 20).

[25] *Recueil* I.1, 157–59, nos. 1–9. Heraclea's influence in this region was probably not confined to Cromna since the coins of Cromna provided the model for the earliest issues of Tium (*Recueil* I.3, 615; 616, nos. 1–3) and Sesamus (*Recueil* I.1, 177, nos. 1–7), so that these three cities formed an economic unit. Moreover, Cromna and Sesamus both appear to have used the Rhodian standard (Cromna: *Recueil* I.1, 157–58, nos. 1–5; Sesamus: *Recueil* I.1, 177, no. 1) which otherwise only Heraclea among the south Pontic cities used.

[26] *Recueil* I.1, 45, no. 1.

V. TIMOTHEUS AND DIONYSIUS

141

INTERNAL DEVELOPMENTS

Under Timotheus' astute government the tyranny regained much of the popular support it had enjoyed at its foundation. The voting of divine honors to him on the one hand and the rearming of his subjects on the other are sufficient proof of this. Indeed, even his personality has been largely obscured by the tendency of Heracleote tradition to portray him solely as a benevolent and gracious monarch. Nevertheless, as the fact that he and his successors continued to rule from Clearchus' citadel on the acropolis shows,[27] this is only one aspect of his reign.

From the beginning, at the same time that he moderated on the personal level his relations with his subjects, Timotheus revealed a new attitude toward his position within Heraclea. We do not know if he continued to hold the office of *stratēgos autokratōr*, but even if he did, it could not have empowered him to issue a general amnesty. Similarly, as Berve noted,[28] no *polis* office could have given him the power to act as a judge, as Memnon says he did. These are acts more suitable to a king than to a magistrate and indicate that Timotheus no longer maintained the fiction that his authority in Heraclea derived from the fact of his holding a particular magistracy. That this was actually his view is made clear by the provisions he made for the succession.

Soon after his accession Timotheus took the unprecedented step of officially designating his brother Dionysius, although he was still a minor, to be his coregent and successor.[29] Even more notable, Timotheus, according to a most plausible suggestion by Berve,[30] issued a remarkable series of coins to commemorate the establishment of the coregency. Struck on the Persian standard instead of the Rhodian favored by Clearchus,[31] these new coins marked a complete break with the previous numismatic history of Heraclea. In place of the traditional Heracles and Hera types they bore on the obverse a head of Dionysius and on the reverse an image of Heracles erecting a trophy. More important, the inscription *HĒRAKLEIA*, which had hitherto identified the city of Heraclea as the minting authority, was replaced by the names of Timotheus and Dionysius in the genitive case. Although Timotheus continued to issue

---

[27] This is clear from Memnon *FGrH* 3B, 434 F6. 2.

[28] Berve 1967 I, 319–20.

[29] Memnon *FGrH* 3B, 434 F3. 1.

[30] *Recueil* I.2, 350, nos. 33–37. Berve 1967 I, 319. The trophy on the reverse suggests that the occasion for proclaiming Dionysius' new role was a victory.

[31] *Recueil* I.2, 350, nos. 33–37. The new coins are staters weighing from 8.01 to 9.81 g. and quarter-staters weighing 1.81 to 2.44 g. The adoption of the Persian standard for the new coins is paralleled by the replacement of the Rhodian by the Persian standard in western Anatolia and the Propontis after 350 (Le Rider 1963, 58, n. 1). Franke 1966, 139.

142   PART I: BOOK

coins bearing the inscription *HĒRAKLEIA* also, the implications of this new series are striking.[32] Issuing coinage was a privilege that belonged to the sovereign authority in a state.[33] If Timotheus placed the names of himself and his brother on these coins instead of that of Heraclea, a step neither Clearchus nor Satyrus had dared to take, that can only mean he considered himself and not the assembly to be the sovereign authority within Heraclea, and the tyranny itself to be hereditary within his own family.

Timotheus' reign, therefore, marked a major transition in the history of the tyranny: the democratic facade Clearchus and Satyrus had used to conceal their autocracy was dropped. Almost three decades of rule by him and his predecessors had accustomed the Heracleotes to the domination of the government by one man. The significance of Timotheus' actions lay not so much in his having abandoned the pretense that no tyranny existed as in his having strengthened the regime and made his usurpations of *polis* authority both accepted and acceptable by his moderate manner and the personal rapport he established with his subjects.[34]

The new situation was quickly reflected in the decline of the role played by the assembly in the conduct of Heraclea's affairs. It continued to meet during the reigns of Timotheus and his successors, but only to deal with minor matters.[35] Clearchus had allowed it to receive embassies, but now foreign affairs were the exclusive concern of the tyrant, as can be seen from an Athenian decree of 330, only seven years after Timotheus' death, which records the dispatch of an embassy to Dionysius.[36]

Timotheus died in 337 after only about nine years of rule.[37] Since he was apparently still childless at the time of his death, his brother Dionysius succeeded him. Although Dionysius hitherto had probably played only a minor role in governing Heraclea, the transfer of power took place smoothly without any challenge being presented to his succession.

---

[32] Seltman 1955, 21. Franke (1966, 138–39) noted that the radical character of this step was cushioned somewhat by the fact that the coins involved were of relatively large denominations and hence had only a limited circulation within Heraclea.

[33] This is proved by the fact that Heracleote tradition, as reflected in Memnon, praised Timotheus for precisely these usurpations.

[34] For the reign of Timotheus, see above n. 9. For the reign of Dionysius, see Diogenes Laertius 5. 91 (= Heracleides F14a Wehrli); *APIH* IX, X (= Heracleides F14b, 15). As Wehrli recognized (63 *ad* F14), the basis for this tendentious account was the awarding of a crown to Heracleides.

[35] *SIG*[3] 1 304, lines 39–40. The inscription contains decrees in honor of Heracleides of Salamis between 330 and 325.

[36] Diodorus 16. 88. 5.

[37] Memnon *FGrH* 3B, 434 F3. 3.

V. TIMOTHEUS AND DIONYSIUS

THE REIGN OF DIONYSIUS: 337 TO 305

As a result of his brother's policies Dionysius, on his assumption of sole power, found the tyranny stronger than ever and Heraclea a powerful and prosperous city whose political influence extended throughout the Pontus. For much of his own reign Dionysius followed these same policies and built on the success achieved by Timotheus. The first task facing him as tyrant, however, was organizing the funeral of his brother. Within Heraclea grief at the death of Timotheus was widespread and Dionysius spared no expense in making the occasion a major public event which would be at once an expression of fraternal affection, a worthy tribute to the dead monarch, and an auspicious beginning of his own reign. When Timotheus' corpse was cremated, Dionysius led the mourners; but he had prepared more than a funeral. The cremation marked the initial celebration of a Heracleote festival in honor of the deified Timotheus which was established then by Dionysius and which continued to be held with increasing splendor throughout his long reign. Initially the central feature of the festival was an equestrian contest, but during later celebrations Dionysius added also gymnastic, dramatic and musical contests.[38]

FOREIGN AFFAIRS: ALEXANDER AND THE EXILES: 334 TO 323

Shortly after Dionysius' accession the open struggle for power in Asia between Persia and Macedon began. When Alexander invaded Anatolia in the spring of 334, Heraclea maintained her traditional allegiance to the Persian crown. Indeed, if the recent dating of a much discussed Athenian inscription (*IG* 2² 363) honoring Dionysius to Anthesterion (February) 334 is correct, he had even established contact with the anti-Macedonian faction at Athens.[39]

Even after the battle of the Granicus River, which left Alexander in control of Hellespontine Phrygia and Persian rule in the rest of western Anatolia weak and disorganized, Dionysius did not change his policy nor did he have any reason to do so. The Macedonian line of march was south, away from Heraclea, and the decisive confrontation with the main forces of the Persian empire

---

[38] Meritt 1964, 213–17. Previously this inscription has been dated to 324 (*IG* 2² 363), 326 (Meritt 1941, 48–49), and 331 (Meritt 1961, 91–94). In fact, no evidence remains on the badly damaged stone which would allow it to be dated (Pritchett 1963, 283–85). Historical considerations however, namely, the improbability that Dionysius would have allowed himself to be publicly connected with such anti-Macedonian politicians as Polyeuctus of Sphettus, the mover of the decree (lines 7–8; for his career, see Berve 1926 II, 323, no. 650) much later than 334, tend to support the date given in the text. Apropos of this it should be noted that the sharp tone of *SIG*³ 1, 304, lines 41–43, becomes more intelligible if the Athenians previously honored Dionysius.

[39] Arrian *Anabasis* 1. 18. 1–2. Chios: *GHI* 2 192; Theopompus *FGrH* 2B 115 T2.

144   PART I: BOOK

was still in the future. Likewise, Alexander's policy of supporting the democratic factions in the cities of western Anatolia, a policy that included forcing
Chios to agree to the return of her exiles, can only have strengthened Dionysius' hopes for a Persian victory.[40] This same policy, however, raised the
expectations of the Heracleote exiles. Once Alexander's final victory had
become obvious, that is, probably soon after the battle of Gaugamela in the fall
of 331, he received a delegation from them requesting that he arrange their
return to Heraclea and the restoration of the city's ancestral democracy (*patrios
demokratia*).[41] Behind the cant phrase was the appeal that Alexander use his
power to overthrow Dionysius.[42]

In Photius' epitome of Memnon the nature of Alexander's reply is not
stated, but his narrative implies that he acceded to the exiles' request and
issued orders for their return and the installation of a democratic government
at Heraclea. Since he intended to continue eastward, enforcement of this order
and a similar one issued on behalf of exiles from Amisus depended on action
by one of his Anatolian satraps.[43]

Such action, however, would be possible only at great expense and diffi-
culty. Officially, Alexander claimed authority over all northern and central
Anatolia.[44] Between 333 and 330 he appointed satraps in Hellespontine
Phrygia,[45] Cappadocia,[46] and Armenia,[47] and accepted the submission of the
Paphlagonians, whom he assigned to Hellespontine Phrygia.[48] Actually, this
organization existed only on paper. Mithrines, the satrap of Armenia, seems

---

[40] Memnon *FGrH* 3B, 434 F4. 1. Decisive for the date is the phrase *periphanōs ēdē tēs Asias
Kratounta:* Plutarch *Alexander* 34. 1; and Hamilton 1969, 90, note *ad loc.* Possibly the flute
player Dionysius whom Chares says (*FGrH* 2B, 125 F4) performed at the mass weddings at Susa
was one of the Heracleote exiles (*cf.* Chamaeleon F3 Wehrli = Athenaeus 5. 184c).

[41] For the political significance of *patrios politeia* in the Hellenistic period, see Tarn 1913,
107, 437–38 (with particular reference to the 3rd and 2nd centuries).

[42] Dionysius may have been included in the tyrannies Alexander claimed to have suppressed
(Plutarch *Alexander* 34. 2; Hamilton 1969, 91, note *ad loc.*). Amisus: Appian *Mithridatica* 8. 83.

[43] Although Alexander exercised no power on the north coast of Anatolia, he did view its
inhabitants as his unsubdued subjects as can be seen from the description of Eumenes' satrapy
(Diodorus 13. 3. 1; Arrian *FGrH* 2B, 156 F1. 5; Dexippus *FGrH* 2A, 100 F8. 2; Plutarch
Eumenes 3. 2; Justin 13. 4. 16; Curtius Rufus 10. 10. 3). For Heraclea and the immediately
adjacent area of Paphlagonia, see Porphyry *FGrH* 2B, 260 F41; Curtius Rufus 3. 1. 22–23; and
Callisthenes *FGrH* 2B, 124 F53; and the discussion of the latter two passages by Pearson 1960,
43–44. These claims are probably behind the invention of a Pontic expedition by Alexander that
we find in the *Itinerarium Alexandri* 26. 1, and Ps.-Callisthenes 1. 44. 2.

[44] Arrian *Anabasis* 1. 17. 1; 2. 4. 2.

[45] Memnon *FGrH* 3B, 434 F12. 4.

[46] Arrian *Anabasis* 2. 4. 2.

[47] Arrian *Anabasis* 3. 16. 5; Curtius Rufus 5. 1. 44; Diodorus 17. 64. 5.

[48] Arrian *Anabasis* 24. 1–2; Curtius Rufus 3. 1. 23–24. 49. Darius' satrap Orontes held Armenia throughout Alexander's reign (Berve 1926 I, 290; II, 295, nos. 23–25).

V. TIMOTHEUS AND DIONYSIUS

never to have even attempted to assume his post,[49] and throughout Alexander's reign Ariarathes, who like Dionysius never recognized him, held Cappadocia Pontica and the adjacent coast of Paphlagonia.[50] Cappadocia proper also fell to him after a revolt (instigated by elements of Darius' army that had escaped from the battle of Issus) drove Alexander's forces out of that area and threatened to do the same in inland Paphlagonia.[51] Macedonian authority was, in fact, secure only in Hellespontine Phrygia, but even there it was in the main confined to the area of the Hellespont proper. The upper Propontic cities,[52] and Chalcedon,[53] seem to have remained independent and an attempt to subdue the Bithynians in 327 ended with the death of Calas, the Macedonian satrap.[54] It is not surprising, therefore, that Alexander found on his return from India in 324 that his instructions concerning the Heracleote exiles had not been followed.

Dionysius himself was not inactive in his own cause. Although he faced a number of problems during the years after Alexander's invasion,[55] the increased popular support for the tyranny within Heraclea resulting from his brother's policies enabled him to concentrate his attention on meeting the threat to his survival posed by Alexander's support of the exiles. Preparations were made to resist an attack should the situation deteriorate to that extent, and on several occasions that eventuality seemed about to materialize.[56] That it never did was due, in part, to the difficulties of the Macedonian satraps, described above, and to Dionysius' own astute diplomacy. Dionysius, judging from Memnon's laconic account, entered into direct negotiations with the exiles and their Macedonian patrons. His conduct of the negotiations was masterful. He affected a reasonable and conciliatory tone, yielding on the nonessential points, but always managing to defer a final decision. While Dionysius quieted the exiles' sense of urgency in this way, he sought and found important foreign support

---

[49] Berve 1926 II, 262–63, no. 524.

[50] Berve 1926 II, 59, no. 113.

[51] Curtius Rufus 4. 1. 35–36. For this revolt, see Tarn 1948 II, 11.

[52] Cyzicus was a free ally: Diodorus 18. 52. 3. Cius: ruled by Mithridates II from 337 to 302 (Diodorus 16. 90. 2; 20. 111. 4), who probably did not recognize Alexander since Cius issued an autonomous coinage (Le Rider 1963, 39–40; Head 1911, 513) instead of the silver staters minted by cities subject to him (Bickermann 1934, 349–50). For Alexander's alleged offer of the revenues of Cius to Phocion (Plutarch *Phocion* 18. 5; Aelian *VH* 1. 25), see Tarn 1948 II, 222–23.

[53] Chalcedon remained loyal to Darius 111 until his death (Arrian *Anabasis* 3. 24. 5).

[54] Memnon *FGrH* 3B, 434 F12. 4. Berve 1926 II, 188, no. 397.

[55] Memnon *FGrH* 3B, 434 F4. 1. Aristotle (*Meteorologica* 2. 8, 367a1–2) mentions a serious earthquake as a recent occurrence at Heraclea, i.e. with reference to the composition of the work which Lee (1952, xxiii–xxv) dates to after 340 and Düring (1966, 51) to between 347 and 334. Moreover, the seizure of the ship of Heracleides of Salamis in 330 by the Heracleotes (*SIG*[3] 1 304, lines 37–38) suggests that the city suffered during the famine of that year.

[56] Memnon *FGrH* 3B, 434 F4.1.

146   PART I: BOOK

for his own position. Despite his not having made his submission to Alexander and, implicitly at least, having been condemned by him, Dionysius was able to establish close relations with Antipater's government in Macedonia and, his most important diplomatic achievement, with Cleopatra, Alexander's sister, after her return from Epirus in the early 320s.[57]

Meanwhile, Dionysius took advantage of the collapse of Persian power in Anatolia and the subsequent confusion to expand the territory under his control. Memnon, unfortunately, reports only the bare fact without furnishing details concerning the area in which these new conquests were made, their extent, or the amount of time necessary to accomplish them.[58] At the time of his death in 305, Dionysius' power extended eastward into Paphlagonia as far as the city of Cytorus and westward into Bithynia as far as the Rhebas River, encompassing approximately the region called Thynian Thrace.[59] Since Ariarathes apparently held the Paphlagonian coast until his death in 322, Dionysius probably made his first move westward across the Sangarius River into Bithynian territory where, at least until 327, the Bithynian ruler Bas was unable to concentrate his forces against Heraclea because of the possibility of an attack on his southern and south-western frontiers by Calas.

With the return of Alexander from India in 324, however, Dionysius' position became more difficult. Rumors of a Pontic expedition were in the air[60] and the exiles were pressing Alexander again to bring about their return to Heraclea.[61] Worse yet, the contemporary decree ordering all the cities of European Greece to receive back their exiles must have made the threat that Alexander might take similarly decisive action with regard to Heraclea only too real.[62] Still, there was a slight possibility that Alexander, now that he

---

[57] Memnon *FGrH* 3B, 434 F4. 1. In 330 she was still in Epirus (*GHI* 2 196, line 10) but she had returned to Macedon before Alexander's death (Plutarch *Alexander* 68. 3). For her relations with Antipater, see Hamilton 1969, 190 *ad* 68. 3, and Berve 1926 II 212, no. 433.

[58] Memnon *FGrH* 3B, 434 F4. 1.

[59] *Contra* Ed. Meyer (1897, 512), who identified *tēn Thunida gēn* (Memnon *FGrH* 3B, 434 F9. 4) with the island of Thynias. As Niese recognized (1893–1903 II, 75, n. 5), however, Apollonius of Rhodes 2, lines 788–789, which probably derive from Nymphis, imply that Heraclea controlled the whole region. This is supported by the fact that the walls of the Heracleote colony on Thynias were built with stones quarried on the opposite mainland (Fıratlı 1953, 16).

[60] Arrian *Anabasis* 7. 1. 1. Alexander is said to have considered such a plan while he was in Hyrcania (Arrian *Anabasis* 4. 15. 4–5; *cf.* C. Robinson 1940, 410–11, and Tarn 1948 II, 399, n. 5). Zopyrion's unsuccessful siege of Olbia about 326 or 325 (Justin 2. 3. 4; 12. 1. 4; 12. 2. 16–17; 37. 3. 2; Curtius Rufus 10. 1. 44; Macrobius *Saturnalia* 1. 11. 33; Niese 1893–1903 I, 171, n. 2, 498–500; Berve 1926 II, 164, no. 340) would have warned Dionysius of the reality of the danger.

[61] Memnon *FGrH* 3B, 434 F4. 1. Cleopatra's assistance (below n. 64) points to problems with the exiles late in Alexander's reign.

[62] Diodorus 17. 109. 1; Curtius Rufus 10. 2. 4; Justin 13. 5. 2. For the scope and purpose of the decree, see Lane Fox 1973, 413–16.

V. TIMOTHEUS AND DIONYSIUS   147

considered himself the successor of the Achaemenids, might not be completely unsympathetic to a ruler and potential ally whose principal sin was his steady loyalty to Darius III.[63] To better plead his cause Dionysius turned for assistance to Cleopatra, and her intercession led Alexander to delay his taking decisive action on behalf of the exiles until his own death in June 323 seemingly ended the matter. According to Memnon, Dionysius received the news of Alexander's death and the apparent end of the threat that had hung over his regime for almost a decade with such delirious relief that he founded, at Heraclea, a cult to the goddess Euthymia – that is, to Joy.[64]

FOREIGN AFFAIRS: DIONYSIUS AND THE DIADOCHI: 323 TO 305

His confidence was premature. Almost immediately after Alexander's death Perdiccas, the regent for his successors Philip Arrhidaeus and the unborn Alexander IV, revealed his intention of completing the conquest of northern Anatolia by assigning the still unsubdued satrapy of Cappadocia together with Paphlogonia to Eumenes.[65] Shortly thereafter the Heracleote exiles approached him just as they previously had Alexander and presented him with the same petition asking that he arrange their return to Heraclea.[66]

Although Heraclea probably fell within the boundaries of the satrapy of Hellespontine Phrygia, which Perdiccas had assigned to Leonnatus,[67] and not Cappadocia-Paphlagonia, reduction of the latter region would place Macedonian power on the Pontus just to the east of Heraclea, leaving Dionysius open to an attack from that quarter should Perdiccas decide to take aggressive action on behalf of the exiles. Time and the growing tensions between the Macedonians, however, came to Dionysius' aid. The assistance Eumenes was supposed to receive from Leonnatus and Antigonus,[68] the satrap of Phrygia Maior, in the task of subduing Ariarathes did not materialize, so that it was not until the late summer or early fall of 322, over a year after Alexander's death, that Perdiccas himself installed Eumenes in his satrapy after defeating and executing Ariarathes.[69] Dionysius used the time thus gained to good advantage.

---

[63] Compare his pardon of Sinope after the death of Darius III (Arrian *Anabasis* 3. 24. 4).
[64] Memnon *FGrH* 3B, 434 F4. 1–2.
[65] For Eumenes' satrapy and its significance, see above n. 44.
[66] Memnon *FGrH* 3B, 434 F4. 3.
[67] Diodorus 18. 3. 1; Arrian *FGrH* 2B, 156 F1. 6; Justin 13. 4. 16; Curtius Rufus 10. 10. 2; Dexippus *FGrH* 2A, 100 F8. 2.
[68] Plutarch *Eumenes* 3. 2–3.
[69] Diodorus 18. 16. 1–3; Plutarch *Eumenes* 3. 6–7; Appian *Mithridatica* 8; Justin 13. 6. 1. For the chronology of the years 323 to 320 I have adopted that of Errington 1970, 75–77. For the date of the conquest of Cappadocia, see Errington 1970, 76–77.

148 PART I: BOOK

With Perdiccas he employed the same careful, apparently conciliatory, but always delaying diplomacy he had used with such success during the reign of Alexander, and with similar results.[70] Meanwhile Dionysius' Macedonian contacts culminated in a brilliant and politically advantageous marriage. In the winter of 322, shortly after Perdiccas finally installed Eumenes in Cappadocia, Antipater arranged a marriage between his daughter Phila and Craterus, who had furnished him valuable support during the Lamian War.[71] But Craterus was already married. At Susa in 324 Alexander had given him as his bride Amastris, the daughter of Oxathres, the brother of Darius III.[72] Since Antipater would hardly tolerate Phila's occupying the lowly position of a secondary wife, Craterus divorced Amastris and she then married Dionysius, who was most likely a widower at this time.[73]

Marriage to Amastris brought Dionysius increased prestige and, more important, powerful friends. Memnon notes that she married Dionysius *gnōmēi tou lipontos* (sc. Craterus) and that his rule was strengthened *ploutou te peribolēi dia tēs epigamias prostetheisei*. This should most probably be understood to mean that Craterus arranged the marriage with Amastris and that he equipped her with a sizable dowry to make the match even more attractive to Dionysius.[74] In short, a marriage alliance between Dionysius on the one hand and Antipater and Craterus on the other had been concluded. Under these circumstances, so long as Perdiccas wished to avoid an open break with Antipater and Craterus – and his marriage to another of Antipater's daughters, Nicaea, early in 321 showed this to be the case – he would hesitate to do more than provide verbal support to the Heracleote exiles.[75]

But with this marriage the survival of the tyranny ceased to be in any important way a Heracleote problem. Memnon aptly characterized Dionysius as balancing on the edge of a razor.[76] Hitherto he had achieved his diplomatic success largely because of his freedom to maneuver; attached to no one of the Macedonian leaders, he had been able to balance them off against each other. But this situation no longer existed. The exiles were already clients of Perdiccas and now Dionysius was an ally of his most important potential enemies. The future of Heraclea had become, and would henceforth remain, an issue

---

[70] Memnon *FGrH* 3B, 434 F4. 3.

[71] Diodorus 18. 18. 7.

[72] Memnon *FGrH* 3B, 434 F4. 4; Diodorus 20. 109. 7; Arrian *Anabasis* 7. 4. 4.

[73] Memnon *FGrH* 3B, 434 F4. 4. Previous marriage: Memnon *FGrH* 3B, 434 F4. 6. That Dionysius was a widower was suggested by Schneiderwirth 1882, 30.

[74] Memnon *FGrH* 3B, 434 F4. 5. Seibert 1967, 25, n. 2, noted that this could have been the dowry provided her in 324 by her father or Alexander.

[75] Diodorus 18. 23. 1–3.

[76] Memnon *FGrH* 3B, 434 F4. 3.

V. TIMOTHEUS AND DIONYSIUS

149

connected with the far greater question of the final disposition of Alexander's empire, which would be decided eventually by the success or failure of the respective parties' Macedonian supporters. The guarantee of Dionysius' security was not his own power and ability but the continued existence of peace between the various Macedonian leaders.

This precarious situation lasted only until the winter of 321, when Antigonus informed Antipater of Perdiccas' plans to invade Macedonia after repudiating Nicaea and marrying Alexander's sister Cleopatra.[77] The struggle was joined during the first half of 320. Antipater and Craterus crossed into Anatolia while Perdiccas, after leaving Eumenes to guard against this threat, moved against their ally Ptolemy.[78] Although Eumenes was victorious over Craterus, who died in the battle, the conflict was decided in Egypt with the murder of Perdiccas by his own officers. Shortly afterwards, the Macedonian army that had fought Perdiccas condemned Eumenes and at Triparadeisos Antipater assigned Antigonus the task of dealing with him.[79] Dionysius probably had taken little if any part in the actual fighting, although Eumenes' activities had caused him considerable difficulty and anxiety,[80] but now with Perdiccas dead and Eumenes a hunted outlaw – and with himself a friend of the victorious Antipater – his hold on Heraclea was finally secure. In Memnon's phrase, the hopes of the exiles had been extinguished by the death of Perdiccas.[81]

Dionysius took advantage of his new freedom to resume, in the years following 320, the aggressive foreign policy of the beginning of his reign. Essentially an interested onlooker in the struggle with Perdiccas, Dionysius seems to have actively supported the coalition of Antigonus, Ptolemy, Seleucus, Lysimachus, and Cassander against Polyperchon and Eumenes, which ended with the death of the latter in 316. While Antigonus' troops occupied Cappadocia and Antigonus himself pursued Eumenes into the upper satrapies, Dionysius seized the opportunity to expand and crossed the Billaeus river into Paphlagonia. His thrust stopped well short of Sinopean territory, but still resulted in the addition to his small empire of the Greek cities of Tium, Cromna, Sesamus, and Cytorus.[82]

---

[77] Diodorus 18. 25. 3.
[78] Diodorus 18. 29. 1; Plutarch *Eumenes* 5. 1–2; Justin 13. 6. 14–15; Nepos *Eumenes* 3. 2.
[79] Diodorus 1840. 1; Plutarch *Eumenes* 8. 2; Justin 13. 8. 10.
[80] Memnon *FGrH* 3B, 434 F4. 3. The reference by Nicephorus Gregoras (Letter 45, p. 161) to Eumenes' relying on Heracleote support may refer to his having a contingent of exiles with him.
[81] Memnon *FGrH* 3B, 434 F4. 3.
[82] Memnon *FGrH* 3B, 434 F4. 6; Strabo 12. 3. 10.

150 PART I: BOOK

Meanwhile, with Eumenes dead, the coalition of his enemies foundered. Even before Antigonus returned to the Mediterranean area from Media, Cassander's troops ejected his men from Cappadocia and laid siege to Amisus.[83] War became inevitable when in 315 Antigonus rejected the ultimatum presented him by his former allies[84] and issued instead a general call for new allies.[85] At the same time he sent his nephew Polemaeus to assume control of Hellespontine Phrygia after reestablishing his authority in Cappadocia and lifting the siege of Amisus.[86] For Dionysius neutrality was hardly possible; only the decision which side to join was to be made and that was largely determined by events. When Polemaeus accomplished his task with ease and arranged alliances with the cities of Chalcedon and Astacus – and with Zipoetes, Bas' successor in Bithynia[87] – Dionysius also agreed to an alliance with Antigonus, and then sent a Heracleote force to assist him in pressing the siege of Tyre.[88]

When, after 14 months, the siege of Tyre was finally brought to a successful conclusion in 314, Antigonus further strengthened his ties with Dionysius by arranging that his nephew Polemaeus, now *stratēgos* in Hellespontine Phrygia, marry a daughter of the Heracleote tyrant by his first wife.[89] This marriage alliance formed a successful climax to Dionysius' diplomatic and military activity. After having pushed Heraclea's power to its maximum extent, he had now gained official recognition of his tyranny from Antigonus and enhanced security against a possible attempt by Zipoetes to recover his lost territory. Naturally, the improving of his relations with Antigonus was matched by the deterioration of those with his enemies. Indeed, Cassander may even have tried to revive again the hopes of the Heracleote exiles in order to intimidate Dionysius, or at least this would seem to be the most probable explanation for the interesting fact that sometime during the reign of Demetrius of Phaleron his agent at Athens, Demetrius' close friend Menander[90] produced a play entitled

[83] Diodorus 19. 57. 4.
[84] Diodorus 19. 57. 1–2; Justin 15. 1. 1–3; Appian *Syriaca* 53.
[85] Diodorus 19. 57. 3–5.
[86] Diodorus 19. 57. 3–5.
[87] Diodorus 19. 60. 2–3.
[88] Memnon *FGrH* 3B, 434 F4. 6. Droysen 1883–85 II, 317, n. 1) emended the manuscript reading *Kupron* to *Turon*. That Dionysius fought at Tyre is based on the assumptions (*a*) that *Summachēsas* should be understood in its literal sense and (*b*) that *philotimias amoibēn* implies that he rendered Antigonus an actual service. For the siege of Tyre in general, see Diodorus 19. 58–59. 3; 19. 61. 5.
[89] Memnon *FGrH* 3B, 434 F4. 6; Diodorus 19. 61. 5. Seibert 1967, 26, dates the marriage to 315, but Memnon's reference to its being in exchange for Dionysius' *philotimia* at Tyre points toward 314. Polemaeus and Hellespontine Phrygia: Memnon *FGrH* 3B, 434 F4. 6; Diodorus 20. 19. 2; Bengtson 1937, 204–05.
[90] Diogenes Laertius 5. 79.

V. TIMOTHEUS AND DIONYSIUS

151

Halieis about the Heracleote exiles.[91] The fragments are too few to permit reconstruction of the plot, but it clearly was sympathetic to the exiles and treated Dionysius in an exceptionally hostile manner, portraying him as a hideously fat and decadent monarch.[92] Nevertheless, Dionysius apparently avoided committing Heraclea to further military action on behalf of Antigonus in the period between the end of the siege of Tyre and the Peace of 311.[93]

The years from 311 to his death in 305 are the least adequately documented of Dionysius' reign. For the whole period only one event is mentioned by the sources, his assumption of the title of king in 306 or 305, but this is sufficient to establish the important fact that by then his relations with Antigonus had deteriorated to the point of an open break.[94] Antigonus himself had taken the title of king after the victory of his forces over those of Ptolemy at Cyprus in 306, to signify his claim to rule all of Alexander's empire.[95] His pretensions threatened Dionysius as much as his Macedonian contemporaries, and, as was true of their similar proclamations, his assuming the title of king was a direct challenge to Antigonus' claims, a declaration that Dionysius was his equal and not his subject.

These events, however, represented only the climax of a gradual process of estrangement between Antigonus and Dionysius. The alliance between them can never have been completely secure because Dionysius must always have known that Antigonus could use his policy of supporting the freedom of all Greek states against him as easily as against Lysimachus or Cassander.[96] The murder of Antigonus' nephew Polemaeus by Ptolemy in 310, after the former's abortive revolt, weakened the alliance still further by severing the personal tie

---

[91] Menander Ff 13–29 (Edmonds). F13 indicates that the action of the play was set in Heraclea. For dating the key is the reference to the gold of Cyinda in F24 (= Athenaeus 11. 484c–d). The only occasion during Dionysius' lifetime when a topical connection of Cyinda and Heraclea would be possible would be sometime soon after 315 when Antigonus removed 10,000 talents from the fortress (Diodorus 19. 56. 5). For Cyinda in general, see Simpson 1957.

[92] Menander Ff 21–23 (Edmonds) = Nymphis *FGrH* 3B, 432 F10 = Athenaeus 12. 549a–d.

[93] Apel (1910, 51–52) suggested that Dionysius supported Callatis in its revolt against Lysimachus in 313 (Diodorus 19. 73), but Diodorus' account indicates that beside the Thracians and Scythians the only direct assistance Heraclea's colony received came from Antigonus.

[94] Memnon *FGrH* 3B, 434 F4. 6. For the justification of a tyrant such as Dionysius taking the title, see Diodorus, 20. 54. 1, apropos of Agathocles.

[95] Diodorus 20. 53. 1–4; Plutarch *Demetrius* 18. 1–2; Justin 15. 2. 10–13. For the exclusive attitude of Antigonus and Demetrius toward the kingship, see Plutarch *Demetrius* 25. 4, and Phylarchus *FGrH* 2A, 81 F31.

[96] Diodorus 19. 61. 3–4. *OGIS* 1 5, lines 53–61. For Antigonus' policy toward the Greeks, see C. Wehrli 1968, 103–29, and Simpson 1959. The favorable treatment Antigonus receives in Heracleote tradition (Memnon *FGrH* 3B, 434 F4. 9; *cf.* Laqueur 1937, 1614) indicates that he had influential supporters in Heraclea. Moreover, in such men as the Heracleote *metic* who served as a trierarch with Demetrius (Wilhelm 1942b, 69, lines 1–3) or Philetaerus of Tium, then serving Docimus, one of his officers (Pausanias 1. 8. 1; Strabo 12. 3. 8), he had potential agents to use against Dionysius.

152   PART I: BOOK

between them.[97] As we would expect, the sources indicate that at the same time his relations with Antigonus were worsening Dionysius sought friends among his former enemies, and in particular that a rapprochement took place between him and Lysimachus.[98] Indeed, this developing friendship with Lysimachus probably encouraged him to defy Antigonus by proclaiming himself king. Only his death soon afterwards forestalled the inevitable confrontation with Antigonus on this matter.[99]

INTERNAL HISTORY AND THE DEATH OF DIONYSIUS

In the main, the internal history of Heraclea under Dionysius was marked by the continuation of the basic political and economic trends established by his brother. The role of the tyrant in all aspects of public affairs continued to increase at the expense of the assembly and other institutions of Clearchus' restored democracy. Like his brother, Dionysius made little attempt to conceal this growing autocracy – he also issued coins bearing only his name[100] – but instead strove to make it appear inoffensive and even desirable by the moderation and graciousness with which he exercised his power. He was accessible to his subjects and took care that he did not monopolize civic honors.[101] For these qualities he earned the sobriquet *Chrestos*, or the Good, and this, together with the general success of his policies, brought him the public support he needed during the difficult period that opened with Alexander's invasion of Anatolia.[102]

---

[97] Diodorus 20. 19. 2; 20. 27. 3. It would be interesting to know if Dionysius was involved in this revolt.

[98] The existence of friendship between Lysimachus and Dionysius is required by the device Lysimachus used in 284 to gain access to Heraclea (Memnon *FGrH* 3B, 434 F5. 3) and implied by Memnon's statement (*FGrH* 3B, 434 F4. 9) that Lysimachus cared for Heraclea *palin* in 302. The fact that Eumelus of Bosporus and not Dionysius received refugees from Callatis after the failure of that city's second revolt against Lysimachus *ca.* 310/09 (Diodorus 20. 25. 1; Saitta 1955, 115–16) suggests that total abandonment of her colony was part of the price Dionysius paid for that friendship.

[99] Diodorus, 16. 88. 5; 20. 77. 1, places his death in 306/5 after 32 years of rule. The 32 years of Nymphis (*FGrH* 3B, 432 F10) are almost certainly reckoned inclusively and hence do not support Beloch's proposal (1912–27 III, 2, 95) to lower the date to 304. The 30 years of Memnon (*FGrH* 3B, 434 F4. 8) are probably the result of a textual omission.

[100] *Recueil* I.2, 350, nos. 38–41.

[101] See above n. 35 for the awarding of a civic crown to Heracleides. In this connection one should also mention the Athenian proxeny decree for a Heracleote named Hermo – from the year 317 (Schweigert 1939, 30–32; Wilhelm 1942a, 175–83; and Raubitschek 1945, 106–07).

[102] Memnon *FGrH* 3B, 434 F4. 8. The goodwill of his subjects: Memnon *FGrH* 3B, 434 F4. 1; 4. 6.

V. TIMOTHEUS AND DIONYSIUS

153

The prosperity of Heraclea during this period probably contributed significantly to the further consolidation of this popularity. Again, the basic policies were laid down by Timotheus, but Dionysius reaped the benefits of them. From both archaeological and literary sources it is clear that Heraclea's trade with the Aegean and especially with the north coast of the Euxine – that with the west coast apparently remained relatively insignificant[103] – increased considerably. For Athens we have evidence of the continued import of Heraclea's traditional products, fish, nuts, and grain,[104] and now also a certain amount of wine.[105] Inscriptions, furthermore, indicate a growth in the number of Heracleotes living at Athens[106] and in the importance of their role in the city's grain trade.[107] The most impressive growth, however, took place at the other end of the grain route in Heraclea's economic relations with the cities of southern Russia. Here, also, in the form of epitaphs[108] and proxeny decrees,[109] we find evidence of the growing importance of Heracleotes in the area's economic life. Excavation has shown that from the middle of the 4th century until well into the 3rd these cities imported from Heraclea a small amount of manufactured goods, such as roofing tiles,[110] and an increasing volume of cheap wine for their poor and for the natives of their hinterlands.[111]

Dionysius' marriage to Amastris and the collapse of the threat from the exiles brought a change in style but not in basic policies. The simple life-style characteristic of Timotheus' reign and the first years of his own was not suitable to the enhanced status of a ruler who was the husband of a Persian princess and the master of a small but respectable empire. Again the tyrant became the center of a rich court life, and Amastris' dowry allowed him to indulge his taste for elegance and provide an appropriately splendid setting for his court by purchasing the household furnishings of his namesakes, Dionysius I and Dionysius II of Syracuse.[112]

---

[103] Canarache 1957, 357–58.

[104] Grain: *IG* 2² 363. Nuts: Athenaeus 2. 53b–54c. Fish: Athenaeus 8. 331c; Pliny *NH* 9. 176–178; Ps.-Aristotle *De Mirabilibus auscultationibus* 73, 853b15–23.

[105] Athenaeus 1. 32b.

[106] *IG* 2²–3² pt 2, f3 contains 17 epitaphs of Heracleotes from the beginning of the 3rd century (8570, 8614, 8639, 8682, 8705, 8706, 8719, 8722, 8729, 8737, 8759, 8768, 8770, 8784, 8803, 8811, 8816). In addition, I counted 41 epitaphs belonging to the 3rd century proper, which indicates that the process of settlement continued to gain momentum.

[107] *IG* 2² 408. Schweigert 1940, 332, 333. Wilhelm 1942b, 69, lines 4–14.

[108] Epitaphs of foreigners are admittedly too rare to provide a reliable statistical sample. Still, it is worth noting that four are known from the 4th and early 3rd centuries (*IOSPE* 444 = *CIRB* 1193; *IOSPE* 2 289 = *CIRB* 246; *IOSPE* 2 288 = *CIRB* 923; *IOSPE* 4 399 = *CIRB* 925).

[109] Levi 1958, 238–39.

[110] Zeest 1951, 106–09; Canarache 1957, 365.

[111] Zeest 1948, 47–48; Canarache 1957, 191.

[112] Memnon *FGrH* 3B, 434 F4. 5. The furniture and other possessions of Dionysius had been seized by Timoleon in 343 (Diodorus 16. 70. 1–2; Plutarch *Timoleon* 13. 3). *Cf.* Menander F24 (Edmonds).

154 PART I: BOOK

This same period also saw the conquest and organization of the greater part of Heraclea's empire. Details are lacking, but sufficient evidence exists to determine in outline the relationship Dionysius established between Heraclea and her new subjects. The area involved was substantial, extending from the Rhebas River in Bithynia to Cytorus in Paphlagonia, and marked by strong contrasts. The western district, Thynias, was essentially a continuation of Mariandynia, a country of native villages with no Greek cities.[113] The Paphlagonian coast, on the other hand, contained both a native population and the four old Milesian colonies of Tium, Sesamus, Cromna, and Cytorus. Clearly the same administrative system could not be applied to both areas. Although the evidence clearly indicates that both areas were considered by the Heracleotes to be in a juridical sense their property,[114] it is only with regard to the Greek cities that we can form some idea of the system devised to rule them. It is probable that the natives were assimilated to the status of the Mariandynian *perioeci*, but certainty is not possible.[115] As for the cities, Niese suggested that they were connected to Heraclea by treaty only, and that they retained their internal autonomy.[116] Niese based his interpretation on the fact that Cierus and Tium were, along with Heraclea, parties to the treaty signed by Nicomedes I with the Gauls in 279.[117] The right to sign a treaty, however, is one of the essential characteristics of an independent state in Greek thought and cannot be reconciled with Heraclea's claim to own these cities.[118] As far as the treaty is concerned, it rather proves, as A.H.M. Jones pointed out, that Heraclea did not rule them at all at the time it was signed.[119] That the actual relationship was much harsher is clearly indicated by Amastris' later union of Tium, Sesamus, Cromna, and Cytorus to form her new city of Amastris. This would only be possible if Dionysius had both claimed and exercised complete authority

---

[113] Xenophon *Anabasis* 6. 3. 1; 6. 4. 3; 6. 4. 5. Theopompus *FGrH* 2B, 115 F15, does, however, suggest that the Bithynians established a sizable settlement at Calpe during the 4th century. The Heracleote *emporium* at Calpe was probably a Hellenistic foundation (Anonymous *Periplus* 8r46–47; Menippus *Periplus* D5707–5708; Marcian *Epitome Peripli Menippei* 8 [*GGM* I 569]). The remains are all of Roman date (Fıratlı 1953, 18–19).

[114] Memnon *FGrH* 3B, 434 F9. 4; 19. 1.

[115] A possible indicator of this may be the story in the late 4th century historian Andron of Teos (*FGrH* 3C, 802 F1; Berve 1926 II, 40, no. 81) that Heracles during his stay at Heraclea had a son named Poimenus by Dardanis the daughter of king Acheron and that two places near Heraclea were named Dardanis and Poimen after them. The former is unidentifiable, but the latter is probably connected with the mountain near Amastris mentioned by Stephanus of Byzantium *s.v. Poimēn*. If this is so, it may reflect a late 4th century tendency to assimilate the peoples up to the Parthenius River to the Mariandynoi.

[116] Niese 1893–1903 II, 75, who is followed by Ernst Meyer 1925a, 109.

[117] Memnon *FGrH* 3B, 434 F11. 2.

[118] Bickerman 1939, 345–46.

[119] Jones 1971, 419, n. 6.

V. TIMOTHEUS AND DIONYSIUS

over the internal and external lives of these cities. This supposition is confirmed, moreover, by two pieces of evidence: Memnon's reference to Tium as being subject to Heraclea (*hupēkoos*) and the minting by Tium after the battle of Corupedium of a series of coins bearing the inscription *ELEUTHERIA*.[120] In terms of Greek political terminology, this would commemorate the end of a period of *douleia* or in other words a period in which Tium was completely subject to the dictates of another state in both her domestic and foreign policies.[121] Presumably the cities paid Heraclea tribute, but whether Dionysius ruled them by imposing governors and garrisons or through governments dominated by his supporters is not known.

The fact of the empire is crucial to a proper understanding of the implications of Dionysius' taking the title of king for his relations with Heraclea. The key question in this matter is what constituted his kingdom, and Memnon fortunately provides the evidence that enables us to answer it when, in connection with Dionysius' will, he notes that Amastris became *tōn holōn despoinan* and again when he describes her *archē* at the time of her death as including Heraclea, Tium, and Amastris.[122] Like his Macedonian contemporaries, on whose similar proclamations his was based, therefore, Dionysius claimed to be king not of Heraclea but of all the territory he ruled.[123] As Nymphis noted, this was a radically new departure which signaled the end of the tyranny as established by Clearchus and redefined by Timotheus.[124] His predecessors' pretensions and official position were restricted to Heraclea, whereas those of Dionysius and Amastris, his successors', were based – as were those of any other Hellenistic monarch – on their ruling a territory that happened to include a number of Greek cities of which Heraclea was only the most important. Henceforth, the relationship between the Heracleotes and Dionysius was the same as that which existed between him and, for example, the Tians – they were simply his subjects.

Meanwhile, excessive obesity undermined Dionysius' health and steadily impaired his ability to effectively govern.[125] Finally, in 305, shortly after his becoming king and after 32 years of a brilliantly successful reign, Dionysius

---

[120] Memnon *FGrH* 3B, 434 F19. 1. *Recueil* I.3, 615, 616, no. 4.

[121] C. Wehrli 1968, 104. *Cf.* Gomme *et al.* 1944–70 III, 645–46.

[122] Memnon *FGrH* 3B, 434 F4. 8; 5. 4.

[123] *Cf.* Diodorus 20. 54. 1. Porphyry (*FGrH* 2B, 260 F4I) calls his kingdom Heraclea, but this probably only reflects the city's importance compared to his other possessions. Dionysius struck no coins as king but those issued later by Amastris bore the inscription *AMASTRIOS BASILISSES* (*Recueil* I.1, 135, nos. 1–3).

[124] Memnon *FGrH* 3B, 434 F4. 6.

[125] Memnon *FGrH* 3B, 434 F4. 7; Nymphis *FGrH* 3B, 432 F10; Aelian *VH* 9. 13; Menander Ff 21–23 (Edmonds); Palladas in Paton 1916–18, 10. 54.

156 PART I: BOOK

died.[126] He was survived by his queen Amastris and by the three children she had borne him, Clearchus, his eldest son, another son named Oxathres, and a daughter named Amastris after her mother.[127] A popular ruler, like Timotheus, his funeral and deification also took place amid general public mourning.[128]

Dionysius had previously made plans for the succession, and on his death these were implemented smoothly. Amastris assumed the kingship with the title *basilissa* and overall responsibility for the government of all of Dionysius' dominions. Clearchus and Oxathres succeeded jointly to the rule of Heraclea itself under the suzerainty of Amastris. But since they were still minors, a regency council headed by Amastris took over the task of actually governing Heraclea until they attained their majority.[129]

---

[126] Memnon *FGrH* 3B, 434 F4. 8; Diodorus 16. 88. 5; 20. 77. 1. According to Memnon he was 55 at the time of his death, which was presumably from natural causes (Palladas [Paton 1916–18, 10. 54] attributed it to his obesity). The account in the Scholia to Ovid's *Ibis* (Ovid, *Ibis*, ed. R. Ellis [Oxford 1881], 61) that he was driven from power by a Mithridates and died abandoned by his followers on the island called Achilles' Race Course is the result of a misinterpretation of *Ibis* lines 329–330: *Aut ut Amastriacis quondam Lenaeus ab oris/ Nudus Achillea destituaris humo*. La Penna (1957, 78–80) showed that the lines actually refer to Mithridates VI of Pontus.

[127] Memnon *FGrH* 3B, 434 F4. 8.

[128] Memnon *FGrH* 3B, 434 F4. 8–9. Berve (1967 I, 322; II, 681) pointed out that the phrase *met a ten ekeinou ex anthrōpōn anachoresin* in F4. 9 implies deification. His cult was apparently still being observed in 284 (Memnon *FGrH* 3B, 434 F5. 3).

[129] Memnon *FGrH* 3B, 434 F4. 8; 5. 1.

CHAPTER VI

AMASTRIS, CLEARCHUS II, AND OXATHRES: THE END OF THE TYRANNY: 305 TO 281

The Regency of Amastris: 305 to *ca.* 300

Antigonus quickly took advantage of the death of Dionysius to reassert his influence in Heraclea while Amastris' government was still new and her power not yet fully consolidated. Memnon's phraseology is vague, but it seems to hint at a personal appearance in Heraclea during which Antigonus made a show of his concern for the continued welfare of the Heracleotes and of Dionysius' children as well. There was clearly no violence, but his declaration, and the influence of his friends within the city sufficed to accomplish his purpose. Unable to resist, Amastris acquiesced in the protectorate Antigonus offered – in the meantime awaiting the opportunity to escape from his influence.[1]

That opportunity came in 302. Antigonus' plans to reunite all of Alexander's empire under his control and his ultimatum to Cassander that year finally brought all his enemies – Ptolemy, Cassander, Lysimachus, and Seleucus – together in a new alliance.[2] In the summer of the same year, before Antigonus could move against them, Lysimachus invaded northwest Anatolia with an army of over 40,000 men.[3] Initially, much of western Anatolia went over to him,[4] and it was probably at this time that Amastris established contact with him. Her support for his cause only became public, however, in the winter of 302, when she furnished supplies to his army while it was in winter quarters in the Salonian Plain south of Heraclea. The alliance between Heraclea and Lysimachus was then formally sealed by the marriage of Amastris and the Thracian monarch soon after his army arrived in Paphlagonia.[5]

---

[1] Memnon *FGrH* 3B, 434 F4. 9.
[2] Diodorus 20. 106; 21. 1. 2.
[3] According to Plutarch (*Demetrius* 28. 3), Seleucus and Lysimachus had 64,000 infantry at Ipsus. Diodorus (20. 113. 4) gives Seleucus 20,000 infantry while about a third of 12,500 men sent by Cassander to Lysimachus in the winter of 302 reached him (Diodorus 20. 112), so that his original force was about 40,000 men.
[4] Diodorus 20. 107, 108. 3.
[5] Diodorus 20. 109. 6–7; Memnon *FGrH* 3B, 434 F4. 9.

158 PART I: BOOK

In Lysimachus Amastris had gained a powerful ally and assured Heraclea a privileged position in any future division of Antigonus' empire. Meanwhile, although Lysimachus like Antigonus before him professed that he entertained only the best of intentions toward the Heracleotes and his new wife and step-children, considerations of military expediency determined his treatment of the city. At the approach of Antigonus his gains in western Anatolia had evaporated and Demetrius' fleet held the Bosporus;[6] so continued control of Heraclea was vital to Lysimachus since it was the only port still open to him through which he could maintain contact between his army wintering in Paphlagonia and his European base. Lose it and he would be cut off from his allies, reinforcements, supplies, and money. Therefore, although he spent the winter with his troops, Lysimachus stationed a strong detachment of soldiers in Heraclea to strengthen the city's defenses and his own influence there.[7]

Early the next spring Lysimachus led his army south to effect a junction with that of Seleucus, which had spent the winter in Cappadocia after completing its long march from the borders of India.[8] But while Lysimachus was still in winter quarters Cassander had ordered his general Pleistarchus to reinforce him by leading to Asia a force of 12,000 infantry and 500 cavalry. The project ended disastrously, however, with only about a third of the troops managing to reach Lysimachus. Unable to cross at the Bosporus because of Demetrius' fleet, Pleistarchus led his force north along the Thracian coast to Odessus where, because of a lack of adequate shipping facilities, he had to divide his men into three sections for the voyage across the Black Sea to Heraclea. Only the first division reached its destination safely. Demetrius' cruisers intercepted and captured the second, and a sudden winter storm overwhelmed the third at sea causing severe losses of both ships and men. Even the flagship, a six, foundered, although Pleistarchus himself survived to reach Lysimachus after having been washed ashore near Heraclea.[9]

The combined armies of Lysimachus and Seleucus and that of Antigonus met at Ipsus in Phrygia in the spring of 301. At the end of the battle Antigonus' dreams of empire were in ruins, he himself lay dead on the field and Demetrius was in flight.[10] The division of his empire by his enemies followed, and in that process Lysimachus particularly profited, taking as his share of the spoils all of

---

[6] Diodorus 20. 108. 3, 111. 3, 112. 3.

[7] Diodorus 20. 112. 2. For the importance of Heraclea as a possible retreat, see Diodorus 20. 113. 1.

[8] Diodorus 20. 113. 4; Justin 15. 4. 21–23; Memnon *FGrH* 3B, 434 F4. 9.

[9] Diodorus 20. 112.

[10] Plutarch *Demetrius* 29–30; Appian *Syriaca* 55; Diodorus 21. 1. 2–4b.

VI: AMASTRIS, CLEARCHUS II, AND OXATHRES: THE END OF THE TYRANNY 159

Anatolia north of the Taurus Mountains.[11] Demetrius still held a number of the major Ionian cities,[12] and in the north Lysimachus' influence was still limited to Heraclea, but even so, his kingdom, which now extended from the Danube River to the passes of the Taurus range, was a formidable power and likely to become more so as he strengthened and expanded his hold on his new territories.

Amastris had remained in Heraclea during the campaign and only joined her husband after the battle of Ipsus, when Lysimachus summoned her to Sardis to take up her rightful place as his consort and queen.[13] Amastris could, at this point, well consider that the results of her marriage to Lysimachus were satisfactory. Because of it Heraclea had not suffered in the collapse of Antigonus' empire and, more important, her sons' positions were secure since the city was not a subject but a free ally bound to Lysimachus only by the ties established by his marriage to her. Hardly had she arrived at Sardis, however, than her position was undermined by the radical realignment of political forces in the Near East that occurred after the battle of Ipsus.

Only their common fear of Antigonus had united his enemies, so after his death the grand alliance disintegrated. In particular, relations between Lysimachus and Seleucus, whose territories now marched side by side along the Taurus range, quickly became strained and marked by mutual suspicion.[14] The first move was made by Lysimachus. Probably in 300 he and Ptolemy, who was already at odds with Seleucus because of his occupation of Coele Syria, concluded an alliance which was sealed by the marriage of Lysimachus to Ptolemy's daughter Arsinoe.[15] Although it is possible that Nymphis' assertion that Lysimachus actually loved Amastris may have some truth in it, mutual political advantage had provided the basis for their marriage.[16] In the new political situation, therefore, the Heracleote alliance, although still of value to Lysimachus, could not compare in importance with the alliance with Ptolemy, so he did not hesitate to divorce Amastris in order to fulfill the terms of the agreement he had made with the Egyptian monarch.[17]

---

[11] Geyer 1930, 10–11; Saitta 1955, 145–48.

[12] Manni 1951, 120–21; Saitta 1955, 146. Lysimachus seized Demetrius' holdings in Anatolia in 294 (Plutarch *Demetrius* 35. 3).

[13] Memnon *FGrH* 3B, 434 F4. 9.

[14] See Plutarch *Demetrius* 31; and Justin 15. 4. 24–25.

[15] Memnon *FGrH* 3B, 434 F4. 9 (he mistakenly calls her the daughter of Ptolemy II); Plutarch *Demetrius* 32. 3; Pausanias 1. 10. 3. For the date, see Seibert 1967, 74.

[16] Memnon *FGrH* 3B, 434 F4. 9; *cf.* Jacoby *FGrH* 3B *Texte*, 273 *ad* F4. 9.

[17] Memnon *FGrH* 3B, 434 F4. 9. On the basis of Polyaenus 6. 12, Wilcken (1894, 1750; *cf.* Melber, *apparatus ad* Polyaenus 6. 12) suggested that Amastris may have borne Lysimachus a son named Alexander. Jacoby's objection (*FGrH* 3B *Texte*, 273 *ad loc.*) that Pausanias (1. 10. 4) says that Alexander's mother was an Odrysian is not cogent since, as Geyer pointed out (1930, 30), Lysimachus could easily have had two sons named Alexander by different women.

160 PART I: BOOK

The parting was cordial, however, and in fact left undisturbed the alliance between Heraclea and Lysimachus. Amastris herself returned to Heraclea to resume her position as queen of the kingdom created by Dionysius.[18]

THE GOVERNMENT OF CLEARCHUS II AND OXATHRES: 301 TO 284

The return of Amastris to Heraclea in 300 created an impossible situation. While she was still at Sardis, Clearchus had already come of age and begun to govern Heraclea without the further assistance of his regency council.[19] Now the presence of his mother, the queen, effectively deprived him of his recently acquired authority. Had this arrangement continued for any length of time serious friction and bitterness would inevitably have developed between Amastris and her children. She eventually might even have had to deal with plots against her formed by partisans of her sons, perhaps even with their consent. Faced with this problem, Amastris resolved it soon after 300 by dividing the administration of her realm and allowing Clearchus and Oxathres, when he attained his majority, to govern Heraclea and Cierus under her authority.[20]

Amastris herself left Heraclea to make her residence at Sesamus, which had become the center (*akropolis*) of a new city named Amastris after her. She founded the city at this time by the union of Sesamus and the other three Paphlagonian cities conquered by Dionysius, Tium, Cromna, and Cytorus.[21] Despite the use of the verb *sunoikizō* by Memnon and Strabo to describe this act, Amastris did not follow the example of her Macedonian contemporaries who founded their name cities by destroying the cities that composed them and transferring their populations to the site of the new foundation. Instead, the four cities that formed Amastris continued to physically exist, but politically they were no longer separate *poleis* but rather districts of the new city of Amastris. Likewise, although their citizens remained in their old homes, they were now citizens of the new city of Amastris instead of Tians, Cromnians, and so on.[22] Although

[18] Memnon *FGrH* 3B, 434 F4. 9.

[19] Memnon *FGrH* 3B, 434 F5. 1.

[20] Memnon *FGrH* 3B, 434 F5. 4. The fact that the coins of Clearchus II and Oxathres bear only the inscription *HERAKLEŌTAN* (*Recueil* I.2, 351–52, nos. 42–46) while their mother's have the title *basilissa* (*Recueil* I.1, 135, nos. 1–3) indicates their relatively inferior position as compared to her.

[21] Memnon *FGrH* 3B, 434 F4. 9; Strabo 12. 3. 10; Ps.-Scymnus, lines 1005–1011 (= 961–967); Anonymous *Periplus* 8v20–23; Stephanus of Byzantium *s.v. Amastris*; *Schol. Ap. Rhod.* 195 *ad* 2. 941–942a; *Schol. ad Ovid Ibis*, lines 329–331.

[22] Continued existence of Cromna: Pliny *NH* 6. 5; Anonymous *Periplus* 8v23; Menippus *Periplus* D5817; Arrian *Periplus* 14. 1. Continued existence of Cytorus: Anonymous *Periplus* 8v24; Menippus *Periplus* D5818; Arrian *Periplus* 14. 2. For the status of Cromna, see Stephanus of Byzantium *s.v. Krōmna: tines de chōrion Amastridos* (*cf.* Anonymous *Periplus* 8v23, and

VI: AMASTRIS, CLEARCHUS II, AND OXATHRES: THE END OF THE TYRANNY 161

Tium withdrew from the new city shortly after its foundation and resumed her separate existence,[23] Amastris survived, grew, and prospered as a result of its splendid commercial location near Cape Carambis, the point at which ships struck out for or returned from the north coast of the Euxine.[24]

Even after Oxathres came of age sometime during the 290s, Clearchus continued to play the dominant role in the governance of Heraclea. Although he was an ambitious and aggressive ruler, his foreign policy had to be conducted within the limits imposed upon him by Amastris. As her representative he was committed to act in accordance with the alliance between Heraclea and Lysimachus that she had concluded at the time of her marriage and maintained after her divorce. Because of this alliance Clearchus personally accompanied Lysimachus in 292 on his ill-fated campaign across the Danube against the Getae which ended with the slaughter of his army and the capture of himself, his staff, and Clearchus by the Getan king Dromichaetes. When Dromichaetes released Lysimachus in return for the cession of his Transdanubian territory and a marriage alliance, Clearchus remained for a brief time with the Getan ruler as a hostage until the Thracian king procured his release also.[25] In spite of his captivity, relations between Clearchus and Lysimachus remained close. Accordingly, when Demetrius was building his great fleet in preparation for his invasion of Anatolia in 287, it was probably in Heracleote shipyards that Lysimachus had constructed a great galley to rival Demetrius' giant 15 and 16 called the Leontophorus, apparently a huge catamaran composed of two eights yoked together, manned by 1600 rowers, and carrying 1200 marines.[26]

Menippus *Periplus* D5817–5818, where the term *chōrion* is used for both Cromna and Cytorus). Sesamus was the heart of the city and later became identified with it (Strabo 12. 3.10; Pliny *NH* 6. 5). The artificiality of the new foundation is indicated by the known names of four of its tribes: Demetrias (Kalinka 1933, 67, no. 16, line 8); Dioscourias (Kalinka 1933, 68, no. 18, line 17); Asclepias (Kalinka 1933, 81, no. 39, line 3); and Amastrias (Kalinka 1933, 71, no. 19, lines 5–6). For the novelty of this foundation, see Robert 1937, 263, n. 1; and Magie 1950 II, 1193, n. 28, who suggested calling it a *sumpoliteia*.

[23] Strabo 12. 3. 10.

[24] Sesamus' strong defensive position on its landward side (*cf.* Ainsworth 1842 I, 54) probably led Amastris to choose it as the center of her new city. As for the site's commercial possibilities, the epitaph of a Cromnian at Panticapaeum (*IOSPE* 2 291 = *CIRB* 199), the amphora on the coins of Cromna (*Recueil* I.1, 1158, nos. 6–9), and the drinking cup on those of Sesamus (*Recueil* I1, 177, nos. 6–7) indicate that trade between them and the north coast of the Black Sea already existed before the foundation of Amastris.

[25] Memnon *FGrH* 3B, 434 F5. 1. For the date of Lysimachus' campaign against the Getes, see Beloch 1912–27 IV.2, 248; and for the campaign itself, see Geyer 1930, 15–16, and Saitta 1955, 86–89.

[26] Memnon *FGrH* 3B, 434 F8. 5. The reconstruction is that proposed by Casson (1971, 112–14). For the circumstances of its construction, see Tarn 1913, 131, n. 42, and Casson 1971, 138–39 and 138, n. 1. This ship is probably behind Nicephorus' statement (Letter 45. 163) that historians say that eights and tens were first built at Heraclea.

162   PART I: BOOK

In Anatolia, Clearchus' ties with Amastris and Lysimachus meant of necessity that Heraclea incurred the hostility of Zipoetes in Bithynia[27] and Mithridates Ctistes, whose attempts to expand the principality he had carved out around Mount Olgassys in Paphlagonia north to the Black Sea threatened the security of Amastris.[28] Although Clearchus probably assisted his mother to defend her eastern frontier against Mithridates,[29] the main theater for his military activities was in the west where he actively supported Lysimachus in his long and ultimately futile attempt to subdue Bithynia.

Because of the expansionist policies of Zipoetes, Bithynia constituted a formidable danger to the cities of Hellespontine Phrygia and, together with her ally in Europe, Byzantium, she formed a block of hostile territory dividing the Asiatic and European halves of Lysimachus' kingdom, and denying his safe use of the Bosporus.[30] The history of Lysimachus' attempt to eliminate this bottleneck is lost, but the fighting was fierce with outbreaks as late as the middle of the 280s.[31] According to Memnon, one of his generals was killed during an abortive invasion of Bithynia, another routed, and even Lysimachus himself finally suffered defeat at Zipoetes' hands.[32] Lysimachus' failure was total and humiliating. Nicaea fell to Zipoetes[33] and only the destruction of Astacus by the Thracian monarch prevented its permanent occupation also.[34] As Lysimachus' principal ally in the struggle Heraclea also suffered severely as a result

[27] Memnon *FGrH* 3B, 434 F6. 3.

[28] Diodorus 20. 111. 4; Appian *Mithridatica* 9; Strabo 12. 3. 41; Plutarch *Demetrius* 4. 3. Ed. Meyer 1879, 40, and Ernst Meyer 1925a, 117, point out that the surrender of Amastris to Ariobarzanes after Corupedium (Memnon *FGrH* 3B, 434 F9. 4) presupposes that the coast east of that city was already in Pontic hands.

[29] Military activity by Amastris, probably against Mithridates, is implied by the seated female figure holding a Nike that appears on the city's coins (*Recueil* I.1, 135, no. 3). Amastris and Lysimachus are probably intended by Memnon's statement (*FGrH* 3B, 434 F5. 1) that Clearchus II waged war in 'alliance with others'.

[30] Plutarch *Greek Questions* 49, 302E–F. Plutarch's reference to Zipoetes as king would date the alliance to after 297/6 if we could be sure that the assumption of the royal title was the reason for the beginning of the Bithynian era in that year (Reinach 1888, 95; Perl 1968). Beloch (1912–27 IV.2, 234, n. 1) said, however, that Diodorus (19. 60. 3) also called Zipoetes king in 315 and suggested that the title might, therefore, be traditional in Bithynia as it was in Thrace.

[31] Justin 16. 3. 3; Trogus Prologue 16. For the date, see the Appendix.

[32] Memnon *FGrH* 3B, 434 F12. 5.

[33] G. Mendel (1904, 380–82) published the epitaph of a Bithynian named Menas who was killed at Corupedium (*cf.* Keil 1892; and Beloch 1912–27 IV.2, 458–61). Since the inscription was found at Nicaea and Menas (line 12) is said to have died fighting for his *patrēs*, Nicaea must have been Bithynian in 281 (*cf.* Ernst Meyer 1925a, 109–10).

[34] Strabo 12. 4. 2. Ernst Meyer (1925a, 109–10) pointed out that its destruction by Lysimachus implied a prior seizure by Zipoetes. This capture may be behind Pausanias' peculiar statement (5. 12. 7) that Zipoetes founded Nicomedia, the successor to Astacus (Memnon *FGrH* 3B, 434 F12. 1).

VI: AMASTRIS, CLEARCHUS II, AND OXATHRES: THE END OF THE TYRANNY 163

of the debacle. Sometime before 284 Zipoetes invaded her territory; although Clearchus managed to save Heraclea itself, the Bithynian monarch reconquered Thynian Thrace and drove Heracleote power from the valley of the Hypius by bringing the city of Cierus under his influence.[35]

During the 17 years Clearchus and Oxathres governed Heraclea the city continued to grow and prosper economically.[36] These same years, however, saw the tyranny gradually lose the broad base of popular support that Timotheus and Dionysius had regained for it. Abroad, the brothers' military activity had resulted only in humiliation and severe losses for Heraclea, especially in the west where by 284 the city's border with the hostile kingdom of Bithynia stood east of the Hypius for the first time since the early 5th century. At home, their harsh and arbitrary manner of rule alienated their subjects – including, judging from subsequent events, many of those who stood closest to the government – and provoked comparisons with the gentle and gracious style of their father, which were at once nostalgic and bitterly critical of the present regime.[37]

Their tactless behavior eroded their authority, but it was the death of Amastris under mysterious circumstances during a sea voyage about 284 which brought their ruin.[38] Not surprisingly, even after her departure from Heraclea, considerable tension continued to characterize relations between Amastris and her sons;[39] so it is understandable that immediately after her death rumors began to circulate charging that she had been murdered on orders from Clearchus and Oxathres.[40] Whether true or not they found wide acceptance and the revulsion produced by the brothers' alleged crime

---

[35] Zipoetes is presumably among those Memnon says (*FGrH* 3B, 434 F5. 1) attacked Heraclea. Loss of Cierus and Thynias: Memnon *FGrH* 3B, 434 F9. 4. Memnon (*FGrH* 3B, 434 F5. 4) indicates that the city had been lost before 284; the fact that Cierus signed the treaty with the Galatians in 279 (Memnon *FGrH* 3B, 434 F11. 2) implies that Cierus was an ally of Bithynia and not a subject.

[36] Indicative of Heraclea's wealth is the gold she sent Byzantium in 279 (Memnon *FGrH* 3B, 434 F11. 1). Likewise, the expansion of a money economy in Heraclea during the early 3rd century is revealed by the fact that the city first issued bronze coins on a large scale at this time (*Recueil* I.2, 353–54, nos. 49–53; *cf.* Kapossy 1971, who describes a recently discovered hoard of 68 bronze coins bearing 14 hitherto unknown mint marks, i.e. new issues). The competition of Thasian wine is implied by the adoption of a type of amphora modeled on those of Thasos during the early 3rd century (Zeest 1948, 51; Canarache 1957, 195) but is unlikely to have seriously affected Heraclea's prosperity.

[37] Memnon *FGrH* 3B, 434 F5. 2.

[38] Memnon *FGrH* 3B, 434 F5. 2. For the date, see the Appendix.

[39] The tension is probably hinted at in Memnon's reference (*FGrH* 3B, 434 F5. 2) to *tēn gar mētera mēden peri autous mega plēmmelēsasan*. For a similar view, see Beloch 1912–27 IV.1, 233.

[40] B. Lenk (1928, 20) first pointed to the suspicious circumstances surrounding Amastris' death.

164   PART I: BOOK

completed the disenchantment of their subjects and left them weak and vulnerable. Although his friendship with Clearchus was of long standing,[41] Lysimachus did not scruple to take advantage of his ally's weakness. Influential figures within Heraclea had probably already indicated to him that his intervention would not be unwelcome,[42] and the tyrant's wealth and the chance of bringing Heraclea and the rest of Amastris' realm under his direct control were temptations too strong to resist. Lysimachus, however, managed to keep his plans secret. When, therefore, he and a force of soldiers arrived at Heraclea for the ostensible purpose of assisting the brothers, perhaps by helping them to suppress their critics, and to pay his respects to the memory of his friend Dionysius, Clearchus and Oxathres readily admitted him and his men into the city. But once safely inside Lysimachus quickly dropped his mask and ordered his hosts seized for the murder of their mother. Taken by surprise, Clearchus and Oxathres could offer no resistance; their trials followed immediately. When they were convicted, Lysimachus had first Clearchus and then Oxathres executed while he appropriated their fortune for his own purposes.[43] Eighty years of rule by the family of Clearchus I had come to an end, but for Heraclea this meant only a change of masters and the loss of the city's independence.

Lysimachus remained in Heraclea only long enough to complete the process of annexation and organize the administration of his new territories. As the basis of the new organization Lysimachus retained the administrative pattern established by Amastris, according to which Heraclea was governed separately from Tium and Amastris. In accordance with his normal policy, Lysimachus allowed all three cities to retain their own political institutions unchanged and to enjoy a considerable degree of internal autonomy.[44] This autonomy was tempered in Amastris by the appointment of a royal governor in the person of

---

[41] Memnon *FGrH* 3B, 434 F5. 3.

[42] This is suggested by the note that after the death of Clearchus II and Oxathres Lysimachus allowed the Heracleotes to set up the democracy they desired (*thou ephiento*: Memnon *FGrH* 3B, 434 F5. 3) and by the generally favorable treatment he receives in Memnon.

[43] Memnon *FGrH* 434 F5. 3; Justin 16. 3. 3; Trogus Prologue 16. The reference to a war against Heraclea in Justin (*Inde Thraciae ac deinceps Heracleae bellum intulerat*) is probably the result of Justin's compressing Trogus' account of Lysimachus' actions in Bithynia and Heraclea into one sentence. Prologue 16 speaks only of Lysimachus' occupying the city (*in Ponto Heracleam occuparit; occupavit urbem*). One indication of Lysimachus' attempt to court Amastris' supporters in Heraclea by posing as her avenger is provided by the fact that his mint at Heraclea issued a copper coin with her portrait on it after her death (Mamroth 1949). For the date of these events, see the Appendix.

[44] For Lysimachus' policy toward the Greek cities, see Bengtson 1937, 215–19.

VI: AMASTRIS, CLEARCHUS II, AND OXATHRES: THE END OF THE TYRANNY 165

Eumenes, the brother of Philetaerus of Tium,[45] but no such action was taken in the case of Heraclea, although that city was Lysimachus' chief prize and soon became an important administrative and military center, the site of a royal mint,[46] and home port of a strong division of his fleet which included the Leontophorus and a number of fives and sixes.[47] He apparently placed a garrison in the tyrant's old fortress on the acropolis, but its commander's authority was solely military in character –[48] Lysimachus acceded to the desires of his Heracleote friends and allowed the citizens to form a democratic government which would govern the city in his name.[49]

The position of the new government, dependent as it was for its existence on a concession that could be retracted by Lysimachus at any time, was weak; in fact, it remained in power for only a brief time. Immediately on his return to Europe the future of Heraclea along with that of Tium and Amastris became an issue in the bitter struggle over his succession that divided his court in the 280s. Arsinoe, who was striving to displace Agathocles, the eldest son and heir apparent, and secure the throne for her own children, began pressing Lysimachus to make her a gift of these cities.[50] According to Memnon, Arsinoe's interest in these cities was roused by the praise Lysimachus lavished on them. Indeed, from her point of view, possession of them would give her a compact and wealthy base of power in Anatolia to which she and her sons might retreat or from which a revolt might be organized should her schemes fail.[51] For a time Lysimachus refused to thus betray his supporters in Heraclea, but eventually he yielded to Arsinoe's persuasive arguments and granted her request. For her part, now that Heraclea was hers to rule as she pleased, Arsinoe ignored completely the privileges previously conceded to the Heracleotes and instead appointed an individual by the name of Heracleides of Cyme, a man of severe character and considerable ability who was devoted to her interest, to act as her governor of Heraclea.[52]

---

[45] Memnon *FGrH* 3B, 434 F9. 4. For the identification, see Hansen 1947, 16–17. He was most likely *epistates* of the city, a post that combined command of its garrison with supervisory powers over its internal affairs (Préaux 1954, 98–99; Jones 1940, 105–07). In view of the bad feelings between Arsinoe and Eumenes' brother Philetaerus (Pausanias 1. 10. 4), he is not likely to have been appointed after she gained control of Amastris.

[46] Thompson 1968, 166, 178.

[47] This is the most probable explanation of how Heraclea was in a position to gain possession of these ships after Lysimachus' death (Memnon *FGrH* 3B, 434 F8. 5).

[48] Memnon *FGrH* 3B, 434 F6. 2.

[49] Memnon *FGrH* 3B, 434 F5. 3.

[50] Memnon *FGrH* 3B, 434 F5. 5.

[51] Memnon *FGrH* 3B, 434 F5. 5. She also received control of Cassandrea about this time (Justin 24. 2. 1; 24. 3. 3).

[52] Memnon *FGrH* 3B, 434 F5. 4–5.

166 PART I: BOOK

The Administration of Heracleides of Cyme: 284/3 to 281

Heracleides administered Heraclea for about two years, a period in which, according to Memnon, the Heracleotes lost the happiness that had recently appeared to be in their grasp.[53] The political atmosphere within the city quickly came to resemble that during the worst days of the tyranny. With the support of Lysimachus' garrison on the acropolis, which had been placed under his authority, Heracleides governed Heraclea with a heavy hand. Heracleotes who fell afoul of the governor for their suspected opposition to the interests of his mistress, or any other reason, were quickly accused and placed on trial by Heracleides – and not a few suffered stiff punishment or exile as a result.[54]

Meanwhile, political conditions in the Near East changed to the advantage of Heraclea. Following Arsinoe's triumph and the execution of Agathocles by Lysimachus at her instigation in 282, revolts broke out among the Greek cities of Asia.[55] Seleucus then moved west to attack Lysimachus before he could restore order among his subjects; the armies of the last two survivors of Alexander's generation collided at Corupedium in Lydia in February 281. At the end of the battle Seleucus was master of all of Alexander's empire save Egypt and Lysimachus lay dead on the field, struck down by a javelin hurled by a Heracleote named Malacon[56] serving in Seleucus' army.

Despite widespread discontent in Heraclea, Heracleides had been able to prevent the city from going over to Seleucus during the campaign, although Zipoetes to the west did so[57] and Tium to the east of the city seized the opportunity to regain her independence.[58] After the news of Corupedium reached the

---

[53] Memnon *FGrH* 3B, 434 F5.

[54] Memnon *FGrH* 3B, 434 F5.

[55] Memnon *FGrH* 3B, 434 F5. 6; Justin 17. 1. 4; Trogus Prologue 17; Pausanias 1. 10. 3; Appian *Syriaca* 64; Porphyry *FGrH* 2B, 260 F3. 8. For the date, Heinen 1972, 17–20. For the revolts, see Memnon *FGrH* 3B, 434 F5. 7; Justin 17. 1. 6–8; Pausanias 1. 10. 4–5. Agathocles' support in Asia was probably based on his having administered that area for his father (*cf.* Bengtson 1937, 227–29).

[56] Memnon *FGrH* 3B, 434 F5. 7; Justin 17. 2. 1; Trogus Prologue 17; Appian *Syriaca* 62; Pausanias 1. 10. 5; Porphyry *FGrH* 2B, 260 F3. 8; Polybius 18. 51. 4; Nepos *De Regibus* 3. 2. For the date of the battle, see Heinen 1972, 20–24; and for its location, see Keil 1892, 260–61, and Heinen 1972, 28. Nothing further is known about Malacon unless he is to be identified with the Malacon whose name appears on an early 3rd-century Heracleote amphora recently discovered in the Taman Peninsula (Beletsky and Yakovenko 1969, 160) which would indicate that he returned to Heraclea after the battle and probably held the office of *agoranomos*.

[57] Menas inscription, lines 12–13 (see above n. 33; Keil 1892, 261, and Heinen 1972, 36).

[58] The *ELEUTHERIA* series of coins belongs here (*Recueil* I.3, 615; 616, no. 4). The fact that Tium signed the treaty with the Galatians in 279 (Memnon *FGrH* 3B, 434 F11. 2) indicates that Tium was not subject to Zipoetes as suggested by, for example, Schneiderwirth 1885, 6, and Ernst Meyer 1925a, 110. More probable is the suggestion of Vitucci (1953, 22, n. 4) that a local dynast seized control of the city as Eumenes did at Amastris (Memnon *FGrH* 3B, 434 F9. 4).

VI: AMASTRIS, CLEARCHUS II, AND OXATHRES: THE END OF THE TYRANNY   167

Pontus, however, his position became precarious. Not only was he isolated, but now that Lysimachus was dead and Arsinoe a fugitive[59] Heracleides was no longer able to continue the pay of the garrison on which his power and security depended.[60] Meanwhile, the fact that it was a Heracleote who killed Lysimachus emboldened his subjects. Nevertheless, Heracleides decided to maintain his control of Heraclea: when a delegation of Heracleotes offered him splendid gifts and a promise of safe conduct out of the city if he would agree to its becoming free, he rejected their proposal out of hand and seized and severely punished the group's leaders. But his bravado was in vain. Rebuffed by Heracleides, the Heracleotes approached the *phrourarchs* and easily concluded an agreement with them according to which the soldiers would receive their back pay and enjoy the privileges of *isopoliteia* in Heraclea. Heracleides' arrest and imprisonment followed swiftly, and then in delirious relief at their liberation the Heracleotes rushed to Clearchus' citadel on the acropolis, the most visible and hated symbol of their recent subjection, and leveled it to the ground. A new government, probably a democracy, was installed and shortly thereafter Heracleides was freed and allowed to leave Heraclea.[61]

AN END AND A BEGINNING

The fall of Heracleides opened a new period in the history of Heraclea. Eighty-three years after Clearchus had founded the tyranny a free government was once more in full control of Heraclea, but the city it ruled and the political environment in which it had to survive differed greatly from those he had known. The long decades of rule by his dynasty had effectively consolidated the changes in Heracleote society that had resulted from his revolution, so the leadership of the new government was composed of the descendants of his partisans.[62] Moreover, although Heraclea had temporarily lost all her foreign possessions, she was still the wealthiest and strongest of the south Pontic cities, and this was particularly true now that the soldiers of the garrison had been added to her citizen levy and Lysimachus' ships, including the great Leontophorus, to her fleet.

Yet Heraclea was only a third-class power compared to the great monarchies of the period. The death of Lysimachus had enabled her to regain her freedom; retaining it was the one overriding goal of her new leaders. To that

---

[59] Polyaenus 8. 57.

[60] Memnon *FGrH* 3B, 434 F6. 2.

[61] Memnon *FGrH* 3B, 434 F6. 1–2. For archaeological evidence of the destruction, see Hoepfner 1966, 25.

[62] This follows from the terms of the final settlement with the exiles (Memnon *FGrH* 3B, 434 F7. 3).

168   PART I: BOOK

end they had, immediately after deposing Heracleides, appointed Phocritus, a Heracleote, to serve as *epimelētēs* of the city and dispatched an embassy to announce their recognition of his suzerainty to Seleucus personally.[63] Hardly had their decision to recognize Seleucus become known, however, than Zipoetes, whose own alliance with him had foundered after Corupedium invaded and began ravaging Heracleote territory.[64] His attack was repulsed, but worse was still to come.

About the same time that the Heracleote embassy left for Seleucus' camp he sent Aphrodisius, his *doikētēs*, to exact recognition of his authority from the cities of Hellespontine Phrygia and the south coast of the Pontus.[65] Although his demands were acceded to without question elsewhere, this clearly was not the case at Heraclea – even before the arrival of the city's embassy Seleucus had received from Aphrodisius a report stating that its attitude was unsatisfactory.[66] The nature of the difficulty is not stated, but it probably concerned the appointment of Phocritus as *epimelētēs* and its implications: *epimelētēs* was one of the titles of a royal governor of a city.[67] The fact that the Heracleotes chose Phocritus, one of their fellow citizens, for such a post could only mean that their recognition of Seleucus' authority was purely formal. Unlike Lysimachus, he would have the semblance of authority within Heraclea, but no real power, since his representative would be a Heracleote chosen by and responsible to his fellow Heracleotes instead of Seleucus. Such conditions could not be accepted. When, therefore, the Heracleote embassy was presented to him, Seleucus received it with obvious contempt and sought only to terrify it into submission by his furious threats. The philosopher, Chamaeleon, one of the ambassadors, tried to impress him with Heraclea's strength by menacingly replying that Heracles was the stronger, but Seleucus could not understand his Doric and instead angrily terminated the audience.[68]

The ambassadors chose to go into exile rather than return home to report the failure of their mission, so some time elapsed before the Heracleotes learned of Seleucus' hostile attitude toward them. But when the information finally did reach Heraclea, preparations were made to receive a possible attack and embassies were sent to arrange alliances with the cities of Byzantium and

---

[63] Memnon *FGrH* 3B, 434 F6. 2.

[64] Memnon *FGrH* 3B, 434 F6. 3.

[65] Memnon *FGrH* 3B, 434 F7. 1. For the geographical implications of *huper* in Memnon, see Memnon *FGrH* 3B, 434 F20. 1.

[66] Memnon *FGrH* 3B, 434 F7. 1.

[67] Préaux 1954, 98–99.

[68] Memnon *FGrH* 3B, 434 F7. 1 (= Chamaeleon, F1 [Wehrli]). For the identification of the ambassador and the philosopher, see Wehrli, 69 *ad* Chamaeleon F1, and Jacoby *FGrH* 3B *Texte*, 274 *ad* F7. 1.

VI: AMASTRIS, CLEARCHUS II, AND OXATHRES: THE END OF THE TYRANNY 169

Chalcedon and with Mithridates Ctistes.[69] While the stage was thus being set for the struggle between Heraclea and the Seleucids that would last for at least a quarter of a century,[70] a reconciliation with the descendants of the men exiled by Clearchus finally took place.

Negotiations concerning the terms on which it might be possible for the exiles to return to Heraclea were undertaken with the city's new government about this time by one of their leading figures, the future statesman and distinguished historian Nymphis, the son of Xenagoras.[71] Initially, the new Heracleote leadership had been almost as little inclined to consider the return of the exiles as the tyrants had been before them, since the exiles' claims threatened their own wealth and position. The hostility of Seleucus, however, and probably also the memory of the difficulties the existence of the exiles had caused for Dionysius, induced them to moderate their attitude. Nymphis was made to understand that there would be no difficulty if the exiles, for their part, would agree to abandon all claims to the estates confiscated from their ancestors. Time and events had eroded both the exiles' numbers and their hopes so that Nymphis easily persuaded them to accept the conditions offered. When they reentered Heraclea soon afterwards, the Heracleotes greeted them graciously and undertook to provide them with everything necessary to begin new and prosperous lives.[72] As the man responsible for this event, Nymphis henceforth played an important role in the city's government. With the return of the exiles and their reintegration into Heracleote society, the period that had begun with the seizure of power by Clearchus 83 years before finally drew to a close.

---

[69] Memnon *FGrH* 3B, 434 F7. 1–2. Mithridates had already repulsed an attack by one of Seleucus' generals (Trogus Prologue 17) and proclaimed himself king (Perl 1968, 326–29).

[70] The last recorded confrontation took place about 250 (Memnon *FGrH* 3B, 434 F15; for the date, see Niese 1893–1903 II, 138).

[71] Memnon *FGrH* 3B, 434 F7. 3. For his later career, see Memnon *FGrH* 3B, 434 F16. 3.

[72] Memnon *FGrH* 3B, 434 F7. 3–4.

CONCLUSION

281 marked the beginning of a new era for Heraclea. The death of Lysimachus at Corupedium freed the city from foreign suzerainty for the first time in almost three centuries. Heraclea was prosperous and militarily strong. The problem of the exiles, the most dangerous legacy of her tyrants, had been solved by Nymphis' astute diplomacy, thus depriving her enemies both of any pretext for intervention in the city's affairs and of allies to assist them. In the future a new problem would dominate the policies of Heraclea's leaders, the preservation of her newfound independence in the face of the threats to be posed by the ambitions of the Seleucids and the other heirs of Lysimachus' Asian domains.

The emergence of Heraclea as an independent power in northern Anatolia was a significant development in Greek, not merely Pontic, history. In her struggle to maintain her freedom during the 3rd century, Heraclea would be instrumental in assisting the other cities and peoples of northern Anatolia to also assert their independence. Again and again it would be Heraclea's military forces or diplomats that would frustrate the plans of the Seleucids to extend their power over the whole of the Anatolian peninsula. The purpose of this monograph was to trace the rise of Heraclea to this influential position. The rich remains of Heracleote historiography enabled this to be done in considerable detail, and at the same time they illuminated conditions in one of the least known areas of the Greek world, the south coast of the Black Sea.

The process of emergence as revealed in this study was long and difficult. The site of Heraclea, with its fertile soil, abundant fishing, and superb commercial location, must have seemed a guarantee of the success of the new city, but for many the hope of land and a better life that attracted settlers to the colony proved empty. A century of struggle with the Mariandynoi was required merely to secure the physical survival of the city. Internally, *stasis* racked Heraclea repeatedly. Social divisions, widened and embittered as growing population outstripped the available land in the 6th and early 5th century, became great chasms with the conquest of the Mariandynoi and the appropriation of their land by Heraclea's aristocracy. Four governments fell victim to revolution before Clearchus put an end to free political life for 80 years in 364. Tyranny finally brought the city political stability, but these centuries saw no satisfactory solution to Heraclea's social problems, as can be seen from her extensive colonial activity and the steady rise in the number of Heracleotes who chose to live abroad.

172 PART I: BOOK

The harsh realities of life in northern Anatolia gave a special character to the Hellenism of early Heraclea. For a small *polis* isolated amidst numerous and hostile natives, the slogans of 5th-century Aegean Greece had little meaning. The homeland Greeks, emboldened by the defeat of the invasion of 480, might scorn the Persians as Asiatic aggressors, enemies of freedom; the Heracleotes found in the Great King their only possible protector against the Mariandynoi or the even more formidable Bithynians. Accordingly, while the Greeks of the Aegean became ever more restive under Persian rule, recognition of Persian suzerainty in return for a guarantee of Heraclea's internal autonomy became the cornerstone of Heracleote foreign policy – a foreign policy, indeed, that survived the fall of Persia in the form of alliances with the new masters of Anatolia, Antigonus the One-Eyed and Lysimachus. Only Seleucus' refusal after Corupedium to respect the city's traditional privileges forced her leaders to formulate new guidelines for foreign affairs.

If the isolation of the frontier forced Heraclea to embrace Persian overlordship, it also fostered cultural conservatism. By itself, the haphazardness of communication between Heraclea and the Aegean contributed to this by enabling archaic usages to survive there long after they disappeared in the homeland. An even more potent factor, however, was the peculiar relationship that developed between the Heracleotes and the Mariandynoi. The conquest and enslavement of the Mariandynoi divided Heraclea into two separate societies. To be Greek was to belong to the society of masters, not that of slaves. A heightened sense of Greek identity and, judging from Posidonius' picture of Heraclea's subjects as contented 'Sambos', a denigration of the Mariandynoi as racial inferiors followed. Their subjects' seeming acquiescence in their slavery encouraged the latter attitude; the former was actively cultivated. Saga was rewritten to justify Greek domination of Mariandynia and to erase as much as possible any reminders of Mariandynian influence within Heraclea herself. Ties with European Greece were maintained and strengthened. The Panhellenic shrines of Olympia and Delphi were patronized and used as stages to display Heraclea's achievements to the Greek world at large. The sons of the city's aristocracy increasingly were sent to the Aegean for their education and Heraclea offered a warm welcome to such homeland intellectuals and artists who chose to visit it. Yet for most of this period Heraclea remained a provincial city whose cultural achievement was mediocre at best. The roll call of 5th- and 4th-century Heracleote intellectuals is impressive, but the evidence indicates that prior to the return of Heracleides Ponticus from Athens in 338 they all did their work in the Aegean. As in foreign affairs, so in culture, Heraclea's great period was only beginning in 281.

APPENDIX

THE DATE OF LYSIMACHUS' OCCUPATION OF HERACLEA

Modern scholars are divided in their opinions between 289/8 (or 288/7) and *ca.* 284 as the date when Lysimachus occupied Heraclea.[1] The majority support 289/8 and cite as the authority for their position Diodorus' statement that on the death of Dionysius in 305 Clearchus and Oxathres succeeded him and ruled for 17 years.[2] The minority base their interpretation on the apparently contradictory evidence of Memnon and Trogus/Justin.[3]

According to Memnon, Lysimachus was king of Macedon at the time he seized Heraclea.[4] Moreover, although allowance must be made for possible distortion resulting from the brevity of Photius' epitome, he appears to imply that the execution of Agathocles took place within a relatively short time after the fall of Clearchus and Oxathres.[5] Since Lysimachus became king of Macedon in 284[6] and his son's death occurred during 282, his actions at Heraclea should, in Memnon's view, belong to the period between these two events – most likely to late 284 so as to allow for the interval indicated by him before Lysimachus gave the city to Arsinoe and for the administration of it by Heracleides of Cyme. The death of Amastris presumably occurred earlier in 284, as suggested in the text, or possibly even in 285.

Trogus/Justin fully agree with this version and provide further chronological precision. From the Prologue it is clear that Trogus' 16th book treated the histories of Demetrius and Lysimachus at length and that of Ptolemy I briefly during the period after the death of Cassander in 296. The Prologue contains the following summary of the account of Lysimachus: *Ut Lysimachus in Ponto captus ac missus a Dromichaete rursus in Asiae civitates quae sub Demetrio fuerant, et in Ponto Heracleam occuparit. Repetitae inde Bithyniae et Heracleoticae origines.* Lysimachus was captured by Dromichaetes in 292, so that his

---

[1] E.g. Niese 1893–1903 I, 396 n. 6; Tarn 1913, 117; Saitta 1955, 127–28; Geyer 1930, 16. 287: Beloch 1912–27 III.2, 95, IV.1, 233, n. 1; Berve 1967 I, 322–23; Lenk 1928, 20, n. 2.

[2] Diodorus 20. 77. 1.

[3] E.g. Apel 1910, 84–88; Schneiderwirth 1882, 37 (286 on the mistaken belief that Lysimachus became king of Macedon in that year).

[4] Memnon *FGrH* 3B, 434 F5. 3.

[5] Memnon *FGrH* 3B, 434 F5. 5–6.

[6] Beloch 1912–27 IV.2, 107.

174 PART I: BOOK

operations against the cities in Asia controlled by Demetrius and Heraclea must have occurred after that date. But since he had already seized Demetrius' Anatolian possessions in 294[7] and still controlled them in 289/8,[8] these cities can only be the ones that defected to Demetrius during his invasion of Asia in 287.[9] Their reoccupation would have taken place after that date so that, according to the Prologue, the *terminus post quem* for the seizure of Heraclea is 287. If we turn to Justin, further exactitude can be obtained from the following passage: *Victor Lysimachus, pulso Pyrrho, Macedoniam occupaverat. Inde Thraciae ac deinceps Heracleae bellum intulerat.*[10] As already mentioned, Lysimachus became king of Macedon in 284 and Justin's use of *inde* and *deinceps* indicates that his actions against Thrace – that is, Bithynia – and Heraclea were chronologically subsequent to that event.

Confirmation of the above is furnished by the following considerations. The latest events mentioned in Prologue 16 and Justin are the deaths of Demetrius and Ptolemy I, both of which took place in the year 283.[11] A priori, we would expect that Trogus carried his history of Lysimachus to approximately the same point; that is, the latest event of his reign mentioned in book 16, the occupation of Heraclea, should be roughly contemporary with these occurrences instead of having happened almost six years earlier. That this is actually the case is indicated by the fact that book 17 began with the death of Agathocles, which according to Justin took place *brevi post tempore*, a strange expression if Heraclea was captured in 289.[12] Trogus/Justin, therefore, just as Memnon does, requires a date about 284. Since, moreover, Memnon and Trogus followed the contemporary Heracleote historian Nymphis, their evidence should be preferred to that of Diodorus, whose references to the tyranny seem to be taken from a now unidentifiable chronological handbook.[13]

Any attempt to explain the discrepancy between Memnon and Trogus/Justin on the one hand and Diodorus on the other is bound to be somewhat speculative,

---

[7] Plutarch *Demetrius* 35. 3.

[8] *SIG*³ 1 368.

[9] Plutarch *Demetrius* 46. 3–4.

[10] Justin 16. 3. 3. The identification of *Thraciae* with Bithynia is assured by the reference to *Bithyniae ... origines* in Trogus Prologue 16.

[11] Trogus Prologue 16; Justin 16. 2. 6–7; Beloch 1912–27 IV.2, 169–70.

[12] Trogus Prologue 17; Justin 17. 1. 4. Justin, it is true, actually opens book 17 with a reference to an earthquake that leveled Lysimachia 22 years after its foundation in 309/8 (Diodorus 20. 29. 1; Marmor Parium *FGrH* 2B, 239 FB19), which he says occurred *per idem ferme tempus* (*sc.* as the capture of Heraclea; 17. 1. 1). At first sight this would suggest 287/6 as the date, but, as *ferme* indicates, the synchronism is only approximate. Moreover, the earthquake was only mentioned because it seemed a portent of the disaster that would overwhelm Lysimachus (17. 1. 3), i.e. it is introductory to the death of Agathocles which was the true beginning of book 17.

[13] Schwartz 1905, 664–69.

APPENDIX: THE DATE OF LYSIMACHUS' OCCUPATION OF HERACLEA   175

but there is a strong possibility that it is actually only apparent. The key is the fact that Diodorus' source for the Heracleote tyrants clearly omitted Amastris. Since Satyrus was also not named and his years of power were included with those of Timotheus,[14] a similar explanation for the exclusion of Amastris is, at first sight, attractive. The cases, however, are not the same. Satyrus ruled only as regent for Timotheus, but Amastris was queen in her own right as well as head of her sons' regency council. They only began to actually rule when Clearchus came of age about 301. Fortunately, the manner in which Diodorus dealt with this type of situation is readily ascertainable. Thus, although both Leucon I[15] and Paerisades I[16] of Bosporus ruled jointly with their children, Diodorus only reckons their sons' reigns from the date of their fathers' deaths.[17] Similarly, Diodorus' figures for the length of the reign of Dionysius of Heraclea do not include the years of his coregency with his brother Timotheus.[18] If we assume that the same was true in the case of Clearchus and Oxathres and their mother, then the contradiction between Diodorus and the other sources disappears. Their 17 years would have been calculated, as we would expect, from Clearchus' attaining his majority in 301. Diodorus, misled by the omission of Amastris by his source, mistakenly assumed that Clearchus and Oxathres' reign began immediately after death of their father and entered his notice about them accordingly.[19]

[14] Diodorus 16. 88. 5; *cf.* Berve 1967 II, 681.

[15] *SIG*[3] 1 212, line 1.

[16] *IOSPE* 2 1, line 2 (= *CIRB* 1, line 2).

[17] Diodorus 16. 31. 6; 20. 22. 1–2; 20. 100. 7.

[18] Diodorus 16. 88. 5; 20. 77. 1.

[19] Three further points tend to confirm this position: (1) the date Clearchus came of age is emphasized in Memnon (*FGrH* 3B, 434 F5. 1); (2) the method of calculating the length of reigns described above was used by Nymphis (*cf. FGrH* 3B, 432 F10), the most probable source for a Hellenistic chronographer to use for the Heracleote tyrants; and (3) the type of misplacements postulated for Clearchus and Oxathres do occur in Diodorus' treatment of the Spartocids (*cf.* Werner 1955, 416, 418–21).

BIBLIOGRAPHY

Ainsworth, W.F. 1842: *Travels and Researches in Asia Minor, Mesopotamia, Chaldea, and Armenia*, 2 vols. (London).

Akurgal, E. 1956: 'Recherches faites à Cyzique et à Ergili'. *Anatolia* 1, 15–24.

Akurgal, E. and Budde, L. 1956: *Vorläufiger Bericht über die Ausgrabungen in Sinope* (Türk Tarih Kurumu Yayınları, ser. 5, no. 4) (Ankara).

Alföldi, A. 1955: 'Gewaltherrscher und Theaterkönig: Die Auseinandersetzung einer attischen Ideenprägung mit persischen Representationsformen im politischen Denken und in der Kunst bis zur Schwelle des Mittelalters'. In Weitzmann, K., Der Nesessian, S., Forsythe, G.H., Kantorowicz, E.H. and Mommsen, T.E. (eds.), *Late Classical and Medieval Studies in Honor of A.M. Friend, Jr.* (Princeton), 15–55.

Amandry, P. 1950: *La Mantique apollonienne à Delphes* (Paris).

Andrewes, A. 1961: 'Thucydides and the Persians'. *Historia* 10, 1–18.

—. 1967: *The Greeks* (New York).

Apel, H. 1910: *Die Tyrannis von Heraklea* (Dissertation, Halle).

Asheri, D. 1966: *Distribuzioni di terre nell'antica Grecia* (Memoria dell'accademia delle scienze di Torino, Classe di scienze, morali storiche e filologiche, ser. 4a, no. 10) (Turin).

—. 1972: 'Über die Frühgeschichte von Herakleia Pontike'. In Asheri *et al.* 1972, 11–34.

Asheri, D., Hoepfner, W. and Erichsen, A. 1972: *Forschungen an der Nordküste Kleinasiens* 1 (Denkschriften der Österreichischen Akademie der Wissenschaften 106, Ergänzungsbande zu den Tituli Asiae Minoris 5) (Vienna).

Atenstadt, F. 1925: 'Ein Beitrag zu Stephanos von Byzanz'. *Philologus* 80, 312–30.

Badian, E. 1961. Review of Lionel Pearson, *The Lost Histories of Alexander the Great*. *Gnomon* 33, 660–67.

Balsdon, J.P.V.D. 1950: 'The Divinity of Alexander'. *Historia* 1, 363–88.

Beletsky, A.A. and Yakovenko, E.V. 1969: 'Novye epigraficheskie nakhodki v skifskikh kurganakh Kerchenskogo poluostrova'. *VDI* 109, 152–60.

Belin de Ballu, E. 1972: *Olbia: cité antique du littoral nord de la mer Noire* (Leiden).

Beloch, K.J. 1912–27: *Griechische Geschichte*, 4 vols. in 8, 2nd ed. (Strassburg/Berlin).

Belov, G.D. 1948: *Chersonesus Taurica* (Leningrad).

Bengtson, H. 1937: *Die Strategie in der hellenistischen Zeit* (Münchener Beiträge zur Papyrusforschung und antiken Rechtsgeschichte 26) (Munich; repr. 1964).

Bérard, J. 1960: *L'Expansion et la colonisation grecques jusqu'aux guerres médiques* (Paris).

Berve, H. 1926: *Das Alexanderreich auf prosopographischer Grundlage*, 2 vols. (Munich).

—. 1967: *Die Tyrannis bei den Griechen*, 2 vols. (Munich).

Bickermann, E. 1934: 'Alexandre le Grand et les villes d'Asie'. *Revue des études grecques* 47, 346–74.

178 PART I: BOOK

—. 1939: 'Notes et discussions: La Cité grecque dans les monarchies hellénistiques'. *Revue de philologie*, ser. 3, 65, 335–49.

Bilabel, F. 1920: *Die ionische Kolonisation: Untersuchungen über die Gründungen der Ioner, deren staatliche und kultliche Organisation und Beziehungen zu den Mutterstädten* (*Philologus* Suppl. 14) (Leipzig).

Birmingham, J.M. 1961: 'The Overland Route across Anatolia in the Eighth and Seventh Centuries B.C.'. *Anatolian Studies* 11, 185–95.

Boardman, J. 1963: 'Greek Archaeology on the Shores of the Black Sea'. *Archeological Reports for 1962–63*, 34–51.

—. 1964: *The Greeks Overseas* (Baltimore).

Bore, E. 1840: *Correspondance et mémoires d'un voyageur en orient*, 2 vols. (Paris).

Bosi, F. 1967: 'Note epigrafiche bosporane'. *Epigraphica* 29, 131–44.

Boultounova, A. 1969: 'L'épigraphique en U.R.S.S.'. *Klio* 51, 299–309.

Bowie, E.L. 1970: 'Greeks and their Past in the Second Sophistic'. *Past and Present* 46, 3–41.

Boysal, Y. 1959: 'Über die älteren Funde von Sinope und die Kolonisationsfrage'. *Archäologischer Anzeiger* 74, 8–20

Brandis, C. 1899: 'Chersonesos'. *RE* 3, 2254–69.

Brashinskii [Brašinskij], I.B. 1965: 'Keramicheskie kleima Geraklei Pontiiskoi'. *Numizmatika i Epigrafika* 5, 10–30.

—. 1967: 'Die Beziehungen Athens zu den Griechenstädten des nördlichen Schwarzmeergebietes zur Zeit der Perserkriege'. *Klio* 49, 53–61.

—. 1968: 'Athen und die Gebiete an der nördlichen Schwarzmeerküste zwischen dem 6. und 2. Jahrhundert v.u.Z.'. *BCO* 1, 78–84.

Breitenbach, H.R. 1967: 'Xenophon von Athen'. *RE* 9A2, 1569–2052

Broughton, T.R.S. 1938: *An Economic Survey of Ancient Rome 4: Roman Asia* (Baltimore).

Burn, A.R. 1935: 'Dates in Early Greek History'. *JHS* 55, 130–46.

—. 1960: *The Lyric Age of Greece* (New York).

—. 1962: *Persia and the Greeks: The Defense of the West, c. 546–478 B.C.* (New York).

Burstein, S.M. 1974a: 'The War between Heraclea Pontica and Leucon I of Bosporus'. *Historia* 23, 401–16.

—. 1974b: 'Sceptre or Thunderbolt: Plutarch, *Moralia* 338B'. *California Studies in Classical Antiquity* 7, 89–92.

—. 1976: 'Fragment 53 of Callisthenes and the Text of *Iliad* B 850–855'. *Classical Philology* 71.4, 339–41.

Busolt, G. and Swoboda, H. 1926: *Griechische Staatskunde* (Handbuch der Altertumswissenschaft 4.1–2), 2nd ed., 2 vols. (Munich)

Butler, D. 1962: 'Competence of the Demos in the Spartan Rhetra'. *Historia* 11, 387–96.

Cameron, G.C. 1943: 'Darius, Egypt, and the Lands beyond the Sea'. *Journal of Near Eastern Studies* 2, 207–313.

—. 1973: 'The Persian Satrapies and Related Matters'. *Journal of Near Eastern Studies* 32, 47–56.

Canarache, V. 1957: *Importul Amforelor Stampate la Istria* (Bucharest).

Capelle, W. 1932: 'Griechische Ethik und römischer Imperialismus'. *Klio* 25, 86–113.

Cary, M. 1935: Review of K. Hanell, *Megarische Studien. JHS* 55, 96.

BIBLIOGRAPHY 179

Casson, L. 1971: *Ships and Seamanship in the Ancient World* (Princeton).

Cloché, P. n.d.: *Thèbes de Béotie: des origines à la conquête romaine* (Paris).

Cook, R.M. 1960: *Greek Painted Pottery* (London).

Cozzoli, U. 1968: *I Cimmeri* (Studi pubblicati dall'istituto italiano per la storia antica 20) (Rome).

Danov, C.M. 1960: 'Thracian Penetration into the Greek Cities on the West Coast of the Black Sea'. *Klio* 38, 75–80.

—. 1962: 'Pontos Euxinos'. *RE* Suppl. 9, 865–1176.

de Ste Croix, G.E.M. 1972: *The Origins of the Peloponnesian War* (Ithaca).

Deonna, W. 1908: 'Fouilles de Délos'. *BCH* 32, 5–176.

Desideri, P. 1967: 'Studi di storiografia eracleota, I: Promathidas e Nymphis'. *Studi classici et orientali* 16, 316–416.

—. 1970–71: 'Studi di storiographia eracleota, II: La guerra con Antioco il Grande'. *Studi classici et orientali* 19–20, 487–537.

Detschew, D. 1957: *Die thrakischen Sprachreste* (Österreichische Akademie der Wissenschaften, Philosophisch-historische Klasse, Schriften der Balkankommission, Linguistische Abteilung 14) (Vienna).

Diehl, E. 1929: 'Spintharos'. *RE* 3A, 1813

Diest, W. v. 1889: *Von Pergamon über den Dindynmos zum Pontus* (Ergänzungsheft 94 zu Dr. A. Petermanns Mitteilungen aus Justus Perthes' geographischer Anstalt) (Gotha).

Diller, A. (ed.). 1952: *The Tradition of the Minor Greek Geographers* (London).

Doenges, N. 1953: *The Letters of Themistocles* (Dissertation, Princeton).

Dörner, F.K. 1952: *Bericht über eine Reise in Bithynien ausgeführt im Jahre 1948 am Auftrage der Österreichischen Akademie der Wissenschaften* (Denkschriften der Österreichischen Akademie der Wissenschaften, Philosophisch-historische Klasse 75) (Vienna).

—. 1957: 'Prusias ad Hypium'. *RE* 23.1, 1128–48.

—. 1962: 'Vorbericht über eine im Herbst 1961 ausgeführte Reise in Bithynien'. *Anzeiger der Philosophisch-Historische Klasse* 99, 3–35.

—. 1963: 'Vorbericht über eine Reise in Bithynien und im bithynisch-paphlagonischen Grenzgebiet, 1962'. *Anzeiger der Philosophisch-Historische Klasse* 100, 132–39.

Dörner, F.K. and Hoepfner, W. 1962: 'Vorläufiger Bericht über eine Reise in Bithynien, 1961'. *Archäologischer Anzeiger*, 564–93.

Doublet, G. 1889: 'Inscriptions de Paphlagonie'. *BCH* 13, 293–319.

Dow, S. 1941: 'Studies in the Athenian Tribute Lists III'. *TAPA* 72, 70–84.

Drews, R. 1969: 'The Fall of Astyages and Herodotus' Chronology of the Eastern Kingdoms'. *Historia* 18, 1–11.

Droysen, J.G. 1883–85: *Histoire de l'hellénisme*, 3 vols. (Paris).

Dunker, M. 1885: 'Des Perikles Fahrt in den Pontus'. *Sitzungsberichte der Deutschen Akademie der Wissenschaften zu Berlin. Klasse für Sprache, Literatur und Kunst* 27, 533–50.

Düring, I. 1966: *Aristoteles: Darstellung und Interpretation seines Denkens* (Heidelberg).

Edmonds, J.M. (ed.). 1931: *Greek Elegy and Iambus with the Anacreonta*, 2 vols. (London).

—. (ed.). 1957–61: *The Fragments of Attic Comedy: After Meineke, Berg and Kock, Augmented, Annotated and Translated into Verse*, 3 vols. in 4 (Leiden).

180 PART I: BOOK

Ehrenberg, V. 1960: *The Greek State* (New York).
Errington, R.M. 1970: 'From Babylon to Triparadeisos, 323–320 B.C.'. *JHS* 90, 49–77.
Evelyn-White, H.G. 1936: *Hesiod, The Homeric Hymns, and Homerica*, new and rev. ed. (London).
Finley, M.I. 1962: 'The Black Sea and Danubian Regions and the Slave Trade in Antiquity'. *Klio* 40, 51–59.
Fıratlı, N. 1953: 'Bitinya Arastirmalarina Birkaç İlave'. *Turk Tarih Kurumu Belleten* 17, 15–25.
Forrest, W.G. 1957: 'Colonization and the Rise of Delphi'. *Historia* 6, 160–75.
Franke, P.R. 1966: 'Zur Tyrannis des Klearchos und Satyros in Herakleia am Pontos'. *Archäologischer Anzeiger* 81, 130–39.
Fritz, K. v. 1934: 'Theaitetos'. *RE* 5A2, 1351–72.
Gall, H. v. 1966: *Die paphlagonischen Felsgräber: eine Studie zur kleinasiatischen Kunstgeschichte* (Istanbuler Mitteilungen, Beih. 1) (Tübingen).
Gardner, P. 1918: *A History of Ancient Coinage 700–300 B.C.* (Oxford).
Gernet, L. 1909: 'L'approvisionnement d'Athènes en blé au Ve et au IVe siècle'. In *Melanges d'histoire ancienne* 25 (Paris), 271–391.
Geyer, F. 1930: 'Lysimachus'. *RE* 14, 1–31.
Gigon, O. 1962: 'Plato und politische Wirklichkeit'. *Gymnasium* 69, 205–19.
Gissinger, F. 1929: 'Zur Geographie bei Hesiod'. *Rheinisches Museum für Philologie* n.F. 78, 315–28.
Glotz, G. and Cohen, R. 1925–38: *Histoire grecque, Histoire générale: Histoire ancienne II*, 4 vols. (Paris).
Goetze, A. 1957: *Kulturgeschichte des alten Orients 1: Kleinasien* (Handbuch der Altertumswissenschaft 3.3.1), 2nd ed. (Munich).
Golenko, K.W. and Shelow, D.B. 1965: 'Münzen aus Pantakapaion von den Ausgrabungen der Jahre 1945–1961'. *BCO* 10, 197–98.
Gomme, A.W., Andrewes, A. and Dover, K.J. 1944–70: *A Historical Commentary on Thucydides*, 4 vols. (Oxford).
Graham, A.J. 1958: 'The Date of the Greek Penetration of the Black Sea'. *Bulletin of the Institute of Classical Studies, University of London* 5, 25–42.
—. 1964: *Colony and Mother City in Ancient Greece* (Manchester).
Griffith, G.T. 1935: *The Mercenaries of the Hellenistic World* (London; repr. Chicago 1968).
Grote, G. 1907: *A History of Greece*, 12 vols. (London).
Guillland, R. 1926: *Essai sur Nicéphore Grégoras: l'Homme et l'œuvre* (Paris).
—. (ed.) 1927: *Correspondence de Nicéphore Grégoras* (Paris).
Gundel, H.G. 1942–43: 'Die Krim in Altertum'. *Das Gymnasium* 3, 117–38.
Gwynn, A. 1918: 'The Character of Greek Colonization'. *JHS* 38, 88–123.
Habicht, C. 1956: *Gottmenschentum und griechische Städte* (Zetemata 14) (Munich).
Hamilton, J.R. 1969: *Plutarch, Alexander: A Commentary* (Oxford).
Hampl, F. 1939: 'Poleis ohne Territorium'. *Klio* 32, 1–60.
Hanell, K. 1934: *Megarische Studien* (Dissertation, Lund).
Hansen, E.V. 1947: *The Attalids of Pergamon* (Cornell Studies in Classical Philology 29) (Ithaca).
Hasebroek, J. 1933: *Trade and Politics in Ancient Greece* (London).
Head, B.V. 1911: *Historia Numorum: A Manual of Greek Numismatics*, new and enlarged ed. (Oxford).

BIBLIOGRAPHY 181

Heinen, H. 1972: *Untersuchungen zur hellenistischen Geschichte des 3. Jahrhunderts v. Chr.: Zur Geschichte der Zeit des Ptolemaios Keraunos und zum Chremonideischen Krieg* (*Historia* Einzelschriften 20) (Wiesbaden).

Hemberg, B. 1952: 'Die idaiischen Daktylen'. *Eranos* 50, 41–59.

Hester, D. 1957: 'Pre-Greek Place Names in Asia Minor'. *Revue Hittite et Asianique* 15, 107–19.

Highbarger, L. 1927: *The History and Civilization of Ancient Megara* (Baltimore).

Hignett, C. 1963: *Xerxes' Invasion of Greece* (Oxford).

Hirschfeld, G. 1888: 'Inschriften aus dem Norden Kleinasiens besonders aus Bithynien und Paphlagonien'. *Sitzungsberichte der Deutschen Akademie der Wissenschaften zu Berlin. Klasse für Sprache, Literatur und Kunst* 36, 863–90.

Hoepfner, W. 1966: *Herakleia Pontike – Ereğli: Eine baugeschichtliche Untersuchung* (Forschungen an der Nordküste Kleinasiens 2.1, Denkschriften der Österreichischen Akademie der Wissenschaften 89, Ergänzungsbande zu den Tituli Asiae Minoris 2.1) (Vienna).

Hollaux, M. 1898: 'Epigraphica IV: Fragments de decrets de Mégare'. *Revue des études grecques* 11, 267–73.

Hommarie de Hell, X. 1854: *Voyage en Turquie et en Perse*, 4 vols. (Paris).

Homolle, T. 1890: 'Comptes et inventaires des temples déliens en l'année 279'. *BCH* 14, 389–511.

Hudson-Williams, C.T. 1903: 'Theognis and his Poems'. *JHS* 23, 1–23.

Hunter, L.W. (ed.). 1927: *Aeneas On Siegecraft: A Critical Edition*, rev. S.A. Handford (Oxford).

Huxley, G.L. 1969: *Greek Epic Poetry: From Eumelus to Panyassis* (London).

Jaeger, W. 1948: *Aristotle: Fundamentals of the History of his Development*, 2nd ed. (Oxford).

Janke, M. 1963: *Historische Untersuchungen zu Memnon von Herakleia: Kap. 18–40, FgrHist Nr. 434* (Dissertation, Würzburg).

Jaubert, P.-A. 1821: *Voyage en Arménie et en Perse fait dans les années 1805 et 1806* (Paris).

Jones, A.H.M. 1940: *The Greek City from Alexander to Justinian* (Oxford).

—. 1971: *The Cities of the Eastern Roman Empire*, 2nd ed. (Oxford).

Judeich, W. 1892: *Kleinasiatische Studien* (Marburg).

—. 1894: 'Anytus'. *RE* 1, 2656.

Kagan, D. 1969: *The Outbreak of the Peloponnesian War* (Ithaca).

Kalinka, E. 1933: 'Aus Bithynien und Umgegend'. *Jahreshefte des Österreichischen Archäologischen Institutes in Wien* 28 Beiblatt, 44–111.

Kämmel, O. 1869: *Herakleotika: Beiträge zur älteren Geschichte der griechischen Kolonisation im nördlichen Kleinasien* (Plauen).

Kapossy, B. 1971: 'Hellenistische Bronzemünzen aus Heraclea Pontica'. *Schweizer Münzblätter* 21, 21–22.

Keil, B. 1892: 'KORUPEDION'. *Revue de Philologie* 26, 257–62.

Kent, R.G. 1953: *Old Persian: Grammar Texts Lexicon* (American Oriental Series 33), 2nd ed. (New Haven).

Kirchhoff, A. 1878: 'Zur aristotelischen Oekonomie'. *Hermes* 13, 139–40.

Kirk, G.S. 1962: 'The Structure and Aim of the Theogony'. In *Hésiode et son Influence* (Entretiens sur l'antiquité classique 7) (Brussels), 63–95.

Knipovich, T.N. and Levi, E.I. (eds.). 1965: *Inscriptiones Olbiae (1917–1965)* (Leningrad).

182   PART I: BOOK

Kocevalov, A. 1932: 'Die Einfuhr von Getreide nach Athen'. *Rheinisches Museum für Philologie* n.F. 81, 321–23.

Köppner, F. 1892: 'Der Dialekt Megaras und der megarischen Kolonien'. *Jahrbuch für classischen Philologie, Suppl.* 18 (Leipzig), 529–63.

Kraay, C.M. 1964: 'Hoards, Small Change and the Origin of Coinage'. *JHS* 84, 76–91.

Kraay, C.M. and Hirmer, M. n.d.: *Greek Coins* (New York).

Krumbholtz, P. 1883: *De Asiae Minoris satrapis Persicis* (Dissertation, Leipzig).

La Penna, A. (ed.). 1957: *Ovidi Ibis* (Biblioteca di studi superiori 34) (Florence).

Labaree, B.W. 1957: 'How the Greeks Sailed into the Black Sea'. *American Journal of Archaeology* 61, 29–33.

Lacey, W.K. 1968: *The Family in Classical Greece* (Ithaca).

Lane Fox, R. 1973: *Alexander the Great* (London).

Lapin, W.W. 1965: 'Ökonomische Characterisierung der Siedlung auf Beresan'. *BCO* 10, 91–94.

Laqueur, R. 1927: 'Lokalchronik'. *RE* 13, 1098–1102.

—. 1937: 'Nymphis'. *RE* 17, 1608.

Latyschew, B. 1885: 'La Constitution de Chersonésos en Tauride: d'après des documents épigraphiques'. *BCH* 9, 265–300.

Le Rider, G. 1963: *Deux trésors de monnaies grecques de la propontide (IVe siècle avant J.-C.)* (Bibliothèque archéologique et historique de l'institut français d'archéologie d'Istanbul 18) (Paris).

Lee, H.D.P. (ed.). 1952: *Aristotle, Meteorologica* (London).

Legrand, P.-E. 1954: *Hérodote: Index analytique* (Paris).

Lehman-Hartleben, K. 1923: *Die antiken Hafenanlagen des Mittelmeeres. Beiträge zur Geschichte des Städtebaues im Altertum (Klio* Beih. 14) (Leipzig), 130–31.

Lehmann-Haupt, C. 1921: 'Satrap'. *RE* 2A1, 82–188.

Lenardon, R.J. 1959: 'The Chronology of Themistocles' Ostracism and Exile'. *Historia* 8, 22–48.

Lenk, B. 1927: 'Die Tyrannen von Herakleia am Pontos'. *Verein klassischer Philologen in Wien, Mitteilungen* 4, 77–83.

—. 1928: 'Die Tyrannen von Herakleia am Pontos: Fortsetzung und Schluss'. *Verein klassischer Philologen in Wien, Mitteilungen* 5, 13–21.

Leskow, A.M. 1960: 'Die Taurer auf der Krim'. *BCO* 5, 346–49.

Lesky, A. 1966: *A History of Greek Literature* (New York).

Lessen, O. 1884–1937: 'Phineus'. In Roscher, W.H. (ed.), *Ausführliches Lexicon der griechischen und römischen Mythologie*, 10 vols. (Leipzig), 2357–75.

Leuze, O. 1935: *Die Satrapieneinteilung in Syrien und im Zweistromlande von 520–320* (Halle).

Levi, E.I. 1958: 'K istorii torgovykh snoshenii Ol'vii v IV–III vv. do n. e. (Po epigraficheskim pamyatnikam agory)'. *Sovetskaya Arkheologiya* 28, 234–47.

Linton, D.L. and Moseley, F. 1970: 'The Geological Ages'. *CAH* I.1³, 1–34.

Lotze, D. 1959: *METAXU ELEUTHERŌN KAI DOULŌN. Studien zur Rechtsstellung unfreier Landbevölkerungen in Griechenland bis zum 4. Jahrhundert v. Chr.* (Berlin).

Magie, D. 1950: *Roman Rule in Asia Minor to the End of the Third Century after Christ*, 2 vols. (Princeton).

Mamroth, A. 1949: 'Ein Bildnis der Königin Amastris auf Münzen des Lysimachos'. *Berliner numismatische Zeitschrift* 1, 81–86.

BIBLIOGRAPHY

Maksimova [Maximowa], M.I. 1956: *Antichnye goroda iugo-vostochnogo Prichernomor'ya: Sinopa, Amisus, Trapezunt* (Moscow/Leningrad).
—. 1959: 'Der kurze Seeweg über das Schwarze Meer im Altertum'. *Klio* 37, 101–18.
Mattingly, H.B. 1966: 'Periclean Imperialism'. In *Ancient Society and Institutions: Studies Presented to Victor Ehrenberg on his 75th Birthday* (Oxford), 193–223.
Meiggs, R. 1972: *The Athenian Empire* (Oxford).
Meiggs, R. and Lewis, D. (eds.). 1969: *A Selection of Greek Historical Inscriptions to the End of the Fifth Century B.C.* (Oxford).
Mendel, G. 1904: 'Inscriptions de Bithynie'. *BCH* 24, 361–426.
Meritt, B.D. 1941: 'Greek Inscriptions'. *Hesperia* 10, 38–64.
—. 1961: *The Athenian Year* (Sather Classical Lectures 32) (Berkeley).
—. 1964: 'Athenian Calendar Problems'. *TAPA* 95, 200–60.
Meritt, B.D. and West, A.B. 1934: *The Athenian Assessment of 425 B.C.* (Ann Arbor).
Merlin, P. 1959: 'Zur Biographie des Speusippus'. *Philologus* 103, 198–214.
Meyer, Ed. 1879: *Geschichte des Königreichs Pontos* (Leipzig).
—. 1897: 'Bithynia'. *RE* 3.1, 510–11.
—. 1965–69: *Geschichte des Altertums*, ed. H.E. Stier, 5 vols. in 8 (Darmstadt).
Meyer, Ernst. 1925a: *Die Grenzen der hellenistischen Staaten in Kleinasien* (Zürich/ Leipzig).
—, 1925b: 'Megara'. *RE* 15.1, 152–205.
Mihailov, G. 1961: 'La Thrace aux IVe siècle av. notre ère'. *Athenaeum* n.s. 39, 33–44.
Miller, M. 1970: *The Sicilian Colony Dates* (Studies in Chronography 1) (Albany).
Miltner, F. 1939: 'Die erste milesische Kolonisation im Südpontus'. In Calder, W.M. and Keil, J. (eds.), *Anatolian Studies Presented to William Hepburn Buckler* (Manchester), 191–95.
Minns, E.H. 1913: *Scythians and Greeks: A Survey of Ancient History and Archaeology on the North Coast of the Euxine from the Danube to the Caucasus* (Cambridge).
Mitchell, H. 1957: *The Economics of Ancient Greece*, 2nd ed. (Cambridge).
Momigliano, A. 1933: 'Dalla spedizione scitica de Filippo alla spedizione scitica di Dario'. *Athenaeum* n.s. 11, 336–59.
Moretti, L. 1953: *Iscrizioni agonistiche greche* (Rome).
Mossé, C. 1960: 'Le rôle des esclaves dans les troubles politiques du monde Grec à la fin de l'époque classique'. *Cahiers d'histoire* 6, 353–60.
—. 1962a: *La Fin de la démocratie athénienne: Aspects sociaux et politiques du déclin de la cité grecque au IVe siècle avant J.-C.* (Paris).
—. 1962b: 'Un aspect de la crise de la cité grecque au IVe siècle: La recrudescence de la tyrannie'. *Revue philosophique de la France et de l'etranger* 152, 1–20.
Natrop, P. 1899: 'Bryson'. *RE* 3, 927–29.
Neubauer, H. 1960: 'Die griechische Schwarzmeerkolonisation in der sowjetischen Geschichtsforschung'. *Saeculum* 11, 132–56.
Neumann, K.J. 1906: 'Die Enstehung des spartanischen Staates in der Lykurgischen Verfassung'. *Historische Zeitschrift* 11, 1–80.
Newman, W.L. (ed.). 1887–1902: *Aristotle, Politics*, 4 vols. (Oxford).
Niese, B. 1893–1903: *Geschichte der griechischen und makedonischen Staaten seit der Schlacht bet Chaeronea*, 3 vols. (Gotha; repr. Darmstadt 1963).
Nilsson, M.P. 1906: *Griechische Feste von religiöser Bedeutung mit Ausschluss der attischen* (Stuttgart; repr. 1957).

184 PART I: BOOK

—. 1961–67: *Geschichte der griechischen Religion* (Handbuch der Altertumswissen-schaft, 5.2.1–2), 3rd ed., 2 vols. (Munich).

Nowack, E. 1931: 'Journeys in Northern Anatolia'. *Geographical Review* 21, 70–92.

Oliver, J.H. 1957: 'The Peace of Callias and the Pontic Expedition of Pericles'. *Historia* 6, 254–55.

Osborne, M.J. 1973: 'Orontes'. *Historia* 22, 515–51.

Pape, W. and Benseler, G.E. 1875: *Wörterbuch der griechischen Eigennamen* (Hand-wörterbuch der griechischen Sprache, 3.I–II), 3rd ed., 2 vols. (Brunswick).

Pargoire, J. 1898: 'Inscriptions d'Heraclée du Pont'. *BCH* 22, 492–96.

Parke, H.W. 1933: *Greek Mercenary Soldiers: From the Earliest Times to the Battle of Ipsus* (Oxford).

—. 1939: *A History of the Delphic Oracle* (Oxford).

Parke, H.W. and Wormell, D.E.W. 1961: *The Delphic Oracle*, 2 vols. (Oxford).

Paton, W.R. (ed.). 1916–18: *The Greek Anthology*, 5 vols. (London).

Pearson, L. 1960: *The Lost Histories of Alexander the Great* (London).

Pease, A.S. 1917: 'Notes on the Delphic Oracle and Greek Colonization'. *Classical Philology* 12, 1–20.

Pečirka, J. 1970: 'Country Estates of the Polis of Chersonesos in the Crimea'. In de Rosa, L. (ed.), *Richerche storiche ed economiche in memoria de Corrado Barba-gallo*, vol. 1 (Naples), 459–73.

Perl, G. 1968: 'Zur Chronologie der Königreiche Bithynia, Pontos und Bosporos'. In Harmatta, J. (ed.), *Studien zur Geschichte und Philosophie des Altertums* (Amster-dam), 299–330.

Perrot, G., Guillaume, E. and Delbet, J. 1872: *Exploration archéologique de la Galatie et de la Bithynie: D'une partie de la Mysie, de la Phrygie, de la Cappadoce et du Pont*, 2 vols. (Paris).

Pick, B. and Regling, K. 1898–1910: *Die antiken Münzen von Dacien und Moesien* (Die antiken Münzen Nord-Griechenlands 1.1–2) (Berlin).

Pippidi, D.M. 1969: 'Note de lectura'. *Studii Clasice* 11, 223–49.

—. 1971: *I Greci nel basso Danubio: dall'età arcaica alla conquista romana* (Milan).

Pohlenz, M. 1916: 'Kronos und die Titanen'. *Neue Jahrbücher* 37, 549–94.

Popescu, E. 1964: 'Zeus Soter à Callatis'. *Studii si Cercetari de Istorie Veche* 15, 545–49.

Powell, J.E. 1938: *A Lexicon to Herodotus* (Cambridge).

Powell, J.U. (ed.). 1970: *Collectanea Alexandrina. Reliquiae Minores Poetarum Grae-corum Aetatis Ptolemaicae 323–146 A.C. Epicorum, Elegiacorum, Lyricorum, Ethicorum* (Oxford).

Préaux, C. 1954: 'Les Villes hellénistiques principalement en Orient: leurs institutions administratives et judiciaires'. In *La Ville* (Recueils de la Société Jean Bodin 6) (Brussels), 69–134.

Preda, C. 1961: 'Archaeological Discoveries in the Greek Cemetery of Callatis-Man-galia (IVth–IIIrd Centuries before Our Era'. *Dacia* n.s. 5, 275–303.

—. 1968: *Callatis*, 2nd ed. (Bucharest).

Premerstein, A. v. 1911: 'Athenischer Ehrenbeschluss für einer Grosskaufmann'. *Mitteilungen des Kaiserlich deutschen archäologischen Instituts, Athenische Abteilung* 36, 75–86.

Pritchard, J.B. (ed.). 1955: *Ancient Near Eastern Texts Relating to the Old Testament*, 2nd ed. (Princeton).

BIBLIOGRAPHY   185

Pritchett, W.K. 1963: *Ancient Athenian Calendars on Stone* (University of California Publications in Classical Archaeology 4) (Berkeley).

Radet, G. 1892: *La Lydie et le monde Grec au temps des Mermnades (687–546)* (Paris).

Rădulescu, A. 1964: 'Inscriptii inedite din Dobrogea'. In *Noi monumente epigrafice din Scythia Minor* (Constanţa), 139–77.

Raubitschek, A.E. 1945: 'The Pyloroi of the Akropolis'. *TAPA* 76, 104–07.

Reinach, T. 1888: *Trois royaumes de l'Asie Mineure: Cappadoce, Bithynie, Pont* (Paris).

Robert, L. 1936: 'Études d'épigraphie grecque'. *Revue de philologie de litérature et d'histoire anciennes* 62, 113–70.

—. 1937: *Études anatoliennes*. (Études orientales publiées par l'institut français d'archéologie de Stamboul 5) (Paris; repr. Amsterdam 1970).

—. 1963: *Noms indigènes dans l'Asie Mineure Gréco-Romaine* (Bibliothèque archéologique et historique de l'institut français d'archéologie d'Instanbul 13) (Paris).

—. 1970: 'Épigraphie et antiquités grecques'. *Annuaire, Collège de France, Paris* 70, 451–62.

Robinson, C.A. Jr. 1940: 'Alexander's Plans'. *AJPh* 61, 402–11.

Robinson, D.M. 1906a: 'Ancient Sinope: First Part'. *AJPh* 27, 125–53.

—. 1906b: 'Ancient Sinope: Second Part'. *AJPh* 27, 245–79.

Robinson, E.S.G. 1920: 'A Find of Coins of Sinope'. *NC*, ser. 4, 20, 1–16.

—. 1921: 'Greek Coins from the Dardanelles'. *NC*, ser. 5, 1, 1–25.

Roebuck, C. 1959: *Ionian Trade and Colonization* (New York).

Rohde, E. 1881: 'Studien zur Chronologie der griechischen Literaturgeschichte'. *Rheinisches Museum für Philologie* ser. 3, no. 36, 524–75.

Rostovtzeff [Rostowzew], M.I. 1910: *Studien zur Geschichte des römischen Kolonates* (Leipzig).

—. 1922: *Iranians and Greeks in South Russia* (Oxford).

—. 1930: 'The Bosporan kingdom'. *CAH* VIII, 561–89.

—. 1931: *Skythien und der Bosporus 1: Kritische Übersicht der schriftlichen und archäologischen Quellen* (Berlin).

—. 1941: *The Social and Economic History of the Hellenistic World*, 3 vols. (Oxford).

Ruge, W. 1930: 'Mariandynoi'. *RE* 14.2, 1747–49.

Sachs, A.J. and Wiseman, D.J. 1954: 'A Babylonian King List of the Hellenistic Period'. *Iraq* 16, 202–11.

Saitta, G. 1955: 'Lisimaco di Thracia'. *Kokalos* 1, 62–154.

Sathas, C.-N. 1880: 'Nicéphore Grégoras, Éloge de la ville d'Héraclée du Pont d'après Memnon et autres historiens inconnus'. *Annuaíre de l'association pour l'encouragement des études grecques en France* 14, 217–24.

Sauciuc-Saveanu, T. 1924: 'Callatis: Ier rapport préliminaire: fouilles et recherches de l'année 1924'. *Dacia* 1, 108–65.

Schachermeyr, F. 1934: 'Theagenes'. *RE*, ser. 2, 5, 1341–45.

Schaefer, A. 1885: *Demosthenes und seine Zeit*, 2nd ed., 3 vols. (Leipzig).

Schaefer, H. 1949: 'Pasion'. *RE* 18.4, 2064–68.

—. 1963: 'Die Autonomieklausel des Kalliasfriedens'. In Weideman, U. and Schmitthenner, W. (eds.), *Probleme der alten Geschichte* (Göttingen), 253–68.

Scheele, M. 1932: *Stratēgos Autokratōr: staatsrechtliche Studien zur griechischen Geschichte der 5. und 4. Jahrhunderts* (Dissertation, Leipzig).

Schmid, W. and Stahlin, O. 1929: *Geschichte der griechischen Literatur* (Handbuch der Altertumswissenschaft 1.1) (Munich).

186 PART I: BOOK

Schmitt, H.H. 1969: *Die Staatsverträge des Altertums: Die Verträge der griechisch-römischen Welt von 338 bis 200 v. Chr.* (Munich).

Schmitt, R. 1972: 'Die achaimenidische Satrapie *TAYAIY DRAYAHYA*'. *Historia* 21, 522–27.

Schneiderwirth, H. 1882: *Heraclea am Pontus* (Heiligenstadt).

—. 1885: *Das pontische Heraklea* (Heiligenstadt).

Schwart, E. 1894: 'Amphitheos'. *RE* 1, 1963.

—. 1905: 'Diodorus'. *RE* 5, 663–704.

Schweigert, E. 1939: 'Greek Inscriptions'. *Hesperia* 8, 3–47.

—. 1940: 'Greek Inscriptions'. *Hesperia* 9, 309–57.

Sealey, R. 1969: 'Probouleusis and the Sovereign Assembly'. *California Studies in Classical Antiquity* 2, 247–69.

Seibert, J. 1967: *Historische Beiträge zu den dynastischen Verbindungen in hellenistischer Zeit* (*Historia* Einzelschriften 10) (Wiesbaden).

Seltman, C. 1955: *Greek Coins: A History of Metallic Currency and Coinage down to the Fall of the Hellenistic Kingdoms*, 2nd ed. (London).

Shelov, D.B. 1950: 'Feodosiya, Gerakleya i Spartokidy'. *VDI* 3, 168–78.

Sherman, C.L. (ed. and trans.). 1952: *Diodorus of Sicily, 7: Books XV.20–XVI.65* (London).

Short, G.A. 1937: 'The Siting of Greek Colonies on the Black Sea Coast of Bulgaria and Rumania'. *Liverpool Annals of Archaeology and Anthropology* 24, 141–55.

Simpson, R.H. 1957: 'A Note on Cyinda'. *Historia* 6, 503–04.

—. 1959: 'Antigonus the One-Eyed and the Greeks'. *Historia* 8, 385–409.

Six, J.P. 1885: 'Sinope'. *NC*, ser. 3, 5, 15–65.

—. 1894: 'Monnaies grecques, inédites et incertaines'. *NC*, ser. 3, 14, 297–338.

Skudnowa, W.M. 1959: 'Ein Fundkomplex von den Ausgrabungen des kabiren Heiligtums in Nymphaion'. *BCO* 4, 99–100.

—. 1961: 'Zur Frage der Handelsbeziehungen zwischen Sinope und dem kimmerischen Bosporos im 5. Jahrhundert v.u.Z.'. *BCO* 6, 102–04.

Smith, S. 1944: *Isaiah Ch. XL–LV: Literary Criticism and History* (Oxford).

Sokolowski, F. 1955: *Lois sacrées de l'Asie Mineure* (Paris).

Sölch, J. 1925: 'Bithynische Städte im Altertum'. *Klio* 19, 140–88.

Sordi, M. 1953: 'La Guerra tessalofocese del V secolo'. *Rivista di Filologia Classica* n.s. 31, 235–58.

Stadter, P.A. 1965: *Plutarch's Historical Methods: An Analysis of the Mulierum Virtutes* (Cambridge, MA).

Stein, H. 1893–1908: *Herodot*, 4th–6th ed., 5 vols. (Berlin).

Stern, Ernest v. 1909: 'Die griechische Kolonisation am Nordgestade des Schwarzen Meeres im Lichte archäologischer Forschung'. *Klio* 9, 139–52.

—. 1915: 'Die politische und soziale Struktur der griechischen Colonien am Nordufer der Schwarzmeergebietes'. *Hermes* 50, 161–224.

Stroheker, F.K. 1958: *Dionysius I: Gestalt und Geschichte des Tyrannen von Syrakus* (Wiesbaden).

Sykutris, J. 1931: 'Epistolographie'. *RE* Suppl. 5, 185–220.

Syme, R. 1939: *The Roman Revolution* (Oxford).

Tarn, W.W. 1908: 'The Fleet of Xerxes'. *JHS* 28, 202–33.

—. 1913: *Antigonus Gonatas* (Oxford; repr. 1969).

—. 1948: *Alexander the Great*, 2 vols. (Cambridge).

BIBLIOGRAPHY 187

Thompson, M. (ed.). 1962: *Sylloge Nummorum Graecorum: The Burton Y. Berry Collection. Part II: Megaris to Egypt* (New York).

—. 1968: 'The Mints of Lysimachus'. In Kraay, C.M. and Jenkins, G.K. (eds.), *Essays in Greek Coinage Presented to Stanley Robinson* (Oxford), 163–82.

Toepffer, J. 1896: 'Astakos'. *Hermes* 31, 124–36.

Tomaschek, W. 1894: *Die alten Thraker: Eine ethnologische Untersuchung. II: Die Sprachreste, 1. Hälfte: Glossen aller Art und Götternamen* (Sitzungsberichte der philosophisch-historischen Klasse der kaiserlichen Akademie der Wissenschaften 130.2) (Vienna).

Trever A.A. 1925: 'The Intimate Connections between Economic and Political Conditions as Illustrated in Ancient Megara'. *Classical Philology* 20.2, 115–32.

Turk, G. 1895: *De Hyla* (Breslauer philologischer Abhandlungen 7.4) (Breslau).

Turkey 1942–43: *Turkey* (Geographical Handbook Series. Naval Intelligence Division, Br. 507–507a), 2 vols. (Oxford).

Tyumenev [Tjumenev], A. 1938: 'Khersonesskie etyudy'. *VDI* 2, 245–75.

—. 1956: 'Chersonesitanische Studien IV. Chersonesos und Kerkinitis'. *BCO* 1, 172–76.

van der Kolf, M.C. 1954: 'Priolas'. *RE* 22.2, 2315–18.

van Effenterre, H. 1948: *La Crète et le monde Grec de Plato à Polybe* (Paris).

Van Groningen, B.A. (ed.). 1933: *Aristote, Le second livre de l'Économique* (Leiden).

Vitucci, G. 1953: *Il Regno di Bitinia* (Studi pubblicati dall'istituto italiano per la storia antica 10) (Rome).

Vryonis, S. jr. 1971: *The Decline of Medieval Hellenism in Asia Minor and the Process of Islamization from the Eleventh through the Fifteenth Century* (Publications of the Center for Medieval and Renaissance Studies 4) (Berkeley).

Wade-Gery, H.T. 1958: 'The Peace of Kallias'. In Wade-Gery, H.T., *Essays in Greek History* (Oxford), 200–32.

Walbank, F.W. 1957–79: *A Historical Commentary on Polybius.* 3 vols. (Oxford).

Wasowicz, A. 1966: 'À l'époque grecque: le peuplement des côtes de la mer Noire et de la Gaule méridionale'. *Annales, Économies, Sociétés, Civilisations* 21, 553–72.

Wehrli, C. 1968: *Antigone et Démétrios* (Geneva).

Wehrli, F. (ed.). 1967–69: *Die Schule des Aristoteles, Texte und Kommentar*, 2nd ed., 10 vols. (Basel).

Werner, R. 1955: 'Die Dynastie der Spartokiden'. *Historia* 4, 412–44.

—. 1957: 'Schwarzmeerreiche im Altertum'. *Die Welt als Geschichte* 17, 221–44.

West, A.B. 1935: 'Prosopographical Notes on the Treaty between Athens and Haliai'. *AJPh* 56, 72–76.

West, M.L. (ed.). 1966: *Hesiod, Theogony* (Oxford).

Wilamowitz-Moellendorff, U. v. 1886: 'Oropos und die Graer'. *Hermes* 21, 91–115.

Wilamowitz-Moellendorff, U. v. and Niese, B. 1910: *Staat und Gesellschaft der Griechen und Römer* (Die Kultur der Gegenwart 2.4.1) (Berlin/Leipzig).

Wilcken, U. 1894: 'Amastris'. *RE* 1.2, 1750.

Wilhelm, A. 1892: 'Bemerkungen zu griechischen Inschriften'. *Archaeologisch-Epigraphische Mitteilungen aus Oesterreich-Ungarn* 15, 1–25.

—. 1894: 'Zu griechischen Inschriften'. *Archaeologisch-Epigraphische Mitteilungen aus Oesterreich-Ungarn* 17, 34–45.

—. 1903: Review of W. Dittenberger, *Sylloge inscriptionum graecarum*, 2nd ed., vol. 1. *Göttingische Gelehrte Anzeigen* 163, 769–98.

188 PART I: BOOK

—. 1942a: 'Attische Urkunden. V. Teil'. *Sitzungsberichte der philosophisch-historischen Klasse der Akademie der Wissenschaften* 22.5, 3–192.

—. 1942b: 'Beschluss der Athener zu Ehren eines Herakleoten'. *Anzeiger der Philosophisch-Historische Klasse* 79, 65–73.

Wilson, D.R. 1960: *The Historical Geography of Bithynia, Paphlagonia, and Pontus in the Greek and Roman Periods: A New Survey with Particular Reference to Surface Remains Still Visible* (Dissertation, Oxford).

Wirth, G. 1967: 'Zum Volksstamm der Treren'. *Klio* 49, 47–51.

Wroth, W. (ed.). 1889: *Pontus, Paphlagonia, Bithynia and the Kingdom of Bosporus* (Catalogue of Greek Coins in the British Museum 13) (London).

Zeest, I.B. 1948: 'O tipakh gerakleiskikh amfor'. *Kratkie soobshcheniya o dokladakh i polevykh issledovaniyakh instituta istorii material'noi kultury akademii nauk SSR* 22, 48–52.

—. 1951: 'Novye dannye o torgovykh svyazyakh Bospora Yuzhnym Prichernomor'em'. *VDI* 2, 106–16.

Zgusta, L. 1964: *Kleinasiatische Personennamen* (Tschechoslowakische Akademie der Wissenschaften, Monografie Orientálního ústavu 19) (Prague).

Ziegler, K. 1937: 'Thynias'. *RE* 2.6, 718–20.

Zograf, A.N. 1951: *Antichnye monety* (Materialy i issledovaniya po arkheologii SSSR 16) (Moscow).

PART II

ARTICLES

FRAGMENT 53 OF CALLISTHENES AND THE TEXT OF *ILIAD* 2. 850–55[*]

The only evidence for substantial Greek knowledge of, and hence possible contact with, any of the coasts of the Black Sea during the 8th century BC is provided by the Paphlagonian entry in the catalogue of Troy's allies (*Iliad* 2. 850–855). Particular significance in this connection attaches to lines 853–855, since they seemingly supply precise data about the coast of Paphlagonia at a time when non-Greek populations still occupied the sites of the later cities of Cromna, Seasmus, and Cytorus.[1] Recent scholars, however, especially those writing in English,[2] contend that lines 853–855 are Late Hellenistic interpolations and thus of no value in reconstructing the history of the Greek penetration of the Black Sea. The purpose of this note is to point out that evidence furnished by fragment 53 of Callisthenes renders such a position untenable.

The condemnation of these three lines dates from the publication of T.W. Allen's book, *The Homeric Catalogue of Ships*.[3] Allen based his attack on a statement by Strabo to the effect that Apollodorus of Athens, following the views of Eratosthenes, had maintained that Homer was ignorant of the coasts of the Black Sea, since he would otherwise have mentioned them (Strabo 12. 3. 26 = Apollodorus *FGrH* 244 F157b).[4] Since lines 853–855 explicitly mention places and features of the Paphlagonian coast, Allen concluded that these lines cannot have been in the texts of the *Iliad* used by Eratosthenes and Apollodorus. On the other hand, since Strabo[5] accepted them as Homeric, they had clearly entered the text by his time: that is, the interpolation probably occurred some time between the publication of Apollodorus' Περὶ τοῦ νεῶν καταλόγου in the 2nd century BC and Strabo's *Geography* in the

---

[*] Acknowledgment should be made to Prof. T.S. Brown and Prof. M.H. Chambers of UCLA and Prof. A.R. Baca of California State University at Northridge for their criticism of earlier versions of this paper. Paper first published in *Classical Philology* 71 (1976), 339–41.

[1] 11. 2. 853–855: [*sc.* Ἐνετῶν] οἵ ῥα Κύτωρον ἔχον καὶ Σήσαμον ἀμφενέμοντο / ἀμφί τε Παρθένιον ποταμὸν κλυτὰ δώματα ναῖον / Κρωμάν τ' Αἰγιαλόν τε καὶ ὑψηλοὺς Ἐρυθίνους, ed. D.B. Monro and T.W. Allen, 3rd ed. (Oxford 1920).

[2] E.g. Bolling 1925, 77–78; Page 1959, 147; Thomas and Stubbings 1962, 304, 309, n. 1; and Hope Simpson and Lazenby 1970, 182, n. 3. Among continental scholars only V. Burr (1944, 149) appears to accept this position.

[3] Allen 1921, 156–59.

[4] Ed. and trans. H.L. Jones, 8 vols. (London 1917–32).

[5] Strabo 12. 3. 10.

192   PART II: ARTICLES

early 1st century AD. Finally, Allen rounded out his case by suggesting that the interpolator took the three lines in question from the catalogue of Trojan allies in the *Cypria*.

The fact that the *Cypria* contained no such catalogue obviously weakens Allen's theory somewhat, by depriving it of one of its most attractive features, an identifiable source for the interpolated lines.[6] A still more serious difficulty is provided by the echoing of 855 in the *Argonautica* of Apollonius of Rhodes.[7] Apparently, either Apollonius used the same source as Allen's hypothetical interpolator, or copies of the *Iliad* containing line 855 (at least) were already in circulation during the 3rd century BC. Nevertheless, Allen's initial inference remains valid. The most natural interpretation of the passage of Strabo cited by Allen is that Eratosthenes and Apollodorus both used texts of the *Iliad* that omitted lines 853–855. By itself, however, this fact does not suffice to prove that these lines were interpolated in the Hellenistic period, since there is another equally satisfactory explanation not considered by Allen that would account both for Eratosthenes' and Apollodorus' ignorance of these three lines and for Apollonius' knowledge of line 855: Eratosthenes and Apollodorus could have accepted the judgment of an editor of the *Iliad* who rejected these lines as un-Homeric despite their being found in pre-Hellenistic texts of the *Iliad*.[8] Probability, moreover, supports this latter suggestion, since it is difficult to believe such an interpolation could have been made without being noticed, let alone have won universal acceptance, as late as the 2nd or 1st centuries BC.[9] Fortunately, there is no need to rely on mere probability, since fragment 53 of Callisthenes provides the evidence necessary to decide the question.

According to Strabo, Καλλισθένης δὲ καὶ ἔγραφε τὰ ἔπη ταῦτα εἰς τὸν Διάκοσμον, μετὰ τὸ

Κρῶμνάν τ' Αἰγιαλόν τε καὶ ὑψηλοὺς 'Ερυθίνους

τιθεὶς

Καύκωνας δ' αὖτ' ἦγε Πολυκέος υἱὸς ἀμύμων,
Οἵ περὶ Παρθένιον κλυτὰ δώματ' ἔναιον.

[6] Bethe 1929, 216.

[7] Apollonius Rhodius, *Argonautica* (ed. H. Frankel [Oxford 1961]) 2. 941–942: Σήσαμον αἰπεινούς τε παρεξενέοντ' 'Ερυθίνους, / Κρωβίαλον Κρῶμνάν τε καὶ Κύτωρον.

[8] They would have found such a text acceptable because of their belief that Greeks did not sail the Black Sea before the beginnings of colonization (Apollodorus *FGrH* 244 F157a = Strabo 7. 3. 6; *cf.* Strabo 1. 3. 2), a process which began much later than the 11th-century date Eratosthenes (*FGrH* 241 F9) assigned to Homer or the 10th-century date favored by Apollodorus (*FGrH* 244 F63).

[9] This is made all the more difficult to believe by Strabo's reference (12. 3. 10) to the controversy among Homerists as to whether or not line 855 should be emended to read Κρῶμναν Καβίαλόν τε, a reading of which, as the lines of Apollonius quoted in n. 7 indicate, a variant was already known as early as the 3rd century BC.

FRAGMENT 53 OF CALLISTHENES AND THE TEXT OF *ILIAD* 2. 850–55 193

παρήκειν γὰρ ἀφ' Ἡρακλείας καὶ Μαριανδυνῶν μέχρι Λευκοσύρων, οὓς καὶ ἡμεῖς Καππάδοκας προσαγορεύομεν, τό τε των Καυκώνων γένος τὸ περὶ Τίειον μέχρι Παρθενίου καὶ τὸ τῶν Ἐνετῶν τὸ συνεχὲς μετὰ τὸν Παρθένιον τῶν ἐχόντων τό Κύτωρον, καὶ νυν δ' ἔτι Καυκωνίτας εἴναι τινας περὶ τὸν Παρθένιον.[10]

Although Callisthenes' lines appeared in some Hellenistic copies of the *Iliad*[11] and were even accepted as Homeric by Apollodorus (Apollodorus *FGrH* 244 F170 = Strabo 14. 5. 23),[12] they early disappeared from the text, surviving henceforth only as curiosities in the scholarly literature about Homer.[13] Today, of course, no scholar doubts their spuriousness, and it is probably this unanimity that accounts for the tendency to ignore the implications of fragment 53 as a whole for the textual history of the Paphlagonian entry. Of particular importance in this regard is Strabo's statement that Callisthenes added his lines after Κρῶμνάν τ' Αἰγιαλόν τε καὶ ὑψηλοὺς Ἐρυθίνους, that is, after the present line 855. If Allen's reconstruction of the development of the text were correct, Callisthenes should have placed his lines after line 852. By itself, therefore, Strabo's report of Callisthenes' placement of his lines is sufficient to prove that line 855 at least was in the latter's text of the *Iliad*. But there is more. Not only is the second of the Callisthenic lines itself only a variant of 854 but, more importantly, Callisthenes' description of the Eneti as τὸ των Ἐνετῶν ... τῶν ἐχόντων τὸ Κύτωρον in his explanation of his proposed reading clearly reflects a text in which both lines 852 and 853 were present.[14] There can, therefore, be no doubt that the text of the *Iliad* used by Callisthenes contained the Paphlagonian entry in the same form as does ours. One final point Fragment 53 almost certainly comes from Callisthenes' history of Alexander, a work intended for as broad a reading public as possible.[15] Inclusion of a textual discussion of the sort contained in fragment 53 in such a work presupposes that Callisthenes expected it to be intelligible to his audience. In other words, the text of the *Iliad* he wished to modify cannot have been an unusual one, but instead one that was in general circulation during the 4th century BC.[16] It is thus clear that lines 853–855 were

[10] Strabo 12. 3. 5 = Callisthenes *FGrH* 124 F53.
[11] Bolling 1925, 78.
[12] Allen (1921, 159) noted this.
[13] For the scholia, see Bolling 1925, 77–78. In addition to Strabo, Eustathius (G. Stallbaum [ed.], *Commentarii ad Homeri Iliadem et Odysseam* [Leipzig 1825–30; repr. 1960], I, 294 and IV, 162) also knows of the lines.
[14] That Strabo adhered closely to Callisthenes' wording in 12. 3. 5 is revealed by his appending to the latter's mention of the Leucosyrians the gloss οὓς καὶ ἡμεις Καππάδοκας προσαγορεύομεν.
[15] Pearson 1960, 43–44.
[16] Further evidence pointing to the general inclusion of these lines in copies of the *Iliad* before 300 BC is provided by a Cromnian inscription, published by E. Kalinka (1933, 60, no. 6), and discussed by L. Robert (1937, 262–65), which reads Ὅμηρος / Κρομνεύς. The claim is

194 PART II: ARTICLES

not added to the *Iliad* during the Hellenistic period, but rather deleted from it during the 3rd century BC by some editor, most likely Zenodotus.[17] Accordingly, since there are neither textual nor historical grounds for rejecting these lines,[18] historians in the future may not justify their failure to consider the implications of lines 853–855 in their reconstructions of the process of Greek penetration of the Black Sea simply by referring to Allen's discussion.

BIBLIOGRAPHY

Allen, W. 1921: *The Homeric Catalogue of Ships* (Oxford).
Bethe, E. 1929: *Homer: Dichtung und Sage*, 2nd ed., vol. 2 (Stuttgart).
Burr, V. 1944: ΝΕΩΝ ΚΑΤΑΛΟΓΟΣ: *Untersuchung zum homerischen Schiffskatalog* (*Klio* Beiheft 49) (Leipzig).
Bolling, G.M. 1925: *The External Evidence for Interpolation in Homer* (Oxford).
Carpenter, R. 1948: 'The Greek Penetration of the Black Sea'. *American Journal of Archaeology* 52, 1–10.
Graham, A.J. 1958: 'The Date of the Greek Penetration of the Black Sea'. *Bulletin of the Institute of Classical Studies* 5, 25–42.
Kalinka, E. 1933: 'Aus Bithynien und Umgegend'. *Jahreshefte des Österreichischen Archäologischen Institutes* Beiblatt 28, 44–111.
Labaree, B.W. 1957: 'How the Greeks Sailed into the Black Sea'. *American Journal of Archaeology* 61, 29–33.
Pearson, L. 1960: *The Lost Histories of Alexander the Great* (New York).
Page, D.L. 1959: *History and the Homeric Iliad* (Sather Classical Lectures 31) (Berkeley).
Robert, L. 1937: *Études anatoliennes* (Études orientales publiées par l'institut français d'archéologie de Stamboul 5) (Paris).
Simpson, R.H. and Lazenby, J.F. 1970: *The Catalogue of the Ships in Homer's Iliad* (Oxford).
Thomas, H. and Stubbings, F.H. 1962: 'Lands and Peoples in Homer'. In Wace, A.J.B. and Stubbings, F.H. (eds.), *A Companion to Homer* (London), 283–310.

---

obviously based on the mention of Cromna in line 855, and although the inscription is undated, the tradition is most likely to have arisen before *ca.* 300 BC when Cromna became part of the new city of Amastris (Memmon *FGrH* 434 F4. 9; Strabo 12. 2. 10) and lost its independent identity.

[17] Two facts point to Zenodotus' edition as the one that omitted lines 853–855: (1) the use of such a text by both Eratosthenes and Apollodorus; and (2) Apollodorus' approval of Zenodotus' reading Ἐνετῆς instead of Ἐνετῶν in line 852 (Apollodorus *FGrH* 244 F171 = Strabo 12. 3. 24–25).

[18] Only proof that the Greeks could not have sailed the Black Sea in the 8th century BC would suffice to impeach these lines. Carpenter's attempt (1948) to provide such proof, by showing that the Greeks could not have overcome the problems of sailing through the Bosporus before the invention of the pentecounter *ca.* 700 BC, has been refuted by Labaree (1957) and Graham 1958, 26–31.

HERACLEA PONTICA: THE CITY AND SUBJECTS*

Colonization always involves the interaction of two groups of peoples, the indigenous inhabitants of the area to be settled and the settlers themselves. This is particularly true in the earliest days of a successful colony. Then the presence of natives near the prospective settlement is an attraction since they offer both the possibility of trade and assistance for the colonists during the difficult period before the colony becomes self-supporting. Only after its continued existence has been assured are relations between the two peoples likely to turn hostile as the colonist's need for additional land begins to threaten the welfare of their native neighbors. This pattern, whose full significance is now being explored by historians of 17th-century North America,[1] applies also to the Greek colonization of the shores of the Black Sea. Literary tradition, philology and archaeology all confirm that the majority of Greek cities in the area were founded on or near the sites of earlier non-Greek settlements.[2] The common finds of imported Greek wares on native sites contemporary with the early period of Greek settlement attest to the intense interaction of the Greeks and their native neighbors.

Such interaction and on a relatively equal basis is particularly well illustrated by discoveries made in the cemetery of the mid-7th century Milesian colony of Histria in the North Dobruja in Romania. There five rich 6th-century burials of chieftains were found, each marked by a non-Greek ritual including horse and human sacrifice – in one case involving 35 human victims – and containing both native wares and fine imported Greek pottery of various types.[3] By the Hellenistic period the situation had changed. Histria had annexed all of the territory between her and Tomis, her nearest Greek neighbor to the south.[4] Her now extensive *chora* was inhabited and worked by both Greek and non-Greek farmers, and it was on the secure exploitation of this territory that the city's prosperity depended. Thus during the 2nd century Thracian raids into Histria's *chora* just before the harvest put the citizens in great distress. In response to such threats Histria hired mercenaries, paid protection money to nearby petty chieftains and tribute to more distant powerful rulers who

---

* First published in *The Ancient World* 2 (1979), 25–28.
[1] *Cf.*, for example, Morgan 1975, 72–73; Nash 1974, 88–155; Jennings 1975, 85–104.
[2] Danov 1976, 355; Boardman 1973, 240–54.
[3] Alexandrescu 1965; 1966,
[4] This seems to follow from Memnon *FGrH* 3B, 434 F13. *Cf.* Pippidi 1971, 204–06.

196 PART II: ARTICLES

promised the city protection against raids by their vessals.[5] Such measures assured a modicum of security to the Greek and native farmers of Histria's *chora* as well as being one of the principle means by which Greek luxury goods and coins found their way into the interior.

But what were the relations between the Greeks of Histria and the natives who inhabited the city's *chora*? The description of the latter as *barbaroi* in *SEG* 24, 1095 makes it clear that they had neither been assimilated nor were they citizens of Histria.[6] Despite their evident political inferiority, D.M. Pippidi has suggested that they were active collaborators with the Greeks in the exploitation of Histria's territory, a relationship he characterizes as a 'Greco-Thracian symbiosis'.[7] The excavations of the native settlement of Tariverde, about 15 km from Histria, however, suggest a less happy relationship. Greek luxury goods, relatively common in the 6th- and 5th-century levels, are almost totally absent in the Hellenistic levels in which Greek influence is evident mainly in the style of utilitarian wares and housebuilding techniques and in the ubiquitous wine amphoras.[8] The impression is that the Hellenistic inhabitants of Tariverde were little more than peasants farming the *chora* of Histria. Similar conditions are suggested by material from Olbia[9] and Chersonesus Taurica,[10] but by far the clearest and most revealing evidence for Greek-native relations in the Black Sea basin is provided by the north Anatolian city of Heraclea Pontica.

The history of the relations between Heraclea Pontica and the Mariandynoi, a people of mixed Anatolian and Thracian origin, conforms closely to the pattern outlined for Histria. Initial relations between the Mariandynoi and the Megarian and Boeotian colonists who settled near one of their villages about 560 BC were peaceful. Colonial growth, however, quickly led to hostilities which ended in the mid-5th century with the conquest of the Mariandynoi and the appropriation of their land by the Heracleotes. By the 3rd century Heraclea had become an important power in the Pontus, controlling the coast of northern Anatolia from eastern Paphlagonia to central Bithynia and taking an active role in military affairs to the east and west of her small empire. Nevertheless, the key to her power and prosperity remained her control of Mariandynia and the Mariandynoi who worked the estates of her upper class and rowed the ships of her fleet; and like Histria Heraclea sometimes found it necessary to

---

[5] *SEG* 24, 1095, 11. 8–55. *Cf*. Pippidi 1975a.
[6] 11. 43–44.
[7] Pippidi 1975b, 79–80.
[8] Condurachi *et al*. 1953; Stephan *et al*. 1954.
[9] Pippidi 1975b, 74–75.
[10] Pippidi 1975b, 72–74.

HERACLEA PONTICA: THE CITY AND SUBJECTS

buy protection from raids on her territory by her enemies, particularly the Galatians.[11]

Also as at Histria, there is no evidence of significant assimilation between the Heracleotes and the Mariandynoi. Quite the contrary. The settlement that ended overt hostilities between them established a virtual caste system at Heraclea that reminded ancient scholars strongly of conditions at Sparta and Thessaly and lasted until at least the 1st century BC.[12] As was true of the Helots and Penestai, conquest transformed the Mariandynoi into a caste of hereditary agricultural workers. Legally they were slaves of the *polis* of Heraclea, guaranteed only protection against sale outside of Mariandynia. In practice they continued to farm their ancestral land, but now they paid tribute to those Heracleotes to whom it had been allotted.[13]

By itself the system ensured the survival of the Mariandynoi as a distinct people, and in fact they are attested as such with their own language and cults as late as the 1st century BC.[14] At the same time, however, the gap in attitudes and culture between the Mariandynoi and their Heracleote masters could only broaden and deepen as time passed. Archaeological confirmation of this is lacking because of the absence of significant excavation at Heraclea, but this deficiency in the material evidence is compensated for by the remains of Heracleote historiography.

The culture of the Mariandynoi and their contacts with Greek beginning with Heroic times were important themes in Heracleote historiography and are relatively well represented in the fragments of the local historians. Of particular importance in this regard is the material dealing with the Mariandynian summer harvest festival in honor of Bormus and with the exploits of Heracles and the Argonauts at Heraclea.

The Bormus festival was the best known feature of Mariandynian culture, and its conduct is attested from the 5th century to the 1st century BC.[15] Its central rite was the mournful search by the Mariandynian celebrants for a disappearing god, Bormus, the son of Titias, the son of Zeus – presumably a local manifestation of one of the Anatolian weather gods – who was supposed to have increased the power and prosperity of the Mariandynoi, to have founded

---

[11] For Heraclea and the Galatians, see Memnon *FGrH* 3B, 434 Ff 14. 3; 16. For the history of Heraclea in general, see Burstein 1976.

[12] For the main texts, see Athenaeus 6. 263c and Plato *Laws* 776B. Strabo 12. 3. 4 points to the survival of the system in the late Hellenistic period.

[13] *Cf.* Burstein 1976, 28–30. A portion of them seems to have lived on public land and paid their tribute to Heraclea itself.

[14] Implied by Strabo 12. 3. 4.

[15] Aeschylus *Persians* 939; Nymphis *FGrH* 3B, 432 F5; Domitius Callistratus *FGrH* 3B, 433 F3.

198   PART II: ARTICLES

a town named Tition after himself and finally to have been deified by them.[16] Most commonly his son Bormus is said to have disappeared while hunting.[17] The 3rd-century Historian Nymphis, however, collected the following version of the story two centuries after the subjugation of the Mariandynoi (*FGrH* 3B, 432 F5; trans. C.B. Gulick):

> Similarly, one may note some of the songs which they (*sc.* the Mariandynoi) sing during a certain festival that is held in their country, in which they repeatedly invoke one of their ancient heroes, addressing him as Bormus. They say that he was the son of [Titias],[18] an eminent rich man, and that in beauty and perfection of loveliness he far surpassed all others; he, when superintending work in his own fields, desiring to supply drink for the reapers, went to get water and disappeared. And so the people of countryside sought for him to the strains of a dirge with repeated invocation, which they all continue to use to this very day.

The most remarkable feature of this version of the story is the suppression of the heroic element. Instead of the son of a great hero who disappears while hunting, a suitable occupation for such a figure, Bormus has been transformed into the model master of a great estate, the son of an important rich man, who disappears while performing a kindly deed for his field hands, who then search for him. Clearly Nymphis' informants recast the background of the traditional story to reflect their historical experience. Being themselves agricultural laborers on the estates of rich Heracleotes, they transformed Bormus and Titias into idealized versions of their masters while they saw themselves as re-enacting the actions of the ancient reapers. Equally clearly, the source of the reapers' affection for Bormus is his considerate behavior, presumably the sort of behavior they would expect of a Heracleote, whom they would characterize as a 'good master'. Thus, this 3rd-century variant of the Bormus story reflects two developments, the adjustment of the Mariandynoi to their servitude and the development of a set of standards by them to judge their masters, standards that approximate those of a client to his patron.

The adjustment of Mariandynian myth to reflect current social reality is not surprising. After two centuries of such servitude, the life of agricultural laborers was the only life the Mariandynoi knew, and the tendency to project it back into their past must have been strong. Equally unsurprising is the myth's suggestion that as dependents the Mariandynoi judged their masters according

---

[16] Domitius Callistratus *apud* Promathidas *FGrH* 3B, 430 F1; Burstein 1976, 102, n. 91. For Tition, see *Scholia in Apollonium Rhodium Vetera*, ed. C. Wendel (Berlin 1935), 187, *Scholium ad* B 780–783a.

[17] Domitius Callistratus *FGrH* 3B, 433 F3; Pollux 4. 54. *Cf.* Burstein 1976, 10–11 for the cult in general.

[18] For the introduction of the name Titias at this point see Nymphis *FGrH* 3B, 432 F5a.

HERACLEA PONTICA: THE CITY AND SUBJECTS 199

to how well they treated them and provided for their basic needs. Similarly there is evidence that as time passed and the system became firmly established, the Heracleotes themselves developed a distinctly paternalistic attitude toward their subjects. This is suggested by the 2nd-century scholar Callistratus' observation (*FGrH* 348, F4) that the Heracleote term for the Mariandynoi, *dorophoroi* or gift-bearers, 'took away the sting of the appelation slave' and is readily apparent in the accounts of the relations between the Marandynoi and Heracles and the Argonauts.

The clearest account of Heracles' adventures at Heraclea is provided by Ps.-Appolldorus (*Bibliotheca* 2. 5. 3) who states that while seeking the girdle of Hippolyte

> he came to Mysia to Lycus the son of Dascylus and while his guest [the forces] of the king of the Bebrycians attacked. Heracles came to the aid of Lycus and killed many among whom was the king Mygdon the brother of Amycus. He then took away much[19] land from the Bebrycians and gave it to Lycus who called it all Heraclea.[20]

Needless to say, this story does not reflect Mycenaean contact with the Mariandynoi nor is it simply an invention intended to explain the reason the city was called Heraclea. The similarity between this story in which Heracles, a deified son of Zeus, was ultimately responsible for both the founding of Heraclea and the settlement of the Mariandynoi there and the Titias story alluded to earlier suggests that the Heracleotes identified the two figures and then transferred the deeds of the native hero to Heracles.[21] In the process, however, the meaning of the story changed. Instead of celebrating the deeds of a Mariandynian hero, it now became a charter myth, justifying both Greek settlement at Heraclea and rule of the Mariandynoi by transposing to the time of initial Greek contact with the site of Heraclea and Mariandynian settlement there the pattern of relations that existed between the two people after the defeat of the

---

[19] Reading *pollen* instead of *polin* (*Cf.* Apollodorus, *The Library* 1, ed. J.G. Frazer [London, 1921], 204, n. 3). The corruption is old since it was already present in Stephanus' text of Ps.-Apollodorus (*apud* John Tzetzes *Historiarum variorum chiliades* 3. 11. 806–817).

[20] Ps.-Apollodorus' source was probably the late 5th-century Heracleote mythographer Herodorus (*cf.* Burstein 1976, 103, n. 96; and Jacoby *FGrH* 1a, 508 n. *ad* 31 F49). For Heracles as the true founder of Heracleas, see Pomponius Mela 1. 103; Menander, *Rhetores graeci*, ed. C. Walz, 9 (Stuttgart 1836), 178, 192; Himerius 41. 9; and Head 1911, 516. Nymphis as preserved by Apollonius of Rhodes (*Argonautica* 2, lines 774–791; for Nymphis as Apollonius' source, see Desideri 1967, 380–87) seems to have concentrated on Heracles' territorial benefactions to the Mariandynoi and played down or ignored his role in bringing them to Heraclea.

[21] Such identifications of figures of Greek myth and saga with native figures are attested in the fragments of the Heracleote historians (Promathidas *FGrH* 3B, 430 F3; Amphitheus *FGrH* 3B, 431 F1).

200 PART II: ARTICLES

Mariandynoi by the Heracleotes in the mid-5th century.[22] At the very beginning of their settlement of Heraclea the Mariandynoi are shown to have been dependent on the protection of Heracles, a Greek, for their survival and on his benefactions for their home and future prosperity.

The Mariandynoi's dependence on Greek protection for survival was also the main theme of Nymphis' account of the visit of the Argonauts to Heraclea, which Apollonius of Rhodes followed in the second book of his *Argonautica*. According to Apollonius, Lycus, the king of the Mariandynoi, received the Argonauts graciously because the Dioscouroi had killed their enemy Amycus, king of the Bebrycians. After recounting Heracles' benefactions to his people, Lycus describes their present sad state now that he is gone (*Argonautica* 2, lines 792–801: trans. R.C. Seaton):

> But now the Bebrycians and the insolence of Amycus have robbed me, since Heracles dwells far away, for they have long been cutting off huge pieces of my land until they have set their bounds at the meadows of deep-flowing Hypius. Nevertheless, by your hands have they paid the penalty... Wherefore, whatever requital I am now able to pay, gladly will I pay it, for that is the rule for weaker men when the stronger begin to help them.

The last line says it all. In its immediate context it refers to Lycus' promise to aid the Argonauts and to establish a *temenos* for the Dioscouroi (lines 802–807), but in a broader sense it points up the moral of the whole episode. Hardly had Heracles left than the Mariandynoi began to lose what he had given them. Only the opportune arrival of the Agonauts preserved their territory for them. Again, therefore, the Mariaadynoi and shown to have been dependent on the protection of Greeks for their welfare from the earliest days of their history.

Unfortunately direct evidence is lacking for the continuation of the story and in particular for the manner in which the Heracleote historians treated the final subjugation of the Mariandynoi. The following fragment from the eleventh book of Posidonius' histories, however, gives a hint (*FGrH* 2A, 87 F8):

> Many people, unable to govern themselves because of the weakness of their understanding, give themselves into the service of the more intelligent in order that those might take care for their necessities in return for whatever services they might be able to render to them. In just this way the Mariandynoi became subject to the Heracleotes, promising to serve as agricultural laborers those who furnished them with necessities...

Posidonius' general rule is essentially Aristotle's doctrine of the natural slave. His use of the Mariandynoi as a concrete example of its application, however,

---

[22] For a good discussion of this subject as it involves Heracles, see Asheri 1975. Less satisfactory is the historicizing treatment by Sjoquist 1962.

suggests that the Heracleote historians treated the struggle for domination in Mariandynia as an aberration and the establishment of the system of servitude that prevailed after its end as a reaffirmation of the paternalistic relationship between the Greeks and their Mariandynian dependents that they described in their accounts of the exploits of Heracles and the Argonauts at Heraclea.

The purpose of this paper has not been to argue that by the Hellenistic period interaction between Greeks and non-Greeks ceased in the territories of the Pontic cities. The opposite is obviously true. Greeks worshipped non-Greek deities[23] and married non-Greek women[24] although not necessarily women of local origin. Likewise individual non-Greeks, again not necessarily of local origin, Hellenized, settled in the cities and became citizens.[25] All this is true, but the evidence still indicates that the conditions at Heraclea Pontica were typical of the general situation, that is, the native population of the *chora* of a city constituted little more than a disfranchised, dependent caste of agricultural laborers. Whether or not the harshness of this condition was moderated elsewhere by the emergence of paternalistic attitudes similar to those attested at Heraclea is not known.

BIBLIOGRAPHY

Alexandrescu, P. 1965: 'Les rapports entre indigènes et Grecs à la lumière des fouilles de la nécropole d'Histria'. In Demargne, P. (ed.), *Le rayonnement des civilisations grecque et romaine sur les cultures périphériques* (Paris), 336–39.

—. 1966: 'Necropola tumulară: Şapături 1955–1961'. In Condurachi, E. (ed.), *Histria* II (Bucharest), 143–59.

Asheri, D. 1975: 'Eracle, Eraclea e I Cyclicranes; mitología e decolonizzazione nella Grecia del IV se. B.C.'. *Ancient Society* 6, 33–50.

Boardman, J. 1973: *The Greeks Overseas*, 2nd ed. (Harmondsworth).

Burstein, S.M. 1976: *Outpost of Hellenism: The Emergence of Heraclea on the Black Sea* (University of California Publications: Classical Studies 14) (Berkeley).

Condurachi, E. *et al.* 1953: 'Santierul Histria'. *Studii si cercetări di istorie veche* 4, 129–35.

Danov, C.M. 1976: *Altthrakien* (Berlin).

Desideri, P. 1967: 'Studi Storiografia Eracleota I: Promathidas e Nymphis'. *Studi Classici et Orientali* 16, 366–416.

Head, B.V. 1911: *Historia Numorum*, 2nd ed. (London).

---

[23] For examples, *cf.* Danov 1976, 359 and Pippidi 1975c, 92.

[24] For examples of such mixed marriages, see *IGBR* I² 108, 115, 116, 127, 130, 141*bis*, 171*bis*, 172, 176*ter*, 178*bis*, and 200. Outside of such diplomatic marriages as those of the Scythian kings Ariapeithes and Scylas (Herodotus 4. 78) the marriage of Greek women to non-Greek men seems to have been extremely rare.

[25] On this whole subject, see Danov 1976, 348–68.

202 PART II: ARTICLES

Jennings, F. 1975: *The Invasion of America: Indians, Colonialism, and the Cant of Conquest* (New York).

Morgan, E.S. 1975: *American Slavery American Freedom: The Ordeal of Colonial Virginia* (New York).

Nash, G.B. 1974: *Red, White, and Black: The Peoples of Early America* (Englewood Cliffs, NJ).

Pippidi, D.M. 1971: *I Greet nel Basso Danubio: dall'età arcaica alla conquista romana* (Biblioteca storica dell'antichità 8) (Milan).

—. 1975a: 'Istros et les Gètes au IIe siècle. Observations sur le décret en l'honneur d'Agathoclès, fils d'Antiphilos'. In Pippidi 1975d, 30–55.

—. 1975b: 'Le problème de la main d'oeuvre agricole dans les colonies grecques de la mer Noire'. In Pippidi 1975d, 65–80.

—. 1975c: 'Pour une histoire des cultes d'Istros: Documents d'époque hellénistique'. In Pippidi 1975d, 81–95.

—. 1975d: *Scythica Minora: Recherches sur les colonies grecques du littoral roumain de la mer Noire* (Bucharest).

Sjoquist, E. 1962: 'Heracles in Sicily'. *Opuscula Romana* 4, 117–23.

Stephan, G. *et al.* 1954: 'Santierul Histria'. *Studii si cercetări de istorie veche* 5, 100–08.

THE BLACK SEA: AN ACHAEMENID FRONTIER ZONE[*]

Two facts about the Persian Empire are uncontroversial. It was the last and greatest of the Ancient Near Eastern world empires, and like its various predecessors – Babylonian, Assyrian and Akkadian – it was not truly universal despite its claims of world rule, being bounded by frontier zones that were outside the administrative structure provided by the system of satrapies. One such zone was the Black Sea, especially its south coast, where relations between the Great King's government and its Greek and Anatolian subjects were particularly complex. The aim of this paper is to consider how Achaemenid authority was exercised in this region in the final decades of the empire's existence 'on the basis of evidence provided' by an important new inscription, *I. Sinope* 1.

It is not an easy story to tell, since the Black Sea occupies little space in histories of ancient Persia. The reasons are twofold. First, although the Black Sea was recognized as belonging to the broader Persian sphere of influence down to the end of the empire in the late 4th century BC, its location on the northwest periphery of the Achaemenid Empire means that sources for the history of the Black Sea in the Persian period are particularly poor. The sources are limited to scattered references in a handful of Greek and Latin literary texts, a few inscriptions, and, most importantly, archaeological evidence. Second, although in an important passage Herodotus (3. 97), distinguished between satrapies that paid tribute and peoples on the empire's peripheries who sent the Great King gifts, such as the kingdom of Kush south of Egypt and Colchis and its immediate neighbors,[1] Achaemenid ideology treated all peoples within the claimed boundaries of the empire including those on its most distant frontiers as equally subject to the Great King.[2] This is clear from the lack of distinction between the figures in Achaemenid throne bearer reliefs and from the list of

---

[*] First published in T. Daryaee and R. Rollinger (eds.), *Iran and its Histories: From Earliest Times Through the Achaemenid Empire* (Classica et Orientalia 29) (Harrassowitz, Wiesbaden 2021), 369–78.

[1] According to Herodotus (3. 97. 4), the Colchians were required to send 100 boys and 100 young women every four years and continued to do so until his own time. Archaeological finds including evidence for a Persian style palace at Gumbati confirm the strong Persian presence in Colchis (Tsetskhladze 2018a, 522–33; 2019, 138–42). For a convincing analysis of how Persian influence in Colchis was exercised, see Brosius 2010.

[2] *Cf.* Wiesehöfer 1996, 59–61.

204 PART II: ARTICLES

border peoples in inscriptions such as DPh, two of which Herodotus listed as tribute payers and one as a gift bringer:

> Saith Darius the King: This is the kingdom which I hold, from the Scythians who are beyond Sogdiana, thence unto Ethiopia; from Sind, thence unto Sardis, which Ahuramazda, the greatest of the gods, bestowed upon me.[3]

As a result, contemporary Persian evidence for the unique character of relations between the peoples of the south coast of the Black Sea and their Achaemenid suzerain is lacking, leaving us no choice but to rely on Greek sources of which two are particularly important.

The first is the fifth book of Xenophon's *Anabasis*, which provides a vivid snapshot of conditions in northern Anatolia at the end of the 5th century BC. The second is a substantial epitome of a local history of the city of Heraclea Pontica on the southwest coast of the Black Sea by an otherwise unknown historian named Memnon, which exists thanks to the survival to the 9th century AD of a codex containing Books 9 to 16 of his work, when it was read and summarized by the Byzantine patriarch Photius.[4]

About the life of Memnon all that can be said for certain is that he wrote some time after Julius Caesar's defeat of Pompey in 48 BC.[5] It has long been recognized, however, that for his account of the rise and fall of the 4th century BC Heracleote tyranny Memnon relied on the *Peri Herakleias* of the local historian Nymphis, whose life extended from the late 4th to some time after the mid-3rd century BC.[6] Consequently, we have a near contemporary account, albeit at third hand, of relations between one of the principal Greek cities of northern Anatolia and Persia during the decades immediately before its conquest by Alexander in the late 330s BC.

This is not the first time I have examined Persian relations with the peoples of the Black Sea. I worked through the fifth book of Xenophon's *Anabasis* and Memnon's account of Heraclea and the other relevant sources over 40 years ago in my first book,[7] *Outpost of Hellenism: The Emergence of Heraclea on the Black Sea*. Almost half a century is a long time in scholarship, however, and new evidence has appeared in the meantime that justifies reconsideration of my analysis of these issues.

---

[3] Kent 1953, 137 = DPh 2. 3–10.

[4] Photius *Bibl.* 224. The most recent edition with translation and commentary is by A. Keaveney and J.A. Madden in Brill's *New Jacoby* (434).

[5] The latest datable reference in Photius' epitome of Memnon is Caesar's victory in the civil war in the early 40s BC (Memnon *BNJ* 434 F 1. 40. 3; *cf.* Janke 1963, 128).

[6] Nymphis: *FGrH* 3B, no. 432 with *FGrH* 3B, 259–65. Memnon's sources: Desideri 1967; Jacoby *FGrH* 3B, 269–70; Burstein 1976, 2–3.

[7] Burstein 1976, 72–78.

THE BLACK SEA: AN ACHAEMENID FRONTIER ZONE

Because of the limitations of the literary sources, however, the new evidence is overwhelmingly archaeological and epigraphical. Moreover, since none of the cities of the south coast of the Black Sea has been excavated or is likely to be because of their being overlaid by modern construction, both civil and military, the bulk of the new evidence deals with the Greek cities of the west, north, and east coasts of the Black Sea. Still, despite the lack of proper excavations in northern Anatolia, archaeological evidence relevant to our problem has been discovered there including Achaemenid style luxury silver vessels being discovered in illicit excavations at Sinope and Ünye (ancient Cotyora),[8] the head of a life size statue, most likely of a Persian official, at Heraclea, and Persian style tombs in the interior of Paphlagonia.[9] Combined with the more extensive discoveries of Persian and Persianizing material found elsewhere in the region, it clearly implies that[10] Achaemenid cultural influence was pervasive throughout the Black Sea basin during the 5th and 4th centuries BC, not only extending over the whole region, but also influencing the elite culture of both of the Greek cities and their non-Greek neighbors.

The most unexpected of the recent discoveries and remarkable in its implications, however, is a fragment of a monumental Old Persian inscription of Darius I that was found during excavations at Phanagoria in the Taman Peninsula on the east coast of the Straits of Kerch.[11] Despite its poor state of preservation, the

[8] Dusinberre 2013, 180.

[9] Rehm 2010; Treister 2010. Rare examples of Persian influence on the south coast of the Black Sea are rock tombs in Paphlagonia (Summerer and von Kienlin 2010) and the head of a life size statue with diadem of a Persian king or official discovered at modern Ereğli, ancient Heraclea Pontica (Summerer 2005).

[10] *Cf.* above n. 2. For a full list of Achaemenid objects found on the north coast of the Black Sea, see Tsetskhladze 2018b, 476–80.

[11] The inscription was assigned to Xerxes in the original publication (Kuznetsov and Nikitin 2017), but re-examination indicated that it belonged to the reign of Darius I (Tsetskhladze 2019, 113–20; Shavarebi 2019; Schmitt 2019). It should be noted that Shavarebi (2019, 13) and Schmitt (2019, 42–43) have suggested that the stele was not erected originally at Phanagoria, but that it is a fragment of one of the two stelae Herodotus (4. 87) claims that Darius I set up at the Bosporus, which was subsequently transported to Phanagoria, perhaps as ballast on a ship. This is, however, speculative and three considerations make it more likely that Phanagoria was the original location of the stele: first, the Phanagoria fragment has a secure archaeological *terminus ante quem* of the mid-5th century BC (Tsetskhladze 2019, 117–18, 122), while, according to Herodotus (4. 87. 2), Darius' stelae, except for one block, were built into the altar of Artemis the Savior in Byzantium, and there no evidence that the altar was subsequently dismantled; second, Herodotus (4. 87. 2) claims that the omitted block was preserved at the Temple of Dionysus in Byzantium, and his description of it being 'full of Assyrian letters' suggests that he saw it there; and, third, his (4. 87. 1) description of Darius' stelae suggests that they contained lists of subject peoples, while the restoration *a]dam: aku[navam*, '(I) did/made/built', in the fifth line of the Phanagoria fragment (Shavarebi 2019, 10; Schmitt 2019, 40) implies, if correct, that it commemorated the construction of a building, not military activity. For possible connections between the new inscription and Achaemenid ideas of universal rulership, see Rollinger and Degen 2021, 13–16.

206 PART II: ARTICLES

presence of such an inscription at Phanagoria suggests that for an undetermined period of time, extending at a minimum from sometime in the late 6th century BC into the first two decades of the 5th century BC, the cities of at least part of the north coast of the Black Sea were subject to Persian overlord-ship. Similarly, Persian authority in the region was still recognized in the mid-5th century BC in the Peace of Callias ending hostilities between Persia and the Delian League[12] and again a little over a century later in 330 BC, when Alexander pardoned captured envoys to Darius III from Sinope on the ground that 'the Sinopeans did not belong to the Greek league and, being subject to the Persians, they did not seem to do anything inappropriate in sending ambassadors to their king' (Arrian *Anabasis* 3. 24. 4). In short, Persian authority in the Black Sea, albeit not necessarily exercised equally in all portions of the region, was recognized by the Greeks throughout almost the whole history of the empire.

At the same time, while Persian authority in the Black Sea was recognized by contemporaries, actual evidence of direct Persian governance on the south coast is lacking. In the 430s and 420s BC Athens intervened in the region, founding colonies at Sinope[13] and Amisus[14] and levying tribute on a substantial number of Greek cities on the south, west, and north coasts without encountering, so far as we can tell, significant Persian resistance.[15] Similarly, at the end of the 5th century BC Xenophon's account in the fifth book of the *Anabasis* contains no evidence of Persian authority in northern Anatolia, but reveals instead a crazy quilt of local alliances and hostilities with, for example, the Sinopean colony of Trapezus seeking to protect friendly tribes from the Ten Thousand while encouraging them to raid their enemies, the Drilae (Xenophon *Anabasis* 5. 2. 2), although presumably they all were Persian subjects. Likewise, when the army reached Paphlagonia, Xenophon claims that Sinope was threatened by another Persian subject, the Paphlagonian chieftain Corylas, who had recently refused to obey a Persian order to muster his cavalry for a campaign (Xenophon *Anabasis* 5. 6. 6). The pattern continued into the 4th century BC with hostilities being attested *ca.* 370 between Sinope and Datames, the satrap of Cappadocia, and between Heraclea and a certain Mithridates, most likely Mithridates Ctistes, the founder of the Pontic royal house and probably a member of the family of the satraps of Hellespontine Phrygia, *ca.* 364.[16]

[12] See Wade-Gery 1958, 213.

[13] Plutarch *Pericles* 20. 1–2.

[14] Theopompus *FGrH* 115, F 389; Plutarch *Lucullus* 19. 7; Appian *Mithridates* 83; Anonymous *Periplus of the Black Sea* 9r1.

[15] Meiggs 1972, 328–29; Burstein 1976, 32–34.

[16] Bosworth and Wheatley 1998.

THE BLACK SEA: AN ACHAEMENID FRONTIER ZONE 207

Because recognition of the extent of Persian influence in the Black Sea is recent, attempts to explain the nature of the relationship between Persia and its various peoples are as yet few. Maria Brosius, however, has suggested that frontier regions like the Black Sea, because of their lack of organized kingdoms like, for example, Lydia, were only 'loosely linked', to existing satrapies without further integration into the Achaemenid administrative system;[17] while Gocha Tsetskhladze has argued for an even weaker connection, maintaining that:

> the Great King allowed the Greek cities of the latter [*sc.* Black Sea] to keep their own laws and institutions until the beginning of the 4th century BC, additionally prohibiting his officials and satraps from meddling in their internal affairs – his principal concern being that the Greek cities and local people paid the taxes and tributes demanded of them and furnished him with troops and provisions as and when required to do so.[18]

Ignored, however, in both these discussions is an important passage of Memnon (*BNJ* 434 F 1. 4. 1), that refers to conditions on the south coast of the Black Sea after Alexander's victory in 334 BC in the battle of Granicus and points to a more active role for the Great King in the affairs of the region than allowed for by either of these theories:

> Succeeding to the rule [*sc.* of Heraclea], Dionysius added to it. For the battle of Granicus between Alexander and the Persians enabled those who wished to do so to increase their holdings, since the Persian strength, which always stood in the way, was removed.

The implications of Memnon's account are clear. Despite the absence of satraps able to directly impose order in northern Anatolia, Persian power still restrained the ambitions of the various groups that occupied the south coast of the Black Sea until Alexander's victory at the Granicus River destroyed Persian authority throughout northern and western Anatolia. Unfortunately, Photius' epitome of Memnon contains no further information, but *I. Sinope* 1 provides insight into how that restraint was exercised.

I. Sinope 1 was discovered during the construction of a building at modern Sinop, ancient Sinope, and published in 2004 by David French in *The Inscriptions of Sinope*.[19] Although the inscription is broken at the top and bottom and badly abraded in places, internal evidence, specifically the mention of Satyrus, tyrant of Heraclea from 352 to 346 BC, allows *I. Sinope* 1 to be dated to the late 350s or early 340s BC. As a result, it has thrown a flood of new light directly on relations between the two most important of the south coast cities,

[17] Brosius 2010, 30–33.
[18] Tsetskhladze 2018b, 484.
[19] French 2004, 1–4.

208   PART II: ARTICLES

Heraclea and Sinope, and Persia and indirectly on conditions in the region as whole in the decades immediately before Alexander's campaign.

I. Sinope 1 contains the Sinopean copy of a treaty of alliance that was concluded between Sinope and the tyrant Satyrus and his nephews Timotheus and Dionysius, who ruled Heraclea jointly after the assassination of Satyrus' brother and their father Clearchus, the founder of the Heracleote tyranny, in 352 BC. The text is as follows:

- (line 1) On these (terms) the Sinopeans and Satyros and the sons of Klearchos made an oath and alliance:
- That if anyone attacks Satyros or the son of Heraklia or its territory, except the King, the Sinopeans are to help with all their strength according to their ability and if anyone attacks Sinope or its territory, except the King, Satyros and the (line 5) sons of Klearchos are to help with all their strength according to their ability;
- And if the one who is attacking Satyros or the sons of Klearkhos or Heraklia or its (line 10) territory or Sinope or its territory says that he is attacking with the King, (the parties to the treaty) are to send, jointly with the attacker, envoys to the King and to request him (the attacker) to leave the territory;
- And if the attacker does not choose to send envoys and to leave the territory, (the parties) are to help one another with all their strength according to their (line 15) ability; that the pay of the soldiers is to be 2½ staters a month; and those who are giving help are to provide in advance one month's pay;
- And repayment of the expenses is (to come) from the party requesting help within 6 months after peace has been made;
- That as many as have fled Sinope or Heraklia, to them it is permitted to remain in (line 20) the cities if they do no wrong;
- And if they in any way seem to do wrong from the [time] when the treaty has come into being, the (parties) are to send envoys and to banish them, provided that it is decided by the Sinopeans and Satyros and the sons of Klearkhos to banish them;
- That the people of Kromna and Sesamos are (included) in the treaty, if they wish;
- (line 25) That each party is to [maintain] the alliance, if on the one hand [anyone attacks] within twenty days from the days when those in charge call for help;
- If on the other hand anyone of those [in the cities] works to overthrow the people of Sinope or [to divide them], or conspires against Satyros or the sons of Klearkhos, (theparties) [are to help one another]

THE BLACK SEA: AN ACHAEMENID FRONTIER ZONE 209

– (line 30) With all their strength according to their ability within ten days of the day when those in charge call for help; …[20]

I. Sinope 1 is without doubt the most important addition to the sources for the history of the Greek cities of the southern Black Sea to have been discovered in decades. Needless to say, while its primary focus is diplomatic and military relations between Heraclea and Sinope and their respective internal politics and military organization, it is clear that those relations are assumed to take place in an environment similar to that described by Xenophon a half century earlier in which the possibility of conflict between Persian subjects is not unusual but expected. What is new, however, is the revelation of the Great King's[21] active role in managing such situations (lines 2 to 14):

> That if anyone attacks Satyros or the sons of Klearkhos or Heraklia or its territory, except the King, the Sinopeans are to help with all their strength according to their ability and if anyone attacks Sinope or its territory, except the King, Satyros and the sons of Klearchos are to help with all their strength according to their ability;

> And if the one who is attacking Satyros or the sons of Klearkhos or Heraklia or its territory or Sinope or its territory says that he is attacking with the King, they (the parties to the treaty) are to send, jointly with the attacker, envoys to the King and to request him (the attacker) to leave the territory; and if the attacker does not choose to send envoys and to leave the territory, (the parties) are to help one another with all their strength according to their ability…

What is particularly noteworthy is that the treaty envisions a right of self-help by its signatories against cities or peoples not partners to it even if they are Persian subjects except in two circumstances: an attack by the Great King himself in which case the provisions of the treaty are no longer in force or when the attacker claims to be a royal agent and 'says that he is attacking with the King' – in which case both sides are to refer the conflict to the Great King for resolution. Should the attacker, however, refuse to send envoys to the king to verify his claim to be carrying out the Great King's orders or, although it is not explicitly stated, to obey a royal order to break off his attack, the treaty's self-defense provisions could be activated with impunity and, again although it is not explicitly stated, the attacker presumably henceforth would be considered a rebel against the king. Nor were these provisions merely theoretical.

---

[20] The final three lines (lines 31–33) seem to deal with the procedure for mobilizing troops and amending the treaty, but they are too fragmentary for certain translation. French suggests: That [the callup] is to be made by both parties from [the ages from] 20 to [39], And it is permitted (for it) to be amended in whatever way [is decided by the Sinopeans and Satyros and] the sons of Klearkhos…

[21] For Heraclea's close ties to the Persian king, see Justin 16. 3. 9 and Memnon *BNJ* 434 F 1. 4 and F 4. 1. For Sinope, see Arrian *Anabasis* 3. 24. 4.

210   PART II: ARTICLES

Several passages survive concerning a war *ca.* 370 BC between Sinope and Datames, satrap of Cappadocia, who had already seized control of Paphlagonia and the city of Amisus.[22] According to the texts, Datames deceived Sinope by promising to turn the city of Sesamos over to it in return for Sinopean assistance in besieging the city, only to lay siege to Sinope instead. The 2nd-century AD rhetorician Polyaenus preserves the account of the unexpected sequel in his *Strategemata*:[23]

> Datames, while he was besieging Sinope, received a letter from the king, forbidding him from conducting the siege. After reading it, he performed *proskynesis* to the letter and sacrificed for good tidings, as though he had received many good things from the king. At night, however, he boarded a ship and sailed away.

Clearly, Polyaenus' anecdote, although compressed, presupposes the same procedure as that outlined in *I. Sinope* 1, that is, the Great King, Artaxerxes II in this case, had been notified, presumably by envoys from the combatants, that Sinope had been attacked by Datames, one of his satraps, and ordered him to lift the siege, an order that he obeyed.

The fact that at a later date Datames did succeed in occupying Sinope does not lessen the significance of this passage as confirmation of the evidence provided by *I. Sinope* 1 for how the Persians exercised the restraint on their Black Sea subjects mentioned by Memnon, since by then Datames was, in all likelihood, one of the rebels in the so-called Great Satrap's Revolt of the late 360s BC. Similarly, in 364 BC, a little less than a decade after Datames' failed siege of Sinope, Clearchus, the first tyrant of Heraclea, humiliated a Persian dynast, probably, as already mentioned, Mithridates Ctistes, who had tried to seize Heraclea, and then succeeded in insulating himself against the Persian's revenge by obtaining recognition from Artaxerxes II and Artaxerxes III as ruler of Heraclea.[24]

In a famous passage Herodotus (6. 42) describes how the Satrap of Sardis imposed peace on the Ionians after the Ionian Revolt. At first glance, conditions in northern Anatolia as depicted in Xenophon and other 4th-century BC sources seem the opposite: In the absence of local satrapal authority conditions in the region seems chaotic, and racked by chronic hostility between the Greek cities and their neighbors, whose only tie to the empire was a direct but loose connection to the Great King. *I. Sinope* 1 and Memnon's account of conditions in the Black Sea before Alexander's invasion, however, suggest that this impression is misleading and that the Great King could and did intervene to limit the violence and prevent significant changes in the existing

---

[22] Aeneas Tacticus *Poliorketika* 40. 4–5. Polyaenus *Strategemata* 7. 21. 2, 5.
[23] Polyaenus *Strategemata* 7. 21. 5.
[24] Burstein 1976, 51–52.

THE BLACK SEA: AN ACHAEMENID FRONTIER ZONE 211

political and territorial relationships in the region. How effective that intervention could be against an isolated rebel is revealed by the fate of Datames who was driven from his satrapy and continually harassed by superior forces loyal to the Great King until he was assassinated trying to arrange a truce with representatives of Artaxerxes II.

BIBLIOGRAPHY

Bosworth, A.B. and Wheatley, P.V. 1998: 'The Origins of the Pontic House'. *JHS* 118, 155–64.

Brosius, M. 2010: 'Pax Persica and the Peoples of the Black Sea Region: Extent and Limits of Achaemenid Imperial Ideology'. In Nieling and Rehm 2010, 29–40.

Burstein, S.M. 1976: *Outpost of Hellenism: The Emergence of Heraclea on the Black Sea* (University of California Publications: Classical Studies 14) (Berkeley).

Desideri, P. 1967: 'Studi di storiografia eracleota, I: Promathidas e Nymphis'. *Studi classici et orientali* 16, 366–416.

Dusinberre, E.R.M. 2013: *Empire, Authority, and Autonomy in Achaemenid Anatolia* (Cambridge).

French, D.H. (ed.) 2004: *The Inscriptions of Sinope, Part I: Inscriptions* (Inschriften Griechischer Städte Kleinasiens 64) (Bonn).

Janke, M. 1963: *Historische Untersuchungen zu Memnon von Herakleia: Kap. 18–40, FGrHist Nr. 434* (Dissertation, Würzburg).

Kent, R. 1953: *Old Persian Grammar Texts Lexicon* (New Haven).

Kuznetsov, V.D. and Nikitin, A.B. 2017: 'Drevnepersidska Nadpis iz Phanagorii'. In Kuznetsov, V.D. (ed.), *Phanagoriya* 6 (Moscow), 154–59.

Meiggs, R. 1972: *The Athenian Empire* (Oxford).

Nieling, J. 2010: 'Persian Imperial Policy Behind the Rise and Fall of the Cimmerian Bosporus in the Last Quarter of the Sixth to the Beginning of the Fifth Century BC'. In Nieling and Rehm 2010, 123–36.

Nieling, J. and Rehm, E. (eds.) 2010: *Achaemenid Impact in the Black Sea: Communication of Powers* (Black Sea Studies 11) (Aarhus).

Rehm, E. 2010: 'The Classification of Objects from the Black Sea Region Made or Influenced by the Achaemenids'. In Nieling and Rehm 2010, 161–94.

Rollinger, R. and Degen, J. 2021: 'Conceptualizing Universal Rulership: Considerations on the Persian Achaemenid Worldview and the Saka at the "End of the World"'. In Klinkott, H., Luther, A. and Wiesehöfer, J. (eds.), *Beiträge zur Geschichte und Kultur des alten Iran und benachbarter Gebiete. Festschrift für Rüdiger Schmitt* (Oriens et Occidens 36) (Stuttgart), 1–38.

Schmitt, R. 2019: 'Überlegungen zu zwei neuen Altpersischen Inschriften (Phanagoria, Naqš-i Rustam)'. *Nartamongæ* 14.1–2, 34–49.

Shavarebi, E. 2019: 'An Inscription of Darius I from Phanagoria (DFa): Preliminary report of a work in progress'. *Achaemenid Research on Texts and Archaeology* (ARTA) 2019.005, 1–16.

Summerer, L. 2005: 'Achämeniden am Schwarzen Meer: Bermerkungen zum spätarchaischen Marmorkopf aus Herakleia Pontike'. *Ancient Near Eastern Studies* 42, 231–52.

Summerer, L. and von Kienlin, A. 2010: 'Achaemenid Impact in Paphlagonia: Rupestral Tombs in the Amnias Valley'. In Nieling and Rehm 2010, 195–222.

Treister, M. 2010: '"Achaemenid" and "Achaemenid Inspired" Goldware and Silverware, Jewellery and Arms and their Imitations to the North of the Achaemenid Empire'. In Nieling and Rehm 2010, 223–79.

Tsetskhladze, G.R. 2018a: 'The Colchian Black Sea Coast: Recent Discoveries and Studies'. In Manoledakis, M., Tsetskhladze, G.R. and Xydopoulos, I. (eds.), *Essays on the Archaeology and History of the Black Sea Littoral* (Colloquia Antiqua 18) (Leuven/Paris/Bristol, CT), 425–546.

—. 2018b: '"The Most Marvellous of All Seas": The Great King and the Cimmerian Bosporus'. In Pavúk, P., Klontza-Jaklova, V. and Harding, A. (eds.), *ΕΥΔΑΙΜΩΝ: Studies in Honour of Jan Bouzek* (Opera Facultatis philosophicae Universitatis Carolinae Pragensis 18) (Prague), 467–90.

—. 2019: 'An Achaemenid Inscription from Phanagoria: Extending the Boundaries of Empire'. *AWE* 18, 113–51.

Wade-Gery, H.T. 1958: 'The Peace of Kallias'. In Wade-Gery, H.T., *Essays in Greek History* (Oxford).

Wiesehöfer, J. 1996: *Ancient Persia from 550 BC to 650 AD* (London).

THE GREEK CITIES OF THE BLACK SEA[*]

1. INTRODUCTION

The emergence of the *polis* system in Greece coincided with the beginning of an extraordinary emigration of Greeks from the Aegean homeland. This emigration began about the middle of the 8th century and continued for over two centuries. When it ended around 500, the Greek world extended from eastern Spain in the west to Colchis in the east. The primary causes of this remarkable expansion were twofold: the search for sources of metal to satisfy the Greeks' growing need and the hope of acquiring the land required to live the life of a citizen in the new *poleis*, as opportunities for land at home dwindled.

The Black Sea was the last major area colonized by the Greeks. Attracted first by the rich fishing and agricultural potential of the Hellespont and the Pontus and then by its remoteness, which offered refuge from Lydian and Persian pressure, various Ionian and Aeolian states founded colonies in the area. The most active of these was Miletus, credited by the ancient sources with 70 colonies, though the actual number was probably much smaller. Among Miletus' numerous colonies were such important cities as Cyzicus (675) near the entrance of the Hellespont, Sinope (*ca.* 631) on the north coast of Anatolia, Olbia (*ca.* 550) at the mouth of the Bug River in the south-western Ukraine, and Panticapaeum (*ca.* 600) in the Crimea. Megara also colonized in this area, occupying the important sites of Byzantium and Chalcedon on both sides of the Bosporus as well as founding the city of Heraclea Pontica (560) in north-west Anatolia near one of the reputed entrances to Hades.

Because they had no rivals in this area, the Greeks were able to establish new colonies throughout the Archaic and Classical periods until the Black Sea was almost entirely ringed by prosperous Greek cities equipped with fine public buildings and temples and linked by steadily growing ties of trade. The Black Sea seemed to be on the verge of becoming a Greek lake like the Aegean. Instead, the 5th century opened with unprecedented threats to the survival of the Greek cities of the region that resulted in fundamental changes in their organization and relations to each other and the world around them.

---

[*] First published in K. Kinzl (ed.), *A Companion to the Classical Greek World* (Blackwell Publishing, Oxford 2006), 137–52.

214 PART II: ARTICLES

Reconstruction of the history of these developments is difficult, not least because of the lack of sources that plagues the historian of Greek colonies everywhere.

2. SOURCES FOR THE HISTORY OF THE GREEK CITIES

The literary sources for the history of the Black Sea in the 5th and 4th centuries are limited in quantity and uneven in coverage. Although evidence exists for local historical traditions dealing with the Bosporan kingdom in the eastern Crimea and the Taman Peninsula and the city of Heraclea Pontica and its colony Chersonesus, only fragments remain. References to the Black Sea cities occur also in numerous classical authors such as the historians Herodotus, Xenophon, and Diodorus, the geographer Strabo, and the Athenian orators, especially Isocrates and Demosthenes. Their value for the history of the Black Sea cities is limited, however, by their strongly Athenocentric biases. As a result, while relatively full evidence survives concerning the dates, founding cities (*metropoleis*), and founders of the Black Sea cities as well as the legends that were invented to connect them to the Heroic Age and to establish divine sanction for their foundation, the evidence for the 5th and 4th centuries primarily concerns issues related to Athenian history, such as the return of the Ten Thousand and the grain trade, rather than the internal history of the cities themselves.

Fortunately, archaeology has compensated for much of the deficiencies of the literary sources. Although excavation of the cities of northern Turkey has barely begun, there is a long and rich archaeological tradition dealing with those of the west and north coasts of the Black Sea. Almost a century of excavation of cities such as Histria, Olbia, Chersonesus, and Panticapaeum has produced a wealth of epigraphical and material evidence illuminating their society and economy, culture, institutions, and urban development. Moreover, since studying the Greek cities in their geographic and ethnographic contexts is a hallmark of the Black Sea archaeological tradition, archaeology has also involved the exploration of the cities' hinterlands, producing a wealth of information about the structure and history of their *choras* (rural hinterlands) and their relations with their non-Greek neighbors, and illuminating basic trends in the history of the region as a whole.

3. GREEKS AND NON-GREEKS IN THE BLACK SEA

The history of the Greek cities of the Black Sea is usually written in terms of the spread of Greek life and culture in the region, and there is some truth in such reconstructions. Cities such as Heraclea Pontica, Sinope, and Olbia proudly affirmed their 'Greekness' by working their foundations into Panhellenic saga, maintaining close ties with their metropolis, patronizing the Delphic oracle, celebrating their military triumphs at Olympia, and keeping abreast of cultural developments in the Aegean. Such Hellenocentric accounts, however, ignore an equally important truth: these cities formed a thin fringe on the edges of a vast 'barbarian' world. Although a few cities such as Heraclea Pontica succeeded in dominating their non-Greek neighbors, most were not so fortunate and had to find accommodations with their 'barbarian' neighbors, trading and intermarrying with them and sometimes even seeking their protection in order to survive. The negotiation and renegotiation of these accommodations is central to the history of the Greek cities of the Black Sea, especially during the 5th and 4th centuries, when they assumed the form that they would maintain for the rest of antiquity.

During the 6th century the cities had grown and prospered, building their first stone temples and expanding and settling their *choras*. Olbia, for example, founded over a hundred subsidiary agricultural settlements in its *chora* in the lower reaches of the Dnieper and Bug rivers. The good times ended, however, in the first third of the 5th century. Although literary evidence is lacking, evidence of the change is clear in the archaeology of the cities. The situation is clearest at Olbia, where the city acquired new defensive walls at the same time that virtually all the settlements in its *chora* were abandoned. New walls and evidence of widespread destruction have also been found at Histria in levels dated about 500 by the excavators. Finally, there are remains of an extensive system of fortifications intended to defend the cities of the Kerch Peninsula dating to this period. Russian and Ukrainian scholars explain these development by the efforts of powerful non-Greek states located in the hinterlands of the Black Sea – those of the Odrysian Thracians in the Balkans and the 'Royal Scythians' in the Ukraine – to extend their control over the Greek cities on their coasts, and their view is supported by the character and extent of the changes.[1]

For much of the late 6th century the Persian Empire had protected the Greek cities of the south and west coasts of the Black Sea, albeit at the price of their paying tribute and providing troops for Persian military campaigns. Unsuccessful efforts by Cyrus the Great (*ca.* 530) and Darius I (*ca.* 513) to extend Persian power north of the Black Sea were followed by withdrawal of Persia from the region in the wake of the defeat of Xerxes' invasion of Greece in 480/79 and its aftermath. In northern Anatolia the result was political fragmentation as various local populations vied for control of the coast and its

---

[1] Vinogradov 1997c, 20–21.

216 PART II: ARTICLES

hinterlands, while elsewhere the Odrysians and Scythians hastened to fill the vacuum created by the collapse of Persian power. Herodotus (4. 80) refers to hostilities – probably in the 470s – between the Thracians and Scythians near Olbia that ended with the mutual surrender of rival claimants to the thrones of the two peoples and recognition of the Danube as the boundaries between their kingdoms, thereby freeing them to turn their attention to the Greek cities of the coasts of Thrace and Scythia.

The cities' responses to the changed political environment of the Black Sea varied according to the peculiarities of their local situation. The lack of a dominant non-Greek power in northern Anatolia to replace the Persians encouraged the cities there to try to expand their influence over their neighbors. First to take advantage of these possibilities was Heraclea Pontica. Founded about 560 by colonists from Megara and Boeotia near the mouth of the Lycus River about 150 km east of the Bosporus, Heraclea had coexisted uneasily with the natives of the region – a people of probably Thracian origin called the Mariandynoi – for most of the first century of its existence, recognizing Persian suzerainty and possibly even participating in Xerxes' ill-fated Greek campaign.

The weakening of Persian power in the area, however, freed the city to turn on the Mariandynoi, and by the second half of the 5th century at the latest, Heraclea had conquered its neighbors, a victory it celebrated with a monument in Olympia. Following their victory, the Heracleotes reduced their new subjects to a form of agricultural servitude that reminded other Greeks of the condition of Sparta's helots and the Thessalian *penestai*. Henceforth the Mariandynoi were bound to the soil as hereditary tenants protected only by the guarantee that they would not be sold out of their homeland.

The conquest of the Mariandynoi enriched Heraclea and provided the city with a strong foundation for future economic growth. References by Aristotle and other sources to demands tor redistribution of land, conflicts between 'oligarchs' and 'democrats', and a short-lived tyranny by an otherwise unknown Euopios suggest, however, that it was Heraclea's aristocracy that had profited most from the city's victory. The result was *stasis* and political instability that probably contributed to the city's decision to colonize outside its *chora*, first in the late 420s when it founded Chersonesus near modern Sevastopol in the south-western Crimea, and again in the early 4th century when it founded Callatis on the site of modern Mangalia in the Dobruja.[2] Equally important, domination of Mariandynia provided Heraclea with an extensive labor force to

---

[2] Graham 1994, 6.

THE GREEK CITIES OF THE BLACK SEA 217

work the citizens estates and numerous lowers to man its fleet, making it the most powerful of the cities of northern Anatolia.

The situation was more complex east of Heraclea. Sinope was the principal city on the Paphlagonian coast. Founded by Miletus in the second half of the 7th century, Sinope had flourished, founding a series of colonies of her own further east on land seized from the Paphlagonians, including Cotyora, Cerasus, and, most importantly, Trapezus. Not surprisingly, relations between Sinope and her colonies and the Paphlagonians were tense throughout the city's history. Xenophon (*Anabasis* 5. 5. 7–12) reveals that by the end of the 5th century Sinope had been able to exploit that tension and bind her colonies tightly to her, forcing them to accept Sinopean harmosts and pay tribute to Sinope. Epigraphic and archaeological evidence indicates Sinope's influence was not limited to northern Anatolia but that the city established economic and political ties with the cities of the north and west coasts of the Black Sea, most notably with Olbia, where Sinopean pottery and decrees honoring Sinopeans and granting special trading privileges have been found. At the same time, the presence of a tyranny at Sinope in the 430s suggests that the city had experienced internal tensions similar to those documented at Heraclea Pontica and elsewhere in the Black Sea.

Significantly different from the experience of Heraclea Pontica and Sinope was that of the cities of Colchis – modern Georgia – at the eastern end of the Black Sea. Unlike their kinsmen to the west, whose neighbors were small-scale polities capable of being conquered as Heraclea had done or held at bay as was the case at Sinope, the Colchian Greek cities had been founded on the coast of rich states with a long tradition of urbanism and close ties with the various empires of their hinterlands, such as Urartu, Assyria, and, of course, Persia.

Three cities are mentioned in the sources as founded in this remote area – Dioscourias, Gyenos, and Phasis – while archaeology has added two more, whose ancient names are still unknown, one at the important site of Pichvnari and another nearby at Tsikhisdziri. The sources suggest, therefore, that the Colchian Greek cities were virtual dependencies of the various kingdoms of the interior, whose precarious survival depended on their usefulness as commercial gateways to the outside world, Phasis is even described as an *emporion* – a market – for the Colchians. Although the earliest written sources for the Colchian cities date to the 4th century, archaeological evidence indicates Greek activity in the region began as early as the 6th century. Excavations at Pichvnari and interior sites such as Vani indicate that by the late 5th century there was an unusually high degree of intermingling of Colchian and Greek traditions in the region, so 'that the culture of the

218 PART II: ARTICLES

gymnasium coexisted at Pichvnari with a local culture exemplified by its tools, wares, and dwellings'; while 'deep in the hinterland, at least some of the elite sported an identity that was both Colchian and Greek.'[3]

The central theme of the history of the west coast of the Black Sea in the 5th century was the emergence of the Odrysian Thracians as the dominant power in the region. Freed from Persian suzerainty, the Odrysian kings rapidly expanded their power in the Balkans. The details of the process are unknown, but Thucydides (2. 96–97) describes their empire in the 420s as extending over the whole of the eastern Balkans from the Propontis to the Danube and including both the tribes of the interior and the Greek cities of the Black Sea coast, all of whom paid tribute to the Odrysian high king. The amount of their tribute is unknown, but it is likely to have been substantial since Thucydides says that Sitalces realized an income of 400 talents a year in gold and silver, a sum almost comparable to that of the Athenian Empire at the beginning of the Peloponnesian War. Although evidence concerning relations between the Greek cities and their Odrysian suzerains is lacking, it is likely that, just as would be the case in the Hellenistic period, the burden of their tribute was offset by the protection afforded them against raids on their *choras* by neighboring tribes and increased trading opportunities with the peoples of the interior.

For the cities of the coasts of the Ukraine and the Crimean and Taman peninsulas, the central fact of the early 5th century was the pressure put on them by the kingdom of the Royal Scythians, which dominated the steppes north of the Black Sea. As elsewhere in the Black Sea, the responses of the South Russian cities to the new situation were not uniform. The evidence is fullest for Olbia.[4] In a famous passage of his fourth book Herodotus (4. 78–79) tells the pathetic story of the Scythian king Skyles, who resided in Olbia for half of the year in a Greek-style palace with his Olbian wife, until his nobles learned of his participation in the rites of Dionysus and assassinated him. Herodotus' purpose in telling the story of Skyles is to illustrate the Scythians' hostility to foreign customs. The fact that Skyles had a Greek wife and regularly spent part of the year in Olbia, however, suggests that the Olbian aristocracy had recognized Scythian authority in return for a privileged position for the city in the kingdom, perhaps as one of the royal residences where the kings would stay during their annual migrations throughout their vast territories.

Olbia's function as a royal residence probably ended with the death of Skyles but not the city's subjection to the Scythians. Initially the Scythians ruled through the agency of Greek tyrants who governed the city in the interests of

[3] Braund 1994, 116, 118.
[4] Vinogradov and Kryžikij 1995, 130–34.

their Scythian masters, such as the Tymnes who Herodotus says was *epitropos* of Olbia for Skyles' predecessor Ariapeithes, or a certain Pausanias who held the eponymous office of *aisymnetes* of the Molpoi, suggesting that as elsewhere Olbia's tyrants governed by manipulating rather than suppressing the city's *polis* institutions. Thereafter, however, Olbian coins with non-Greek names such as Arichos and Eminakos suggest that the Scythians replaced their Greek puppet tyrants and imposed their own administrators on the city. But whatever the modalities of Scythian rule, the evidence for substantial public building, including a new temple for Apollo Delphinios, suggests that Olbia prospered during much of the 5th century thanks to Scythian protection and her function as the primary center for the export of the products of the Scythians' steppe subjects and the provision of Greek manufactured goods to the peoples of the interior.

The most original response to the rise of Scythian power, however, was that of the cities bordering the Straits of Kerch at the entrance to the Sea of Azov, which united in a military alliance led by the Milesian colony of Panticapaeum about 480/79.[5] Unfortunately, the sole evidence for this important development is provided by a brief note that the historian Diodorus (12. 31) entered under the year 438/7: 'In Asia the dynasty of the Cimmerian Bosporus, whose kings were known as the Archaeanactidae, ruled for 42 years: and the successor to the kingship was Spartokos, who reigned seven years (438/7–432/1).' It has long been recognized that this note taken from Diodoros' chronological source anachronistically treats the founders of the Bosporan state as kings, a status they first acquired in the Hellenistic period. Although scholarship is divided as to whether the origin of the Archaeanactidae should be sought in Mytilene or Miletus, it is agreed that their rule took the archaic form of the collective rule of an aristocratic lineage like the Corinthian Bacchiads that monopolized key political and military offices, and not a simple tyranny. Information about the internal organization of the Archaeanactid state is lacking, but the existence of coins minted by Phanagoria suggests that it was organized as a loose alliance rather than an integrated territorial state. Its extent is also unknown, but the fact that the cities of Nymphaeum (south) and Theodosia (west) of Panticapaeum remained independent throughout the 5th century points to its initially being limited to a few cities on either side of the Straits of Kerch, most probably including Panticapaeum, Hermonassa, Kepoi, and, possibly, Phanagoria. Finally, while the manner in which the rule of the Archaeanactidae came to an end is unknown, the fact that their successors bear Thracian names such as Spartocus and Paerisades, well attested among

---

[5] Vinogradov 1997c, 21.

220 PART II: ARTICLES

members of the Odrysian dynasty, suggests that the new dynasty was Thracian in origin, possibly being descendants of the leaders of Thracian military units, who originally came to Panticapaeum as allies against the Scythians.

4. ATHENIAN INTERVENTION IN THE BLACK SEA

For most of the 5th century relations between the Black Sea cities and the Aegean were limited. Trade increased, particularly with Athens, but political involvements were avoided. The Aegean and Black Sea basins formed two relatively self-contained political universes, a situation that Athens recognized when it conceded the Black Sea to Persia in the Peace of Kallias (most commonly dated to 449). The situation changed, however, in the 430s when Pericles led a powerful Athenian fleet into the Black Sea. The evidence for this event is limited to a single passage in Plutarch's *Life of Pericles* (20):

> He once made a naval expedition into the Euxine Sea with a large and exceptionally well-equipped fleet, where he saw to it that the Greek cities got what they wanted and treated them kindly, made the surrounding non-Greek tribes and their kings and chieftains aware of the extent of Athenian power, proved their fearlessness and courage, in that they sailed wherever they wished and made themselves masters of the whole sea, and left thirteen ships along with Lamachus and troops to help the people of Sinope against their tyrant Timesilaus. Once Timesilaus and his supporters had been overthrown, he got a decree passed to the effect that 600 volunteers would leave for Sinope and settle there alongside the Sinopians, taking over the houses and estates which had previously belonged to the tyrant and his men (trans. R. Waterfield [Oxford 1998], 163).

Plutarch's source for his account of Pericles' Pontic Expedition is unknown, but attacks on its historicity have not been convincing. More contentious has been the question of the expedition's date and purpose. For over a century scholars have argued that it should be dated to 437/6 and connected to Spartokos' assumption of power at Panticapaeum, maintaining that Pericles' goal was to establish cordial relations between Athens and the new ruler of Panticapaeum and secure for Athens a privileged position in the Black Sea grain trade, similar to that enjoyed by the city in the 4th century. Despite its wide acceptance, this interpretation is seriously flawed. The problems are twofold: first, epigraphic evidence suggests a date later than 437/6 for the expedition;[6] and, second, it rests on an anachronistic overestimation of Athenian dependence on Black Sea grain, retrojecting late 5th- and 4th-century conditions into the 430s, when Athens was able to import grain freely from a wide variety of Mediterranean sources.[7] More

[6] Clairmont 1979.
[7] Noonan 1973; Burstein 1999.

THE GREEK CITIES OF THE BLACK SEA

probable is the explanation provided by Plutarch's source, namely, that Pericles opportunistically responded to appeals for help from factions in the Black Sea cities. Certainly, the most tangible result of the expedition was an expansion of Athenian influence in the region with its center on the south coast at Sinope and Amisus, both of which received substantial bodies of Athenian colonists and the latter even renamed itself Peiraieus after Athens' port.

Athenian influence in the Black Sea basin increased with the outbreak of the Peloponnesian War in 431. As the region did not become a significant theatre of military operations, references in the sources are few, but the trend is clear. The Assessment Decree (*IG* 1^3 71) reveals the existence in 425 of a Euxine district containing at least 40 cities on the south, west, and north coasts of the Black Sea; and the fact that Nymphaeum was still paying tribute and had an Athenian garrison throughout most of the Peloponnesian War indicates that doubts concerning the reality of the Euxine district are unjustified. It is likely, however, that as in the Aegean the reaction of Pontic cities to the growth of Athenian power was pragmatic.

Cities threatened by the ambitions of more powerful neighbors such as Theodosia and Nymphaeum probably welcomed Athenian protection, while by the same token cities with expansionist aspirations of their own, such as Panticapaeum, Olbia, and Heraclea, were less enthusiastic, if not openly hostile. So the new Thracian rulers of Panticapaeum are described as 'enemies' in Athenian sources. Likewise, Heraclea refused to pay her assessment, maintaining her long-standing policy of loyalty to Persia. The situation at Olbia is less clear, but the fact that the city had already given sanctuary to the exiled tyrants of Sinope in the 430s points to the existence of a desire to maintain Olbian independence.[8] At the same time, however, numismatic and epigraphic evidence suggests that Olbia's aristocrats took advantage of Athenian protection to escape from Scythian rule and replace the city's Scythian governor with a native tyrant.

Athenian power in the Black Sea – as elsewhere – quickly declined after the Syracusan disaster. Although the details are unknown, the decision in 410 to raise revenue by levying a 10% toll at Chalcedon on shipping in and out of the Black Sea suggests that tribute collection in the region had effectively ceased. Athens' final defeat and surrender in 404 left the remaining Athenians in the Black Sea to fend for themselves. Despite the peace treaty's requirement that Athenian colonists and cleruchs return to Athens, some Athenians clearly decided to remain in the region. So Demosthenes' maternal grandfather Gylon surrendered Nymphaeum to Satyrus, the tyrant of Panticapaeum, in exchange for the city of Kepoi on the Taman Peninsula, while the tact that Amisus was

---

[8] Vinogradov 1997d, 172–89.

222   PART II: ARTICLES

still known as Peiraieus in the 4th century suggests that some of the Athenian colonists decided to stay there as well.

More important in the long run than the continued residence of a few Athenians in the region were the effects of Athenian intervention in the Black Sea on the life of the Black Sea cities. Some changes were cultural, such as the strong influence of Athenian sculptural and epigraphic styles on local workshops and the growing interest of local elites in intellectual developments in the Aegean, as indicated by Xenophon's (*Anabasis* 7. 5. 14) reference to books in the cargoes of ships wrecked on the west coast of the Black Sea about 400, and the appearance of evidence about the same time for students coming from the region to study at Athens. More fundamental, however, was the growth in trade between Athens and the Black Sea and its influence on the economic life of the Pontic cities.

Trade between Athens and the Black Sea Greek cities grew steadily during the 5th century, but for most of the century it was primarily a trade in luxuries, as is indicated by the prominence of Athenian painted pottery of all types and other manufactured goods in the archaeological record. As the Peloponnesian War turned against Athens, however, the city lost access to her traditional Mediterranean grain sources, becoming as a result increasingly dependent on Black Sea grain to survive. The result was a fundamental change in the nature of trade between Athens and the Black Sea cities. From a luxury trade it changed to a trade in staples with grain as its primary focus. Although the Spartan blockade of the Hellespont in 405/4 interrupted the growth of the grain trade, it quickly resumed its growth with the conclusion of peace, reflecting Athens' continuing dependence on Black Sea grain. The Black Sea cities responded by increasing grain production to meet the new demand. Clear evidence of the changed character of Black Sea trade with the Aegean is provided by the sharp increase in the number of agricultural settlements in the cities' hinterlands beginning in the late 5th and 4th centuries, as documented by archaeological surveys at Olbia, Chersonesus, and in the Kerch and Taman peninsulas.[9] Not surprisingly, it was the major cities such as Panticapaeum and Heraclea Pontica that most benefited from the new situation.

5. THE FOURTH CENTURY

From 432 to 389 Panticapaeum was ruled by Spartocus' eldest son, Satyrus I. Although evidence for Satyrus' reign is limited to brief notes dealing with events just before his death, it is clear that he had already established the foreign policy framework that his successors would follow for the rest of the century:

---

[9] Noonan 1973, 233–35; Saprykin 1994; Vinogradov and Kryžickij 1995, 67–74.

THE GREEK CITIES OF THE BLACK SEA   223

expanding Panticapaean power over the Greek cities and native populations on both sides of the Straits of Kerch while cultivating good relations with Athens by providing grain on favorable terms in times of shortage. Satyrus' success in implementing this policy was, however, limited. Thus, while the Athenians responded to his generous gifts of grain by granting him privileges, which are, unfortunately, unspecified,[10] his attempts to extend his influence east and west of the Straits of Kerch ended in failure. Polyaenus (8. 55) recounts how Satyrus' bid to gain control of the Sindians by forcing their king Hecataeus to replace his Maeotian queen Tirgatao with his daughter resulted in a war with the Maeotians that only ended after Satyrus' death, when his son Gorgippus accepted Tirgatao's terms for peace. Equally unsuccessful was his attack on the city of Theodosia in 389, which ended with his death.

Although Satyrus seems to have been succeeded jointly by his sons Leucon I and Gorgippus, Leucon (389/8–349/8) was clearly the dominant figure and his 40-year reign was remembered as being of decisive importance for the history of the dynasty, so much so, indeed, that historians named it after him: the Leuconidae (Strabo 7. 3. 8; Aelian *Varia Historia* 6. 13). The emphasis on the epochal significance of Leucon's reign, however, should not obscure the continuities between his policies and those of Satyrus, particularly in the area of foreign policy. So his first major foreign policy achievement was the conquest of Theodosia. After an initial failure, most likely in the 370s, caused by the intervention of Heraclea Pontica, which probably feared for the safety of its colony Chersonesus,[11] Leucon succeed in conquering the city. The date of Theodosia's conquest is unknown, but it occurred sometime before 354, when Demosthenes (20. 33) refers to it as being under Leucon's control.

Leucon also resumed his father's expansionist policy in the Taman Peninsula. A recently published inscription reveals that Leucon, like Satyrus, first sought to bring the Sindians under his influence by supporting Hecataeus against Tirgatao and her children.[12] Diplomacy soon was replaced by force, and by the end of his reign Leucon had conquered and made himself king of the Sindians and their neighbors, the Toretai, the Dandarioi, and the Psessoi. Unfortunately, epigraphic evidence indicates only that these important events, which extended Leucon's power over the peoples of the Taman Peninsula and their neighbors immediately to the north and south, occurred sometime after the conquest of Theodosia.

[10] Burstein 1993.
[11] Burstein 1974, 416.
[12] Graham 2002, 95–99.

Leucon's reign was also marked by a dramatic political reorganization that is reflected in his adoption for the first time of a formal titulary for the tyranny: Archon of Bosporus and Theodosia. Although scholars have argued that the title 'Archon' as opposed to 'Basileus' reflects Leucon's desire to disguise his real position by claiming to be holding a normal *polis* office, this is unlikely since none of the cities under his rule used the term 'Archon' for their chief political office. Rather, as has long been recognized, Leucon's new title reflects a political conception similar to that embodied in his contemporary Dionysius I of Syracuse's title Archon of Sicily, namely, autocratic rule of a territorial state centered at Panticapaeum in which the subject Greek cities had lost their independent identity. Confirmation of this interpretation is provided by three facts. First, in contemporary epigraphic and literary sources all the political decisions of the Bosporan state are treated as the result of personal decisions by Leucon and his successors, and only they represent Bosporus in diplomatic relations with other states. Second, signs of *polis* sovereignty such as the minting of coins by cities ruled by Leucon cease. Third, and finally, individuals from the region are consistently described as Bosporans and not citizens of a particular *polis* in non-Bosporan documents. The distinction between the titles used by Leucon to describe his rule of his Greek and non-Greek subjects in the final form of his titulary – Archon of Bosporus and Theodosia and King of the Sindians, Toretai, Dandarioi, and Psessoi – are to be explained, therefore, not so much by a difference in the nature of his rule of the two groups of subjects as by the previous use of the title 'Basileus' or its equivalent by the native rulers he supplanted.

As has long been recognized, the effect of Leucon's reforms was to create a multiethnic quasi-monarchy centered on the Straits of Kerch that foreshadowed the Hellenistic kingdoms in many ways, including treating important aspects of the economy as governmental monopolies – most notably, the export of grain from Bosporan territory. Thus, Demosthenes notes that Leucon and successors personally granted tax exemptions and priority loading of grain for ships bound for Athens, while inscriptions attest grants of similar privileges to other cities (*Sylloge Inscriptionum Graecarum*[3] 212: Mytilene). Moreover, although Demosthenes' claim (20. 32–33) that Leucon provided Athens with 400,000 *medimnoi* of grain per year, or half its annual imports, or Strabo's (7. 4. 6) that he made the city a one-time gift of 2,100,000 *medimnoi* of grain, are controversial, it is clear that Leucon and his successors grew rich on the revenues generated by the grain trade. Archaeological evidence of the growth of the trade and the extent of the wealth it generated is provided by the expansion of agricultural settlements, particularly in the Taman Peninsula and by the monumental tombs of the dynasty and extensive building projects undertaken by the tyrants at Panticapaeum and elsewhere in their realm.

Nor was their role in the trade passive. As already mentioned, Demosthenes (20. 33) also remarked that Leucon transformed Theodosia into a major grain exporting center, and he probably also encouraged expansion of agricultural settlement in the hinterlands of the Greek cities of his realm, particularly in the Taman Peninsula. It is unfortunate, therefore, that neither the date nor the circumstances in which Leucon's reforms took place are known. The fact that Leucon is still called a Panticapaean and not Bosporan in a decree of the Arcadian League (*CIRB* 37) may, however, provide a *terminus post quem* of 369 for their completion, while Polyaenus' (6. 9. 2–3) references to conspiracies against Leucon by his 'friends' and 'trierarchs' and his reliance on non-Greek troops during the war with Heraclea Pontica suggests that his plans met strong resistance among his Greek subjects.

Leucon was succeeded in 349/8 jointly by his sons Spartocus II (349/8–344/3) and Paerisades I (349/8–311/10), who followed their father's policies, exploiting their control of the export of Bosporan grain to maintain good relations with Athens, while continuing to extend Bosporan power eastward until by the end of Paerisades' rule it included all the Maeotians and the Thateis and reached, according to a Bosporan poet, the Caucasus Mountains (*CIRB* 113). Panticapaeum was not the only Greek city to build an empire by conquering other Greek cities. Another was Chersonesus, which carved out a place for itself in the grain trade by annexing Kerkinitis and Kalos Limen in the western Crimea, and reorganizing their *choras* by dividing them into regular plots protected from Scythian and Taurian raids by rural fortresses. Even more successful was Chersonesus' mother city, Heraclea Pontica.

Heraclea's emergence as the pre-eminent Greek city on the south coast of the Black Sea was delayed until the late 4th century. Although the city did intervene on the side of Theodosia in its struggle with Leucon and founded a colony at Callatis in the Dobruja, severe *stasis* dominated Heraclea's political life for much of the first half of the century. The problem was rooted in the unequal division of the land conquered from the Mariandynoi and led to increasingly serious agitation for cancellation of debts and redistribution of land. By 364 the situation had become so threatening that in desperation the leaders of Heraclea's ruling oligarchy invited a political exile named Clearchus, who was serving as a mercenary commander for a nearby Persian military official, to return and bring order to the city. Once in the city, however, Clearchus turned on his putative employers and used his mercenaries to become tyrant. The estates of the oligarchs were confiscated and their slaves freed, while those members of Heraclea's aristocracy who managed to escape Clearchus' purge, and their descendants, were to remain in exile until 281.

226 PART II: ARTICLES

The dynasty founded by Clearchus lasted for 80 years, until it was overthrown and Heraclea was annexed by Lysimachus in 284. After a period of consolidation under the rule of the first two tyrants, Clearchus (364–352) and Satyrus (352–346), Heracleote foreign policy became openly expansionist during the reigns of Timotheus (346–337) and Dionysius (337–305), resulting in the creation of an empire that extended eastward along the north Anatolian coast from the Rhebas River in Bithynia to central Paphlagonia and included the cities of Ticion, Sesamus, Cromna, and Cytorus, giving Heraclea control of the principal ports along the route followed by grain ships sailing from the Crimea to the Hellespont. Numismatic evidence indicates that the expansion of Heracleote territory in northern Anatolia was accompanied by an extension of the city's diplomatic influence beyond the limits of its empire to include Amisus in northern Anatolia and the cities of the western Crimea, while the abundance of Heracleote amphora stamps found on sites throughout the Black Sea attests to the city's emergence as one of the principal wine-exporting centers in the region.

The Greek cities were not the only powers to take advantage of the withdrawal of Athens from the Black Sea. Pressure on the Greek cities of the region by the non-Greek states of their hinterlands also revived in the 4th century. As was true a century earlier, the greatest of these states was that of the Royal Scythians, which threatened Bosporus and Chersonesus and its neighbors from its center north of the Crimea. Unfortunately, the sources preserve only scattered references to hostilities between the Scythians and Bosporus and Chersonesus, with little indication of their scale or seriousness. A clearer indication of the magnitude of the threat posed by the Scythians is provided, however, by the elite residences, monumental tombs, and spectacular gold and bronze art works that were created by Greek craftsmen for Scythian kings and aristocrats.[13]

These wonderful objects have primarily been viewed as works of art and ethnographic documents since they were first discovered in the 18th century. They have been and continue to be admired for their superb craftsmanship and their illuminating depiction of Scythian life, and treated as evidence for the closeness of cultural interaction between Greeks and Scythians, with little concern for their political implications. All of this is undeniably true, but such interpretations ignore an important fact: the most likely mechanism by which these objects reached the Scythians is diplomatic gift exchange. Their abundance and richness is, therefore, also clear evidence of the high price Bosporus and the other Greek cities that provided them had to pay for protection against raiding by their Scythian neighbors.

[13] Tsetskhladze 1998.

THE GREEK CITIES OF THE BLACK SEA   227

Although the price the north Pontic Greek cities paid for protection from Scythian raiding was high and the security they gained was precarious, it was still worth the expense. Safety for the new settlements in the cities' hinterlands was essential to the expansion of agricultural production that fed the growing grain trade with the Aegean and the trade in wine between the cities that is well documented both archaeologically and epigraphically. Even more important, however: it opened the interior of Scythia to trade with the Pontic cities. How far into the interior that trade actually reached is suggested by the remarkable discovery of a boat that had sunk with its cargo of fifteen fine bronze vessels and the body of its owner about 350 km north of the coast of the Black Sea on one of the tributaries of the Dnieper River.[14] Unfortunately, the ethnicity of the boat's owner cannot be determined, but the existence at major Scythian settlements scattered between the Dnieper and the Don of what can only be called Greek quarters, complete with Greek-style fortifications and houses and large amounts of Greek pottery, is clear evidence that Greek traders settled for long periods in the Scythian interior.[15] Unfortunately, what they traded for is nowhere made clear, but the recognition that the prime source of grain for the grain trade was the Pontic cities' own hinterlands suggests that it probably consisted of typical steppe products such as animal hides and tallow, fine textiles, and especially slaves for which the Black Sea is known to have been a major source.[16]

Similar conditions faced the Greek cities elsewhere in the Black Sea cities. Most difficult was the situation of south-coast cities such as Heraclea Pontica and Sinope, which attempted to maintain a delicate balance between local independence and loyalty to Persia in an environment dominated by ambitious satraps freed from central control by the chronic instability that characterized the long reign of Artaxerxes II. Equally complicated but far more dangerous was the situation of the cities of the west coast, which found themselves after the withdrawal of Athens increasingly serving as both pawns and prizes in an ongoing struggle for domination between the Odrysians in the south and recently emerged Getic and Scythian states in the north. Because of the lack of sources it is impossible to reconstruct in detail the history of this struggle, but the fact that by the middle of the century major cities throughout the area were ruled by non-Greeks – Apollonia Pontica by the Odrysians, Histria by the Getae, and Callatis by the Scythians – strongly suggests that most had lost their independence by that time. What the ultimate result of these developments

[14] Graham 1984, 8.
[15] Tsetskhladze 2000, 236–38.
[16] Finley 1962.

228   PART II: ARTICLES

would have been is, however, unknown, because the political environment of the Black Sea was changed fundamentally by the sudden and forceful intervention of a new power into the region in the 340s: Macedon.

Two factors induced Philip II of Macedon (360–336) to intervene in the Black Sea: his hope of finally ending Odrysian meddling in Macedonian affairs and his desire to secure the rich land and mineral resources of Thrace for Macedon. By the late 340s Philip had decisively defeated the Odrysians and annexed Thrace, thereby extending Macedonian power north to the Danube, where it threatened both the Getae and the Scythians. Divide and conquer had been the key to Philip's success in northern and central Greece, and the same policy served him well in the Black Sea. Finding the Scythians and Getae at loggerheads over control of the city of Histria, Philip initially responded favorably to the Scythian king Atheas' offer to make him his heir in return for his support against the Getae, only to betray his would be ally's hopes by agreeing to an alliance, brokered by the city of Apollonia Pontica, that was sealed by marriage to the Getic king's daughter. Philip then followed up his diplomatic success with an equally decisive military campaign against now isolated Atheas in 339 that left the Scythian king dead on the field and Macedon the dominant power in the northern Balkans and ruler of the west coast Pontic cities from the Bosporus to the Danube.

Philip's triumph was short-lived, however. Less than a decade later his achievements were undone as a result of his son Alexander's dramatic conquest of the Persian Empire. The south-coast cities suddenly found themselves in a new and particularly threatening environment, since the collapse of Persian power in Anatolia freed their non-Greek neighbors from the last vestiges of Persian authority and facilitated the emergence of new and potentially dangerous states such as the kingdoms of Bithynia and Pontus. A similarly unstable situation was created on the west and north coasts, where the death of Zopyrion, Alexander's governor of Thrace, and the destruction of his army under the walls of Olbia in 326 by the Scythians,[17] was followed by a major Thracian revolt and the reestablishment of an Odrysian kingdom by Seuthes III (ca. 326–300) that was to last well into the Hellenistic period, and once again to threaten the independence of the west Pontic cities.[18] Although some of his ancient biographers suggested that Alexander may have intended to campaign in the Black Sea after returning from India, his sudden death in 323 aborted any such plans, leaving it to his successors to try to restore Macedonian power in the region; but that is another story.

---

[17] Vinogradov 1997a.
[18] Burstein 1986, 21–24.

THE GREEK CITIES OF THE BLACK SEA

6. Conclusion

The 5th and 4th centuries were formative in the life of the Black Sea Greek cities. During these two centuries they emerged as full-fledged *poleis* with rich and dynamic cultures. They were not, however, simply replicas of the cities of their Aegean homelands. Archaic features remained part of their culture, such as funerary blood sacrifice and feasts at Bosporus, and the epigraphical use of the Doric dialect at Chersonesus long after ceasing to be current practice in the Aegean. But as the events treated in this chapter make clear, the hallmark of their political and cultural environment was intense and ongoing interaction between the Greek cities and the native peoples of their hinterlands. Although that interaction was often turbulent and dangerous, it decisively shaped the culture and politics of the Pontic cities.

The result is most obvious in art, where, for example, the empathy for Scythian life evident in the objects created for the Scythians by Black Sea Greek artisans has no parallel in Aegean Greek art, with its stereotyped portrayals of barbarian 'others'. It is evident also in the Pontic cities' ready acceptance of intermarriage between Greek and non-Greek and their willingness to include local deities in pantheons of *polis* deities. Obvious examples are the 'Parthenos', a Taurian goddess once claimed to have demanded the sacrifice of all Greek sailors wrecked on the coasts of Taurian territory, which became the principal deity at Chersonesus, and a Scythian goddess syncretized with Aphrodite Ourania at Panticapaeum. Not surprisingly, the Pontic cities strongly resisted involvement in the affairs of the Aegean and readily invoked the aid of the city's non-Greek neighbors against extra-Pontic powers, as Olbia did when threatened by Alexander's general, Zopyrion. The Black Sea, in other words, was not merely an extension of Aegean Greece but home to an original and distinctive form of Hellenism. It is not surprising, therefore, that the accounts of visitors to the region, from Herodotus in the 5th century BC to Dion Chrysostom in the 1st century AD, reveal a certain puzzlement and ambivalence about the Greekness of the society and culture of the Black Sea cities.

Further reading: books

Archibald, Z.H. 1998: *The Odrysian Kingdom of Thrace: Orpheus Unmasked* (Oxford) – Comprehensive archaeologically based history of Thrace from the early 5th century to the early Hellenistic period.

Boardman, J. 1999: *The Greeks Overseas: Their Early Colonies and Trade*, 4th ed. (London) – Standard archaeological history of Greek colonization.

Braund, D. 1994: *Georgia in Antiquity: A History of Colchis and Transcaucasian Iberia 550 BC–AD 562* (Oxford) – History of ancient Georgia based on Soviet- and post-Soviet-period archaeological discoveries.

230 PART II: ARTICLES

Burstein, S.M. 1976: *Outpost of Hellenism: The Emergence of Heraclea on the Black Sea* (University of California Publications: Classical Studies 14) (Berkeley) – Text-based history of Heraclea Pontica from its foundation to the early Hellenistic period.

Christian, D. 1998: *A History of Russia, Central Asia and Mongolia*, vol. 1: *Inner Eurasia from Prehistory to the Mongol Empire* (Oxford) – Standard textbook of the ancient and medieval history of the Eurasian steppe countries and their peoples.

Davis-Kimball, J., Bashilov, V.A. and Yablonsky, L.T. (eds.) 1995: *Nomads of the Eurasian Steppes in the Early Iron Age* (Berkeley) – Volume of translations of articles by leading Russian archaeologists and historians of steppe nomads and their cultures.

Gajdukevič, V.F. 1971: *Das Bosporanische Reich*, 2nd ed. (Berlin) – Comprehensive history of the Bosporan kingdom with emphasis on its society and economy by the leading Soviet historian of Bosporus.

Graham, A.J. 2001: *Collected Papers on Greek Colonization* (*Mnemosyne* Suppl. 214) (Leiden) – The collected papers of the principal English historian of Greek colonization.

Hind, J.G.F. 1994: 'The Bosporan kingdom'. *CAH* VI², 476–511 – Lucid and up-to-date survey of the history of Bosporus.

Krapivina, V.V. *et al.* 2001: *Ancient Greek Sites of the Northwest Coast of the Black Sea/Antichnye pamiatniki Severo-Zapadnogo Prichernomor'ya* (Kiev) – Well-illustrated and up-to-date survey of the archaeology and history of the cities of the northwest coast of the Black Sea from Odessus to Olbia (contributions in Russian and English).

Minns, E.H. 1913: *Scythians and Greeks: A Survey of Ancient History and Archaeology on the North Coast of the Euxine from the Danube to the Caucasus* (Cambridge) – Large scale and still valuable survey of Czarist-period Russian scholarship on the archaeology and history of the cities of the north coast of the Black Sea and their hinterlands.

Pippidi, D.M. 1971: *I Greet nel Basso Danubio: dall'età arcaica alla conquista romana* (Biblioteca storica dell'antichità 8) (Milan) – Standard history of the Greek cities of the Dobruja by a leading Romanian historian.

Reeder, E.D. (ed.) 1999: *Scythian Gold: Treasures from Ancient Ukraine* (New York) – Lavishly illustrated catalogue of an exhibition of Scythian art at the Walters Gallery in Baltimore with essays on various aspects of Scythian culture by leading scholars.

Rolle, R. 1989: *The World of the Scythians* (Berkeley) – Lucid general survey of Scythian history and culture.

Rostovtzeff, M.I. 1930: 'The Bosporan kingdom'. *CAH* VIII, 561–89 – Still valuable synthesis by a major pre-Soviet historian.

Saprykin, S.J. [S.Y.] 1994: *Ancient Farms and Land-plots on the Khora of Khersonesos Taurike (Research in the Herakleian Peninsula, 1974–1990)* (Antiquitates Proponticae, Circumponticae et Caucasicae 1; McGill University Monographs in Classical Archaeology and History 16) (Amsterdam) – Valuable synthesis of the results of archaeological surveys of the *chora* of Chersonesus by Soviet archaeologists.

—. 1997: *Heracleia Pontica and Tauric Chersonesus before Roman Domination (VI–I Centuries B.C.)* (Amsterdam) – General history of Heraclea Pontica and Chersonesus with particular emphasis on social and economic history.

THE GREEK CITIES OF THE BLACK SEA 231

Struve, V.V. (ed.) 1965: *Corpus Inscriptionum Regni Bosporani (CIRB)/ Korpus bosporskikh nadpisei: polnoe sobranie vsekh do sikh por izvestnykh epigra ft-cheskikh tekstov, naidennykh za poslednie poltorasta let* (Leningrad).

Tsetskhladze, G.R. (ed.) 1998: *The Greek Colonisation of the Black Sea area: Historical Interpretation of Archaeology* (*Historia* Einzelschriftcn 121) (Stuttgart) – Valuable collection of articles on all aspects of the history and archaeology of Greek colonization of the Black Sea by leading contemporary Russian and Western scholars.

Vinogradov, J.G. [Y.G.] 1997: *Pontische Studien: Kleine Schriften zur Geschichte und Epigraphik des Schwarzmeerraumes* (Mainz) – Volume of German translations of the major articles of a leading contemporary Russian historian and epigraphist.

Vinogradov, J.G. [Y.G.] and Kryžikij, S.D. 1995: *Olbia: Eine altgriechische Stadt im nordwestlichen Schwarzmecrraum* (*Mnemosyne* Suppl. 149) (Leiden).

FURTHER READING: ARTICLES

Burstein, S.M. 1974: 'The war between Heraclea Pontica and Leucon I of Bosporus'. *Historia* 23, 401–16.

—. 1986: 'Lysimachus and the cities: the early years'. *The Ancient World* 14: 19–24.

—. 1993: 'The origin of the Athenian privileges at Bosporus: a reconsideration'. *Ancient History Bulletin* 7, 81–83.

—. 1999: '*IG* 1³ 61 and the Black Sea grain trade'. In Mellor, R. and. Tritle, L. (eds.), *Text and Tradition: Studies in Greek History and Historiography in Honor of Mortimer Chambers* (Claremont, CA), 93–104.

Clairmont, C. 1979: 'New light on some public Athenian documents of the 5th and 4th century'. *Zeitschrift für Papyrologie und Epigraphik* 36, 123–26.

Finley, M.I. 1962: 'The slave trade in antiquity: the Black Sea and Danubian regions'. *Klio* 40, 51–59.

Graham, A.J. 1984: 'Commercial interchanges between Greeks and natives'. *The Ancient World* 10, 3–10.

—. 1994: 'Greek and Roman settlements on the Black Sea coasts: historical background'. In Tsetskhladze, G.R. (ed.), *Greek and Roman settlements on the Black Sea Coast: A Workshop held at the 95th Annual Meeting of the Archaeological Institute of America, Washington, D.C., USA, December 1993* (Colloquenda Pontica 1) (Bradford), 4–10.

—. 2002: 'Thasos and the Bosporan kingdom'. *AWE* 1.1, 87–101.

Noonan, T.S. 1973: 'The grain trade of the northern Black Sea in antiquity'. *AJPh* 94, 231–42.

Tsetskhladze, G.R. 1998: 'Who built the Scythian and royal élite tombs?'. *Oxford Journal of Archaeology* 17, 55–92.

—. 2000: 'Pistiros in the system of Pontic emporia (Greek trading and craft settlements in the hinterland of the northern and eastern Black Sea and elsewhere)'. In Domaradzki, M. (ed.), *Pistiros et Thasos: structures économiques dans la péninsule balkanique aux VIIe–IIe siècles avant J.-C.* (Opole), 233–46.

Vinogradov, J.G. [Y.G.] 1997a: 'Eine neue Quelle zum Zopyrion-Zug'. In Vinogradov 1997b, 323–35.

—. 1997b: *Pontische Studien: Kleine Schriften zur Geschichte und Epigraphik des Schwarzmeerraumes* (Mainz).

—. 1997c: 'Pontos Euxeinos als politische, ökonomische und kulturelle Einheit und die Epigraphik'. In Vinogradov 1997b, 1–73.

—. 1997d: 'Zur politischen Verfassung von Sinope und Olbia im fünften Jahrhundert v. u. Z.'. In Vinogradov 1997b, 165–229.

IG 1³ 61 AND THE BLACK SEA GRAIN TRADE*

The Black Sea and its vast grain resources runs like a bright thread through modern histories of Athens. Control of the routes to the Black Sea is assumed to have been one of the linchpins of Athenian foreign policy throughout the classical period.[1] Indeed, inclusion of the grain supply as a required item on the agenda of the *kyria ekklesia* in the 4th century BC is clear proof of the city's concern for its food supply.[2] For over a hundred years, however, scholars have also maintained that in the 5th century BC Athenian policy was intended not only to secure the city's food supply but also to control her allies by rationing their grain imports. Mort Chambers has always taught his students to be skeptical of grandiose theories, so I hope he will find interesting this reconsideration of *IG* 1³ 61, the key piece of evidence underpinning contemporary reconstructions of Athenian imperial policy in the Hellespontine region.

IG 1³ 61 is a stele of pentelic marble discovered in the Theater of Dionysus and first critically published by A. Boeckh in the second edition of his great *Die Staatshaushaltung der Athener*.[3] When the stele was complete, it must have been an unusually impressive monument. Surmounted by a carefully carved and balanced relief of a seated female figure extending her hand protectively toward a central standing figure flanked by a dog,[4] it originally contained a dossier of at least four decrees detailing Athenian support for the city of Methone – located just north of Pydna at the head of the Thermaic Gulf – in its struggles with Perdiccas II of Macedon. Unfortunately, only the lower portion of the relief, the first two decrees, and the prescript of the third survive on the extant fragment of the stele.

Information concerning the specific occasion that prompted the erection of this impressive monument has been lost with the lower portion of the stele. Nevertheless, *IG* 1³ 61 has attracted the attention of historians since its initial publication for good reason. It provides valuable information about some of

---

* First published in R. Mellor and L. Tritle (eds.), *Text and Tradition: Studies in Greek History and Historiography in Honor of Mortimer Chambers* (Regina Press, Claremont, CA 1999), 93–104.

[1] *Cf.*, for example, de Ste Croix 1972, 46–49. The blanket denial that Athenian policy was affected by concerns about her food supply by Edmund Bloedow (1971) is unconvincing.

[2] Aristotle *Analytica Posteriora* 42. 4. *Cf.* Thucydides 6. 20. 4; and Xenophon *Memorabilia* 3. 6. 13 for the 5th century BC.

[3] Boeckh 1851 II, 748–64.

[4] Illustrated in *IG* 1 15.

234 PART II: ARTICLES

the most important historical questions of the early 420s BC. The first decree (lines 3–32) provides unique insight into the complexities of the diplomatic duel between Athens and Perdiccas II as well as important evidence for the functioning of the tribute assessment process. It is the first provision of the second decree, however, passed in early 426/5 BC, that has generated the most scholarly interest and has had the greatest impact on the interpretation of Athenian policy in the Hellespontine region during the Archidamian War:

> The M[ethonaians] *shall be permitted to import* grain from Byzantium up to the amount of [...] *thousand medimnoi* each year. The [Hellesp]ontine guards shall not themselves prevent them from exporting it or allow anyone else to prevent them, or (if they do,) they are to be liable to a fine of ten thousand *drachmas* each. After giving notice to the Hellespontine guards they shall export up to the permitted amount. Exemption *shall also apply to* the ship carrying it (lines 34–42; trans. Fornara 1983, 145–46).

The intent of this provision is clear. In order to help Methone recover from the effects of the harassment by Perdiccas II detailed in the first decree – blockade by land and sea and ravaging of Methone's *chora* (lines 18–23) – Athens granted Methone a partial exemption from restrictions imposed on the export of grain from Byzantium. In order to exercise their privilege, Methone was required first to notify the Hellespontine guards of their intention and then to load the amount of grain allocated to them from stocks at Byzantium. The Hellespontine guards, for their part, were ordered to prevent anyone from interfering with the Methonaians on pain of a heavy fine. So long as the Methonaians limited their grain exports to the amount provided in the decree, their ship would not be liable to any penalty. The exact amount of Methone's grain allocation is not preserved on the stone. It is not likely to have been large since the city of Aphytis in the Chalcidice was granted permission in a nearly contemporary decree[5] to export (presumably from Byzantium) 10,000 *medimnoi* per year – approximately 400 tons or one large ship load[6] – 'on the same terms as the Methonaians'.

Much still remains unclear about the system of controls established by Athens in the Hellespont, particularly with regard to the Hellespontine guards including the date of their establishment, their base of operations, and their functions.[7] The clear implication of *IG* 1[3] 61, however, is that Athens restricted the export of grain from Byzantium during the Archidamian War.[8] The exact

---

[5] *IG* 1[3] 62, lines 3–5; *cf.* Meritt 1944, 216–17.

[6] A *medimnos* of grain equals about 40 kg; *cf.* Casson 1971, 172, n. 25.

[7] Particularly unclear is their possible connection with the 'ten percent' tax mentioned in *IG* 1[1] 52, line 7 and often assumed to be identical with the ten percent toll on shipping through the Bosporus in 410 BC (Xenophon *Hellenica* 1. 1. 22; *cf.* Hopper 1979, 75–76).

[8] The suggestion that Athens also controlled the price of grain sold at Byzantium rests solely on an erroneous restoration of *IG* 1[3] 62 by B.D. Meritt (1944, 216; *cf.* Mattingly 1997, 525).

nature of the restrictions is not stated, but the close similarity between the provisions of *IG* 1³ 61 and those governing the 4th-century BC Athenian monopoly of Cean ruddle suggests that Byzantium was required to limit its grain exports to Athens alone.[9] That represented a significant addition to our knowledge of Athenian foreign policy in the Archidamian War, since neither Thucydides nor any other 5th-century source suggested that Athens intervened in the grain trade in this way, despite the city's well documented concern for its grain supply and the 'Old Oligarch's' reference to the routine use of such trade monopolies.[10]

From its initial publication in the 19th century, however, scholars have maintained that *IG* 1³ 61, in actuality, reflected much more extensive Athenian interference with trade in the Hellespontine region than mere regulation of grain exports from Byzantium. Specifically they have argued that Athenian policy envisaged using Byzantium as a 'choke-point' in order 'to make a "closed sea" of the Aegean, by ensuring that she controlled incoming supplies of food'.[11] In its most extreme form the theory credits Athens with plans to create a full-blown mercantilism in which all merchant ships had to obtain exit permits from Athens prior to sailing from any Aegean harbor.[12] This expansive interpretation of the significance of *IG* 1³ 61 was already present *in nuce* in the analysis of Athenian policy in the Hellespont that August Boeckh offered in *Die Staatshaushaltung der Athener*:[13]

> While the power of Athens was at its height, during the Peloponnesian War the Hellespont was guarded by the Athenians... No grain could be exported from the Pontus, or from Byzantium, to any place without permission of the Athenians. In case permission was granted, it was determined to what amount annually the importation should be allowed to the favored state, and a manifest of what was to be imported was required to be handed in to the Athenian officers above mentioned (*sc.* the Hellespontine guards).

The essential elements of Boeckh's reconstruction recur in most later interpretations of *IG* 1³ 61. But while accepting Boeckh's overall interpretation of Athenian policy in the Hellespont, most subsequent scholars have placed special emphasis on the implications of *IG* 1³ 61 for Athenian relations with her allies during the early years of the Peloponnesian War. So Russell Meiggs and David Lewis suggested that 'reserve stocks (*sc.* of grain), under Athenian

---

[9] Particularly significant are the similarities between *IG* 1³ 61, lines 34–36 and 40–41 and Tod 1948, 162, lines 27–33.

[10] Ps.-Xenophon *Ath. Pol.* 2. 11–12.

[11] *Cf.*, for example, Hornblower and Greenstock 1988, 134; and Isaac 1986, 225.

[12] Andreades 1933, 303–05.

[13] Boeckh 1857, 77–78.

control, were stored at Byzantium' and noted that in addition to 'helping to ensure Athenian supplies it gave her a useful hold over her allies who depended for their corn on imports'.[14] R.J. Hopper argued that 'it would seem from the decree that trade in corn was permitted within the Athenian Empire only on special conditions and was otherwise forbidden',[15] while Peter Garnsey dryly observed that 'it was one thing to cut off the flow of grain to hostile states, and quite another to set limits on the grain imports of a privileged ally'.[16] Louis Gernet was blunter in his assessment, asserting that *IG* 1[3] 61 indicated that Athenian policy in the Hellespont aimed at controlling her allies through 'extortion'.[17]

Boeckh offered no specific date for the beginning of the policy he believed was reflected in *IG* 1[3] 61, merely characterizing it as a war measure. Later scholars have been more precise, viewing it as a response to Mytilene's success in getting grain and supplies from the Pontus prior to her revolt in 428 BC. They have dated the formulation and imposition of the policy, therefore, sometime between the outbreak of the Mytilenean revolt in summer 428 BC and early 426/5 BC, when *IG* 1[3] 61 reveals the system of controls already in place and functioning.[18]

It is surprising that a theory with such potentially far-reaching historical implications has reigned virtually unchallenged for so long in a field as thoroughly studied as 5th-century BC Athenian history, especially when neither Thucydides nor any other contemporary source even hints at the existence of a system of trade controls as extensive as that envisaged by it. Two considerations, I believe, account for this surprisingly persistent scholarly consensus.

First, the policy of actually controlling the Black Sea grain trade could be seen as the logical conclusion to a long series of Athenian actions beginning in the 6th century BC which focused on the north Aegean and Hellespontine region and are usually understood as intended to secure control of the grain route to the Pontus. These actions include the acquisition of Sigeum, the colonization of the Thracian Chersonesus, the foundation of the cleruchy at Carystus on Euboea, and the occupation of the islands of Lemnos, Imbros, and Scyros.[19] Second, the ruthless exploitation of the allies 'need for imported grain implied by the theory also could be treated as just another example of the

---

[14] Meiggs and Lewis 1969, 180.
[15] Hopper 1979, 77.
[16] Garnsey 1988, 122.
[17] Gernet 1909, 357.
[18] *Cf.* Meiggs 1972, 206; Hopper 1979, 75; Garnsey 1988, 121.
[19] E.g. Miltner 1935, 5, 10; Hopper 1979, 72; Keen 1993.

'tyrannical' treatment of her allies that Harold Mattingly[20] has long maintained characterized Athenian governance of her empire in the years following Pericles' death in 429 BC. As for the most obvious objection to the theory – the failure of contemporary sources and especially Thucydides to mention such a policy – that could simply be added to the list or Thucydides' puzzling omissions of such significant Athenian actions as the Peace of Callias and the Reassessment of 425 BC.[21] Nevertheless, the view that *IG* 1³ 61 provides evidence of Athenian efforts to pressure her allies by controlling the Black Sea grain trade is fundamentally flawed, despite its general acceptance since it was first promulgated by Boeckh almost a century and a half ago.

Part of the problem is the assumption, already evident in Boeckh's discussion of *IG* 1³ 61 and pervasive among the theory's later supporters, that the Black Sea played the same prominent role in the grain trade in the 5th century BC that it did in the 4th century BC. Archaeological evidence, however, has made it clear that the great expansion of the Black Sea grain trade occurred in the late 5th and early 4th centuries BC.[22] Moreover, as Louis Gernet demonstrated convincingly almost a century ago, the Black Sea – far from being the principal source of grain exports to the Aegean cities – was only one of a number of competing sources of grain used by Greeks in the 5th century BC.[23] Any attempt by Athens to manipulate Black Sea grain in the manner postulated by Boeckh and his successors, therefore, could not have succeeded, since her allies would have had many other potential sources of grain available to them in the Mediterranean including Sicily, Libya, Egypt, and the north Aegean.

A second and almost equally important difficulty is the fact that the theory assumes that Byzantium was, in Benjamin Isaac's phrase[24] 'the major cornmarket' on the sea route from the Black Sea to the Aegean. This is to fundamentally misunderstand, however, Byzantium's role in the Black Sea grain trade. No ancient source indicates that Byzantium served as an important market for the distribution of Black Sea grain for the very good reason that Byzantium herself was a significant producer of grain. In addition to possessing large estates worked by helot-like subjects in Bithynia,[25] Byzantium also had an extensive and fertile *chora* on the European side of the Bosporus. So,

---

[20] Mattingly 1997, *passim*.

[21] *Cf*. the survey of such omissions in Gomme 1945, 25–29.

[22] *Cf*. Noonan 1973; and Tsetskhladze 1998, 54–63. For the expansion of farming settlements in the Crimea and neighboring regions in the late 5th and especially the 4th centuries BC, see Gajdukevič 1971, 112–13.

[23] Gernet 1909, 302–26.

[24] Isaac 1986, 225.

[25] Phylarchus *FGrH* 81 F 8; *cf*. Lotze 1959, 57–58.

238   PART II: ARTICLES

Polybius observes in his famous digression on the city that the Byzantines possess 'a most fertile country, that produces an abundant harvest of high quality, when they cultivate it'.[26] As was true of its medieval successor, Constantinople, ancient Byzantium could draw substantial amounts of grain from its hinterlands and even sometimes had a surplus to export.[27] To bring Black Sea grain to Byzantium, therefore, would be the proverbial case of 'bringing coals to Newcastle'.

Not surprisingly, in the 4th century BC, when the Athenian fleet convoyed the grain fleet from the Black Sea to the Aegean, the fleet passed directly through the Bosporus and Hellespont without stopping at Byzantium.[28] Only in times of *sitodeia* would Byzantium require imported grain; and, indeed, one of the duties of the Athenian squadron escorting the grain ships was to prevent the ships from being forced to stop at Byzantium during food shortages.[29] Athens could control the grain trade in the manner postulated by Boeckh and his successors, therefore, only if grain ships exiting the Pontus could be forced to stop at Byzantium. But that only became possible in 410 BC, when the Athenians first permanently based naval forces at the fortress of Chrysopolis near Chalcedon[30] long after the passage of the Methone decrees. The most serious flaw in the accepted reconstruction of Athenian policy, however, is that it is contradicted by *IG* 1^3 61 itself.

Central to the prevailing interpretation of *IG* 1^3 61 is the assumption that Athens sought to control her allies by restricting their access to imported grain, but that is precisely what is not provided for in the Methone decrees. As the first decree makes clear (lines 18–23), Athens granted Methone permission to export grain from Byzantium because Perdiccas II had cut the city off from her normal sources: Methone's own *chora* and neighboring Macedonian territories.[31] Moreover, the first decree also allows no doubt that Athens' diplomatic intervention with Perdiccas was intended to restore Methone's access to those same sources of grain, sources which, of course, Athens did not control (*ibid.*).[32] In other words, in the one instance in which we can observe dealings with an ally's grain supply, Athens sought to reduce, not increase that ally's vulnerability to Athenian manipulation of her grain supply: the exact opposite

---

[26] Polybius 4. 45. 7; Dionysius of Byzantium *Anaplus Bospori* 11, 19. *Cf.* Cary 1949, 300.

[27] Polybius 4. 38. 9; Agathocles *Hist.* 5. 16. *Cf.* Teall 1959, 135; and Magdalino 1995.

[28] Demosthenes 50. 4–6; Philochorus *FGrH* 328 F 162.

[29] Demosthenes 50. 6; *cf.* Ps.-Aristotle *Oecon.* 2. 3c, 1346B.

[30] Xenophon *Hellenica* 1. 1. 22: Polybius 4. 44. 4; Diodorus 13. 64. 2.

[31] For the close connection between the first and second Methone decrees, see Mattingly 1961 and 1997, 525–27.

[32] Mattingly 1961, 164.

of the result scholars have assumed for over a century was the overriding goal of Athenian policy in the Hellespontine region.

The depressing saga of the scholarship concerning *IG* 1³ 61 is a prime example of one of the major problems of Greek historiography: the reluctance to reexamine long-entrenched theories, in this case the importance of the Black Sea grain trade in the 5th century BC. Obsession with the Black Sea grain trade despite clear evidence that for most of the century Athenian involvement with the region was extremely limited[33] has had more unfortunate effects, however, than merely encouraging forced interpretations of texts such as *IG* 1³ 61. It also has distorted understanding of an important aspect of Athenian foreign policy by obscuring the fact that Athens did attempt to ensure her food supply by securing control of significant grain sources. These were, however, located not in the Black Sea, but in the Aegean and the Hellespontine regions, most notably, Euboea,[34] Lemnos,[35] the Thracian Chersonesus,[36] and, as *IG* 1³ 61 indicates, Byzantium and its Thracian hinterland. It was only in the last years of the Peloponnesian War, when Athens had lost control of these sources, that the Black Sea emerged as the city's major source of grain.[37] Then, and only then, did the Hellespont and Bosporus truly become Athens' lifeline; and her fate was sealed when Lysander's victory at Aegospotami severed this lifeline.

BIBLIOGRAPHY

Andreades, A. 1933: *A History of Greek Public Finance*, vol. 1 (Cambridge).
Bloedow, E.F. 1975: 'Corn Supply and Athenian Imperialism'. *L'Antiquité Classique* 44.1, 20–29.
Boeckh, A. 1851: *Die Staatshaushaltung der Athener*, 2nd ed. (Berlin).
—. 1857: *The Public Economy of the Athenians* (Boston).
Burstein, S.M. 1993. 'The Origin of the Athenian Privileges at Bosporus: a Reconsideration'. *The Ancient History Bulletin* 7, 81–83.
Cary, M. 1949: *The Geographic Background of Greek and Roman History* (Oxford).
Casson, L. 1971: *Ships and Seamanship in the Ancient World* (Princeton).
de Ste Croix, G.E.M. 1972: *The Origins of the Peloponnesian War* (Ithaca).
Fornara, C.W. 1983: *Archaic Times to the End of the Peloponnesian War*, 2nd ed. (Cambridge).
Gajdukevič, V.F. 1971: *Das Bosporanische Reich* (Berlin).
Garnsey, P. 1988: *Famine and Food Supply in the Graeco-Roman World: Responses to Risk and Crisis* (Cambridge).

---

[33] *Cf.* in particular Mattingly 1996.
[34] Thucydides 7. 28. 1.
[35] For Lemnos as a source of grain, see Garnsey 1988, 99–101; and Stroud 1998.
[36] Lysias 32. 15.
[37] *Cf.* Tuplin 1982 and Burstein 1993.

240 PART II: ARTICLES

Gernet, L. 1909: 'L'approvisionnement d'Athènes en blé au Ve et au IVe siècle'. In *Mélanges d'histoire ancienne* 25 (Paris), 271–391.

Gomme, A.W. 1945: *A Historical Commentary on Thucydides*, vol. 1 (Oxford).

Hornblower, S. and Greenstock, M.C. 1988: *The Athenian Empire*, 3rd ed. (London).

Hopper, R.J. 1979: *Trade and Industry in Classical Greece* (London).

Isaac, B. 1986: *The Greek Settlements in Thrace until the Macedonian Conquest* (Studies of the Dutch Archaeological and Historical Society 10) (Leiden).

Keen, A.G. 1993: '"Grain for Athens": Notes on the Importance of the Hellespontine Route in Athenian Foreign Policy before the Peloponnesian War'. *Electronic Antiquity* 1.6 (November) (*https://scholar.lib.vt.edu/ejournals/ElAnt/*).

Lotze, D. 1959: *ΜΕΤΑΞΥ ΕΛΕΥΘΕΡΩΝ ΚΑΙ ΔΟΥΛΩΝ: Studien zur Rechtsstellung unfreier Landbevölkerungen in Griechenland bis zum 4. Jahrhundert v. Chr.* (Berlin).

Magdalino, P. 1995: 'The Grain Supply of Constantinople, Ninth-Twelfth Centuries'. In Mango, C. and Dagron, G. (eds.), *Constantinople and its Hinterland* (Papers from the Twenty-seventh Spring Symposium of Byzantine Studies, Oxford, April 1993) (Aldershot/Brookfield, VT), 35–47.

Mattingly, H.B. 1961: 'The Methone Decrees'. *Classical Quarterly* 55, 154–65.

—. 1996: 'Athens and the Black Sea in the Fifth Century BC'. In Lordkipanidzé, O. and Lévêque, P. (eds.), *Sur les traces des Argonautes* (Actes du 6e symposium de Vani, Colchide, 22–29 septembre 1990) (Annales Littéraires de l'Université de Besançon 613) (Besançon), 151–57.

—. 1997: *The Athenian Empire Restored: Epigraphic and Historical Studies* (Ann Arbor).

Meiggs, R. 1972: *The Athenian Empire* (Oxford).

Meiggs, R. and Lewis, D.M. 1969: *A Selection of Greek Historical Inscriptions to the End of the Fifth Century B.C.* (Oxford).

Meritt, B.D. 1944: 'Greek Inscriptions'. *Hesperia* 13, 211–29.

Miltner, F. 1935: 'Die Meerengenfrage in der griechischen Geschichte'. *Klio* 28, 1–15.

Noonan, T.S. 1973: 'The Grain Trade of the Northern Black Sea in Antiquity'. *AJPh* 94, 231–42.

Stroud, R.S. 1998: *The Athenian Tax Law of 374/3 B.C.* (*Hesperia* Suppl. 29) (Princeton).

Teall, J.L. 1959: 'The Grain Supply of the Byzantine Empire, 330–1025'. *Dumbarton Oaks Papers* 13, 89–139.

Tod, M.N. 1948: *A Selection of Greek Historical Inscriptions*, vol. 2 (Oxford).

Tsetskhladze, G.R. 1998: 'Trade on the Black Sea in the Archaic and Classical Periods: Some Observations'. In Parkins, H. and Smith, C. (eds.), *Trade, Traders and the Ancient City* (London), 51–74.

Tuplin, C. 1982: 'Satyros and Athens: *IG* ii^2 212 and Isokrates 17.57'. *Zeitschrift für Papyrologie und Epigraphik* 49, 121–28.

CHERSONESUS BETWEEN GREECE AND SCYTHIA[*]

The important role played by the Black Seal in the history of ancient Eurasia receives surprisingly little recognition in World History texts and courses.[1] For much of antiquity and the Middle Ages, however, the Black Sea was the link between the world of the Eurasian steppe and the Mediterranean basin. The critical intermediaries in the interaction between these two worlds were the Greek cities that occupied the north coast of the Black Sea and its extension, the Sea of Azov.

The Black Sea was the last major area settled by Greeks during the extraordinary migration that resulted in the foundation of Greek cities from southern Spain to the mouth of the Don River at the eastern end of the Sea of Azov. Identifying the causes that drove Greeks from their Aegean homeland is one of the great themes of Greek historiography. Land hunger, trade, and refuge from expanding imperial powers such as Lydia and Persia have all been proposed. While historians cannot agree on the ultimate cause or causes of Greek overseas settlement, there is no dispute concerning the significance of Greek colonization for the history of the Black Sea basin.[2]

Although Greek mariners probably entered the Black Sea and made contact with its inhabitants as early as the 8th century, archaeological evidence makes it clear that the bulk of Greek settlement in the region occurred in the late 7th and 6th centuries, when Miletus and other Greek cities from the west coast of Anatolia together with the city of Megara from southern Greece founded settlements in the Black Sea basin, first on its south coast, and then on its north and west coasts. Unlike the Mediterranean, where the Phoenicians proved to be formidable competitors for prime settlement sites, the Greeks had no rivals in the Black Sea so that by the early 5th century the Black Sea was almost entirely ringed by prosperous Greek cities that were equipped with fine public buildings and linked to each other, their non-Greek neighbors, and their Aegean homeland by complex political and economic ties. The most important of these cities, however, were concentrated on the north coast of the Black Sea between Olbia near the mouth of the Bug River in the west and Panticapaeum on the Straits of Kerch in the north-eastern Crimea.

---

[*] This article is a revised version of a paper delivered at the 2015 meeting of the World History Association in Savannah, Georgia. Unless otherwise noted, translations are by the author. First published in *World History Connected* 14.1 (February 2017 [electronic]).

[1] The most recent general history of the Black Sea is King 2004.

[2] For Greek colonization of the Black Sea, see Tsetskhladze 2013.

242   PART II: ARTICLES

Reconstructing the history of these of these cities is difficult because relevant ancient sources are few, forcing historians to rely on scattered references in Greek and Latin literature, inscriptions, and especially archaeology. The source problems, moreover, have been aggravated by scholars' tendency to reconstruct the histories of the cities and their relationships with their non-Greek neighbors on the basis of misleading analogies between ancient Greek colonies and 19th-century European colonies with their often overwhelming military and economic superiority to local populations,[3] when the actual situation was more similar to that of the 16th- and early 17th-century colonies, whose survival often depended on their ability to find allies among local populations.

Despite these problems, reconstructing the history of the Greek cities of the Black Sea and their relations with the peoples – both nomadic and settled – of the western Eurasian steppe was one of the triumphs of Czarist and Soviet-era scholarship. The bulk of that scholarship focused, however, on the history of Bosporus, a kingdom formed in the late 5th century BC by the unification of the Greek cities and non-Greek peoples living on both sides of the Straits of Kerch that survived until the 6th century AD.[4] The focus of this paper is a different but particularly revealing piece of this vast and complex history: the history of the principal rival of Bosporus, the city of Chersonesus Taurica in the south-western Crimea, the ancestor of modern Sevastopol, and the strategies that enabled the city to survive and prosper as a critical intermediary between the nomadic populations of the Ukrainian steppe and the states of the Black Sea and Mediterranean basins.

Chersonesus was one of the last founded and longest lived of the Greek cities of the Crimea.[5] Indeed, it survived as a center of Greek culture under its Byzantine name of Cherson as late as the 15th century AD, and was the location of some of the key events of early Russian history. Cyril and Methodius prepared there for their unsuccessful mission to the Khazars in the mid-9th century AD that was the forerunner of their later missions to the Slavic peoples of the Balkans, Moravia, and Pannonia; and Vladimir, Prince of Kiev, was baptized there in AD 988, thereby beginning the process of Christianizing Russia.

Until recently archaeologists believed that Chersonesus was founded in 422/1 BC jointly by the north Anatolian city of Heraclea Pontica, modern Ereğli, about 100 miles east of the Bosporus, and exiles from the island of Delos. Since Chersonesus, like its modern successor, Sevastapol, is located on Quarantine Bay, the best harbor at the northern end of the shortest direct

---

[3] *Cf.* De Angelis 1998; Tsetskhladze and Hargrave 2011.
[4] The fullest treatment of the kingdom of Bosporus in English is Hind 1994.
[5] For the history of Chersonesus, see Saprykin 1997.

CHERSONESUS BETWEEN GREECE AND SCYTHIA

sailing route between the north and south coasts of the Black Sea, its late foundation was surprising. Historians tried to explain the late date of the city's establishment by citing the hostility of the Tauri, the local non-Greek population, who were famous as pirates and supposedly sacrificed shipwrecked Greek sailors to their patron goddess, the Parthenos or Virgin. Thus, according to Herodotus (4. 103. 1–3) writing in the 5th century BC:

> The Tauri ... sacrifice to the Virgin all who are shipwrecked and any Greeks they seize at sea. After beginning the sacrificial ritual, they crush in the victim's head with a club ... (and) then impale the head on a stake... They treat prisoners of war as follows. Each man cuts off one of their heads, brings it home, and then he sticks it on a long pole and raises it high above his house.

Despite their fearsome reputation, however, the Tauri were unlikely to have been the reason for Chesonesus' supposed late foundation. Virtually all Pontic Greek cities actually were founded with the co-operation of local populations, and the foundation of Chersonesus in their territory indicates that the Tauri were also open to relations with Greeks. This suggestion has been confirmed by recent archaeological discoveries that indicate that such co-operation began much earlier than scholars had believed, and that an Ionian settlement, probably Milesian in origin like the other colonies in the region, already existed on the site in the late 6th century BC. Historical Chersonesus, therefore, was a refoundation and expansion of an already existing settlement. Moreover, the existence of non-Greek burials and settlement sites near Chersonesus combined with the adoption of the Parthenos, the 'Virgin', as the city's chief deity and the presence of non-Greek names – primarily Iranian – among its elite suggests that, as was the case elsewhere in the Black Sea, the city was founded with the co-operation of the Tauri. Moreover, the identification of the Tauri's virgin goddess with Iphigenia, the daughter of the Homeric hero Agamemnon, also already attested in Herodotus (4. 103. 2), further suggests that the early co-operation between the Tauri and the Greek settlers was facilitated by the sort of creative misunderstanding typical of what historians call 'Middle Ground' situations.[6]

History was to prove that the Heracleotes had chosen well when they decided to found Chersonesus in the south-western Crimea. The new city grew rapidly and prospered throughout the 4th century and into the early 3rd century BC. Although literary sources are lacking for Chersonesus' early history, inscriptions and archaeological evidence have gone far to remedy that deficiency. Most revealing is a large inscription containing the text of an oath sworn by all Chersonesite citizens on coming of age.[7]

---

[6] For the 'Middle Ground' in antiquity, see Wolf 2011, *passim.*
[7] See now Stolba 2005.

244 PART II: ARTICLES

Historians date the inscription to *ca.* 280, and the oath's detailed imprecations against those persons and their allies who intended to overthrow the democracy or betray the city, its institutions, or its secrets suggest that it was instituted after an unsuccessful attempt to establish an oligarchy or a tyranny at Chersonesus. Particularly revealing, however, is the citizens' promise that 'I will not betray Chersonesus, nor Kerkinitis nor Kalos Limen (Beautiful Harbor) nor the other forts or the other territories the Chersonesites inhabit or have inhabited' (*IOSPE* 1 401, lines 7–12). As these settlements were located well to the north of Chersonesus, the oath indicates that sometime before the oath was composed in the early 3rd century the city had expanded its territory northward from its original site at Quarantine Bay to include almost the whole west coast of the Crimea.

Archaeology allows us to fill in the details of the process.[8] Ukrainian archaeologists call Chersonesus a Slavic Pompeii with some justification. Much of the city's Medieval street plan still survives. Equally important, the most compliete example of planned land division survives at Chersonesus,[9] and this fact enabled Soviet archaelologists to reconstruct in detail the agricultural settlement plan of the 4th-century BC city. The evidence revealed by decades of excavation indicates that the city's agricultural territory was systematically divided and re-distributed by the city's government in the mid-4th century. Stone paved roads and stone retaining walls marked out the territory into roughly equal rectangular plots sufficient for at least 2400 families. The plots themselves included internal stone terracing and planting walls for grape vines, and in some cases the remains of well-built farmhouses and other farm buildings still survive. Wine producing facilities on many of the farms and large scale local production of amphorae for the transportation of wine beginning in the late 4th century suggest, moreover, that the main purpose of this development was commercial and not subsistence agriculture.

So radical a change in the pattern of land division and usage in the territory of Chersonesus must have seriously impacted the life of the Tauri. Until recently, the dominant view among scholars has been that Chersonesus followed the example of its mother city Heraclea Pontica, and obtained the needed labor force to work its farms by reducing the Tauri to the status of a dependent agricultural laboring population, whose society remained intact but subject to the rule of the Greek city.[10] Recent excavations in Chersonesus'

---

[8] The archaeological evidence for the history of Chersonesus is summarized in *Crimean Chersonesos* 2003.

[9] *Crimean Chersonesos* 2003, 120–34.

[10] The classic expression of this view is Pippidi 1962.

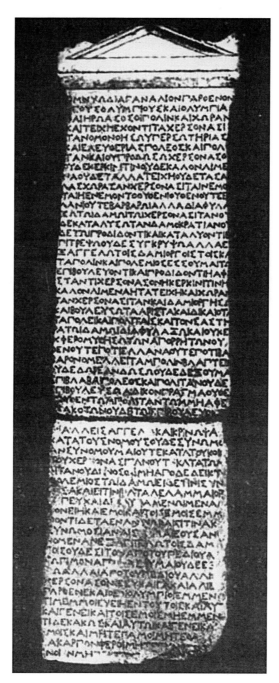

Fig. 1: The Oath of Chersonesus.

246 PART II: ARTICLES

agricultural hinterland suggest a different scenario, however, revealing that (1) the Kizil-Koba culture, which scholars identify with the material culture of the Tauri, disappeared from the territory of Chersonesus in the late 4th century; and (2) many of the new Greek farms were superimposed on the burned out remains of settlements of the Kizil-Koba culture. Taken together, these developments indicate that the 4th-century expansion of Chersonesus' territory was accompanied by the forcible expulsion of the Tauri from the city's rural hinterland. Moreover, the remains of towers on some of the farm plots, which have recently been shown to have functioned as jail-like barracks for workers,[11] suggest that slaves and other impoverished laborers provided much of the city's needed work force instead of a serf-like Tauri population.

The 'good times' for Chersonesus and the other cities of the north coast of the Black Sea ended, however, in the early and mid-3rd century BC. Archaeological evidence of the crisis is clear. Fortifications at Chersonesus and its dependencies of Kerkinitis and Kalos Limen were strengthened, more distant farms were abandoned as the area under cultivation retreated closer to the protection of the city's walls, while surviving farm houses were fitted with anti-ramming belts to protect them against attack by raiders. The most likely cause of the sudden increase in insecurity, according to Russian and Ukrainian scholars, was a dramatic change in the balance of power among the nomadic populations of the Pontic steppe and their relationship to the Greek cities of the north coast of the Black Sea.

For most of their early history, the central fact of life for Greek cities of the northern Black Sea like Chersonesus was their relationship to the kingdom of the Royal Scythians in the Pontic steppe, which dominated the southern Ukraine from the 6th to the 4th centuries.[12] Information about how the Scythians exercised their influence over cities like Chersonesus is limited, but it is clear that the survival of Chersonesus and its neighbors depended on accommodating the Scythians' need for trading outlets to the Black Sea and the Mediterranean while at the same time profiting from the protection the Scythians could provide against raids by peoples living in the city's Crimean hinterlands. The most tangible evidence of the cities' efforts to establish good relations with the Scythians are the splendid gold and bronze objects found in royal tombs and elite graves throughout the region that most likely were either diplomatic gifts or part of the cities' tribute payments instead of trade goods as was assumed in the old view of relations between the Greeks and their non-Greek neighbors.[13]

[11] Morris and Papadopoulos 2005.
[12] Burstein 2006, 141–42.
[13] See now Trofimova 2007.

BLACK SEA

Fig. 2: the Crimea in Antiquity.

The system collapsed, however, in the early 3rd century as a result of population movements in the Pontic steppe. Specifically, a new people, Iranian speaking nomads Greek and Roman authors call Sauromatae or Sarmatians, moved westward into the Pontic steppe from their home east of the Volga River and broke the power of the Royal Scythians.[14] The 1st-century BC historian Diodorus (2. 43. 67) summarizes the result as follows: 'Many years later this people [*sc.* the Sarmatians] grew strong and overran much of Scythia, completely destroying those they had conquered and turning most of the land into a desert.' Normally an account of generalized destruction such as this would arouse skepticism. In this case, however, archaeological evidence confirms the broad picture drawn by Diodorus, indicating that Scythian settlement and the construction of royal and elite graves both ceased in the Pontic steppe in the early 3rd century BC with the survivors retreating into the Crimea where they founded a new kingdom with its capital at Neapolis ('New City'), modem Simferopol, that survived until the early 1st century AD.[15]

The causes of the Sarmatian migration and the resulting upheavals in the Pontic Steppe and the Crimea are unknown. The usual suspects have been suggested including climate change and pressure from nomadic peoples further east, but evidence is lacking to confirm any of the proposed explanations. What is clear is

---

[14] The fullest account of the Sarmatians in English is Sulimirski 1970.
[15] Cunliffe 2015, 181–82.

248   PART II: ARTICLES

that the irruption of the Sarmatians into the Pontic steppe and the consequent disintegration of Scythian power resulted in a crisis that threatened the survival of Chersonesus as the rump kingdom of the Scythians in the Crimea sought to expand its territory at the expense of Chersonesus and the neighboring Bosporan kingdom. While Chersonesus initially sought to solve the problem by forming an alliance with the Scythians' Sarmatian enemies,[16] that strategy failed because of the unreliability of their new Sarmatian allies as is revealed by a Chersonesian decree (*IOSPE* 1 343) honoring the Parthenos for having saved the people

> from the greatest dangers and now [*sc.* did so] when the free men together with their children and wives had gone out to collect the harvest in the month of Dio nysus and the neighboring barbarians unexpectedly made an attack and a force of Sarmatians was preparing to invade (?) ... and the free people were in danger of being sold by the barbarians into Sarmatian territory...

The severity of the Sarmatian menace is indicated by the fact that Sarmatian continued to be used as a generic designation in Chersonesian tradition for hostile nomads in the Pontic steppe long after the real Sarmatians had disappeared.[17] Still, Chersonesus survived and even prospered thanks to its strategic position on the trade route from the Pontic steppe to northern Anatolia and the Mediterranean by adopting a new strategy, namely, seeking the protection of powers outside the north coast of the Black Sea and its steppe hinterland. The first evidence of the new strategy is an alliance concluded in the first half of the 2nd century BC with Pharnaces I, the ruler of the kingdom of Pontus in northeast Anatolia. When Pontus was conquered by Rome, similar relations were established with Rome and then with its Byzantine successor state. Security, however, came at a price. For the rest of its history, Chersonesus was a client state of its various protectors, first Pontus, then Rome, and finally the Byzantine Empire.

As the dynamics of the system did not change throughout the city's long history, it is fitting that the clearest exposition of its implications for the city is found near the end of that history in a remarkable work, the *On the Administration of the Empire*, a manual of statecraft compiled by the 10th-century AD Byzantine emperor Constantine VII Porphyrogenitus (913–957 AD) for his son Romanus II (959–963 AD). According to Constantine,[18] the Pechenegs, who dominated the Pontic Steppe

> trade with the Chersonites, and perform services for them and for the emperor in Russia ... and ... they receive from the Chersonites a prearranged remuneration in respect of this service proportionate to their labor and trouble in the form of

---

[16] Polyaenus *Strategemata* 8. 56 with Burstein 2002.

[17] Jenkins 1962, 206.

[18] Constantine Porphyrogenius *De Administrando Imperio*, ed. and trans. G. Moravcsik and R.J.H. Jenkins (Budapest 1949), 6.

pieces of purple cloth, ribbons, silks, gold brocade, pepper, scarlet or 'Parthian' leather, and other commodities which they require.

Constantine[19] is clear about the implications of these relationships for Chersonesus:

If the Chersonesites do not journey to the land of the Romans and sell the hides and wax that they get by trade from the Pechenegs, they cannot live. If grain does not pass across [*sc.* to them] from [*sc.* the land of the Romans], they cannot live.

In other words, from the crisis of the 3rd century BC to the end of its history, Chersonesus survived and prospered, but only by walking a fine line between the demands of its two masters: nomads such as the Pechenegs and their predecessors who dominated the Pontic steppe and whose elites needed Mediterranean luxury goods and the city's Anatolian protectors who needed the products of the steppe Chersonesus provided thanks to its role of intermediary between Greece and Scythia.

While the details of Chersonesus' long and complex history were peculiar to it, its historical experience was not unique. In his classic study of ports of trade, 'Ports of Trade in Early Societies', the economic historian Karl Polanyi[20] noted that the Black Sea was an area, where ports of trade were common; and Chersonesus probably began its long history as a typical 'port of trade', being located on the interface between two ecological zones, the Pontic steppe and the Black Sea and founded with its permission in the territory of a strong local population, the Tauri. Chersonesus' existence as a port of trade was temporary, however, and for most of its long history it was an independent city, while continuing to perform the functions of a port of trade. Still, as Constantine VII's perceptive description of the city's situation shows, its independence and prosperity were always precarious, requiring constant negotiation and renegotiation with its more powerful neighbors in the Pontic steppe and the Black Sea basin. Equally important, Chersonesus' experience can be paralleled among the other Greek colonies of the Black Sea and many of the Greek and Phoenician colonies of the Mediterranean basin including Massalia – modem Marseilles – and Carthage, as well as similarly situated cities in other regions and periods of history.

BIBLIOGRAPHY

Burstein, S.M. 2002: 'The Date of Amage, Queen of the Sarmatians: A Note on Polyaenus, *Strategemata* 8.56'. *AWE* 1.1, 173–77.
—. 2006: 'The Greek Cities of the Black Sea'. In Kinzl, K.H. (ed.), *A Companion to the Greek World* (Malden, MA), 137–52.

[19] *De Administrando Imperio* 53.
[20] Polanyi 1963, 30.

250 PART II: ARTICLES

Crimean Chersonesos 2003: *Crimean Chersonesos: City, Chora, Museum, and Environs* (Austin).

Cunliffe, B. 2015: *By Steppe, Desert, and Ocean: The Birth of Eurasia* (Oxford).

De Angelis, F. 1998: 'Ancient Past, imperial present: the British Empire in T.J. Dunbabin's *The Western Greeks*'. *Antiquity* 72, 539–49.

Hind, J.G.F. 1994: 'The Bosporan Kingdom'. *CAH* VI², 476–511.

Jenkins, R.H.M. (ed.) 1962: *Constantine Porphyogenitus, De Administrando Imperio: A Commentary* (London).

King, C. 2004: *The Black Sea: A History* (Oxford).

Morris, S.P. and Papadopoulos, J.K. 2005: 'Greek Towers and Slaves: An Archaeology of Exploitation'. *American Journal of Archaeology* 109, 155–225.

Pippidi, D.M. 1962: 'Die Agrarverhältnisse in den griechschen Städtcn dcr Dobrudscha in vorrömischer Zeit'. In Pippidi, D.M., *Epigraphische Beiträge zur Geschichte Histrias in Hellenistischer und Römischer Zeit* (Deutsche Akademie der Wissenschaften zu Berlin. Sektion für Altertumswissenschaft. Schriften 34) (Berlin), 60–74.

Polanyi, K. 1963: 'Ports of Trade in Early Societies'. *Journal of Economic History* 23, 30–45.

Saprykin, S.J. [S.Y.] 1997: *Heraclea Pontica and Tauric Chersonesus before Roman Domination (VI–1 Centuries B.C.)* (Amsterdam).

Stolba, V.F. 2005: 'The Oath of Chersonesos and the Chersonesean Economy in the Early Hellenistic Period'. In Archibald, Z.H., Davies, J.K. and Gabrielsen, V. (eds.), *Making, Moving and Managing: The New World of Ancient Economies, 325–31 BC* (Oxford), 298–321.

Sulimirski, T. 1970: *The Sarmatians* (London).

Trofimova, A.A. (ed.) 2007: *Greeks on the Black Sea: Ancient Art from the Hermitage* (Los Angeles).

Tsetskhladze, G.R. 2013: 'The Black Sea'. In Raaflaub, K.A. and van Wees, H. (eds.), *A Companion to Archaic Greece* (Malden, MA), 330–46.

Tsetskhladze, G.R. and Hargrave, J.F. 2011: 'Colonisation from Antiquity to Modern Times: Comparisons and Contrasts'. *AWE* 10, 161–82.

Woolf, G. 2011: *Tales of the Barbarians: Ethnography and Empire in the Roman West* (Malden, MA).

THE ORIGIN OF THE ATHENIAN PRIVILEGES AT BOSPORUS:
A RECONSIDERATION[*]

In 355 BC an Athenian politician named Leptines proposed that the practice of granting exemptions from liturgies be ended and that existing exemptions be revoked. In his maiden speech on public affairs, Demosthenes opposed Leptines' motion, arguing that it risked grievous harm to Athens. In particular, he pointed out that it would constitute a severe insult to Leucon I, the contemporary ruler of Bosporus, whose territory supplied half of the city's imported grain and who had recently extended to the city of Theodosia in the Crimea the same commercial privileges Athens already enjoyed at his capital, Panticapaeum, namely: priority in loading grain for ships bound for Athens and exemption from the one-thirtieth export tax on grain.[1]

The value of these privileges is obvious.[2] Priority in loading assured Athens bound ships full cargoes of the highest quality grain while exemption from export taxes significantly reduced the cost of shipping grain to Athens. Unfortunately, except for vague allusions to traditional Spartocid benevolence toward Athens in *In Leptinem* 33 and *IG* II[2] 653, line 9, an Athenian decree of 284/3 BC honoring Spartocus II, no ancient source provides clear evidence concerning the date these privileges originated. Not surprisingly, therefore, two widely discrepant dates for the origin of the privileges have been proposed by historians, namely, 437 BC by K.J. Beloch[3] and the late 390s BC by M.I. Rostovtzeff.[4]

Most 20th-century scholars have followed Beloch in assuming that these privileges were established by a treaty negotiated by Pericles with Spartocus I, the founder of the Spartocid dynasty, in 437 BC during his Pontic expedition.[5] Nevertheless, despite its wide acceptance, Beloch's theory is essentially an arbitrary construct based on little more than a selective use of evidence and the belief that Bosporan grain was so essential to Athens that Pericles must have

---

[*] First published in *Ancient History Bulletin* 7 (1993), 81–83.

[1] Demosthenes *In Leptinem* 29–40. Demosthenes' connections with the rulers of Bosporus were well known and controversial (Aeschines 3. 171–172; Dinarchus 1. 43; *cf.* Burstein 1978, 433–35; and Worthington 1992, 206–07).

[2] For a discussion of their significance, see Hopper 1979, 88–89. For their later history, see Burstein 1978.

[3] Beloch 1916, 216; 1922, 133–34.

[4] Rostovtzeff 1930, 567.

[5] E.g. Gomme 1944, 367–68; Meiggs 1972, 198; and Hopper 1979, 54.

252 PART II: ARTICLES

visited Panticapaeum and established contact with Spartocus I, whose accession Diodorus dates to 437 BC.[6] Already when Beloch proposed this reconstruction, evidence existed that strongly suggested a later date for the establishment of good relations between Athens and Bosporus. Thus, Aeschines characterized the 5th-century Spartocids as πολέμιοι (enemies) of Athens,[7] a description that rings true since Spartocid ambitions in the Crimea were effectively frustrated for almost two decades by the inclusion of the Crimean cities in the Athenian Empire.[8] Equally important, Plutarch (*Pericles* 20) and Theopompus (*FGrH* 115 F389), the principal sources for the Pontic expedition, ignore the area of Bosporus entirely, clearly indicating instead that Pericles' goal was to strengthen Athenian ties with the Greek cities of the south coast of the Black Sea, particularly Sinope and Amisus, both of which received significant numbers of Athenian colonists. The *coup de grâce* to Beloch's theory, however, was provided by the publication in 1979 of a new fragment of *IG* I² 944 that made clear that the Pontic expedition must be dated significantly later than 437 BC,[9] thereby severing the connection between it and the accession of Sprartocus I. But does rejection of Beloch's date for the granting of Athens' trade preferences at Bosporus automatically entail accepting for them a date in the late 390s BC as suggested by Rostovtzeff?

The evidence in favor of Rostovtzeff's theory is impressive at first glance. Most important is *IG* II² 212, an Athenian decree of 347 BC honoring the sons of Leucon I for caring for the export of grain to Athens just as their father had done (lines 14–15: ἐπιμε[λ]ήσεσθαι τῆς ἐκ[π]ομπῆς τοῦ [σ]ίτ[ου] καθάπερ ὁ πατέρ αυτῶν ἐπεμελεῖτο) and giving to Athens the same gifts which Satyrus and Leucon had given (lines 20–22: [τὰ]ς δω[ρει]ὰς διδόασιν Ἀθηναίοις, ἅσ]περ Σ[άτ]υ[ρ]ος καὶ Λεύκων ἔδοσαν). Further support is provided by Isocrates' reference in the late 390s BC (17. 57) to the granting of export preferences to Athens by Satyrus, Leucon's predecessor, and by archaeological evidence pointing to the early 4th century BC as a period of significant expansion of agricultural activity in Bosporan territory.[10] Closer analysis, however, suggests doubts.

---

[6] For the invalidity of the assumption that 4th-century accounts of the Black Sea grain trade can be applied to 5th-century conditions, see Gernet 1909.

[7] Aeschines 3. 171, *apropos* of the condemnation of Demosthenes' maternal grandfather for surrendering the Crimean city of Nymphaeum to the Spartocids.

[8] First attested in the Assessment Decree of 425 BC (*cf. IG* I³ 71, IV lines 163–172). Craterus (*FGrH* 342 F8) found Nymphaeum still listed as tributary sometime *ca.* 407 BC.

[9] C. Clairmont (1979, 123–26), confirming that Athenian casualties at Sinope, presumably incurred during the Pontic expedition and its aftermath, were listed on a casualty list most probably to be dated *ca.* 431 BC.

[10] Gajdukevič 1971, 112; and Noonan 1973, 233–34.

The problems are twofold. First, the sources clearly indicate that the privileges enjoyed under Leucon I were permanent grants good for the reign of the tyrant[11] while Isocrates refers only to temporary guarantees of full cargoes afforded Athens during periods of grain shortage. Second, and more important, the situation described by Demosthenes and later Athenian sources is one in which the Bosporan grain trade was centralized at designated ports, specifically Panticapaeum and Theodosia,[12] and controlled directly by Leucon I and his successors.[13] Isocrates' account, by contrast, clearly presupposes a less tightly controlled grain trade, one in which Satyrus was a major grain exporter but other Bosporan citizens could also sell grain directly from their own estates.[14] The implications are clear. Athens' commercial privileges reflect a major reorganization of the Bosporan grain trade that must have occurred sometime between the late 390s and 355 BC when their existence is first attested by Demosthenes. Unfortunately, the sources do not allow further precision, although Polyaenus' references to tension between Leucon I and the merchants and landed aristocracy of Bosporus in the 370s BC might provide a possible context for the sort of major reorganization of the grain trade implied by Demosthenes.[15]

Be that as it may, the evidence discussed in this paper suggests that the history of relations between Athens and Bosporus was more complex than that depicted in current accounts. Instead of a simple story of a harmonious relationship based on a mutual interest in the grain trade, Atheno-Bosporan relations clearly went through several phases, beginning with an initially hostile one that ended only with Athens' withdrawal from the Crimea in the last decade of the 5th century BC. Thereafter, relations gradually improved until sometime in the 380s or 370s BC when Leucon I granted Athens the commercial privileges at Panticapaeum referred to by Demosthenes and Athens reciprocated by making Leucon an Athenian citizen, albeit one exempt from the obligation to undertake liturgies. Still unexplained are Leucon's reasons for so favoring Athens, although evidence of a similar grant by Leucon to the city of Mitylene (SIG^3 212) suggests that his action may have been part of a general policy of seeking recognition for his regime in the Aegean world as a whole.

---

[11] This is clear from the need to have them reconfirmed at the beginning of the reign of Pairisades I (Ps.-Demosthenes 34. 36–37); cf. Demosthenes *In Leptinem* 31–34.

[12] Demosthenes *In Leptinem* 32–33. A similar policy of centralization, presumably to maximize the revenue from export taxes, was pursued by Bosporus' chief Crimean rival in the grain trade, the city of Chersonesus, in the late 4th or early 3rd century BC (*IOSPE* 4. 79, lines 47–50).

[13] According to Demosthenes (*In Leptinem* 31) Leucon was κύριος of the grain trade.

[14] Note that the father of Isocrates' client exported grain to Athens directly from his own estate and is said to have granted Athens the same privileges as Satyrus during grain shortages (Isocrates 17. 3–4; 57).

[15] Polyaenus 8. 2–3. For the probable date and historical context of these events, see Burstein 1974.

254   PART II: ARTICLES

BIBLIOGRAPHY

Beloch, K.J. 1916: *Griechische Geschichte* II.2 (Strassburg).

—. 1922: *Griechische Geschichte* III².1 (Berlin).

Burstein, S.M. 1974: 'The War between Heraclea Pontica and Leucon I of Bosporus'. *Historia* 22, 401–16.

—. 1978: '*IG* II² 653, Demosthenes and Athenian Relations with Bosporus in the Fourth Century B.C.'. *Historia* 27, 428–36.

Clairmont, C. 1979: 'New Light on Some Public Athenian Documents of the 5th and 4th Century'. *Zeitschrift für Papyrologie und Epigraphik* 36, 123–30.

Gajdukevič, V.F. 1971: *Das bosporanische Reich* (Berlin).

Gernet, L. 1909: 'L'approvisionnement d'Athènes en blé au Ve et au IVe siècles'. In *Mélanges d'histoire ancienne* 25 (Paris), 271–391.

Gomme, A.W. 1944: *A Historical Commentary on Thucydides* I (Oxford).

Hopper, R.J. 1979: *Trade and Industry in Classical Greece* (London).

Meiggs, R. 1972: *The Athenian Empire* (Oxford).

Noonan, T.S. 1973: 'The Grain Trade of the Northern Black Sea in Antiquity'. *AJPh* 94, 231–42.

Rostovtzeff, M.I. 1930: 'The Bosporan Kingdom'. *CAH* VIII, 561–89.

Worthington, I. 1992: *A Historical Commentary on Dinarchus: Rhetoric and Conspiracy in Later Fourth-Century Athens* (Ann Arbor).

THE DATE OF AMAGE, QUEEN OF THE SARMATIANS:
A NOTE ON POLYAENUS, *STRATEGEMATA* 8. 56[*]

Abstract

The textual sources for the history of Chersonesus are few and often lack clear indications concerning the date and historical context of the events described in them. Historians have tried to use archaeological evidence to date such events by trying to identify archaeological contexts in which they 'seem to fit'. The purpose of this note is to show that the currently accepted mid-2nd century BC date of one such archaeologically dated event – the intervention of Amage, queen of the Sarmatians, on behalf of Chersonesus against the Scythians – is not supported by the text of Polyaenus.

As is true of most of the Pontic Greek cities, textual sources for the history of Chersonesus are few and all too often lack clear indications concerning the date and historical context to which the events described in them belong. Not surprisingly in these circumstances, historians have tried to remedy this deficiency by resorting to archaeological evidence, asserting that the events mentioned in this or that text can only refer to one particular archaeological context and no other because that is where they 'seem to fit'.[1]

Despite the frequency with which it occurs in the historiography of the ancient Black Sea, this approach is methodologically unsound and its results insecure. Archaeology deals primarily with socio-economic structures and their transformations over the *longue durée*. Absent some specific trace in the material record, it cannot provide precise dates for short-term political events such as are found in the ancient literary sources. A good example of this practice and its problems is provided by efforts to date the dramatic story of Chersonesus' rescue from Scythian attack by the intervention of the Sarmatian queen Amage recounted in Chapter 56 of the 8th Book of the *Strategemata* of the 2nd-century AD Macedonian writer Polyaenus:[2]

> Amage was the wife of Medosakkos, the king of the Sarmatians, whose territory extended to the shore of the Pontus. When she saw that her husband was sunk in luxury and drunkenness, she judged most matters, established guards for their land, repelled attacks of their enemies, and fought in alliance with those of their neighbors who had been wronged. Her fame was great among all the Scythians so

---

[*] First published in *Ancient West and East* 1.1 (2002), 173–77.
[1] The phrase is Minns's (1913, 518, n. 3).
[2] For Polyaenus, see now Buraselis 1993–94, 121–40.

256   PART II: ARTICLES

that even the Chersonesians, who inhabited Taurica, and were suffering ill treatment at the hands of the king of the nearby Scythians, asked to become her allies. At first she sent a message bidding the king to leave Chersonesus alone. But since the Scythian held her in contempt, she assembled a force of 120 warriors who were among the bravest in spirit and body, assigned three horses to each man, raced over a distance of 1200 stades in a night and a day, and launched a sudden attack on the royal palace, and killed all the guards at the gates. While the Scythians had been thrown into confusion by the unexpected attack, thinking that the attackers were not as few as those they saw but were far greater in number, Amage burst into the palace with the force accompanying her, and killed the Scythian king, his kinsmen, and his friends. She returned their land to the Chersonesians and entrusted the kingdom to the son of the slain ruler, having exacted a promise from him that, having seen the end of his father, he would rule justly and refrain from attacking the neighboring Greeks and barbarians.

With a few notable exceptions,[3] historians of Chersonesus date these events to the mid-2nd century BC on the basis of archaeological criteria, and view them as evidence for the existence of an alliance between Chersonesus and the Sarmatians during the first half of the 2nd century BC.[4] At first glance, this reconstruction has considerable plausibility. The tactic of appealing to a more remote people to counter a threat from a neighboring population is well attested among the Pontic Greek cities, and was employed by Chersonesus and her neighbors repeatedly in the 2nd century BC, when they sought the aid of the kingdom of Pontus against the Scythian kingdom of Scilurus. Moreover, archaeological evidence suggests that settlement of the Sarmatians in the northern Black Sea region likewise began in the early 2nd century BC, and this has seemed to preclude substantially earlier dates for the story.[5] Nevertheless, this interpretation is seriously flawed, and a reconsideration of the evidence indicates that Amage's reign should, in fact, be dated much earlier, to the early 3rd or even the 4th century BC.

The problems are threefold. First, Scythian threats to Chersonesus and her territories, such as those described by Polyaenus were not unique to the 2nd century BC, so an earlier date for these events cannot be excluded on the grounds that the situation described by Polyaenus was unique to the mid-2nd century BC. Second, although Sarmatian settlement in the northern Black Sea region may have begun only in the early 2nd century BC, Sarmatian military activity in the region began much earlier, being already alluded to by the philosopher Plato in the 4th century BC.[6] More important, Sarmatian military

---

[3] Rostowzew 1931, 123–24; and Saprykin 1997, 182. Both place it in the 3rd century BC.
[4] E.g. Minns 1913, 518, n. 3; Harmatta 1950, 11; Sulimirski 1970, 135; Gajdukevič 1971, 312; Boffo 1989, 234, n. 98; Hind 1994, 505.
[5] Moshkova 1995, 87.
[6] Plato *Laws* 7, 804–805.

THE DATE OF AMAGE, QUEEN OF THE SARMATIANS 257

activity – albeit hostile rather than friendly is attested near Chersonesus in *IOSPE* 1[2] 343 – a Chersonesian inscription of the early 3rd century BC – as Y.G. Vinogradov[7] convincingly demonstrated in one of his last articles. Third, and most important, however, internal evidence provided by Polyaenus' work itself, but largely ignored by historians of the Pontic Greeks, clearly excludes a date as late as the mid-2nd century BC for the story of Amage.

Scholarship on Polyaenus mostly consists of largely futile attempts to identify the sources of the *Strategemata*.[8] For example, in the case of Polyaenus 8. 56 equally plausible cases have been made for both the 3rd century BC Athenian historian Phylarchus[9] and the 1st century BC philosopher historian Posidonius[10] as the source of the Amage story depending on the archaeological context to which the story was believed to belong. The situation changes dramatically, however, when the Amage story is considered in the light of the chronological framework of the *Strategemata* itself.

Although E.L. Bowie[11] in his fundamental study of Greek attitudes to history in the Second Sophistic described the *Strategemata* as concentrating 'almost entirely on the Classical and Hellenistic world of Greece' and showing little interest in Roman history, the reality is different. In actuality, Polyaenus' interest in Greek history did not include the whole of Greek history through the 1st century BC, but was limited to the Classical and early Hellenistic periods only. The historical context for all stratagems in the *Strategemata* that refer to events of Greek history after 200 BC, that is, events of the 2nd and 1st centuries BC, is Roman expansion in the eastern Mediterranean.[12] A 2nd-century BC date for the story of Amage, therefore, would mean that it is the sole stratagem in the *Strategemata* referring to an event in Greek history datable to the period after 200 BC that was unconnected with Roman history, and that is highly improbable. Moreover, there is additional evidence pointing to an even earlier date for the reign of Amage, one possibly as early as the 4th century BC. As has long been recognized, the story of Amage has clear literary affinities with that of Tirgatao contained in the immediately preceding chapter of Polyaenus (8. 55),[13] and the Tirgatao story, like the remaining stratagems in the

---

[7] Vinogradov 1997.

[8] The fullest discussion remains Melber 1885, 419–688. For more recent discussions, see Stadter 1965, 13–29; Phillips 1972; Hammond 1996.

[9] Rostowzew 1931, 124.

[10] Boffo 1989, 234, n. 98.

[11] Bowie 1974, 189.

[12] The relevant passages are Polyaenus 4. 21; 5. 27; 6. 4, 17; 7. 29, 41.

[13] *Cf.* Rostowzew 1931, 118–24, who recognizes their stylistic affinities but ascribes 8. 55 to Duris of Samos and 8. 56 to Phylarchus on historical criteria, i.e. Duris wrote too early for his dating of the Amage story.

258   PART II: ARTICLES

Strategemata dealing with Bosporus and other Pontic cities, concerns events of the 4th century BC.[14]

Be that as it may, the lesson of this brief study of the Amage story is clear. The history of the Greek cities of the Black Sea rests on the integration of textual and archaeological evidence, the interpretation of each which has its own distinctive methodological requirements. Ignoring that fact in the case of the story of Amage has distorted the study of a critical period in the history of Chersonesus for almost a century. Far from marking the beginning of a period of close relations between Chersonesus and the Sarmatians, the internal evidence of Polyaenus' work suggests that the intervention of Amage into Chersonesian affairs was an isolated event with little long term significance, an interpretation that is strengthened by the indications of hostilities between Chersonesus and the Sarmatians in the early 3rd century BC provided by the recently revised text of *IOSPE* 1² 343.

BIBLIOGRAPHY

Boffo, L. 1989: 'Grecità di Frontiera: Chersonasos Taurica e i Signori del Ponto (*SIG*³ 709)'. *Athenaeum* 78, 211–60.

Bowie, E.L. 1974: 'Greeks and Their Past in the Second Sophistic'. In Finley, M.I. (ed.), *Studies in Ancient Society* (London), 166–209.

Buraselis, K. 1993–94: 'The Roman World of Polyainos. Aspects of a Macedonian Career between Classical Past and Provincial Present'. *Archaiognosia* 8, 121–40.

Burstein, S.M. 1974: 'The War between Heraclea Pontica and Leucon I of Bosporus'. *Historia* 23, 401–16.

Gajdukevič, V.F. 1971: *Das Bosporanische Reich*, 2nd ed. (Berlin).

Harmatta, J. 1950: *Studies on the History of the Sarmatians* (Budapest).

Hammond, N.G.L. 1996: 'Some Passages in Polyaenus' *Stratagems* concerning Alexander'. *Greek, Roman, and Byzantine Studies* 37, 23–53.

Hind, J.G.F. 1994: 'The Bosporan kingdom'. *CAH* VI², 476–511.

Melber, J. 1885: *Über die Quellen und den Wert der Strategemensammlung Polyäns: Ein Beitrag zur griechischen Historiographie (Jahrbucher für classische Philologie* Suppl. 14) (Leipzig).

Minns, E.H. 1913: *Scythians and Greeks: A Survey of Ancient History and Archaeology on the North Coast of the Euxine from the Danube to the Caucasus* (Cambridge).

Moshkova, M.G. 1995: 'A Brief Review of the History of the Sauromatian and Sarmatian Tribes'. In Davis-Kimball, J., Bashilov, V.A. and Yablonsky, L.T. (eds.), *Nomads of the Eurasian Steppes in the Early Iron Age* (Berkeley), 85–89.

Phillips, R.J. 1972: 'The Sources and Methods of Polyaenus'. *Harvard Studies in Classical Philology* 76, 297–98.

Rostowzew, M. 1931: *Skythien und der Bosoporus* (Berlin).

---

[14] All passages in Polyaenus concerning Bosporus and Heraclea Pontica refer to events of the 4th century BC; *cf.* Burstein 1974.

THE DATE OF AMAGE, QUEEN OF THE SARMATIANS 259

Saprykin, S.J. 1997: *Heracleia Pontica and Tauric Chersonesus before Roman Domination (VI–I Centuries B.C.)* (Amsterdam).
Stadter, P.A. 1965: *Plutarch's Historical Methods: An Analysis of the Mulierum Virtutes* (Cambridge, MA).
Sulimirski, T. 1970: *The Sarmatians* (London).
Vinogradov, Y.G. 1997: 'Khersonesskii dekret o "nesenii Dionisa" *IOSPE* I^2 343 i vtorzhenie Sarmatov v Skifiyu'. *VDI* 3, 104–24.

THE WAR BETWEEN HERACLEA PONTICA AND LEUCON I OF BOSPORUS[*]

The Problem and the Sources

During the first half of the 4th century BC the Spartocid tyrants of Panticapaeum brought under their control the Greek cities and native peoples of the eastern Crimea together with those of the Taman Peninsula. The greatest prize, however, was the Greek city of Theodosia in the south-eastern Crimea with its splendid harbor and rich grain growing hinterland.[1] Control of it placed the great bulk of the profitable grain trade in Spartocid hands and had also the political advantage of eliminating a refuge for Panticapaean exiles.[2] The annexation of this important city was not without difficulty. The tyrant Satyrus died in 389 during a futile attempt to conquer it,[3] thus leaving its reduction to his son Leucon I (389–347) who, as is revealed by Demosthenes' speech *In Leptinem*, succeeded in bringing Theodosia under his authority sometime between 389 and the delivery of the speech in 354.[4]

Control of Theodosia opened the way for further expansion in the Crimea by Leucon or his successors should they be so inclined. The primary target of any such aggression would be the city of Chersonesus so that it is not surprising that her *metropolis*, Heraclea Pontica, came into conflict with the Spartocids[5] and that

---

[*] Acknowledgment is due at this point to Prof. T.S. Brown and Prof. M.H. Chambers of UCLA and Prof. L. Okin of California State University at Humboldt who read earlier drafts of this paper and to Miss S. Breit and my colleague Prof. J. Zimmerman who kindly translated for me the Russian material used in its preparation. First published in *Historia* 23 (1974), 401–16.

[1] Strabo, 7. 4. 4, 6; Demosthenes, 20. 33. See also Minns 1913, 556–57.

[2] Ps.-Arrian *Periplus Ponti Euxini*: *GGM* I, 415, Ch. 51: ἐν ταύτῃ δὲ τῇ Θευδοσίᾳ λέγεταί ποτε καὶ φυγάδας ἐκ τοῦ Βοσπόρου οἰχῆσαι. Rostovtzeff (1931, 65) and Latyschev (*IOSPE* II²), xxix, connect this with the hostilities between Bosporus and Heraclea. Shelov (1950, 170), however, has questioned the validity of any conclusions drawn from this passage because of its vagueness.

[3] Harpocration *s.v.* Θευδοσία. Diodorus' (14. 93. 1) date of 393 for Satyrus' death is four years too early. *Cf.* Werner 1955, 418–19.

[4] Demosthenes 20. 33. For the date of the *In Leptinem*, see Blass 1887–98 III.1, 264.

[5] That Chersonesus' safety was Heraclea's primary concern is generally conceded (see, for example, Minns 1913, 515–16; Brandis 1899, 764–65; and Shelov 1950, 174, who also notes that Heraclea may have had interests in the Taman Peninsula to defend). The economic interpretations of Rostovtzeff (1930, 569) and Maximowa (1959, 115–16), who both believe Heraclea fought to maintain or even increase her share in the Pontic grain trade are unconvincing since they ignore the key facts that Heraclea could neither gain control of the grain producing areas nor determine the sailing routes of the ships engaged in the trade.

262 PART II: ARTICLES

on one occasion a Heracleote general named Tynnichus frustrated an attempt by them to seize Theodosia either before her conquest or during a subsequent rebellion.[6] Equally unsurprising is the fact revealed by numismatic evidence, namely the issuing of coins with the type of a butting bull borrowed from the coinage of Heraclea, that Theodosia[7] and probably Phanagoria[8] on the Taman Peninsula, another city threatened by Spartocid expansionism, concluded alliances with Heraclea sometime during the first half of the 4th century. Scholarly opinion, however, is strongly divided as to whether Heraclea fought one or several wars with Panticapaeum as a result of this involvement in the affairs of the Greek cities of South Russia. Since the main difficulty lies in the interpretation of the literary sources relevant or believed to be relevant to it, an anecdote in the Pseudo-Aristotelian *Oeconomica* and four in Polyaenus' *Strategemata*, the following discussion will be more easily understood if these texts are provided at this point:[9]

> Ἡρακλεῶται πέμποντες ναῦς τεσσαράκοντα ἐπὶ τοὺς ἐν Βοσπόρῳ τυράννους, οὐκ εὐπορούμενοι χρημάτων παρὰ τῶν ἐμπόρων συνηγόρασαν τόν τε σῖτον πάντα καὶ τὸ ἔλαιον καὶ τὸν οἶνον καὶ τὴν ἄλλην ἀγορὰν χρόνου διισταμένον ἐν ᾧ ἔμελλον ἀποδώσειν τὴν τιμήν. Τοῖς δὲ δὴ ἐμπόροις καλῶς εἶχε μὴ κοτυλίζειν, ἀλλ' ἀθρόα τὰ φορτία πεπρᾶσθαι. Ἐκεῖνοί τε διαδόντες διμήνου μισθὸν παρῆγον {ἀλλὰ} τὴν ἀγορὰν ἐν ὁλκάσιν, ἄνδρα <τε> ταμίαν ἐπέστησαν ἐφ' ἑκάστῃ τῶν νεῶν. Ἀφικομένων δ' εἰς τὴν πολεμίαν αὐτῶν ἠγόραζον οἱ στρατιῶται παρὰ τούτων ἅπαντα. Πρότερον <οὖν> συλλεγέντι ἀργυρίῳ ἐδίδοσαν οἱ στρατηγοὶ πάλιν τὸν μισθόν, ὥστε συνέβαινε ταὐτὸ{τὸ} ἀργύρων δίδοσθαι ἕως εἰς οἶκον ἀπῆλθον.

The Heracleotes, being about to send 40 ships against the tyrants in Bosporus but not having sufficient money, bought up all the grain, olive oil, wine and other staples from the merchants and set a date on which they would pay for them. The merchants were pleased to have disposed of their cargoes all at once instead of having to sell them item by item. The Heracleotes distributed two months' pay in advance[10] and brought along the supplies in cargo ships on each of which they stationed a financial officer. On arriving in enemy territory the soldiers purchased everything from these men. There, the generals paid their salaries again with the money collected previously so that the same funds were distributed until they returned home (Ps.-Aristotle *Oeconomica* 2. 2. 8).

---

[6] Polyaenus *Strategematon libri VIII*, ed. E. Woelfflin and J. Melber (Leipzig 1887), 5. 23.

[7] For the coins, see Zograf 1951, pl. 39 nos. 3–4. Zograf (1951, 244) dates them to the mid-4th century. For their significance see Minns 1913, 559, and Shelov 1950, 175–76. See *Recueil* I.2, pl. 55 nos. 5–9.

[8] Zograf 1951, pl. 39, no. 44. He dates it (1951, 244) to the period 400–350. For the connection with Heraclea, see Shelov 1950, 174.

[9] All translations are by the author. For the *Oeconomica* I followed the text of van Groningen 1933.

[10] The text is uncertain at this point. For the problems of it as printed, see Griffith 1935, 270, n. 2; and Burstein 1972, 295, n. 77. As it does not affect the topic of this paper, no attempt to resolve these difficulties is offered here.

THE WAR BETWEEN HERACLEA PONTICA AND LEUCON I OF BOSPORUS 263

Τύννιχος Θευδοσίας τῆς ἐν τῷ Πόντῳ πολιορκουμένης ὑπὸ τῶν πλησίον τυράννων καὶ κινδυνευούσης ἁλῶναι τὴν πολιορκίαν ἔλυσεν. ὁρμηθεὶς μὲν ἐξ Ἡρακλείας νηὶ στρογγύλῃ καὶ τριήρει μιᾷ, δεξάμενος δὲ στρατιώτας ὅσους οἷόν τε ἦν, καὶ σαλπιγκτὰς τρεῖς καὶ σκάφας τρεῖς μονοξύλους, ἑκάστην ἄνδρα ἕνα δέξασθαι δυναμένην, νυκτὸς ἐπιπλεύσας, τῆς πόλεως ἐγγὺς γενόμενος, ἐξελὼν τὰς σκάφας, ἐμβιβάσας ἑκάστῃ σαλπιγκτὴν ἕνα συνέταξεν ἀποσχόντας ἀλλήλων διάστημα σύμμετρον, ἐπειδὰν ἐκ τῆς τριήρους καὶ τῆς στρογγύλης ὑποσημήνῃ, διαδεξαμένους σημαίνειν παραλλάσσοντας τοῖς χρόνοις, ὡς μὴ σάλπιγγος μιᾶς προσπίπτειν ἦχον, ἀλλὰ πλειόνων, οἱ μὲν ἐσήμηναν ἤχῳ σαλπίγγων τὸν περικείμενον ἀέρα τῇ πόλει πληροῦντες, οἱ δὲ πολιορκοῦντες νομίσαντες ἐπίπλουν εἶναι στόλου μείζονος οὐδενὶ κόσμῳ τὰς φυλακὰς ἐκλιπόντες ᾤχοντο. Τύννιχος δὲ προσπλεύσας τὴν Θευδοσίαν ἠλευθέρωσε τῆς πολιορκίας.

When Theodosia, a city on the Pontus, was under siege by the nearby tyrants and in danger of being captured, Tynnichus lifted the siege. He had set out from Heraclea with one merchant-ship and one trireme after having embarked as many soldiers as possible, three trumpeters and three dugouts each able to hold one man. He sailed at night and when near the city, he lowered the dugouts, having placed in each a trumpeter whom he had ordered to take up a position separated from the others by an appropriate distance. When the signal was given from the trireme and the merchant-ship, they were to pick it up and repeat it at differing intervals so that the sound, not of one trumpet, but of many would be heard. They gave the signal and filled the air around the city with the sound of trumpets. The besiegers, thinking that a larger force was approaching, abandoned their posts in disorder and fled. Thus, Tynnichus, having sailed to Theodosia, freed it from siege (Polyaenus 5. 23).

Λεύκων ἐν τῷ πρὸς Ἡρακλεώτας πολέμῳ αἰσθόμενος τῶν τριηράρχων τινὰς προδιδόντας καὶ αὐτομολεῖν μέλλοντας συλλαβὼν αὐτοὺς ἀκοῦσαι μὲν ἔφη περὶ αὐτῶν λόγους οὐκ ἐπιτηδείους, οὐ πιστεῦσαί γε μήν. ὅπως οὖν μὴ κατὰ τύχην ἥττης γενομένης αὐτοὶ δοκοῖεν αἴτιοι τοῦ σφάλματος, αὐτοὺς μὲν ἡσυχάζειν ἐκέλευσεν, ἄλλους δὲ τριηράρχους ἀπέδειξε, τοῖς δὲ οἰκείοις τῶν ὑπόπτων ἀρχὰς καὶ ἐπιμελείας ἐνεχείριζε κωμῶν, ὡς δὴ φιλοφρόνως ἔχων πρὸς αὐτούς. ἐπεὶ δὲ τὸν πόλεμον κατελύσατο, δίκαιον ἔφη κριθῆναι τοὺς ὑπόπτους, ἵνα μὴ δόξῃ ἀλόγως αὐτοῖς ἀπιστῆσαι. παρελθόντων δὲ εἰς τὸ δικαστήριον ὁμοῦ τοῖς οἰκείοις περιστήσας ὡπλισμένην δύναμιν ἅπαντας αὐτοὺς ἀναιρεθῆναι προσέταξεν.

During the war against the Heracleotes Leucon, learning that some of his trierarchs were disaffected and intending to desert, arrested them and said that he had heard unfavorable statements about them, but that he placed no trust in these. Therefore, he ordered them to be relieved and appointed other trierarchs so that, should by chance a defeat occur, they should not appear to have been the cause of the failure. And he entrusted to the relatives of the suspects their offices and the management of their villages as though he were well intentioned towards them. But when he had brought the war to an end, he said that it was just that the suspects stand trial in order that he should not seem to have distrusted them unreasonably. When, however, they and their relatives entered the court which he had surrounded with an armed force, he ordered them all to be executed (Polyaenus 6. 9. 3).

264 PART II: ARTICLES

Λεύκων ἐπιστρατευσάντων Ἡρακλεωτῶν ναυσὶ πολλαῖς καὶ ἀποβαινόντων ὅποι τῆς χώρας ἐβούλοντο, ὁρῶν τοὺς αὑτοῦ στρατιώτας ἐθελοκακοῦντας καὶ οὐκ ἀνείργοντας ἔταξε τοὺς ὁπλίτας πρώτους πρὸς τὴν ἀπόβασιν τῶν πολεμίων, ἐπὶ δὲ τούτοις ὄπισθεν τοὺς Σκύθας. καὶ φανερῶς παρήγγειλε τοῖς Σκύθαις, ἐὰν οἱ ὁπλῖται ὀκνῶσι καὶ τοὺς πολεμίους ἀποβαίνοντας παρέχωνται, τηνικαῦτα τοξεύειν καὶ κτιννύειν αὐτούς, τοῦτο μαθόντες οἱ ὁπλῖται εὐρώστως τοὺς πολεμίους ἀποβαίνειν ἐκώλυον.

When the Heracleotes were attacking with many ships and making landings at whatever point in his territory that they wished, Leucon, observing that his sol-diers were showing signs of cowardice and hanging back, stationed his hoplites as the first to meet the landing of the enemy, and behind them he placed the Scyth-ians. And he openly gave orders to the Scythians that, if the hoplites shrank back and allowed the enemy to disembark, at that moment they should shoot them down and kill them. On learning this, the hoplites manfully prevented the enemy from making a landing (Polyaenus, 6. 9. 4).

Μέμνων ἐπιτιθέμενος Λεύκωνι τῷ Βοσπόρου τυράννῳ, βουλόμενος καταμαθεῖν τὰ μεγέθη τῶν πολεμίων <πόλεων> καὶ τὰ πλήθη τῶν ἐνοικούντων ἔπεμψεν Ἀρχιβιάδην Βυζάντιον ἐπὶ τριήρους πρεσβευτὴν πρὸς Λεύκωνα ὡς ὑπὲρ φιλίας καὶ ξενίας διαλεξόμενον. συνέπεμψε δὲ αὐτῷ καὶ Ὀλύνθιον κιθαρῳδὸν Ἀριστόνικον, εὐδοκιμοῦντα μάλιστα δὴ πάντων τότε παρὰ τοῖς Ἕλλησιν, ὅπως ἐν τῷ παράπλῳ προσορμιζομένων, ἐπιδεικνυμένου τοῦ κιθαρῳδοῦ, τῶν ἐνοικούντων εἰς τὰ θέατρα σπουδῇ συνιόντων τὸ πλῆθος τῶν ἀνθρώπων κατάδηλον τῷ πρεσβευτῇ γένοιτο.

Memnon, making plans for an attack on Leucon, the tyrant of Bosporus, and desiring to find out the size of the enemy cities and population, sent a trireme bearing Archibiades of Byzantium as ambassador to Leucon ostensibly to discuss the establishment of friendly relations and ties of guest friendship. He also sent with Archibiades the Olynthian cithara player Aristonicus, then enjoying among the Greeks the highest reputation of all such musicians. He expected that once their ship had anchored near the coast and the presence of the cithara player became known, the size of the population would become clear to the ambassador as the inhabitants hastily collected at the places from which they could get a view (Polyaenus 5. 44. 1).

Examination of these texts reveals only two points that can serve as guideposts in their interpretation. The first is the constant reference to Heracleotes which indicates that Heraclea was not ruled by a tyrant during the hostilities, a fact that excludes the possibility of dating any of these events to the period between 364 and 281. The second is the use of τύραννοι in the plural which implies the existence of a collegiate government in the Spartocid territories at the time of the incidents described in the anecdote from the *Oeconomica* and in that con-cerning Tynnichus. Fifty years ago K.J. Beloch contended,[11] correctly as I

---

[11] Beloch 1912–27 III.1, 134 and 134, n. 3.

THE WAR BETWEEN HERACLEA PONTICA AND LEUCON I OF BOSPORUS   265

intend to show, that the most probable interpretation of the passages is that all but that about Memnon refer to a single war between Heraclea and Leucon I prior to the fall of Theodosia that ended in a Heracleote victory.

ONLY ONE WAR

As Beloch merely stated his thesis without offering supporting arguments, his contribution to the debate was ignored. Instead scholars before and after him have adhered, albeit with slight differences in detail, to one of three alternative reconstructions all based on the assumption that Heraclea and Panticapaeum fought several wars during a period that may have been as short as a third of a century or as long as a century and a third. Of these the first and most widely accepted is that espoused among others by H. Schneiderwirth,[12] C. Brandis,[13] V.V. Latyschev,[14] V.F. Gajdukevič[15] and Helmut Berve[16] according to which Heraclea fought two wars with Panticapaeum, one against Satyrus in 389 to which the Tynnichus episode and the Ps.-Aristotle anecdote belong, and another against Leucon I some years later with which the anecdotes about his stratagems and possibly that about Memnon are connected. The second was advanced by E.H. Minns[17] and D.E. Wormell[18] and differs from the above only in the belief that the Memnon passage refers to a third war between Heraclea and Panticapaeum that broke out about 350. Finally, there is what can be called the long conflict theory which originated in J.G. Droysen's[19] suggested dating of Tynnichus' exploit to the mid-3rd century and which has since been elaborated in different ways by M.I. Rostovtzeff[20] and D.B. Shelov.[21] According to Rostovtzeff, Leucon I conquered Theodosia in the 360s after a long struggle with Heraclea, but that about a century later during the joint reign of Leucon II and Spartocus V the war broke out of which the Tynnichus episode and the fiscal measures of Ps.-Aristotle formed part. Shelov's version is similar only in his agreeing with Rostovtzeff that the Ps.-Aristotle anecdote should be dated to the reign of Leucon II and Spartocus V. Uniquely, however, he

---

[12] Schneiderwirth 1882, 17.

[13] Brandis 1899, 764–65.

[14] *IOSPE* II, xix, xxi (Latyschev).

[15] Gajdukevič 1949, 58–59. I have not as yet been able to see the new edition of this work (Gajdukevič 1971).

[16] Berve 1967 I, 326.

[17] Minns 1913, 556, 574, 576.

[18] Wormell 1946, 52, 54.

[19] Droysen 1883–85 III, 275.

[20] Rostovtzeff 1931, 121–23.

[21] Shelov 1950, 172–73.

266   PART II: ARTICLES

also dates the texts referring to a war between Heraclea and a Leucon to this same period. Moreover, he retains the connection of Tynnichus with Satyrus' attack in 389 and agrees with Minns and Wormell in seeing in the Memnon passage evidence of an outbreak of fighting about 350. In other words, Shelov argues that three wars between Heraclea and Panticapaeum took place between 389 and approximately 260.

Fortunately, the long chronology favored by Rostovtzeff and Shelov can be quickly eliminated. The basis of Rostovtzeff's position was his belief that the situation implied by Pseudo Aristotle, namely an extensive campaign conducted by a strong Heracleote fleet in Bosporan waters at a time when Heraclea was ruled by a free government and more than one tyrant was in power at Bosporus could not be reconciled with the conditions of the reign of Leucon I but would fit those of the co-regency of Spartocus V and Leucon II which he dated to the mid-3rd century. To these considerations Shelov has added those of numismatics, pointing to the fact that a rare issue of Theodosian coinage, which he dates to the mid-3rd century, bears on its reverse a club similar to that found on Heracleote coins of the same period.[22] Arguing from the analogy of the butting bull type that Theodosia used in the 4th century, he contends that these coins also indicate an alliance between that city and Heraclea which should be dated about 260. This would constitute strong support for the long chronology theory except for two points, first, that the dating of these coins is based solely on stylistic considerations, and second, that the club type also appears on the roughly contemporary coinage of Chersonesus, a city which boasted of the assistance it lent other cities during the 3rd century.[23] In other words, the numismatic evidence can only be used at all in a discussion of a Heracleote-Bosporan conflict in the mid-3rd century if the existence of such a struggle at that time can be independently established on the basis of other data as Rostovtzeff attempted to do.

On purely *a priori* grounds there has long been good reason to doubt the possibility of such a war about 260 since there are strong indications that friendly relations existed between Panticapaeum and Heraclea's colonies of Callatis and Chersonesus beginning as early as the last quarter of the 4th century and lasting in the case of the latter until at least the second half of the

---

[22] Shelov 1950, 176. For the Theodosian coin, see Zograf 1951, pl. 39, no. 5; and for the Heracleote parallels, see *Recueil* I.2, 56, nos. 15–17, 20, 22, 24.

[23] Zograf (1951, 244) dates the Theodosian issue to *ca.* 225–200. For the Chersoncsian parallels, see Zograf 1951, pl. 35, nos. 2, 3, 6–7, 9, 13, and pl. 36, nos. 1 and 15. For Chersonesus' relations with other cities, see *IOSPE* I, 344, lines 4–7, 17–19 = Syriscus *FGrH* 3C, 807, T1. Latyschcv (*IOSPE* I, 291) dates the inscription to the late 3rd century.

THE WAR BETWEEN HERACLEA PONTICA AND LEUCON I OF BOSPORUS   267

3rd century.[24] Furthermore, both Rostovtzeff and Shelov ignored Ulrich Wilcken's[25] discovery that the anecdotes in the *Oeconomica* are arranged chronologically, a fact which enables its composition to be placed with great probability in the late 4th century and which provides us with a *terminus post quem* of 409 and a *terminus ante quem* of 364 for the war between Heraclea and the tyrants of Bosporus mentioned in it.[26] Since Rostovtzeff's low dating of the Tynnichus episode is tied to that of the Ps.-Aristotle passage, there remains no reason to deny that it too belongs to the period between 409 and 364. Actually, however, Robert Werner gave the theory its *coup de grâce* by showing that the reigns of Leucon II and Spartocus V should be dated to the second instead of the 3rd century, thus eliminating the possibility of a co-regency at Panticapaeum about 260 as assumed by Rostovtzeff and Shelov.[27] With this also falls Shelov's belief that Polyaenus 6. 9. 3–4 refers to Leucon II and not Leucon I.[28] Instead it is clear that these texts as well as the Tynnichus anecdote and that in the *Oeconomica* concern hostilities between Heraclea and Panticapaeum that took place before 364.

Equally unsubstantiated is Minn's and Wormell's theory that Heraclea fought two wars with Leucon I. It is based on the belief that Memnon was in the pay of Heraclea when he plotted against Leucon which would necessitate a date about 350 since he would be most unlikely to have entered Heracleote service until after the beginning of his exile in 353.[29] This, in turn, would have to have been during a second war with Leucon because, as already mentioned, Polyaenus' use of Heracleotes in his anecdotes about Leucon must be taken as referring to a conflict that took place before the establishment of Clearchus' tyranny at Heraclea in 364. Although, as Beloch pointed out,[30] one weakness in this theory is the lack of any evidence that Memnon's plot was followed by actual fighting, the

---

[24] Callatis: Diodorus, 20. 25. 1. Chersonesus: *IOSPE* I, 344 lines 4–7, 17–19 = Syriscus *FGrH* 3C, 807, T1. The reference in line 5 to τούς Βοσ[π]όρου [β]ασιλεῖ[ς …] indicates that friendly relations with Bosporus had existed for some time.

[25] Wilcken 1901, 188–90. See also van Groningen 1933, 35; and Cracco Ruggini 1966, 216–21.

[26] Date of the work: van Groningen 1933, 41–44; and Ruggini 1966, 205–06. The chronological limits are provided by the anecdote on Lampsacus (Ps.-Aristotle *Oeconomica* 2. 2. 7), which refers to events of the year 409 (van Groningen 1933, 83) and the first of three anecdotes concerning Mausolus of Caria (2. 2. 13a) which belongs to the year 364 (van Groningen 1933, 97).

[27] Werner 1955, 422–23.

[28] Shelov's (1950, 172) arguments in support of this theory, namely the incompatibility of Polyaenus' picture of Leucon as a suspicious tyrant in 6. 9. 3–4 and the account of his fiscal problems in 6. 9. 1–2 with the general ancient picture of him as a benevolent ruler (e.g. Strabo 7. 4. 4) of a rich and powerful state are too subjective to justify abandoning without further evidence the obvious view that Polyaenus is referring to the famous Leucon and not to an obscure successor of the same name.

[29] *Cf.* Shelov 1950, 173.

[30] Beloch 1912–27 III.1, 134, n. 4. This has also been noted by Werner 1955, 440, n. 2.

268 PART II: ARTICLES

key point is obviously the contention that Heraclea hired him, a fact which is not mentioned by Polyaenus whose account contains no hint that he had an employer. Indeed, the reference to Archibiades being sent to Leucon ὡς ὑπὲρ φιλίας καὶ ξενίας διαλεξόμενον is difficult to account for on that assumption since, while ξενία or guest-friendship could exist between any two individuals, φιλία in diplomacy normally referred to friendly relations between diplomatic equals and could hardly apply to any ties which might be arranged between Leucon and a hired mercenary.[31] In support of his thesis Minns[32] himself could only offer the argument that 'we do not know in what other war he [sc. Memnon] should have opposed Leucon', which is merely to beg the question at issue and hardly convincing in view of the gaps in our knowledge of Pontic affairs in the 4th century. Almost certainly decisive against this theory, however, is a hitherto unnoticed note in Polyaenus 6. 9. 3. Since Polyaenus' source for his anecdotes about Leucon I in 6. 9 was clearly an account of that monarch's reign,[33] his use of the definite article τῷ in stating that Leucon's difficulties with his trierarchs occurred ἐν τῷ πρὸς Ἡρακλεώτας πολέμῳ can only mean that his source contained information about only one war with Heraclea which cannot have involved Memnon since it took place before 364. Having thus shown that no evidence exists pointing to a clash between Heraclea and Panticapaeum after 364, we can now turn to consider the last two items to be accounted for, the anecdote about Tynnichus and that in the *Oeconomica*.

These, as already indicated, are usually interpreted to mean that Heraclea supported Theodosia during the siege of the city by Satyrus in 389. Since, however, Satyrus had no co-regent at that time, the use of the plural τύραννοι in both texts makes this impossible. Werner,[34] who first recognized this difficulty, attempted to evade it by postulating that Satyrus and his co-regent Seleucus had attacked Theodosia shortly before the death of the latter in 393/2, and that it was on this occasion that Heraclea had come to Theodosia's

---

[31] *Cf.* the close parallel in Xenophon *Agesilaus* 8. 3–5. For this meaning of φιλία see also LSJ *s.v.* φιλία 1; and the passages cited by Bengtson 1962, index *s.v.* φιλία.

[32] Minns 1912, 556. The argument is repeated by Shelov 1950, 173.

[33] This is clear from the perspective of the anecdotes. Leucon is simply named without further identification being supplied, his plans and personal reflections are described in detail while, on the other hand, the Heracleotes are only mentioned as his enemies who are attacking his territory. Despite the ascription of these passages to Duris by Rostovtzeff (1931, 117, 121–22) and Wormell (1946, 67–68), any attempt to identify the source would be futile. Their assertion, however, that the anecdote about Memnon comes from the same source is almost certainly incorrect since, unlike the others, it is written from Memnon's and not Leucon's point of view – notice that the latter is here specifically identified as tyrant of Bosporus – and is correctly placed at the head of a chronologically arranged series of anecdotes about his career (Polyaenus 5. 44) and thus, is unlikely to have come from a narrative of Leucon's reign.

[34] Werner 1955, 436–37. See also Werner 1957, 221–23, 237–38.

THE WAR BETWEEN HERACLEA PONTICA AND LEUCON I OF BOSPORUS   269

assistance. Such a reconstruction is certainly possible as the Spartocids were in position to launch such an assault from the moment that Nymphaeum was handed over to them by Gylon, its Athenian commander, most likely during the last years of the Peloponnesian War.[35] Given the lacunae in our knowledge of Bosporan history, the silence of our sources about such an earlier attack is no proof that it did not take place. Still, it is worth noting that the glimpses of Pontic conditions about 405 and 400 provided by Lysias[36] and Xenophon[37] give us no reason to assume that a major conflict such as that implied by Ps.-Aristotle took place during these years. As for Werner's own date of the 390s, it is possible, but it raises the puzzling question of the silence of Isocrates about such a war in the *Trapeziticus*, a speech delivered sometime between 394 and 390 that describes Panticapaean affairs in the 390s in some detail and specifically mentions Satyrus' difficulties with exiles whose support by Theodosia has been plausibly suggested to have been one of the reasons for the hostility between her and the Spartocids.[38] Moreover, one would expect that such a war would have seriously disrupted the Pontic grain trade on which Athens largely depended by the beginning of the 4th century to maintain her food supplies at an adequate level, yet we hear of no such problems between the blockade imposed by Lysander in 405 and that established by Antalcidas in 387.[39] Finally, and perhaps more important, Satyrus seems to have had to devote much of his attention during the latter part of his reign to defending Spartocid interests in the Taman Peninsula which were threatened by the deterioration of relations between Panticapaeum and the important tribe of the Sindoi.[40] None of these considerations, of course, suffices to disprove the theory of an unsuccessful attack on Theodosia prior to 389, but, taken together, they render it doubtful.

Actually, however, Werner had no need to advance so complicated a hypothesis since he, like Latyschev and Beloch before him, had no difficulty in showing that Leucon I did, in fact, have a co-regent for part of his reign, namely, his brother Gorgippus who seems to have administered the dynasty's possessions

---

[35] Aeschines 3. 171. For the date, see Minns 1913, 561; *IOSPE* 2, xix (Latyschev); Werner 1955, 437; 1957, 237. It is confirmed by Craterus *FGrH* 3B, 342 F8, which indicates that Nymphaeum was still officially under Athenian control in 410 (*cf.* Jacoby *FGrH* 3B *Texte*, 103).

[36] Lysias 16. 4.

[37] Xenophon *Anabasis* 6. 2, clearly suggests that Heraclea was at peace in 400.

[38] Isocrates *Trapeziticus* 5. For the date see Blass 1887–98 II, 230.

[39] Xenophon *Hellenica* 5. 1. 25–29. For the kind of difficulties in the Pontus that drove grain prices up at Athens see Lysias 22. 14. For the effect of wars in Bosporan territory on commerce, see Demosthenes 34. 8.

[40] Polyaenus 8. 55. For the historicity of this anecdote, see Werner (1955, 437–39), who effectively answers the objections raised by Minns (1913, 573–74).

270 PART II: ARTICLES

in the Taman Peninsula until his death.[41] Thus, the use of the plural τύραννοι in these texts would be appropriate if the war with Heraclea took place while Gorgippus was still alive. The fact that Polyaenus does not mention him in 6. 9. 3–4 is of no importance in this connection for two reasons, first, because his purpose in these passages was to illustrate Leucon's cleverness in resolving his difficulties and not to narrate the history of the war, and second, because his silence can at the very most only be taken as evidence that Gorgippus was not involved in these particular events. On the other hand, as the anecdote about Tynnichus and that in the *Oeconomica* both clearly have as their source an account of the history of Heraclea,[42] it is perfectly natural that they should refer to Heraclea's enemy as the 'tyrants', that is, the Spartocid house as a whole, whether or not the main theatre of operations was to be in the territory of Leucon instead of that of his brother. That these texts do, in fact, belong to the same war as that mentioned in Polyaenus 6. 9. 3–4 is all the more probable because the impression given in the latter, of Leucon being on the defensive in the face of Heraclea's naval supremacy, corresponds exactly to the situation implied by Ps.-Aristotle. Thus, in default of persuasive evidence to the contrary, we should accept Beloch's theory that Heraclea and Leucon I fought only one war as providing the most satisfactory interpretation of these texts.

THE WAR AND ITS RESULTS

With our sources confined to four disconnected anecdotes, only the most general reconstruction of the course of the war is possible. In view of the meagerness of the forces at Tynnichus' disposal in contrast to the considerable size of those credited to the Heracleotes in the other passages, his exploit most likely belongs to the beginning of the war prior to the full mobilization of Heraclea's fleet. This, in turn, suggests that Leucon opened the hostilities with a surprise attack on Theodosia that succeeded to the extent of allowing him to draw his siege lines around the city tightly enough to bring it to the point of surrender before Heraclea could assemble a full scale relief expedition. Likewise, the fact that Tynnichus took with him as many soldiers as his two ships would carry indicates that his primary mission was to reinforce Theodosia's defenses and that his actually lifting the siege of the city was an unexpected success. Presumably the actual purpose of his stratagem was to confuse the besiegers

[41] Werner 1955, 438–41; *IOSPE* 2, xx (Latyschev); and Beloch 1912–27 III.2, 93.

[42] As in the case of the anecdotes about Leucon (n. 33), the key is the perspective of the author which is in this case Heracleote with Heraclea's actions being given in detail while the Spartocids arc merely mentioned as being their enemies.

THE WAR BETWEEN HERACLEA PONTICA AND LEUCON I OF BOSPORUS   271

sufficiently to allow him to safely land his forces at Theodosia. The remaining texts indicate that the Heracleotes followed up the relief of Theodosia by carrying the war into Leucon's own territory where their fleet of 40 warships gave them naval superiority and permitted them to land and raid at will while disaffection among Leucon's subjects after his humiliation at Theodosia hindered his attempts at defense and forced him to rely on the support of his Scythian allies. Beyond this, however, we can only say that this second phase of the war lasted more than one month and probably extended over several since Ps.-Aristotle notes that the Heracleotes paid their troops' *misthos* more than once.[43]

Unfortunately, direct evidence concerning the outcome of the war is lacking. Clearly, Leucon was able to beat off at least one Heracleote landing in his territory with the aid of his Scythian troops and to eventually make peace on terms that did not compromise his hold on Panticapaeum. But this is hardly sufficient to justify Rostovtzeff's contention that the war ended with Leucon victorious and in control of Theodosia and Heraclea in turmoil as a result of her defeat.[44] Actually, since the cause of the war was Leucon's attempt to seize Theodosia, the question of who won it can be answered if we can determine its date and the date Theodosia came under Spartocid control. If the two are the same, then Leucon was the probable victor, but if not, then Heraclea was victorious. Fortunately, circumstantial evidence does exist which permits these chronological problems to be resolved with sufficient precision for our purposes.

Until recently it was only possible to place the fall of Theodosia sometime between 389 and 354, since there was no way to closely date the reorganization of Leucon's realm caused by that event and reflected in his adoption of the titulary ἄρχων Βοσπόρου καὶ Θεοδοσίης[45] beyond saying that it belonged to an earlier period than that in which the longer form ἄρχων Βοσπόρου καὶ Θεοδοσίης καὶ βασιλεὺς Σινδῶν, Τορετέων, Δανδαρίων, Ψησσῶν[46] was in use. The discovery of a new inscription at Hermonassa in 1965 employing the short titulary and recording a dedication by a certain Phaenippus has, however,

---

[43] *Misthos* was normally paid monthly (see Griffith 1935, 265–66).

[44] Rostovtzeff 1930, 569–70. Similar opinions were expressed also by Wormell (1946, 54), and Gajdukevič (1949, 59).

[45] For the Bosporan inscriptions, see now *CIRB* 1111 = *IOSPE* II, 232 = *SIG*³ 210.

[46] E.g. *CIRB* 6 = *IOSPE* II, 6 = *SIG*³ 211. See Shelov (1950, 171) for a survey of the various proposed dates. His own preference is for a date in the 380s on the ground that the harbor facilities mentioned by Demosthenes (20. 33) as existing in 354 require us to assume that Leucon had controlled Theodosia long enough to complete them. The validity of this observation is beyond question, but it is questionable if the period required need have been as long as three decades.

272   PART II: ARTICLES

changed this situation.[47] As Fernando Bosi[48] pointed out, this person is to be
identified with a Phaenippus whose son was prominent during the last years of
Leucon's reign and who was himself still active well into the period of sole
rule of Leucon's son Paerisades I which began in 344/3.[49] While it is clear that
a considerable period of time separates the inscriptions concerning Phaenippus
himself, that interval is, as Bosi noted,[50] hardly likely to have exceeded thirty
years if it was even that much; and this in turn points to a date around 370 as
the *terminus post quem* for the adoption of the short titulary and, hence, for
the conquest of Theodosia. By themselves these considerations might not be
strong enough to decide the issue, but, fortunately, this dating is confirmed by
the fact that an inscription of the Arcadian League, which was only organized
in 370, in honor of Leucon merely identifies him as a citizen of Panticapaeum,
a designation which would only be appropriate in the period before he began
to use the short titulary, so that we again find the year 370 as the *terminus post
quem* for the annexation of Theodosia.[51] On the other hand, it is highly unlikely

---

[47] Belova 1967.

[48] Bosi 1967, 134–35.

[49] The relevant inscriptions are *CIRB* 1038, which employs the long form of Leucon's titulary
and *CIRB* 9 = *IOSPE* II, 8 = *SIG*³ 213, which is shown to belong to the second period of Paerisades's sole reign by the inclusions of Θατέων in the titulary (*cf.* Minns 1913, 577). For the date
of Paerisades' reign, see Werner 1955, 418. It should be noted, however, that the dating of *CIRB*
9 = *IOSPE* II, 8 = *SIG*³ 213 after 344/3 is disputed because of the omission of Βοσπόρου in
Paerisades' titulary. Although this has been taken as indicating that it belongs to the period of
Paerisades' joint rule with his brother Spartocus II (349/8–344/3; *cf. SIG*¹1, 291; *IOSPE* II 7–8
[Latyschev]; and *CIRB* 22), I have been persuaded by the arguments of Minns (1913, 577) and
Bosi (1967, 134, n. 8), that the irregularity of the titulary is the result of a mason's error and can-
not be used as the basis for dating the inscription.

[50] Bosi 1967, 135.

[51] *CIRB* 37 = *IOSPE* II, 4 = *SIG*³ 209. Against the view maintained in *SIG*³ (289 *ad* 209) that
this was a decree passed by Arcadian mercenaries in Leucon's service, Gajducevič (1966, 26–30)
has shown that Ἀρκάσιν (line 1) refers to the Arcadian League organized by Epaminondas in
370. On the other hand, he attached no significance to the identification of Leucon in the decree
as [τὸν Σατυ]ρο Παντικαπαίταν beyond noting (Gajducevič 1966, 29) that it was common practice for other states (*cf. SIG*³ 206 and 212) to omit the titulary of the Bosporan rulers. In the
4th century, however, Bosporus was not synonymous with Panticapaeum, but denoted instead a
group of several cities of which Panticapaeum was only one (*cf.* Minns 1913, 569, n. 9; Berve
1967 I, 327; and Neubauer 1960, 146). Even more important, the use of Bosporus as a place
name in Athenian decrees (*SIG*³ 206, line 52) and the designation of persons from that area resident at Athens as Bosporans from as early as the mid-4th century (*IG* 2–3² 8424–8432) indicate
that foreign states viewed Bosporus as a distinct political entity with its own citizenship. Accordingly, had Leucon already adopted the title ἄρχων Βοσπόρου καὶ Θεοδοσίης when the Arcadian
League honored him, they would most likely have identified him as a Bosporan and not as a
Panticapaean precisely as the Athenians were to do in 288 in the case of [King] Spartocus III
(*SIG*³ 370, line 35). Admittedly, this conflicts with the view current in Soviet scholarship that
Bosporus was organized in the 5th century (Neubauer 1960, 146). The evidence for so early a
date, however, is weak. The only examples of the use of Bosporus in connection with the period

THE WAR BETWEEN HERACLEA PONTICA AND LEUCON I OF BOSPORUS 273

that Heraclea would have or, indeed, could have been able to engage in a major war on the north coast of the Black Sea at any time between 370 and 364 since the first half of the 360s was a period of serious danger for the city. Internally, it experienced severe and prolonged *stasis* that climaxed in the *coup d'état* of Clearchus in 364[52] while externally it was threatened by the ambitions of a certain Mithridates, most likely the son of Ariobarzanes,[53] the satrap of Hellespontine Phrygia and one of the leaders of the Satraps Revolt that broke out soon after 370.[54] In these circumstances we would hardly expect Heraclea to engage in foreign adventures during these years, and this is confirmed by Justin's indicating that the city had already been at peace for a considerable period at the time of Clearchus' revolution in 364.[55] In view of these considerations, circumstantial though they are, it is probable that the truth is the opposite of what Rostovtzeff assumed, namely, that Heraclea succeeded in its primary military objective, the frustrating of an attempt by Leucon I to seize Theodosia sometime between 389 and 370.[56]

---

prior to the reign of Leucon I are Aeschines 3. 171, Diodorus 12. 36. 1 and 14. 93. 1 apropos of the deaths of Spartocus I and Satyrus I, and the passage of the *Periplus Ponti Euxini* quoted in n. 2; and none of these can be considered reliable on matters of constitutional detail for the following reasons: (1) Aeschines' speech *Against Ctesiphon* was delivered after the reign of Leucon I when Bosporus was in common use and he would naturally use the term familiar to his audience irrespective of the situation in the late 5th century; (2) Diodorus anachronistically treats all of the Spartocids as kings of Bosporus although they did not adopt the title βασιλεύς Βοσπόρου until the end of the 4th century (Werner 1955, 444; Porphyry *FGrH* 2B, 260 F 41); and (3) in the early Byzantine period when the *Periplus Ponti Euxini* was composed (*cf.* Aubrey 1952, 109–13), Bosporus had replaced Panticapaeum as the name for the city (Minns 1913, 569, n. 9). On the other hand the fact that our sources contemporary with Satyrus do not refer to him as ruler of Bosporus but use a circumlocution such as ὁ ἐν τῷ Πόντῳ (Lysias 16. 4; *cf.* Isocrates *Trapezititus* 3. 5, *passim*) whereas during and after the reign of Leucon I, except for Dinarchus 1. 43, we always find Bosporus (Demosthenes 20. 33 from 354 is the earliest example) strongly supports my suggestion that the political use of the term Bosporus was introduced sometime during the reign of Leucon I.

[52] Aeneas Tacticus 11. 10a. For the date, see Aeneas *On Siegecraft*, ed. L.W. Hunter, rev. S.A. Handford (Oxford 1927), 139–40; and Burstein 1972, 298, n. 81. Justin 16. 4. 2–5. *Suda s.v.* Κλέαρχος.

[53] Justin 16. 4. 7–9; *Suda s.v.* Κλέαρχος. For the identification of him with the son of Ariobarzanes, see Burstein 1972, 300, n. 7.

[54] For the Satraps' Revolt the most useful account remains that of Judeich 1892, 190–225.

[55] This is indicated by the fact that Trogus (Justin 16. 4. 3) took over from the 3rd-century Heracleote historian Nymphis (*cf.* Jacoby *FGrH* 3B *Texte*, 255; and Desideri 1967, 391, n. 123) the argument that the *stasis* leading to the establishment of the tyranny was caused by the unreasonable demands of the Heracleote poor who had been corrupted by too much peace (*plebem nimio otio lascivientem*; for *otium* meaning peace and its significance, see Fraenkel 1957, 211–14).

[56] The silence of the sources on the outcome of the war is to be ascribed to their fragmentary character and not to the inconclusiveness of the conflict as suggested by Werner (1957, 238). In this connection, however, it should be noted that an important victory is commemorated on Heraclea's coinage of this period. Peter Robert Franke (1966, 132–37) has shown that some of a

274 PART II: ARTICLES

Despite the deficiencies of our sources, it seems clear that Heraclea's success had only a limited impact on the subsequent course of events on the north coast of the Pontus. Doubtless, her prestige among the Greek cities increased sharply for a short period, and perhaps even the alliances with Theodosia and Phanagoria mentioned earlier and possibly one with Tyras[57] as well were formally concluded soon after her victory. Nevertheless, the logical conclusion to be drawn from the previous discussion is that no lasting Heracleote political involvement in the affairs of the region east of Chersonesus resulted from it, or, put more precisely, the fact that Heraclea fought only one war with Leucon means that she did nothing to assist her allies Theodosia and Phanagoria when Leucon annexed them to the Spartocid empire sometime after 370.[58] The reason for this inactivity on Heraclea's part is, of course, unknown, but speculation is possible. Ps.-Aristotle clearly indicates that her victorious campaign severely strained Heraclea's financial resources, and that may have been a factor in discouraging any later expeditions of a similar type. Equally possible, Leucon may have struck at a time when local problems such as, for example, the difficulties attendant on the establishment of the tyranny by Clearchus and his struggle to retain power, foreclosed the possibility of an effective Heracleote response. Two items, however, the fact that Leucon and his successors concentrated their imperial activity north and east of the Straits of Kerch after the fall of Theodosia[59] and the aforementioned friendship of the Spartocids and Heraclea's colonies in the late fourth and third centuries, suggests another and more positive explanation. As Heraclea had most likely been drawn into

series of obols and diobols with obverse Hera or Heracles heads and reverse trophy (*Recueil* I.2, pl. 55 nos. 17, 22–23) must be dated before 364. Likewise, Colin Kraay has dated a rare Heracleote type, obverse beardless Heracles in lionskin helmet and reverse Nike writing *HPAKΛEIA* (Kraay and Hirmer 1966, no. 726; Six 1885, 62, no. 65) to the period 380–360 on the basis of style (Kraay and Hirmer 1966, 370); the 3rd-century dates proposed by Franke (1966, 139, n. 40) and Six (1886, 62, No. 65) are improbable since Heracleote coins of that period always bear the inscription HPAKΛEΩTAN. *Cf. Recueil* I.2, pls. 56, nos. 9–27, and 57, nos. 1–2.

[57] Tyras issued coins about the mid-4th century (Zograf 1951, pl. 28, no. 2; 240) with a butting bull similar to the issues of Theodosia and Phanagoria. Given Tyras' geographical position, however, this might also indicate ties with Macedon which struck coins with this type during the reign of Perdiccas III (364–359) (Gaebler 1935, 161, n. 4, pl. 30, no. 4).

[58] Maximowa (1959, 117–18) suggested that the detaining of the ship of a certain Protomachus by Heraclea in 361 (*IG* 2² 117) was connected with an attempt to assist Theodosia by interrupting the grain trade. The inscription, however, like the similar text involving Heracleides' of Salamis difficulties at Heraclea in 330 (*SIG*³ 304, lines 41–43) gives no reason to believe that the incident was part of an organized program of seizures. More likely, it reflected a local problem like the inscription edited by von Premerstein (1911), which mentions (p. 75, lines 14–16) the attempt by some Pontic city about 175 to prevent a ship carrying a cargo of olives from sailing because of a temporary shortage.

[59] *Cf.* Rostovtzeff 1930, 570–71.

THE WAR BETWEEN HERACLEA PONTICA AND LEUCON I OF BOSPORUS 275

the war against Leucon because of fear for the safety of Chersonesus, it is likely that a guarantee of Chersonesus' independence would have been one of the terms on which the hostilities would have been brought to an end. But this would also have removed the incentive for further Heracleote opposition to his plans, and, hence, would satisfactorily account for the at first glance puzzling fact that Heraclea later abandoned her allies when Leucon renewed his activity against them.

CONCLUSION

The implications of this study for the histories of Bosporus and Heraclea can be summarized as follows. Of primary importance is the clarification brought to the account of the incorporation of Theodosia into the Spartocid realm. It is now clear that this took place in three phases, namely, the unsuccessful attack on the city by Satyrus in 389, a second attempt on the city by his sons Leucon I and Gorgippus sometime between 389 and 370 which was frustrated by the forceful intervention of Heraclea, and then finally the reduction of the city by Leucon following the withdrawal of Heracleote support from Theodosia at a still undetermined date between 370 and 354. Almost equally significant, however, is the revised picture of the course of relations between Heraclea and Bosporus during the 4th and 3rd centuries that is implicit in these results. Far from reflecting a consistent Heracleote policy of opposition to Spartocid ambitions as has been maintained by previous scholars,[60] her militant support of Theodosia now appears as an isolated incident which did not lead to long term hostility between her and Panticapaeum, a picture which is in striking agreement with that provided by Russian archaeologists who have shown that the second half of the 4th and the first half of the 3rd centuries were marked by increasingly close commercial relations between Heraclea and Bosporus.[61] On the other hand, the demonstration that Polyaenus' anecdote concerning Memnon's plotting against Leucon is not connected with the latter's war with Heraclea is a sobering reminder of the gaps still remaining in our knowledge of the history of Bosporus since our sources give no hint as to what historical context it does belong.[62]

---

[60] See, for example, Minns's (1913, 577) characterization of the Heracleotes as 'the consistent foes of the Bosporan kings'.
[61] Zeest 1951, 106–09.
[62] For a suggestion along these lines, see Momigliano 1934, 123, n. 1.

276   PART II: ARTICLES

BIBLIOGRAPHY

Beloch, K.J. 1912–27: *Griechische Geschichte*, 4 vols. in 8, 2nd ed. (Strassburg/Berlin).

Belova, N.S. 1967: 'Novaya nadpis iz Germonassy'. *VDI* 1, 60–69.

Bengtson, H. (ed.) 1962: *Die Staatsverträge des Altertums* 2: *Die Verträge der griechisch-römischen Welt von 700 bis 338 v. Chr.* (Munich/Berlin).

Berve, H. 1967: *Die Tyrannis bei den Griechen*, 2 vols. (Munich).

Blass, F. 1887–98: *Die attische Beredsamkeit*, 3 vols. in 4, 2nd ed. (Leipzig).

Bosi, F. 1967: 'Note epigrafiche bosporane'. *Epigraphica* 29, 131–44.

Brandis, C. 1899: 'Bosporus'. *RE* 3, 757–89.

Burstein, S.M. 1972: *A Political History of Heraclea Pontica to 281 B.C.* (Dissertation, UCLA).

Cracco Ruggini, L. 1966: 'Eforo nello Pseudo-Aristotle, Oec. II? (Parte I)'. *Athenaeum* n.s. 44.3–4, 199–237.

Desideri, D. 1967: 'Studi Storiografia Eracleota I: Promathidas e Nymphis'. *Studi Classici et Orientali* 16, 366–416.

Diller, A. 1952: *The Tradition of the Minor Greek Geographers* (Lancaster, PA).

Droysen, J.G. 1883–85: *Histoire de l'hellénisme*, 3 vols. (Paris).

Fraenkel, E. 1957: *Horace* (Oxford).

Franke, P.R. 1966: 'Zur Tyrannis des Klearchos und Satyros in Herakleia am Pontos'. *Archäologischer Anzeiger* 81, 130–39.

Gaebler, H. 1936: *Die antiken Münzen Nord-Griechenlands 3.1: Makedonia und Paionia* (Berlin).

Gajdukevič, V.F. 1949: *Bosporskoe tsarstvo* (Moscow).

—. 1966: 'Bosporos und Arkadien'. *BCO* 11, 26–30.

—. 1971: *Das Bosporanische Reich*, 2nd ed. (Berlin).

Griffith, G.T. 1935: *The Mercenaries of the Hellenistic World* (Cambridge).

Judeich, W. 1892: *Kleinasiatische Studien: Untersuchungen zur gr.-pers. Geschichte des iv. Jahrhunderts v. Chr.* (Marburg).

Kraay, C. and Hirmer, M. 1966: *Greek Coins* (New York).

Maximowa, M.I. 1959: 'Der kurze Seeweg über das Schwarze Meer im Altertum'. *Klio* 37, 101–18.

Minns, E.H. 1913: *Scythians and Greeks: A Survey of Ancient History and Archaeology on the North Coast of the Euxine from the Danube to the Caucasus* (Cambridge).

Momigliano, A. 1934: *Filippo il Macedone, Saggio sulla storia greca del IV secolo A.C.* (Florence).

Neubauer, H. 1960: 'Die griechische Schwarzmeerkolonisation in der sowjetischen Geschichtsschreibung'. *Saeculum* 11, 132–56.

Premerstein, A. von 1911: 'Athenischer Ehrenbeschluss für einen Großkaufmann', *Mitteilungen des kaiserlich-deutschen archäologischen Instituts, Athenische Abteilung* 36, 73–86.

Rostovtzeff, M.I. 1930: 'The Bosporan kingdom'. *CAH* VIII, 561–89.

—. [Rostowzew] 1931: *Skythien und der Bosporus 1: Kritische Übersicht der schriftlichen und archäologischen Quellen* (Berlin).

Schneiderwirth, H. 1882: *Heraclea am Pontus* (Heiligenstadt).

Shelov, D.B. 1950: 'Feodosiya, Gerakleya i Spartokidy'. *VDI* 3, 168–78.

Six, J.P. 1885: 'Sinope'. *NC* ser. 3, 5, 15–66.

Van Groningen, B.A. (ed.) 1933: *Aristote, Le second livre de l'Économique* (Leiden).

Werner, R. 1955: 'Die Dynastie der Spartokiden'. *Historia* 4, 412–44.

—. 1957: 'Schwarzmeerreiche im Altertum'. *Die Welt als Geschichte* 17, 221–44.

Wilcken, U. 1901: 'Zu den pseudo-aristotelischen Oekonomika'. *Hermes* 36, 187–200.

Wormell, D.E.W. 1946: 'Studies in Greek Tyranny II: Leucon of Bosporus'. *Hermathena* 68, 49–71.

Zeest, I.B. 1951: 'Novye dannye o torgovykh svyazyakh Bospora Yuzhnym Prichernomor'em'. *VDI* 2, 106–16.

Zograf, A.N. 1951: *Antichnye monety* (Moscow).

SCEPTRE OR THUNDERBOLT: PLUTARCH, *MORALIA* 338B*

Καίτοι τί ἂν περί τούτων λέγοι τις, οἷς ἐξῆν δι' 'Αλέξανδρον μέγα φρονεῖν, ὅπού Κλέαρχος 'Ηράκλειας τύραννος γενόμενος σκηπτὸν ἐφόρει καί τῶν υἱῶν ἕνα Κεραυνόν ὠνόμασε;

And yet why should one speak of these [*sc.* Cleitus, Demetrius Poliorcetes and Lysimachus] who might be haughty because of Alexander, when Clearchus, after he had become tyrant of Heraclea, used to carry a thunderbolt and named one of his sons Ceraunus?

This reference to Clearchus, tyrant of Heraclea Pontica from 364 to 352 BC occurs in the midst of a discussion by Plutarch of the contrast between Alexander's sobriety in the management of his great power and the excesses of men whose outrageous behavior was justified neither by their achievements nor their position in the world. Instead of σκηπτόν, 'thunderbolt', all manuscripts read at this point σκῆπτρον, 'scepter', although two 15th-century manuscripts, Voss. qu. 2 and Paris 2076, are reported to contain marginalia suggesting the reading σκῆπτον, a synonym of σκῆπτρον, which occurs in the Doric form σκᾶπτόν but is otherwise only attested in compound words (LSJ s.v. σκῆπτον).[1]

The emendation σκηπτόν was first proposed by L.C. Valckenaer on the grounds that *de Clearcho tyranno non scripserat Plutarch ... σκῆπτρον, sed σκηπτόν ut igneum Iovis telum gestare videretur: nam et filiorum quendam dici voluit* Κεραυνόν.[2] The argument is a non sequitur, but the emendation was nevertheless approved by Daniel Wyttenbach, who cited in support of it

---

* I should like to thank Prof. T.S. Brown, Prof. P. Clement, Prof. H. Hoffleit, and Prof. J. Puhvel of the Departments of History and Classics at UCLA for reading and criticizing earlier drafts of this paper. First published in *California Studies in Classical Antiquity* 7 (1974), 89–92.

[1] Plutarch *De Alexandri Magni fortuna aut virtute, Moralia*, ed. W. Nachstädt, W. Sieveking and J. Titchener, vol. 2 (Leipzig 1934), 337F–338C. The marginalia were reported by Daniel Wyttenbach (1796, 384), in his note on this passage: σκηπτόν *Legendum ita ex G*. [= Paris 2076] *et Voss, qui ita in margine habent: Corriget item Meg. et Valckenaerius...* The marginalia in Voss. qu. 2 are the work of G. Budé (Nachstädt, Sieveking and Titchener, *apparatus ad loc.*). There is some question, however, about the marginalia in Paris 2076 since Nachstädt, Sieveking and Titchener omit any reference to them although they used that manuscript in establishing their text (*Praef.* IX). Finally, Nachstadt, Sieveking and Titchener's citation of a third manuscript, Voss. fol. 3 (*apparatus ad loc.*) as containing the reading σκῆπτον is incorrect since examination of a microfilm of it furnished me by the library of the Rijksuniversiteit Leiden revealed that it actually reads σκῆπτρον at this point.

[2] Valckenaer 1768, 200–12.

280 PART II: ARTICLES

the above mentioned marginal notes; and his decision has been followed by subsequent editors of the *De Alexandri Magni fortuna aut virtute*[3] until at present Clearchus' having wielded a thunderbolt has attained the status of an accepted fact that can itself be used as evidence for Greek religious practices in the 4th century.[4]

The assumed corruption of an original σκηπτόν to σκῆπτρον is possible, but that possibility is by itself insufficient to justify the emendation in the face of the historical problems raised by it. Had Clearchus identified himself with Zeus as Wyttenbach and other scholars have believed,[5] the bizarre behavior suggested by the text of Plutarch as usually printed – behavior virtually unparalleled before the death of Alexander[6] – might be acceptable. Our other sources for his reign, however, forbid any such interpretation since they state unequivocally that he proclaimed himself to be, not Zeus, but son of Zeus.[7] Moreover, none of them mention a thunderbolt in connection with the regalia he adopted on declaring his divine filiation, although we would certainly expect something so spectacular to be noted by them. Instead, they concentrate their attention on his ornate dress, with Memnon[8] referring to the various χιτῶνας he wore to impress visitors and Aelian[9] to his wearing στολὰς ... θεοῖς συνήθεις καὶ τοῖς ἀγάλμασι τοῖς ἐκείνων ἐπιπρεπούσας. The fullest and most illuminating account, however, is that of Justin[10] who, after recording Clearchus' claim to be son of Zeus, continues as follows: *eunti* (*sc. Clearcho*) *per publicum aurea aquila, velut argumentum generis praeferebatur, veste purpurea et cothurnis regum tragicorum et aurea corona utebatur...* Two points are to be noted. First, the costume of a tragic king was modeled on that of the Persian Great King[11] and accordingly had as one of its elements a scepter and not a thunderbolt.[12] Second, Justin clearly implies that Clearchus' relation to Zeus

---

[3] See n. 1. Σκηπτὸν in Wyttenbach's note suggests that he misread the accent of the marginalia. Scott (1929, 123–24) rejected the emendation in his translation of the passage.

[4] See Kleinknecht 1937, 299, who, after remarking that in the 4th century it became usual for men to raise themselves to the level of the gods by wearing their costumes and carrying their symbols, cites Clearchus and his thunderbolt as his sole example for the period before Alexander.

[5] Wyttenbach 1810, 129, on the basis of a misreading of Memnon *FGrH* 3B, 434 F 1.1. Among later scholars see, for example, Taylor 1931, 12; and Jacoby *FGrH* 3B *Noten*, 173, n. 38.

[6] All other pre-Alexander examples belong to the circle of the eccentric Syracusan doctor Menecrates, but he and his followers actually identified themselves with the gods whose symbols they carried (Athenaeus 7. 289 a–f; Clement *Protr.* 4. 48; *Suda s.v.* Μενεκράτης).

[7] Memnon *FGrH* 3B, 434 Fl. 1; Justin 16. 5. 8.

[8] Memnon *FGrH* 3B, 434 Fl. 1.

[9] F. 85 (Hercher) = *Suda s.v.* Κλέαρχος.

[10] Justin 16. 5. 9–10.

[11] Alföldi 1955, 32–54.

[12] Alföldi 1955, 41.

was not indicated by his carrying the god's thunderbolt but by the gilt eagle that preceded him in public processions. Our other sources, thus, strongly suggest that the manuscript reading σκῆπτρον is correct and that it should be retained.

Reading σκῆπτρον means that Plutarch accused Clearchus, a tyrant, of wrongfully assuming the symbols of kingship, a not uncommon *topos*[13] and one especially likely in this instance since the tyrants mentioned in this passage, Clearchus, Dionysius I and Dionysius II, had long been used as stereotypes of the violent tyrant as opposed to the gentle king.[14] But does this *topos* fit the overall context of *De Alexandri Magni fortuna aut virtute* 337–338C, where all but one of the other examples[15] seem to involve an unjustified claim to divinity or divine power, and where the coupling of Clearchus' wielding a scepter with his naming one of his sons Ceraunus implies that something similar was intended in his case also?[16] Could the use of a scepter by a tyrant have appeared particularly shocking to Plutarch?

The answer is that it most certainly would when viewed in the light of Plutarch's ideas on kingship. For him the office of king was not merely a secular but also a religious function. Although always remaining a human being, the true king was νόμος ἔμψυχος, Animate Law, and he owed his position to God whose representative and image he was on earth.[17] The scepter, the main symbol of his office, belonged, therefore, to God just as much as the thunderbolt and its improper use was a folly that aroused both enmity and divine wrath as is revealed by the following passage from the essay *Ad principem ineruditum*:[18] [*sc.* as God established the sun and moon as his images in heaven, so a ruler establishes intelligence] οὐ σκῆπτρον οὐδέ κεραυνόν οὐδέ τρίαιναν, ὡς ἔνιοι πλάττουσιν ἑαυτοὺς καὶ γράφουσι τῷ ἀνεφίκτῳ ποιοῦντες ἐπίφθονον τὸ ἀνόητον. νεμεσᾷ γὰρ ὁ θεὸς τοῖς ἀπομιμουμένοις, βροντὰς καὶ κεραυνοὺς καὶ ἀκτινοβολίας ...

The assimilation of the scepter to the other divine symbols is obvious in the above quotation. Likewise, it is clear that, although the immediate targets of Plutarch's wrath were artistic works such as Apelles famous portrait of Alexander wielding a thunderbolt, his sentiments were also applicable to actual

---

[13] *Cf.* Diodorus 19. 9. 7; Dion Chrysostom *Orat.* 1. 70–75, 78–79.

[14] Aristotle(?) *Mag. Moral.* 2. 6. 33, 1203a 22–23; Aelian *N.A.* 5. 15. *Cf.* Plutarch, *Ad principem ineruditum* 781 D–E.

[15] The accusation against Dionysius I (338C) appears to be hypocrisy.

[16] For the implications of Ceraunus in Plutarch's eyes, see *Aristides* 6. 2.

[17] Scott 1929, 124–25, 127–29; and Delatte 1942, 150.

[18] *Ad prinicipem ineridutum* 780 F. See also Plutarch *De Iside et Osiride* 371 E for the interpretation of the scepter as symbolic of divine power.

282 PART II: ARTICLES

behavior such as the use of a scepter by a tyrant. As the reading σκῆπτρον is thus not only supported by the evidence of the manuscripts and the other sources for the reign of Clearchus but is also appropriate to its context, there remains no reason why future editors of the *De Alexandri Magni fortuna aut virtute* should not restore it at this point and banish from the religious history of Greece in the 4th century BC the strange image of the tyrant of Heraclea carrying a thunderbolt through his city's streets.

BIBLIOGRAPHY

Alföldi, A. 1955: 'Gewaltherrscher und Theaterkönig'. In Weitzmann, K. *et al.* (eds.), *Late Classical and Medieval Studies in Honor of Albert Mathias Friend Jr.* (Princeton), 15–55.

Delatte, L. 1942: *Les Traités de la royauté d'Ecphante, Diotogène et Sthénidas* (Paris).

Kleinknecht, H. 1937: 'Zur Parodie des Gottmenschentums bei Aristophanes'. *Archiv für Religionswissenschaft* 34, 294–313.

Scott, K. 1929: 'Plutarch and the Ruler Cult'. *Transactions of the American Philological Association* 60, 117–35.

Taylor, L.R. 1931: *The Divinity of the Roman Emperor* (Middletown).

Valckenaer, L.C. (ed.) 1768: *Euripidis Tragoedia Hippolytus* (Leiden 1768; repr. Leipzig 1823).

Wyttenbach, D. (ed.) 1796: *Plutarchi Chaeronensis Moralia*, vol. 2.2 (Oxford).

—. (ed.) 1810: *Plutarchi Chaeronensis Moralia*, vol. 7 (Oxford).

IG II² 653, DEMOSTHENES AND ATHENIAN RELATIONS
WITH BOSPORUS IN THE FOURTH CENTURY B.C.[*]

Beginning in the last quarter of the 5th century, South Russia and particularly the area around the Straits of Kerch ruled by the Spartocid dynasts of Panticapaeum became not merely an important but a primary source of grain for Athens.[1] As the assurance of a steady supply of grain was one of the few areas of trade which actively interested the governments of Greek cities,[2] it is not surprising that ancient literary and epigraphical sources provide evidence of successful attempts by Athens to obtain from the Spartocids guarantees of special treatment for grain exported to her. Leucon I (389/8–344/3)[3] formally granted the city the right to import grain duty-free and ordered that ships bound for Athens were to be allowed to load their cargoes before all others.[4] *IG* II² 212, lines 13–23 indicates that similar grants of privilege were made by Leucon's predecessor Satyrus I (433/2–389/8) and his sons and joint successors Spartocus II and Paerisades I (349/8–344/3). Previous scholars who have dealt with this problem have usually assumed that relations between Athens and Bosporus remained close and cordial throughout the 4th century, and that Athens continued to enjoy these privileges during the whole century.[5] The purpose of this paper is to reconsider the subject of Atheno-Bosporan relations during the 4th century in the light of evidence provided by *IG* II² 653.

At first glance *IG* II² 653, a decree passed early in 284[6] for the purpose of requesting that Spartocus III (304/3–284/3) send military aid to Athens seems to confirm the prevailing opinion. In the course of a summary of past (lines 8–20):

... ἐπειδὴ [πρότερόν τε οἱ πρόγονοι οἱ]
Σπαρτόκου χρείας [παρέσχηνται τῶι δήμωι καὶ]
νῦν Σπάρτοκος πα[ραλαβὼν τὴν εἰς τὸν δῆμον οἰ]-
κειότητα κοινῆι [τε τῶι δήμωι χρείας παρέχε]-

---

[*] Acknowledgment should be made at this point of the help afforded me by Prof. J.A.S. Evans of the University of British Columbia, Prof. A. Raubitschek of Stanford University and Prof. M. Wallace of the University of Toronto who read and criticized earlier versions of this paper. Research for this study was made possible by a fellowship from the National Endowment for the Humanities. First published in *Historia* 27 (1978), 428–36.

[1] This was pointed out by Gernet (1909, 314–19), on the basis of literary evidence and has now been confirmed archaeologically. *Cf.* Brašinskij 1968, 106–07; and Gajdukevič 1971, 102–03.

[2] Aristotle *Rhetoric* 1. 4, 1360A 12–15. Hasebroek 1933, 146–50.

[3] For the chronology of the Spartocids I follow Werner 1955.

[4] Bengtson 1962, no. 306 = Demosthenes *In Leptinem* (20) 31, 36–37.

[5] E.g. Minns 1913, 574–76; Rostovtzeff 1930, 566–67; Brašinskij 1968, 106–07.

[6] For the correct date of the archonship of Diotimos see Dinsmoor 1954, 287, 314.

284 PART II: ARTICLES

ται καὶ ἰδίαι Ἀθη[ναίων τοῖς ἀφικνουμένοις]
πρὸς αὐτόν ἀνθ' [ὧν καί ὁ δῆμος ὁ Ἀθηναίων αὐτοὺς]
πολίτας ἐποιή[σατο καί ἐτίμησ]εν [εἰκόσιν χαλ]-
καῖς ἔν τε τῆι [ἀγορᾶι καί] ἐν τῶι ἐμπορίωι [καί]
ἄλλαις δωρεα[ῖς, αἷς προσή]κει τιμᾶσθαι τοὺ[ς]
ἀγαθοὺς ἄνδρ[ας, καί διέθε]το, ἐάν τις βαδίζε[ι]
ἐπὶ τὴν ἀρχήν τ[ὴν τῶν προγόνω]ν αὐτοῦ ἢ⁷ τὴν Σπα[ρ]-
τόκου, βοηθε[ῖν παντὶ σθένε]ι κ[α]ὶ κατὰ γῆν καὶ
κατὰ θάλατ[ταν ....]

Since formerly the ancestors of Spartocus rendered services to the people and now Spartocus, taking up their friendship toward the people, renders services to the people as a whole and to those Athenians who come individually to him and in return for services the Athenian people made them citizens and honored them with bronze statues in the *agora* and in the *emporion* and with other gifts by which it is proper that good men be honored; and the people agreed that if anyone marched against the realm of his ancestors or that of Spartocus, they would come to help in full force both by land and by sea...

The inscription then goes on to record the favorable reception Spartocus gave to an embassy which notified him of Athens' successful recovery of the city in 286 and acknowledges his gift to the city on that occasion of 15,000 *medimnoi* of grain (lines 20–24). It then notes his promise to continue his friendly attitude toward Athens and the city's grant of honors to him (lines 24–42) and finally concludes with the arrangements for the dispatch of the present embassy requesting military aid and the instructions for the setting up of the stele (lines 42 to the end). In other words, it reviews relations between Athens and Spartocus III during his reign until 284, noting both his general policy toward the city and the special favors he had bestowed on Athens up till the time of the present decree. The passage quoted above contains the account of Spartocus' general policy, and as it emphasizes that policy's continuity with that of his ancestors (οἱ πρόγονοι), it is clear that Athens continued to enjoy during his reign essentially the same privileges that it had during the reigns of his predecessors.[8] At the same time, however, this section of the inscription contains two hitherto neglected references, one

[7] Thanks to the courtesy of Mr B.F. Cook, Keeper of Greek and Roman Antiquities in the British Museum, I was able to examine *BMI* 15 during the summer of 1977 and confirm that its editor E.L. Hicks correctly read an *eta* at this point. I have corrected the reading of *IG* II² 653, 18 accordingly.

[8] Rostovtzeff (1930, 579) argued that *IG* II² 653 proved that the privileges were no longer in force because they were not mentioned explicitly in the decree; he did not recognize that *IG* II² 653 itself presupposed previous dealings between Athens and Spartocus III. In fact, Spartocus himself seems to have initiated relations with Athens in the first years of his reign as is indicated by his sending the city a crown sometime during the last years of the 4th century (*IG* III² 1485A, line 22). The reading Spartocus, proposed by Droysen (*apud IG* II² 1485, note *ad loc.*), was

to the existence of bronze statues of Spartocus' ancestors in the *agora* and the *emporion* and the other to a defensive alliance or *epimachia* between Athens and Bosporus.[9] Neither of these items is mentioned in our sources for the period before 346. Indeed their existence is positively excluded by the combined evidence of Demosthenes' *In Leptinem* and *IG* II[2] 212 which clearly indicates that Athens had concluded no formal military alliance with Bosporus and that the only public honors she had awarded to the joint rulers Spartocus II and Paerisades I and their predecessors were citizenship and crowns, not statues.[10] By revealing the existence both of the statues and of an alliance, therefore, *IG* II[2] 653 shows that Atheno-Bosporan relations were actually significantly improved sometime after 346. The question to be answered is when and under what circumstances did this improvement in the relations between the two states take place?

Given the prevailing belief that relations between Athens and Bosporus remained cordial throughout the 4th century and the fact that the privileges had to be renewed with each change of ruler at Panticapaeum,[11] one would naturally assume that it occurred shortly after Paerisades I (344/3–311/10) became sole ruler of Bosporus in 344/3. In fact, however, this is unlikely to be correct since there is evidence pointing to a worsening of relations between Athens and Bosporus during the early part of Paerisades' reign. In the oration against Phormio which was delivered in 327,[12] Ps.-Demosthenes informs us that Paerisades had proclaimed during that year that grain exported to Athens was to be shipped duty-free.[13] As this privilege was one of those granted to Athens by Leucon I, the fact that Paerisades specifically renewed it in 327 can only mean that it had been canceled or allowed to lapse sometime before that year. V.G. Gajdukevič,[14] who recognized this, attempted to minimize its importance by suggesting that Paerisades had briefly canceled the privilege shortly before 327 as a revenue measure to

---

confirmed by me through personal examination of the inscription in the Epigraphical Museum at Athens. I will discuss the reading and its implications in detail elsewhere.

[9] Schmitt (1969, no. 401) recognized that lines 17–20 referred to an alliance concluded before the accession of Spartocus III. For the special characteristics of an *epimachia*, see Adcock and Mosley 1975, 191.

[10] Leucon I received Athenian citizenship with immunity from its obligations (Demosthenes *In Leptinem* [20] 29–30, 36–40). Crowns were first given to his sons in 346 as is implied by the καί which introduces the reference to them in *IG* II[2] 212, line 24.

[11] *Cf. IG* II[2] 21, lines 13–17. This aspect of the privileges was pointed to by Rostovtzeff 1930, 567.

[12] Blass 1893, 578; Isager and Hansen 1975, 169.

[13] Ps.-Demosthenes 34. 36.

[14] Gajdukevič 1971, 98–99. Brashinsky (1971, 120–21) claims that the decree merely confirmed existing Athenian privileges, but this cannot be so since Ps.-Demosthenes, 34. 36, clearly implies the opposite by noting that Lampis registered for the *ateleia* only *after* the proclamation of Paerisades.

286 PART II: ARTICLES

raise money for the Scythian war also mentioned in the oration against Phormio,[15] and that he then reinstated it in 327 because of his desire to help Athens cope with the severe famine that afflicted her and other Greek cities during the early 320s.[16] Despite its attractiveness, however, this suggestion is almost certainly not correct for several reasons. Certainly, the casual manner of the reference to the Scythian war of 327 points to its being only a brief outbreak of border hostilities which would not require the taking of extraordinary fiscal measures by Paerisades.[17]

More important, however, are two other points. First, although Athens' need to import foreign grain steadily increased during the 4th century, Soviet archaeologists have established that there was no parallel steady increase in the importation of Athenian goods into Bosporus. On the contrary, the volume of Athenian imports peaked during the first half of the century, not during the second half as one would expect.[18] As grain for export was apparently available in South Russia at this time,[19] this surprising discrepancy between the growth in Athens' need for foreign grain and the volume of her trade with Bosporus, one of her main suppliers, suggests that there was a worsening of the conditions under which Athenian trade with Bosporus had to be conducted during the second half of the 4th century. Second, the fact that both Aeschines in 330 and Dinarchus in 324 believed that they could prejudice a jury against Demosthenes by emphasizing the ties between him and his family and the Spartocids[20] clearly implies that by the third quarter of the 4th century a considerable amount of ill feeling toward the dynasty

---

[15] Ps.-Demosthenes 34. 8.

[16] For a good brief analysis of the famine see Isager and Hansen 1975, 200–06. In a recent and still unpublished PhD thesis John McK. Camp (1977, 144–59), adduces convincing evidence that the great famine was the result of prolonged drought conditions in Greece during the second half of the 4th century.

[17] Two facts lead to this conclusion: (1) 34. 8 allows no doubt that Phormio did not expect the market disruption caused by the Scythian war so that it cannot have begun long before his arrival at Bosporus, and (2) 34. 36 shows that Paerisades was back in Panticapaeum and grain was available for export while Phormio was still in Bosporus, that is, the war's effects and presumably the war itself seem to have been confined to the spring of 327, the period of Phormio's stay in the area (Isager and Hansen 1975, 169).

[18] Brašinskij 1968, 107.

[19] Polybius (4. 38. 5) refers to the occasional occurrence of grain shortages in the Black Sea basin and Isocrates *Trapeziticus* (17) 57 seems to allude to such shortages in the late 5th century. Ps.-Demosthenes 34. 36, however, indicates that this was not the case in 327. Soviet archaeologists also have documented an increase in the cultivation of land in the Crimean area during the 4th century (*cf.* Gajdukevič 1971, 112; and Pečirka 1973, 142).

[20] Aeschines *Against Ctesiphon* (3) 171–172 where he refers to the Spartocids as τοῖς πολεμίοις apropos of the surrender of Nymphaeum to them by Demosthenes' grandfather Gylon. Dinarchus 1. 43.

existed at Athens, a development that is easily understood if Athens had lost her privileged position in the Pontic grain trade and hence could not count on Bosporan grain to alleviate the bitter famine conditions of this period.[21] Taken together, the drop in the volume of Athenian exports to Bosporus at a time of increasing need for grain and the existence of considerable popular antipathy toward the Spartocids already by 330 – antipathy, moreover, which seems to have lingered for much of the following decade despite Paerisades' proclamation of 327 – suggest that the suspension of the duty-free status of grain bound for Athens was not a temporary revenue measure in force for a brief period as assumed by Gajdukevič but rather a settled policy for much of Paerisades' reign as sole ruler of Bosporus, quite possibly, in fact, from his accession in 344/3.

Contrary to the accepted view, therefore, Paerisades' policies, far from being beneficial to Athens, were for many years actually detrimental to her interests; and, judging by the indications of popular antipathy towards his house, were perceived as such by a significant number of Athenians. The erection of statues and especially the erection of a pair of statues as is indicated by *IG* II² 653, however, was a rare and signal honor granted by the Athenians only to notable benefactors of the city.[22] Accordingly, although the use of the plural in referring to the statues in *IG* II² 653, lines 14–15 and 41 combined with the evidence adduced above for Athenian practice prior to the reign of Paerisades and the fact that only one reign, that of Eumelus, intervened between his reign and that of Spartocus III, allows no doubt that one of the statues was of Paerisades I, that statue clearly cannot have been set up nor the *epimachia* have been concluded before his reinstatement of Athens' trade privileges in 327. That year, therefore, is the *terminus post quem* for the modification of Atheno-Bosporan relations implied by *IG* II² 653. Fortunately, in this case a formal *terminus ante quem* is not needed since the unlikelihood of there having been more than one bronze statue of Paerisades in the *agora* allows us confidently to identify at least some of the statues referred to in *IG* II² 653 with the group of bronze statues of Paerisades I and two of his sons, Satyrus and Gorgippus, which Demosthenes

---

[21] That Athens was seeking alternative sources of grain in these years is suggested by her presence among the recipients of a gift of grain from Cyrene (Tod 1948, no. 196, line 5); and explicitly stated as one of the purposes of her project to found a colony in the Adriatic in 325/4 (*IG* II² 1629a, lines 217–220).

[22] Demosthenes 23. 143. For the significance of the erection of statues in general, see Walsh 1904–05; and for that of multiple statues in particular, see Dow 1963, 83–84.

288   PART II: ARTICLES

had set up in the *agora* sometime between 330 and 324,[23] most likely during his second *sitonia* in the early 320s.[24]

The coincidence in timing between the renewal of the *ateleia* for grain shipped to Athens by Paerisades in 327 and the erection of the bronze statues of him and his sons on the motion of Demosthenes suggests that it was, in fact, about this time that the relations between Athens and Bosporus were put on the new footing that we find in *IG* II² 653, and there is one piece of evidence which tends to confirm this theory. In addition to claiming that Demosthenes set up statues of such 'unworthies' as the Bosporan tyrants, Dinarchus charges that in return for so doing Demosthenes received not money as he did from other persons for whom he obtained honors,[25] but an annual gift of 1000 *medimnoi* of grain.[26] By itself, of course, this is an easily understandable appeal to the emotions of the jurors in a time of famine and one, moreover, that is paralleled elsewhere in the Demosthenic corpus,[27] but it gains particular point if the statues were erected in conjunction with the renegotiation of the old trade agreement, since then Dinarchus would be implying that Demosthenes and not the Athenian people as a whole had received the anticipated benefit from their being set up. If this be so, then it does tend to strengthen the suggestion offered above that the pact was not in force during much of the first part of Paerisades' sole reign, but instead was at least partially reinstated in the early 320s through the agency of Demosthenes. By 284, however, Athens' ties to Bosporus also included the *epimachia*. Can it also have been concluded in the early 320s?

Unfortunately, definite evidence for dating the conclusion of the *epimachia* is lacking, although the use of the plural τ[ῶν προγόνω]ν (line 18) in referring to it does suggest a policy extending over more than one reign, and the fact that it was not yet in existence during the joint reigns of Spartocus II and Paerisades I indicates that it too dates from Paerisades' sole reign. The early 320s when some parts of the old agreement were reinstated would certainly seem a probable date for its negotiation also, and there is one consideration which

---

[23] The date of the erection of these statues is not attested. The view presented in the text is based on the following considerations: (1) Demosthenes' relations with the Spartocids were subject to hostile comment in 330 and 323; (2) Aeschines did not cite the statues in this connection in 330, using instead the obscure story of Gylon's alleged treason while Dinarchus could cite both the statues and Demosthenes' rumored private grain subsidy in 323. Taken together these two points suggest that the statues were set up between 330 and 324.

[24] Ps.-Plutarch *Moralia* 851B. For the date of the *sitonia* and the probable connection of the statues with it, see Schaefer 1887, 295–96.

[25] 1. 41–42.

[26] 1. 43.

[27] *Cf.* Ps.-Demosthenes 56. 7–8 with its reference to the speaker's opponents' ties with Cleomenes of Naucratis. For the limited validity of the charges made against Cleomenes, see Seibert 1969, 45–46.

does point toward that being the case. Since all of our evidence for Atheno-Bosporan relations comes from Athens, it understandably emphasizes the privileges granted by Bosporus to Athens instead of any commitments to Bosporus made by Athens, thus conveying the impression that Athens received from the Spartocids substantial and valuable trade preferences in exchange for only grants of citizenship and public honors. Although found in modern studies of the subject,[28] this situation is both inherently improbable and almost certainly incorrect. On the contrary, in *IG* II² 212, lines 17–20 we find that the Bosporan envoys of Spartocus II and Paerisades I are instructed to tell their masters that if they continue to protect Athens' interests in the grain trade, οὐδενὸ[ς] ἀτυχήσ[ο]υσιν τοῦ δήμου ᾽Αθηναίων. Vague though it is, this remark clearly implies a reciprocal Athenian commitment to promote Spartocid interests at Athens, and this is confirmed later in the decree (lines 53–65) when the Athenians assure Spartocus and Paerisades that they will take steps to have debts owed to them at Athens paid[29] and agree to comply with their request that Athens δοῦναι δ[ὲ τὰ]ς ὑπη[ρεσί]/[α]ς, perhaps to send them a number of skilled public slave rowers.[30] Far from being virtual unilateral grants of valuable trade preferences by Bosporus, the original agreements thus did involve reciprocal undertakings by Athens to promote Bosporan interests so long as the Spartocids maintained Athens' preferential position in the grain trade. In this regard it is to be noted that the *epimachia* is included in *IG* II² 653 precisely among those actions taken by Athens in response to the benevolent deeds of Spartocus' ancestors, that is, it seems to correspond to the more general promise to watch over Spartocid interests found in *IG* II² 212. Accordingly, since there are likely to have been some reciprocal undertakings by Athens when the agreement with the Spartocids was renegotiated by Demosthenes in the early 320s, it is tempting to suggest that the old vague Athenian commitment to promote Bosporan interests was transformed, presumably at the insistence of Paerisades, into the formal *epimachia* attested in *IG* II² 653. Although this would have involved a major departure from her previous policy which avoided such binding ties, Athens' weakness and her desperate need for foreign grain in large quantities to cope with the great famine would have made it extremely difficult for her to refuse such a demand.

---

[28] See, for example, Rostovtzeff 1930, 567; and Finley 1973, 162.

[29] Apropos of the usefulness of these privileges to the Spartocids and the significance of the Athenian pledge to protect their interests, note Demosthenes' significant remark (*In Leptinem* [20] 40) that there is always property of Leucon's at Athens.

[30] For this interpretation of ὑπερε[σίας], see the full and convincing discussion by Jordan 1975, 240–59.

290 PART II: ARTICLES

Viewed in the perspective provided by *IG* II² 653, Demosthenes' diplomacy must be considered to have been successful. Admittedly in return for greater public honors than had previously been granted to the Spartocids and perhaps a more formal pledge of Athenian support to them than had existed before, Demosthenes regained for Athens at a time of severe crisis the most important of the privileges given her by Leucon I, the *ateleia* for grain exported to the city, and re-established the cordial relationship between the two states that had characterized the period prior to the accession of Paerisades I to sole power in 344/3. If his diplomacy was successful in the long term, however, Dinarchus' malicious remark about his having corruptly persuaded the Athenians to honor such 'unworthy' characters as Paerisades I and his sons clearly indicates that the tangible benefits of the renewed relationship were not yet apparent to many of Demosthenes' contemporaries at the time of his trial in 323. Soon after his conviction, the situation was different. An important but badly damaged inscription found in the Athenian *agora* records a decree of the year 323 honoring a group of Bosporans[31] for a previous gift of grain and for a new contribution, apparently, to the financing of the Lamian War.[32] The thaw in Atheno-Bosporan relations had finally set in.

BIBLIOGRAPHY

Adcock, (Sir) F.E. and Mosley, D.J. 1975: *Diplomacy in Ancient Greece* (London).
Bengtson, H. (ed.) 1962: *Die Staatsverträge des Altertums 2: Die Verträge der griechisch-römischen Welt von 700 bis 338 v. Chr.* (Munich).
Blass, F. 1893: *Die attische Beredsamkeit*, 2nd ed., vol. 3.1 (Leipzig).
Brašinskij, I.B. 1968: 'Athen und die Gebiete an der nördlichen Schwarzmeerküste zwischen dem 6. und 2. Jahrhundert v.u.Z.'. *BCO* 13, 102–08.
Brashinsky, J.B. 1971: 'Epigraphical Evidence on Athens' Relations with the North Pontic Greek States'. In *Acta of the Fifth International Congress of Greek and Latin Epigraphy, Cambridge, 1967* (Oxford), 119–23.
Camp, J.McK. 1977: *The Water Supply of Ancient Athens from 3000 to 86 B.C.* (Dissertation, Princeton).
Dinsmoor, W.B. 1954: 'The Archonship of Pytharetos'. *Hesperia* 23, 284–316.
Dow, S. 1963: 'The Athenian Honors for Aristonikos'. *Harvard Studies in Classical Philology* 67, 78–92.
Finley, M.I. 1973: *The Ancient Economy* (London).
Gajdukevič, V.F. 1971: *Das bosporanische Reich* (Berlin).
Gernet, L. 1909: 'L'approvisionnement d'Athènes en blé au Ve et au IVe siècles'. In *Mélanges d'histoire ancienne* 25 (Paris), 271–391.

---

[31] First published by Schweigert 1939, no. 70; and republished by him with an improved text in 1940, no. 42.
[32] For this interpretation of lines 14–16, see Schweigert 1939, 28.

Hasebroek, J. 1933: *Trade and Politics in Ancient Greece* (London).

Isager, S. and Hansen, M.H. 1975: *Aspects of Athenian Society in the Fourth Century B.C.* (Odense).

Jordan, B. 1975: *The Athenian Navy in the Classical Period: A study of Athenian Naval Administration and Military Organization in the Fifth and Fourth Centuries B.C.* (University of California Publications: Classical Studies 13) (Berkeley).

Minns, E.H. 1913: *Scythians and Greeks: A Survey of Ancient History and Archaeology on the North Coast of the Euxine from the Danube to the Caucasus* (Cambridge).

Pečirka, J. 1973: 'Homestead Farms in Classical and Hellenistic Hellas'. In Finley, M.I. (ed.), *Problèmes de la terre en Grèce ancienne* (Paris), 113–47.

Rostovtzeff, M.I. 1930: 'The Bosporan Kingdom'. *CAH* VIII, 561–89.

Schaefer, A. 1887: *Demosthenes und seine Zeit*, 2nd. ed., vol. 3 (Leipzig).

Schmitt, H.H. 1969: *Die Staatsverträge des Altertums 3: Die Verträge der griechisch-römiscben Welt von 338 bis 200 v. Chr.* (Munich).

Schweigert, E. 1939: 'Greek Inscriptions'. *Hesperia* 8, 1–70.

—. 1940: 'Greek Inscriptions'. *Hesperia* 9, 309–57.

Seibert, J. 1969: *Untersuchungen zur Geschichte Ptolemaios' I.* (Munich).

Tod, M.N. 1948: *A Selection of Greek Historical Inscriptions 2: From 403 to 323 B.C.* (Oxford).

Walsh, M.K. 1904–05: 'Honorary Statues in Ancient Greece'. *Annual of the British School at Athens* 11, 32–49.

Werner, R. 1955: 'Die Dynastie der Spartokiden'. *Historia* 4, 412–44.

MENANDER AND POLITICS:
THE FRAGMENTS OF THE *HALIEIS**

The accepted view of New Comedy in general and of the plays of Menander in particular is that they were 'primarily entertainments'.[1] Political satire in the manner of Old Comedy was eschewed in favor of safe themes such as the loves and other foibles of the Athenian middle class. Allusions to contemporary events were infrequent and unimportant.[2] On the whole the spectacular papyrological discoveries of the 20th century have confirmed the essential validity of this picture of Menander's work. The fragments of the *Halieis*,[3] however, indicate that occasionally Menander used his art to influence Athenian opinion on a political issue which interested him.

At first glance the fragments of the *Halieis* are discouraging. August Meineke identified 17 fragments of the play – none of them exceeding four lines in length – and no additional ones have been discovered since.[4] One fragment indicates that the set contained only two houses.[5] Others contain a bit from a narrative of a pirate attack,[6] a eulogy of his home by someone returning to it after a long absence,[7] a complaint that a daughter is a troublesome possession,[8] some sententious moralizing to the effect, on the one hand, that the poor would be better off dead[9] and, on the other, that riches make men benevolent[10] and a number of allusions to the material aspect of a luxurious life style.[11] On the basis of such meagre evidence little more can be said than

---

[*] First published in S.M. Burstein and L.A. Okin (eds.), *Panhellenica: Essays in Ancient History and Historiography in Honor of Truesdell S. Brown* (Lawrence, Kansas 1980), 69–76.

[1] Gomme and Sandbach 1973, 26.

[2] Gomme and Sandbach 1973, 23–24, 24 n. 1. *Cf.* Webster 1974, 23; 1964, 12; and Handley 1965, 3.

[3] The title is uncertain as it occurs in the fragments in the generally accepted plural form and also in the singular (Edmonds 1957–61), Ff 14, 16, 17, 19, 24, 27, and 28: the fragments are cited below according to the numbering of Edmond's edition. In a 2nd-century AD list of Menander's plays it is entered as *Halieus* (P. Oxy. 2462). *Cf.* Webster 1974, 144.

[4] Meineke 1839–41 IV, 74–78.

[5] F 17.

[6] F 15.

[7] F 13. *Cf.* Austin 1969–70, lines 101–105. For parallels see Gomme and Sandbach 1973, 555 *ad Samia*, line 101.

[8] F 18.

[9] F 14.

[10] F 19.

[11] Ff 20, 24, 29.

294 PART II: ARTICLES

that the *Halieis* probably had a typical Menandrian plot centering on the problems involved in arranging the marriage of an apparently poor girl and that it contained social criticism about riches and poverty of a type familiar in the work of Menander.[12] Even this bit of information is significant, however, since it clearly indicates that the *Halieis* was not primarily a political play.

These conclusions are neither surprising nor remarkable, but they do serve to highlight the unique character of a group of fragments preserved by Athenaeus:[13]

> Menander, by no means a railer [*hekista g'on loidoros*], mentions him [sc. Dionysius of Heraclea] in *The Fishermen* after promising the story of some exiles from Heraclea [*ton muthon hupostēsamenos huper tinōn phugadōn ex Herakleias*]. 'For a fat hog lay upon his snout'; and again [*kai palin*]: 'He was living in luxury so as to not luxuriate for long.' And further [*kai eti*]: 'I desire this only for myself – only this death seems a happy death – that I should lie on my back with my great fat stomach, barely talking or breathing, while I eat and say, "I'm being corrupted by pleasure".'

These bits of the *Halieis* survive because Athenaeus found in them confirmation of a spectacular description of the obesity of Dionysius, the fourth tyrant of Heraclea Pontica, by the Heracleote historian Nymphis.[14] That Menander's portrayal of Dionysius was hostile is obvious, but analysis of the fragments reveals more. Athenaeus appears to have excerpted the items that interested him in the order they occurred in the play. This, at least, is suggested by *ton muthon hupostēsamenos huper tinōn phugadōn ex Herakleias* which probably refers to the prologue and by the *palin* and *kai eti* which separate the several quotes. Of the three direct quotations, two are barbed allusions to Dionysius by another party, either the speaker of the prologue or a character or both, while the third is a short speech or portion of a speech by Dionysius himself. The latter by itself is remarkable since it implies that Dionysius, the contemporary ruler of Heraclea, was a character in the *Halieis*, a situation that has no parallel elsewhere in the remains of Menander's work. Moreover, the fact that Dionysius was a character in the play must mean that its action was set in Heraclea.[15] Finally, the scenario suggested by the sequence of the fragments is interesting. What was almost certainly a sympathetic account of some Heracleote exiles in

---

[12] Webster 1960, 59–67; Sherk 1970, 341–42.

[13] Athenaeus 12. 549 c–d = Ff 21–23.

[14] Athenaeus 12. 549 a = Nymphis *FGrH* 3B, 432 F10. For Dionysius, see Burstein 1976, 72–80.

[15] A setting in the Black Sea is also suggested by F 25; 'And a muddy sea which nourishes a great tunny'. For the great tunny runs along the south coast of the Black Sea, see Strabo 12. 3. 19; and Aelian *N.A.* 15. 5, for the tunny fishing at Heraclea. *Cf. Samia*, line 98 for the abundant fish of the Black Sea. F 13 points to Heraclea in particular. Conceivably the story involved the accidental return of some exiles to the city, perhaps as a result of the pirate attack indicated in F 15.

MENANDER AND POLITICS: THE FRAGMENTS OF THE *HALIEIS* 295

the prologue and the following references to Dionysius' corruption would have aroused expectations in the audience which Menander then fulfilled with the decadent sentiments he placed in Dionysius' mouth. This is more than a passing satiric allusion to a notorious foible such as Menander's jokes about Athenian parasites or Alexander's drinking and divine pretensions.[16] Rather it is a deliberate attempt by Menander to prejudice his Athenian audience against the ruler of another city, and the deliberateness of it is to be emphasized. As already noted, the *Halieis* seems to have had a typical New Comedy plot, that is, a plot built around a non-political theme which could have been set anywhere. Even the decision to build it around the story of some Heracleote exiles need not have forced Menander to locate the play's action in Heraclea or to have made Dionysius a character or to have portrayed him in the fashion that he did. In other words, vilification of Dionysius was one of Menander's purposes, albeit probably a subordinate one, in writing the *Halieis*. No analogy to this treatment exists in the other fragments of his plays, and, judging from Athenaeus' parenthetical remark that Menander was *hēkista g'ōn loidoros*, it probably was, in fact, highly unusual.

Furthermore, Menander took a certain risk in writing a play dealing with Heracleote exiles, particularly a play set in Heraclea. He could hardly avoid the problem of the exiles' inability to return home and that might irritate a raw Athenian nerve. The exiles were members of Heraclea's aristocracy who had fled the city when Dionysius' father Clearchus seized power there in 364.[17] A little more than three decades after the beginning of their exile, Alexander and then Perdiccas ordered Dionysius to allow them to return home. Only Dionysius' astute diplomacy and the death of Perdiccas in 320 frustrated their hope. The parallel between their plight and that of the Samians exiled by Athens in 365 is striking. Just as[18] the Heracleotes did, the Samians sought and received support from Alexander and Perdiccas. Unlike the Heracleotes, however, Samian hopes had been followed by the expulsion of the Athenian cleruchs from Samos and the restoration of the Samians to their homes by Perdiccas, a bitter blow to both Athenian power and pride.[19]

---

[16] E.g. F 319 (Callimedon), F 117 (Hipparchia), Ff 56–57 and *Samia*, line 603 (Chaerophon), F 293 and F 924 (Alexander). For further examples see Webster 1960, 103–04; and 1974, 3–11. Webster (1970, 102, n. 3) arbitrarily dismisses Ff 21–23 as merely a similar allusion to 'a glutton of international reputation'. His later suggestion (1974, 10) that Menander had Heracletoe exiles tell stories about Dionysius which were known already in Athens ignores the complex structure of the fragments.

[17] Justin 16. 4. 7; Isocrates Letter 7 *passim*. *Cf.* Burstein 1976, 52–53.

[18] Memnon *FGrH* 3B, 434 F4. 1–3.

[19] Hicks 1882, no. 135. Diodorus 18. 8. 7; 18. 9; 18. 56. 7. For a possible Athenian attack on Samos during the reign of Demetrius of Phalerum, see Habicht 1957, 172, no. 19.

296 PART II: ARTICLES

Menander may have hoped that Dionysius' being a tyrant would make an attack on him acceptable to be Athenians, but even so he risked awakening memories of Athens' recent humiliation and thereby prejudice in his audience against the Heracleote exiles. In these circumstances, while it is likely enough that the harsh picture of Dionysius resulted from Menander's personal sympathy for the cause of the Heracleote exiles, his decision to write the play at all requires explanation.

Support for the exiles may have been common among the Heracleote metics living in Attica,[20] but there is no reason believe that it was widespread among the Athenians themselves. Quite the contrary. Early in his reign at least Dionysius had had friends among the Athenian democratic leaders,[21] and in the one area of Athenian society where the exiles had enjoyed considerable sympathy, the rhetorical and philosophical schools, support for their cause seems to have declined after the mid-340s.[22] Under these conditions only a period of strong political opposition between Athens and Dionysius could have provided Menander with the occasion to write the *Halieis*.

The *terminus post quem* for the composition of the *Halieis* is 321, the date of the production of the *Orge*, Menander's first play;[23] and the *terminus ante quem* is the death of Dionysius in 305.[24] The key to a more precise dating of the play, however, is provided by another fragment preserved by Athenaeus:[25]

> We're rich, and not at all moderately so; we have gold from Cyinda; Persian robes and purple rugs are laid out. Embossed wares are inside, gentlemen, and drinking cups, and other silver plate, and masks in high relief, goat stag drinking horns, and *labronioi*.

---

[20] For Heracleote metics at Athens see Burstein (supra n. 14) 139, n. 96; 140 n. 106. A striking example of the prosperity and prominence attained by some Heracleotes resident in Athens in the mid-4th century is provided by the fine family tomb of Agathon and Sosicrates on the Street of Tombs (*cf.* Karo 1943, 32; Ohly 1965, 342–45).

[21] *IG* II², 363. For the date, see Burstein 1976, 137, n. 39. *SIG*³ 1, 304, lines 41–43 does not indicate a permanent break in good relations. Friendly if not necessarily close relations between Athens and Heraclea during the brief period of democratic government permitted by Polyperchon are suggested by an Athenian proxeny decree in honor of a Heracleote named Hermo – dated to the year 317 (Raubitschek 1945, 106–07).

[22] For the hostility of the schools to Clearchus see *Suda s.v. Klearchos* and Isocrates Letter 7, 12–13. For the softening of the attitude after the accession of Timotheus in 346 see Isocrates Letter 7, 1–2 and Aristotle's favorable characterization of the city in *Politics* 7. 5. 7, 1327b 9–16.

[23] Lesky 1966, 645.

[24] Diodorus 20. 77. 1. Burstein 1976, 141, n. 126.

[25] Athenaeus 11. 484c = F 24. Webster (1974, 144) suggests that this refers to booty brought back by the exiles, but it is unlikely that Menander would portray his sympathetic characters in this fashion. Rather the reference is probably to the luxurious life style of Dionysius, characterized as dominated by *truphē* in Ff 21–23 and in actuality known to have presided over a splendid court after his marriage to the Persian princess Amastris (Memnon *FGrH* 3B, 434 F4. 4–5).

MENANDER AND POLITICS: THE FRAGMENTS OF THE *HALIEIS*   297

Scholars have long recognized that the reference to gold from the Macedonian treasury at Cyinda must be topical, and, hence, that the *Halieis* must be roughly contemporary with the putting into circulation of a sizeable portion of the treasure stored there. Three such occasions are known during the career of Menander, one by Eumenes in 318[26] and two by Antigonus the One-Eyed, one in the winter of 316[27] and the other in 302.[28] The last of these can be ignored, however, since Dionysius was already dead in 302 and the fragments of the *Halieis* clearly imply that he was alive at the time of its composition. Largely, it seems, on the strength of Strabo's statement that Eumenes removed the treasures of Cyinda, previous scholars have assumed that the reference is to Eumenes' withdrawal in 318 and have dated the play accordingly.[29] But Strabo was clearly exaggerating since sufficient funds remained there for Antigonus to exploit later.[30] Moreover, the fact that the *Halieis* was set in Heraclea requires that the play be dated to a period when 'gold from Cyinda' could have reached or could plausibly be said to have reached that city. That could not have been in 318 because Eumenes and Dionysius were on opposite sides during the wars of the Diadochoi.[31] On the other hand, the situation is different with regard to Antigonus' withdrawal in 316. Dionysius supported Antigonus during his siege of Tyre the following year, and in 314 he and Antigonus sealed an alliance by the marriage of Dionysius' daughter to Polemaeus, Antigonus' nephew and *stratēgos* in Hellespontine Phrygia.[32] At the same time Athens, governed by Menander's friend Demetrius of Phalerum,[33] was a client state of Cassander, Antigonus' bitter enemy. The political situation in 314, therefore, was precisely that suggested by the allusion to gold from Cyinda and the hostile treatment accorded Dionysius in the *Halieis*.

Dating the *Halieis* to 314 also has the advantage of providing a plausible reason for Menander's decision to take up the cause of the Heracleote exiles after the apparent destruction of all their hopes in 320 Precisely at that time the outbreak of hostilities between Antigonus and his former allies – Cassander, Ptolemy, Lysimachus and Seleucus – had made the whole question of exiles again something of a public issue. In response to the ultimatum of his enemies that he surrender the gains he had made through his victory over Eumenes,

---

[26] Diodorus 18. 62. 2.

[27] Diodorus 19. 56. 5.

[28] Diodorus 20. 108. 2–3.

[29] Strabo 14. 5. 10. Meineke 1839–41 IV, 75; Edmonds 1957–61 III.2, 555 n. c (Edmonds wrongly dates Eumenes' withdrawal to 320).

[30] This was pointed out by Simpson 1957.

[31] Burstein 1976, 76.

[32] Memnon *FGrH* 3B, 434 F4. 6. For the date see Burstein 1976, 77, 139, n. 89.

[33] Diogenes Laertius 5. 79.

298 PART II: ARTICLES

Antigonus issued his famous proclamation of the freedom of the Greeks and, more importantly for our purposes, a series of specific charges against Cassander which included the complaint that he had restored the exiles of Olynthus and Thebes to their homes despite the fact that these peoples were bitter enemies of the Macedonians.[34] How did Cassander respond to these charges? Unfortunately, we do not know, but it is hard to believe that he did not at least publicly note the contradiction between Antigonus' professions and his subsequent marriage alliance with Dionysius, a ruler who had defied a direct order from Alexander to allow the Heracleote exiles to return home. If he did so, then it becomes understandable that Menander would have taken advantage of this change in the political environment and attempted to arouse public sympathy for the exiles by writing a play favorable to them and hostile to their enemy Dionysius. The scantiness of the fragments of the *Halieis* forbids certainty on this point, but there is one suggestive piece of evidence that tends to strengthen this theory. As already mentioned, Antigonus charged that Cassander had allowed the Olynthians to return home. In 314, two years after the foundation of Cassandrea, the new city into which Cassander incorporated the Olynthian exiles, Menander wrote a play entitled *Olynthia* in which the principal sympathetic character was an Olynthian woman.[35] By itself the title would have been sufficient to remind the Athenians of the recent good fortune of the Olynthians; and that is significant because it indicates that in 314 Menander was interested in the fate of yet another group of exiles who, just as the Heracleotes, were hostile to Antigonus.

Despite their necessarily tentative character, several conclusions of interest emerge from this study of the fragments of the *Halieis*. First, the play can be dated to about the year 314,[36] a useful addition to our limited knowledge of the chronology of Menander's career. Second and more important, these fragments allow us a glimpse of Menander's interests at that time, and the manner in which they influenced his drama. That he alluded to contemporary events in order to provide a realistic background for his plays[37] has long been known as has also his willingness to poke fun at the moral reforms of his friend Demetrius of Phalerum[38] or to mock various notorious Athenian figures such as the

[34] Diodorus 19. 61. 2–3.
[35] Ff 356–358. For the date and tone, see Webster 1974, 2, 167–68.
[36] Webster (1974, 10) suggests *ca.* 308–306 for the date of the *Halieis* but he offers no supporting evidence. The only stylistic criterion Webster accepts for dating, the presence of trochaic tetrameters in F 23, points to an earlier date since except for the *Sikyonios* (1974, 9–10) no Menandrian play employing that meter can be dated later than *ca.* 311 (1974, 1–2). The weakness of the metrical criterion in general, however, has been pointed out by Dedoussi 1970, 159.
[37] Webster 1974, 2.
[38] F 272.

parasite Chaerophon.[39] The fragments of the *Halieis* reveal, however, that occasionally Menander went beyond such incidental uses of contemporary references and made a particular issue in which he was interested, such as the plight of the Heracleote exiles, an important even if not a dominant theme in a play if the atmosphere at Athens seemed favorable to such a course.

BIBLIOGRAPHY

Austin, C. 1969–70: *Samia, Menandri Aspis et Samia*, 2 vols. (Berlin).
Burstein, S.M. 1976: *Outpost of Hellenism: The Emergence of Heraclea on the Black Sea* (University of California Publications: Classical Studies 14) (Berkeley).
Dedoussi, C. 1970: 'The Samia'. In *Ménandre* (Entretiens sur l'antiquité classique 26) (Geneva), 157–70.
Edmonds, J.M. (ed.) 1957–61: *The Fragments of Attic Comedy*, 3 vols. in 4 (Leiden).
Gomme, A.W. and Sandbach, H.F. 1973: *Menander: A Commentary* (Oxford).
Habicht, C. 1957: 'Samische Volksbeschlüsse der hellenistischer Zeit'. *Mitteilungen des Deutschen Archäologischen Instituts, Athenische Abteilung* 72, 152–274.
Handley, E.W. (ed.) 1965: *The Dyskolos of Menander* (London).
Hicks, E.L. 1882: *A Manual of Greek Historical Inscriptions* (Oxford).
Karo, G. 1943: *An Attic Cemetery* (Philadelphia).
Lesky, A. 1966: *A History of Greek Literature* (New York).
Meineke, A. (ed.) 1839–41: *Fragmenta Comicorum Graecorum*, 4 vols. in 5 (Berlin).
Ohly, D. 1965: 'Kerameikos-Grabung Tätigkeitsbericht 1956–1961'. *Archäologischer Anzeiger* 2, 277–376.
Raubitschek, A.E. 1945: 'The Pyloroi of the Akropolis'. *Transactions of the American Philological Association* 76, 104–07.
Sherk, R.K. 1970: 'Daos and Spinther in Menander's *Aspis*'. *AJPh* 91, 341–43.
Simpson, R.H. 1957: 'A Note on Cyinda'. *Historia* 6, 503–04.
Webster, T.B.L. 1960: *Studies in Menander*, 2nd ed. (Manchester).
—. 1964: *Hellenistic Poetry and Art* (London).
—. 1970: *Studies in Later Greek Comedy*, 2nd ed. (Manchester).
—. 1974: *An Introduction to Menander* (Manchester).

---

[39] For Chaerophon, see Gomme and Sandbach 1973, 613 *ad Samia*, line 603.

LYSIMACHUS AND THE CITIES: THE EARLY YEARS[*]

W.W. Tarn[1] once remarked apropos of the two decades following the death of Alexander the Great in 323 BC that 'the more the period is studied, the stronger the conviction grows of the presence of a great lost writer behind it.' His allusion was to the lost history of Hieronymous of Cardia, and subsequent scholarship has by and large confirmed Tam's essentially intuitive assessment of the reliability of the Hieronymean tradition, particularly as it is reflected in Diodorus Books 18–20. Unfortunately, scholars have too often forgotten, however, that of necessity that tradition also reflects Hieronymous' biases, his partiality for the Antigonid house, already notorious in antiquity (Pausanias 1. 9. 8), and his tendency to use the freedom of the Greeks as the standard against which to measure the actions and policies of Alexander's successors rather than their success in coping with the particular problems they faced in the governing of their various satrapies and, later, kingdoms.[2] Most adversely affected has been the reputation of Lysimachus, first satrap and then King of Thrace and ultimately of much of Anatolia from 323 to 281, and bitter enemy of the early Antigonids and the 'destroyer' of Cardia, Hieronymous' birthplace (Pausanias 1. 9. 8). Not surprisingly judgments of Lysimachus' policies toward the Greek cities based on sources derived from Hieronymous have been harsh. Thus, according to T. Lenschau[3] he was the king 'qui Graecorum libertate fuit inimicissimus', the one most hostile to the freedom of the Greeks, while D.M. Pippidi,[4] in his standard history of the Greek cities of the west coast of the Black Sea, *I Greci nel Basso Danubio*, characterized his policy toward the cities of the Dobruja simply as 'tyranny'.

There is, to be sure, considerable evidence that seems to support this interpretation of Lysimachus' policy toward the Greek cities of his realm. Most important is the presence of garrisons in various Greek cities and the subjection of their governments to the oversight of royal agents (*epistates*), a situation implied

---

[*] Research for this paper was made possible by a grant from the National Endowment for the Humanities. An earlier version was read at the 1986 meeting of the Pacific Coast Branch of the American Historical Association in Honolulu, Hawaii. First published in *The Ancient World* 14 (1986), 19–24.

[1] Tarn 1961, 284,

[2] Hornblower 1981, 171–79.

[3] Lenschau 1890, 175.

[4] Pippidi 1971, 93.

302   PART II: ARTICLES

for the Greek cities of the Dobruja in 313[5] and attested for Heraclea Pontica in northern Anatolia and probably also Cassandrea in the 280s.[6] Further, Lysimachus issued no declaration supporting the principle of the freedom of the Greeks in response to that of Antigonus the One Eyed in 315 nor did he implement in his territories the relevant provisions of the Peace of 311 dealing with that subject.[7] Not surprisingly, cities subject to him, again chiefly those in the Dobruja, proved responsive to such proclamations by his rivals, rising in rebellion in 313 (Diodorus 19. 73) following that of Antigonus the One Eyed and probably again (Diodorus 20. 25. 1) subsequent to that of Ptolemy I in 310 (Diodorus 20. 19. 4). Add to these facts the figurative 'destruction' of cities such as Cardia in 309 and Ephesus in 294 through their enforced inclusion in Lysimachus' newly founded capitals of Lysimachia in Europe[8] and Arsinoea in Asia[9] and the actual physical destruction of Astacus in northwest Anatolia in the 280s,[10] and the characterization of Lysimachus' policy toward the Greek cities as unusually harsh in comparison with that of his contemporaries seems plausible.

The evidence that Lysimachus subjected the cities of his realm to a tyrannical regime, therefore, seems compelling, but is it? The anecdotal and often fragmentary sources for Hellenistic history encourage scholars to ignore chronology and, instead, to use evidence drawn from the whole of a king's reign – in Lysimachus' case a reign that spanned four turbulent decades – to construct a generalized synchronic analysis of his policies. But if the evidence concerning Lysimachus' treatment of the Greek cities subject to him is considered chronologically, it becomes clear that his policies toward them changed markedly after the battle of Ipsus in 301 and his acquisition of vast new territories in Anatolia.[11] Thus, the evidence pointing to a consistent policy of tightly controlling his subject cities, principally those of the Dobruja, is concentrated in the period prior to 301, while the situation in the 290s and 280s is much more complex. Examples of harsh treatment of individual cities after 301 are attested, but they are balanced by a considerable list of concessions

---

[5] This is implied by Diodorus' remark (19. 73. 1–2) that the cities τῆς αὐτονομίας ἀντείχοντο; *cf.* Orth 1977, 3–5.

[6] Heraclea Pontica: Memnon *FGrH* 3B, 434 F 5. 6–6. 2. Cassandrea: Polyaenus 6. 7. 2; for Lachares as an agent of Lysimachus, see Polyaenus 3. 7. 2–3.

[7] Diodorus 19. 105; *RC* 1, lines 53–55.

[8] Tscherikower 1927, 1–2.

[9] Arsinoea: Tscherikower 1927, 25. That Arsinoea/Ephesus was Lysimachus' Asiatic capital is not explicitly stated in the sources but is likely in view of the recent discovery of the remains of a monumental statue of the king there (Atalay and Türkoğlu 1972–75) and Arsinoe's residence in the city during the Corupedium campaign (Polyaenus 8. 57).

[10] Strabo 12. 4. 2, C 563.

[11] For the results of a similar analysis of Lysimachus' fiscal policies, see Burstein 1984a.

LYSIMACHUS AND THE CITIES: THE EARLY YEARS 303

and privileges granted to other cities.[12] Moreover, during the Ipsus campaign and again in the 280s but not before, Lysimachus, like his rivals, did invoke the principle of the freedom of the Greeks.[13] Most revealing, however, is the change in his policies regarding garrisoning the cities of his kingdom and limiting their internal self-government. Again, both practices are attested in the decades after 301, but they seem clearly to be exceptions provoked by special circumstances to a general policy of permitting considerable freedom of action to local city governments. The situation is clearest with regard to the north Anatolian city of Heraclea Pontica. There, it is true, Lysimachus did ultimately install a garrison and *epistates* following his overthrow in 284 of the dynasty of tyrants that had ruled the city since the 360s, but this was probably one of the security measures he took in the wake of the upheavals that followed the execution of his popular son Agathocles and the purging of his supporters from the court and the Anatolian territories he had apparently administered for his father.[14] In 284, however, he left it ungarrisoned and governed by its own local officials;[15] and he seems to have followed the same policy a decade earlier in dealing with the Ionian cities he seized from Demetrius Poliorcetes in 294.[16] This more flexible policy toward the Greek cities during and after 301 raises, therefore, the question whether there were particular circumstances that would account for Lysimachus' far less generous treatment of the west Pontic cities during the early years of his reign.

Two such circumstances can, in fact, be identified with regard to these cities. The first concerns the manner in which they became subject to Lysimachus. On paper, the satrapy of Thrace in 323 when it was assigned to him at Babylon was enormous, including the Chersonesus, that is, the present day Gallipoli Peninsula, and all of the north Balkans from the Nestos River[17] east to the Black Sea and north to the Danube River. The reality was far different. Early in the 320s the death of Lysimachus' predecessor Zopyrion and the loss of his army while campaigning north of the Danube had been followed by a general uprising of Macedon's Thracian subjects led by Seuthes III, the ruler of the most important of them, the Odrysians. The magnitude of the resulting disaster is clear from Arrian's (*FGrH* 2B, 156 F1. 7) description of Lysimachus'

---

[12] For such lists, see Burstein 1980, 74–76.

[13] Ipsus campaign: Diodorus 20. 107. 2. 280s: *IG* II² 656, lines 31–38. For the context, see Burstein 1984b, 41.

[14] Suggested by Ghione 1903–04, 628.

[15] Memnon *FGrH* 3B, 434 F5. 3; *cf.* Burstein 1976, 85–86.

[16] I have discussed this question in Burstein 1986.

[17] That the Nestos River was the western boundary of Lysimachus' kingdom is suggested by Pausanias 1. 10. 2.

304 PART II: ARTICLES

satrapy as including 'the Chersonesus and the peoples bordering Thrace as far
as the sea at Salmydessus', a barren stretch of coast extending north for about
seventy miles from the Bosporus (Strabo 7. 6. 1). In other words, virtually all
of Philip II's gains in Thrace had been lost. Equally important, none of the
west Pontic cities fell within the boundaries of Lysimachus' satrapy as defined
in 323. The presence of his garrisons in these same cities in 313, therefore,
must mean that they were forcefully subdued by him sometime after 323. In
such circumstances, a policy of respect for the freedom of the Greeks would
have been impractical, all the more so, since recent studies have made it clear
that declarations in support of Greek freedom were not so much statements of
strongly held principles as propaganda devices used by various kings, including Lysimachus later in his reign, to induce cities subject to one king to defect
to another and, therefore, hardly useful in the case of genuinely independent
cities being forcefully deprived of their freedom.[18]

The second is the well attested tradition of close ties between the west Pontic Greek cities and the principal non-Greek states of the Thracian interior. The
west coast of the Pontus was a frontier zone in which the few and isolated
Greek cities maintained a precarious existence 'full of anxiety and fear' and
'hedged about on all sides by warlike tribes, the enemy almost pressing against
my side' as the despondent Roman poet Ovid (*Tristia* 3. 11 lines 10–14)
described his life in exile at Tomis, modern Constantia, in the early 1st century
AD. Natives in the immediate vicinity of the cities might be and were conquered and reduced to a type of servitude similar to that of Sparta's helots.[19]
Beyond the borders of the city's territories, however, were other groups, independent or vassals of the powerful chieftains of the interior states whose raids,
actual or potential, produced that state of 'anxiety and fear' alluded to by
Ovid.[20] Survival, therefore, required protection and the coastal cities obtained
it by recognizing the suzerainty of and, sometimes, paying tribute to the Thracian or Getic overlords of the raiders. The system is most clearly documented
in a series of 2nd- and 1st-century BC inscriptions such as the Histrian decree
honoring a certain Agathocles for his repeated and only partially successful
missions seeking military aid from a probably Getic king named Rhemaxus,
overlord of Histria, against raids by the city's native neighbors.[21] That it

---

[18] For realistic assessments of declarations supporting the 'freedom of the Greeks', see Simpson 1959; and Seager 1981, 107.

[19] Pippidi 1975.

[20] *Cf.* the similar situation of Byzantium (Polybius 4. 45), which, however, was complicated
by the lack of a paramount chief in the city's hinterland.

[21] For text and commentary: Pippidi 1975b. For the general situation in the Dobruja: Pippidi
1962, 77–81.

existed already in the 4th century, however, is suggested by an early 3rd-century inscription from Mesembria, likewise within Lysimachus' territory, which refers to that city's ties with a chief name Sadalas and his four predecessors.[22]

Protection against attack by their non-Greek neighbors was the chief benefit the west Pontic cities gained from such ties, but not the only one. Thus, before the outbreak of their revolt in 313 the Dobruja cities secured the alliance of Thracian and Scythian populations. Again in the early 320s the destruction of Zopyrion, Lysimachus' predessor as Macedonian governor of Thrace, and his army at the hands of the Scythians[23] followed his unsuccessful siege of Olbia at the mouth of the Bug River in the northwest Black Sea (Macrobius, *Saturnalia* 1. 11. 33). That the Scythians were acting as allies of Olbia is not explicitly attested, but likely in view of Olbia's previous relations with that people.[24] Finally, a little over a decade earlier in 341 Odessus successfully invoked the aid of the Getes against Philip II.[25] Clearly central, therefore, to any assessment of Lysimachus' policies toward the west Pontic Greek cities is the question of the extent of his authority over the various Thracian populations of his satrapy and, especially, over the most powerful of them, the Odrysians and their king Seuthes III, the mastermind of the successful Thracian revolt of the early 320s.

It is particularly unfortunate, therefore, that the sources are unclear with regard to this particular issue. Thus, after briefly describing a hard fought battle in 323 between Lysimachus and Seuthes III in which Lysimachus, heavily outnumbered by his Thracian opponent, barely managed to escape total defeat, Diodorus (18. 14. 2–4) remarks that 'then both armies withdrew from the area and (*sc.* the kings) began to collect greater forces for the decisive encounter.' No account of any further battle between Lysimachus and Seuthes, however, is to be found in Diodorus or in our other two sources for these events, Arrian (*FGrH* 2B, 156 F1. 10) and Pausanias (1. 9. 6), both of which seem to have emphasized Lysimachus' unexpected escape from disaster in the first battle. Scholars, nevertheless, generally have assumed that he did ultimately subdue Seuthes III and re-establish firm Macedonian control over all Thrace.[26] A considerably different scenario, however, is suggested by three pieces of, admittedly, circumstantial evidence, namely: (1) Diodorus' twice referring to

---

[22] *IGB* I² 307, lines 2–16.

[23] Berve 1926, *s.v.* Ζωπυρίων (no. 340).

[24] *Cf.* Herodotus 4. 77–78.

[25] Theopompus *FGrH* 2B, 115 F 216; Jordanes *Getica* 65.

[26] E.g. Possenti 1901, 57; Geyer 1930, 3; and Saitta 1965, 65. In support Geyer cites the claim of the Heidelberg Epitome (*FGrH* 2B, 155 F1. 4) that Antipater was unable to remove Lysimachus as satrap of Thrace in 321, a statement whose evidential value is limited in view of the lack of any evidence indicating that Antipater wished to remove Lysimachus at that time.

306 PART II: ARTICLES

Seuthes III as king, first in his account of the battle between him and Lysimachus in 323 (Diodorus 18. 14. 2) and again in his narrative of the revolt of the Dobruja cities in 313 (19. 73. 8); (2) Lysimachus' having an Odrysian wife (Pausanias 1. 10. 4); and (3) Appian's statement (*Syriaca* 1. 1) that Lysimachus founded Lysimachia in 309 as an ἐπιτείχισμα, a bulwark against the Thracians. Taken together these items suggest that, far from subduing the Odrysian king, Lysimachus' recognized his de facto independence, concluded a marriage alliance with him, and then took steps to defend against possible future hostilities should the alliance fall.

Until recently interpretations along these lines have found little favor with scholars, the evidence on which they are based being either ignored or dismissed;[27] and this despite the closely parallel situation in the late 290s when Lysimachus was forced to conclude just such a marriage alliance with the transdanubian Getic ruler Dromochaetes as part of a treaty recognizing the Danube as the border between their respective territories after two attempts to gain the same objective by military means had failed disastrously.[28] Particularly welcome, therefore, is the recent discovery of archaeological evidence tending to confirm this reconstruction as a result of the excavation of Seuthes III's capital of Seuthopolis, located on the upper reaches of the Tundja River north of the Sredna Gora Mountains and controlling the vital Shipka Pass, the key to northern Thrace.[29]

The evidence is both numismatic and epigraphic. The former consists of a number of bronze coins of Cassander and Lysimachus minted after 306 but overstruck with the name of Seuthes, clearly indicating that as late as the last decade of the 4th century Seuthes still enjoyed autonomy in his own territory.[30] Equally important is the evidence provided by the so-called Great Inscription (*IGB* 1731) from Seuthopolis:[31]

> Good Fortune. Oath given by Berenice and her sons to Epimenes. Since Seuthes is safe and well, she has turned Epimenes and his property over to Spartocus and Spartocus has given pledges concerning these matters on behalf of Epimenes, it

---

[27] E.g. Tscherikower's remark (1927, 2) that Lysimachia was founded 'nicht so sehr gegen die Thraker als vielmehr gegen Antigonos'; and the characterization of his Odrysian wife as probably only a 'Nebenfrau' by Seibert 1967, 95–96.

[28] Diodorus 21. 11–12; Polyaenus 7. 25; Pausanias 1. 9. 6; *cf.* Pippidi 1971, 92–93.

[29] Dimitrov and Čičikova 1978. For a brief account, see Hoddinott 1975, 93–103. For historical reconstructions based on the new evidence see Bengston 1962; Mihailov 1969, 35–36; and Dimitrov and Čičikova 1978, 4–5.

[30] Youroukova 1976, 24, 78–79.

[31] Although discovered in 1953, the Greek text of *IGB* 1731 has still not been published. The translation in the text is based on the Latin version published by G. Mihailov in *IGB*. For a German translation, see Danov 1962, 1376.

LYSIMACHUS AND THE CITIES: THE EARLY YEARS

has been decided by Berenice and her sons – Ebryzelmus, Teres, Satocus and Sadalas – and her grandsons, should any be born, that Epimenes shall remain alive and the property handed over to Spartocus shall be secure and that Epimenes shall serve Spartocus as faithfully as he can or anyone (*sc.* Spartocus) orders him to. The sons of Berenice shall lead Epimenes out from the temple of the Samothracian gods on this condition, that they harm him in no way, but turn him and his property over to Spartocus, and if Epimenes inflicts no injury on them, they will seize nothing of his property, but should it be clear that they have suffered some harm, let Spartocus be the judge. This oath shall be inscribed on stone steles and set up, one in Cabyle in the Phosphorion and another in the agora by the altar of Apollo and in Seuthopolis, one in the shrine of the Great Gods and one in the agora in the shrine of Dionysus.

Neither the exact historical context of this inscription nor its date are known. The known facts of Seuthes' life, however, suggest the last decade of the 4th century or, at the latest, the 290s.[32] Likewise, the fact that affairs apparently were being managed by Seuthes' queen acting as regent for him and his sons and the reference to him being safe and well as a condition of Epimenes' safe conduct points to his having been the victim of an unsuccessful assassination plot. What is of particular importance to the present discussion, however, are not the precise circumstances that resulted in the agreement detailed in *IGB* 1731 but two incidental facts referred to in the inscription, namely, that Seuthes had a Macedonian queen, most likely a daugher of Lysimachus,[33] just as the interpretation proposed above requires, and that the town of Cabyle was ruled by another independent Thracian dynast named Spartocus.[34] The latter is particularly important since Cabyle, located east of Seuthopolis, and like it occupying a strategic location on the upper Tundja River, had been colonized by Philip II[35] and served during his reign and that of Alexander as one of the anchors of Macedonian rule in Thrace. Taken together with the virtual independence of Seuthes III during the last quarter of the 4th century, the simultaneous occupation of a key Macedonian

---

[32] Since Seuthes already had at least two adult sons in 330 (*GHI* 193; Berve 1926 *s.v.* Σεύθης [no. 702]), he would have been at a minimum close to seventy in the last decade of the 4th century.

[33] This has been denied by G. Mihailov (*IGB* 3 148 *ad* 1731) who suggests that Berenice was a daughter of Antigonus married to Seuthes as part of the terms of the alliance concluded between them in 313 (Diodorus 19. 73. 8), but this is unlikely for two reasons. First, it is most improbable that such a marital alliance between Seuthes and Antigonus could have survived after the defeats inflicted in that same year on Seuthes and Antigonus' general Pausanias by Lysimachus (Diodorus 19. 73. 9–10); and, second, the active role played by Berenice's four sons in the events described in *IGB* 1731 suggests that they were too old to have been the products of a marriage concluded in 313.

[34] Spartocus' independence is implied by coins of his with the inscription [Σ]ΠΑΡΤΟΚΟΥ [ΒΑ]ΣΙΛΕΩΣ (Dimitrov 1980, 78).

[35] *Cf.* Griffith in Hammond and Griffith 1979, 557–58 and 673 for the importance of Cabyle. For a brief description of the site, see Hoddinott 1975, 103–04.

308   PART II: ARTICLES

stronghold such as Cabyle by Spartocus can only mean that Lysimachus never succeeded in reestablishing Macedonian authority over the interior of Thrace prior to the Ipsus campaign of 302/1.

The implications of this conclusion are clear. In view of the fact that Lysimachus apparently never enjoyed more than nominal authority over the various people of the interior of Thrace, actions such as the garrisoning of the west Pontic cities and the consolidation of the small and weak cities of the Gallipoli Peninsula into his fortress capital of Lysimachia should not be viewed as reflecting a policy of arbitrary hostility to Greek freedom but as sensible security precautions taken by the satrap of a satrapy that was deficient in both manpower and financial resources[36] and faced the constant threat of attack along a lengthy frontier by powerful chiefdoms with traditional ties to those same cities. Nor is this surprising. Although historians tend to treat Lysimachus as one of the major actors in the events of the years between 323 and 302/1, one who even himself once briefly in 308 toyed with the idea of seeking the rule of the whole of Alexander's empire by marrying Cleopatra, Alexander's sister and then the sole surviving member of his immediate family (Diodorus 20. 37. 4), a close reading of the sources provides little support for such an interpretation. A follower rather than a leader in the disputes that broke out among his generals at Babylon after Alexander's death in 323,[37] Lysimachus, like Eumenes, was assigned a satrapy that had still to be conquered or, in his case, reconquered. The result is clear in the sources. Between 323 and 302/1 Lysimachus campaigned only against the Thracians and Transdanubian Getes (Pausanias 1. 9. 6) and the rebellious cities of his satrapy and their allies while avoiding anything beyond the most perfunctory involvement in the affairs of Macedon and the Aegean. Establishing his authority in Thrace, not the succession to Alexander's empire, was Lysimachus' first priority in the first two decades of his reign. Only in the aftermath of the battle of Ipsus in 301 and his acquisition of vast new territories in Anatolia would he emerge as a king of equal stature with his contemporaries, Cassander, Ptolemy, Seleucus and Demetrius.

BIBLIOGRAPHY

Atalay, E. and Türkoğlu, S. 1972–75: 'Ein frühhellenistischer Porträtkopf des Lysimachos aus Ephesos'. *Jahreshefte des Österreichischen Archäologischen Institutes* Beiblatt 50, 123–50.

---

[36] Note the attempts to reinforce the population of Thrace by Antipater (Diodorus 18. 18. 4–5; Plutarch *Phocion* 28. 4) and Cassander (Diodorus 20. 19. 1). For Lysimachus' fiscal problems in the early years of his reign see Burstein 1984a, 59.

[37] Arrian *FGrH* 2B, 156 F1. 2.

LYSIMACHUS AND THE CITIES: THE EARLY YEARS 309

Bengston, H. 1962: 'Neues zur Geschichte des Hellenismus in Thrakien und in der Dobrudscha'. *Historia* 11, 18–28.

Berve, H. 1926: *Das Alexanderreich auf prosopographischer Grundlage* (Munich).

Burstein, S.M. 1976: *Outpost of Hellenism: The Emergence of Heraclea on the Black Sea* (University of California Publications: Classical Studies 14) (Berkeley).

—. 1980: 'Lysimachus and the Greek Cities of Asia: The Case of Miletus'. *The Ancient World* 3, 73–79.

—. 1984a: 'Lysimachus the *Gazophylax*: A Modem Scholarly Myth?'. In Heckel, W. and Sullivan, R. (eds.), *Ancient Coins of the Graeco-Roman World: The Nickle Numismatic Papers* (Waterloo, Ontario), 57–68.

—. 1984b: 'Bithys, Son of Cleon from Lysimachia: A Reconsideration of the Date and Significance of *IG* II², 808'. *California Studies in Classical Antiquity* 12, 39–50.

—. 1986: 'Lysimachus and the Greek Cities: A Problem in Interpretation'. *Ancient Macedonia* 4, 133–38.

Danov, C. 1962: 'Seuthopolis'. *RE* Suppl. 9, 1370–78.

Dimitrov, D.P. and Čičikova, M. 1978: *The Thracian City of Seuthopolis* (BAR Suppl. Series 38) (Oxford).

Dimitrov, K. 1980: 'New Types of Thracian Coins from the Excavations in Seuthopolis'. *Bulgarian Historical Review* 8, 76–84.

Geyer, F. 1930: 'Lysimachus'. *RE* 14, 1–31.

Ghione, P. 1903–04: 'Note sul regno di Lisimaco'. *Atti della Reale Accademia delle scienze di Torino* 39, 628.

Hammond, N.G.L. and Griffith, G.T. 1979: *A History of Macedonia 2: 550–336 B.C.* (Oxford).

Hoddinott, R.F. 1975: *Bulgaria in Antiquity: An Archaeological Introduction* (New York).

Hornblower, J. 1981: *Hieronymous of Cardia* (Oxford).

Lenschau, T. 1890: *De rebus Prienensium* (Leipziger Studien zur Klassischen Philologie 12) (Leipzig).

Mihailov, G. 1969: 'La Thrace aux IVe et IIIe siècles avant notre ère'. *Athenaeum* n.s. 39, 33–44.

Orth, W. 1977: *Königlicher Machtanspruch und städtische Freiheit* (Munich).

Pippidi, D.M. 1962: 'Die Beziehungen Histrias zu den Geten im 3. Jh. v. u. Z.'. In Pippidi, D.M., *Epigraphische Beiträge zur Geschichte Histrias in hellenistischer und romischer Zeit* (Deutsche Akademie der Wissenschaften zu Berlin. Sektion für Altertumswissenschaft. Schriften 34) (Berlin), 75–88.

—. 1971: *I Greci nel basso Danubio: dall'età arcaica alla conquista romana* (Biblioteca storica dell'antichità 8) (Milan).

—. 1975a: 'Le problème de la main d'œuvre agricole dans les colonies grecques de la mer Noire'. In Pippidi 1975c, 65–80.

—. 1975b: 'Istros et les Gètes au IIe siècle: Observations sur le décret en l'honneur d'Agathocles, fils d'Antiphilos'. In Pippidi 1975c, 31–55.

—. 1975c: *Scythica Minora: Recherches sur les colonies grecques du littoral Roumain de la mer Noire* (Bucharest).

Possenti, G.B. 1901: *Il re Lisimaco di Tracia* (Florence).

Saitta, G. 1965: 'Lisimaco di Tracia'. *Kokalos* 1, 62–154.

Seager, R. 1981: 'The Freedom of the Greeks of Asia: From Alexander to Antiochus'. *Classical Quarterly* 31.1, 106–12.

310   PART II: ARTICLES

Seibert, J. 1967: *Historische Beiträge zu den dynastischen Verbindungen in hellenistischer Zeit* (*Historia* Einzelschriften 10) (Wiesbaden).
Simpson, R.H. 1959: 'Antigonus the One-Eyed and the Greeks'. *Historia* 4, 385–409.
Tarn, W.W. 1961: *Hellenistic Civilization*, rev. ed. by G.T. Griffith (New York).
Tscherikower, V. 1927: *Die hellenistischen städtegründungen von Alexander dem Grossen bis auf die Römerzeit* (*Philologus* Suppl. 19) (Leipzig).
Youroukova, Y. 1976: *Coins of the Ancient Thracians* V (BAR Suppl. Series 4) (Oxford).

IG II² 1485A AND ATHENIAN RELATIONS WITH LYSIMACHUS*

IG II² 1485 (= EM 7899) is a badly abraded fragment of an opisthographic sto-ichedon stele of Pentelic marble (38 cm in height and 22 cm in width at its widest point) which belongs to the series of inscriptions containing the inventories of the objects cared for by the treasurers of Athena and the other gods. Side A contains a list of crowns which is generally dated to the last decade of the 4th century because of the presence in it of a crown awarded to the hipparchs of the year of Anaxicrates, 307/6 (lines 5–6). The majority of the crowns listed were awarded to Athens by other cities or, in one case, by a ruler from the Black Sea. Particular interest, however, adheres to the crown mentioned in lines 28–29: cτέφ]α[v]- | [οc ἐφ᾽ ὧι τὸ]: Γ´ : ὁ [δῆ]μο[c] ὁ [᾽Α]θ[ην]- | [αίων Λυ]cίμαχον. It has been long recognized that the Lysimachus in question is the well-known ruler of Thrace.[1] Because of the omission of the title βαcιλεύc and of the earlier entry for the crown for the hipparchs of the year of Anaxicrates, Lysimachus' crown has also been dated to the year of Anaxicrates.[2]

The implications of an Athenian crown for Lysimachus in 307/6 would be important and have not escaped the notice of scholars. For Athens to have conferred a crown on Lysimachus would imply that he had previously been the source of a benefit of some sort for the city; and since Athens was closely allied with Antigonus and Demetrius in 307/6, such a crown would imply, as F. Geyer pointed out,[3] that Lysimachus enjoyed good relations with Antigonus at that

---

* I should like to thank Prof. A.E. Raubitschek and Prof. M. Walbank for their help in the examination of EM 7899, and Dr Dina Peppas-Delmousou, Director of the Athens Epigraphical Museum, for allowing me to examine EM 7899. Research for this paper was made possible by a Fellowship from the National Endowment for the Humanities. First published in *Zeitschrift für Papyrologie und Epigraphik* 31 (1978), 181–85.

[1] *CIA* II.2, p. 88 n. *ad* 731, lines 27–29. *IG* II² 3, p. 86 n. *ad* 1485A, line 29.

[2] In *CIA* II.2, p. 88 n. *ad* 731, lines 27–29 and *IG* II² 3, p. 86 n. *ad* 1485A, line 29, the crown is dated only to the period before Lysimachus assumed the royal title. Geyer (1930, 6) and Momigliano (1935, 315) both date the crown to 307/6.

[3] Geyer 1930, 6. Momigliano (1935, 315–16) cites in this connection the fact established by Ettore Bignone (1936, 490) that Epicurus appealed to Lysimachus' dioiketes Mithres to intercede on his behalf with Demetrius about 306 as proof of the existence of good relations between Lysimachus and Demetrius at this time. As Mithres, however, is known to have been a benefactor of Demetrius' wife Phila and his half-brother Craterus (Epicuro, *Opere*, ed. G. Arrighetti [Turin 1960], F 57) and Phila was also in Athens at this time (*cf.* Ferguson 1911, 114, n. 7), it is likely that Epicurus appealed to him as a personal friend of Demetius' house and, hence, his appeal has no bearing on the question of the state of relations between Lysimachus and Demetrius and his father.

312   PART II: ARTICLES

time. Equally clearly, this interpretation would require Lysimachus to have broken sometime between 311 and 307/6 with his former ally Cassander who was then at war with Athens. Likewise the cordial relations between the two Balkan rulers later in the decade would have to represent a resumption of ties between Lysimachus and Cassander after a new rupture between the former and Antigonus, a sequence of events that is not even hinted at in any source for the period and is seemingly excluded by Diodorus' allusion in his account of events in 303 to Cassander's long established habit of calling on Lysimachus for assistance.[4] So radical a revision of the accepted interpretation of the diplomacy of the last decade of the 4th century is a heavy burden to be borne by a single dated crown and the omission of the title βαcιλεύc. In fact, of course, the crown for the hipparchs of 307/6 indicates no more than the general period to which the crowns listed on *IG* II² 1485A belong; and close examination of the list itself points clearly to the conclusion that the items inventoried on Side A were not dedicated during the single year 307/6 but over a period of years.

First and foremost, the list of crowns on Side A falls into two distinct groups. The first group (lines 1–7), now reduced to references to two crowns, closes with the crown for the hipparchs of 307/6 and is distinguished from the second (lines 8–35), which includes the Lysimachus crown, by the fact that the items in the latter are entered according to the Lycurgan system of alphabetic enumeration of the objects, beginning in line 8 with an A.[5] This difference in the clerical systems used in listing items of the same general type would alone suffice to indicate that the list of crowns on Side A extended over more than one year, and this is confirmed by the fact that the first item in the second group of crowns is an aristeion crown dedicated by the Ephesians to Athena (lines 8–11). In view of the hostile relations between Ephesus' overlord Antigonus and Cassander and the fact that aristeion crowns were dedicated only during years in which the Great Panathenaia was celebrated,[6] the earliest possible date for this crown is 306/5, the year of the first Great *Panathenaia after the expulsion* of Demetrius of Phalerum. That year, therefore, must be considered the *terminus post quem* for the crowns of the second group in general and for the Lysimachus crown in particular, the eighth in the group. Unfortunately for Geyer's interpretation of the significance of this crown, however, it is precisely beginning with the year 306/5 that we have clear evidence for the existence of hostility between Antigonus and Lysimachus on the one hand and cordial

---

[4] Diodorus 20. 106. 2: αἰεὶ γὰρ εἰώθει τοῦτον (*sc.* Lysimachus) ... εἰc τὴν βοήθειαν προολαμβάνεοθαι...

[5] Lehner 1890, 118; and Ferguson 1932, 123.

[6] Ferguson 1932, 118, n. 1.

IG II² 1485A AND ATHENIAN RELATIONS WITH LYSIMACHUS   313

relations between the latter and Cassander on the other hand.[7] Accordingly, in the hope of clarifying the question of the date of the Lysimachus crown A.E. Raubitschek of Stanford University, M. Walbank of the University of Calgary and I examined EM 7899 in the Athens Epigraphical Museum during the spring of 1977. Particular attention was devoted to identifying the Pontic ruler listed as crowning Athens in lines 21–23: cτέφανοc ἐφ' [ὧι τὸ: Ε´] | Ί/P.OIOC ἐ[κ] τοῦ Πό[ντου[8] τὸ]- | [ν δῆμον] τὸν 'Αθηναίων ...

Already at the time of the publication of this inscription in *CIA*. J.G. Droysen[9] pointed out that the random letters and traces registered by U. Köhler in line 22 were compatible with the restoration of the name Cπαρτόκοc, presumably Spartocus III, ruler of Bosporus from 304 to 284. As Spartocus could not have sent a crown to Athens before his accession to power in 304 on the death of his father Eumelus, verification of his name would confirm the essentially chronological ordering of the list of crowns on Side A and thereby establish the year 304 as the absolute *terminus post quem* for the Lysimachus crown.[10] Moreover, it would sharply reduce the importance of the omission of the title βαcιλεύc in the entry for the Lysimachus crown since the parallel omission of any title for Spartocus[11] and the use of the clumsy circumlocution ἐκ τοῦ Πόντου instead of the official Βόcπορος normal in Athenian inscriptions dealing with the Spartocids[12] would allow little doubt that the official responsible for this list was interested only in the clear identification of any mentioned individuals and not in constitutional

---

[7] Ptolemy announced his victory over Antigonus and Demetrius at Pelusium to Seleucus, Cassander and Lysimachus (Diodorus 20. 76. 7). As Cassander was then at war with Athens (*cf.* Ferguson [1911, 112] for the Four Years War from 307 until 304), Lysimachus is unlikely to have made overtures to Athens at this time.

[8] The reading ΠΌ[ΝΤΟΥ] is assured by the duplicate of *IG* II² 1485A, *IG* II² 1486 (= EM 7900) line 15.

[9] *Apud CIA* 11.2, p. 88 n. *ad* 731, lines 21–24; and repeated at *IG* II² 3, p. 86 n. *ad* 1485A, line 22. The reading has been accepted as probable and the whole list of crowns dated to 307/6 by J.B. Brashinsky, 'Epigraphical Evidence on Athens's Relations with the North Pontic Greek States', *Acta of the Fifth International Congress of Greek and Latin Epigraphy, Cambridge 1967* (Oxford, 1971) 121.

[10] As Lehner pointed out (1890, 105), the tendency in the fourth century was to devote particular care to the listing of crowns in the chronological order of their dedication with only occasional minor deviations being allowed. In fact, a survey of the examples of objects listed out of proper chronological order reveals no instance in which the observed deviation is more than one year from the correct chronological sequence (*cf. IG* II 1424, lines 21–26; 1436, line 41; 1438, line 21; 1441, lines 4–5; 1443, lines 92 and 104; 1479, line 30). To postulate a greater error in the single case of the Lysimachus crown would, therefore, be arbitrary in the extreme in the light of this evidence.

[11] The parallel would be even more striking if it could be established that this crown was received after Spartocus assumed the title βαcιλεύc (*cf.* Porphyry *FGrH* 2B, 260 F 41 and *IG* II² 653, lines 33 and 42). It is clear, however, from *CIRB* 18 that Spartocus reigned for an unknown period of time without the royal title so that the relative dates of these two events now be determined.

[12] E.g. *IG* II² 212, line 51; 653, line 33; and Schweigert 1940, no. 42, line 9.

314 PART II: ARTICLES

precision. Given the letters and traces already read by Köhler in line 22 and confirmed in our examination of EM 7899, establishment of only one additional letter would have sufficed to assure the correctness of Droysen's proposed reading. In the second stoichos, where Köhler read only a vertical, autopsy revealed to the right of the first vertical a second shorter vertical descending from a point level with the top of the first. At the top of this second vertical there can still be seen the right hand tip of what was once a horizontal stoke. There can, therefore, be no doubt that the letter is to be read as Π. Similarly, in the seventh stoichos, where Köhler again read only a vertical, autopsy revealed traces to the right of that vertical of the upper diagonal stroke of a K, thereby assuring the correctness of Droysen's suggestion that the name be read as Σπαρ[τ]όχος.

The fact that Spartocus III sent a crown to Athens in 304/3 at the earliest – probably on learning that Athens intended to continue the close relations between herself and Bosporus that had been reestablished in the early 320s after a period of estrangement[13] – requires that the Lysimachus crown be dated no earlier than that year while the political realities of the period exclude a date before the battle of Ipsus in 301. Furthermore, once it is realized that this particular crown must postdate the battle of Ipsus, there can be little doubt as to the occasion for it. In the year 299/8, at about the same time that Athens *resumed friendly relations with* Cassander,[14] Lysimachus sent the city a sizable gift of grain together with a new mast and sail for the Panathenaic ship.[15] Such distinguished gifts would have to be acknowledged, and it is difficult not to see in this crown part of the honors voted to Lysimachus at that time.

Dating of the Lysimachus crown to the year 299/8 removes a significant obstacle to our understanding of the diplomacy of the last decade of the 4th century. Contrary to Geyer, there is, in fact, no evidence for good relations between Lysimachus and Athens or Antigonus between the expulsion of Demetrius of Phalerum in 307 and the battle of Ipsus in 301. It also provides a small but useful addition to our knowledge of the history of the treasurers of Athena and the other gods since the inclusion of the Lysimachus crown among those listed in *IG* I[2] 1485A means that that inscription must be the remains of the report of the board for 299/8 or one of the subsequent years. *IG* I[2] 1485A, therefore, provides the first identified example of a 3rd-century inventory of the treasures of Athena and the other gods and the latest evidence in our possession for the continued functioning of the board of treasurers itself.[16]

---

[13] For this see Burstein 1978.
[14] *IG* II[2] 641.·
[15] *IG* II[2] 657 = *Sylloge*[3] 374 = Pouilloux, Choix 1, lines 10–16.
[16] *Cf.* Ferguson 1932, 126.

BIBLIOGRAPHY

Bignone, E. 1936: *L'Aristotele perduto e la formazione filosofica di Epicuro*, vol. 1 (Florence; repr. 1973).

Brashinsky, J.B. 1971: 'Epigraphical Evidence on Athens' Relations with the North Pontic Greek States'. In *Acta of the Fifth International Congress of Greek and Latin Epigraphy, Cambridge, 1967* (Oxford), 119–23.

Burstein, S.M. 1978: '*IG* II² 653, Demosthenes, and Athenian Relations with Bosporus in the Fourth Century B.C.'. *Historia* 27, 428–36.

Ferguson, W.S. 1911: *Hellenistic Athens: An Historical Essay* (London).

—. 1932: *The Treasurers of Athena* (Cambridge, MA).

Geyer, F. 1930: 'Lysimachus'. *RE* 14, 1–31.

Lehner, H. 1890: *Über die athenischen Schatzverzeichnisse des vierten Jahrhunderts* (Strassburg).

Momigliano, A. 1935: 'Su alcuni dati della vita di Epicuro'. *Rivista di filologia e di istruzione classica* 63, 302–16.

Schweigert, E. 1940: 'Greek Inscriptions'. *Hesperia* 9, 309–57.

SYRISKOS OF CHERSONESUS:
A NEW INTERPRETATION OF *IOSPE* 1² 344*

Abstract

IOSPE 1² 344 contains a decree by Chersonesus Taurica honoring a local historian named Syriskos for recording the epiphanies of the city's chief deity, the Parthenos, and benefits given various cities and the kings of Bosporus. This article surveys the current state of scholarship on *IOSPE* 1² 344 and proposes a new interpretation of Syriskos' work that reconciles the apparent contradiction of the simultaneous presence in it of religious and political content.

INTRODUCTION

Unlike the case with regard to Sicily and Italy,[1] the Greek cities of the Black Sea did not produce a significant number of local historians. Only the history of Heraclea Pontica was recorded by a series of historians extending from the 4th century BC to the early centuries AD.[2] Otherwise, the evidence for local historiography in the Pontus is scanty.[3] References in scholia and the *Suda* refer to historians of Odessus (*FGrH* 808) and Olbia (*FGrH* 804), and it has been suggested that Diodorus' account of the reign of Eumelus of Bosporus derives from a Bosporan court history (Diodorus 20. 22–26. 2).[4] Only one non-Heracleote local historian, however, is documented in a contemporary source: Syriskos, son of Herakleidas, from Heraclea's colony of Chersonesus Taurica.

IOSPE 1² 344

The evidence for Syriskos and his work is provided by a fragmentary inscription – *IOSPE* 1² 344 – from Chersonesus, proposing honors for him for researching and publicly reading his account of the manifestations of Chersonesus'

---

* I would like to thank Dr Dobrinka Chiekova for reading and commenting on an earlier draft of this article. First published in *Ancient West and East* 21 (2022), 273–78.

[1] *Cf. FGrH* 554–577.

[2] *Cf. FGrH* 430–435.

[3] The evidence is collected in Dana and Dana 2001–03, 91–111.

[4] *Cf.* Blawatsky 1968, 73-77.

318 PART II: ARTICLES

chief deity, the Parthenos or 'Maiden', and narrating the benefits conferred on the kings of Bosporus and unspecified cities.[5]

The inscription consists of three fragments – the first discovered by L. Jurgiewicz in 1881 and the final two by R. Löper in 1908 – and is dated by letter forms to the early 3rd century BC.[6] The most recent edition of the text edited by M. Cuypers in *Brill's New Jacoby* is as follows:

> [ἐπειδὴ] Συρίσκος Ἡρακλείδα τὰ[ς]
> [ἐπιφαν]είας τᾶς Πα[ρ]θένου φιλ[ο]-
> [πόνως] γράψας ἀ[νέ]γνω καὶ τ[ὰ]
> [ποτὶ τ]οὺς Βοσ[π]όρου [β]ασιλεῖ[ς] (5)
> [διηγήσα]το, τά [θ' ὑ]πάρξαντα φ[ι]-
> [λάνθρωπα ποτὶ τὰ]ς πόλεις ἰστ[ό]-
> [ρησεν ἐπιεικ]έως τῶι <δ>άμω[ι],
> [ἵνα λάβοι τιμὰ]ς ἀξίας, δεδόχθ[αι]
> [τᾶι βουλᾶι καὶ τῶι δάμωι ἐ]παινέσα[ι] (10)
> [τε αὐτὸν ἐπὶ τούτοις καὶ στεφ]αν[ῶ]-
> [σαι τοὺς συμμνάμ]ονας [χρυσέωι στεφ]-
> [άνωι τῶν Διονυ]σίων μιᾶι ἐφ' ἱκ[άδι],
> [καὶ τὸ ἀνάγγ]ελμα γενέσθαι· ὁ δ[ᾶ]-
> [μος στεφα]νοῖ Συρίσκον Ἡρακλε[ί]- (15)
> [δα, ὅτι τὰ]ς ἐπιφανείας τᾶς Π[αρ]-
> [θένου ἔγρα]ψε καὶ τὰ ποτὶ τὰς [πό]-
> [λεις καὶ τοὺς] βασιλεῖς ὑπάρξ[αν]-
> [τα φιλάνθρωπα] ἱστόρησε ἀλαθιν[ῶς]
> [καὶ ἐπιεικέως] τᾶι πόλει· ἀνα[γρά]- (20)
> [ψαι δὲ τοὺς συμμ]νάμονας εἰ[ς] στ[άλαν]
> [λιθίναν τὸ ψ]άφισμα καὶ θέμε[ν ἐν]-
> [τὸς τοῦ προ]νάου τᾶς Παρθέν[ου· τὸ δὲ]
> [γενόμενον ἀνά]λωμα δόμ[εν ...]
> [... τὸν τα]μίαν τῶν [ἱερῶν]. (25)
> [ταῦτ' ἔδοξε βουλᾶι κ]αὶ δάμ[ωι μηνὸς]
> ...] δεκα[ται ... / ...]

Since Syriskos, the son of Herakleidas, having written up with great care the manifestations of the Parthenos, gave a public reading of them, and narrated the affairs concerning the kings of Bosporus and he recorded the previous benefits for the cities appropriately to the demos, in order that he receive worthy honors, it has been resolved by the boule and the demos that it praise him for this things and that the *symmnamones* crown him with a gold crown on the twenty-first of the Dionysia (?) and there take place the following proclamation. The demos crowns Syriskos, the son of Herakleidas, because he wrote up the manifestations of the Parthenos and recorded truthfully and appropriately to the city the previous benefits for the cities and the kings. And the *symnamones* will record the decree on a

---

[5] Important recent editions are Chaniotis 1988, 300–01; and Cuypers 2012 in *BNJ* 807.
[6] For the history of the text, see Latyschev at *IOSPE* 1² 344, p. 289.

SYRISKOS OF CHERSONESUS: A NEW INTERPRETATION OF *IOSPE* 1² 344   319

stone stela and place it within the *pronaos* of the Parthenos. And the treasurer of the sacred affairs shall pay the incurred costs. These things were decreed by the boule and the demos in the month … tenth…[7]

STATE OF SCHOLARSHIP

Syriskos was introduced to scholarship outside Russia in a brief article by M.I. Rostovtzeff[8] published in *Klio* in 1919 in which he identified the major issues that have dominated subsequent discussion of *IOSPE* 1² 344. His conclusions were threefold. First, he identified Herakleidas, probably the father of Syriskos, with Herakleidas, son of Parmenon, who moved a decree contained in an unfortunately fragmentary inscription, *IOSPE* 1² 343, proposing some form of civic thanks for the Parthenos because she had saved the women and children from an attack through an epiphany.[9] Second, he suggested that Syriskos had written one or more works dealing with the recent history[10] of Chersonesus that focused on epiphanies of the Parthenos and diplomatic relations between Chersonesus and other cities in the Black Sea and Bosporus. Third, and most important, he pointed out parallels between Syriskos' work or works and the *Lindos Chronicle*[11] and other similar works that also treated epiphanies of various deities and other aspects of the histories of Greek cults and temples.

Little has changed since Rostovtzeff published his article in 1919, although three developments are particularly noteworthy. First, John Dillery[12] convincingly argued that Syriskos' work belong to a subcategory of local historiography that he called 'Sacred History' that sought to enhance a city's or region's importance in the general Greek world through a focus on the history of city's cults and the temples connected to them. Second, Angelos Chaniotis[13] pointed out that the benefits documented by Syriskos were conferred by Chersonesus on other cities and the kings of Bosporus and not the reverse as implied by Rostovtzeff. Third and finally, Martine Cuypers[14] clarified the subject matter

---

[7] Translated by Cuypers 2012 in *BNJ* 807.

[8] Rostovtzeff [Rostowzew] 1919, 203–06.

[9] Rostovtzeff 1919, 205–06. For the most recent edition, see *SEG* 48.1168.

[10] The reference to 'kings of Bosporus' suggests that the focus was on recent history since the earliest Bosporan ruler known to have used that title was Spartocus III, who reigned *ca.* 304/3 BC to 284/3 BC (*cf.* Werner 1955, 444). Civic honors for rulers, which might be considered 'benefits', usually were limited to crowns and statues such as, for example, Athens awarded Spartocus III (*SEG*⁴ 370. 35 and 40–42).

[11] For the *Lindos Chronicle*, see now the edition by Higbie 2003.

[12] Dillery 2005, 520–21. *Cf* Thomas 2019, 62.

[13] Chaniotis 1988, 300–01.

[14] Cuypers 2012 in *BNJ* 807: commentary on T 1.

320 PART II: ARTICLES

of Syriskos' work, noting that the text of the decree honoring him quoted in *IOSPE* 1² 344 indicated that he recorded benefits conferred on cities and the kings of Bosporus by Chersonesus and not relations between Chersonesus and various cities and benefits accorded by the kings of Bosporus to Chersonesus as Rostovtzeff[15] had suggested.

Nevertheless, the core of Rostovtzeff's interpretation has remained largely intact. Whether Syriskos wrote one or two works,[16] it is assumed that the religious content was confined to his account of the epiphanies of the Parthenos while the rest of his work was historical in character, focusing on recent political relations between Chersonesus and other Greek cities and Bosporus. As to what cities were involved, opinions differ. Rostovtzeff was cautious, only suggesting that Heraclea Pontica and other south coast cities were meant. Other scholars have been less restrained with the most recent list proposed by Sergei Saprykin including: Olbia, Callatis, Istros/Histria, Delos, Delphi, Rhodes, Sinope, and Heraclea Pontica.[17]

Moreover, there also are two considerations that tend to support Rostovtzeff's interpretation. First, the early 3rd century BC was a difficult period for Chersonesus, and the city might well have needed to seek help from other Pontic cities and Bosporus, particularly to counter the pressure on it caused by the foundation of a powerful Scythian kingdom in the Crimea with its capital at Neapolis.[18] Second, benefits could be political in character. So, in 336 BC Demosthenes (*On the Crown* 186) justified aid to Thebes against Philip II by using almost identical language in *On the Crown* to characterise Athenian assistance to Thebes, admittedly, in the mythical period: καὶ ἕτερα πολλὰ ἡμῖν ὑπάρχει φιλάνθρωπα καὶ ἔνδοξα πρὸς Θηβαίους ('and we have conferred many other distinguished benefits on the Thebans'). Nevertheless, the fundamental contradiction in Rostovtzeff's interpretation also has remained unresolved. If, as is probable, Syriskos' work was part of the honours for the Parthenos authorised in *IOSPE* 1² 343, it is difficult to understand the presence

---

[15] Rostovtzeff 1919, 205.

[16] For the question of how many works Syriskos wrote, see, for example, Latyschev at *IOSPE* 1² 344, p. 291; Rostovtzeff 1919, 206; Chaniotis 1988, 300.

[17] Saprykin 1997, 217–27.

[18] Rostovtzeff 1919, 205; Saprykin 1997, 191; Molev 2003, 209–12; and Vinogradov 2003, 217–20. *Cf.* Clarke (2008, 344–45), for the suggestion that 'in the context of such an intricate set of intra-polis negotiations ... the significance of Syriscus' work reaches beyond his home city'. While local histories might be cited as evidence in disputes between cities as in the case of that between Samos and Priene in the 280s BC (Welles 1934, 7, lines 11–13), the evidence is clear that the primary audience for works such as that of Syriskos was local, not international (*cf. IOSPE* 1² 344, lines 19–20: [*sc.* he wrote his account] ἀλαθιν[ῶς] [καὶ ἐπιεικέως] τᾶι πόλει).

in it of two unrelated themes – an account of the epiphanies of the Parthenos and a survey of the recent diplomatic history of Chersonesus – instead of his writing a unified work focusing on the Parthenos.[19]

RESOLUTION AND CONCLUSION

The solution to the difficulty was provided by Dillery's[20] description of Syriskos' work as 'a history of the relations between Chersonesus and neighboring powers ... organized around a list of epiphanies of his city's patron god, the Maiden', provided, however, that we understand that the Parthenos was also the source of the benefits for the cities and the kings of Bosporus. Such is surely implied by the probability that Syriskos' work was one of the honors for the Parthenos authorised by *IOSPE* 1[2] 343. Equally important, this interpretation is supported by the fact that such a benefit is implied by a well-known passage in *IOSPE* 1[2] 352, the decree in honor of Diophantos of Sinope, the general of Mithridates VI:[21] 'the Parthenos, who ever stands over the Chersoneseans and who on that occasion was with Diophantos, foretold the action that was about to happen by the signs that occurred in the sanctuary and inspired the whole army with courage and daring' (lines 23–26). Rostovtzeff interpreted the passage as referring to an epiphany of the Parthenos,[22] but that ignores the fact that the only visible actions of the Parthenos took place in her shrine and not on the battlefield, namely the signs that prophesied Diophantos' victory. In other words, therefore, the prophetic signs were a benefit given to Diophantos by the Parthenos.

Recognition that Syriskos' work treated both the epiphanies and benefits of the Parthenos makes clear the underlying unity of his work. Just as the *Lindos Chronicle* provided a history of the cult and temple of Athena Lindia told through a record of dedications and her epiphanies, so Syriskos celebrated the power of the Parthenos through an account of her epiphanies and the benefits she conferred not only on Chersonesus but also on other cities and even the kings of Bosporus. Like the authors of other sacred histories, therefore, Syriskos' purpose was not to seek aid for Chersonesus during a time of troubles but to celebrate his local deity and her shrine and the city that she protected, and it was because he fulfilled that task 'truthfully and appropriately to the city' that Syriskos was honored.

---

[19] This was to be the theme of the, unfortunately, still unpublished paper of I. Makarov, as revealed by the abstract (Makarov 2013, 429).

[20] Dillery 2005, 521.

[21] Translation by Bagnall and Derow 204, 103.

[22] Rostovtzeff 1919, 204.

PART II: ARTICLES

BIBLIOGRAPHY

Bagnall, R.S. and Derow, P. (eds.) 2004: *The Hellenistic Period: Historical Sources in Translation* (Malden, MA).

Blawatsky, W.D. 1968: 'Anschauungen des Bosporanischen Anonymus vom Ende des IV. Jahrhunderts v.u.Z.'. In Harmatta, J. (ed.), *Studien zur Geschichte und Philosophie des Altertums* (Budapest), 73–77.

Chaniotis, A. 1988: *Historie und Historiker in den griechischen Inschriften: Epigraphische Beiträge zur griechischen Historiographie* (Heidelberger althistorische Beiträge und epigraphische Studien 4) (Stuttgart).

Clarke, K. 2008: *Making Time for the Past: Local History and the Polis* (Oxford).

Dana, D. and Dana, M. 2001–03: 'Histoires locales dans le Pont-Euxin ouest et nord. Identité grecque et construction du passé'. *Il Mar Nero* 5, 91–111.

Dillery, J. 2005: 'Greek Sacred History'. *AJPh* 126, 505–26.

Higbie, C. 2003: *The Lindian Chronicle and the Greek Creation of their Past* (Oxford).

Makarov, I.A. 2013: 'Les rois du Bosphore et le culte chersonésien de la déesse Parthénos (sur l'interpretation de *IOSPE* I² 344)'. In Tsetskhladze, G.R., Atasoy, S., Avram, A., Dönmez, Ş. and Hargrave, J. (eds.), *The Bosporus: Gateway between the Ancient West and East (1st Millennium BC–5th Century AD)* (BAR International Series 2517) (Oxford), 429.

Molev, E.A. 2003: 'Bosporos and Chersonesos in the 4th–2nd Centuries BC'. In Bilde, P.G., Højte, J.M.H. and Stolba, V.F. (eds.), *The Cauldron of Ariantas: Studies Presented to A.N. Ščeglov on the Occasion of his 70th Birthday* (Black Sea Studies 1) (Aarhus), 209–15.

Rostovtzeff [Rostowzew], M.I. 1919: 'Ἐπιφάνειαι'. *Klio* 16, 203–06.

Saprykin, S.J. [S.Y.] 1997: *Heracleia Pontica and Tauric Chersonesus before Roman Domination (VI–I Centuries B.C.)* (Amsterdam).

Thomas, R. 2019: *Polis Histories, Collective Memories and the Greek World* (Cambridge).

Vinogradov, J.A. [Y.A.] 2003: 'Two Waves of Sarmatian Migrations in the Black Sea Steppes during the Pre-Roman Period'. In Bilde, P.G., Højte, J.M.H. and Stolba, V.F. (eds.), *The Cauldron of Ariantas: Studies Presented to A.N. Ščeglov on the Occasion of his 70th Birthday* (Black Sea Studies 1) (Aarhus), 217–26.

Welles, C.B. 1934: *Royal Correspondence in the Hellenistic Period: A Study in Greek Epigraphy* (London).

Werner, R. 1955: 'Die Dynastie der Spartokiden'. *Historia* 5, 412–41.

THE AFTERMATH OF THE PEACE OF APAMEA: ROME AND THE PONTIC WAR[*]

The signing of the Peace of Apamea in 188 BC marks the beginning of a new era in the history of Anatolia. Almost a century of Seleucid influence in the affairs of the peninsula had been ended by Roman power. Henceforth no Seleucid force was to enter an area north of the Taurus Mountains and west of the Halys River. Roman power had expelled the Seleucids from the peninsula; Roman diplomacy in 188 aimed at preventing their return. In the absence of a permanent Roman military presence east of the Aegean, responsibility for upholding the terms of the Peace of Apamea fell to Rome's chief allies in the war against Antiochus III, Rhodes and especially Eumenes II, the king of Pergamum. To that end Rome transformed Pergamum into a major power, awarding her (in addition to the bulk of the former Seleucid holdings in western Anatolia) Hellespontine Phrygia, Phrygia Epictetus and Galatia. Alliances with Ariarathes IV of Cappadocia and Mithridates, perhaps one of Antiochus Ill's rebel satraps in Armenia, extended Eumenes' influence across the Halys River into central and eastern Anatolia.[1]

Although intended to stabilize the new order in Anatolia, the aggrandizement of Pergamum had exactly the opposite effect. Eumenes' gains had been at the expense of Bithynia and Pontus, and two wars involving almost a decade of fighting were required before they accepted the settlement of 188. The first, which broke out soon after 188 and lasted until 183, pitted Eumenes against Prusias I of Bithynia and his ally, the Galatian dynast Ortiagon.[2] Its course and

---

[*] This study was originally prepared as my contribution to a National Endowment for the Humanities Summer Seminar on the topic of 'Roman Imperialism', conducted by Prof. William V. Harris at Columbia University in the summer of 1979. A revised version of it was delivered to the 1980 meeting of the Pacific Coast Branch of the American Historical Association, held at the University of Southern California in Los Angeles. I should like to express my thanks to Prof. Harris, and to Prof. R. Mellor, Prof. E. Gruen and Prof. C. Habicht for their comments on earlier drafts, and, in particular, to the editor and readers of the *American Journal of Ancient History* and to Prof. Robert K. Sherk for their suggestions, which were of great value in the preparation of the final text. First published in the *American Journal of Ancient History* 5 (1980), 1–12.

[1] For a detailed analysis, see Liebman-Frankfort 1969, 41–75. For the reading *Halys* at Livy 38. 3. 8, see Liebmann-Frankfort 1969, 50–64.

[2] Trogus (Prologue 32) includes Pharnaces I of Pontus among the allies of Prusias. This has been denied, most recently by Walbank 1979, 254 *ad* 24. 1. 2; but strongly defended by Hopp 1977, 41, n. 37.

324   PART II: ARTICLES

significance have recently been clarified by Christian Habicht in two studies.[3] At the root of the war was Prusias' refusal to accept the decision of Cn. Manlius Vulso awarding Phrygia Epictetus to Eumenes, in defiance of promises made to him by the Scipios in 190 in order to gain his neutrality in the war against Antiochus III. The war ended in 183 with Prusias' acceptance of the settlement of 188, as a result of a combination of Pergamene military victories and strong Roman diplomatic pressure exerted in the form of an embassy to Bithynia headed by T. Quinctius Flamininus. Much, however, remains unclear about its sequel, the Pontic War, about Rome's role in bringing it to an end and especially about its implications for Roman relations with Eumenes of Pergamum in the late 180s.

I. The Pontic War

Prior to the winter of 183/2 Roman contact with Pontus was limited. Despite a marital alliance with the Seleucids, Pontus had avoided direct involvement in the campaign of 190, and this, combined with the kingdom's remote location, probably accounts for its being unaffected by the Peace of Apamea.[4] The Senate, therefore, can hardly have anticipated the arrival in Rome in the winter of 183/2 of three separate embassies from Rhodes, Eumenes, and Pharnaces I of Pontus, all seeking Senatorial intervention in Pontic affairs.[5]

The Rhodians had come to Rome at the behest of the citizens of Sinope. Annexation of the Greek cities of the Paphlagonian coast had been a goal of the Pontic kings since achieving full independence in 281. Amastris and Amisus had been occupied in the third century but the great prize was Sinope.[6] An earlier attack on the city by Mithridates II in 220 had been foiled by Rhodian intervention,[7] and now again the Sinopeans had turned to Rhodes for aid, when Pharnaces took advantage of the distraction of the Bithynian War and its aftermath to seize the city in 183.[8]

While the nature of the Rhodian complaint against Pharnaces is clear, the opposite is true of the embassies from Eumenes and Pharnaces. Polybius (23. 9. 3) only refers to 'matters in dispute between the kings' without specifying exactly what questions the kings had agreed to submit to the Senate for

---

[3] Habicht 1956, 90–100; 1957.

[4] Ed. Meyer 1879, 71; Reinach 1895, 34. For marital relations between Pontus and the Seleucids, see Seibert 1967, 118–19.

[5] Polybius 23 .9. 1–3; Livy 40. 2. 6, 8. For the date, see Walbank 1979, 254 *ad* 24. 1. 2.

[6] Memnon *FGrH* 3B, 434 F9. 4 for Amastris and F 16. 2 for Amisus.

[7] Polybius 4. 56.

[8] Strabo 23. 3. 11. For the date, see Walbank 1979, 227 *ad* 23. 9. 2.

THE AFTERMATH OF THE PEACE OF APAMEA: ROME AND THE PONTIC WAR   325

judgment. In view, however of the prominence of Galatia in the Pontic War and in the treaty of 179 ending it, and of the possibility that Pharnaces had hereditary claims in the area,[9] it is possible that the points at issue were conflicting territorial claims in Galatia resulting from Eumenes' successful extension of Pergamene authority over the region in 183. Be that as it may, the Senate informed the embassies that a commission of inquiry[10] would visit the area to examine the Sinopean problem and the issues in dispute between the kings.

The commissioners' mission, however, was unsuccessful since serious fighting had already broken out in Cappadocia even before their arrival on the scene in the spring of 182.[11] Equally unsuccessful was a second commission of inquiry dispatched – in response to new embassies in the winter of 182/1 from Eumenes, Anarathes and Pharnaces – with instructions to investigate the matter more thoroughly: fighting in 181 spread from Cappadocia into Galatia, where Pharnaces succeeded in detaching two Galatian dynasts, Cassignatus and Gaizatorigus, from Eumenes. A truce between Eumenes and Pharnaces for the purpose of requesting decisive action by the Senate to end the war likewise had no effect, as a Pontic offensive in the winter of 180 extended the war deeper into Galatia and Paphlagonia, where Pharnaces' general Leocritus seized from Eumenes the coastal city of Tium.[12] The winter of 180, however, marked the peak of Pharnaces' success. A Pergamene counter-offensive in the spring of 180, which regained for Eumenes the territory lost in Galatia the year before, was followed by a joint invasion of Pontus itself by the forces of Eumenes and Ariarathes. Only the urging of the new Roman commissioners that nothing be done to prejudice their attempts at a negotiated settlement prevented the allies from forcing a decisive military confrontation on Pharnaces. When the Pontic ambassadors rejected the terms offered to their master at a Roman-sponsored peace conference at Pergamum in 180, however, fighting resumed. An attempt to deprive Pharnaces of supplies by closing the Hellespont to navigation failed because of Rhodian opposition, but a new Pergamene drive into Pontus in the spring of 179, supported by both Prusias II of Bithynia

[9] Suggested by Hopp (1977, 45) and Staehelin (1907, 63, n. 3), on the basis of Justin 38. 5. 3. *Cf.* Polybius 25. 2. 3–4.

[10] Only the *praenomen* of its leader, Marcus, is known (Polybius 24. 1. 2; *cf.* Walbank 1979, 254 *ad* 24. 1. 2).

[11] The main sources for the war are Polybius (24. 1. 1–3; 5. 1–8, 14–15; 25. 1. 1–15; 27. 7. 5) and Diodorus (29. 22–24). For reconstructions of it, see Meyer 1879, 71–80; Hopp 1977, 44–48; and Olshausen 1978, 410–14.

[12] Diodorus 29. 23. For the date, see Walbank 1979, 267 *ad* 24. 14. 1 and Ed. Meyer 1879, 74. Ἀποδοῦναι in Polybius 25. 2. 7 can only mean that Pharnaces seized Tium from Eumenes (*cf.* Ernst Meyer 1925, 149–51).

326   PART II: ARTICLES

and Ariarathes, forced the now-isolated Pontic king to sue for peace,[13] a peace which was concluded by a treaty whose text is preserved by Polybius.[14]

With his enemies encamped in Pontus, Pharnaces had little choice but to accept terms which reflected the decisiveness of Eumenes' victory Basically the treaty required a restoration of the *status quo ante* at Pharnaces' expense, in effect, a recognition by him of the Peace of Apamea and the concession of all questions in dispute between him and Eumenes. All his gains in the interior of Paphlagonia and Cappadocia were to be surrendered in the condition in which he found them, and he was to withdraw from Galatia, sever all existing relations with Galatian dynasts and desist from any future activity in the region. He was to bear the costs of the war and give hostages as a pledge of his intention to abide by the treaty. Of his once-considerable conquests, his victors allowed Pharnaces to retain only Sinope and probably her two colonies of Cerasus and Cotyora;[15] but then the fate of that unfortunate city had been the particular interest of Rhodes, and after her break with Eumenes in 180, it is not surprising if he in turn abandoned her ally. Otherwise, however, Pharnaces emerged from the war stripped of the bulk of his gains and financially embarrassed.[16]

II. ROMAN DIPLOMACY IN THE PONTIC WAR

Rome's role in the Pontic War, it would seem, was singularly inglorious, with the dispatch of three commissions of inquiry, each with more comprehensive instructions and goals than its predecessor and each totally ineffective.[17] Only decisive action by Eumenes brought the war to an end, a fact which would at first glance seem to justify Roger McShane's emphasis on the success of

[13] Pharnaces did unsuccessfully attempt, with an offer of a 500-talent payment, to induce Seleucus IV to come to his aid (Diodorus 29. 2. 4; Polybius F 96 [BW], with Walbank 1979, 274 *ad* 25. 2. 14). For the date, see Meyer 1879, 79. Scholars often ascribe Seleucus' refusal to direct Roman intervention (*cf.*, for example, Liebmann-Frankfort 1969, 77; Will 1967, 143; and Magie 1950 I, 192); but this is unlikely, since Diodorus mentions no embassy, but only ascribes his action to reflection on the consequences (ἔννοιαν δέ λαβών) of his breaking the Peace of Apamea, consequences that are likely to have been pointed out to him in 183 when Flamininus visited him (Polybius 23. 5. 1).

[14] Polybius 25. 2. 3–14.

[15] Pharnaces' retention of Sinope is implied by Strabo 13. 3. 11. His possession of Cerasus and Cotyora is indicated by their synoecism into his eponymous city of Pharnakeia (*cf.* Herrmann 1938, 1848 for full references).

[16] For Pharnaces' financial problems in the decades after the Pontic War, see *OGIS* 771. 16–20 with Dittenberger's note *ad loc.*

[17] *Cf.* Hopp 1977, 46, who characterizes them as 'symbolisch'. The weakness of the commissions as diplomatic tools in general is noted by Sherwin-White (1977, 66), who, however, also points to the Senate's willingness to intervene to preserve the *status quo* in Anatolian affairs.

THE AFTERMATH OF THE PEACE OF APAMEA: ROME AND THE PONTIC WAR   327

Pergamene military and diplomatic action independent of Rome as the most significant aspect of the entire episode.[18]

In truth the apparent ineptness of Roman action in this war is surprising, especially since the list of combatants indicates that the prolongation of the conflict led to the involvement in it of participants from the whole of the Anatolian peninsula, while the inclusion in the treaty of 179 of *adscripti*[19] from Armenia and the north and west coasts of the Black Sea[20] indicates a concern for its settlement throughout the Black Sea basin. Clearly, continuation of the war carried with it the potential of disrupting the new regime in Anatolia established by the Peace of Apamea. In these circumstances it is understandable that scholars have seen, in the seeming lack of effective Roman support for Eumenes, evidence of a fundamental change in the Senate's attitude toward the Pergamene monarch. F.W. Walbank[21] has observed that 'the Senate let the war drag on for four years… ; perhaps they were not averse to seeing Eumenes checked'; while Edouard Will[22] has gone even further and suggested that the Senate actually welcomed the expansion of Pontus as a counter-balance to the power of Pergamum. As confirmation of their interpretation of the duplicitous character of Roman diplomacy in the Pontic War, both Walbank and Will point to *IOSPE* 1[2] 402, an inscription from Chersonesus Taurica published by R. Loeper in 1908 and dated by him to the late spring of 179:

> […] but we shall attempt to preserve his ki]ngd[om to the best of our ability so long as he remains in friendship] with us and preserves friendship [with the Rom]ans and does [nothin]g against them. May all be well with us if we do not violate our oath and the opposite if we do. This oath was sworn on the fifteenth day of the month Herakleios when Apollodorus son of Herogeiton was king and Herodotus son of Herodotus secretary.
> The oath which king Pharnaces swore when Matris and Heracleius went on embassy to him. I swear by Zeus, Ge, Helius and all the Olympian gods and goddesses. I will be a friend to the Chersonesites for all time. If the neighboring barbarians march against Chersonesus or the territory ruled by Chersonesus or injure the Chersonesites and they summon me, I will come to their aid if I can, and I will not plot against the Chersonesites nor will I do anything against the Chersonesites which might harm the Chersonesites, but I will attempt to preserve the democracy to the best of my ability so long as they remain in friendship with

---

[18] McShane 1964, 163.

[19] For *adscripti* as interested non-belligerents, see Bickermann 1932. The sources for the Pontic War provide no support for Dahlheim's thesis (1968, 209–17) that they are secondary belligerents with whom peace has to be made for a war to be completely ended.

[20] As *adscripti* Polybius (25. 2. 12–14) lists in Asia Artaxias, the ruler of most of Armenia, and Acusilochus, and in Europe the Sarmatian Gatalus; as well as the free cities of Heraclea Pontica, Chersonesus Taurica, Mesembria and Cyzicus.

[21] Walbank 1979, 277 *ad* 23. 9. 3.

[22] Will 1967, 243–44.

328   PART II: ARTICLES

me and swear the same oath and preserve friendship with the Romans and do nothing against them. May all be well with me if I do not violate my oath and the opposite if I do. This oath was sworn in the one hundred fifty-seventh year, in the month Daisios, on king Pharnaces' year-count.

IOSPE 1² 402 contains the oaths exchanged by Chersonesus and Pharnaces in ratifying an *epimachia* or defensive alliance. Each pledges aid to the other in case of attack, provided they have maintained *philia* not only between themselves but also with Rome, and, most significantly, have committed no acts prejudicial to Roman interests. The reference to *philia* with Rome and the emphasis on the primacy of Roman interests in the oath formulae clearly point to both Chersonesus and Pharnaces being Roman clients at the time of the treaty's negotiation,[23] a fact which is of particular interest, since it is likely that both Chersonesus and her metropolis, Heraclea Pontica – both *adscripti* to the treaty of 179 and the latter an ally of Rome's as well[24] – were sympathetic to Pharnaces and not to Eumenes during the Pontic War.[25] In 179, it would seem, Rome effected a reconciliation with Pharnaces and approved of military cooperation in the future between him and one of the states friendly to him during the Pontic War. This, together with the lack of apparent opposition to his continued occupation of Sinope and her colonies, and the blunting of Eumenes' offensive in 180 by the Senate's commissioners, would appear to provide strong support for the theory that Rome's dilatory diplomacy reflected a Roman 'tilt' toward Pharnaces as a result of a 'cooling', to use Walbank's phrase,[26] of the relations between the Senate and Eumenes.

Despite the attractiveness of this interpretation, particularly in the light of the worsening of relations between Rome and Pergamum in the 160s,[27] it is both

---

[23] Clearly the traditional picture of Pharnaces as consistently intransigent in dealing with Rome (*cf.*, for example, Badian 1958, 99; and Sherwin-White 1977, 64, n. 15) must be revised to take account of *IOSPE* 1² 402 (*cf.* Olshausen 1978, 414).

[24] Memnon *FGrH* 3B, 434 F18. 10; for the circumstances, see Janke 1963, 31–32.

[25] Scholars usually assign the Greek *adscripti* to Eumenes and the non-Greek to Pharnaces (*cf.*, for example, Will 1967, 243; Liebmann-Frankfort 1969, 81–82; and Dahlheim 1968, 215, n. 85). In the case of Chersonesus this has been based on the arbitrary belief that the allusion to attacks by neighboring barbarians in *IOSPE* 1² 402. 14–16 refers to attacks by Gatalus made at the behest of Pharnaces, instead of to the well-documented threat to the city posed by her Scythian and Taurian neighbors (*IOSPE* 1² 401. 12; 343. 14; 352 *passim*; 353; *cf.* Hopp 1977, 47, n. 71, and Walbank 1979, 273 *ad* 25. 2. 13). Relations between Chersonesus and her metropolis Heraclea Pontica, however, were close throughout her history (Seibert 1963, 160–88); and two items strongly point to Heraclea's hostility toward Eumenes during the Pontic War: Eumenes' attempt to close the Hellespont to navigation (which would certainly hurt Heraclea) and his return to Tium to Prusias II after the war (Polybius 25. 2. 7), which would enable him to threaten the city from both the east and the west, as had his father Prusias I (*cf.* Memon *FGrH* 3B, 434 F19. 1; De Sanctis 1923, 264).

[26] Walbank 1979, 257 *ad* 24. 5. 1, and *cf.* his remarks at 254 *ad* 24. 1. 3.

[27] *Cf.* Hopp 1977, 57–58 and McShane 1964, 182–86 for details.

THE AFTERMATH OF THE PEACE OF APAMEA: ROME AND THE PONTIC WAR   329

unlikely and unsupported by the evidence. Polybius and Justin[28] together allow no doubt that Roman diplomatic support for Pergamum during the Pontic War was both strong and consistent. The report of the first commission of inquiry was wholly supportive of Eumenes' position and condemned Pharnaces' aggressive behavior.[29] The embassy of Eumenes' brother Attalus in the winter of 181/0 was well received by the Senate,[30] and the refusal of Pharnaces' ambassadors to accept the terms offered by the Roman commissioners at the peace conference at Pergamum in 180, after their master's explicit promise to do so, is explicable only on the assumption that they were perceived as being too favorable to Eumenes – as indeed they are likely to have been, since the treaty of 179, which presumably reflects them, favors Pergamum and its allies on all significant points in contention in Anatolia save the fate of Sinope.[31] Most importantly, however, *IOSPE* 1[2] 402, the one supposedly contemporary document assumed to reflect Roman partiality toward Pharnaces, actually points to the opposite conclusion.

The interpretation of *IOSPE* 1[2] 402 as indicating Roman sympathy toward Pharnaces is based solely on the belief that it is dated according to an otherwise unattested Pontic era beginning with the accession of Mithridates of Cius in 336, so that Daisios of year 157 would fall in the late spring of 179. This dating was proposed by the inscription's first editor, R. Loeper,[32] and accepted by subsequent scholars,[33] because a dating according to the more familiar Pontic era beginning in 297[34] was impossible since Pharnaces was dead by year 157 of that era. Although generally accepted, Loeper's interpretation was seriously flawed from the beginning: first, because it assumed that the accession of Mithridates of Cius was an epochal event in Pontic history, when Pontic tradition ignored him and traced the fortunes of the dynasty to the establishment of Mithridates I Ctistes as ruler in northern Cappadocia in 302;[35] and second, because it seriously distorted the evidence of Diodorus on the chronology of the rulers of Cius. Loeper's dating implies that Mithridates

---

[28] Justin 38. 6. 2: *Sic et avum suum Pharnacen per cognitionum arbitria succidaneum regi Pergameno Eumeni datum.* For the interpretation of this text, see Niese 1903, 74, n. 5.

[29] Polybius 24. 1. 2–3.

[30] Diodorus 29. 22.

[31] Polybius 24. 15. 11.

[32] Loeper's argumentation is known to me only through its summary by Diel 1938, 1850–51; and Rostovtzeff 1932, 217–18.

[33] The literature on *IOSPE* 1[2] 402 is summarized by Perl 1968, 301, n. 10.

[34] For the Pontic era, see Perl 1968, 300–05.

[35] Plutarch *Demetrius* 4. 4; Appian *Mith.* 9. The significance of this point was brought to my attention by Mr. Brian McGing of the Department of Classics of the University of Dublin. The attempt by Rostovtzeff (1932, 218) to strengthen the theory by assigning one of the five royal tombs at Amasia (*cf.* Reinach 1895, 288) to Mithridates of Cius is unconvincing; more likely the five tombs are for Mithridates I, Ariobarzanes, Mithridates II and Pharnaces I, with the fifth ruler

330 PART II: ARTICLES

became ruler of Cius in 336/5, while Diodorus clearly places his accession in the year 337/6, which would result in a date of spring, 180[36] (not spring, 179) for the Chersonesus treaty. This is a manifest improbability since the treaty suggests friendly relations between Pharnaces and Rome, while spring, 180 is precisely the period of the strongest and most open Roman support of Pharnaces' enemy Eumenes. Evasion of this difficulty by redating Mithridates' accession to 336/5, however, is difficult, as Diodorus' dates for the dynasty of Cius are internally consistent, so that alteration of that for Mithridates of Cius would be justified only if there were strong evidence, which there is not, that Diodorus systematically antedated by one year the reigns of all the rulers of that dynasty.[37] Clearly, an interpretation which does not require such gross distortions of the sources is desirable, and evidence pointing to one exists.

In 1902 Loeper also published an inscription of Pharnaces' son Mithridates V, found at Ineboli (ancient Abonuteichos) in Paphlagonia and dated to 1 Dios of year 161 of an era which was naturally assumed to be the known Pontic era beginning in 297 BC, or, in other words, to the fall of the year 137/6 BC.[38] Despite its paradoxical implication that year 161, in the reign of Mithridates V, was not four but 42 years later than year 157, still in the reign of his father Pharnaces, publication of *IOSPE* 1[2] 402 did not lead to a serious reconsideration of Loeper's dating of the Ineboli inscription.

Nevertheless, it has long been clear that an alternative dating of the Ineboli inscription by the Seleucid era of 312/11 was possible.[39] On that assumption it would date from fall, 152 BC, a date that is fully compatible with the known fact that in 149 Mithridates V had already been king of Pontus for an unknown period of time.[40] By the same system *IOSPE* 1[2] 402 would date to spring, 155, thus eliminating both the historical and the source problems posed by the accepted dating of this inscription, and the puzzling 42-year gap between year 157 in the reign of Pharnaces and year 161 in the reign of his son Mithridates V.

---

being Mithridates III, whose reign should be inserted between those of Mithridates II and Pharnaces (Ed. Meyer 1879, 54–56; Magie 1950 II, 1088, n. 39).

[36] The alternatives are clearly stated by Walbank 1979, 20.

[37] As assumed by Perl (1968, 306, n. 33). The key passages are Diodorus 15. 90. 3, 16. 90. 2 and 20. 111. 4; for their interpretation, see Ed. Meyer 1879, 34–38.

[38] Cited according to the edition of Théodore Reinach (1905, 114–15). It is clear from Reinach's remark (118) that the date 161 must certainly be reckoned according to the 'royal Pontic era' that this was only an unconfirmed assumption. In fact, the 'royal Pontic era' is not attested before the 90s BC (*cf.* Perl 1968, 300–01).

[39] *Cf.* Rostovtzeff 1932, 217.

[40] Appian *Mith.* 10. Perl (1968, 301, n. 10), erroneously dates his accession to 149.

THE AFTERMATH OF THE PEACE OF APAMEA: ROME AND THE PONTIC WAR 331

Is this solution possible? Opposition has relied on two assumptions, which are now known to be erroneous: namely, that Pharnaces died in 170;[41] and that Polybius 33. 12. 1 indicated that his successor, Mithridates IV, was already king in the winter of 156/5.[42] In fact Polybius 33. 12. 1 refers to events of winter, 155/4,[43] and hence does not preclude Pharnaces' still being king in the spring of 155, while *OGIS* 771 reveals Pharnaes as still alive in the spring of 159[44] and, moreover, gives a plausible reason for his adopting the Seleucid era, since it refers to his recent renewal of the marital alliance between his house and the Seleucids through his marriage to Nysa, the daughter or grand-daughter of Antiochus III.[45] For these reasons, therefore, the dating of *IOSPE* 1^2 402 to the spring of 179 should be abandoned, and with it Loeper's hypo-thetical Pontic era of 336 BC. The inscription should be redated according to the Seleucid era to the spring of 155, 24 years later.

The theory that the apparent ineffectiveness of Roman diplomacy in the Pontic War reflected Roman displeasure with Eumenes and sympathy for Pharnaces rested ultimately on the belief that *IOSPE* 1^2 402 proved the existence of close relations between Rome and Pharnaces when the treaty of 179 was singed. Dating of this inscription to the spring of 155 – that is, to a period known to be marked by good relations between Rome and Pergamum[46] – materially alters its significance. It does attest to the establishment of *philia* between Rome and Pharnaces sometime between the end of the Pontic War and 155,[47] but that by itself is neither surprising nor indicative of a change in relations between Rome and Pergamum in the late 180s, since by signing the treaty of 179 Pharnaces signaled his acceptance of the terms of the Peace of Apamea, and in so doing removed the principal obstacle to friendship with Rome. What is striking, how-ever, is that when Pharnaces and Chersonesus did negotiate, in 155, an alliance they believed only so long as both sides maintained *philia* with Rome, and hence useless in the event Pharnaces should attempt to attack Pergamum or her allies.

---

[41] The belief that Pharnaces died in 170 rested on the assumption that Polybius 27. 17 was part of the obituary notice on him (*cf.* Ed. Meyer 1879, 81; Reinach 1895, 27, n. 4).

[42] E.g. Reinach 1895, 36; Rostovtzeff 1932, 218; Magie 1950 II, 1090, n. 46.

[43] *Cf.* Habicht 1956, 107 and Walbank 1977, 555 *ad* 33. 12. 1.

[44] For the dating of the archonship of Tychandros to 160/59 and hence of *OGIS* 771 to that year, see Ferguson 1932, 145; and Walbank 1979, 318 *ad* 27. 17.

[45] *OGIS* 771. 28–29. Daughter: Walbank 1977, 318 *ad* 27. 17. Granddaughter: Mørkholm 1966, 54; Seibert 1967, 69. The appearance of months Dios and Daisios in the Abonuteichos stele and *IOSPE* 1^2 402 indicates adoption of the Seleucid calendar by the kings of Pontus (*cf.* Reinach 1905, 119).

[46] For details, see McShane 1964, 186–92; and Sherwin-White 1977, 62–63.

[47] Appian *Mith.* 10, it is true, claims that Mithridates V was the first Pontic king to be a *philos* of Rome, but he is clearly mistaken, since Mithridates IV was already a *philos* of Rome, as Mellor (1978, 326–27) showed.

332   PART II: ARTICLES

IOSPE 1² 402 thus provides no evidence of a 'cooling' of Roman relations with Eumenes during the Pontic War. Quite the contrary. In the treaty of 179 Eumenes consolidated the gains he had made in the Peace of Apamea by forcing Pharnaces to accept the borders of the various Anatolian states as defined by Manlius Vulso and his colleagues in 188,[48] and *IOSPE* 1² 402 reveals that 24 years later Pharnaces' freedom of action in northern Anatolia was still restricted by the terms of the treaty of 179.

Viewed in this light, Roman diplomacy in the Pontic War was neither notably inept nor hostile to the interests of Pergamum. There was, moreover, no reason for the Senate to be displeased with its results: Rome avoided direct military involvement in the conflict, while Eumenes, the principal champion of her settlement of Anatolia, enforced recognition of the Peace of Apamea on Pontus, the one power not include in it, and thereby stabilized relations in northern Anatolia for much of the next half-century.[49] The price was recognition of Pharnaces' annexation of Sinope and her colonies, but so long as he abided by the terms of the treaty of 179, Rome raised no objection to that or to his other activities in the Black Sea basin.[50] Roman tolerance, however, was not unlimited. Thus, while she ignored the annexation of the Crimean cities by Mithridates VI later in the century,[51] war and ultimately the destruction of his kingdom followed Mithridates' refusal to adhere to the restraints imposed by the treaty of 179 on Pontic activity in central and northern Anatolia.[52]

BIBLIOGRAPHY

Badian, E. 1958: *Foreign Clientelae 264–70 BC* (Oxford).
Bickermann, E. 1932: 'Rom und Lampsakos'. *Philologus* 87, 278–83.
Dahlheim, W. 1968: *Struktur und Entwicklung des römischen Vökerrechts im dritten und zweiten Jahrhundert v. Chr.* (Vestigia 8) (Munich).
De Sanctis, G. 1923: *Storia dei Romani* 4.1 (Turin).
Diel, E. 1938: 'Pharnakes'. *RE* 19, 1850–51.
Desideri, P. 1973: 'Posidonio e la Guerra mitridatica'. *Athenaeum* 51, 3–29, 237–69.

---

[48] Pointed out by Liebmann-Frankfort 1969, 80.

[49] Broken only by the Bithyno-Pergamene war of the mid-150s, on which see now Habicht 1956, 101–10.

[50] For evidence of Pharnaces' diplomatic activity on the west coast of the Black Sea, see *IGBR* I² 40 with G. Mihailov's comments *ad loc.* (p. 89).

[51] Strabo 7. 4. 3; *IOSPE* 1² 352.

[52] For the background to the First Mithridatic War, see now Sherwin-White 1977, 70–75 and Glew 1977, 380–404. According to Appian (*Mith.* 43), Sulla ignored Nicomedes IV's charge that Pontic expansion in the Crimea violated the Peace of Apamea (*cf.* Desideri 1973, 3, n. 3) and confirmed Mithridates' possession of those territories in the Peace of Dardanus (Appian *Mith.* 55 with 58 and 64).

THE AFTERMATH OF THE PEACE OF APAMEA: ROME AND THE PONTIC WAR 333

Ferguson, W.S. 1932: *Athenian Tribal Cycles in the Hellenistic Age* (Cambridge, MA).

Glew, D.G. 1977: 'Mithridates Eupator Rome: A study of the background of the First Mithridatic War'. *Athenaeum* 65, 380–404.

Habicht, C. 1956: 'Über die Kriege zwischen Pergamon und Bithynien'. *Hermes* 84, 90–110.

—. 1957: 'Prusias I'. *RE* 23.1, 1098–1103.

Herrmann, A. 1938: 'Pharnakeia'. *RE* 19, 1848.

Hopp, J. 1977: *Untersuchungen zur Geschichte der letzten Attaliden* (Vestigia 25) (Munich).

Janke, M. 1963: *Historische Untersuchungen zu Memnon von Herakleia Kap. 18–40, FGrHist. Nr. 434* (Dissertation, Würzburg).

Liebman-Frankfort, T. 1969: *La frontière orientale dans la politique extérieure de la République romaine* (Brussels).

McShane, R.B. 1964: *The Foreign Policy of the Attalids of Pergamum* (Urbana).

Magie, D. 1950: *Roman Rule in Asia Minor: to the End of the Third Century after Christ*, 2 vols. (Princeton).

Mellor, R. 1978: 'The dedications on the Capitoline hill'. *Chiron* 8, 319–30.

Meyer, Eduard 1879: *Geschichte des Königreichs Pontos* (Leipzig).

Meyer, Ernst 1925: *Die Grenzen der hellenistischen Staaten in Kleinasien* (Zürich).

Mørkholm, O. 1966: *Antiochus IV of Syria* (Copenhagen).

Niese, B. 1903: *Geschichte der griechischen und makedonischen Staaten seit der Schlacht bei Chaeronea 3: Von 188 bis 120 v. Chr.* (Gotha).

Olshausen, E. 1978: 'Pontos'. *RE* Suppl. 15, 396–442.

Perl, G. 1968: 'Zur Chronologie der Königreiche Bithynia, Pontos und Bosporos'. In Harmatta, J. (ed.), *Studien zur Geschichte und Philosophie des Altertums* (Amsterdam), 299–330.

Reinach, T. 1895: *Mithridates Eupator König von Pontos* (Leipzig).

—. 1905: 'A Stele from Abonuteichos'. *NC* ser. 4, 5, 113–19.

Rostovtzeff, M.I. 1932: 'Pontus and its Neighbours: The First Mithridatic War'. *CAH* IX, 211–60.

Seibert, J. 1963: *Metropolis und Apoikie; historische Beiträge zur Geschichte ihrer gegenseitigen Beziehungen* (Dissertation, Würzburg).

—. 1967: *Historische Beiträge zu den dynastischen Verbindungen in hellenistischer Zeit* (*Historia* Einzelschriften 10) (Wiesbaden).

Sherwin-White, A.N. 1977: 'Roman involvement in Anatolia, 167–88 B.C.'. *Journal of Roman Studies* 67, 62–75.

Staehelin, F. 1907: *Geschichte der kleinasiatischen Galater bis zur Errichtung der römischen Provinz Asia*, 2nd ed. (Leipzig).

Walbank, F.W. 1979: *A Historical Commentary on Polybius*, vol. 3 (Oxford).

Will, E. 1967: *Histoire politique du monde hellénistique, 323–30 av. J.-C.*, 2 vols. (Nancy).

GO-BETWEENS AND THE GREEK CITIES
OF THE BLACK SEA[*]

The growth in World History at the expense of Western Civilization since the 1980s has been nothing short of remarkable. Inevitably, however, the process has been uneven with many important topics being incompletely reformulated in World historical terms, and much of the old Western Civilization framework surviving in the new courses and, of course, the textbooks even to the present. A good example is ancient Greece where Classical Athens remains the center of most accounts instead of increased emphasis being placed on topics involving interconnections between Greeks and non-Greeks.[1] Particularly striking is the lack of attention given to the frontiers of the Greek world such as the Black Sea and the accommodations Greeks had to make to survive there.

At first glance this is surprising. Greek settlement in the Black Sea was part of one of the most extraordinary migrations in ancient history, a migration that began about the middle of the 8th century BC and continued for over 200 years. The causes of this emigration of Greeks from their Aegean homeland are disputed: land hunger, trade, and refuge from expanding imperial powers such as Lydia and Persia have all been suggested. What is not in doubt, however, is the result. When the waves of emigration finally ended about 500 BC, the area of Greek settlement had expanded from the Aegean to cover a vast area that extended from eastern Spain in the west to the mouth of the Don River in the east.[2]

The Black Sea was the last major area settled by the Greeks. Various Greek cities from the west coast of modem Turkey and southern Greece founded colonies in the area. The most prominent, however, was Miletus, which ancient sources credited with 70 colonies including Odessus, modem Varna, Olbia at the mouth of the Bug River, Panticapaeum in the Crimea, and Sinope, modem Sinop, in northern Turkey. Unlike the Mediterranean, where the Phoenicians proved to be formidable competitors for prime settlement sites, the Greeks had no rivals in the Black Sea so that by the end of the 6th century BC, the Black

---

[*] An earlier version of this paper was delivered at the 2012 meeting of the World History Association in Albuquerque, New Mexico. First published in *World History Connected* 10.3 (October 2013 [electronic]).

[1] The problems involved in rethinking ancient history in terms of World History are discussed in Burstein 2007.

[2] The standard account of Greek colonization is Boardman 1999.

336   PART II: ARTICLES

Sea was almost entirely ringed by prosperous Greek cities that were equipped
with fine public buildings and linked to each other, their non-Greek neighbors,
and their Aegean homelands by steadily growing ties of trade.

At this point the story of the Greeks in the Black Sea as told in textbooks
usually ends, although, of course, history did not. The reasons are threefold.
The first is simple inertia, the reluctance to rethink the traditional Aegean centered narrative of Greek history to fit a world historical framework. The second is disciplinary. The bulk of the evidence for the later history of the Black
Sea in antiquity is archaeological and epigraphical, and the relevant scholarship is in unfamiliar languages: Russian, Romanian, and Bulgarian to name
only the most important. The third and final reason is politics. During the Cold
War Western scholars did not have easy access to archaeological sites and
museum collections in Eastern Europe and the Soviet Union and scholars on
both sides of the 'Iron Curtain' had great difficulty in obtaining the publications of their opposite numbers.[3]

The result was a view of the history of the Black Sea that foregrounded the
activity of the Greeks and limited the role of their 'barbarian' neighbors to
being passive recipients of Greek cultural influences that still survives in the
few World History textbooks that treat the topic.[4] Two examples will suffice.
So, according to *Worlds Together, Worlds Apart*[5] 'Whether they wished it or
not ... the Scythians to the north of the Black Sea, who were living in nomadic
bands, isolated settlements, and small villages became integrated into the
expanding cities' networks of violence, conquest, and trade.' The story in
Traditions & Encounters[6] is fuller but essentially the same:

> During the eighth and seventh centuries B.C.E., Greeks ventured into the Black
> Sea in large numbers and established colonies all along its shores. These settle-
> ments offered merchants access to rich supplies of grain, fish, timber, honey, wax,
> gold, and amber as well as slaves captured in southern Russia and transported to
> markets in the Mediterranean... As Greek merchants brought wealth into these
> societies, local clan leaders built small states in ... the Crimean peninsula and
> southern Russia where trade was especially strong.

Interestingly, the same view of Greek-non-Greek relations was also common
in the Soviet Union. So, in F. Korovkin's prize-winning secondary school textbook, *History of the Ancient World*,[7] which went through 20 editions before

---

[3] Soviet scholarship on the ancient history of the Black Sea is surveyed in Shelov 1980.

[4] Of 13 world history textbooks I examined, only four included more than a bare mention of
Greek colonization of the Black Sea.

[5] Tignor *et al.* 2011, 196.

[6] Bentley and Ziegler 2008, 238–39.

[7] Korovkin 1985, 140.

being translated into English in 1985, students learned that 'trade also grew in the countries where the colonies arose and Greek culture spread there; local tribes moved more quickly from the primitive communal system to slave-owning society'. Meanwhile, however, the Cold War ended and the barriers inhibiting collaboration between Western and Eastern scholars collapsed, making possible the development of a new and very different view of relations between Greeks and non-Greeks in the ancient Black Sea.

Central to the new interpretation is recognition of an important truth: the Greek cities formed a thin fringe on the edges of a vast non-Greek world.[8] In the new view of Black Sea history the implications of that reality became clear in the 5th century BC with the emergence of powerful kingdoms in the hinterlands of the Greek cities of the west and north coasts of the Black Sea. The dominant state on the west coast of the Black Sea – essentially European Turkey, Bulgaria, and Romania – was the kingdom of the Odrysian Thracians, whose power extended by the late 5th century from the Propontis to the Danube and included both the tribes of the interior and the Greek cities of the Black Sea coast, all of whom paid tribute to the Odrysian high king. The extent of the Odrysian kingdom's wealth is unknown, but, according to the 5th-century Athenian historian Thucydides, the tribute alone was approximately equal to that realized by Athens from its empire at the beginning of the Peloponnesian War. Although detailed evidence concerning the relations between the Greek cities and the Odrysian overlords is lacking, it is likely that the burden of their tribute was offset by the protection afforded them against raids on their territory by neighboring tribes and increased trading privileges in the territories of the Odrysian kingdom.

The evidence for the north coast of the Black Sea is poorer than that for the west coast, but what there is suggests that the situation was similar with the central fact of life for the Greek cities being the pressure put on them by the kingdom of the Royal Scythians, which dominated the steppes of the southern Ukraine. Information about how the Scythians exerted their influence over the Greek cities of the northern Black Sea is limited. In the case of Olbia, however, it suggests that the Scythians first tried to rule the city through Greek tyrants, who were then replaced in the mid-5th century by resident administrators of Scythian origin. Be that as it may, with few exceptions, the over-riding reality for the Greek cities of the Black Sea was that in order to survive they had to find accommodations with their non-Greek neighbors by trading and intermarrying with them, and, most importantly, by seeking their protection. The dominant 'barbarian' populations that Greeks had to deal with – Thracians, Getes, Dacians, Scythians, or Sarmatians – may have changed over the

---

[8] Burstein 2006.

338 PART II: ARTICLES

centuries, but from the late 5th century BC to the early 2nd century AD, when the Roman conquest of the Dacians put an end to the last and greatest of the Pontic kingdoms, the negotiation and renegotiation of these accommodations were central to the life of the Black Sea Greek cities.

The most tangible evidence of the results of these negotiations are the splendid gold and bronze objects found in elite graves throughout the region that most likely were either diplomatic gifts or part of the cities' tribute payments instead of trade goods as was assumed in the old view of relations between the Greeks and their non-Greek neighbors.[9] The negotiations themselves, however, were only possible because of the services of individuals the Latin Americanist Alida C. Metcalf[10] calls 'go-betweens', men or women, who were facilitators of 'social interaction between worlds; translators, cultural brokers, negotiators'.

Unlike the go-betweens in early modem European empires, however, who were often socially marginal figures, and, therefore, invisible in the sources, despite the critical importance of their ability to live in two worlds and facilitate communication between them because of their fluency in multiple languages, the go-betweens in the ancient Black Sea usually were aristocrats. The reason is clear. The Black Sea Greeks were political dependents negotiating from positions of weakness with powerful kingdoms that were ruled by warrior aristocracies who would deal only with their social equals. Hence, go-betweens tended to be drawn from the upper classes of the Greek cities, particularly those with family connections to the Thracian and Scythian aristocracies.

The Athenian historian Thucydides, himself a member of such a family, gives an illuminating account of such an individual and his role in facilitating relations between Greeks and Thracians, noting that in the summer of 431 BC

> Nymphodorus son of Pythes, an Abderite, whose sister [sc. the Thracian king] Sitalces had married, was made their *proxenos* by the Athenians. They had hitherto considered him their enemy, but he had great influence with Sitalces, and they wished the prince to become their ally (Thucydides *History of the Peloponnesian War* 2. 29).[11]

Here the Athenians use a traditional Greek institution, *proxenia*, guest friendship with the moral obligation of watching over the city's interest, in the hope of gaining the support at the Thracian court of the king's influential Greek brother-in-law.

---

[9] *Cf.* Archibald 1994, 461–62.
[10] Metcalf 2005, 12.
[11] Trans. R. Crawley.

GO-BETWEENS AND THE GREEK CITIES OF THE BLACK SEA

The literary sources mention similar figures in the 4th century BC, but the heyday of the go-betweens in the Black Sea was the Hellenistic period, when attempts by the successor states of Alexander's empire to expand their influence in the region combined with renewed nomadic migrations in the Ukrainian steppes and the northern Balkans destabilized the Thracian and Scythian kingdoms on which the Greek cities depended for their security. Not surprisingly in view of the turbulent conditions throughout the Black Sea, decrees passed by Greek cities honoring such individuals are common. Some were courtiers, both Greek and non-Greek, like the Nymphodorus mentioned by Thucydides, whose influence the cities sought to gain through the award of honors like the *proxenia* and valuable privileges such as tax exemptions and guarantees of expedited court proceedings. More important, however, were individuals from the cities themselves whose ability to move in both Greek and non-Greek societies enabled them to function as brokers in negotiating the terms governing relations between the Greek cities and their non-Greek overlords. The best known of these figures is Agathocles, son of Antiphilus, from the city of Histria on the north coast of the Dobruja in modem Romania, whose career is outlined in a Histrian decree of the late 3rd or early 2nd century BC.[12]

The situation facing Histria as described in the Agathocles decree was not unusual in the Hellenistic Black Sea. Put simply, the city was trapped between the proverbial rock and hard place, caught in a power struggle between its overlord, the Getic king Rhemaxos, whose territory was located across the Danube in Dacia, and a Thracian dynast named Zoltes, who was trying to detach the Dobrujan cities from Rhemaxos by using his war-bands to intimidate them into paying tribute for the privilege of working their agricultural hinterlands.[13] As the decree indicates, Agathocles had to find a way to protect Hstria's interest by brokering a deal with Zoltes to guarantee the security of its farmland while not alienating the city's overlord Rhemaxos until the conflict between the two rival kings could be decided. Although the decree contains no dates, the process was clearly lengthy and complex. In the process Agathocles organized the city's defense against Zoltes' raiders on two occasions and undertook five separate embassies. Three were directed to Zoltes' camp during which Agathocles arranged for the ransom of flocks that had been rustled by the king's raiders while negotiating agreements to protect Histria's farmland. The other two involved long journeys through hostile territory to Rhemaxos' court to plead, ultimately successfully, for troops to protect Histria's territory. Much, of course, is left unsaid in the decree. What stands out, however, is that,

[12] Burstein 1985, no. 68.
[13] For the details, see Pippidi 1975.

340   PART II: ARTICLES

like all successful go-betweens, Agathocles' success in brokering deals between Histria and its powerful neighbors depended on his ability to function in two world, that of the Greek cities of the Dobruja and that of the royal courts of the Thracian and Getic states in their hinterlands, an ability that even allowed him to discover and frustrate a plot being hatched against Histria during one of his visits to Zoltes' camp.

The go-between system illustrated in the Agathocles decree is only one of the many features of the culture of the Greek cities of the Black Sea that set them apart from the more familiar cities of the Greek homeland. The hallmark of their political and cultural environment was intense and ongoing interaction between the Greek cities and the non-Greek peoples of their hinterlands. Although that interaction was often turbulent and dangerous as the Agathocles decree makes clear, it decisively shaped the life of the Black Sea cities. The result is most evident in art, where the empathy for Scythian life evident in the often spectacular gold objects found in Thracian and Scythian elite graves has no parallel in Aegean Greek art with its stereotyped portrayals of barbarian 'others'. It is also evident in their ready acceptance of intermarriage between Greeks and non-Greeks and their willingness to incorporate local deities in the pantheons of their cities and even to adopt elements of steppe dress such as leggings. Moreover, despite problems such as those between Histria and its Thracian and Getic neighbors, the cities clearly thought good relations with their 'barbarian' neighbors were worth cultivating both for the security they provided and the military support they could bring the cities when they were threatened by hostile neighbors such as Zoltes and his Thracians or powers from outside the region as, for example, happened when Olbia was attacked by one of Alexander's generals and rescued by Scythian forces. It is not surprising, therefore, that visitors to the Pontus from the Aegean homeland from Herodotus in the 5th century BC to the end of antiquity express a certain ambivalence about the Greekness of the society and culture of the Black Sea Greek cities.

BIBLIOGRAPHY

Archibald, Z.F. 1994: 'Thracians and Scythians'. *CAH* VI², 444–75.
Bentley, J.H. and Ziegler, H.F. 2008: *Traditions & Encounters: A Global Perspective on the Past*, 4th ed. (Boston).
Boardman, J. 1999: *The Greeks Overseas: Their Early Colonies and Trade*, 4th ed. (London).
Burstein, S.M. 1985: *The Hellenistic Age from the Battle of Ipsos to the Death of Kleopatra VII* (Cambridge).
—. 2006: 'The Greek Cities of the Black Sea'. In Kinzl, K. (ed.), *A Companion to the Classical Greek World* (Oxford), 137–52.

GO-BETWEENS AND THE GREEK CITIES OF THE BLACK SEA   341

—. 2007: 'Ancient History and the Challenge of World History'. *Syllecta Classsica* 18, 225–40.

Korovkin, F. 1985: *History of the Ancient World* (Moscow).

Metcalf, A.C. 2005: *Go-betweens and the Colonization of Brazil: 1500–1600* (Austin).

Pippidi, D.M. 1975: 'Istros et les Gètes au IIe siècle. Observations sur le décret en l'honneur d'Agathoclès, fils d'Antiphilos'. In Pippidi, D.M., *Scythica Minora: Recherches sur les colonies grecques du littoral roumain de la mer Noire* (Bucharest), 31–55.

Shelov, D.B. 1980: 'Der nördliche Schwarzmeerraum in der Antike (1977)'. In Heinen, H. (ed.), *Die Geschichte des Altertums im Spiegel der sowjetischen Forschung* (Darmstadt), 341–402.

Tignor, R. *et al.* 2011: *Worlds Together, Worlds Apart: A History of the World, from the Beginnings to the Present*, 3rd ed. (New York).

INDEX

Abderites, 338
Abonuteichos, 330
Achaeans, 92
Achaemenid (*see* Persia)
Acherousian Peninsula, 4, 29
Aconae port, 72
Aegean, 99, 127, 172, 213, 323
    art/culture, 215, 340
    Athens and, 87, 221
    basin, 94
    Black Sea area interactions/trade with, 23, 220, 222, 336
    Clearchus' personal reputation in, 119
    Delian League success in, 74
    grain source/trade, 227, 235, 237, 238
    Greeks' emigration from, 335
    Heraclea's communications/relations/ trade with, 82, 153, 172
    Lysimachus avoided involvement in affairs of, 308
    north, 34, 65, 236
    Pericles to strengthen position in, 76
    Pontus and, 84, 229
Aegospotami, 84, 87, 92, 238
Aelian, 31, 93, 124, 145, 155, 280, 281
Aeneas Tacticus, 54, 57, 72, 86, 99, 101, 104, 105, 107, 109, 113, 210, 273
    on Heraclea's *hekatostues*/tribes, 58, 59, 63
Aeolis, 66, 89, 213
Aeschines, 78, 83, 107, 108, 251, 252, 269, 273, 286
Aeschylus, 40, 73, 197
Agamemnon, 243
Agamestor, 39, 53
Agatharchides, 126
Agathocles, 174, 238, 304, 339, 340
    execution of, 166, 173, 303
Agenor, 32
Agesilaus, 94, 106
Akkadia, 203
Alcibiades, 83

Alexander, 166, 206, 280–82, 301, 307
    Apelles portrait of wielding a thunder-bolt, 281
    conquests of, 145, 204, 228
    death of, 147, 308
    empire of, 148–49, 157, 339
    histories of, 25, 144, 193, 208, 279
    invasions of, 143, 152, 210
    supports Heracleote exiles, 144–46, 295, 298
    victory in Battle of Granicus, 207
Alexander IV, 147
Alyatta, 50
Alyattes, 50
Amage, 255, 256
Amastris, 148, 154, 155, 175
    death of, 163, 173
    Dionysius and, 153, 156
    Lysimachus and, 158, 159
    regency of, 157–60
Amastris (city), 160–62, 166, 324
    autonomy tempered by royal gover-nor, 164–65
Amisus, 45, 47, 140, 144, 150, 226
    Athens and, 206, 221, 252
    Datames controls, 105, 210
    double founding of, 46, 75
    freed from Cappadocian ruler, 74–75
    known as Peiraieus, 221–22
    occupied in 3rd century, 324
    Persian authority in, 90
Ammianus Marcellinus, 31, 39, 44
Amphitheus, 5, 24, 25, 39, 199
amphorae (Heracleote, stamps, etc.), 3, 9, 10, 85, 123, 138, 161, 163, 166, 196, 226, 244
Amyclas, 93, 117
Amycus, 200
Amyntas I, 8, 9, 64
Amyntas III, 8, 64
Anarathes, 325
Anatolia, 6, 114, 162, 172, 214, 332

360s BC a dangerous period for, 105
Anabasis (Xenophon) on conditions in, 204
Arsinoe's power base in, 165
Cassander invades, 157
central, 30, 105, 106, 332
cities of northern, 27, 131, 204
Heraclea and northern, 131, 171, 196, 204, 226
Heraclea and western, 30, 94, 95
Heraclea's relations with, 29
invasions of, 34, 46, 94, 143, 152, 161
Lysimachus rules/seizes, 31, 158–59, 301, 302, 308
Mariandynoi in, 33–34, 47–48
among Miletus' colonies, 213
northern, 147, 158–59, 216, 217, 248
north-western, 37, 68, 128
ordered to build warships, 68
Peace of Apamea, 323, 327
peninsula, 171, 327
Persian rule in, 66, 73, 143, 146, 207, 228
political situation, 89, 138, 139, 215
royal authority in, 104, 115
western, 37, 106, 144, 157, 335
Xenophon on conditions in, 204, 206, 210
Anatolians, 5, 41, 203
Anaxicrates, 311
Andron of Teos, 154
Antalcidas, 269
Anthesterion, 143
Antigonids, 301
Antigonus the One Eyed, 147, 149, 150, 158, 172, 297, 302, 312
Athens closely allied with, 311
Dionysius' estrangement with, 151, 152
empire collapses, 159
proclamation of freedom of Greeks, 298
reasserts influence in Heraclea, 157
Antiochus III, 323, 324, 331
Antipater, 146, 148, 149, 308
Antiphilus, 339
Antoninus Liberalis, 33, 39
Anytus, 92–93

Apamea, Peace of, 323–32
Apelles, 281
Aphrodisius, 168
Aphrodite Ourania, 229
Aphytis, 234
Apollo, 137, 219, 307
Apollodorus of Athens, 191–93, 199, 327
Apollonia Pontica, 44, 77, 228
Apollonius Rhodius/of Rhodes, 24–26, 30–37, 39, 40, 49, 53, 54, 73, 84, 92, 131, 146, 160, 198–200
Appian, 75, 144, 147, 150, 158, 162, 206, 329–32
Arcadian League, 225, 272
Arcadians, 92
Archaeanactidae, 219
Archaic period, 213
Archemachus, 71
Archibiades, 264, 268
Archidamian War, 234, 235
Archilochus, 43, 46–47
Argonauts, 5, 25, 32, 33, 192, 197, 199, 200
Argos, 82–83, 94
Ariapeithes, 219
Ariaramnes, 66, 67
Ariarathes, 145–47
Ariarathes IV, 323, 325–26
Arichos, 219
Ariobarzanes (satrap of Hellespontine Phrygia), 104–07, 112, 114, 115, 273
brings Hellespontine cities under his control, 105
supports Council of Three Hundred, 112
Aristides, 74
Aristonicus, 264
Aristophanes, 75, 80
Aristotle, 38, 54–56, 62, 63, 69, 71–73, 76, 86, 105, 107, 108, 115, 121, 138, 139, 145, 200, 216, 233, 281, 283, 296
on Heraclea, 62, 63, 86, 121, 216
Arkiroessa, 35, 72
Armenia, 89–90, 144, 323
Armenians, 327
Arrian, 29, 30, 33–36, 39, 49, 54, 67, 115, 126, 139, 143–48, 160, 261, 303–05, 308

INDEX

345

Arsaces, 81
Arsinoe, 159, 165–67, 173
Arsinoea (*see* Ephesus)
Artaxerxes I, 79
Artaxerxes II, 105, 210, 211, 227
  Clearchus and, 114, 115
Artaxerxes III, 115, 139, 210
Artemisium, 68
Artystone, 69
Asia, 89, 94, 143, 174, 219
  Greek cities of, 166
  Lysimachus domains in, 171
Asiatic coast, 66
Asiatic Thrace, 34
Assessment Decree, 221
Assos, 105
Assyria, 203, 217
Astacus, 52, 74, 150, 162, 302
  Clearchus attacks, 112, 115–16, 122
Atheas, 228
Athena, 311, 314
Athenaeus, 30, 31, 47, 62, 70, 71, 76, 93,
  108, 125, 126, 144, 151, 153, 197,
  280, 294–97
Athenian Empire, 95, 218, 252
Athenian Tribute Lists, 64, 77, 78, 83
Athenians, 76, 220, 287, 296, 338
  colonists, 75, 221–22, 252
  expel Delians from Delos, 81
  grant Satyrus I privileges, 223
  Heracleotes' relations with, 80, 94
  Lysimachus' relations with, 311–14
Athens, 76, 82, 117, 299, 313, 335
  Amisus' refounding, 75
  annual revenue of, 99
  Archidamian War foreign policy, 235
  Black Sea and, 220–22, 226, 236, 237
  Bosporus' relations/trade with, 252–
    53, 283–90
  Clearchus' stay in, 108
  client state of Cassander, 297
  crowns awarded to, 311
  Dionysius and, 142, 143, 296
  falls in 404, 84
  grain trade, 92, 118, 236–37, 251,
    253, 269, 283, 286
  Hellespontine region policy, 233, 234,
    238

Heraclea and, 73–74, 80, 86–87, 92,
  119, 153
Heracleotes and, 80, 85
Lamachus and, 79
Leucon I and, 224
Lycon a merchant in, 93
orators, 214
Panticapaeum's relations with, 223
Peloponnesian War defeat, 89
Perdiccas II's diplomatic duel with,
  234, 238
Pontic cities' trade with, 44
Sinope and Amisus colonies founded
  by, 206
Spartocus III's relations with, 284
Spartokos' relations with, 220
Atramyttium, 81
Attalus, 329
Attica, 296
Augustus, 126
Aulus Gellius, 125
Autocrator, 137
Autophradates, 105, 106, 114
Axsăina, 43

Babylon, 308
Babylonia, 203
Bacchiads, Corinthian, 219
Balkans, 6, 218, 242
  northern, 228, 303, 339
  Baton, 126
Bas, 146
Bebrycians, 33, 37, 200
Berenice, 306–07
Billaeus River, 149
Bithynia, 146, 174, 228, 237, 323
  Alyattes founds city in, 50
  central, 196
  coast, 84
  colonization of, 45
  Heraclea and, 162, 163, 226
  Heracleotes and, 69, 85, 92
  Persia and, 68, 90
  Roman embassy to, 324
  Zipoetes succeeds Bas in, 150
Bithynian War, 324
Bithynians, 5, 6, 69, 116, 145
  culture and language, 35

346 INDEX

enter Anatolia, 34
Great King protects Heraclea from, 172
Mariandynoi's relationship with, 33
recognize Persia's overlordship, 66
Thracian origin of, 36
threaten Astacus, 74
Black Sea/Euxine/Pontus, 23, 30, 43, 69, 74–76, 78, 115, 117, 140, 220, 227, 337, 338, 340
Aegean's trade with, 84
Athens and, 83, 87, 220–22, 226
basin, 47, 205, 221, 332
Bosporus, 68, 74, 80, 237
cities, 1–4, 6–7, 10–12, 23, 73, 77, 200, 229, 303–05, 308, 319, 320
coasts, 95, 98, 140, 153, 161, 191, 195
coinage, 128
colonization in basin, 43, 44, 46, 48, 327
conditions after Battle of Granicus, 207
conditions in, 335, 339
Corupedium, news of reaches, 166–67
culture/politics, 138, 139, 229
Delians establish colony on, 81
Euxine district in 425 BC, 221
geological origin of, 28
grain route to, 236
Great King's relations with subjects, 203
Greek cities of, 11, 215, 229, 246, 317, 335–36, 340
historiography/history/historians, 24, 214, 241, 242, 255, 258, 317
last major area settled by Greeks, 213, 335
Miletus' primacy in colonization, 47
north coast, 7, 95, 98, 227, 256, 273, 274, 305, 327, 337
Old Persian inscription discovered, 6
Persian influence/overlordship, 206, 207
rich fishing and agricultural potential of, 213
Royal Scythians pressure Greek cities of, 337
scholarship on, 2–3
shipping through Bosporus, 76, 83, 84, 99, 162

Sinope's ties with cities of north coast, 217
south coast, 7, 66–67, 73, 89, 167, 168, 171, 204, 205, 209, 214, 335
trade, 29, 89, 92, 220, 222, 233, 237–38, 246, 249
weather of, 43
west coast, 2, 64, 65, 139, 214, 217, 218, 228, 305, 327, 337
Boeotia, 10, 45, 51, 82
war with Phocis, 49, 50
Boeotian League, 48, 49, 50, 51, 57
Boeotians, 44, 62, 196
colonizing, 50, 51, 64
Bolu, plain of, 29
Boreis, 45
Bormus, 39, 40, 41, 197, 198
Bosporus (kingdom), 224, 272, 274, 275
Chersonesus and, 226, 319, 320
Demetrius' fleet holds, 158
funerary blood sacrifice and feasts at, 229
grain for Athens, 283–90
history of, 242, 275
kings of, 317, 318, 320, 321
Leucon I represents in diplomatic relations, 224
Macedon rules extends to, 228
a military monarchy, 120
relations/trade with Athens, 238, 252, 253, 283–90, 314
Royal Scythians threatened, 226
rulers of, 34, 251
shipping and, 127
tyrants of, 266, 267
Boteiras, 90
Bryson (son of Herodorus), 93
Bug River, 213, 215, 241, 305, 335
Byzantium, 51, 52, 59, 65, 107, 139, 205
440 BC revolt, 76–77
ally of Bithynia, 162
Chersonesus a client state of, 248
grain trade in, 119, 234–38
Heraclea seeks alliance with, 168–69
Spartans place garrisons in, 89

Cabyle, 307, 308
Calas, 145, 146

INDEX   347

Cales River, 29, 30, 69, 79
Callatis, 4, 39, 55–57, 65, 152
    foundation of, 7–8, 9, 64, 216, 225
    relations with other cities, 98, 266,
        320
    scholarship on, 2, 7–9
Callias, Peace of, 74, 76, 206, 220, 237
Callippus, 93, 106
Callisthenes, 144, 191–94
Callistratus (see Domitius Callistratus)
Calpe, 92, 154
Calpe Limen, 136
Cape Baba, 29
Cape Carambis, 81, 84, 161
Cape Shabla, 9
Cappadocia, 115, 139, 158, 326, 329
    Alexander and, 144, 145
    Antigonus and, 149, 150
    Datames as satrap of, 210
    fighting in, 325
    hostilities with Sinope, 206
    Paphlagonia and, 66, 147
    rebellion in, 105
Cappadocians, 66, 69
Cardia, 301, 302
Carthage, 249
Carystus, 236
Cassander, 149, 158, 173, 306
    Antigonus and, 150, 151, 157, 298
    Athens and, 297, 314
    Lysimachus and, 308, 312
    Cassandrea, 298, 302
Cassignatus, 325
The Catalogue (Ps. Hesiodic), 32, 37
Caucasus Mountains, 43, 225
Cerasus, 90, 217, 326
Ceraunus, 136, 279, 281
Cerbatis, 65
Cerberus, 82
Chaeron of Pellene, 113
Chaerophon, 298–99
Chalcedon, 52, 79, 89, 119, 221, 238
    council of, 56
    hekatostues of, 58
    Heraclea seeks alliance with, 168–69
    Polemaeus arranges alliance with, 150
    remains independent, 145
Chalcidice, 106, 234

Chamaeleon, 168
Charon, 53
Chersonesites, 244, 321, 327
Chersonesus, Thracian, 236, 238, 239
    in Lysimachus' satrapy, 303, 304
Chersonesus Taurica (Cherson/Sevas-
    topol), 56, 80, 87, 96, 196, 216, 242,
    317–21
    4th-century BC expansion of territory,
        246
    archaeological   surveys/excavations,
        57, 214, 222
    built empire by conquering other
        Greek cities, 225
    coinage of, 266
    colonization of, 10
    epigraphical use of Doric dialect, 229
    fortifications strengthened, 246
    founding of, 7–8, 9, 46, 81, 86, 242
    fully developed polis, 8
    Heraclea and, 82, 95, 223, 274–75
    inscriptions, 55, 243–44, 327
    local historical traditions in, 214
    mnamones, 57
    Parthenos principal deity at, 229
    Pharnaces alliance negotiated, 331
    Pharnaces exchanged oaths with, 328
    relations with its metropolis, 65
    Royal Scythians threaten, 226
    Sarmatians' relation with, 258
    Scythia-Greece intermediary, 249
    security of, 98
    Spartocids and, 96, 98
    survival threatened, 248
    target of expansion, 261
    textual sources for history of, 255–58
    treaty, 330
Chion, 80, 93, 125, 130, 131
Chios, 144
Chirisophus, 91, 92
Chortaitus monastery, 28
Chrysopolis, 83, 238
Cierus, 70, 72–73, 86, 116, 154, 160
    inscriptions, 57
    tribes of, 58
    Zipoetes brings under his influence,
        163
Cimmerian Bosporus (see Kerch Straits)

348 INDEX

Cimmerians, 34, 43, 46
Cimmeri(-con?) near Kerch Straits, 77
Cimmerius, 32, 34
Cimon, 76
Cius, 104–05, 145, 330
Clearchus of Heraclea, 10, 11, 98, 104–33 passim, 135, 141, 142, 171, 208–10
   assassinated, 124, 130
   campaign against Astacus, 116
   citizenship grant dating, 118
   coinage, 123, 128
   coup d'état in 364 BC, 10, 55, 98, 109–12, 126, 273
   dynasty lasts 80 years, 226
   exile of, 104, 108–09
   exiles and, 12, 25, 107–08, 169
   foreign policy of, 117
   Heraclea and, 113, 120, 208, 209, 225, 295
   Heracleotes level citadel of, 167
   land goes to his supporters, 122
   Mariandynoi not freed, 121
   military monarchy founding, 123
   Mithridates (satrap) and, 111
   Plato's and Isocrates' student, 93
   pretensions and official position of, 155
   reforms of, 127
   in Great Satraps' Revolt, 114
   self-deification, 125
   sources for reign of, 282
   Timotheus rules differently from, 136
   tyranny of, 67, 137, 267, 274, 279, 281
   wielded a thunderbolt, 280
Clearchus of Soli, 36
Clearchus II, 156, 160–65, 173, 175
Cleisthenes, 101
Cleitus, 279
Clement, 126, 280
Cleomenes of Naucratis, 288
Cleommis, 138
Cleon, 77, 78
Cleopatra (5th century), 146, 147, 149, 308
Cn. Manlius Vulso, 324, 332
Cnidus, 90

Coele Syria, 159
coins/coinage, 6, 23, 49, 56, 65, 70, 75, 80, 83, 85–87, 91, 95–99, 105, 115–16, 123, 127–28, 136, 139–42, 155, 158, 160–64, 166, 195, 262, 266, 273–74, 286, 288, 306–07
Colchians, 217, 218
Colchis, 25, 203, 213, 217
Cold War, 3, 336, 337
Constantia, 304
Constantine VII Porphyrogenitus, On the Administration of the Empire, 32, 51, 248–49
Constantinople, 238
Corcyra, 108
Corinth, 44
Corinthian Bacchiads, 219
Corupedium, 155, 162, 166–68, 171, 302
Corylas, 90
Cotyora, 91, 205, 326
Cotys, 115, 130
Council of Three Hundred (Heraclea), 55, 103, 104, 111–13, 122, 123, 126
Craterus, 78, 83, 148, 149, 252, 269
Crimea, 4, 96, 218, 247, 252, 332, 336
   Athens withdraws from, 253
   Bosporus, 275
   Chersonesus and, 226, 319, 320
   Chersonesus foundation in, 7, 242
   Demetrius' fleet holds, 158
   eastern, 114, 214, 261
   funerary blood sacrifice and feasts at, 229
   history of, 242, 275
   kings of, 317, 318, 320, 321
   Leucon I represents in diplomatic relations, 224
   Macedon rules extends to, 228
   Miletus' colony, 213
   a military monarchy, 120
   northeast, 241
   relations/trade with Athens, 238, 252, 253, 283–90, 314
   routes to/from, 81–82, 226
   rulers of, 34, 251
   Scythian kingdom in, 320
   shipping and, 127
   southeast, 242, 261

INDEX 349

south-western, 216, 243
Theodosia in, 251
tyrants of, 266, 267
western, 225, 244
Criumetopon, 81
Croesus, 50, 65
Cromna, 140, 149, 154, 160, 191, 226
Ctesias, 66, 68, 79
Curtius Rufus, 115, 144–47
Cyanean Rocks, 74
Cybele, 39
Cyinda, 151, 296–97
The *Cypria*, 46–47, 192
Cyprian Salamis, 119
Cyprus, 151
Cyril, 242
Cyrus I the Great, 44, 65–67, 215
Cythera, 77
Cytorus, 146, 149, 160, 191
in Heraclea's empire, 154, 226
Cyzicus, 46, 106, 119, 128, 145, 213

Dacia, 339
Dacians, 337, 338
Daisios, 329
Damis, 51
Dandarioi, 223, 224
Danube, 216, 218, 228, 337
Lysimachus' kingdom extends to, 159, 303, 306
Darius I, 6, 66, 68, 205, 215
Darius III, 145, 147, 206
Dascyleum, 47, 66, 74
Dascylus, 37
Datames, 106, 114, 115, 211
Sinope and, 105, 206, 210
Delian League, 67, 73–75, 79, 83, 206
Delians, 9, 81, 82
Delion, 10
Delos, 10, 81, 242, 320
Delphi, 49–50, 81, 82, 172, 215, 320
Demeter, 39, 65
Demetrius, 158–59, 161, 173–74, 308, 311
Demetrius of Callatis, 8
Demetrius of Phalerum, 150, 298, 312, 314
Demetrius Poliorcetes, 279, 303

Demosthenes, 92, 96, 97, 99, 104–06, 108, 109, 115, 118, 119, 127, 221, 238, 251, 253, 261, 269, 271, 285–89, 320
on Atheno-Bosporan relations, 285
on Athens's annual revenue, 99
on Bosporan grain trade, 238, 253
on Leucon I, 98, 223–25, 261
On the Crown, 320
opposes Leptines motion, 251
refers to Black Sea cities, 214
regains important privilege for Athens, 290
Dexippus, 144, 147
Diadochi, 25, 147–52
Diadochoi wars, 297
Dinarchus, 251, 286, 288, 290
Diodorus (Siculus), 29, 43, 49, 57, 68, 79, 81–83, 89, 91, 96, 98, 99, 105–07, 113, 115, 116, 124, 125, 130, 142, 144–56, 157, 158, 162, 173, 175, 214, 219, 238, 261, 267, 273, 281, 296–98, 302, 303, 305–08, 312, 313, 325, 326, 329, 330
Books 18–20, 301
on Cius rulers chronology, 329–30
on Eumelus of Bosporus' reign, 317
on Lysimachus-Seuthes battle, 305
on Sarmatians overrunning Scythia, 247
on Seuthes III as king, 305–06
on Spartocus I's accession, 252
on tyranny in Heraclea, 174
Diogenes Laertius, 80, 93, 117, 122, 130, 142, 150, 297
Dion Chrysostom, 229, 281
Dion of Prusa, 139
Dionysias, 58
Dionysius of Byzantium, 51, 238
Dionysius of Heraclea, 11, 153–54, 169, 173, 175, 294–95
Alexander and, 145–47
Antigonus and, 150, 151, 157
Athens' feelings toward, 296
born in 361/60 BC, 125
death of, 155–56, 297
Heraclea and, 141, 152, 155
hopes for Persian victory, 144

350 INDEX

marries Amastris, 148, 153
a minor at father's death, 131
policies of, 149, 226
Timotheus and, 139, 141–43, 208
Dionysius I of Syracuse, 113, 116, 124, 153, 224, 281
Dionysius II of Syracuse, 153, 281
Dionysus, 39, 58, 130, 218, 307
Dionysus, Theater of, 233
Diophantos of Sinope, 321
Dioscourias, 217
Dioscouroi, 200
Dnieper River, 215, 227
Dniester River, 96
Dobruja, 4, 225, 301–02, 339, 340
    Callatis in, 7, 216
    cities revolt in 313 BC, 305, 306
    North Dobruja, 195
Domitius Callistratus, 5, 24, 26, 27, 32, 36, 40, 41, 70, 72, 73, 197–99
Don River, 227, 241, 335
Dorians, 9
Doric (dialect), 8, 168, 229, 279
Doric tribes, 57
Drilae, 206
Dromichaetes, 161, 173, 306
Duris of Samos, 124, 257

Eastern Europe, 2, 3, 336
Ebryzelmus, 306–07
Egypt, 139, 237
Eminakos, 219
Eneti, 193
Epaminondas, 107
Ephesians, 312
Ephesus, 302, 312
Ephippus, 93
Ephorus, 31, 43, 49, 71
Epigoni, 25
epigraphical evidence, 4, 6, 7, 10, 11, 17, 23, 39, 45, 52, 54–57, 72, 77, 78, 80, 82, 83, 85, 86, 115, 117–19, 123, 137, 141–43, 146, 152, 153, 155, 160, 162, 166, 193, 195, 203–07, 214, 217, 220–24, 227, 229, 233–39, 242–49, 257, 266, 271–72, 274, 283–90, 304–07, 311–14, 317–21, 327–31
Epimenes, 306–07

Epirus, 146
Epistles of Chion, 31, 80, 108, 110, 113, 117, 124, 125, 129, 130, 132
Eratosthenes, 191, 192
Euboea, 236, 238, 239
Eucleides, 93
Eumelus, 25, 46–47, 152, 287, 313
Eumenes (satrap) 115, 147–50, 297, 308
Eumenes (brother of Philetaerus of Tium), 165, 166
Eumenes II of Pergamum, 323, 332
    embassy to Rome, 324, 325
    in Pontic War, 326, 328, 329
Euopios, 216
Euphorion, 48, 49, 70
Eupolis, 78, 80
Eurasian steppe, 241, 242
Euripides, 82
Eurytion, 86–87, 100–01, 108
Eusebius, 31, 43, 44, 46, 52, 64
Eustathius, 40, 70, 193
Euthymia, 147
Euxine (*see* Black Sea)

Gaizatorigus, 325
Galatia, 323, 325, 326
Galatians, 196–97
Gallipoli Peninsula, 303, 308
Gaugamela, 144
Gauls, 154
Ge, 327
Georgia, 217
Gerania, 52
Getae, 161, 227, 228
Getes, 305, 308, 337
Getics, 340
Gnesiochus, 49, 51, 53, 62
    divides Heraclea unevenly, 54, 55
Gobryes, 69
Gordion, 6
Gorgippus, 223, 275
grain trade, 92, 96, 153, 214, 220, 222, 224–27, 251–53, 261, 262, 268, 283–90
Granicus, Battle of, 207
Granicus River, 143
Great Gods, 307
Great Inscription, 306

INDEX

351

Great King, 7, 89, 203, 210, 280
 Heraclea and, 67, 172
 in Peace of Callias, 74
 Persia and, 94, 209
Great Mother, 39
Great Panathenaia, 312
Great Satraps' Revolt, 114, 210, 273
Greece, 31, 33, 35, 249, 335
 eastern, 43
 European, 89, 93, 146, 172
 history of, 5, 26, 282
 northern, 2, 85, 228
 Persian invasion of, 69
 polis system in, 213
 provincial culture, 23
Greeks, 172, 191, 200, 206, 226
 from Aegean homeland, 213
 disaffected with Leucon I, 96
 freedom of, 298, 301, 304
 hekatostues, 58
 of Heraclea, 120
 history in Black Sea, 336
 interactions with non-Greeks, 229, 335,
  339
 kinship groups, 57
 mythology/religion, 24, 37, 280
 relations with Great King, 203
 scholars, 2, 32, 33, 36
 settlements, 12, 195–96, 227, 241,
  338
Gyenos, 217
Gyges, 43, 50
Gylon, 221, 269, 288

Habrondas, 46
Hades, 213
Halys River, 323
Harpocration, 96, 115, 261
Hattusas, 6
Hecataeus, 38, 223
Helius, 327
Hellanicus, 32
Hellespont, 66, 68, 213, 226, 238
 passage through, 76, 325
 Spartans hold, 89, 222
Hellespontine Phrygia, 105, 150, 162, 168,
 297
 Alexander and, 143, 144

authority/power/control in, 66, 89–90,
 145, 147, 323
satrapy of, 104, 115, 139, 206, 273
Hellespontine regions, 119, 234–36, 238
Helots, 70, 197, 216, 304
Hera, 128
Heraclea Pontica (Ereğli), 2, 4, 10, 11,
 117, 242, 267
 Alexander and, 146, 148–49
 Anatolia and, 29
 Anatolia, northern and, 131, 171, 196,
  204, 226
 Anatolia, western and, 30, 94–95
 ancient historians on, 24, 26, 27, 54,
  76, 110, 172, 174
 archaeological/textual evidence for
  history of, 4, 6–7, 23, 275
 Aristotle on, 54, 62, 63, 71, 86, 121,
  216
 Athens and, 73–74, 77–78, 80, 86–87,
  92, 119, 153, 221–22
 Bithynia and, 162, 163, 226
 Black Sea and, 44, 143, 196
 Chersonesus and, 82, 95, 223, 242–
  44, 274–75
 Clearchus and, 10, 55, 98, 103, 104,
  109–13, 120, 122, 123, 126, 208,
  225, 273, 279, 282, 295
 coinage, 95, 128, 139–41
 colonies founded by, 8
 colonization/settlement of, 5, 6, 45, 48,
  52, 53, 199
 communications/relations/trade with
  Aegean, 82, 153, 172
 Council of Three Hundred, 55, 103,
  104, 111–13, 122, 123, 126
 Delian League, 67, 79, 83
 democracy of, 12, 63, 87
 Dionysius rules, 150, 152–53, 155,
  294–95
 double founding of, 46, 47
 economy of, 10, 85, 153
 empire's extent, 136, 149, 154, 155,
  226
 foreign policy, 94, 138
 founding of, 44–45, 48–51, 61–62, 82,
  213
 freedom regained, 167

INDEX

geography of, 28–30
Gnesiochus divides unevenly, 54, 55
government of, 56, 103, 120, 302
Great King and, 67, 172
hekatostues/tribes, 57–59, 63
Heracles at, 37, 199, 200
history, 4, 12, 26, 152–53, 275, 317
history, early, 5, 6, 7
history, pre-Greek, 24
intellectual activity at, 125
Lamachus and, 79, 80
Leucon I's war with, 225, 264–66
Lysimachus and, 157–58, 160, 162–
    65, 167, 171, 173, 226, 303
Mariandynia becomes territory of, 70,
    72, 84, 154, 196, 216–17
Mariandynoi relations with, 53–54,
    61, 69, 70, 72, 84, 171, 196, 216
Memnon on, 5, 25, 54, 140, 144, 149,
    155, 157, 165, 173, 204, 265
Milesian colony at, 44, 45
E.H. Minns on, 265, 266–67
Mithridates I's ambitions toward, 104,
    162, 168–69, 206, 273
natural resources, 30, 31
Near East political conditions advan-
    tage, 166
Nymphis on, 25, 26, 79, 294
Oxathres rules, 156, 163
in Panhellenic sagas, 214–15
Panticapaeum war with, 96–97, 140,
    262, 265, 268, 270, 275
patronizes shrine at Delphi, 82, 172
patronizes shrine at Olympia, 82, 172,
    216
Persia and, 6–7, 65–68, 76, 79, 94,
    204, 221
Persia, loyalty to, 143, 172, 227
Phanagoria alliance with, 98, 262, 274
Photius on, 144, 204
Pontic War and, 328
power of, 44, 69, 98, 143, 196, 274
prosperity/wealth, 27, 84, 99, 129,
    135, 171
Ps.-Aristotle on, 96–98, 262, 265–66,
    270, 274
revenue sources, 127
Satyrus and, 131, 226, 265

scholarship on, 1–12
Seleucus and, 168–69, 171–72
Sinope's relations with, 207–08
Sparta's victory makes free, 90
Spartocids' conflict with, 261
Strabo on, 31–32, 45–47, 67
The Ten Thousand and, 62, 84, 92
Thebes assists, 107
Theodosia and, 262, 268, 273, 274
Timotheus rules, 140, 208
Trogus/Justin on, 48, 49, 54, 63, 67,
    79, 173, 273
Xenophon on, 29, 48–49, 84, 92
Zipoetes and, 150, 162, 163, 168
Heracleides of Cyme, 165–67, 172, 173
Heracleides Ponticus, 34, 51, 93, 117,
    122, 125, 142
Heracleides of Salamis, 119, 125, 142, 145
Heracleius, 327
Heracleotes, 10, 11, 30, 199, 226, 274
    amphorae, 3, 10, 128
    Antigonus, 298
    Athenians/Athens, 80, 93
    Bosporus tyrants attack, 262
    Clearchus' behavior toward, 110, 113,
        116, 122–24
    Clearchus II and Oxathres' rule alien-
        ates, 163–64
    debt among poor, 103, 135
    democracy, 12, 55, 165
    Dionysius, 155
    exiles, 145, 169, 295, 296
    found Callatis, 64
    found Chersonesus, 243
    hekatostues/tribes, 57–59, 101
    Heracleides offered safe conduct, 167
    historians, 4–5, 26, 36, 45, 52, 294
    historians, early, 25
    historians on Mariandynoi, 33, 39,
        200–01
    historiography lost, 38
    history, 1, 3, 5, 10, 28, 33
    influence among cities of southern
        Russia, 96
    influence on Pontic north coast, 95
    inscriptions, 4, 23, 54, 56
    interpersonal affairs, 28, 34, 63, 100,
        120

INDEX

353

Lamachus, 79
Leucon I, 97, 264, 271, 275
living abroad, 153, 171
Lycus, 54
Mariandynoi under rule of, 23, 61, 69, 71–72, 172, 197–99
merchants/trade, 3, 84–85, 91
military, 12, 150, 266, 270
Posidonius, 47–48
Protomachus, 118
Ten Thousand's breaking up advantageous to, 92
Thebes epitaph of, 93–94
Theodosia support withdrawn from, 275
Timotheus, 136, 139
Tyndaridae temple constructed by, 84
Heracleotis, 5, 6, 10, 44, 92
Heracles, 24, 33, 49, 51
adventures at Heraclea, 37, 199, 200
on Heraclea's coins, 128, 139, 141
Herakleidas, 317, 319
Hērakleios, 51
Heraklia (*see* Heraclea)
Hermippus, 76
Hermonassa, 219, 271
Herodorus, 5, 24, 25, 30, 37, 53, 84, 93, 199
Herodotus, 38, 39, 43, 44, 50, 51, 57, 62, 66–69, 74, 82, 201, 203, 205, 210, 214, 216, 305
on border peoples in DPh, 204
in Chersonesus Taurica inscription, 327
on culture of Black Sea cities, 229
on Scythian king Skyles, 218–19
on Tauri sacrifices to Parthenos, 243
visits Pontus, 340
Herogeiton, 327
Heroic Age, 214
Hesiod, 32, 37, 46–47
Hesychius, 39–41, 70
Hieronymous of Cardia, 301
Himerius, 199
Hipparchus, 131
Hippolyte, 199
Histria, 44, 195, 196, 214–15, 228, 320, 339, 340

Hittites, 6, 35
Hodioupolis, 73
Homer, 25, 34, 35, 46–47, 191–94
Hydra, 82
Hylas, 41
Hypius River/valley, 29, 30, 35, 69, 70, 72–73, 116, 163

IG 1³ 61, 233–39
I. Sinope 1, 10, 11, 207–10
Iliad, 46, 70, 191–94
Imbros, 236
India, 146
Ineboli, 330
Inönü Cave, 4, 6
Ionia, 68, 89, 159, 213
Ionian Revolt, 210
Ionians, 33, 43, 44, 47, 210
contact with Mariandynoi, 36, 45
pottery, 9, 10
Iphigenia, 243
Ipsus, 158–59, 302–03, 308, 314
Battle of, 308
Isidore, 125
Isocrates, 78, 90, 93, 105–08, 116, 117, 122, 124, 126–28, 136–38, 214, 252, 253, 269, 273, 286, 295, 296
Callippus is friend, 93, 106
on Heracleotes, 128, 137, 138
students of, 93, 108
Istros (*see* Histria)
Italy, 317
Itinerarium Alexandri, 144

John Lydus, 52
John Tzetzes, 33, 37, 199
Jordanes, 305
Julius Caesar, 131
Justin/Trogus, 24, 29, 55, 61, 63, 67, 79, 103–07, 109–13, 121, 123–27, 130, 132, 139, 144, 146, 147, 149–51, 158, 159, 162, 164, 166, 169, 173–74, 209, 273, 280, 295, 323, 329
on Boeotians, 48, 49
on Clearchus, 107, 111–13, 121, 130, 280–81
on Greek settlers, 53
on Heraclea, 50, 54, 273

354 INDEX

on Lamachus, 79

Kalos Limen, 225, 244, 246
Kaska, 6
Kepoi, 219, 221
Kerch Peninsula, 215, 222
Kerch Straits, 98, 205, 219, 223, 241–42
Kerkinitis, 82, 140, 225, 244, 246
Khazars, 242
King's Peace, 94
Kizil-Koba culture, 246
Kizil Tepe Mountains, 29, 31
Klearkhos (*see* Clearchus)
Kromna, 11, 208
Kush, 203
Kynosouris, 58

Lamachus, 75, 79, 80, 220
Lamian War, 148, 290
Lampsacus, 58, 267
Lemnos, 236, 238, 239
Leocritus, 325
Leonnatus, 147
Leontophorus, 161, 165, 167
Leptines, 251, 261, 285
Leucon I, 224, 251, 253, 270, 271, 274
    Athens and, 252, 283, 285, 290
    Diodorus on, 175
    executes deserting trierarchs, 263
    Greek subjects' disaffection, 96
    Heraclea and, 264–66, 273
    Panticapaeum reign lasts forty years, 224
    Theodosia, refit and opened, 127
    Theodosia, surprise attack on, 97, 270
    Theodosia abandoned to, 114
    Theodosia and Phanagoria annexed, 274
    Theodosia attacked with Gorgippus, 275
    Theodosia brought under authority of, 98, 261
    Theodosia transformed, 225
Leucon II, 265
Libya, 237
Ligyes, 69
Lindos Chronicle, 319, 321
Livy, 124, 323, 324

Lycon, 93
Lycus (king of the Mariandynoi), 54, 200
Lycus River, 29, 30, 39, 53
Lydia, 65–66, 166, 213, 241, 335
    kings of, 43, 50
    Tantalid dynasty of, 37
Lysander, 84, 92, 126, 238, 269
Lysias, 78, 93, 269, 273
Lysimachia, 302, 306, 308
Lysimachus, 149, 162, 165, 174, 301–08
    Anatolia, 158–59, 172
    Antigonus and, 151, 157, 297
    Athenians' relations, 311–14
    death of, 166, 167, 171
    Dionysius' rapprochement with, 152
    Getae, campaign against, 161
    Greek cities, Arsinoe, 302
    Heraclea alliance, 157, 160
    Heraclea occupation, 164, 173, 226, 303
    history of, 173
    marriage, 159, 306
    in Plutarch's *Moralia*, 279
    Pontic Greek cities policies, 305
    Seuthes' queen probably daughter of, 307
    Thrace, 308

Macedon, 139, 143, 145–47, 149, 228, 303
    Amyntas I ascends throne of, 64
    Lysimachus and, 173, 308
Macedonians, 147, 298
Macrobius, 30, 146
Maeotians, 223, 225
Maiden (*see* Parthenos)
Malacon, 166
Mangalia, 2, 64, 216
Marcian, 154
Mariandynia, 31, 68, 71, 86, 172
    fertility of, 38
    Heraclea and, 61, 70, 72, 84, 154, 196, 216–17
    historical period, 35
    under Lydian authority, 50, 65
    struggle for domination in, 200
Mariandynoi, 5, 6, 31–41, 54, 171–72, 200, 216

INDEX

355

chieftains, 39
Clearchus determines status of, 120
culture, 35, 38–40
ethnicity, 32, 34
Greek conquest of, 5
Greek protection of, 200
Heraclea's subjects, 23, 61, 69–70, 72–73, 84, 198–99
Heracleotes' relations with, 53, 54, 62, 63, 196, 197
heroes fighting for Troy, 33
Ionians familiar with, 45
land conquered from, 225
language, 35
legend, 37
in light infantry corps, 69
lose what Heracles gave them, 200
Milesians conquer, 47
military equipment of, 39
Mysians settled in classical, 35
Persia's overlordship, 66
poleis, 38
political systems, 39
population not a unity in historical times, 35
rowers, 69
royal family, 37
servitude of, 121
settled farming population, 38
status as slaves, 71
Thynians settled in classical, 35
Mariandynus, 32, 34, 36, 41, 44–45
Massalia/Marseilles, 249
Matienoi, 69
Matris, 327
Mausolus, 105, 106, 114
Maximus, 28
Media, 44
Mediterranean, 150, 222, 246, 248, 335, 336
basin, 241
eastern, 139, 257
Medosakkos, 255
Megara, 51–53, 62, 93, 213, 241
founded Heraclea, 45, 48, 61, 82
hekatostues, 57–59
Megarians, 8, 44, 53, 62, 196
Megaris, 58

Memnon, 5, 7, 24, 26, 27, 49, 51, 53, 55, 64, 65, 68, 70, 73, 74, 86, 90, 108, 110, 113–17, 120–25, 127–33, 135–37, 139–42, 144–51, 153–56, 157–69, 173–75, 194, 195, 197, 204, 209, 280, 295–97, 302, 303, 324, 328
on Alexander's democratic government at Heraclea, 144
on Amastris founding her name city, 160
on Antigonus' visit to Heraclea, 157
on Arsinoe's interest in Heraclea, Tium, and Amastris city, 165
on Clearchus' dress, 124, 280
on Dionysius, 145–48
followed Nymphis, 25, 174
on Great King's role in Black Sea, 207
on Heraclea, 5, 54, 149, 166, 204, 267
on Lysimachus, 162, 173
Oeconomica on, 264–65
plot against Leucon, 275
Polyaenus mentions, 210
on Satyrus, 11, 132
on Timotheus, 136, 137, 139–41
Menander, 150–51, 153, 155, 199, 293–99
Menecrates, 126
Menippus, 65, 81, 154, 160, 161
Mermnad dynasty, 43
Mesembria, 305
Methodius, 242
Methonaians, 234
Methone, 233, 234, 238
Methymna, 138
Milesians, 44
Miletus, 9, 45–48, 67, 217, 219
Black Sea colonies of, 43, 213, 241
has 70 Greek colonies, 335
Megara on good terms with, 51–52
Mithridates I Ctistes (of Pontus), 10, 115, 210, 323
Clearchus and, 107, 109–11, 162
Heraclea and, 104, 162, 168–69, 206, 273
as ruler, 329–30
Mithridates II, 324
Mithridates IV, 331
Mithridates V, 330

356 INDEX

Mithridates VI, 321
Mithridatic kings of Pontus, 27
Mithridatic wars, 27, 332
Mithrines, 144–45
Mitylene, 253
Mnoa, 47
Molpoi, 219
Moravia, 242
Mount Olgassys, 162
Mysia, 10
Mysians, 35
Mytilene, 219, 236

Nabonidus Chronicle, 65
Neapolis, 247, 320
Near East, 159, 166, 203
Nepos, 90, 105, 106, 108, 115, 149
Nestos River, 303
Nicaea, 148, 162
Nicander, 38
Nicephorus Gregoras, 28, 91, 149
Nicomedes I, 154
Nicomedes IV, 332
Niconia, 77
Nisaia, 52
Nymphaeum, 78, 81, 83, 219, 221, 269
Nymphis (historian), 5, 24–26, 35–37, 40,
    70, 79, 113, 114, 130, 132, 135, 146,
    151, 152, 155, 159, 174, 175, 197–99,
    204, 273, 294
  astute diplomacy of, 171
  on Bormus, 40, 198
  on Clearchus, 113–14, 125–26
  on Dionysius of Heraclea, 155, 294
  on Heracleote tyranny, 204
  on Mariandynoi, 33, 200
  negotiates with exiles, 169
Nymphodorus, 338, 339
Nysa, 331

Oath of Chersonesus, 245
Odessus, 158, 305, 317, 335
Odrysia, 74
Odrysians (Thracians), 216, 218–20, 227,
    303, 305, 337
Odyssey, 25, 34, 46, 70
OGIS 771, 331
Olbia, 44, 96, 146, 196, 216, 229, 320

  Alexander's army destroyed at, 228
  Alexander's general attacks, 340
  along Russian grain route, 81–82
  archaeological surveys at, 222
  founding of, 44
  historians of, 317
  hostile toward Athenian power, 221
  important Greek cities extend to, 241
  among Miletus' colonies, 213, 335
  in Panhellenic sagas, 214–15
  Royal Scythians pressure, 218
  Sinope's ties with, 217
  tyrants of, 219, 337
  Zopyrion's unsuccessful siege of, 305
Olympia, 82, 172, 215, 216
Olynthus, 298
Orontes, 114
Ortiagon, 323
Otys, 94
Ovid, 64, 156, 160, 304
Oxathres, 148, 156, 163, 173, 175
  begins reign, 160
  comes of age, 161

Paerisades I, 175, 219–20, 225, 272, 283,
    285–90
  Athens and, 283, 285, 287–89
Palladas, 155, 156
Panelus, 64
Pannonia, 242
Panticapaeum, 44, 78, 96, 221, 251, 272,
    275, 286, 335 (*see also* Bosporus;
    Crimea)
  anti-Spartocid elements in, 97
  Aphrodite Ourania at, 229
  empire of, 225
  excavation of, 214
  founding of, 44
  on grain route, 81–82, 118, 253
  Greek cities extend to, 241
  Heraclea's conflicts with, 140, 262,
    265, 268
  Leucon I and, 127, 271, 272
  Miletus' colony, 213
  military alliance leader, 219
  Pericles goes to, 252
  rulers of, 78, 219, 220, 222, 224, 285
  Sindoi and, 95, 269

INDEX

Spartocids of, 82, 261, 283
Paphlagonia, 29, 75, 145, 157, 196, 226, 326
   archaeological evidence in, 205, 330
   Cimmerians active in, 46
   coast, 146, 154, 217, 324
   Dionysius enters, 149
   in Hellespontine Phrygia satrapy, 115, 139
   Heracleote merchants in, 85
   in *Iliad*, 191
   Mithridates Ctistes carved principality in, 162
   Persian authority in, 90
   Pontic War extends into, 325
   rulers of, 34, 94, 146, 206, 210
Paphlagonians, 39, 66, 144, 217
Paris 2076 mss, 279
Parmenon, 319
Parthenius, 131
Parthenos/Maiden, 229, 243, 248, 317–21
Patriarch of Constantinople, 24
Pausanias, 49, 50, 82, 108, 151, 159, 165, 166, 219, 305, 306
Peace of 311 BC, 151, 302
Peace of Apamea, 323–32
Peace of Callias, 74, 76, 206, 220, 237
Peace of Dardanus, 332
Pechenegs, 248–49
Peiraieus, 221–22
Peloponnesian League, 77
Peloponnesian War, 77, 78, 87, 221–22, 235, 238, 269
Penestae, 47, 70, 197
Perdiccas, 147, 148, 149, 295
Perdiccas II of Macedon, 233, 234, 238
Pergamum/Pergamenes, 323–32
Pericles, 74–77, 83, 220, 237, 251
Periplus (anonymous), 29, 31, 35, 39, 44, 49, 54, 65, 75, 81, 83, 160, 206
Persepolis, 114, 117, 139
Persia, 146, 203, 206, 207, 217, 220
   empire, 6–7, 67, 203, 215, 228, 241
   fall of, 172
   Greeks and, 213, 335
   Heraclea loyal to, 68, 79, 221, 227
   Heraclea's relations with, 66, 76, 94, 204
   in *I. Sinope* 1, 208
   Macedon tensions with, 139, 143

Persians, 7, 11, 89, 147, 209, 216, 247
   Clearchus' relations with, 117
   Greeks scorn as Asiatic aggressors, 172
   Heraclea's relations with, 65
Peutinger Table, 29
Phaenippus, 271–72
Phanagoria, 4, 95–96, 98, 205–06, 219, 262, 274
   Old Persian inscription, 205
Pharnabazus, 94
Pharnaces I (of Pontus), 248, 324–32
Phasis, 217
Pherecrates, 71, 76
Pherecydes, 32, 34, 35, 51
Phila, 148
Philip Arrhidaeus, 147
Philip II, 126, 139, 228, 304, 305, 307, 320
Philochorus, 139, 238
Phineus, 32, 34, 36, 44–45
Phocis, 49, 50
Phocritus, 168
Phoenicia, 139
Phoenicians, 44, 241, 335
Phoenix, 32
Phormio, 285–86
Phosphorion, 307
Photius, 24, 27, 70, 144, 173, 204, 207
Phrixus, 32
Phrygia, 158
Phrygia Epictetus, 323, 324
Phrygia Maior, 147
Phrygians, 33
Phylarchus, 151, 237, 257
Pichvnari, 217–18
Piraeus, 75
Plato, 47, 70, 73, 93, 108, 117, 121, 127, 130, 197, 256
Platonists, 125
Pleistarchus, 158
Pliny, 30–32, 38, 43, 44, 65, 81, 83, 153, 137, 160, 161
Plutarch, 23, 52–53, 55, 58, 74–76, 115, 123, 124, 129, 144–47, 149, 151, 153, 157–60, 162, 174, 206, 220, 252, 276, 281, 308, 329
Moralia, 279–82

on Clearchus, 129, 279, 281
on Pericles' Pontic Expedition, 220, 221
Poimen, 154
Polemaeus, 150, 151, 297
Pollux, 36, 40, 41, 70–71, 198
Polyaenus, 54, 55, 59, 67, 95–97, 103, 105, 107, 109–12, 115, 116, 123, 167, 210, 223, 253, 255–58, 261–70, 302, 306
   on Clearchus, 110, 111, 115, 116
   on Datames' siege of Sinope, 210
   on Leucon I, 225, 253, 267
   on Memnon, 275
Polybius, 48, 83, 113, 117, 238, 286, 304, 324–27, 329, 331
Polyeuctus of Sphettus, 143
Pomponius Mela, 8–9, 64, 199
Pontic kingdom/kingdom of Pontus, 115, 248, 256, 324–32, 338
   Chersonesus and, 248, 327–28
   Eumenes and, 323, 332
   Heraclea and, 44, 143, 196
   Mithridatic monarchs 10, 27, 104, 107, 109–11, 115, 162, 168–69, 206, 210, 273, 321, 323, 324, 329–31
Pontic Mountains, 29, 30
Pontic steppe, 246–49
Pontic War, 324–32
Pontus (see Black Sea)
Porphyry, 144, 155, 166, 273, 313
Posidonius, 47–48, 71, 73, 172, 200, 257
pottery/ceramics, 6, 9, 10, 44, 47, 73, 76, 82, 85, 140, 195, 217, 222, 227 (see also amphorae)
Priolas, 36
Proclus, 93
Promathidas, 5, 24, 25, 39, 53, 199
Propontis, 68–69, 105–06, 116, 145, 218, 337
Protomachus, 118, 119, 125
Prusias ad Hypium, 57, 73
Prusias I, 323, 324
Prusias II, 325–26
Psessoi, 223, 224
Ps.-Apollodorus, 33, 37, 199
Ps.-Aristotle, 30, 31, 56, 72, 85, 86, 95–99, 105, 153, 238, 262, 264–71, 274

on Heraclea's war with Panticapaeum, 96
Ps.-Arrian, 261
Ps.-Callisthenes, 144
Ps.-Demosthenes, 80, 83, 93, 94, 253, 285–86, 288
Ps.-Plutarch, 288
Ps.-Scylax, 8, 38, 81, 136–37
Ps.-Scymnus, 8, 9, 10, 31, 35, 43, 44, 46, 49, 64, 81, 136, 160
   on colonization of Chersonesus, 81
   on foundation of Callatis, 64
Ps.-Xenophon, 90, 235
Psilis, 131
Ptolemy (geographer) 32, 73
Ptolemy I, 149, 151, 159, 173, 174, 302, 308
   Antigonus and, 157, 297
Pydna, 233
Pythes, 338

Quarantine Bay, 242, 244
Quintus of Smyrna, 30, 33, 39

Rhebas River, 131, 146, 154, 226
Rhemaxos, 339
Rhemaxus, 304
Rhodes, 320, 323, 326
Rhodians, 324
Romanus II, 248
Rome/Romans, 5, 248, 323–32, 338
Royal Scythians, 215, 226, 246, 247, 337

Sadalas, 305, 306–07
Sagaris, 35
Salamis, 52, 68
Salmydessus, sea at, 304
Salonian Plain, 29, 157
Samians, 295
Samos, 58, 76–77, 295
Sandarace, 31
Sangarius, 38
Sangarius River, 69, 92, 146
Sardis, 81, 159, 210
Sarmatians, 247, 255, 256, 258, 337
Satocus, 306–07
Satyros/Satyrus I, 10, 11, 78–79, 132, 136, 207, 208, 221–23

INDEX 359

Athens' relations with, 252, 283
coinage of, 123
death of, 96, 135
Diodorus does not include regency of, 175
exiles and, 269
as grain exporter, 253
as Heraclea's regent, 11, 131, 133, 226, 265
Rostovtzeff on, 265–66
Theodosia siege, 261, 268, 275
as tyrant, 137, 142
Sauromatae, 247
Scilurus, 256
Scipios, 324
Scyros, 236
Scythia, 66, 74, 216, 221, 227, 249
Scythians, 218–20, 339, 340
  Alexander's army destroyed by, 228
  Amage attacks, 256
  Black Sea Greeks and, 229, 337
  Callatis ruled by, 227
  Chersonesus and, 226, 246, 255
  Darius' defeat by, 68
  Dobrujan cities secure alliance of, 305
  Greek–non-Greek go-betweens, 338
  Leucon I and, 97, 264, 271
  Paerisades I raises revenue for war of, 285–86
  power of, 248, 320
  Thracians and, 216
Sea of Azov, 31, 219, 241
Seasmus, 191
Seleucids, 169, 171, 323, 324, 331
Seleucus I, 149, 157–59, 166, 297, 308
  Heraclea and, 168, 169, 172
Selymbria, 52
Sesamos/Sesamus, 11, 140, 149, 154, 160, 208, 210, 226
Seuthes, 83, 306, 307
Seuthes III, 228, 303, 305–07
Seuthopolis, 306, 307
Sevastopol, 81, 216, 242
Shipka Pass, 306
Sicily, 237, 317
Sigeum, 236
Silenus, 129
Simferopol, 247

Sindians/Sindoi, 95, 223, 224, 269
Sindica, 95, 96
Sinop(e), 4, 6, 7, 9–11, 44, 47, 68, 75, 90, 105, 115, 207–10, 217, 335
  ancient, 4
  archaeological evidence discovered in, 205
  Athenian influence/times, 221, 252
  autonomy of, 67, 115
  Cappadocia satraps control, 139
  Chersonesus Taurica relations with, 320
  colonization of, 43, 206, 213, 335
  Datames and, 105, 210
  double founding of, 46
  good harbor between it and Bosporus, 84
  Heraclea relations with, 207–08
  in Panhellenic sagas, 214–15
  Persia and, 128, 227
  Pharnaces occupies, 326, 328, 332
  Pontic kings wish to annex, 324
  Pontic War's effect on, 329
Sinopeans, 11, 75, 220, 324
Sitalces, 76, 218, 338
Skyles, 218
Socrates, 80, 93
Soonautes, 53
Sophocles, 32, 73
Sotimus, 80
South Russia, 46–47, 153, 218, 242, 262
  as grain source, 81, 92, 283, 286
  Heracleotes and, 96
Spain, 213, 241, 335
Sparta, 77, 89, 90, 95, 197, 304
  Athens' war with, 83
  helots of, 216, 304
Spartans, 87, 94
Spartocids, 78, 82, 98, 269, 273, 274, 286, 287
  Athens and, 252, 283, 289, 313
  Demosthenes' ties with, 286
  dynasty of, 251
  expansionist plans of, 96
  Theodosia comes under control of, 97–98
Spartocus I, 219–20, 222, 251–52, 306–08

360 INDEX

Spartocus II, 225, 251, 283, 285, 288–89
Spartocus III, 283–84, 287, 313, 314
Spartocus V, 265
Spartokos, 219, 220
Sphacteria, 77
Spintharus, 80
Spithridates, 94
Sredna Gora Mountains, 306
Stephanus of Byzantium, 27, 31, 35, 36, 38, 50, 51, 64, 154, 160, 199
Strabo, 23, 29, 30, 34, 35, 43, 50, 51, 64, 67, 68, 70, 71, 74, 81, 82, 96, 115, 149, 151, 160–62, 191–93, 197, 214, 261, 294, 297, 302, 324, 326, 332
  on Heraclea, 31–32, 67
  on the *Iliad*, 191–92
  on Mariandynoi, 5–6, 48, 71
  on Milesians at Heraclea, 45–47
Stratonicus, 93
The *Suda*, 51, 52, 70, 80, 86, 92, 93, 104, 107–09, 123–25, 130, 273, 280, 296, 317
Sulla, 332
Syriscus/Syriskos, 57, 98, 266, 267, 317–21

T. Quinctius Flamininus, 324
Taman Peninsula, 83, 95, 96, 214, 218, 222, 269–70
  Kepoi on, 221
  Leucon I and, 223–25
  Old Persian inscription, 6, 205
  Spartocids and, 261, 269
Tanagra, 10, 50
Tantalid dynasty, 37
Tariverde, 196
Tauri, 10, 82, 243, 244, 246, 249
Taurica, 256
Taurus Mountains, 115, 159, 323
The Ten Thousand, 24, 28, 69, 90, 91, 206, 214
  Heraclea and, 62, 84, 92, 128
Teres, 306–07
Tetukkian, 125
Thateis, 225
Theaetetus, 92
Theagenes, 52
Thebais, 51, 58

Thebes, 50, 93–94, 107, 298, 320
Themistius, 93
Theodosia, 219, 221, 223, 263, 269
  coinage, 95–96, 266
  grain trade and, 81–82, 253
  Heraclea's alliance with, 262, 268, 274
  Leucon I and, 97, 114, 127, 223, 225, 251, 270–72
  Spartocids attempt to conquer, 96, 98, 261, 271, 275
Theognis, 52, 55
Theophanes, 36
Theophrastus, 30, 38
Theopompus, 30, 31, 37, 45, 71, 74, 75, 93, 94, 125, 129, 139, 143, 154, 206, 252, 305
Thermaic Gulf, 233
Thespiae, 51
Thessalia, 216
Thessaly, 197
Thorax, 91
Thoudippus, 77
Thrace, 6, 89, 146, 216, 305, 307
  Chersonesus, 236, 238
  coast, 158
  Lysimachus rules, 174, 301, 303–04, 308, 311
  northern, 306
  Philip II takes, 139, 228
Thracians, 35, 38, 337, 339, 340
  Anatolia invasion, 33
  culture, 38
  Dobruja cities secure alliance of, 305
  Greek–non-Greek go-betweens, 338
  Histria raid, 195–96
  Lysimachus against, 306, 308
  migrations, 34
  Phineus rules, 34
  revolt, 228, 305
  Scythians hostilities, 216
Thracians/Odrysians, 215, 216, 218–20, 227, 303, 305, 337
Thucydides, 29, 38, 69, 74, 77, 79, 81, 83, 89, 218, 233, 235–37, 239, 337–39
Thynians, 35, 36, 146
Thynias, 84, 136, 146, 154

INDEX

Thynus, 32, 34, 36, 44–45
Ticion, 226
Timasion, 91
Timesilaus, 220
Timogenes of Miletus, 5, 23
Timotheus, 11, 106–09, 125, 128, 133, 175
    Clearchus and, 108–09, 123, 131
    Heraclea's coinage under, 140
    Heracleotes and, 121, 138
    policies of, 139, 153, 226
    rule of, 135–37, 141–42, 155, 208
Tiphys, 51
Tirgatao, 223, 257
Tissaphernes, 94
Titias, 36, 39, 40–41, 197–99
Tition, 197–98
Tium, 149, 154–55, 160–61, 165, 166, 226
Tomis, 195, 304
Toretai, 223, 224
Trapezus, 46, 90, 206, 217
Trogus (*see* Justin)
Trojan War, 33
Troy/Trojans, 6, 191, 192
Tsikhisdziri, 217
Tundja/Tondja River, 306, 307
Tymnes, 219
Tyndaridae, 39, 84
Tynnichus, 96–97, 262–66, 270
Tyras, 44, 95–96, 98, 274
Tyre, 150, 297

Ukraine, 213, 215, 218, 242, 246, 337, 339
Ünye, 205
Urartu, 43, 217

Valerius Flaccus, 33, 39
Valerius Maximus, 115
Vani, 217
Vladimir, Prince of Kiev, 242
Volga River, 247
Voss. qu. 2 mss, 279

Xenagoras, 169
Xenophon, 62, 66, 67, 83, 85, 87, 89–92, 94, 106, 115, 127, 128, 217, 222, 233, 234, 238, 268, 269
    Anabasis, 29, 30, 31, 34, 49, 69, 70, 92, 128, 154, 204, 206, 222, 269
    on Asiatic Thrace, 34
    on Black Sea cities, 214
    on conflict between Persian subjects, 209
    on Heraclea, 29, 48–49, 84, 92
    on Mariandynian culture, 35
    on northern Anatolia, 204, 206
Xerxes, 68, 215

Zeus, 39, 44, 64, 123, 127, 197, 280, 327
Zipoetes, 150, 162, 163, 166, 168
Zoltes, 339, 340
Zopyrion, 146, 228, 229, 303, 305

COLLOQUIA ANTIQUA

1. G.R. TSETSKHLADZE (ed.), The Black Sea, Greece, Anatolia and Europe in the First Millennium BC.
2. H. GENZ and D.P. MIELKE (eds.), Insights into Hittite History and Archaeology.
3. S.A. KOVALENKO, Sylloge Nummorum Graecorum. State Pushkin Museum of Fine Arts. Coins of the Black Sea Region. Part I: Ancient Coins from the Northern Black Sea Littoral.
4. A. HERMARY and G.R. TSETSKHLADZE (eds.), From the Pillars of Hercules to the Footsteps of the Argonauts.
5. L. MIHAILESCU-BÎRLIBA, *Ex Toto Orbe Romano*: Immigration into Roman Dacia. With Prosopographical Observations on the Population of Dacia.
6. P.-A. KREUZ, Die Grabreliefs aus dem Bosporanischen Reich.
7. F. DE ANGELIS (ed.), Regionalism and Globalism in Antiquity: Exploring Their Limits.
8. A. AVRAM, Prosopographia Ponti Euxini Externa.
9. Y.N. YOUSSEF and S. MOAWAD (eds.), From Old Cairo to the New World. Coptic Studies Presented to Gawdat Gabra on the Occasion of his Sixty-Fifth Birthday.
10. R. ROLLINGER and K. SCHNEGG (eds.), Kulturkontakte in antiken Welten: vom Denkmodell zum Fallbeispiel.
11. S.A. KOVALENKO, Sylloge Nummorum Graecorum. State Pushkin Museum of Fine Arts. Coins of the Black Sea Region. Part II: Ancient Coins of the Black Sea Littoral.
12. A.V. PODOSSINOV (ed.), The Periphery of the Classical World in Ancient Geography and Cartography.
13. A.M. MADDEN, Corpus of Byzantine Church Mosaic Pavements from Israel and the Palestinian Territories.
14. A. PETROVA, Funerary Reliefs from the West Pontic Area (6th–1st Centuries BC).
15. A. FANTALKIN and O. TAL, Tell Qudadi: An Iron Age IIB Fortress on the Central Mediterranean Coast of Israel (with References to Earlier and Later Periods).
16. C.M. DRAYCOTT and M. STAMATOPOULOU (eds.), Dining and Death: Interdisciplinary Perspectives on the 'Funerary Banquet' in Ancient Art, Burial and Belief.
17. M.-P. DE HOZ, J.P. SÁNCHEZ HERNÁNDEZ and C. MOLINA VALERO (eds.), Between Tarhuntas and Zeus Polieus: Cultural Crossroads in the Temples and Cults of Graeco-Roman Anatolia.

18. M. MANOLEDAKIS, G.R. TSETSKHLADZE and I. XYDOPOULOS (eds.), Essays on the Archaeology and Ancient History of the Black Sea Littoral.
19. R.G. GÜRTEKİN DEMİR, H. CEVİZOĞLU, Y. POLAT and G. POLAT (eds.), Archaic and Classical Western Anatolia: New Perspectives in Ceramic Studies.
20. C. KÖRNER, Die zyprischen Königtümer im Schatten der Großreiche des Vorderen Orients. Studien zu den zyprischen Monarchien vom 8. bis zum 4. Jh. v. Chr.
21. G.R. TSETSKHLADZE (ed.), Pessinus and Its Regional Setting. Volume 1.
22. G.R. TSETSKHLADZE (ed.), Pessinus and Its Regional Setting. Volume 2: Work in 2009–2013.
23. I. MOGA, Religious Excitement in Ancient Anatolia. Cult and Devotional Forms for Solar and Lunar Gods.
24. G.R. TSETSKHLADZE (ed.), Phrygia in Antiquity: From the Bronze Age to the Byzantine Period.
25. L. MIHAILESCU-BÎRLIBA (ed.), *Limes*, Economy and Society in the Lower Danubian Roman Provinces.
26. M. COSTANZI and M. DANA (eds.), Une autre façon d'être grec: interactions et productions des Grecs en milieu colonial/Another Way of Being Greek: Interactions and Cultural Innovations of the Greeks in a Colonial Milieu.
27. G.R. TSETSKHLADZE (ed.), Ionians in the West and East.
28. G.R. TSETSKHLADZE (ed.), Archaeology and History of Urartu (Biainili).
29. M.-P. DE HOZ, J.L. GARCÍA ALONSO and L.A. GUICHARD ROMERO (eds.), Greek *Paideia* and Local Tradition in the Graeco-Roman East.
30. A.V. BELOUSOV, Defixiones Olbiae Ponticae (*DefOlb*).
31. J. PORUCZNIK, Cultural Identity within the Northern Black Sea Region in Antiquity. (De)constructing Past Identities.
32. M.G. ABRAMZON and V.D. KUZNETSOV, Coin Hoards Volume XI: Greek Hoards, The Cimmerian Bosporus.
33. A. COŞKUN (ed.), Galatian Victories and Other Studies into the Agency and Identity of the Galatians in the Hellenistic and Early Roman Periods.
34. V.D. KUZNETSOV and M.G. ABRAMZON, The Beginning of Coinage in the Cimmerian Bosporus (a Hoard from Phanagoria).
35. A.-I. PÁZSINT, Private Associations in the Pontic Greek Cities (6th century BC–3rd century AD).
36. M. MANOLEDAKIS, An Approach to the Historical Geography of the Southern Black Sea Littoral (First Millennium BC).
37. M.G. ABRAMZON, Y.Y. EFIMOVA, N.V. KOPTSEVA, I.A. SAPRYKINA and T.N. SMEKALOVA, The Metallurgy of Bosporan Silver Coinage: Third Century AD.

38. S.M. BURSTEIN, Greece's Northern Frontier: Studies in the History of the Ancient Greek Experience in the Black Sea.

PRINTED ON PERMANENT PAPER • IMPRIME SUR PAPIER PERMANENT • GEDRUKT OP DUURZAAM PAPIER - ISO 9706

N.V. PEETERS S.A., WAROTSTRAAT 50, B-3020 HERENT